Managing Your Money

ALL-IN-ONE

3rd Edition

by The Experts at Dummies

for dummies®
A Wiley Brand

Managing Your Money All-in-One For Dummies®, 3rd Edition

Published by: **John Wiley & Sons, Inc.,** 111 River Street, Hoboken, NJ 07030-5774, www.wiley.com

For general information on our other products and services, please contact our Customer Care Department within the U.S. at 877-762-2974, outside the U.S. at 317-572-3993, or fax 317-572-4002. For technical support, please visit https://hub.wiley.com/community/support/dummies.

Wiley publishes in a variety of print and electronic formats and by print-on-demand. Some material included with standard print versions of this book may not be included in e-books or in print-on-demand. If this book refers to media that is not included in the version you purchased, you may download this material at http://booksupport.wiley.com. For more information about Wiley products, visit www.wiley.com.

Library of Congress Control Number: 2026949409

ISBN 978-1-394-42198-5 (pbk); ISBN 978-1-394-42199-2 (ebk); ISBN 978-1-394-42200-5 (ebk)

SKY10165586_081426

Contents at a Glance

Table of Contents

Introduction

Welcome to the latest edition of *Managing Your Money All-in-One For Dummies* — a big one-stop shop designed to help you get control over your financial life!

This book tackles a lot of big topics, but it tries to keep things simple, clear, and to the point. We culled the best, juiciest information from a good sampling of *For Dummies* books on personal finance and compiled them into one fat volume. It's absolutely packed with easy-to-grasp advice on all matters having to do with managing your money. Whether you're a stay-at-home parent, a truck driver, a burger flipper, or a CEO — whether you're interviewing for your first job or you retired ten years ago — you can find scads of great tips and sound advice in these pages that can help you get a handle on everything from your credit cards to your health insurance, from your taxes to your will.

About This Book

If it has something to do with your personal relationship to your own money, it's a good bet that this book talks about it. This edition of *Managing Your Money All-in-One For Dummies* offers money-management and personal-finance tips to help assess your true financial situation and take charge of your economic life. You find information on getting the best mortgage, saving for the future (whether for college or retirement), paying off debt, building wealth through triple compounding, creating and sticking to a budget, repairing and improving your credit rating, handling taxes, planning an estate, and protecting your assets.

The facts on the ground aren't pretty at the moment. Many people feel more powerless than ever against mighty and faceless institutions that seem designed for nothing but to confuse and rip off. This book is here to tell you: It doesn't have to be that way. By doing a little homework and taking a renewed interest in your own situation, you can reclaim many rights and advantages you probably didn't know you had. If information is power, then this book is like a gigantic supervitamin.

A quick note: Sidebars (shaded boxes of text) dig into the details of a given topic, but they aren't crucial to understanding it. Feel free to read them or skip them.

You can pass over the text accompanied by the Technical Stuff icon, too. The text marked with this icon gives some interesting but nonessential information about managing your money.

One last point: Within this book, you may note that some web addresses break across two lines of text. If you're reading this book in print and want to visit one of these web pages, simply key in the web address exactly as it's noted in the text, pretending as though the line break doesn't exist. If you're reading this as an e-book, you've got it easy — just click the web address to be taken directly to the web page.

Foolish Assumptions

In order to shovel so much material on such a wide variety of topics into a single book that's actually helpful and inviting, we make a few assumptions about you, the reader. See whether one or more of these shoes fit:

- You can't seem to get out from under credit card debt.
- You'd like to find ways to spend less money, but the idea of sitting down and setting up a budget makes you feel slightly ill.
- You've heard about how great it is to save for retirement in an IRA or 401(k), but the whole concept seems too complicated to deal with.
- You're interested in triple compounding and want to weigh the benefits with the risks.
- When tax time rolls around, you feel frightened and uncertain.
- You can't seem to keep up with mounting bills and wonder where in the world your paycheck goes every month.
- You worry about being able to afford college for your kids.
- You have a vague feeling that you should probably have certain kinds of insurance, but what they might be is a mystery.
- You have health problems and are afraid they are going to end up bankrupting you.

If any (or all) of these descriptions hit the mark, this book is most definitely for you.

Icons Used in This Book

You'll see a number of funny-looking little graphic elements sprinkled throughout this book. Here's what they are and what they mean.

TIP

This icon marks concrete tips and tricks that you can put to use in giving you more control over your financial life.

REMEMBER

This icon highlights passages that are good to keep in mind when it comes time to make money decisions. To siphon off the most important information in each chapter, just skim through these icons.

WARNING

Watch out! This icon alerts you to common mistakes that can trip you up and cause trouble when managing your money.

TECHNICAL STUFF

This icon notifies you that something is a bit more complex than usual, and that you can safely skip it if you're in a hurry or only want to skim the surface of the topic.

Beyond the Book

In addition to the abundance of information and guidance related to managing your money that we provide in this book, you get access to even more help and information online at `Dummies.com`. Check out this book's online Cheat Sheet. Just go to `www.dummies.com` and search for "Managing Your Money All-in-One For Dummies Cheat Sheet."

Where to Go from Here

If you already have a specific interest in one particular area of managing your money or have a sense of what you really need to tackle first, by all means flip to the table of contents or index and zip straight to that section. You certainly are *not* expected to read this book cover to cover. On the other hand, if you're here because you are well and truly lost when it comes to handling your finances, you may as well begin at the beginning with Book 1, Chapter 1, and go from there.

However you end up using this book, we hope you at least gain some insight into better and smarter ways of keeping more and wasting less of what you work so hard for. And we hope you find the determination to apply some of the ideas here to your life. You'll be very glad you did. Just keep in mind that even in tough times like these, you have a surprising number of exploits you can do to beat the system, even if it seems stacked against you.

The idea is to empower yourself. No one is going to stop you if you try, and no one is going to do it for you. So, buck up and steel yourself to look at your life more critically and honestly. We all have bad habits. Recognizing them is half the battle. Get ready to take charge of your life and get more out of it. Good luck!

1 Taking Charge of Your Finances

Contents at a Glance

IN THIS CHAPTER

» Analyzing your spending

» Reviewing your expenses and income

» Setting financial goals

Chapter 1

Assessing Where You Are Financially

Raise your hand if you know where your money went last month. According to a survey published by `Mint.com` in 2020, 65 percent of Americans have no clue where they spent their money in the previous month. Basically, millions of people are saying that their money disappeared without their knowing its whereabouts. No wonder money is considered the number one stressor in today's society! (It's also one of the leading reasons people cite when filing for a divorce.)

Millions of people are in debt, behind in retirement, or just don't have any space in their finances to cover a minor emergency, such as a needed car repair. Many live paycheck to paycheck and don't see a clear way out.

Because you picked up this book, we're going to assume you don't want to be one of those people. One of the key strategies to your newfound success? Finding a budgeting system that works for you. Budgeting is a basic financial concept that doesn't get enough credit for being one of the major parts of financial success.

Having a successful budget helps you accomplish whatever financial goals you may have, whether that's saving money, paying off debt, or something else. Knowing where your money goes and how much you have coming in is key to getting you where you need to be.

REMEMBER

Budgeting tells your money where to go and not the other way around. By properly utilizing a budget, you aren't clueless and wondering where your money goes every month like everyone else.

Taking Inventory of Your Finances: A Spending Analysis

The first part of a new financial you is taking inventory of your finances. You're going to want to know where you're coming from so you can track your progress and pat yourself on the back when you start making actual financial moves.

REMEMBER

By taking inventory of your finances, you can clarify where you stand financially — both good and bad. Here are just a few of the benefits:

- **You have financial data to review anytime.** When you have actual numbers in front of you, you can assess where you're in good standing and where your finances may need a little work. Maybe you've been a rock star with that employer-matched 401(k) but have done little to pay down your student loans.
- **You can set realistic monetary goals.** When you know your income and expenses, you know how much is left for goals such as debt repayment or saving for a vacation. It makes it possible to set a timeline for reaching those milestones.
- **You notice when accounts don't serve your current needs.** You may discover you're paying credit card fees for a card you don't use. An account such as a 529 Savings Plan may no longer be necessary because your child has changed their career goals. Maybe you're not earning enough in an investment vehicle, and that money can better serve you elsewhere. All these small details can add up to money lost.
- **You can try to pay off debt faster, which can save you money.** By looking over your current liabilities, you may find that you can cut years off your payment timeline by making an additional payment or two. You may also realize that you can consolidate a current loan for a better interest rate.
- **You can save time with organized finances.** Having all your accounts in one general place you can see, such as a spreadsheet or an online tool, can save you time and stress from having to always track them down individually. You can monitor due dates for debt repayments and check balances in accounts

before any significant financial purchases are made. You also know which financial institution is in charge of what. You may uncover a forgotten bill or two that can still be saved from going into collections. And when any new accounts or bills come in, you can plug them in with the rest. Find ways to organize your records in the later section "Record-keeping systems."

The following sections are an overview of the first steps of creating your budget.

Make a list of your financial assets and liabilities

Spoiler alert: This step may take a bit longer if you don't already have some kind of net-worth tracker or don't currently have all your financial accounts in one place. The following sections give you the basics of assets and liabilities and your options for corralling your financial info in one place.

Assets

Financial assets are anything with a positive financial value. Lots of facets can qualify as shown in Figure 1-1:

- Checking and savings accounts, the cash you have under the mattress, and any checks you've been meaning to cash
- Money market accounts, your retirement fund at work, pensions, brokerage accounts, company stock shares, treasury bills, and bonds
- Some life insurance policies
- Physical items you can *liquidate* (convert into cash), such as your home; your car or other vehicles such as ATVs, motorcycles, or boats; jewelry; collectibles; and anything else that you can sell for a profit. (That fancy purse you keep in a dust jacket that you can sell tomorrow for a few hundred dollars? Put that on the list, too.)

TIP

Make sure accounts such as financial assets have a beneficiary listed so your heirs have easy access. Having a will or trust is highly recommended because you never know what tomorrow will bring. Still, these can go to probate and can make your assets inaccessible to your beneficiaries for an extended period of time. You also want to ensure that your will is detailed so there's no question of who inherits what. A clear and precise estate plan helps your loved ones focus on healing instead. See Book 7 for more information about estate planning.

Financial Asset Checklist

Traditional Banking

- ☐ Checking account
- ☐ Premium checking account
- ☐ Business checking account
- ☐ Rewards checking account
- ☐ Savings account
- ☐ High-yield savings accounts
- ☐ Money market account
- ☐ Certificates of deposit (CD)
- ☐ Prepaid cards
- ☐ Cash on hand

Retirement

- ☐ Traditional IRA
- ☐ Roth IRA
- ☐ 401(k)
- ☐ SIMPLE 401(k)
- ☐ 403(b)
- ☐ SIMPLE IRA plans
- ☐ SEP Plans (employee pensions)
- ☐ SARSEP Plans
- ☐ Federal government pension
- ☐ 457 plans

Brokerage

- ☐ Stocks
- ☐ Mutual funds
- ☐ Index funds
- ☐ Exchange-traded funds (ETFs)
- ☐ Government-issued bonds
- ☐ Corporate bonds
- ☐ Commodities
- ☐ Real Estate Investment Trusts (REITs)

College

- ☐ 529 Savings Plan
- ☐ Coverdell account
- ☐ Uniform Gift to Minor Accounts (UGMA)

Physical

- ☐ Real estate (primary residence)
- ☐ Real estate (rental properties)
- ☐ Vehicles (both primary and other)
- ☐ Jewelry
- ☐ Art and collectibles
- ☐ Life insurance policies
- ☐ Gold and other precious metals

FIGURE 1-1: A few suggestions of what to consider a financial asset.

Liabilities

Your *financial liabilities* are anything you owe money on. Your home is considered a positive financial asset (see the preceding section), but the mortgage you owe isn't. Other types of housing debt can include a second mortgage, a rental agreement, or property taxes.

Other financial liabilities include the following:

- Loans on other items you financed, such as your car or education
- Personal loans from a financial institution or family friend
- Credit cards that currently have a balance
- Other outstanding debt such as medical bills

Even unpaid taxes, fines you owe a court, or child support can be considered financial liabilities.

Record-keeping systems

After you've made a list of all assets and liabilities off the top of your head (see the two preceding sections), track down any paperwork and/or information necessary to create an online account so that you can log into the accounts. Next, you need to decide how you want to keep all your financial documentation where it's not only safe but also accessible in case of an emergency.

TIP

You may choose to save your information in a spreadsheet program such as Microsoft Excel or enter all your information into an online tool. Another part of your record-keeping system should involve taking care of your physical paperwork. Having stacks of paper everywhere isn't helpful. You can store your paperwork in folders within a file box or filing cabinet; if you prefer a more minimalist approach, you can purchase a scanner, upload your paperwork to your computer, and discard the documents in a safe and secure manner.

Review your spending for the past three months

Anytime you're attempting a new goal, doing some research is a great idea. So for the second step to creating a budget, you need to review (research) the past three months of your spending habits. Where do you even start? Easy: your bank statements. Your bank has a lot of helpful information, including the option to see where your money is coming from and where it's flowing out.

TIP

Check whether your bank has a spending analysis tool. Such tools automatically break spending into categories, show what you spend, and then give an overall percentage of where your money went for the month. This kind of resource can be a great place to start to see your spending in action.

Open a new spreadsheet on your computer or grab a pen and a piece of paper. Start to look over every expense you have. First, write down any expenses that are the same amount every month, such as your rent or mortgage, Internet bill, car payment and insurance, streaming services, and any other expenses that rarely change unless you make a specific change to your service, such as upgrading a tier.

Next, look over your spending that can vary from month to month. Items under this type of spending can be groceries, dining out, gas for your car, and any entertainment expenses while having fun with your friends or family. You can list them individually by category. If this approach seems too overwhelming, or you buy different types of items in one general place, group the transactions by store (see Figure 1-2).

	A	B	C	D	E
1	**Expense**	**Category**	**Amount**		
2	Rent	Living Expenses	1200		
3	Target	Groceries	57.43		
4	Netflix	Entertainment	14.99		
5	Gas	Transportation	20		
6	Target	Household Items	14.87		
7	Amazon	Clothing	35.78		
8	Chewy	Pet Items	40.99		
9	Uber Eats	Dining Out	25		
10					

FIGURE 1-2: A spreadsheet that displays how you track your spending.

TIP

When looking over your spending, don't forget to look at where you're using your credit cards and any apps you use to transfer money, such as Venmo or PayPal. You can easily see these transactions while reviewing your bank statements, but they often don't list the retailer or item. For example, you may use your PayPal account when you buy anything through your favorite food delivery service. Your checking account then has a lot of PayPal transactions but doesn't categorize them automatically into "dining out." You have to review the transaction in your actual PayPal account.

After you go over the past three months of your spending habits, you notice trends. You may see that you spent more money than you imagined on dining out or mindlessly shopping online. You see how those $5 transactions here and there add up over time, and probably to an amount you didn't realize. You may also be pleasantly surprised at how little you spent and are able to congratulate yourself on keeping your expenses down.

REMEMBER

Money can be emotional, and when you realize you wasted some of it, you can quickly feel like crap. But guess what? Money flows in and out. It's not gone forever and can find its way back to you. It's up to you where it goes next.

Seeing Where Your Money Goes: Your Expenses

Your money goes to various places, and hopefully, you've done a spending analysis (as described earlier in this chapter) to show you where. You most likely discovered spending patterns. Some of the patterns may surprise you, while other patterns don't. If you're anything like us, you realized you've spent way too much in a category, such as takeout coffee. (Mmm, lattes.) That's okay.

TIP

If you haven't already completed the spending analysis laid out earlier in this chapter, hit pause on this section and go do that. The info from your analysis makes breaking down your personal expenses so much easier.

Just know that your new budget has three components:

- Expenses (how much money you're spending)
- Income (how much money you have coming in)
- Financial goals (feats you want to accomplish, such as paying down debt or saving for something in the future)

All three are imperative to how your new future budget affects your financial life. In fact, they're equally important to be financially aware of. Your expenses can affect how much income you need to bring in, which determines whether you can accomplish your goals by working one regular full-time job or whether you also need to get a part-time job or a side gig. Your income determines how much money you can spend on your lifestyle or put toward your future, such as retirement. It's all related, so the sooner you figure out what you need to pay and what you want to accomplish, the faster a budget can work for you.

REMEMBER

Like anything in life, you're trying to improve; things may get worse before they get better. Finding where you are in life can be discouraging. Who in their right mind wants to feel discouraged? Not us, and we can imagine the feeling is mutual. But remember this: You're taking positive steps to change your finances. These steps can have a cascading effect and change all areas of your life for the better. We want you to live a good life, and we hope you want that too.

Identifying fixed expenses

Fixed expenses are expenses that are the same amount of money every billing period, such as paying your rent or mortgage. Most fixed expenses are paid monthly, but some are weekly, quarterly, or annually. For example, you pay for your car registration every year, but you pay monthly for car insurance. Weekly fixed expenses may include items such as a parking pass. Figure 1-3 shows various examples of fixed expenses.

Fixed Expenses

Household

- ☐ Rent
- ☐ Mortgage
- ☐ Property taxes
- ☐ HOA fees
- ☐ Rental or Homeowners insurance
- ☐ Internet
- ☐ Electricity
- ☐ Water
- ☐ Cellphone
- ☐ Gas

Debt

- ☐ Auto loan
- ☐ Student loans
- ☐ Personal loans
- ☐ Debt settlements
- ☐ Medical bills
- ☐ Government agencies
- ☐ Court-ordered debt

Financial

- ☐ Automobile Insurance
- ☐ Life Insurance
- ☐ Disability Insurance
- ☐ Retirement contributions
- ☐ Banking fees

Medical

- ☐ Health insurance premiums
- ☐ Insurance co-pays
- ☐ Flexible Spending Account
- ☐ Health Saving Account
- ☐ Therapy
- ☐ Prescriptions

Work

- ☐ Public transportation
- ☐ Parking
- ☐ Professional association fees
- ☐ Professional development classes
- ☐ Conferences/networking events

Personal

- ☐ Gym
- ☐ Subscriptions
- ☐ Memberships
- ☐ Streaming services

Children

- ☐ Childcare
- ☐ Tuition
- ☐ 529 and Coverdell savings accounts
- ☐ After school activities

FIGURE 1-3: Spending categories that are considered fixed expenses.

After you understand what a fixed expense is, you're ready to evaluate what you need to spend money on every month.

1. **Complete a spending analysis (as explained earlier in this chapter).**

   Because you divide your spending into categories, you should see a recurring theme with how much you spend each month on certain items or necessary expenses.

2. **Make a list of your fixed expenses.**

   Examples can include your rent, utilities, gym memberships, or fun purchases such as subscription boxes or streaming services.

3. **Add up the total costs for these fixed expenses each month over the previous three months.**

   You now clearly see how much you spend every month on your fixed expenses. You can even divide this amount per paycheck if you feel like getting creative. (That may hurt your feelings, so be careful how far you want to dig.)

4. **Evaluate whether you need those fixed expenses.**

   Now's the time to see whether all your fixed expenses are necessary. Do you need to be spending money on a gym membership every month, or can you find a cheaper way to work out, such as utilizing local running trails? If you sign up to get monthly items or deliveries, do you have the option to pause them and work through your current supply instead?

   REMEMBER

   Make sure you ask questions about your larger fixed expenses, too — not just the minor ones. Rent may be costing you more of your take-home pay than you realize you're comfortable with. Moving can be expensive, so we're not suggesting you randomly decide to change apartments, but do make a note to research other living arrangements when you get closer to the end of your lease.

TIP

Just because an expense is fixed doesn't mean you can't find a way to lower the costs.

- See whether you can save money by switching to purchasing items quarterly rather than monthly.
- Call your providers, such as cellphone or Internet, to see whether you qualify for any discounts or loyalty rates.
- Research competitors for insurance policies: healthcare, automobile, renters or homeowners, and life.
- Consider switching to different tiers of subscription services, such as home streaming networks.

- Take advantage of apps that provide coupons, cash back on your purchases, and price match for the best deal.
- Install web browser extensions that help you shop a bit more savvily and save you some extra cash.
- Check to see whether your bank offers you cash back for using your debit card.

TIP

Call your service providers to see whether they offer a loyalty rate or discount you may qualify for. Companies want to keep their customers, and if they know you're looking to jump ship, they'll be happy to assist. Some companies and service providers even offer discounts for students, public servants, or those in the military. If your current provider doesn't have anything for you, look to see whether another provider can better fit your needs. A switch may be a way to free up some additional room in your budget so you can breathe. It doesn't hurt to ask. The worst they can do is say no and have you keep paying what you already are.

You can even discuss options with your landlord or mortgage company. Nothing is off the table; the more money you can free up, the more you have to save for your goals or spend on experiences that bring value to your life.

Allowing for variable expenses

Variable expenses, or *variable costs*, are different from fixed expenses (see the preceding section). Variable expenses are different from month to month and may be items you regularly purchase or ones you buy only occasionally (see Figure 1-4). Common variable expenses include the following:

- Groceries
- Gas for your car
- Food for your pets
- Items for any hobbies
- Personal care items such as hygiene products or makeup

These types of expenses can be more challenging for you to track. Depending on the time of year or stage of your life, your spending in these categories can fluctuate. You may spend nearly nothing in a category like household items one month and then easily spend a few hundred dollars there the next month. You may spend a lot more money during the holiday season between purchasing gifts and travel-associated costs.

Variable Expenses

Food

- ☐ Groceries
- ☐ Dining Out
- ☐ Lunch (work and school)
- ☐ Coffee

Transportation

- ☐ Gas
- ☐ Tolls
- ☐ Oil changes and other car maintenance
- ☐ Car repairs
- ☐ Registration and other fees
- ☐ Rideshares

Entertainment

- ☐ Concerts
- ☐ Alcohol
- ☐ Books
- ☐ Hobbies
- ☐ Games for family
- ☐ Admission to movies or museums

Household

- ☐ Pet food
- ☐ Other pet expenses
- ☐ Cleaning supplies
- ☐ Decor
- ☐ Clothing
- ☐ Personal grooming
- ☐ Child expenses such as diapers or formula
- ☐ School field trips and other extracurricular activities

FIGURE 1-4: Spending categories that are variable expenses.

REMEMBER

Because variable expenses are less predictable, assigning a monetary value of what you should spend per month can be frustrating and challenging. You may have control over some of them but not for others, and that's okay. You may get easily flustered when a category spikes and initially throws everything you had planned off course. You're going to figure this all out, too, and we're here to help every step of the way.

Needs and wants

Variable expenses include both needs and wants. You can't just opt out of a lot of your variable spending. You have to purchase items such as medicine, and you have to eat.

Generally speaking, *needs* include food, gas to get to and from work if you commute, clothing, and so on. *Wants* are items such as getting the newest cellphone when your current one is perfectly usable or spending money on experiences like concerts or dining out.

REMEMBER

Just because you can't avoid purchasing some items doesn't mean you can't still save money. One of the ways you can cut your variable expenses is to consider lower-priced alternatives to your usual purchases.

Say you're in the market for foundation because your old bottle is empty. Instead of going to an expensive makeup counter to purchase your usual foundation, try to find a similar product from a different brand that's a lower price. In this example, the high-end foundation is considered a want because you can find less-expensive brands of foundation. But regardless of what some may say, foundation can be a need based on your own comfort and personal preference.

The difference between needs and wants can get murky quickly, especially because one person's want may genuinely be another person's need (see Figure 1-5). Spending money on your wants is perfectly okay; you just need to figure out how to budget for them properly. The 50/30/20 budgeting method, for example, enables you to categorize most of your expenses based on your needs (50 percent of your income) and wants (30 percent of your income); the remaining 20 percent goes toward savings and debt.

Needs versus Wants

Needs

- ☐ Rent
- ☐ Mortgage
- ☐ HOA/property taxes
- ☐ Homeowner/rental insurance
- ☐ Internet
- ☐ Electricity
- ☐ Water
- ☐ Gas for work
- ☐ Public transportation for work
- ☐ Health insurance
- ☐ Prescriptions
- ☐ Therapy
- ☐ Groceries (essentials to feed you and your family)
- ☐ Auto insurance
- ☐ Car payment
- ☐ Other debt with current payment arrangement
- ☐ Pet food and other essentials
- ☐ Child expenses such as diapers or formula
- ☐ Childcare

Wants

- ☐ Dining Out
- ☐ Alcohol
- ☐ Travel
- ☐ Home décor
- ☐ Nonessential clothing
- ☐ Subscriptions
- ☐ Streaming services
- ☐ Admission to museums, concerts, or other events
- ☐ Personal grooming services
- ☐ Travel
- ☐ Nonessential electronics

FIGURE 1-5: A list of what expenses are needs and wants.

REMEMBER

Voluntarily spending money on nonessential items or items that are categorized as wants rather than needs is called *discretionary spending.*

REMEMBER

Be realistic when determining your wants and needs. Suppose you have a specific life situation that requires you to spend a bit more on your variable expenses. Perhaps you have several chronic health conditions. Some expenses may help you manage your quality of life on days when you can't get out of bed, such as ordering takeout so you don't have to spend energy preparing a meal. You may hate admitting that you need to pay more in a specific budget category, such as dining out, than people say you should. But guess what? When you're realistic, that's what keeps you under budget every month.

Value-based spending

One more idea to help save you money and curb your expenses is to evaluate whether your current spending is *value-based* (rooted in the items you value in life) or a result of trying to keep up with your friends and family. Maybe you didn't want to be the only one left out of a vacation, but you really don't want to visit that destination. Or maybe you convinced yourself that life will be infinitely better if you just buy whatever product your favorite influencer recommends. (We're guilty of this; we almost bought cool bathroom containers before we realized what we really needed was just to do a massive purge.)

TECHNICAL STUFF

If you don't know what your values are, that's okay. A lot of free surveys online can help you figure it out. The Barrett Values Centre provides a free Personal Values Assessment quiz online, found at `www.valuescentre.com/tools-assessments/pva`.

Knowing Where Your Money Comes From: Your Income

Your *income* is an essential component of your budget. Knowing how much money you have coming in can ensure your expenses don't exceed your income. It can also help you set realistic goals for all areas of your life that relate to your finances and perhaps even quality of life. You may realize you have more income than you initially thought you had, or a spending deficit that means you need to find ways to either cut back or earn more.

REMEMBER

When discussing your income, one dollar amount you need to keep in mind is your *net pay,* also referred to as *disposable income.* Net pay is the amount of money left over after any withholdings you may be subjected to, such as taxes (federal and state if your residence requires it), Social Security, Medicare, and any wage garnishments you may be paying off. It's important to consider because it's the amount of money you use to budget every month. It's the money you have to put toward your goals, pay your bills, and cover your variable expenses.

Depending on a monthly income

The first type of income you should consider is what you earn monthly to cover all your expenses. *Monthly income* can come from various sources. While it can be consistent dependent on your income type, it can also be different from month to month. Here's a list of different types of monthly income you can earn:

- **Income from full-time and/or part-time employment:** This income you receive from an employer that has you on its payroll and that you regularly trade your time to for money. Some jobs pay a flat amount of money per paycheck, known as a *salary,* and others may pay an hourly *wage*. Hourly income can fluctuate because the hours you work may vary, while a salary doesn't.
- **Income as a self-employed freelancer or consultant:** Freelancers and contractors make variable income depending on what's on their roster. Both are considered self-employed, but the main difference is the number of clients and the type of projects they're currently working on. *Freelancers* balance more than one client and work on projects with a short timeline. *Contractors* take on more significant projects with one main client and do smaller work for several.

  REMEMBER

  At different times in your life, you may prefer different compensation structures, and no one approach is right or wrong.
- **Pensions and other paid retirement plans:** A *pension* is a type of retirement program that an employee, an employer, or both pay into. The plan pays a fixed sum to the employee at regular intervals on retirement. Each employer decides on a compensation formula approved by the U.S. Department of Labor. Some pensions require you to work for the company for a certain number of years before you're eligible (or *vested*). Federal, state, and local government or other public sectors also allow for paid retirement plans.
- **Retirement plans:** Outside of traditional pensions or government-paid retirement plans, you can still receive payments from your retirement accounts if you previously planned. These types of retirement accounts enable you to save for retirement by investing. The most popular ones are 401(k), 403(b), and Roth IRAs, but you can find a complete list on the IRS website (`www.irs.gov/retirement-plans/plan-sponsor/types-of-retirement-plans`).
- **Social Security retirement benefits:** When people talk about receiving Social Security, they're usually referring to retirement benefits. Every year you

remain in the workforce, you can receive up to four work credits. As of this writing, you must earn $1,890 to earn a work credit. This means that you must make at least $7,560 per year to earn all 4 credits you're eligible for. After you earn 40 credits (which you could do over the course of 10 years), you're eligible to collect partial benefits at age 62 and full benefits at age 67. For up-to-date information, please visit `www.ssa.gov/retirement`.

- **Social Security Disability Benefits, Supplemental Security Income, and survivors benefits:** Social Security has three other benefits. If you're disabled, you can receive two different types of benefits.
  - *Social Security Disability Insurance (SSDI)* benefits are granted when you match the Social Security Administration's definition of having a disability and have earned enough workforce credits, depending on the age you become disabled.
  - If you've never worked due to a disability, you can qualify for *Supplemental Security Income (SSI)*.

  Last but not least, if you're a child, a spouse, or a parent who relies on someone in the workforce to support you and they die, you can get *survivors benefits*.
- **Cash benefits from the state:** You may qualify for cash assistance in some states, depending on your situation. Temporary Assistance for Needy Families (TANF) is one example. Along with cash assistance, other benefits you may be eligible for are work assistance, specific training to enter back into the workforce, and help with childcare. Go to `www.benefits.gov/benefit/613` to find out more.
- **Court-ordered payments:** For specific life situations, you may receive court-ordered benefits. Alimony and *court-ordered acceptable for processing (COAP),* which gives a former spouse the rights to retirement annuities, are benefits you may get during a divorce. Other court-ordered benefits include child support and restitution if you were a victim of certain crimes.

TIP

Take time to create a Social Security account at `www.ssa.gov/myaccount/`. Doing so enables you to check your workforce credits, the money you've paid into Social Security, and an estimate of your retirement benefit payment. You can also check to see what other benefits may be available to you, such as disability or survivor, along with the amount you or a loved one would qualify for. This information can help you budget better for life circumstances and save for retirement.

Identifying additional sources of income

Just like your variable expenses (check out the earlier section "Allowing for variable expenses"), variable or irregular income means that your wages fluctuate every month. You can make this type of income yearly, monthly, weekly, or even daily. Variable income, for example from a side gig, is an excellent way to catch up on financial goals or supplement your income. *Side gigs* or *side hustles* are usually jobs that are dependent on task completion. You can freelance for a client or clients, using the skills you learned from current or previous jobs.

REMEMBER

After you start budgeting, you may find that your net pay doesn't cover all your monthly expenses or the goals you set for yourself. In this case, you have to either cut your spending or earn more money.

We feel everyone should have additional income streams. The economy can be downright volatile sometimes. A job may be here one day and outsourced the next. Things happen, which is why being able to budget with the best of them is more important than ever. The following is a short list of common side gigs.

- Becoming a *ride sharer,* a person who drives others in their vehicle for a fee
- Doing/delivering grocery shopping or delivering food purchased through a restaurant
- Selling items you have lying around or buying items for a lower price and then selling them for a profit on sites such as eBay and Amazon
- Creating content online as a writer
- Making and selling crafts on a site such as Etsy or on social media

REMEMBER

Variable income from a side gig can still be considered earned income depending on the source, so check with the IRS to see whether you need to put money aside for taxes. Try to put 25 to 30 percent of any income earned from side gigs aside in a checking account. Pay your estimated taxes quarterly and save anything additional for business expenses. Even better, double-check to ensure you aren't missing expenses that you can use for tax deductions. Software fees, utilities such as Internet, and inventory are all expenses that may be potential tax write-offs. For more information on self-employment taxes, go to the IRS official website at `www.irs.gov`.

You Gotta Have Dreams: Financial Goals

Setting goals enables you to work toward something you want in your life with the end goal of eventually achieving it. Goals can be simple, such as brushing your teeth at night. They can be moderate, such as learning a new language or losing some weight. They can also seem unattainable, such as climbing Mount Everest.

After you're clear on where you want to go, figuring out the steps to get you there is easier. (If Mount Everest is your goal, please send us lots of pictures.)

Having a financial goal can help ensure your budget tells your money where to go. It causes you to look at your spending and evaluate your current lifestyle. It helps you not eat cat food in retirement. It can help you live a life you love and are proud of.

REMEMBER

Setting financial goals can help you live a better quality of life, which can mean the difference in where you can afford to retire or whether you can take a leave of absence from an employer or have a life-changing emergency that causes you to pivot, such as an unexpected death. A budget can be flexible to meet the stage of life you're in, but having a bucket of money can shake things up. Oh, and make your overall life easier.

Saving for your future

We regularly get questions from people who want guidance for a financial situation. Sometimes it's easy, like directing them to a budgeting app. But often, they're more serious than that. One of the more common recurring themes: not saving for the future, mainly retirement (see Book 6). Folks are asking questions not only about their personal retirement plans but also their parents'. Life is short, and every day you don't put money aside for your future is a day you're setting yourself up for risk and, even worse, failure.

You're also better off saving for events you know will eventually happen. You may need a new car for transportation to and from work. The perfect bungalow of your dreams may hit the housing market, and you see yourself establishing some roots! You may even have kids heading off to college — or, better yet, you may want to go back to school yourself to make more money so you can have an even better budget than before. "Someday" can turn into your current day, so you may as well plan for it.

Saving for the future isn't just about retirement or replacing things that break. It can also include fabulous trips you want to experience, such as going to Europe or wine tasting in Napa. Maybe it's establishing a scholarship fund in someone's name at a local nonprofit, redecorating your house in whatever the cool new style is, or buying a muscle car to restore. Your future needs to include fun, and your budget helps you do just that.

REMEMBER

Make sure your goal is actually yours. One of the everyday occurrences seen in the personal finance world is people telling others to become their own bosses. Do you know how hard it is to be your own boss? We're not saying you can't do it, but it's not as easy as many claim. Many people quit their jobs to make money but didn't have a clear plan or realized they didn't want self-employment at all. They let someone's goal become theirs instead of listening to their intuition. Make sure whatever financial goal you choose is one that you want to achieve, so you'll put in the hard work to make it your reality.

Paying down your debt

Another financial goal you can see is paying down your debt. Debt isn't evil if you use it strategically. But having even strategic debt can still be problematic. Who wants to pay thousands of dollars in interest and financing fees?

Setting a financial goal to pay your debt down can help in the long run when budgeting. Because as soon as you pay that debt off, you have more cash flow to do things with, such as saving for retirement or adopting a dog from a shelter. Book 3 gives you some tips to help you eliminate your debt.

Putting your financial goals in place

TIP

Setting financial goals doesn't have to be complicated.

1. **Establish what your goals are.**

   For example, maybe you want to buy a house.

2. **Make the goal as clear as can be.**

   Decide precisely how much money you need to buy that house and when you want to be able to make the purchase.

3. **Take actionable steps toward completing it.**

   Examples of actionable steps may be paying extra on your credit card to reduce debt and free up cash, which can go toward opening a high-yield savings account for the house you want. Every little bit adds up, so don't be discouraged if you have to start small. With every action, you move the needle closer to your goal.

   Celebrate the small wins, and make sure you know you have your own back. We have it, too.

IN THIS CHAPTER

» Exploring categories for your budget

» Finding the budgeting tools that work for you

» Taking a few extra steps toward consistent budgeting success

Chapter 2 Building and Sticking to a Budget

The word has gotten a bad rap over the years, which makes us sad because we love budgets! Budgeting is one of the key financial tools you need to understand to succeed financially. If you have no idea how much money you have coming in or where you're spending it, you can't make a budget work. Proper budgeting gives you more options for how you spend your money. Knowing what you can and can't spend your money on? Option. Being aware of how you're doing with retirement contributions? Option.

When you use a budget, you plan for your future. You're taking charge of your life and leaving fewer things to chance. However, being in control and taking charge of your money can be overwhelming if you've never done it before. Fear of the unknown can paralyze people, especially regarding their finances. Particularly when you grow up without great financial role models, knowing what you're supposed to do or even avoiding picking up those habits is tough.

In this chapter, you discover some budgeting guidelines that have helped millions of people live the lives of their dreams. They may not all apply to you or your situation, and that's okay, too. A famous saying is "Take what you want and leave the rest." That works for all areas of your life, including personal finance. It's personal and yours to call the shots.

REMEMBER

You may already be budgeting without even realizing it. If you send money to your retirement account and live off the remainder of your income, that's the pay-yourself-first budget. If you give yourself a cash allowance for lunch, that's the envelope budgeting method. And if you make a list of categories to track your spending so that every dollar is accounted for, that's zero-based budgeting.

Determining Your Budget Categories

The categories you choose can make or break your budget. When you create categories for your spending, you're creating a spending plan. Creating a spending plan is what's going to get you where you want to be: making your money work for you rather than against you.

Planning ahead for the month

The first step to figuring out what spending categories to use in your budget is to plan ahead for your month. Planning keeps you from wasting time and money, two of your most precious resources. Forgetting events, appointments, or renewal fees can all derail a budget. When you plan, you're fully aware of what you have coming up and can allocate money accordingly. For example, if you have a lot of upcoming get-togethers with friends, you can plan ahead by putting additional money into your entertainment category and cut back elsewhere.

Meal planning is a great example of planning ahead. Every week you make a list of meals to cook and then write out the ingredients you need. You shop for everything at once, meaning you make fewer trips to the grocery store. Knowing what you're eating every night ahead of time also means less money spent dining out.

Similarly, when you know you have something on the horizon, such as a birthday gift, you can shop around for the best deals. Because you aren't making a last-minute purchase, you aren't paying for convenience and forfeiting quality. Bonus: Planning ahead for an event also enables you to save for it a little bit at a time rather than all at once.

Here's how to make sure you have an eye on everything you may need a category for:

1. **Make a list of your fixed expenses.**

   Consider investing in a planner you can write in or using a calendar app.

2. **Add each expense on the due date within the calendar.**

   Look over your expenses to account for any irregular ones you may have forgotten about.

3. **Write down any upcoming appointments, birthdays, and social events that will cost you money and note how much money you'll likely need.**

   The calendar entries give you an idea of how much money you'll need to spend during the month to compare with your monthly income.

REMEMBER

You need to be aware of how much income you'll have so that you can accurately budget your categories. If your categories add up to more than your income, you may need to cut back on your upcoming spending.

TIP

Keep a running list in your Notes app of gifts you need to buy. When you know you need to buy a particular gift ahead of time, you're more likely to spend less money. List each recipient (by name), stuff they like, and the occasion so you're not racking your brain for the details later.

Reflecting on fixed and variable spending

Figuring out where your money goes and seeing where you want it to go can be empowering when determining your budget categories. Your fixed and variable spending can tell you a lot about yourself: your habits, preferences, what you value the most. If you value health, you probably spend money on healthy meals and maybe a gym membership. If your rent is a large percentage of your budget, that may be because where you live is important to you.

TIP

Speaking of rent, a good rule to follow is to not spend more than 25 to 30 percent of your take-home pay. If you live in a big city with high rent, don't feel bad that you're spending more than "recommended." You need shelter and can always balance your budget differently. If you want to aim for 25 to 30 percent, consider living with a roommate.

REMEMBER

Spending your money on experiences you value can help make you happier and more fulfilled. To get a sense of how your money reflects your values and, by extension, what are likely good budget categories for you, consider asking yourself the following questions:

- What am I spending my money on?
- Is my spending productive or helpful?
- Am I happy to see that I spent money on ____?

- What values does my spending reflect?
- What is my money saying to me?
- How do I feel about how much I spent on certain items?
- Do I get emotional when I think about my spending habits?
- Do I shop to make myself feel better?
- Do I hide my purchases from others?
- Am I an impulsive shopper?
- Do I spend more on wants than on needs?
- Do I often pay for convenience?
- Am I planning for my future?
- Is anyone in my life receiving financial assistance from me?
- Am I receiving financial assistance from anyone?

These are all great questions to get you started on your money reflection journey. Be sure to take breaks if you get overwhelmed thinking about where your money goes. Just trust the process. Work your way through so you can develop your financial categories appropriately to make your money work for you.

TIP

If you really want to get in touch with how you spend your money, start a spending journal. Every day, write down your expenses and any emotions or thoughts tied to them. You may be surprised at what feelings come up. For example, when we see a lot of Starbucks purchases in our budget, we know that we're physically exhausted. We use that information to cut back on coffee purchases and take time to rest properly.

Compiling a list of budget categories

You can split your budget among many different categories. Here's a list of some general categories and the kinds of expenses that may fall into them to get you started.

REMEMBER

You don't have to make your budget complicated. The categories that are listed here are just the tip of the iceberg. You may find that this number of categories is too many and want to make it simpler. Do what feels right for you and your money. The important part is that you stick to it.

» **Home**

- Mortgage or rent
- Property taxes and homeowners association fees
- Homeowners or rental insurance
- Warranties
- House maintenance such as landscaping, pool, and cleaning services
- House repairs
- Appliances
- Furniture
- Household decor
- Cleaning supplies
- Security camera services

» **Utilities**

- Electricity
- Water
- Your home's gas bill
- Trash pickup
- Internet
- Cellphone

» **Transportation**

- Gas
- Vehicle payment (if not listed under debt)
- Vehicle insurance
- Vehicle maintenance, such as oil changes and repairs
- Vehicle registration
- Public transportation
- Highway tolls
- Parking fees
- Rideshares such as Uber and Lyft

- **Food**
  - Groceries
  - Meal-prep services such as Blue Apron
  - Personal shopping services such as Instacart
  - Meal delivery such as DoorDash and Postmates
  - Dining out
- **Children**
  - Baby formula and food if outside of regular groceries
  - Daycare
  - Child support
  - Diapers
  - Clothing
  - Personal hygiene items
  - After-school care
  - School fees
  - School supplies
  - Gifts
  - Toys
  - Club or sports fees
- **Medical**
  - Medical, dental, and vision insurance
  - Co-pays
  - Flexible spending account or health savings account
  - Doctor visits
  - Dental exams
  - Hospital stays
  - Medical testing
  - Medications
  - Therapy sessions

- Medical supplies and equipment
- Supplements and other alternative medical visits

» **Pets**
- Pet food
- Veterinarian visits
- Medication and supplements
- Pet insurance
- Grooming such as nails and haircuts
- Boarding or pet sitting
- Cat litter
- Clothing and toys

» **Personal**
- Hygiene products
- Grooming services such as haircuts and aesthetician visits
- Massages and other spa visits
- Makeup and perfume/cologne
- Clothing
- Shoes
- Accessories

» **Entertainment**
- Streaming services like Netflix and HBO Max
- Media subscriptions such as Kindle Unlimited and Spotify
- Alcohol
- Admission fees
- Concerts and other performance shows
- Subscription boxes
- Supplies for hobbies
- Social outings with friends
- Video games and gaming devices
- Movie theater tickets

» **Party planning, gifts, and donations**

- Birthday gifts
- Gifts for special occasions such as weddings, baby showers, and graduations
- Holiday gifts
- Food and decorations
- Cards
- Wrapping paper
- Shipping materials
- Charitable giving
- Fundraising

» **Travel**

- Plane tickets
- Baggage fees
- Hotel accommodations
- House rentals
- Rental cars
- Local transportation
- Food
- Special outings
- Souvenirs

» **Insurance/future-planning**

- Life insurance
- Short-term and long-term disability insurance
- Long-term care insurance
- Caregiving
- Nursing or retirement home
- Estate and trust legal fees
- Burial expenses

- **Savings**
  - Retirement contributions
  - Brokerage accounts
  - Treasury bonds
  - College fund
  - Emergency fund
  - Moving expenses
  - Automobiles
  - House down payments
  - Weddings
  - Graduation (expenses not covered in other categories)
- **Debt**
  - Vehicle payments (if not listed under transportation)
  - Student loans
  - Credit cards
  - Personal loans
  - Medical debt
  - 401(k) loans
  - Payday loans
  - Title loans
  - Debt settlements
  - Court judgments such as restitution or alimony
  - Legal fees
  - Back taxes

Using the Right Tools

One of the key components of budgeting is to make sure you're using the right tools to track where your money goes. Whatever budgeting method you decide to use, you need to know in general where you're spending your money so you can allocate the proper funds for your categories. (For more on figuring out what categories to use, head to the earlier section "Determining Your Budget Categories.")

Tracking your money with budgeting software

An easy way to keep track of your budget is by using budgeting software that you download to your computer desktop or access online. When you use budgeting software, you can relax and have it do the calculations for you. Letting go of manually tracking every monetary transaction can help you free up mental space to focus on something else.

TIP

When picking out budgeting software, make sure it supports a budgeting method you want to try and will stick with in the long run. You also want to ensure the software doesn't share your private information with third parties.

REMEMBER

Don't forget to factor in any associated costs for using budgeting software. A lot of free budgeting software and apps are available, so you don't have to spend money to manage your money. But paid subscriptions to budgeting software and apps can unlock more features to help manage your finances and save money over time.

The budgeting software options in the following list all have downloadable apps from Google Play and the Apple App Store; however, the focus here is on budgeting programs that you can access online or download to your desktop.

- **YNAB (You Need a Budget; `www.youneedabudget.com`):** YNAB is a great software for zero-based budgeting because it stresses that you give every dollar a job. You can see your money all at once by linking the program to all your financial accounts. This overall budget snapshot can help you see whether your money is going where it should be.
- **Mint (`mint.intuit.com`):** Mint is an app but its software is great and has additional features you can use. Like YNAB, Mint has the ability to help you sync all your financial accounts. Mint automatically categorizes your expenses, so that's one less thing you need to do. It also tracks the bills you've paid and alerts you when you're going to be late with a custom setting you can put in place.
- **Quicken (`www.quicken.com`):** Quicken is one of the oldest players in the budgeting software game. It scans your transactions and assigns them to the categories you set up. You can assess your spending to see whether you're hitting your financial goals. Quicken offers a few different tiers of software so you can figure out which one works best for you.

- **Tiller (`www.tillerhq.com`):** If you love spreadsheets, Tiller is for you. The Tiller spreadsheets let you customize them in various ways to reflect your overall spending and daily account balances. You can access the spreadsheets through both Google Sheets and Microsoft Excel. Tiller is also great for couples. When you sign up for Tiller, you can link your and your partner's checking accounts to create shared spreadsheets. This setup enables you and your partner to stay in touch with each other's finances to work as a team.
- **Goodbudget (`goodbudget.com`):** Goodbudget is based on the envelope budgeting method. It makes virtual envelopes for all your budget categories and can help you plan ahead and pay off your debt. If you're budgeting with a significant other, you can share and sync with your partner's categories and see each other's spending in real time, which means you're less likely to go over your budgeted amounts as a couple.
- **PocketGuard (`pocketguard.com`):** Trying to figure out your finances for the first time can be challenging, so PocketGuard is great for college students. With this software, you can easily see how much money you have for whatever you need. PocketGuard negotiates your bills so you can save more money, which is an important life skill.

Looking at budgeting apps

If you don't have time for logging into software (see the preceding section), a budgeting app may be a great alternative. Every budgeting app is different, but they all have the same goal: to help you track your spending and save money. Budgeting apps are a convenient way for you to budget from anywhere. With real-time information, you can access your budget by tapping a few buttons on your phone.

Along with tracking your spending, each app has its own budgeting method. Different apps also allow you different ways to save money toward your financial goals. With some, you can set up automatic transfers into your checking account every time you make a purchase. Others find ways for you to cancel subscriptions and negotiate your bills. If you're finding it hard to remind yourself to transfer money into your savings account, these apps make it easy.

Apps can also pay your bills for you. Whether it's a push notification to pay your bills or being able to set up an automatic payment, an app can help you stay on track. This feature is great if you're new to budgeting or are forgetful. Paying your bills on time helps you avoid late fees or, even worse, service disconnection or disruption. (*Note:* You can link some apps to all your financial accounts, but others you can link to your checking account only.)

Another cool feature with budgeting apps is that they help you learn how to invest and give you opportunities to start investing. They're a great way for new investors to practice without spending much money. Investing is one of the key ways to grow your wealth, and the sooner you start, the better.

The following isn't a complete list of available apps, but it's one to get you started. All these apps are available to download from Google Play and the Apple App Store.

- **Simplifi by Quicken (`www.quicken.com/simplifi`):** If you like the idea of Quicken but don't like sitting down at your computer, don't worry. Simplifi by Quicken is an app that enables you to customize your budget and track your spending just like you can with the Quicken software discussed in the preceding section. The app also finds subscriptions you don't use and helps you cancel them. With features to also help you track your savings goals, it's an easy way to budget.
- **Fudget (`www.fudget.com`):** For a basic way to track your finances, Fudget can't be beaten. You don't have to create categories or eagle-eye your expenses. This app enables you just to keep track of your income and expenses so you can monitor cash flow. Fudget is also available from the Mac App Store and the Windows Store.
- **Honeydue (`www.honeydue.com`):** Are you managing money for the first time as a couple? If you and your partner are just starting your money journey together, Honeydue may be for you. You can sync your checking accounts to review purchases with ease and also coordinate bills with your partner. And it's free!
- **Qapital (`www.qapital.com`):** Qapital has two features to help you save money. One is *microsaving,* where the app rounds up your purchases and transfers the difference into a savings account. The second is an automatic transfer function that works whenever you spend. For example, if you grab a coffee to go, the app automatically transfers a dollar to your savings account.
- **Albert (`albert.com`):** Albert is technically a banking app, but the creators say it's more. This app lets you ask a financial expert for advice directly at no additional cost. You also get cash back when you use the app for your daily spending. And if you're new to investing, Albert helps you start. You just need one dollar.

REMEMBER

Budgeting apps aren't magic. When your app notifies you of a spending trend, you still have to put in the work to reevaluate your allocations or dive deeper into your spending habits. But using an app as a tool can make navigating your finances easier than doing it on your own.

Picking the right app for you

Just because budgeting apps are an easy way to stay accountable doesn't mean you don't have to put some thought and effort into choosing one. You still have to do research to figure out the right budgeting tool for you. When selecting your app, here are a few decisions to consider:

- **Your needs and goals:** Different budgeting apps provide different features, so clarifying why you're using one in the first place is important. Is it to help you remember to pay your bills? Do you need push notifications telling you you're out of money? Figuring out this motivation can keep you from downloading multiple apps that lack the features you need.
- **Style of budgeting:** You can find apps for every budgeting method, so don't feel you have to conform to zero-based budgeting if you're more interested in the pay-yourself-first method.
- **Ease of use:** The app must be relatively easy to use, whatever that means to you. Some apps are more difficult and time-consuming than others. Some won't have enough involvement for your liking. The bottom line is that you're most likely to stick to something if it's easy to use, so keep it simple.
- **Features and benefits:** Every app offers different features and benefits, such as paying your bills or providing cash back. Decide which options are most important to you and your lifestyle. For example, if you're not using credit cards to reap rewards because you're using cash envelopes, consider apps that give rewards.
- **New checking or savings accounts:** Although most budgeting apps enable you to sync to your existing checking account, some take it a step further by providing an opportunity to open a new account with them. Some of these accounts offer great perks, such as paying you interest like traditional high-yield savings accounts (HYSAs). Others let you open accounts with another person while using the app. Consider what ATMs these apps enable you to access for free or at least waive the fee for.

  WARNING

  If you open a new checking or savings account through an app, do your due diligence. Ensure the accounts are backed by the Federal Deposit Insurance Corporation (FDIC). Savings and checking accounts backed by the FDIC are insured up to at least $250,000 if something happens to the financial institution that the app is using. If an app's accounts aren't insured, proceed with caution.
- **Pricing:** Many, but not all, apps are free. Some budgeting apps charge a monthly fee, while others waive a fee if you open a checking or savings account with them. If the benefits of a paid app outweigh those of a free one, consider it money well spent.

Taking the DIY approach

If software and apps aren't for you, you may want to try a more do-it-yourself approach to your budgeting. By being as involved with your money as possible, you're more likely to take care of it.

One of the ways you can become more hands-on with your money is by writing your budget out in a notebook. You can list your income and then keep track of your expenses. Adding a category to each expense can help you keep an eye on your spending to ensure you stay under budget. Consider keeping a running ledger like a checkbook; you can see an example in Figure 2-1.

October — Wells Fargo Account

Date	Expense/Income with Amount Spent	Account Total (starting balance $537.80)
10/1	Netflix (-$14.99)	522.81
10/2	Spotify (-$17)	501.81
10/2	Paycheck (+$1,500)	2005.81
10/7	Starbucks (-$6.49)	1999.32
10/8	Target (-$75.67)	1923.65
10/8	Rent (-$975)	948.65
10/10	Venmo friend for takeout (-$20)	928.65
10/14	Sephora online order (-$36.45)	892.20
10/15	Uber (-$14.99)	877.21
10/15	Safeway (-$122.99)	754.22
10/16	Paycheck (+$1,500)	2254.22
10/20	Student loans (-$400)	1854.22
10/21	Electric company (-$79.55)	1774.67
10/22	Freelance payment (+$350)	2124.67
10/22	Starbucks (-$6.49)	2118.18
10/25	Internet (-$75)	2043.18
10/27	Amazon (Halloween costume) (-$59.33)	1983.85
10/28	Freelance payment (+$500)	2483.85
10/30	Hallow party supplies (-$43.67)	2440.18
10/30	Uber (-$35.66)	2404.52
10/31	Halloween candy (-$14.21)	2390.31
10/31	iTunes movie rental (-$5.99)	2384.32

FIGURE 2-1: A sample page from a budgeting notebook.

If you want to be more creative, you can make a budget binder. You can find free printable PDF worksheets online for your spending, income, saving goals, financial account login information, and anything else you want to keep track of. You can be extra colorful by using various pens and highlighters. A lot of people find success when they use this creative approach.

Paper can come with a lot to keep track of, including clutter. If you still want DIY budget tracking but don't want a bunch of paper floating around, consider making a digital spreadsheet. You can download a budgeting spreadsheet from Google Sheets or Microsoft Excel (see Figure 2-2). Each spreadsheet has embedded math formulas that calculate how much money you have left to spend in each budget category. Spreadsheets can also keep your finances organized with hyperlinks to different financial accounts.

TIP

If you aren't a spreadsheet pro, don't worry! You can still use spreadsheets without knowing fancy formulas. Pop "free budget spreadsheet templates" into your favorite search engine, and thousands of options pop up. Some require you to sign up for a website's newsletter, but you can always unsubscribe after you get your spreadsheet. You can personalize the income sources and categories for easier use to make your money work for you.

Taking advantage of your accounts' resources

Many banks and credit cards offer a spending analysis tool already built into your account. This free resource can be the most accurate way to scrutinize your spending, particularly with specific merchants. It's also an easy way to flag billing errors or fraud in real time.

Simply log into your banking or credit account to see what's available in your account's dashboard. If you can't find anything online, reach out to customer service to see whether the company provides some sort of tool or, if not, what outside option it recommends.

You can monitor not only your spending but also your cash flow and other items of your budget. This tool is great for visual learners because it formats your budget how you need to see it. Figure 2-3 shows you an example.

	A	B	C	D	E
1	**Net Income**	**$3,000**			
2					
3		**Budgeted Amount**			**Actual**
4		Dollars:	% of Income:	Dollars:	% of Income:
5	Rent	1200.00	40%	0.00	0%
6	Car loan	300.00	10%	0.00	0%
7	Utilities	250.00	8%	0.00	0%
8	Cellphone	90.00	3%	0.00	0%
9	Student loans	200.00	7%	0.00	0%
10	Transportation	100.00	3%	0.00	0%
11	Car Insurance	110.00	3%	0.00	0%
12	Groceries/Dining out	300.00	10%	0.00	0%
13	Entertainment	200.00	6%	0.00	0%
14	Personal spending	150.00	5%	0.00	0%
15	Miscellaneous	100.00	5%	0.00	0%
16	**Total**	**3000.00**	**100%**	**0**	**0%**
17				3000	100%

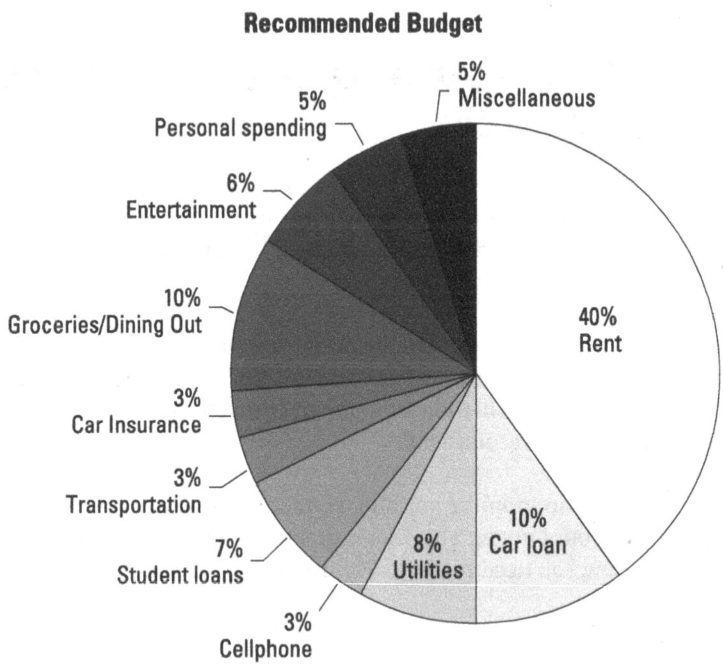

FIGURE 2-2: A Microsoft Excel budget spreadsheet.

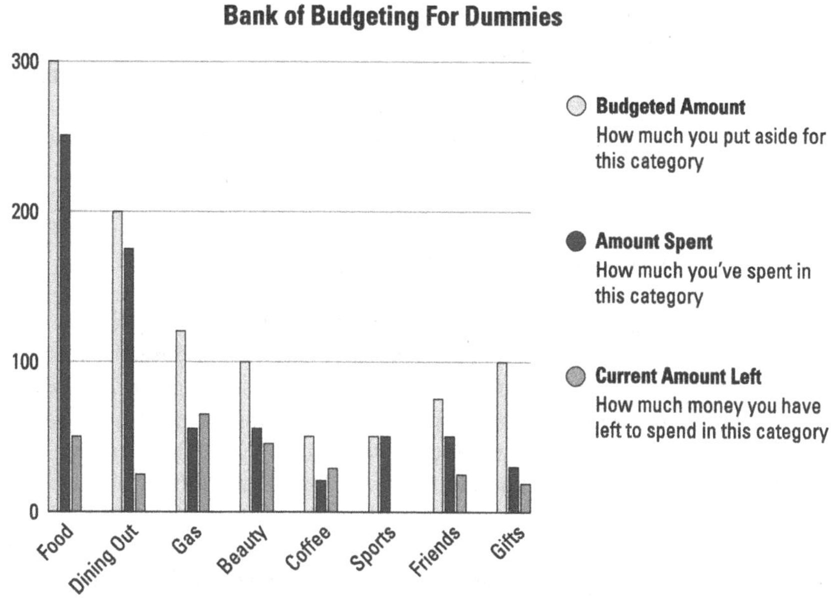

FIGURE 2-3: The result from a bank's spending analysis tool.

Practicing Makes Perfect

Think about budgeting like you would any new skill. It may be difficult at first, but over time it becomes easier to do. Practice makes perfect.

Figuring out how to budget and then sticking with it may be one of the hardest things you do when dealing with your finances. Even if it comes easily to you, you still need self-discipline. But after you put in the blood, sweat, and tears (well, hopefully not blood), the world can be your oyster. The following sections offer a few extra steps to help you ace your budgeting skills and feel liberated to take on your finances with confidence and less (or even no) stress.

Revisit your budget

No matter what budgeting method you choose to implement, regularly revisit it to see whether it's still working for you. Budgeting isn't a Goldilocks situation; the method that's just right for you today may not provide the structure you need down the road.

REMEMBER

Review your spending no less than once a month, even if you're staying within your percentages. This schedule is a way to see whether a bill or subscription price changed and make sure you don't have any erroneous or fraudulent charges.

Your regular budget review is also a great time to see how much progress you're making toward your financial goals. See whether you're on track to hit your target on time. If you're not, you can use this time to strategize to see where you can make a change. If you are making adequate progress, you can use this time to bask in your awesomeness.

Create a cash buffer

Another way you can keep your budget intact is by maintaining a *cash buffer,* an amount of money set aside to cover any bills or purchases that weren't in the budget. Keeping a buffer in your everyday checking account can also help you cover expenses you didn't plan for during a budget cycle and prevent stresses to your budget. For example, if you overspend on your groceries by $50 or your kid forgets to tell you about a field trip, your buffer can soften the blow.

You may say, "Isn't that what my emergency fund is for?" Well, no, not quite. Your emergency fund is strictly for emergencies — events you couldn't have planned for. You got a hole in a tire on the way home? Emergency. Is the dog sick and needs to go to the vet? Emergency. You want to go to a last-minute birthday dinner for a friend? Not an emergency, even though you really want to go. This expense comes out of your cash buffer.

WARNING

You should keep your cash buffer and emergency fund in separate savings or checking accounts from each other. Having your emergency fund in the account you use for everyday spending makes tapping into it way too easy, especially for overspenders.

How much your cash buffer should be depends on your everyday spending. You want it to be sufficient to cover those random expenses without leaving you strapped for cash. If you live below your means, you may be able to get away with having $100 to $200. If you have a family or spend more in general, consider saving at least $500. As you get a feel for your budget and spending, you can adjust the amount as necessary.

You can also practice goal setting by making creating a buffer one of your first financial goals. Whether you designate an amount or a percentage of your income, having a guideline in place can motivate you to get that cash buffer setup taken care of. And because it's a smaller goal, accomplishing it first can build momentum for other goals you have lined up in the queue.

TIP

If you need to, start small. Dedicate $10 or $20 per paycheck toward creating a cash buffer. Even a small amount can be enough to keep you from incurring an insufficient funds fee or dipping into your emergency fund.

Look for ways to make your system easier to follow

The best expert on you is you. You know what makes you feel frustrated or overwhelmed, and you also know when a system feels manageable and satisfying.

One of the ways to make your budgeting system easy is to approach it like you would a work project. Being realistic with how you see your finances can help you find a budgeting method you can easily follow. If an overall picture is easier to visualize than a bunch of tiny steps, use the pay-yourself-first method. If you need a lot of structure in life, try the zero-based budgeting method.

TIP

Another way to make your budgeting system easy is to allow for fun money. When you have money to do whatever you want, sticking to saving the rest is easier. Even if you can't think of anything fun you want to do or buy, still allocate for fun in your budget. The time will come when you want to use it, and having it ready to go will make your heart happy.

IN THIS CHAPTER

- » Understanding why good credit is important
- » Verifying the accuracy of your credit reports
- » Knowing how credit-related laws can help you
- » Disputing and correcting errors on your credit reports
- » Ensuring that your reports contain positive information

Chapter 3

Cleaning Up Your Credit Reports

We live in an information age. Instead of talking, we text, tweet, and Zoom. When we hear the word *Amazon*, we don't think of the rain forest in Brazil, but of a vast online shopping site where we can buy just about anything from just about anywhere. Today, you can research a new car, apply for a loan, and have the car delivered to your driveway without ever leaving the comfort of your couch. You and your couch may be in an apartment with a lease you applied for online, or in a house you refinanced through the Internet. All these relationships and transactions are increasingly impersonal and depend on the flow of vast amounts of information.

Your credit report is a critical part of that information, especially in financial transactions. When it goes right, we all benefit. But with billions of pieces of data floating around, errors can and increasingly do happen. You have a say in how you run your financial life and pay your bills, and that payment information should be reported accurately. Mistakes, misreported information, and identity theft or fraud all can affect your credit reports.

More and more financial decisions are being made from long distances by people who know you only from your credit file. In this environment, where your credit reports can make all the difference in whether you get a job, an apartment, or a loan, you must play an active part in ensuring your credit profile is as accurate as possible.

That's why knowing what's in your credit report and polishing it to its highest luster are vitally important. The tools are yours to use; you just need to know what and where they are. That's what this chapter is all about: helping you look your very best by polishing your credit reports.

Understanding the True Value of Good Credit

Banks and credit unions regularly review your credit profile and use the information largely to decide whether to approve you for a loan or to determine what interest rate to charge you. But banks and credit unions aren't the only ones with a legal right to check your credit report. Employers, landlords, insurance companies, and others are increasingly using the data in your credit reports to make all kinds of decisions, including whether to:

- Extend credit to you and on what terms
- Rent you an apartment
- Grant you insurance coverage or set premium prices
- Hire you for a new job or give you a promotion at work (although it's important to stress that your credit report may be used for employment decisions, employers never get credit scores)
- Award you a professional license in your line of work
- Qualify you for security clearance for your job or in the military

The people who make such decisions know that they're part of an increasingly litigious society. Discrimination on any basis can cost them massive court awards. Consequently, they use independent data — devoid of discrimination, favoritism, or prejudice — to support and validate their decisions. What does this mean to you? If you have negative items on your credit report, you may pay more for an apartment, an insurance policy, or a loan, or you may not qualify at all. That's why having a solid credit report is so important.

REMEMBER

The information in your credit report is a good predictor of future financial and nonfinancial behavior in your life. So if you're borrowing, looking for work or a place to live, seeking career advancement, renewing insurance, or getting licensed, you want to make sure that your credit information is accurate, current, and, yes, about you and not someone else.

WARNING

When you're desperate for a quick credit fix, claims from organizations saying, "We can fix your credit today," sound too good to be true. That's because they are. Predatory "credit repair" companies know that you're looking for any glimmer of hope. What they *really* do is take advantage of your desperation and lack of knowledge to separate you from your hard-earned money, while your credit report goes unchanged. The Federal Trade Commission (FTC) may have said it best: "Credit repair companies can't remove negative information that's accurate and timely from your credit report. Anything a credit repair company can do legally, you can do for yourself at little or no cost. Only time and a personal debt repayment plan will improve your credit."

Reviewing Your Reports for Problems

Discovering what's in your credit report really isn't hard, although the issues you read and hear can make it sound nearly impossible. But it does take a little time, some patience, and occasionally persistence. You don't need to pay anyone to monitor your credit or send you hourly updates on what's happening in your credit universe. You can do so on your own, and for free in most cases. You should watch for potential problems that could indicate you're a victim of identity theft, that information on your report has been confused with someone else, or that mistakes have been made that could cause your application to be declined or pay higher interest rates.

REMEMBER

In the last year, more than 3 million complaints about credit reports were made to the Consumer Financial Protection Bureau, so regardless of whether you find meaningful errors, it's still very important to check your reports, just in case you do. Your credit history is used to make an increasingly large number of decisions about your future, financial and otherwise, from lending to insurance to employment. You want to keep a close eye on your credit reports to make sure they're in good shape and ready to work for you when you need them.

TIP

To begin, arm yourself with the information in your credit reports (one from each of the three major credit bureaus), as well as your credit score from FICO, VantageScore, a lender, or a credit bureau. Along with the credit score, make sure you get a list of the "risk factors" that go with it. The risk factors give you specific information about what's having the most impact on your score from your credit report. The risk factors tell you exactly what to look for in your report to work on.

You almost certainly are not able to get the same exact score your lenders use for a number of reasons. Here are just a few:

- Lenders use hundreds of different credit scores, so the one you get probably won't be exactly the same.
- Lenders have different scores for different types of lending. For example, when you buy a car, the lender uses a score specifically for auto lending, but if you buy a house, the lender will use a score designed to predict the likelihood you'll pay the mortgage on time.
- You are getting your credit report and score at a different time than the lender. Scores reflect information in your credit report at the moment it's requested, so the numbers probably won't match.
- Your lender used a credit report from a different credit bureau to calculate the score. Differences in the credit reports can cause the numbers to be different.

REMEMBER

Don't get freaked out about not having exactly the same score as the lender. Even though the numbers don't match, what the number represents in terms of risk will be about the same. More importantly, the risk factors you get with the credit score tend to be very consistent. Address those factors and all your scores will get better. If you can't find out which score is used, any score will do to establish a benchmark of where your credit report ranks and then to track improvement.

As you study your credit reports, you may be surprised by how many accounts you find. Because your report lists negative information for seven years (with the exception of Chapter 7 bankruptcy, which lasts ten years) and open, active accounts with positive information for much longer, you can see accounts, referred to as *trade lines*, that you've forgotten about, and perhaps even some that you didn't realize you still had. Some creditors, such as retail stores, don't close accounts, even if you haven't used them in years. Your task is to play credit archeologist and sift through the trade lines — current and old, if not ancient — and identify any errors and inaccuracies you find.

Here's what you should look for in particular:

- **Verify that your name, address, birthdate, and Social Security number are correct.** Variations on your name are okay (for example, Stephen and Steve). With all the data moving through the financial reporting system, however, a Jr. or Sr. can easily be missed, or confusion over a II or III designation may occur.

REMEMBER

The variations you can find listed in your name, Social Security number, and addresses are not "mistakes." The credit bureaus list all the variations reported to them to accurately show what your lenders are reporting. If you find variations, the credit bureaus can help you identify the sources and get them corrected.

- **Look to see whether account activity is being reported correctly.** If you see accounts that are familiar but activity that isn't — such as a late-payment notation when you don't recall having been late — report that error to the credit bureau. An account you don't recognize may be a simple misposting of data from someone else's report, or it may be a sign of something more serious, such as identity theft. Contact the bureau and find out.
- **Look out for accounts from banks or stores with which you've never done business.** In the most serious cases, accounts you don't recognize could be a sign of identity theft. Or, it could be the result of someone else's account information being added to your credit report because of a misspelled name, a wrong address, or an incorrect Social Security number. Sometimes a merger or account purchase results in a new trade line showing up on your report. Store credit cards are often reported with the name of the bank that actually owns the account rather than the name of the store. Checking the back of your store card for the bank name can often solve a mystery account. Dispute the account using the instructions on your credit report if you aren't sure about it.
- **Identify and verify any accounts that show negative activity.** *Negative activity* can include anything from a missed or late payment to a charge-off (a debt a lender writes off as unlikely to be collected even though the debt is still owed) or bankruptcy notation. Make sure that this negative information is really yours and is accurate. Also, some negatives are much more serious than others. For example, a 90-day delinquency is more serious than a 30-day delinquency, even though both are negative. Recent negative items are more serious than older ones.
- **Be sure that an account that moved from one source to another is listed as open only once.** Bank and store mergers can result in multiple entries for the same account. Multiple entries can make it look like you have excessive amounts of credit available. Be sure the older account entries are listed as "closed" or have another status indicator that shows they're no longer the active entry.

TIP

If you make a correction to your file, the change may not be reflected in your credit report right away. The dispute process can take up to 30 days, so it could be a while before the updates appear in your credit report. The good news is that most disputes are completed in 10 to 14 business days, and often in just two to three days. Be sure to allow time for information to be updated if you're planning to apply for new credit. If you're already in the process of applying for a loan, ask whether your lender offers a rapid rescore product for sale. Developed by the three major credit bureaus, *rapid rescore* is essentially an unscheduled update to the information on your credit report. If a recent action (such as paying down a balance or closing a card) helps your credit score, then it can be expedited to the bureau as soon as it's made. The credit bureau can then update your file so that you can get an updated report and score in days, not weeks. Expect to pay $25 to $40 per account requested.

Using the Law to Get Your Credit Record Clean and Keep It That Way

Nowadays, you have expanded rights regarding access to your credit report, granting you more empowerment than perhaps at any other time in the modern history of credit. The Fair Credit Reporting Act (FCRA) and the Fair and Accurate Credit Transactions (FACT) Act both help you get the facts about yourself straight. This legislation can help you with tools to fight the growing crime of identity theft. Additionally, the Dodd–Frank Wall Street Reform and Consumer Protection Act offers safeguards to consumers.

TIP

To read the Dodd–Frank Wall Street Reform and Consumer Protection Act, go to `www.congress.gov/111/plaws/publ203/PLAW-111publ203.pdf`. To read the FACT Act, go to `www.congress.gov/108/plaws/publ159/PLAW-108publ159.pdf`.

In addition to requiring lenders and credit bureaus to play a greater role in protecting you, these laws promote consumer rights by enabling you to:

- **Receive your credit report for little or nothing.** You're entitled to a free copy of each of your credit reports once a year under the law. However, the three main credit bureaus have permanently extended a program that allows free weekly credit reports. You can get additional free reports if you believe that your identity has been stolen or if you've had an application declined or did not receive the best terms as a result of information in your credit file. The credit business refers to this as an *adverse action.* Some actions by lenders and some state laws entitle you to multiple free reports each year as well. Check with your state's attorney general's office to find out the laws in your state.

  If you've had adverse action taken, the lender has to tell you what credit bureau provided the report and how to get a free copy from that bureau. Here are the credit bureau websites for requesting a free report if you've been declined or had other adverse action taken within the last 60 days:

- **Equifax:** www.equifax.com/personal/credit-report-services
- **Experian:** www.experian.com/reportaccess
- **TransUnion:** www.transunion.com/credit-reports-disclosures/free-credit-report

» **Limit access to your credit report.** Only people and institutions with a need recognized by the FCRA — usually generated by an application with a creditor, insurer, employer, landlord, or other business — may access your credit report.

» **Have access to all the information in your file.** Ask and you shall receive. You must be given the information in your file, as well as a list of everyone who has recently requested access to it. Creditors are required to give you an early-warning notice and a free credit report or score if they place any negative information on your credit report. Your personal credit report includes "soft inquiries" that lenders don't get. So, you actually get more information in your report than lenders do.

» **Be informed if your report played a part in a negative decision.** People who use information in your credit file as a basis for denying you credit or a job or making an unfavorable rate decision for insurance must tell you that they used the information in your credit report to make the decision. They must also provide the following:

- The name, date, and numerical credit score used in the adverse decision
- The range of possible scores under the model used
- The key factors that adversely affected the credit score

» **Know if alternative data from artificial intelligence (AI) or non-credit bureau sources played a part in a negative decision.** Underwriting models that use AI technologies to automate credit decision making may enable lenders to evaluate other information about credit applicants beyond traditional credit bureau report data. So, under the law, although the creditor must disclose that it used alternative data in any adverse action (such as social media postings), it does not need to specify what the data was.

» **Dispute and have removed any inaccurate or outdated information.** After you file a dispute saying that your report contains inaccurate information, the credit bureau must investigate the items — usually within 30 days — and give you a written report of the investigation and a free copy of your credit report with the revisions made if the investigation results in any changes. If the reported information is later found to be valid, it can be reinserted into your report, in which case you must be given written notice of the reinsertion. The notice must include the name, address, and phone number of the information source. As for outdated info, information that is more than seven years old — ten years for some bankruptcies — should be deleted from your credit report.

TECHNICAL STUFF

The seven-year period for late payments starts from the *original delinquency date* (the date the account was first reported late). For charged-off accounts, the seven years starts from the date the account first became late and was never brought back to current. That can be a bit confusing. If the account isn't automatically removed, you may demand that it be updated. You may also provide documentation to support your request.

- **Place a statement on your report.** You may include a 100-word statement to explain extenuating circumstances or to note your disagreement with items on your report. Including a statement is especially important if you disagree with the results of a dispute. A dispute statement lets you tell your side of the story. For more about this statement, see the later section "Adding a 100-word statement."
- **Exclude your name from lists for unsolicited credit and insurance offers.** Although creditors and insurers may use credit report information as the basis for sending you unsolicited offers of credit or insurance, they must provide a toll-free phone number for you to call if you want your name and address removed from those lists. Such offers can be beneficial if you're shopping for credit. They expand opportunities for you from local banks to a national marketplace. You don't have to accept them — the most powerful word in credit is *no*. But if you're certain you don't want them, you can opt out.

TIP

You can have your name removed from prescreened offer lists from all three national credit reporting agencies by visiting `www.optoutprescreen.com`. If you prefer to call, the opt-out toll-free number is 888-567-8688.

- **Initiate a fraud alert by calling one of the three major credit bureaus.** If you believe that your identity may have been stolen, you just have to make one phone call or visit one credit bureau website (as opposed to contacting each of the three bureaus individually) to initiate an alert. A *fraud alert* warns creditors that you may be a victim of identity theft and requires the creditor to exercise enhanced levels of protection, such as taking additional steps such as calling you at the number you provide in the alert, to verify you are who you claim to be.
- **Freeze access to your credit report.** Freezing your credit report is easy to do and undo. It enables you to lock the door on reviews of your credit report if someone uses your identity to apply for new credit, until you first "thaw" access. A freeze does not prevent identity theft, but it may prevent someone from using your name to falsely apply for a new account after stealing your identity. You have no fee to add, lift, or replace a freeze on your credit report. Just don't forget to lift the freeze before applying or lose your PIN. If you do, your application can be stopped in its tracks.

» **Receive damages from violators.** If anyone violates the law, you can sue that person in state or federal court. Seek legal advice about whether suing makes sense. Some cases have resulted in substantial financial awards, into the millions of dollars, but it's usually much less.

» **Place an active-duty alert to protect your credit as a member of the military.** A business that sees an active-duty alert on your credit report must verify your identity before issuing credit in your name. The business may try to contact you directly, but if you're deployed, doing so may be impossible. Therefore, the law allows you to use a personal representative to place or remove an alert. Active-duty alerts are free, are effective for one year, and may be renewed. When you add the alert, your name is also removed from the nationwide consumer-reporting companies' marketing lists for pre-screened offers of credit and insurance for two years. So, you won't have to worry as much about someone getting credit in your name and running up debt while you're deployed and serving our country.

Identifying and Disputing Inaccurate Information

You can't legally remove accurate and timely info from your credit report, whether it's good or bad. But the law does enable you to request an investigation of any information in your file that you believe is outdated, inaccurate, incomplete, or fraudulent. You're not charged for this investigation, it won't hurt your credit scores, and you can do it yourself.

REMEMBER

Inaccurate data serves no purpose for anyone in the credit chain. The credit bureaus and lenders want the information in your reports to be accurate, just as you do. Accurate information helps lenders say yes to your application, which is what they really want to do — it's how they make money!

In the following sections, we show you how to file a dispute with the credit bureaus as well as with a particular creditor.

Understanding the dispute process

The process for disputing and correcting inaccurate information is simple. Your role is to check your credit reports at least once a year and before making a major credit purchase. If you see information that looks unfamiliar or wrong, you file a dispute with the credit bureau in question. See the later section "Contacting the bureaus" for details on how to notify them of your dispute.

After you notify a bureau of a disputed item, the bureau contacts the source that placed the data in your report. That source has 30 days to respond. If the source can't verify the data within the time allowed — because the information never existed, the info can't be found, or the dispute processing person doesn't hit the Send button — the bureau must remove the information from your report. If, on the other hand, the information is verified, it stays on your report. A third possibility is that the source tells the bureau the information should be updated in some way, which may not be exactly as you disputed. Regardless, you're notified in writing of any actions or nonactions that occur as a result of your dispute.

If you disagree with the findings, you can contact the company that placed the erroneous information yourself and try to get it changed. Be sure to ask how the investigation was conducted and who was contacted. You also have the right to add a statement to your report or to a specific trade line saying why you disagree. See the later section "Adding a 100-word statement" for details on how to write and submit a clear and concise statement.

TIP

If you place a statement on your report, be sure to keep track of the time it's on the report so that it doesn't outlast the negative data it explains and cause you further problems. Today, the bureaus automatically remove account-specific statements when negative information falls off, so it should happen without any action on your part. But it never hurts to check!

Correcting all your credit reports

The credit bureaus don't always have exactly the same information in their credit reports. So, if you look at your Experian credit report, see an inaccuracy, follow the dispute process, and have it corrected, you may not be out of the woods. TransUnion or Equifax may have *different* inaccurate information. Therefore, you need to get all three reports to make sure *all* your information is accurate.

If the same error appears on two or all three reports, you need to dispute it only once. If the source of the information makes a change as a result of your dispute, the source of the information has to tell the other bureaus about the change, too. But we recommend double-checking anyway.

Contacting the bureaus

Correcting all three reports is important, because some lenders and businesses purchase a three-in-one report that includes credit scores and credit history information from each of the three bureaus. Each bureau has slightly different procedures for filing disputes, but all three enable you to dispute inaccurate or out-of-date information by phone, by mail, or online:

- **Equifax:** Call the phone number provided for disputes on your credit report or call 866-349-5191, and be sure to have your ten-digit credit report confirmation number (on your report) available. You can also dispute by mail at Equifax Information Services LLC, P.O. Box 740256, Atlanta, GA 30374 (no confirmation number is required on written correspondence); or online at `www.equifax.com/personal/credit-report-services/credit-dispute`.
- **Experian:** You can dispute by phone by using the toll-free number on your credit report or by calling 888-397-3742; by mail at Experian, P.O. Box 9701, Allen, TX 75013; or online at `www.experian.com/dispute`.
- **TransUnion:** You can dispute information by phone at 800-916-8800; by mail at TransUnion Consumer Solutions, P.O. Box 2000, Chester, PA 19022-2000 (be sure to include the completed request for investigation form found on the website); or online at `www.transunion.com/credit-disputes/dispute-your-credit`.

TIP

Some people recommend that you write to initiate a dispute so that you can maintain a paper trail. Today, when you dispute online, the bureaus provide confirmation throughout the process. Saving or printing the documents along the way also establishes a paper trail for future reference. Either way, be sure to document your interactions.

Disputing online is faster, easier, and more secure than doing it via the mail. Think about sending a letter with all your identification, credit information, and other documents. How many people handle that letter and may be tempted to open it? When you dispute online at Experian, for example, you choose the items you want to dispute with the click of a mouse. You're walked through the process one step at a time. After you finish, you submit the disputes and any documents you upload to support them. You can print the report, the dispute "shopping cart," your documents, and confirmation to make sure you have that paper trail. And it's all free.

If you choose to dispute items on your credit report via mail, write a letter stating which item(s) you're disputing. Include any facts that explain your case, and include copies (not originals) of documents that support your position. Enclose a copy of your credit report with the items in question circled or highlighted. Be sure to provide your complete name and address and tell the company what your desired action is (correction or deletion). Send your dispute letter by certified mail, return-receipt requested, so you can document the fact that the letter was mailed and received. Keep copies of your dispute letter and enclosures.

AVOIDING A FRIVOLOUS DISPUTE

A credit bureau must investigate any disputed items in question — usually within 30 days — unless it considers your dispute frivolous, in which case it's required to notify you within five business days. The bureau must tell you why it considers your dispute frivolous and explain what you must do to convert the dispute to one that will launch the dispute process.

So what is frivolous? If you dispute the same issue exactly the same way multiple times, and the source of the information responds the same way each time, the credit bureaus can eventually declare the dispute frivolous. The credit bureaus and the sources of the information keep thorough records of the disputes that have been made and the results, so disputing the same issue over and over won't cause a different result.

REMEMBER

Make sure your dispute is very clear — for example: "I was never late," "The account is not mine," or "The account is fraudulent."

TIP

You can find a sample letter to a credit bureau that disputes information on a credit report at `www.dummies.com/go/creditrepairkitfd6e`.

Following through with creditors and the bureaus

The credit bureau must forward all relevant data you provide to the company that originally reported the information. When the company receives the request for verification from the credit bureau, it must investigate, review all relevant information, and report the results to the bureau.

- **If the information is found to be accurate,** the source notifies the bureau through which you disputed the information that there should be no change.
- **If the company can't verify the accuracy of the information you're disputing,** the information must be deleted from your file. The source of the information must then notify the other credit bureaus to delete the information, too.
- **If the disputed information is incomplete,** the source of the information will tell the credit bureau to update it. For example, if you were once late in making payments but your file doesn't show that you've since caught up, the source of the information will respond to the dispute telling the bureau that the account is now current and to amend your report to show that you're now on time with your payments.

» **If the information is being disputed as fraudulent,** the bureau will dispute it as such with the source, who will then have it deleted. If you have filed a police report or valid identity theft report, the bureaus can proactively "suppress" the fraudulent account and help you work with the source to update their records.

When the investigation is complete, the credit bureau must give you the written results and an explanation of the results or a free copy of your updated credit report if the dispute results in a change of information. (The bureau may refer to your request for an investigation as a *reinvestigation*; they're the same thing.) If an item is changed or removed, the bureau can't put the disputed information back in your report unless the company providing that information first verifies its accuracy and completeness. Then the credit bureau must give you written notice that includes the name, address, and phone number of the company that provided the verification.

You can request that the bureau send notices of corrections to anyone who received your report in the past six months. If you've applied for a job, you can have a corrected copy of your report sent to anyone who received a copy during the past *two years* for employment purposes.

If you aren't satisfied with the results of your dispute, you can dispute the item directly with the creditor (see the later section "Contacting the creditor"). In fact, the FACT Act requires creditors to initiate a dispute with the credit bureaus directly if you ask them to. Be sure to provide copies of all the information you have. You also have the right to include a 100-word statement of the dispute in your report and in future reports (see the later section "Adding a 100-word statement"). Depending on the bureau's rules, this statement can stay on your report indefinitely, so don't forget about it! When it's no longer relevant, contact the bureau to request that it be removed, if it hasn't been already. Today, such statements are usually deleted automatically, but it never hurts to check.

Knowing the rules on negative information

REMEMBER

When negative information in your report is accurate, only the passage of time can assure its removal. Here's how long information remains in your credit report:

» Open accounts in good standing remain indefinitely.

» Closed accounts with no negative information remain for ten years. This is good because the positive information remains longer than the negative information, and you won't lose the account history when you close an account.

» Late payments remain seven years from the date of the delinquency. If you get behind and never catch up, all the late payments and the charged-off account are deleted seven years from the late payment that led to the charge-off.

- Collection accounts are treated like a continuation of the original debt. They're deleted seven years from the missed payment after which the account was never again current on the original account, called the *date of original delinquency.* Federal law requires collection agencies to report that date and prohibits them from changing it.
- Chapter 13 bankruptcy is deleted seven years from the filing date because you repay part of the debt.
- Chapter 7 bankruptcy remains ten years from the filing date because you don't repay any of the debt.
- Student loan delinquencies that are brought current (up to date) are reported for seven years from the date of the first delinquency and then reported as current thereafter. If the loan is not brought current for seven years, the entire account is dropped from the credit report, and any subsequent positive information is not reported.
- *Inquiries* (records that someone requested your report) remain for two years from the date of the inquiry. Don't panic about them, though. If they have any affect at all on your credit scores, it will be very minimal and only for a few months at most.

TIP

If you're unhappy with the results of your dispute or think that you've been treated unfairly, contact the Consumer Financial Protection Bureau (CFPB) at `www.consumerfinance.gov/complaint`. They have a complaint system that lets you tell them what your issue is. The bureaus work with the CFPB to address those complaints.

WHAT TO DO IF YOU'RE NOT SURE ABOUT YOUR DATA

The law protects the dispute process from abuse, so you don't want to dispute information that you know is accurate or claim that an account listing is the result of identity theft when you know that's not the case. However, you can dispute any information in good faith if you're uncertain of its validity — in other words, if you can't find records that confirm the item, you don't recall the status, or you're simply uncertain that the information has been reported correctly.

Follow the dispute process outlined in this chapter and explain why you believe the item is questionable. Just as you may challenge a word that you aren't familiar with in a game of Scrabble, disputing information that you aren't completely sure about is okay. Disputing information that you know is correct, however, is *not* okay.

Contacting the creditor

Any financial institution that submits negative information about you to a major credit bureau has to tell you so. This heads-up enables you to jump on errors sooner.

You have a right to contact the furnisher of the disputed information directly. The contact process varies; it can be as simple as walking into the credit department and explaining the problem, calling the company's toll-free number, or visiting its website (many companies' websites have information on reporting fraud).

After you contact the creditor, it must investigate the dispute and report the results back to you following the same guidelines that the credit bureaus follow (see the preceding section), including responding within the same time frame as the bureaus.

Best of all, the creditor can't continue to report the negative information without noting that the info is in dispute. If the information that's been disputed was reported as the result of a possible identity theft, then it can't be reported at all while the investigation is pending.

WARNING

One bit of caution: Be sure the creditor tells the bureaus to remove the "account is in dispute" notation after your dispute is complete. Sometimes they forget, and the statement can stall matters such as mortgage loan applications until it's removed.

Again, as with the credit bureaus, the creditor must respond to your request within 30 days. If the creditor doesn't respond, the item in dispute is removed or corrected. If the creditor finds the information to be inaccurate, it must be corrected. If the information is outdated or belongs to someone else, it must be removed. The result must be submitted to each credit bureau with which the creditor has shared the incorrect information. If your dispute isn't found to be valid, you can add a 100-word statement to your report explaining why you dispute the item.

REMEMBER

Be sure to keep good records, including names, dates of contact, and copies of letters and emails. Any company can experience what is called *bureaucratic memory loss*. So, if you get a response such as, "We can't find this in our records; who were you speaking to?" you'll have the answer handy. Good record keeping on your part can keep delays and irritations to a minimum.

Adding Positive Information to Your Credit Report

Insufficient information on your credit report can also cause trouble. The best way to get positive information inserted into your credit report is to pay your creditors on time and in full every month. Do so for a year or more and you'll make great strides in improving your credit history and your credit score.

TIP

Called a *thin file* in the industry, a file that contains very little information may not be able to be scored. To get around this problem, you may be able to request that a FICO XD score be used. An *XD score* uses information from alternative databases (such as National Consumer Telecom and Utilities Exchange for cellphone, landline, and cable records along with LexisNexis for public record and property data) to get enough data to form a valid score. Most recently, FICO announced its UltraFICO score, which lets you include your checking and savings account history to help your traditional credit score. You can read more at `www.fico.com/en/products/ultrafico-score`.

The following sections cover ways to beef up your credit report.

Asking your landlord to report your rent payments

Your landlord can report your positive rent payments to help bolster your credit history. If your landlord doesn't know how to do that, give him information on the following organizations that can work with your landlord to have your rent added to your credit report:

- **eRentPayment:** `www.erentpayment.com`
- **RentTrack:** `www.renttrack.com`

Adding your own rent, utility, and cellphone payments to your report

Utility, insurance, and cellphone companies don't report positive information to the credit bureaus. If your landlord doesn't offer rent payment reporting, you can do it yourself using a rent reporting service. Some services require you to link your bank accounts so that rent payments can be tracked and automatically reported. Be sure to check them out thoroughly before doing this! Some services can report up to 24 months of previous payments. Be sure that any rent reporting services you use only report positive or on-time payments. Check your credit reports to make sure you see a new trade line about 30 days after you sign up.

Here are some payment reporters to get you started:

- **Experian Boost:** Experian has a service called Experian Boost, which lets you have your positive cellphone, cable, rent, insurance, internet, video streaming services, and utility pay added to your Experian credit report. The service is free and permission based, so if you change your mind, you can ask them to stop. You can read more about it at `www.experian.com/boost`.

  REMEMBER

  Experian Boost only reports payments on your Experian credit report. They won't show up on the reports from other credit bureaus.

- **Self:** Free for the basic rent-reporting plan, but the premium plan, which reports other utility payments, costs $6.95 per month. Self also offers loans, but they aren't necessary to get the rent reporting. You can read more about Self at `www.self.inc`.

- **Boom:** Charges $3 per month for ongoing reporting and a one-time $25 payment to include 24 months of past payments from your current residence. You can read more about Boom at `www.boompay.app`.

Opening new credit accounts

Another way to get positive information into your credit file is to open new credit accounts. Opening types of accounts that aren't already on your credit report is particularly helpful. For example, you may have several credit cards, so you could add an installment account, which can enhance your "type of credit used" profile.

ONLY IN CALIFORNIA

If you live in California and have entered into an apartment or property lease on or after April 1, 2025, California housing providers must offer to report positive rental payment information to at least one of the major credit bureaus at least once a year. Other states and cities are looking into or piloting similar programs. Check with your local housing department to see if landlords are required to report payments.

WARNING

Be careful when using this tactic to improve your credit score. You may do more harm than good. More debt may simply drive down scores, especially if you already have a lot of debt or are having difficulty paying existing debts. Also, do so well in advance of applying for a loan, because opening a new account may have a short-term negative effect on your score.

REMEMBER

Don't get carried away with this strategy. Applying for and opening a lot of new accounts in a short period of time is a sign of risk that can *hurt* your credit score. If you're not sure what to do, get a credit score and read the risk factors that go with it. Those factors can tell you if you need to open a new account or just pay down existing debts.

Adding a 100-word statement

Don't like what others are saying about you? You can add a 100-word statement to explain certain items on your credit report. Although a statement doesn't change your credit score, it may help answer questions that are raised when a lender or employer reviews your report. Yes, the score is important, but so is the analysis by the person looking at your record. Your statement can accomplish several feats:

- **Explain your side of the story for a series of late payments, collections, or charge-offs.** These may be due to a life event such as a job loss, divorce, or illness.
- **Document your dispute of information that you believe is incorrect but that the source of the information says should not be removed from your credit report.**
- **Tell your side of a dispute.** For example, you may have ordered a product that wasn't delivered on time or was unsatisfactory and refused to pay for it. Although the situation wasn't resolved in your favor, you may be able to explain it more clearly in your 100-word note.

TIP

You may be able to add more than one statement. Each bureau has its own policy. Experian lets you add several statements: a general statement giving an overview of your credit report woes, as well as individual statements for up to ten items. You may add more, but only after calling Experian. TransUnion lets you file 100 words or fewer in dispute and advises not to include personal, medical, or human trafficking victim status information in a consumer statement. Equifax allows one statement of up to 475 characters.

TIP

You can find a sample 100-word statement at `www.dummies.com/go/creditrepairkitfd6e`. Just plug in your info!

Do these 100-word statements really help? It depends on who reviews your credit report and what you say. The statement stays on your report for at least as long as the disputed item does, so take time to make your statement clear and concise. You can contact the bureau's customer service department for assistance with writing the statement if you need it. The online dispute systems also can help craft a strong statement. If you want to write, send your written statement with your credit report number (see the earlier section "Contacting the bureaus").

WARNING

If you decide to put a statement on your report, don't forget about it. In a year or two, negative information becomes less of a factor in your score, and eventually it drops off your report. Statements don't affect your score but can highlight past payment problems, especially if the credit report shows no recent delinquencies. Your outdated statement could call attention to situations that no longer apply and thus could hurt more than it helps. To remove an outdated statement from your credit report, reach out to the bureaus (see the earlier section "Contacting the bureaus").

One last bit of advice: Make sure your statement is a "statement of dispute" explaining why you disagree with the results of a dispute and why the information is incorrect. "Statements of excuse" aren't helpful. For example, if your statement says you left for vacation in Tahiti and forgot to mail your check, the lender's response would likely be, "We hope you had a nice vacation, but we still need the payment on time."

IN THIS CHAPTER

» Budgeting your money, not pinching your pennies

» Seeing savings as a reward, not a punishment

» Freeing yourself from debt

» Starting to save at any age

Chapter 4

Becoming a Saver

You know you have the will, the desire, and the need to save money — you just seem to be lacking the cash. What can you do? This chapter dissects your life and your spending habits (just a little bit). It shows you that adding more money to this equation isn't the only way you can ever increase the amount of cash you save. Although finding additional money is always nice, you can use a variety of methods to carve some savings out of what you already have.

Focusing on the Family Budget

REMEMBER

You can call it a budget, a financial plan, microeconomics, or a good excuse to pig out on a pint of ice cream every month. Still, whatever name you give it, the most important part of the family economic dynamic isn't *how much* money you have but rather how you *spend* it. By focusing your attention on budgeting, you can gain control over your family's finances and find that extra money you need to start saving.

The mechanics of your family's budget are fairly straightforward — you bring in a certain amount of money through work, entitlement programs such as Social Security or other pensions, or investments. From that income, you need to pay for the basic needs of your family — housing and utility costs, food, clothing, transportation, insurance, and so on. And you also need to pay for the frills your family has come to expect — streaming television services, vacations, and fancy gifts at birthdays and holidays.

While that sounds simple enough, you often find that your family's needs and expectations slightly exceed your monthly income. While you may always intend to push money into your savings, you may sometimes find that you come up short at the end of the month. If you're thinking that saving money is impossible, put that pint of ice cream back in the freezer and check out the following tips on how to dig for the dollars you need in your monthly budget to jump-start your savings program.

Eliminating most of the fat

Your knee-jerk reaction to trying to tighten your budget may be to cancel all television streaming, clamp down on cell phone service, or start looking for a smaller house or apartment.

Before adopting tiny house living for the family, take a giant step back and look at the big picture. You need to know how much money you have coming in, how much is going out, and where that money is headed. To find all the numbers you need, flip to Chapters 1 and 2 in Book 1. With that information, you can see where your money goes and how much of it you actually fribble away.

WARNING

With your income and current spending patterns laid out in front of you, you probably won't have any trouble spotting the expenditure items that are really, really wasteful. Right at the top of the list are bank and finance charges. You may consider these charges to be minimal, but adding those minimal costs up can be another story. Check out the following examples of potential fees you could face, depending on how you manage your money:

- **Minimum balance penalty:** Some banks assess fees if your checking account carries a balance below the minimum for the month. For example, if your checking account balance drops below $750 in any month (even $749), your bank hits us with a $14 per month fee.
- **Insufficient funds penalty:** We don't know of any bank that doesn't slap a fee of at least $35, if not more, on bounced checks.
- **Credit card interest:** Carrying a balance on your credit card can cost you between 10 and 20 percent (or more) per year for the loan of that money in interest alone.
- **Late-payment fees:** If your payment doesn't arrive on time, it'll probably cost you at least $20 for the month. (Late payments also decrease creditworthiness and increase the cost of later loans to you.)

Table 4-1 illustrates how these fees can add up for a typical family.

TABLE 4-1 Examples of Truly Wasteful Spending

What You're Paying	Monthly Amount (Good Credit History)	Annual Amount	Monthly Amount (Slightly Flawed Credit History)	Annual Amount
Bank finance charges	$14	$168	$20	$240
Credit card interest	$25 ($3,000 debt at 10% a year)	$300	$83.33 ($5,000 debt at 20% a year)	$1,000
Late mortgage payment	$80 (5% of $1,600 payment)	$960	$100 (5% of $2,000 payment)	$1,200

Not only can bank and finance charges waste your money, but consider the following examples:

- Paying health club dues to a club you haven't attended for over a year
- Continuing a newspaper subscription that you just haven't gotten around to canceling (and that includes online subscriptions, too)
- Hitting the coffee shop for a cup o' joe in the morning because you don't get up early enough to make your own
- Going out for dinner or lunch rather than eating at home

REMEMBER

Wasteful spending can be curbed if you take the time to assess your spending. We're not advocating punishing your family by getting rid of a health club membership, but we're suggesting ridding yourself of expenses that you don't need or put to use. Add up what you "waste" each month. Start getting payments in on time, maintaining the minimum balance in your checking account, making coffee at home, or canceling memberships or subscriptions that you don't use so that you can begin saving money.

Reorganizing what's left

If you've crossed off all the wasteful spending, or if you had no wasteful spending to begin with, you can still lower your total expenses each month. Check out what's left of your expenses and see whether you can take advantage of additional ways to save that are discussed in the following sections.

Lowering your debt

The biggest piece of most budgets is the amount folks pay to their mortgage company, their car finance company, and their credit card companies. Many people are surprised to find that they pay more than they need to in many of these areas. Check out the following ways to reduce your monthly debt:

- **Consider refinancing your house.** Look at your current housing, car, and credit card payments. You may be able to consolidate all these loans into one mortgage and leave your mortgage closing with one monthly payment that's significantly less than the total of all debt payments you have been making. While this isn't true in every case and is dependent on interest rate fluctuations and the current value of your house, it's certainly worth an afternoon or evening of your time to investigate. Keep in mind, though, that only the mortgage interest that's related to the original purchase price of your house plus the cost of improvements and repairs is deductible, but the ability to drop a credit card interest rate from 20 percent to 5 percent, even without the tax deduction, is well worth it.
- **Consolidate your student loans.** If you're currently paying off student loans and haven't yet consolidated them, you may find that now is the time. Depending on the amount you owe and current interest rates, you may be able to lower your monthly payment significantly.
- **Liquidate your assets.** Another way to lower debt payments is to liquidate assets that you may have and pay down your debt. For example, if you have shares of stock that aren't increasing in value, it may be well worth selling the stock and paying off your credit cards. Other assets that you may want to consider liquidating are some of the household items you've inherited from Great Auntie Marge — Do you really need that sterling silver flatware set? — or perhaps your comic book collection.
- **Lower your credit card interest rate.** If you can't retire your credit card debt entirely, negotiate with your credit card companies for lower rates. You need a history of timely payments; one late payment will muddy the water considerably — two or more, and they'll probably just laugh. If your current company won't negotiate, go shopping. Many banks are eager for your business, often with introductory rates as low as 0 percent for three, six, or nine months. Transfer your high-interest balance and pay it off before the introductory rate expires.
- **Trade down when you trade in.** Take a close look at your car and the size of your car payments. Consider something less than a Mercedes when getting a new vehicle, even if the dealer says you can afford it. The dealer is trying to put their kids through college, but your responsibility extends only as far as you and your family — not theirs. Alternatively, if you absolutely must have that Mercedes, you may try looking for a used car rather than a new one.

Nothing says wasteful spending more than watching the value of your new car shrink as soon as you drive it off the new car lot.

- **Consider debt consolidation.** If you're *really* burdened by debt and can't find *any* reasonable way out (robbing a bank isn't reasonable), making an appointment with a reputable credit counselor isn't the worst idea. Counselors can often negotiate deals with your creditors that you won't be able to get on your own, and through their services, you may be able to eliminate hundreds of dollars from monthly credit card and other loan bills. If you consider this option, note that this may damage your creditworthiness. Of course, it may also help: If you're so deeply in debt that you need to consult with one of these services, you're probably also missing payments, making late payments, and otherwise messing up your credit rating. In the long run, your creditors will likely be relieved to see you gaining some control over your finances. (See Chapter 3 in Book 3 for more information.)

Trimming other costs

Clearly, you need electricity, water, phone service, heat, and so on. And, for most of you, these costs are not negotiable — the utility companies have cultivated a world of monopolies, and in most cases, no bargains are to be found as far as price per unit goes. However, you may be able to reduce costs within your own household, and these are well worth exploring.

TIP

Here are a few ideas to get you thinking about ways you can reduce other monthly costs:

- **Ask for a lower rate.** Phone, internet, and energy companies are highly competitive. Don't hesitate to shop around and ask your current company to meet, or beat, a competitor's lower price.
- **Pay for only what you use.** Don't pay for more cable and/or streaming service than you need or can use. Cut back to a place that still provides the programming you want but doesn't give you many extras you rarely use. And don't be afraid to cancel your cable service if the cable company isn't willing to lower the price. The cable companies are so desperate to retain you as a customer that they will slash their monthly rate the minute you say, "Cancel my service."
- **Practice energy conservation.** Upgrade your house with energy- and water-efficient appliances and improvements. Many of these have small upfront costs (energy-efficient light bulbs and low-flow toilets, for example) but pay off in huge savings over their lifetimes. There are currently credits and rebates for energy improvements to your home.

- **Comparison shop for insurance.** Seek out the most competitive price for all your insurance needs — life, disability, homeowners/renters, car, and medical (if you pay for your own). Just because you've been a loyal customer for years doesn't mean your current company will reward you. In fact, the opposite is usually true, and you can often find comparable, or even better coverage at a lower price from a competitor.
- **Take a hard look at your discretionary spending.** You may not believe how much the $2.99 here to play this online game, $14.99 to rent that new movie that just came out, or the multitude of handy-dandy items that come to us in the mail almost every day from online merchants add up. It all seems like chump change while we're spending it, but at the end of the month, those hundreds, or even thousands, of dollars really add up, and it's hard to figure out what you actually purchased.
- **Trim the grocery bill.** You can reduce your grocery bill by using coupons, store affinity cards, and shopping sales. Also, don't forget that house brands are almost always less expensive than national brands, and the quality remains the same for many items. Just because you've always used a certain brand doesn't mean you have to continue to use it. The manufacturer won't punish you for disloyalty. Note that fresh fruits and vegetables have a season; when you buy in season, the quality is better, and the price is lower, too. If you must have out-of-season produce, frozen is a more cost-effective and nutritious option.

REMEMBER

You can be most successful in your trimming program if you don't slice and dice costs willy-nilly. If you're content with how you're living right now, cutting out the funds to do the activities you love will only create a savings ogre that sucks the joy out of your life in exchange for money in the bank.

Changing Your Perspective and Watching Your Savings Grow

Saving for any purpose, whether for education, retirement, a new home, or that dream vacation of a lifetime, isn't a punishment, nor does it need to be a deferral of pleasure. Some people (and you all know someone like this) squeeze every penny until it squeals and never seem to have any fun. Who can forget Ebenezer Scrooge, after all? He began to live only after he stopped clutching his money quite so tightly. And he is, of course, the epitome of the saver — the miser.

Well, he's a fictional character, and plenty of savers out there still know how to have a good time. And maybe they even have a better time because, at the end of the evening, they know they have the money to pay the bill.

REMEMBER

Saving money can and should be neither painful nor pleasurable; it should just be. You should view putting cash into your savings plans and accounts the same way you view paying your other bills. While it doesn't thrill us to pay bills, we do have real satisfaction knowing that all our bills are paid in full and there's still money in the bank.

Paying yourself first

TIP

You've probably heard this advice more than once but never put it into practice: Pay yourself first. As you look at your income, you should carve a portion out and earmark it for savings.

That money needs to be physically segregated from the rest of your income (so you're not tempted to dip into it, even a little, for that extra something you've wanted to buy). Only after you've subtracted it and put it elsewhere should you figure out how much money you have available for all your other expenses, which need to fit into this smaller amount. If, after putting aside your savings amount, you can't pay the rest of your monthly bills, you need to change something — find a cheaper mortgage, eat out less frequently, or buy fewer books. The choice is yours. The only item not on the table for negotiation is your savings amount.

Systematically saving

You can successfully save if you put the same amount of money into some sort of savings account each and every week or month (depending on when your income is paid to you). Even if the periodic amounts may seem small to you, Table 4-2 illustrates how those savings can add up to considerable nest eggs at the end of one, five, ten, or twenty years.

TABLE 4-2 Systematic Savings (at 1.5 Percent Interest, Compounded Daily)

Amount per Week	1 Year of Savings	5 Years of Savings	10 Years of Savings	20 Years of Savings
$10	$534.00	$2,711	$5,623	$12,144
$25	$1,335	$6,788	$14,057	$30,359
$50	$2,671	$13,556	$28,113	$60,718
$100	$5,341	$27,111	$56,227	$121,436

Earmarking certain pieces of income for savings

Most people not only receive their normal income, paid at regular intervals, but they also have periodic injections of additional cash, whether it's in the form of overtime wages, significant salary increases, holiday bonuses, gifts and/or inheritances, or even income tax refunds.

If you are doing your job and dissecting your budget, you probably already figured out how to live comfortably on what you earn regularly, and you're hopefully saving systematically and regularly.

TIP

So, what should you do when a little extra money comes your way? Of course, from where we're sitting, the answer is obvious. Save, save, save. You figured out how to live nicely without it, and you won't miss it, so put it in a safe place and forget about it!

Ah, but we can see ideas of a vacation, a new piece of jewelry, or redoing the kitchen dancing through your head. Obviously, if your household budget hasn't included money for some glaring need (perhaps your roof is leaking) and you've just been waiting for some extra cash to pay for that project, you can divert at least some of that money for that purpose. But if you've managed to pare your spending to a place where you're managing beautifully with what you have, take a big chunk of that extra money and sock it into your savings plans. What's out of sight is also out of mind, and these additional funds may be just the ticket to beef up a somewhat anemic education savings or retirement account.

Educating yourself about investing

No question about it: The world of investing can be a scary place, and the days when stockbrokers did your buying and selling have mostly gone the way of record albums and 8-track cassettes. Investing is now a do-it-yourself operation that can present many pitfalls for the unwary. Before you even think about sticking your big toe in the investing pool, you need to make sure you have a handle on the following.

Know what you're buying

REMEMBER

Your success with any investment rests squarely on your understanding of what you're buying. Know what you're paying for, whether it's an individual stock or bond, a mutual fund, or even a certificate of deposit. You wouldn't purchase an orange without first making sure it wasn't rotten; don't assume that every security being sold and touted by the so-called experts is as solid as Fort Knox. Do your own research and make your own decisions.

Understand and be able to live with risk

After you move beyond bank savings accounts, certificates of deposit, and mutual fund money market accounts, you enter the world of ever-increasing risk. Whether you invest in individual securities or in mutual funds (which are nothing more than pools of individual securities), the price of those securities can rise (which you hope for) and also fall (which you dread).

Risk is inherent in the investment world. Whether you buy small pieces of companies (stocks or equities) or lend companies and/or governments money (bonds or debt instruments), your money is only as secure as the company or companies you tied it to and the general economic conditions in both the United States and around the world.

WARNING

And then you have digital currency (cryptocurrency or just *crypto*), which is completely unregulated and rises and falls upon the whims of the markets. Of all investment types, digital currency probably carries the highest risk/reward variable, which also means that when it crashes, the effects on your savings will likely be catastrophic.

When it comes to risk, if you can't even contemplate that your savings may be worth less next week, or even next year, than they are today, you may want to reconsider plunging your money into a junk bond fund. (Junk bonds, often referred to as "high yield bonds," are loans to companies Wall Street has serious doubts about, so they're considered risky.) Instead, you may want to consider a mutual fund that purchases nothing but U.S. Treasury bonds and notes (very, very safe).

REMEMBER

If you own an investment that's keeping you awake at night, there's no crime in selling it, whether at a profit or a loss. Even if you don't sell a security at its absolute height, you need never apologize for making a profit. Likewise, if your investment is leaking value, note that this isn't a sinking ship, and you're not the captain. Jump overboard and live to invest another day.

Balance risk and expectations against future monetary needs

Not every great investment is a great investment for you. If you want to gamble on which company will be the next Microsoft or IBM, you need to have the luxury of time to allow that company to develop and grow. You may need to be patient; many start-up companies struggle initially, and the big payoffs, if they do develop, develop over time.

If you need to make that next tuition payment in the not-so-distant future (within the next five years), you may want to temper your level of risk, keeping a larger portion of your savings in cash and cash equivalents such as money market funds or certificates of deposit. We're not saying you can't invest your teenager's college savings funds in Wonder Widget, Inc. However, you may want to only invest a small portion of those savings and keep most of your money invested in less risky ventures.

Identify the cost

Just because you invest directly with a mutual fund company or through an Internet brokerage doesn't mean you avoid paying anything for the privilege of investing your money. Face it: People aren't in this business for their health; they're in it to make money. And they make a lot of it. And as far as purchasing individual securities, the cost of each transaction is usually right there on your confirmation slip.

Still, identifying exactly what a mutual fund costs you may be difficult because the management costs may be buried deep inside the prospectus. Search for it. A company may charge its fee based on a percentage of the value of the assets within a fund or a percentage of income collected. Know how the fees in your accounts are calculated, and then factor that into the total return for that fund.

REMEMBER

Choose your mutual funds carefully. It's not only share price decreases that can cause you to lose money; excessive fees paid can also eat into your savings. Also, be aware that if you're paying someone else to manage your savings, you may be paying fees to more than one player. You could be paying a fee to your financial advisor and a fee to the mutual fund companies in which your advisor invests your money. Every fee takes a slice away from your savings — the more fees you pay, the worse your return will likely be.

Read the fine print about total returns

Every mutual fund company offers literature about how well its fund has performed against other similar funds and about the percentage of increase (or decrease, but those numbers tend to be in much smaller print) the fund has realized over time. The literature probably also touts the expertise of the fund manager (who chooses what to buy and sell within the fund).

REMEMBER

Unless your fund's manager is an expert crystal-ball reader, these numbers are of historical value only. Mutual funds tend to follow the trends of the overall stock and bond markets, and their fortunes rise and fall in concert with the markets. Past performance isn't an indicator of how the fund will do for you, and the bygone wizardry of a fund manager may never be repeated.

Taking advantage of giveaways

You get something for nothing very few times in life, and money-back offers from credit cards and from retailers may or may not qualify as one of those times for you. Still, if you can take advantage of an offer without spending any additional money to do so, well, you would be foolish not to.

Credit card offers

Certain credit cards offer a rebate equaling 1 percent of your total purchases toward a Section 529 plan for you or your child(ren). Sometimes, the rebate is higher for various purchase categories, such as meals at particular restaurants or gas for your car. This plan may be in addition to, or instead of, other incentives that credit cards often offer, such as air miles, travel insurance, rental car insurance, and double warranties.

WARNING

You may want to avoid this offer if you don't handle credit cards well. The one percent incentive can be more than swallowed up by any interest or other fees the credit card company can charge you.

On the other hand, if you use a credit card anyway, you may want to investigate changing card companies to avail yourself of the offer. Doing so won't put your child through school. However, every dollar someone else puts into your savings plan is one less dollar you need to find.

Upromise and `Backer.com`

In a unique twist on the credit card rewards theme, Upromise provides a service that signs up retailers, manufacturers, restaurants, and various sorts of service providers who gift a percentage of your spending into a general account maintained by Upromise. The funds in these accounts can then be invested in a Section 529 plan. For example, a major gasoline company may offer you one cent per gallon, an office supply store may give 2 percent of your total purchases, and the return on a new car or home can be in the hundreds.

Granted, these are all small amounts by themselves, but just as your small weekly savings deposits add up over time, so do these. Your savings could be substantial depending on how many of the associated stores and products you use and how much you spend. You can find out all the details on the Upromise website at `www.upromise.com`.

`Backer.com`, on the other hand, is a way for a group of people to save together for one or more designated students. If you come from a family that tends to give cash gifts to children for savings as opposed to actual presents, Backer.com provides a platform where all your friends and family can chip in what's comfortable for them when it's convenient and/or important to them. There is a small monthly fee to set up your child's 529 plan through Backer.com, but as you find in later chapters, there is an administrator fee for every 529 plan. This one is just a bit more transparent. (For more information on 529 plans, see Chapter 6 in Book 2.)

Dealing with Debt

Your debt is probably the biggest hindrance when it comes to your plans for saving money. You may find it difficult to justify putting money into a college savings or retirement account when you feel swamped by debts that need to be paid, and you may feel like you need to pay off all of your debts before you begin saving for anything. Fortunately for you, you don't need to eliminate all debt before you begin to save. To show you how to save money while drowning in red ink, discover the difference between good debt and bad debt and begin saving right now, regardless of your debt situation. (See Book 3 for more details on handling debt and credit.)

Understanding good debt and bad debt

The good news: Some types of debt are good, are factored into your monthly budget, and shouldn't hinder you from saving. The bad news: Some types of debt are bad and should be paid off as quickly as possible; their presence in your life will effectively stop you from saving for anything.

Clearly, you're not planning on paying off your entire mortgage before you start saving. And you probably feel the same about your car payment, which is factored into your budget as a transportation cost, and any student loans that you may still have outstanding.

REMEMBER

Even after you finish paying off the loan amounts for your house, vehicle, and education, those items should still have value to you. And from a creditworthiness standpoint, because most credit rating companies expect you to have some form of this debt, the fact that you have these sorts of loans actually makes you more attractive as a potential borrower than having no loans at all (provided that you make your payments on time). This is *good debt:* debt you plan for, budget for, and manage appropriately.

On the other hand, your credit cards (if you carry unpaid balances from month-to-month), your rent-to-own accounts, your layaway accounts, and all your so-called consumer debts are considered bad debts. You should reduce or eliminate them if possible. (See the earlier section "Eliminating most of the fat" for ways to reduce and/or eliminate your debt.)

Consumer debt is money you have borrowed to purchase something that is either a consumable (such as groceries) or something that has a very limited life (such as last year's clothes that your teenager won't wear this year because they're no longer fashionable). Basically, after you buy items in these categories, they cease to have any monetary value.

Now, we're not saying you shouldn't buy food, clothing, or even that new television set. You do need to eat, after all, and watching television is still a relatively cheap form of entertainment. What you shouldn't be doing, though, is borrowing money to satisfy these needs. And that is exactly what you do when you carry balances on your credit cards. You're paying interest not only on last night's dinner but also may still be paying for last year's holiday gifts and your wedding dress from ten years ago.

WARNING

However you dig yourself out from under your debt, you also need to break your credit card habit. Stop thinking that just because you still have credit available, you should be free to indulge in anything that crosses your path. If you can't use your cards responsibly and pay them off in full every month, then it's time to make a plastic salad. Sliced and diced credit cards in a glass bowl can make an attractive focal point in a room and also serve as a powerful reminder of spending habits run amok.

Saving while in debt

Being in debt won't preclude you from saving, but it makes doing so more difficult. The following strategies can make saving more manageable even while you start paring down your debt.

- **Understanding the difference between needs and wants:** *Needs* fulfill a necessary function ably but *wants* add other elements — at a price. For instance, you need a new television. The television you need is the one tucked away on the bottom shelf: 32 inches with a flat screen and a remote. But the one you want is on center display: it has every possible bell and whistle available today, and the picture is, well, so sharp that everyone oohs and aahs over it. The first television costs $150; the second setup is a whopping $4,000, and that's before the soundbar, the necessary cables, and the wall mount. Buying the one you need will likely make you just as happy, fulfills your need for a television, and ensures that you don't break the bank or borrow money for it (such as using your credit card) and have to pay it off in installments.

REMEMBER

As you slice away at your consumer debt and hopefully finally retire it, nurture the habit of looking at every potential purchase and expenditure from a need-versus-want perspective. Although denying yourself everything that you want may, in the end, be self-defeating and make you miserable (you're not a monk, after all, and never took a vow of poverty), constant self-indulgence can prove equally disastrous.

- **Discovering to defer gratification until you can afford it:** No matter how badly you want that new television (whether the stripped-down or deluxe version), don't buy it until you've saved enough to pay for it. Most folks see a television as a necessity, but doing without for a period of time won't kill you. You may actually use the extra time you have to rediscover old hobbies, visit with friends, or otherwise spend time pleasurably. When the time comes to plop your hard-saved cash down on the store counter, you'll likely be more pleased with the less expensive TV than you would be with the bells-and-whistles model that you paid for with your charged-to-the-max piece of plastic.
- **Using credit as a tool, not a weapon:** Consumer credit is not, by definition, a bad thing, and used properly, it can be a valuable tool. Paying for purchases using credit cards negates the need to carry large amounts of cash. Also, it enables you to pass unbothered through the checkout line at the grocery store, and at the end of the month or the year, you get an easy way to track your spending habits. Use it improperly, though, and it becomes a weapon that destroys your finances and demolishes good intentions.

REMEMBER

Be responsible: If you can't pay your credit bill in full every month, destroy your cards and use cash instead. Budgeting cash enables you to insert a line item for savings.

Saving for College throughout the Ages

Saving money for college, beginning the instant you know you have a child on the way, is certainly the most effective approach. However, if you couldn't or didn't save money for your child's education back then, you may be behind in the savings game.

REMEMBER

But it's never too late to begin saving for your child's education. The following sections discuss the best ways to start saving today for your children's education, regardless of their age. See Chapter 6 in Book 2 for full details on saving for college.

Beginning at, or even before, birth

Saving for future events in your child's life should begin no later than the day they are born, and many people are starting accounts for this purpose during pregnancy or even as they start trying for a baby, but you shouldn't be the only one putting money away for that purpose. Your child eventually can help fund their college accounts, too. Use the occasion of your child's birth to open up one or more college savings plans and an account in your child's name, into which you can deposit any gifts they receive at birth. You can add birthday gifts and other such sums to it regularly until your child is old enough to begin making their own deposits. You find no better way to show your child the benefits of saving than to have a ready-made example with their name on it.

WARNING

Putting small sums of money aside in your child's name (with you as custodian) is great, but you may want to consider depositing larger sums into an account in *your* name (perhaps as trustee for your child but using your Social Security number to open the account) or even using that money to start a Section 529 plan for your child. Teaching your children about money is key if they're to become successful adults. Still, if your child will need any sort of need-based financial aid down the road, the value of the accounts held in their name will be counted more heavily than one in your name. The assumption here is that all the money your child earns and has is available for their education if that child is still your dependent, whereas only a much smaller portion of your assets should be used for your child's education costs because you have many things you need to be saving for, such as the education of other children and, of course, your own retirement.

TIP

While your child is still young, you may want to consider investing in high-growth stocks instead of bonds or even money market funds. True, the risk is higher than other sorts of investments, and you may see your value drop periodically. However, time is on your side; traditionally, money invested in the stock market has outperformed other investments. If you have the time (usually anything longer than five years) and a stomach that can handle the risk, your investments will probably appreciate significantly.

Getting in gear during the teen years

If you begin your child's college savings accounts at birth, by the time they are a teenager, you should have a tidy sum inside those accounts. Still, you're edging ever closer to that magic matriculation date, and some of your investments may not have been gold-plated. Plus, you may have been accessing some of these funds for private school education if the public school options in your city or town don't have a stellar reputation. Either way, it's time to start super-funding your Section 529 plan, if possible.

Regarding the money you have saved, it doesn't matter if your investments have done spectacularly or tanked. Now is the time to move at least a portion of the value of your investments into less-volatile areas, such as bond and money market accounts. As each year passes, continue to decrease the amount you have invested in riskier stocks, and increase the amount you maintain in bonds, certificates of deposit, and money market funds. Although the potential for growth in these accounts is limited, so is the potential for loss, and at this stage, you want to know that the money you saved is secure for your child's education.

TIP

If the writing is on the wall, and you realize your child will need some financial aid, this is also the time to start moving assets away from your child. If you have a Coverdell account for your child, you may want to convert it into a 529 plan at this point. If you choose this option, the original Coverdell beneficiary must also be the 529 designated beneficiary. If you decide not to roll over the Coverdell funds into a Section 529 plan, now would be the right time to use the money in the account to buy a computer or pay for extra tutoring. At this point, anything you can do to give your child an academic edge may pay off in the long run. Many scholarships are awarded based on merit rather than need. Money spent now in strengthening academics may pay you back many times over down the road.

TIP

You may have been saving in a 529 plan, but your investments have done so poorly that they're now worth less than the amount you initially put into an account. If you want to keep the option of financial aid open, now may be the time to close that 529 plan that has you listed as the owner. You can then gift the funds over to your parent or another relative and have that person open a 529 plan for your child. Because there are no earnings in the account to tax, the fact that you've just taken a nonqualifying distribution won't matter (no income tax and no 10 percent penalty). If you think this scenario may work for you, check with your tax advisor first.

Finding out it's never too late to start saving

Obviously, if you wait until one year before college to set up a college savings account, you probably won't have as much in it as parents who begin saving the day their child is born. You could let that knowledge defeat you: Why bother saving anything if it's too little, too late? But you can fight back.

Forget a Coverdell account at this point (unless you can roll over an existing one from another child to this one). But a Section 529 plan is still the best bet. While there are few prepaid tuition plans still in existence, where you essentially prepay the cost of your child's college tuition using today's dollars, all 50 states and the District of Columbia have 529 plans, which can be used for a much wider range of education-related expenses. They're all just waiting for you to make that first deposit.

And, although putting money into a tax-deferred or exempt account six months before the first tuition payment is due may not make sense, keep in mind that your child will be attending college for the long haul. That money could earn a considerable amount inside that account before the last tuition payment is due. Consider making your first tuition payments using current income or Stafford or PLUS loans and save money in your child's Section 529 plan for their later college or even graduate-school years.

REMEMBER

No matter when you start or how much you manage to accumulate, saving something is better than saving nothing. That something may mean the difference between your child being able to attend college or not or being faced with massive debt or a smaller, more manageable amount.

2 Managing Home and Personal Finances

Contents at a Glance

IN THIS CHAPTER

» Choosing the right type of mortgage

» Understanding fixed, adjustable, hybrid, and other loan options

» Making the 15-year versus 30-year decision

» Dealing with periods of higher mortgage interest rates

Chapter 1

Selecting the Best Home Purchase Loan

As you consider your mortgage options, you may quickly find yourself overwhelmed by the sheer number of choices. Should you choose a 15-year or a 30-year fixed-rate loan? What about mortgages that have variable interest rates — some adjust monthly, others every six or 12 months. Still others have a fixed interest rate for, say, the first one, three, five, seven, or ten years and then convert into some sort of adjustable rate. Or you can choose loans that start out as adjustable-interest-rate mortgages but allow you to elect at some future date to convert into a fixed-rate loan.

Most mortgages come with a number of bells and whistles, which means that literally tens of thousands of loan choices are available. Talk about a mortgage migraine! This chapter goes over the many options you can choose among and helps you select which ones work best for you.

Three Questions to Help You Pick the Right Mortgage

Here's a clutter-busting pain reliever. Each and every possible mortgage you may consider falls into one of two major camps: fixed-rate mortgage or adjustable-rate mortgage. Later in this chapter, we delve into the details of fixed- versus adjustable-rate mortgages.

First, however, we want to help you separate the forest from the trees. Following are three questions you need to ask yourself as you weigh which type of mortgage is best for you.

How long do you plan to keep your mortgage?

From a financial perspective, this is the most important question. Many homebuyers don't expect to stay in their current homes for a long time. If that's your expectation, consider an adjustable-rate mortgage (ARM). Why? Because an ARM starts at a lower interest rate than a fixed-rate loan, so you will save interest dollars in the first few years of holding your ARM.

A mortgage lender takes more risk when lending money at a fixed rate of interest for a longer period of time. The longer the loan term, the more time lenders could experience that interest rates increase and their cost of securing funds from deposits and other sources rise. Thus, compared with an ARM, where the lender is committing to the initial interest rate for a relatively short period of time, lenders charge a premium interest rate for a fixed-rate loan.

TECHNICAL STUFF

The interest rates used to determine most ARMs are short-term interest rates, whereas long-term interest rates dictate the terms of fixed-rate mortgages. During most time periods, longer-term interest rates are higher than shorter-term rates, because of the greater risk the lender accepts in committing to a longer-term rate.

The downside to an ARM, however, is that if interest rates rise, you may find yourself paying more interest in future years than you would be paying had you taken out a fixed-rate loan from the get-go. If you're reasonably certain that you'll hold onto your home for five years or less, however, you may come out ahead with an adjustable-rate mortgage.

If you expect to hold onto your home and mortgage for more than five to seven years, a fixed-rate loan may make more sense, especially if you're not in a financial position to withstand the fluctuating monthly payments that come with an ARM. If you're expecting to stay five to ten years, consider the hybrid loans we discuss in the "Fixed-rate periods on hybrid-ARMs" sidebar, later in this chapter.

How much financial risk can you accept?

Many homebuyers, particularly first-timers, take an adjustable-rate mortgage (ARM) because doing so allows them to stretch and buy a more expensive home. Also, real estate agents and mortgage brokers (also known as salespeople), who derive commissions either from the cost of the home you buy or the size of the mortgage you take on, may encourage you to stretch. So, if you haven't already done so, make sure to understand how much you can really afford to borrow given your other financial needs, commitments, and goals.

If you're considering an ARM, you absolutely, positively must understand what rising interest rates — and, therefore, a rising monthly mortgage payment — can do to your personal finances. Consider taking an ARM only if you can answer yes to all the following questions:

- Is your monthly budget such that you can afford higher mortgage payments and still accomplish other important personal financial goals, such as saving for retirement, your children's future educational costs, vacations, and the like?
- Do you have an emergency reserve or "rainy day" fund equal to at least three to six months of living expenses, which you can tap into to make the potentially higher monthly mortgage payments?
- Can you afford the highest payment allowed on the adjustable-rate mortgage? The mortgage lender can tell you the highest possible monthly payment, which is the payment you'd owe if the interest rate on your ARM went to the lifetime interest-rate cap allowed on the loan.

  WARNING

  Never take an ARM without understanding and being comfortable with your ability to handle the highest payment allowed.
- If you're stretching to borrow near the maximum the lender allows or an amount that will test the limits of your budget, are your job and/or your source of income stable? If you're a two-income household, can you keep making loan payments if one of you loses your job? If you expect to have children in the future, remember that your household expenses will rise and your disposable income may fall with the arrival of those little bundles of joy.
- Can you handle the psychological stresses of dealing with changing interest rates and mortgage payments?

If you're fiscally positioned to take on the financial risks inherent to an ARM, by all means consider one. As we discuss in the previous section, odds are you can save money in interest charges with an ARM. Relative to a fixed-rate loan, your interest rate should start lower and should stay lower if the overall level of interest rates doesn't change.

Even if interest rates do rise, as they inevitably and eventually will, they inevitably and eventually will come back down. So if you can stick with your ARM through times of high and low interest rates, you should still come out ahead.

Although ARMs do carry the risk of a fluctuating interest rate, as we discuss in the "Adjustable-Rate Mortgages (ARMs)" section later in this chapter, almost all adjustable-rate loans limit, or *cap*, the rise in the interest rate allowed on your loan. Typical caps are 2 percent per year *(annual cap)* and 6 percent over the life of the loan *(lifetime cap)*.

REMEMBER

Consider an adjustable-rate mortgage only if you're financially and emotionally secure enough to handle the maximum possible payments over an extended period of time. ARMs work best for borrowers who take out smaller loans than they're qualified for or who consistently save more than 10 percent of their monthly incomes. If you do choose an ARM, make sure you have a significant cash or liquid assets cushion that's accessible in the event that rates go up.

How much money do you need?

One factor that distinguishes the best mortgage from inferior loans is that the best mortgage is the best deal you can get. Why waste your hard-earned money on a mediocre mortgage? That's not why you bought this book. The amount of money you borrow can greatly affect your loan's interest rate. That's why it behooves you to carefully consider how much money you need.

Conventional mortgages that stay within Fannie Mae and Freddie Mac loan limits established each year by Congress are called *conforming loans*. Mortgages that exceed the maximum permissible loan amounts are referred to either as *jumbo conforming loans*, *nonconforming loans*, or *jumbo loans*.

For example, the conforming loan limit for single-family dwellings in the continental United States was $832,750 (up to $1,249,125 in high-cost areas), when this book went to press. Because mortgage maximums change annually, however, be sure to check with your lender for the current Fannie Mae and Freddie Mac loan limits. If the mortgage you need far exceeds the present conforming loan limit, skip the rest of this section. If, however, your loan is within 10 percent or so of the loan limit, keep reading. Our forthcoming advice may save you major money.

Why are we making such a fuss about the loan limit? Because mortgage interest rates for conforming loans typically run anywhere from 1/4 to 1/2 percent *lower* than the interest rates for jumbo loans. Keeping the amount of money you borrow under that all-important loan limit saves you big bucks over the life of your loan.

TIP

If your mortgage slightly surpasses Fannie Mae and Freddie Mac's loan limit, we know three ways to bring it into conformity:

- **Spend less on a home.** This option may seem obvious, but what the heck! The less you pay for a home, the smaller your mortgage.
- **Increase your down payment to reduce the mortgage.** The more money you put down up-front, the less you need to borrow.
- **Use 80-10-10 financing.** This option means you take out a first mortgage for 80 percent of the purchase price, have a second mortgage for 10 percent of the purchase price, and make a down payment of 10 percent. You may be able to use this mode of financing to cut your first mortgage down to size.

Now, get down to the brass tacks of understanding the major features of fixed-rate versus adjustable-rate mortgages. Keeping the previous three questions in mind (How long do you plan to keep your mortgage? How much risk can you handle? How much money do you need?), read the following sections and ponder which mortgage works best for you.

Fixed-Rate Mortgages: No Surprises

As you may have surmised from the name, fixed-rate mortgages have interest rates that are fixed (that is, the rate doesn't change) for the entire life of the loan, which is typically 15 or 30 years. With a fixed-rate mortgage, the interest rate stays the same, and the amount of your monthly mortgage payment doesn't change. Thus, you have no surprises, no uncertainty, and no anxiety over possible changes in your monthly payment as you have with an adjustable-rate mortgage.

Because the interest rate doesn't vary with a fixed-rate mortgage, the advantage of a fixed-rate mortgage is that you always know what your monthly payment is going to be. Thus, budgeting and planning the rest of your personal finances is easier.

That's the good news. The bad news, as we allude to earlier in this chapter, is that with a fixed-rate mortgage, you pay a premium, in the form of a higher interest rate, to get a lender to commit to lending you money at a fixed rate over the full term of the mortgage. The longer the term for which a mortgage lender agrees to accept a fixed interest rate, the more risk that lender is taking.

In addition to paying a premium interest rate when you originally get a fixed-rate loan, another potential drawback to fixed-rate loans is that, if interest rates fall significantly after you have your mortgage, you face the risk of being stuck with your costly mortgage. That could happen if, for example, due to problems with your personal financial situation or a decline in the value of your property, you don't qualify to refinance. Even if you do qualify to refinance, doing so takes time and costs money (appraisal, loan fees, and title insurance).

Here are a couple of other possible drawbacks to be aware of with some fixed-rate mortgages:

- Fixed-rate mortgages aren't generally assumable, so if you sell during a period of high interest rates, your buyers must obtain their own financing. Finding assumable ARMs, however, is difficult.
- As with some adjustable-rate mortgages, some fixed-rate mortgages have prepayment penalties.

Adjustable-Rate Mortgages (ARMs)

Adjustable-rate mortgages (ARMs) have an interest rate that varies over time. On a typical ARM, the interest rate adjusts every six or 12 months, but it may change as frequently as monthly. Popular ARMs include *hybrid loans* where the initial interest rate is locked in for the first three, five, seven, or ten years and then adjusts after that (see the sidebar "Fixed-rate periods on hybrid-ARMs").

As we discuss later in this chapter, the interest rate on an ARM is primarily determined by what's happening to interest rates in general. Keep in mind that interest rates are the "price" for the commodity or product known as cash money. If the price of borrowing money is increasing, then most interest rates are on the rise. In this scenario, the odds are that your ARM will also experience increasing rates, thus increasing the size of your mortgage payment. Conversely, when interest rates fall (as the price of money becomes cheaper, usually due to less demand and more capital available in the market), ARM interest rates and payments eventually follow suit.

If the interest rate on your mortgage fluctuates, so will your monthly payment sooner or later. And therein lies the risk: Because a mortgage payment is probably one of your biggest monthly expenses (if not *the* biggest), an adjustable-rate mortgage that's adjusting upward can wreak havoc with your budget.

You may be attracted to an ARM or hybrid loan because it starts out at a lower interest rate than a fixed-rate loan and thus may enable you to qualify to borrow more. However, just because you can qualify to borrow more doesn't mean you can afford to borrow that much, given your other financial goals and needs.

TIP

The right reason to consider an ARM is because you may save money on interest charges and you can afford the risk of higher payments if interest rates rise. Because you accept the risk of an increase in interest rates, mortgage lenders cut you a little slack. The initial interest rate (also known as the *teaser rate*) should be significantly less than the interest rate on a comparable fixed-rate loan. In fact, even with subsequent rate adjustments, an ARM's interest rate for the first year or two of the loan is generally lower than a fixed-rate mortgage.

Another important advantage of an ARM is that, if you purchase your home during a time of high interest rates, you can start paying your mortgage with the artificially depressed initial interest rate. If overall interest rates then decline, you can capture the benefits of lower rates without refinancing as your ARM adjusts lower.

Here's another situation when adjustable-rate loans have an advantage over their fixed-rate brethren: If, for whatever reason, you don't qualify to refinance your mortgage when interest rates decline, you can still reap the advantage of lower rates. The good news for homeowners who can't refinance and who have an ARM is that they receive many of the benefits of the lower rates as their ARM's interest rate and payments adjust downward with declining rates. With a fixed-rate loan, by contrast, you must refinance to realize the benefits of a decline in interest rates.

The downside to an adjustable-rate loan is that if interest rates in general rise, your loan's interest and monthly payment will likely rise, too. During most time periods, if rates rise more than 1 to 2 percent and stay elevated, the adjustable-rate loan is likely to cost you more than a fixed-rate loan.

Before you make any decision between a fixed-rate mortgage versus an adjustable-rate mortgage, read the following sections for a crash course in understanding ARMs.

FIXED-RATE PERIODS ON HYBRID-ARMS

If you expect to keep your loan for no more than five to ten years, and if you want more stability in your monthly payments than comes with a regular ARM that locks in the initial interest rate only for a year or less, an ARM with a longer fixed-rate period may be for you. These options are called hybrid-ARMs. All such loans start out as fixed-rate loans — the initial rate on the mortgage is actually fixed for three, five, seven, or even ten years — and then the loan converts into an ARM, usually adjusting every six to 12 months thereafter.

The longer the initial rate stays locked in, the higher the rate will be, but the initial rate of a three- to ten-year fixed-rate initial period ARM is almost always lower than the interest rate on a 30-year fixed-rate mortgage. However, because the initial rate of such loans is locked in for a longer period of time than the six-month or one-year term of regular ARMs, three- to ten-year fixed-rate ARMs have higher initial interest rates than regular ARM loans.

To evaluate these mortgages, weigh the likelihood that you'll move before the initial loan interest rate expires. For example, with a five-year ARM, if you're saving, say, 0.75 percent per year versus the 30-year fixed-rate mortgage, but you're quite sure that you'll move within five years, the five-year ARM will probably save you money. On the other hand, if you have a reasonable chance of staying put for more than five years and you don't want to face the risk of rising payments after five years, you should consider a seven- or ten-year hybrid-ARM.

You may occasionally find little difference between short-term and long-term interest rates. For example, we've seen periods when the interest-rate spread between an ARM's initial interest rate and a fixed-rate loan's interest rate was less than 1 percent. We've also seen times when the initial interest rate on a seven- or ten-year ARM was exactly the same as on a 30-year fixed-rate loan. In this type of situation, fixed-rate loans offer the best overall value.

Also, compare the rates for ARMs with varying interest-rate lock periods. You may find very little or even no difference between the five-year and seven-year fixed-rate period ARM loan. In this case, you want to take the loan with the longest fixed-rate period.

Or compare the ARM with a seven-year fixed-rate period to the ten-year fixed-rate period ARM loan, and you may decide that paying a ¼ percent higher rate throughout the entire first ten years is acceptable to prevent a major increase after the first seven years.

How is an ARM's interest rate determined?

Most ARMs start at an artificially low interest rate. Don't select an ARM based on this rate, because you'll probably be paying this low rate for no more than six to 12 months, and perhaps for as little as one month. Like other salespeople, lenders promote the most attractive features of their product and ignore the negatives. The low starting rate on an ARM is what some lenders are most likely to tell you about because profit-hungry mortgage lenders know that inexperienced, financially constrained borrowers focus on this low advertised initial rate.

The starting rate on an ARM isn't anywhere near as important as what the future interest rate is going to be on the loan. How the future interest rate on an ARM is determined is the most important issue for you to understand when evaluating an ARM — if you plan on holding onto your loan for more than a few months.

To establish what the interest rate on an ARM will be in the future, you need to know the loan's index and margin, the two of which are added together.

So ignore, for now, an ARM's starting rate and begin your evaluation of an ARM by understanding what *index* it is tied to and what *margin* it has.

What are the index and margin? We're glad you asked!

Start with the index

The *index* on an ARM is a measure of general interest rate trends that the lender uses to determine changes in the mortgage's interest rate. For example, the one-year Treasury constant maturity index is a common index used for many ARMs (discussed in the next section).

Suppose that the going rate on this index is approximately 2 percent. The indexes used on various ARMs theoretically indicate how much it costs the bank to take in money, for example, from people and companies investing in the bank's various accounts, which the bank can then lend to you, the mortgage borrower.

TIP

The following sections explain the most common ARM indexes. Don't worry about lenders playing games with the indexes to unfairly raise your ARM's interest rate. Lenders don't control any of the indexes we discuss. Furthermore, they're easy to verify. If you want to check the figures, you can usually find these indexes in publications such as the *Wall Street Journal.*

TREASURY SECURITIES

The U.S. federal government is the largest borrower in the world. So it should come as no surprise that some ARM indexes are based on the interest rate that the government pays on some of its pile of debt. The most commonly used government interest rate indexes for ARMs are for one, three, five, and ten-year Treasuries.

The Treasury security indexes are volatile; they tend to be among the faster-moving ones around. In other words, they respond quickly to market changes in interest rates. Treasury indexes are good when interest rates are falling and lousy when rates head higher.

SECURED OVERNIGHT FINANCING RATE (SOFR)

In 2022, the U.S. Congress followed the lead of the United Kingdom regulators and phased out the use of the London Interbank Offered Rate (LIBOR), which had been a common index for a significant portion of ARMs and sub-prime rate loans. On March 15, 2022, President Joe Biden signed the Adjustable Interest Rate (LIBOR) Act into law. This law required that as of July 1, 2023, no new adjustable loans would use the LIBOR index, and all existing adjustable-rate loans would phase out the use of the LIBOR index.

The replacement index for the LIBOR is the *Secured Overnight Financing Rate* (SOFR). It's published daily by the Federal Reserve and reflects the cost for financial institutions to borrow money overnight using U.S. Treasury securities as collateral in the repurchase agreement market. The LIBOR was subject to fluctuation and manipulation as it was based on unsecured loan transactions, whereas SOFR uses overnight rates for loans backed by the U.S. Treasury, which are risk-adjusted and generally lower.

Add the margin

The *margin*, or *spread* as it's also known, on an ARM is the lenders' profit, or markup, on the money that they lend. Most ARM loans have margins of around 2.5 percent, but the exact margin depends on the lender and the index that lender is using. When you compare several loans that are tied to the same index and are otherwise the same, the loan with the lowest margin is better (cheaper) for you.

All good things end sooner or later. After the initial interest rate period expires, an ARM's future interest rate is determined, subject to the loan's interest rate cap limitations as explained later in this section, by adding together the loan's current index value and the margin.

The following formula applies every time the ARM's interest rate is adjusted:

Index + margin = interest rate

For example, suppose that your loan is tied to the *one-year Treasury security index,* which recently was at about 3.5 percent plus a margin of 2.25 percent. Thus, your loan's interest rate is

$$3.5\% + 2.25\% = 5.75\%$$

This figure is known as the *fully indexed rate.* If a loan is advertised with an initial interest rate of, say, 4.5 percent, the fully indexed rate (in this case, 5.75 percent) tells you what interest rate this ARM would rise to if the market level of interest rates, as measured by the one-year Treasury security index, were to stay at the same level.

REMEMBER

Always be sure to understand the fully indexed rate on an ARM you're considering. To avoid any surprises, you also should know what the payment will be for various potentially higher interest rates during the life of your loan, including the maximum rate, so you fully understand what the maximum possible monthly payment is. Ask the lender and/or your mortgage broker to provide this payment information.

How often does the interest rate adjust?

Although some ARMs have an interest rate adjustment monthly, most adjust every six or 12 months, using the mortgage-rate determination formula discussed previously. In advance of each adjustment, the mortgage lender should mail you a notice, explaining how the new rate is calculated according to the agreed-upon terms of your ARM.

REMEMBER

The less frequently your loan adjusts, the less financial risk you're accepting. In exchange for taking less risk, the mortgage lender normally expects you to pay more — such as a higher initial interest rate and/or higher ongoing margin.

What are the limits on rate adjustments?

As discussed earlier in this chapter, despite the fact that an ARM has a formula for determining future interest rates (index + margin = interest rate), a good ARM limits the magnitude of change that can occur in the actual rate you pay. These limits, also known as *rate caps,* affect each future adjustment of an ARM's rate following the expiration of the initial rate period.

Two types of rate caps exist:

» **Periodic adjustment caps:** These caps limit the maximum rate change, up or down, allowed at each adjustment. For ARMs that adjust at six-month intervals, the adjustment cap is generally plus or minus 1 percent. ARMs that adjust more than once annually generally restrict the maximum rate change allowed over the entire year as well. This annual rate cap is typically plus or minus 2 percent.

- **Lifetime caps:** Never, ever, ever take an ARM without a lifetime cap. This cap limits the highest rate allowed over the entire life of the loan. ARMs commonly have lifetime caps of 5 to 6 percent higher than the initial start rate.

WARNING

Without a lifetime cap, your possible loan payment can grow to the moon if interest rates soar again as they did in the early 1980s when rates peaked at more than 18 percent. Be sure you can handle the maximum possible payment allowed on an ARM if the interest rate rises to the lifetime cap.

TIP

You may be wondering why we stress that interest rate adjustments are capped both up and down. Who cares how much rates can go down? You will, if rates drop rapidly and your ARM responds like molasses on a subzero winter morning. A good reason to refinance an ARM is to lower the periodic and lifetime adjustment caps accordingly if interest rates decline significantly.

Does the loan have negative amortization?

On a normal mortgage, as you make mortgage payments over time, the loan balance you owe is gradually reduced through a process called amortization. Some ARMs, however, cap the increase of your monthly payment but don't limit how much the interest rate can increase. Thus, the size of your mortgage payment may not reflect all the interest that you actually currently owe. So rather than paying the interest that's owed and paying off some of your loan principal balance every month, you may end up paying some (but not all) of the current interest that you owe.

Thus, the extra, unpaid interest that you still owe is *added* to your outstanding debt. This process of increasing the size of your loan balance is called *negative amortization.* Negative amortization is like paying only the minimum payment required on a credit card bill. You continue accumulating additional interest on the balance as long as you make only the minimum monthly payment. However, doing this with a mortgage defeats the purpose of your borrowing an amount that fits your overall financial goals.

Some lenders try to hide the fact that an ARM they're pitching you has negative amortization. How can you avoid negative amortization loans?

- **Ask.** As you discuss specific loan programs with lenders or mortgage brokers, *be sure to tell them you don't want a loan with negative amortization.* Specifically ask them if the ARM they're suggesting has it or not.

HOW BAD IS NEGATIVE AMORTIZATION?

Negative amortization loans are also called *option ARMs* because they offer three different options for making mortgage payments. Each month you have the choice of doing one of the following:

- Making a fully amortized payment that includes principal and interest
- Making a smaller payment by paying only the loan's interest charge with no principal
- Lowering your payment even further by making a capped loan payment that doesn't cover all the loan's interest charge and results in negative amortization (an addition to your balance owed)

A disproportionately high percentage of negative amortization ARMs went into foreclosure during the late 2000s real estate market downturn. Some lenders explained this dismal fact by pointing out a disproportionately high percentage of folks who got this type of loan weren't creditworthy borrowers. That may account for part of the problem. However, it's disingenuous for lenders to express shock when people they've led into temptation succumb to the seduction of making the lowest possible monthly payment even if it results in negative amortization.

Good news. It's much harder to find negative amortization ARMs. Most lenders no longer offer them. If you need private mortgage insurance (PMI) because you can't make a 20 percent cash down payment, be advised that PMI companies won't insure negative amortization ARMs. If you currently have a negative amortization loan on your property, it's highly unlikely that you'll find a lender willing to give you a home equity loan.

WARNING

You must be especially wary of being pitched negative amortization loans if you're having trouble finding lenders willing to offer you a mortgage (in other words, you're considered a credit risk). Remember Robert's take on the old adage, "If it's too good to be true, it *is* too good to be true."

» **If the loan has a monthly adjustment, ask again.** Monthly adjusting ARMs are often a warning sign of a negative amortization loan. Another red flag is an ARM with annual payment caps rather than semi-annual or annual interest rate adjustment caps.

See the nearby sidebar "How bad is negative amortization?" for additional details.

Fine-Tuning Your Thought Process

Now that you know darn near everything worth knowing about fixed-rate mortgages and ARMs, you're probably in a veritable frenzy of excitement about getting yourself preapproved for a loan. Not so fast, grasshopper. We have a few more words of wisdom for you.

Finding funds

Before you rush off, wouldn't it be wise to find out where the money is? Here are the big sources for home purchase mortgages:

- **Conventional loans:** Most U.S. residential mortgages are conventional loans originated by lending institutions such as wholesale mortgage lenders, commercial and savings banks, mortgage banks, credit unions, and mortgage brokers.
- **Government loans:** Low-income borrowers or folks with little or no cash for a down payment may be able to qualify for a variety of home loans either insured or guaranteed by an agency of the federal government. Examples include Federal Housing Administration (FHA), Department of Veterans Affairs (VA), and U.S. Department of Agriculture (USDA) Rural Housing loans.
- **Seller loans:** These mortgages, which are generally referred to as *owner-carry financing,* generally represent less than 5 percent of the loan market. They are, however, an extremely important loan source during periods of high mortgage interest rates and properties that may be more challenging to sell where the seller has a lot of equity. Owner-carry financing is usually structured as a home purchase first or second mortgage.

WARNING

Almost all conventional first mortgages and government loans are *fully amortized.* That means they're designed to be repaid in full by the time you make the last regularly scheduled monthly payment. Darn near all owner-carry first mortgages, conversely, come due with a generally quite large unpaid balance. This type of financing is called a *balloon loan.* Balloon loans can be extremely hazardous to your fiscal health if you can't repay or refinance them when they're due and payable — borrower beware!

Making the 30-year versus 15-year mortgage decision

After you decide which type of mortgage — fixed or adjustable — you desire, you have one more major choice to make. Do you prefer a 15-year or a 30-year loan term? (You may run across some odd-length mortgages — such as 20- and 40-year mortgages; however, the issues we discuss in this section remain the same as when comparing 15-year to 30-year mortgages.)

If you're stretching to buy the home of your dreams, you may not have a choice. The only loan you may qualify for is a 30-year mortgage. That isn't necessarily bad and, in fact, has advantages.

The main advantage that a 30-year mortgage has over a comparable 15-year loan is that it has lower monthly payments that free up more of your monthly income for different purposes, such as saving for other important financial goals like retirement. You may want to have more money each month so you aren't a financial prisoner in your abode. A 30-year mortgage has lower monthly payments because you have a longer time period to repay it (which translates into more payments). A fixed-rate, 30-year mortgage with an interest rate of 7 percent, for example, has payments that are approximately 25 percent lower than those on a comparable 15-year mortgage.

What if you can afford the higher payments that a 15-year mortgage requires? Should you take it? Not necessarily. What if, instead of making large payments on the 15-year mortgage, you make smaller payments on a 30-year mortgage and put that extra money to productive use?

If you do make productive use of that extra money, then the 30-year mortgage may be for you. A terrific potential use for that extra dough is to contribute it to a tax-deductible retirement account. Contributions that you add to employer-based 401(k) and 403(b) plans (and self-employed SEP-IRAs) not only give you an immediate reduction in taxes but also enable your money to compound, tax-deferred, over the years ahead. Another vehicle for tax-deductible contributions is the Health Savings Account (HSA) for those with higher deductible health plans. Everyone with employment income may also contribute to an Individual Retirement Account (IRA). Your IRA contributions may not be immediately tax deductible if your (or your spouse's) employer offers a retirement account or pension plan, but they will grow tax-free.

If you exhausted your options for contributing to retirement accounts and an HSA, and if you find it challenging to save money anyway, the 15-year mortgage may offer you a good forced-savings program. If you elect to take a 30-year mortgage, you retain the flexibility to pay it off faster if you so choose. (Just be sure to avoid those mortgages that have a prepayment penalty.) Constraining yourself with the 15-year mortgage's higher monthly payments does carry a risk. If you stumble during tough financial times, you may not be able to meet the required mortgage payments.

Getting a Loan When Rates Are High

Over the years and decades, we've seen interest rates for conforming 30-year fixed-rate loans soar to more than 18 percent in the early 1980s and sink to a low of just over 3 percent in 2012. In the high inflation aftermath of the government-mandated COVID-19 shutdowns, fixed-rate mortgages rose sharply and neared 8 percent in 2023 but have subsequently declined. We can guarantee you with 100 percent certainty that mortgage rates will continue to change. They always do. If we could only figure out a way to forecast how much and when, we'd be rich!

Earlier in this chapter, we point out three places to find a first mortgage with an interest rate *significantly* lower than what you'd pay for a new, 30-year fixed-rate loan. Just to refresh your memory, here's a recap:

- **ARMs:** Lenders charge a premium for fixed-rate loans. If you'll share the lenders' risk of possible future interest rate increases by getting an adjustable-rate mortgage, lenders will reward your adventurous spirit with a lower initial interest rate on your loan. The more often your loan adjusts, the lower your ARM's initial interest rate. ARMs that adjust every six months, for example, generally have a lower start rate than ARMs that adjust annually and so on.
- **Loan assumptions:** It's extremely unlikely that you can find a fixed-rate mortgage you can assume. On the other hand, some ARMs are assumable for creditworthy borrowers. 'Nuff said.
- **Seller financing:** Some long-term homeowners no longer have mortgages on their property. These fortunate folks may offer attractive financing to qualified buyers either to get a higher purchase price or to structure their transaction as an installment sale for preferable tax treatment by the IRS. (An installment sale provides that the buyer pays the purchase price, usually plus interest, in regular payments or installments over multiple tax years to spread out and reduce the tax consequences from the sale.)

Like it or not, you may have the monetary misfortune of buying your home during a period when mortgage rates are on the high side of the cycle. If that happens, don't despair. You can refinance your loan after rates drop.

IN THIS CHAPTER

» Getting acquainted with the specific rules of mortgages

» Finding help for your delinquent mortgage

» Facing grave mortgage problems, including foreclosure

» Coping with a deficiency balance

» Beefing up your credit before a default

Chapter 2
Handling Mortgage Meltdowns

With Gen Y and Gen Z opting for smaller spaces and generations rooming together, many facets have changed about the economics and potential risks of homeownership. Previously, the primary concern was that house values would drop below the mortgage debt, meaning the house became worth less than you owed for it. Today, the issue is not so much price decline, but rather coping with increasing home values coupled with higher interest rate mortgages.

Saying where home prices are going is hard, but as you adjust to higher rates and higher payments, the question remains: What do you do if you can't make your payment? What are the risks to your credit if you have a default? What used to be a no-brainer decision has become more complicated than anyone could have imagined. Millions of people are asking questions about home affordability today. This chapter helps you find the answers.

Assessing the Damage from a Mortgage Meltdown

Credit report and score misinformation is everywhere. What you don't know can and will hurt you if what you don't know is that your credit report and score have been seriously damaged. If you're trying to assess the damage to your score from a mortgage meltdown or even just a mild mortgage sunburn, having the best information available is important. That's what this section is all about.

TIP

Today, credit score simulators can provide you some indication of the impacts of negative events on your credit score. Regardless of which credit score is being used (FICO or VantageScore), you can get a fairly accurate picture. The major credit reporting bureaus (Equifax, Experian, and TransUnion), Credit Karma (`https://creditkarma.com`), and some financial institutions offer credit score simulators as part of your customer experience with no fee associated. All these simulators enable you to use real-life scenarios to gain insight into the impacts certain actions may have on your score. Because they're just a simulation, they don't impact your real scores so you can see the positive and negative impacts before you take any actions.

Seeing which events cause the biggest drops

Mortgage defaults, foreclosures, repossessions, and bankruptcy have some of the most significant negative impacts, underscoring how important it is to resolve any problems as quickly and amicably as possible.

TIP

The terms *default, delinquency,* and *negative event* tend to mean the same thing. Strictly speaking, being *delinquent* (late on a payment) leads to a *default* (based on the legal terms in your mortgage documents). Both are negative credit events that you don't want to experience.

REMEMBER

People with great credit who default on a mortgage see a greater credit-score point drop than those whose credit isn't so great. Why? Because a good score has to fall farther in order to end up at the lower point level that indicates serious credit problems. In general, the higher your starting score, the longer it takes for your score to fully recover from the damage.

Delinquencies and some actions that result in your home being taken back by the lender *(deed-in-lieu)* or sold under distress (as in a *short sale*) cost you big points. However, there's no significant difference in credit-score impact between a short sale or a deed-in-lieu, but a settlement may ding you a little less. Check out Table 2-1.

TABLE 2-1 **Credit Score Penalties**

Action	Typical Score Drop	Credit Report Duration	Severity
Short sale	85–160 points	7 years	High
Deed-in-lieu	85–160 points	7 years	High
Debt settlement	45–125 points	7 years	Moderate
Chapter 7 bankruptcy	130–240 points	Up to 10 years	Extreme
Chapter 13 bankruptcy	100–220 points	Up to 7 years	Extreme

Handling Mortgage Meltdowns

REMEMBER

The actual drop depends on your credit score *before* filing. Those with higher scores usually see *larger* drops.

Mega point drops in your credit score tend to occur when the lender loses money in addition to your being in default, such as in the event of a short sale or a foreclosure, both of which cost the bank money. But the worst and longest lasting of all injury to your credit occurs when you file for bankruptcy. Unlike the other, lesser defaults, a bankruptcy can stay on your credit report for up to ten years.

Considering other repercussions

In addition to credit score penalties, you need to take the collateral damage into consideration:

- Although a score may *begin* to improve sooner, it can take up to seven to ten years to *fully* recover.
- Fannie Mae (the Federal National Mortgage Association) is the nation's largest mortgage buyer. It buys and then resells mortgages on Wall Street, helping to keep mortgage interest rates low. Fannie excludes borrowers who've gone through a foreclosure from obtaining a Fannie-backed loan for seven years. In the case of a deed-in-lieu, the waiting period is typically four years. Post-COVID guideline updates may alter waiting periods, so always check current rules at `www.fanniemae.com`.
- Fannie Mae may not accept a new mortgage application from a person who has had a mortgage delinquency in the last 12 months, if you've been 30 days late twice or 60 days late once.

- If you can't get a Fannie Mae loan, you may have to take a nonconforming loan, which may require expensive mortgage insurance premiums and, for those with lower credit scores, higher interest rates and a larger down payment.

Understanding How Mortgages Differ from Other Loans

Mortgages differ from other consumer loans partly because of their size — a lot of money is on the line — and partly because they're backed by what historically has been the gold standard in collateral: your home. With more at risk, the stakes are greater. Furthermore, mortgages are not only underwritten differently from other types of credit but also have a different collection process, generally called the *foreclosure process.* When you default on a mortgage, the lender *forecloses,* or terminates the mortgage, and your house is taken away from you.

WARNING

From a credit-score and credit-reporting standpoint, mortgage defaults and foreclosures are among the most serious negatives out there, with the exception of bankruptcy.

Obviously, a foreclosure puts a serious hit on your credit history and score. To help you minimize this hit, this section gives you an overview of how mortgages differ from typical credit and how mortgages and credit go hand in hand. Here you can find valuable information to help you understand when a late mortgage payment can quickly cause you problems and what you can do to get help.

Spotting a foreclosure on the horizon

A lender has a lot of money on the line with your mortgage, and the longer you're delinquent, the greater the risk that the lender will lose money on a defaulted loan. The result is that a mortgage lender has a much lower tolerance for delinquency than, say, a credit card issuer. For example, as long as you're less than 180 days past due on a credit card, it's not the end of the world. Generally, you can just pay the minimum due along with a late fee and pick up where you left off, with a small ding to your credit. If you're really lucky, and you've been a good customer in the past, you may get the lender to waive the late fee and not report the delinquency. For a mortgage, however, being just 60 days late puts you well on your way to the edge of a cliff, and you may not even be aware of it.

WARNING

The key number to avoid in a mortgage delinquency is 90 days late. After 90 days, unless you get some help or work out an arrangement, the mortgage servicer generally requires the entire amount that is overdue (the *arrearage*) to be paid at once and may not accept partial payments. A 90-day mortgage delinquency on a credit report is very serious. To make matters worse, many people don't understand when the 90 days is up. The time frame isn't as simple as you may think, so we cover it in detail in the next section.

Mortgage servicers don't call you at work or at night, and they don't yell or threaten you over the phone. On the contrary, the tone of their messages (often letters) is concerned, low-key, and polite. If you ignore these messages, you could lose your home. But if you know where to get help, what to ask for, and what to avoid, your situation can change for the better.

Counting to 90

If you're 30 or 60 days late on your mortgage and you make a partial payment, the servicer usually credits your account with the payment. If you cross the 90-day mark and then send in a month or two's worth of overdue payments rather than the entire amount due, however, the servicer may send the money back and let the foreclosure clock keep ticking.

REMEMBER

After you're late on your first payment, your grace period disappears. (Your *grace period* is the period of time specified in your mortgage loan agreement during which a default can't occur, even though the payment is technically past due.) The grace period applies only to loans that are up-to-date, or current. The following example illustrates how this works.

Say your loan agreement states that your due date is March 1. Assuming that you have a typical two-week grace period, your payment actually has to be in by March 15. If you don't submit your payment by March 15, you miss that window of opportunity and lose your grace period. Your April payment is now due April 1. April 15 is no longer an option. In other words, no more grace period in April. If you pay April's payment on or before April 1, you get your grace period back for May and thereafter, as long as you continue making your payments on time.

If you lose your grace period, the counting of the number of days you're late begins on the 1st of the month rather than the 15th. So if you don't send in a payment on March 15, April 1, or May 1, then on May 2, you need to catch up on the payments for March 1, April 1, and May 1, plus any fees and penalties (which can be hundreds of dollars or more), all at once. This sum is a huge amount for someone in financial difficulty. If you don't pay, then the formal foreclosure process can start within 30 days, and you may incur fees for collection costs, attorneys, title searches, filings, and more. After the foreclosure process begins (it's up to the mortgage servicer when this process actually begins), the mortgage servicer can *accelerate* the loan, meaning that it can ask for the entire loan balance — not just the late part — to stop the foreclosure.

TIP

For a great graph illustrating the timeline for late mortgage payments and what happens each step of the way, see `www.lendingtree.com/home/mortgage/late-mortgage-payment`.

Knowing Where to Turn for Help

If you're having trouble making your mortgage payments, time is of the essence. Getting your mortgage issue resolved quickly is critical. Remember, the mortgage company doesn't want your house; it just wants to keep your loan *performing/up-to-date/current* (different terms for the same thing). But also remember that the mortgage company doesn't care whether it has to take your home. If the rules say to foreclose, the mortgage company will foreclose, without hesitation and without remorse.

Following are a few ideas on where to turn for help (along with some tips on who *not* to turn to!). The essential point, however, is not to wait but to take action. You can work directly with your mortgage servicer, but the servicer may offer you only what it thinks is the easiest solution, not the one you need, because the servicer doesn't know your situation in detail.

Finding good help for free

A number of housing counseling agencies are available to help you work out a solution. We strongly recommend that you use a third-party intermediary that's approved by the U.S. Department of Housing and Urban Development (HUD). These intermediaries are cheap, experienced, and knowledgeable and can help guide you through what can seem like an insurmountable problem. They're experts at getting the right information on the right forms and to the right person at the mortgage servicer — no easy task!

TIP

Although the contact information may change over time and new players are continually offering this service, you can look for resources through Fannie Mae's website (`https://yourhome.fanniemae.com/`) or HUD's website (`www.hud.gov`), contact Money Management International (`www.moneymanagement.org`), or contact 995Hope (`https://995hope.org`). For the fastest service, call or go online for a virtual visit before you visit an office. You can also get good help by contacting the National Foundation for Credit Counseling (`www.nfcc.org/homeowner-guidance`). Many credit counselors are also HUD-certified housing counselors.

Working with your mortgage servicer

If you're unable to make a mortgage payment on time, you can contact your mortgage company for help. If you believe that this may be the beginning of a serious problem that needs serious attention, ask for the *loss mitigation department,* which may be referred to as the *workout department* or the *homeownership retention department.* This department is able to go the extra mile to help you and can deal with complex issues better than the standard collection department, which usually offers only to make catch-up payment arrangements.

TIP

To find the contact information for these departments, you can look in your mortgage loan documents, on your monthly statement, or in the correspondence you received from your mortgage servicer. When you call, get names and extension numbers so that you can try to keep a single point of contact and continuity. Doing so may not be possible, but knowing who you talked to, when you talked, and what you agreed on is important in case matters get really serious. Take good notes!

Keeping the call simple is a blessing to everyone concerned, so do some homework before you call and have a written, well-thought-out proposal prepared that meets your needs and helps solve your problem. Be sure to include what concessions you need and for how long. We also suggest that you write down what happened, what changed, and how to contact you or your counselor if you're working with one. Writing down the facts and options before you call helps you keep from drifting during the conversation and keeps everyone focused on the task at hand. When you ask for what you need, be sure to ask what other options may be available beyond the one that's offered.

TIP

If you want some free help on figuring out what specific help you need to ask for, contact a counselor at 995Hope (`https://995hope.org`) or Money Management International (`www.moneymanagement.org`).

WARNING

If you can't resolve your issue quickly or if you get transferred to multiple people, get expert help quickly. Time is precious, and mortgage servicers can easily pass the buck until you find yourself in a foreclosure situation. See the preceding section for information on where to find free help from experts.

Avoiding help that hurts

REMEMBER

Some people make a living, and a good one, on the backs of folks in trouble. People who offer to help you with a mortgage problem for a fee are only trying to help themselves. So proceed with caution and consider the following tips as you evaluate any prospective source of help:

- Don't decide anything while in a panic.
- Be sure that you're dealing with a HUD-qualified nonprofit organization. Look them up at `www.hud.gov`.
- Don't make payments to anyone other than your mortgage servicer or its designee.
- Be wary of any organization other than your mortgage servicer that contacts you to offer help. It's fine if you call them, but not if they call you!
- Never sign a contract under pressure.
- Never sign away ownership of your property.
- Beware of any company or person who guarantees that they can stop a foreclosure or get your loan modified.
- If English isn't your first language and a translator isn't provided, use your own.
- Get a second opinion from a person or an organization that you know and trust.

WARNING

If you're having trouble paying your mortgage, getting a high-risk, expensive second mortgage won't help. It will only keep you from finding real solutions by wasting critical time and money.

WARNING

If you receive an offer saying that you are preapproved or prequalified for a loan, don't get too excited. Those terms are used very loosely. Read the fine print. You likely haven't been preapproved for the loan at all. More likely, you've been preapproved to *apply* for the loan, not for the loan itself. Don't waste too much time chasing preapproved offers.

Looking at Alternatives to Going Down with the Ship

If you're having trouble making your mortgage payments, you may have a host of options to help you avoid the expense and upset of losing your home through a foreclosure. Even if you can't or don't want to keep your house, you can still lessen the damage to yourself, your family, and your credit by taking positive action.

TIP

Before you take any action, assess your situation as dispassionately as you can. If stress and anxiety make that impossible, seek help first from a third-party professional such as a nonprofit HUD counselor (see the earlier section "Finding good help for free") or an attorney. Your situation may not be as bad as you think it is, or it may be worse. What's important is to know for sure where you stand. You need what's called *loss mitigation counseling,* which is help to develop a solution that enables you to afford to keep your home or lessen the damage caused by a foreclosure.

This section gives you some loss mitigation options to protect your credit.

What to do first

If you already have a plan to resolve your problem, catch up, or at least resume payments in three to six months, consider the following suggestions:

- **Find a good nonprofit housing counseling agency.** We recommend the Hope Hotline (888-995-4673), 995Hope (`https://995hope.org`), or Money Management International (`www.moneymanagement.org`) or another nonprofit credit counseling agency that has a HUD-approved housing counseling program. Expect an assessment of your overall financial picture and whether you can realistically afford your mortgage payments.
- **Ask your mortgage servicer about a repayment plan.** The servicer sets up a structured payment plan (sometimes called a *special forbearance plan*) that gets the mortgage back on track in three to six months by making up past-due amounts in addition to your regular payments. Get all the terms in writing so that you're both clear on the terms. The sooner you do so, the less damage to your credit report and score.
- **Check the HUD (`www.hud.gov`) and Fannie Mae (`https://yourhome.fanniemae.com/`) websites for resources and help.** Both sites have excellent referral resources, information on programs that may be right for you, and warnings to keep you from falling for scams.
- **Don't wait until it's too late!** Talk to your lender about your need for assistance, and do it soon. Some servicers have programs for those who are not yet delinquent and other programs for borrowers who already are delinquent. For the greatest number of options, get started as soon as you know that you have a problem making your mortgage payments as agreed, and be sure to ask for all the options your servicer may have for you.

What to do for more serious problems

For problems that may take longer than three to six months to remedy, ask for mortgage loan forbearance or loan modifications.

A *forbearance* temporarily modifies or eliminates payments that are made up at the end of the forbearance period. This option is where the lender allows you a period of time (usually three to six months), during which time you can make lower or no payments. This option also prevents your credit from being damaged by a string of late payments.

A *repayment plan* is a payment arrangement agreed upon by the lender to accept partial extra payments from you until the delinquent amount is repaid. For example, if the monthly payment is $1,200 and the mortgage is three months delinquent, the lender may allow the borrower to pay $1,800 per month for six months. However, if no agreement is made, lenders will generally reject a partial payment.

A *loan modification* permanently changes one or more terms of the original mortgage in a way that addresses your specific needs. If this option seems intimidating, use a HUD-approved agency to deal with the servicer and offer solutions on your behalf. Clear communication is key here.

Modifications need to be in writing and approved by both the servicer and the borrower. Don't be surprised if the servicer asks for a fee to cover the costs of processing a loan modification.

What to do to end matters

Even when you can't solve your problem or just can't stand it anymore, you're better off staying in control of the process rather than just giving up. Doing so can lessen credit damage and expenses and keep your dignity — and maybe your sanity — intact.

The following are some of the many options available. And don't forget that another reason to use a free professional mortgage counselor is that newer options may be available to you as well. Be sure to check out the resources mentioned in the earlier section "Knowing Where to Turn for Help."

- **Selling your home:** You may be able to sell your home in a short sale if you have no equity left or a pre-foreclosure sale if the value of the house still exceeds the amount due on the mortgage.
- **Short sale:** You get your lender to allow you to sell your home for less than the mortgage value. This option is generally cheaper for the bank and less

stressing for the homeowner than a foreclosure. Because it is good for the lender, you can negotiate a bit. Ask that the loan deficiency be reported to the credit bureau as a zero balance and paid as agreed, rather than a charge-off.

- **Pre-foreclosure sale:** A pre-foreclosure sale arrangement enables you to defer mortgage payments that you can't afford while you sell your house. It also keeps any additional late payments off your credit report.
- **Deed-in-lieu of foreclosure:** If the home can't be sold, you can sign the title over to the lender and move out. To qualify for this option, you usually can't have a second mortgage, a home equity loan, or another lien on the property.
- **Stopping payments as part of a plan:** Not our favorite option, but if your plan is to save money for rent or for the larger down payment you'll need for a new place to live, then setting aside the money you would have paid for your mortgage can accrue several months or even years of savings. The price can be high in credit damage and stress, however. See the later section "Strategic default: Stopping payments."

Managing a foreclosure

TIP

If you're being foreclosed on, you still may have the option to talk to the servicer and try to work matters out, buy more time to come up with a solution, or at least make a more dignified exit from your home. But again, timing is very important, so don't wait!

- **Get a HUD-approved counselor involved and review loss mitigation options with your servicer.** Most want to help. (Check out the earlier section "Knowing Where to Turn for Help.")
- **Remain in contact with the servicer's loss mitigation staff until you get a solution you can live with.** If they don't offer workable suggestions, ask to speak to managers and vice presidents or higher. This is not a time to stand on protocol or accept "I'm sorry" for an answer.
- **See an attorney.** Ask for options. Review all the mortgage and foreclosure documents to be sure they were properly drawn and executed. The technical phrase used here is *truth in lending compliance.* Ask about bankruptcy options and timing so that you know all options available to you.

Strategic default: Stopping payments

A *strategic default* is an intentional mortgage default based on a plan or strategy. Here's an example: A person has a home whose value has fallen so far below what is owed on the mortgage that he will never realistically recover enough equity to break even on the home. Because the house will never be worth what is owed, the homeowner stops paying the mortgage. This option is more popular in states with *nonrecourse mortgages* (meaning that the house is the sole security for the mortgage loan, and the homeowner isn't responsible for any shortage beyond what the house brings at sale). However, you need to understand some of the possible consequences:

- **Credit score:** Any defaulted payments (delinquency) and foreclosure will show up on your credit report and lower your credit score. How much your score will be reduced depends on your score *before* the default and other credit activity. A lower score means you will likely have more difficulty when trying to get approved for credit in the future. If you're able to be approved, you almost certainly will end up with a higher interest rate.
- **Housing:** After foreclosure, buying a new home can be difficult. With a foreclosure on a credit report, you may have to wait three years before you can qualify for a Federal Housing Authority (FHA) mortgage (one year on rare occasions) and two to eight years before you can qualify for a *conforming mortgage* (the most common type of non-government loan), depending on the lender.
- **Deficiency balance:** This balance is the difference between what the lender sells your home for after foreclosure and what you owe on the mortgage. In some states, called *recourse states,* the lender can sue you for the deficiency balance, which may allow them to garnish your wages or take other collection actions against you. In nonrecourse states, the lender generally cannot sue you for the deficiency balance, although there may be some exceptions. For example, nonrecourse protection may not apply to a refinanced loan or second mortgage.

Other factors to consider include how much longer you would like to stay in the home and how far underwater you are. If you're $25,000 underwater and your home suits your long-term needs, it probably makes sense to just stay put and wait for the local market to recover. But if you're $100,000 underwater and your job or family situation requires you to move quickly, you may find strategic default more appealing. At the same time, it may not be your only option. For example, you may be able to rent out your home or get your lender to approve a short sale, where you sell your home for less than what you owe on your mortgage.

Thinking about your goals and the implications of strategic default can help you decide if it's the right choice.

TIP

For a chart that shows each state's timeline for foreclosure based upon the last payment installment in each state, go to `https://singlefamily.fanniemae.com/media/6726/display`.

Strategic default is a high-credit-damage strategy, but it may be cost-effective depending on your situation and plans involving loans or credit use in the future.

Strategic default is an unfortunate reality for the long-term unemployed. The argument goes: After all, this is business, and businesses routinely stop paying on debts that they can't afford or that are worth less than they owe. You probably have been told that you have to pay your bills, honor your obligations, and keep your promises, but some desperate home buyers are taking a business rather than a personal approach to their homes and finances.

Most mortgages detail what happens if you don't pay. Either you pay or your home is taken away. So the question arises: If you tell the bank to go ahead and take the house, are you meeting your obligations? From the bank's perspective, clearly you're not. From your family's perspective, however, the answer may be different.

Some states require all mortgages to be *nonrecourse*, meaning that the lender has recourse to the defaulted property and nothing else.

REMEMBER

Staying in a home you can't afford can deprive your family of your precious savings, empty your retirement accounts, and eventually ruin your credit when you finally default. Many people are willing to put up with the price of any shame or guilt in order to ensure a faster recovery with more money in their bank accounts.

Dealing with Deficiencies

When all is said and done, you may still owe some money. If your home sells for less than the amount you still owe on the mortgage, plus fees, then you may have what's called a *deficiency balance*. For example, say you borrow $500,000 to purchase a home, but you fall behind on payments or walk away from the home, and the bank forecloses. The home ultimately sells for $400,000. The $100,000 that the lender loses on the deal is called a *deficiency*. A first mortgage holder may or may not forgive this amount. Second mortgage holders may go after the borrower for deficiencies.

Your lender can get a deficiency judgment lien against your personal property and any other real estate that you own, giving it a security interest in that property. This means that the bank can foreclose on other real estate if you have enough equity for the bank to think that it may get enough money to make the effort worthwhile. However, just because the lender gets a deficiency judgment does not mean that it will try to collect. The lender may opt to write off the debt and issue you an IRS Form 1099-C. If this happens, you may owe taxes on the forgiven amount over a certain dollar amount.

If a lender comes after you for a large deficiency, consider speaking to an attorney about the benefits of filing for bankruptcy versus trying to work out a payment agreement with the lender. This advice can help to ensure you're making the best possible decision for your situation.

The most important detail is to realize that your problems may not be over after you leave the home. You may need to deal with the IRS if you don't qualify for mortgage debt forgiveness under its rules.

REMEMBER

The following are some potential, and we stress *potential*, situations you may face and what you can do to deal with them:

- **The lender may ask for a note.** Although this practice isn't current among first mortgage holders, we want you to be aware of it for the future, or if your second mortgage holder loses money on your loan. This note isn't written on monogrammed stationery; it's a promise to pay an unsecured amount to cover the mortgage deficiency after the sale. Use an attorney if your lender mentions this to you.
- **The lender may send a demand letter.** A mortgage lender may send a demand for payment of any deficiency following the sale of a home. The lender uses a *demand letter* if it doesn't want to give you an unsecured loan for the balance due. In essence, the problem is all yours, and you need to work out a way to pay the balance. Again, if this happens, get an attorney to advise you.
- **The lender may forgive what you owe.** More likely among first mortgage holders, forgiveness isn't required. This gesture is nice as far as it goes, but the IRS counts forgiven debt as income. Forms 1099-A and 1099-C, which are normally used to document unreported income, are also used to report forgiven debt. The amount of the forgiven debt becomes taxable income in most cases.

  Debt reduced through mortgage restructuring, as well as mortgage debt forgiven in connection with a foreclosure, may qualify for this relief. If you spent the forgiven debt money to pay a car loan, credit card bills, or for any non-real estate purpose, it's not covered, and you'll get a tax bill for it. Debt on second homes, rental property, and business property doesn't qualify.

  TIP

  If you are a foreclosed borrower faced with a sizable 1099-C, you still have hope. If you file IRS Form 982, Reduction of Tax Attributes Due to Discharge of Indebtedness, and you're insolvent at the time of the forgiven debt, the IRS may forgive the liability. (You can find IRS Form 982 at `www.irs.gov/pub/irs-pdf/f982.pdf`.) Again, see your attorney for the details.

  If you receive a Form 1099-C from your mortgage lender for the current tax year, or if you filed a tax return for the prior tax year that included income from mortgage loan forgiveness, this option may be for you. If you meet the requirements of the Qualified Principal Residence Indebtedness (QPRI) exclusion, you don't have to report the forgiven principal as income on your tax return. The QPRI exclusion may allow an exclusion up to $375,000 (up to $750,000 for married couples) of forgiven debt from their taxable income.

- **The state you live in makes mortgages nonrecourse.** If you live in certain states, you may get a break relating to personal mortgage deficiencies. Some states have passed laws saying that you're not responsible for any mortgage deficiencies.

Preparing for "Credit Winter"

After a foreclosure, your credit will be severely damaged — in some cases and for some purposes, for years to come. Knowing that post-foreclosure credit is hard to come by, you're wise to give some thought to how you'll cope with the credit fallout that may seem like the equivalent of a nuclear winter.

When you realize that you may be getting in trouble with your mortgage, you can do some actions to protect your access to credit in the "credit winter" that often follows a foreclosure. Like the biblical farmer who put aside grain for the lean years to come, you can store up some credit in advance. Here's how:

- **Review your credit cards to make sure that you have enough credit available.** Be sure you have enough revolving credit available. If not, consider opening new credit cards before you become delinquent on your mortgage. Doing so ensures that you can lead a more normal credit life while your credit is recovering. Plus, using and paying off multiple cards each month provides new streams of positive data to help repair your damaged credit report.
- **Establish a personal line of credit at your local bank or credit union that is not secured by your home.**
- **If you need to make a large financed purchase such as a car (purchase or lease), major appliance, or furniture down the road, consider making it before you become delinquent on your mortgage, while your credit is still strong.**
- **Prepare a short explanation (called a *consumer statement*) of why you defaulted and what you've done to make sure it won't happen again, and have that statement placed in your credit report.** It's like an exit statement that explains why you left your last job in the best possible light. This explanation may be useful if you need to find a new job that checks your credit report, are up for a promotion at work, or are looking for new housing.

IN THIS CHAPTER

» Looking into life insurance

» Debating disability insurance

» Selecting the best health insurance

Chapter 3

Insurance on You: Life, Disability, and Health

During your working years, multiplying your typical annual income by the number of years you plan to continue working produces a pretty big number. That dollar amount equals what is probably your most valuable asset — your ability to earn an income. You need to protect this asset by purchasing some insurance on *you*.

This chapter explains the ins and outs of buying insurance to protect your income: life insurance in case of death, and disability insurance in case of an accident or severe medical condition that prevents you from working. We tell you what coverage you should have, where to look for it, and what to avoid.

In addition to protecting your income, you also should insure against financially catastrophic expenses — the type of bills that are racked up from a major surgery and a lengthy stay in the hospital. To protect yourself from potentially astronomical medical bills, secure comprehensive health insurance.

Providing for Your Loved Ones: Life Insurance

You generally need life insurance only when other people depend on your income. The following folks don't need life insurance to protect their incomes:

- Single people with no children
- Working couples who can maintain a lifestyle acceptable to them on one of their incomes
- Independently wealthy people who don't need to work
- Retired people who are living off their retirement nest egg
- Minor children (are you financially dependent upon your children?)

If others are either fully or partly dependent on your paycheck (usually a spouse and/or child), you need life insurance, especially if you have major financial commitments such as a mortgage or years of child-rearing ahead. You may also want to consider life insurance if an extended family member is currently or likely to be dependent on your future income.

Determining how much life insurance to buy

Determining how much life insurance to buy is as much a subjective decision as it is a quantitative decision. There's no need to get fancy in your calculations, though. Figuring out how much life insurance you need doesn't have to be complicated.

TIP

The main purpose of life insurance is to provide a lump sum payment to replace the deceased person's income. Ask yourself how many years of income you want to replace. Table 3-1 provides a simple way to figure how much life insurance to consider purchasing. To replace a certain number of years' worth of income, simply multiply the appropriate number in the table by your annual after-tax income.

Another way to determine the amount of life insurance to buy is to think about how much would be needed to pay for major debts or expenditures, such as your mortgage, other loans, and college for your children. For example, suppose you want your spouse to have enough of a life insurance death benefit to pay off your mortgage and half of your children's college education. Simply add your mortgage amount to half of your children's estimated college costs, and then buy that amount of life insurance.

TABLE 3-1 **Life Insurance Calculation**

Years of Income to Replace	Multiply Annual After-Tax Income* By
5	4.5
10	8.5
20	15
30	20

** Roughly determine your annual after-tax income in one of two ways: Get out your last year's tax return (and Form W-2) and subtract the federal, state, and Social Security taxes you paid from your gross employment income; or multiply your gross income by 80 percent if you're a low-income earner, 70 percent if you're a moderate-income earner, or 60 percent if you're a high-income earner.*

Social Security, if you're covered, can provide survivors benefits to your spouse and children. However, depending upon your income, you may owe federal income tax on 50 to 85 percent of your benefits. Single taxpayers may earn up to $25,000 annually without being taxed on these benefits. If your earnings are between $25,000 and $34,000, 50 percent of the survivors benefit is taxable. If you earn above $34,000, 85 percent is taxable. For taxpayers filing their taxes jointly, you may have income up to $32,000 for tax-exempt status on survivor's benefits. For incomes between $32,000 and $44,000, 50 percent is taxable, and 85 percent is taxable for incomes above $44,000.

TIP

You may want to factor your Social Security survivors benefits into how much life insurance to buy, but be sure to consider the taxes you may owe on them. Contact the Social Security Administration by phone at 800-772-1213 or visit its website at `www.ssa.gov` to estimate your benefits.

The Social Security Administration can tell you how much your survivors would receive per month in the event of your death. You should factor this benefit into the amount of life insurance that you calculate in Table 3-1. For example, suppose your annual after-tax income is $25,000 and Social Security provides a survivors benefit of $10,000 annually. Therefore, for the purposes of Table 3-1, you should determine the amount of life insurance needed to replace $15,000 annually ($25,000 – $10,000), not $25,000.

Comparing term life insurance to cash value life insurance

We're going to tell you how you can save hours of time and thousands of dollars. Ready? *Buy term life insurance.* If you've already figured out how much life insurance to purchase and this is all the advice you need, you can jump to the later section "Buying term insurance."

EXAMINING "OTHER" LIFE INSURANCE

Contemplating the possibility of your untimely demise is surely depressing. You'll likely feel some peace of mind when purchasing a life insurance policy to provide for your dependents. However, consider taking matters a step further. Suppose you (or your spouse) pass away. Do you think that simply buying a life insurance policy will be sufficient "help" for the loved ones you leave behind? Surely your contribution to your household involves far more than being a breadwinner.

Do you have a will? See Book 7 for more details on wills and other estate-planning documents. Make sure all your important financial documents — investment account statements, insurance policies, employee benefits materials, small-business accounting records, and so on — are kept in one place (such as a file drawer) that your loved ones know about. You may also want to consider providing a list of key contacts — such as who you recommend calling (or what you recommend reading) in the event of legal, financial, or tax quandaries.

So, in addition to trying to provide financially for your dependents, you should also take some time to reflect on what else you can do to help point them in the right direction on matters you normally handle. With most couples, it's natural for one spouse to take more responsibility for money management. That's fine; just make sure to talk about what's being done so that in the event that the responsible spouse dies, the surviving person knows how to jump into the driver's seat.

If you have kids (and even if you don't), you may want to give some thought to sentimental leave-behinds for your loved ones. These leave-behinds can be something like a short note telling them how much they meant to you and what you'd like them to remember about you.

If you want the details behind this recommendation for term insurance, the following information is for you. Or maybe you heard (and have already fallen prey to) the sales pitches from life insurance agents, most of whom love selling cash value life insurance because of its bigger commissions.

Despite the variety of names that life insurance marketing departments have cooked up for policies, life insurance comes in two basic flavors:

- **Term insurance:** This insurance is pure life insurance. You pay an annual premium for which you receive a particular amount of life insurance coverage. If you, the insured person, pass away, your beneficiaries collect; otherwise, the premium is gone, but you're grateful to be alive!

» **Cash value insurance:** All other life insurance policies (whole, universal, variable, and so on) combine life insurance with a supposed savings feature. Not only do your premiums pay for life insurance, but some of your dollars are also credited to an account that grows in value over time, assuming you keep paying your premiums. On the surface, this type of insurance sounds potentially attractive. People don't like to feel that their premium dollars are getting tossed away.

WARNING

But cash value insurance has a big catch. For the same amount of coverage (for example, for $100,000 of life insurance benefits), cash value policies cost you about eight times (800 percent) more than comparable term policies.

Insurance salespeople know the buttons to push to interest you in buying the wrong kind of life insurance. In the following sections, we give you some of the typical arguments they make for purchasing cash value policies, followed by some perspective on each one.

"Cash value policies are all paid up after X years. You don't want to be paying life insurance premiums for the rest of your life, do you?"

Agents who pitch cash value life insurance present projections that imply that after the first ten or so years of paying your premiums, you don't need to pay more premiums to keep the life insurance in force. The only reason you may be able to stop paying premiums is because you poured a lot of extra money into the policy in the early years. Keep in mind that cash value life insurance costs about eight times as much as term insurance.

Imagine that you're currently paying $500 a year for auto insurance and that an insurance company comes along and offers you a policy for $4,000 per year. The representative tells you that after ten years, you can stop paying and still keep your same coverage. We're sure you wouldn't fall for this sales tactic, but many people do when they buy cash value life insurance.

You also need to be wary of the projections because they often include unrealistic and lofty assumptions about the investment return that your cash balance can earn. When you stop paying into a cash value policy, the cost of each year's life insurance is deducted from the remaining cash value. If the rate of return on the cash balance is not sufficient to pay the insurance cost, the cash balance declines, and eventually you receive notices saying that your policy needs more funding to keep the life insurance in force.

"You won't be able to afford term insurance when you're older."

As you get older, the cost of term insurance increases because the risk of dying rises. But life insurance is not something you need all your life! It's typically bought in a person's younger years when financial commitments and obligations outweigh financial assets. Twenty or thirty years later, the reverse should be true.

After you retire, you don't need life insurance to protect your employment income, because there isn't any to protect. You may need life insurance when you're raising a family and/or you have a substantial mortgage to pay off, but by the time you retire, the kids should be out on their own (you hope!), and the mortgage should be paid down.

In the meantime, term insurance saves you a tremendous amount of money. For most people, it takes 20 to 30 years for the premium they're paying on a term insurance policy to finally catch up to (equal) the premium they've been paying all along on a comparable amount of cash value life insurance.

"You can borrow against the cash value at a low interest rate."

Such a deal! It's your money in the policy, remember? If you deposited money in a savings or money-market account, how would you like to pay for the privilege of borrowing your own money back? Borrowing on your cash value policy is potentially dangerous: You increase the chances that the policy will lapse — leaving you with nothing to show for your premiums.

"Your cash value grows tax-deferred."

Ah, a glimmer of truth at last. The cash value portion of your policy grows without taxation until you withdraw it, but if you want tax-deferral of your investment balances, you should first take advantage of funding 401(k)s, 403(b)s, SEP-IRAs, and other tax-advantaged retirement accounts. Such accounts give you an immediate tax deduction for your current contributions in addition to growth without taxation until withdrawal.

The money you pay into a cash value life policy gives you no up-front tax deductions. If you exhaust the tax-deductible plans, consider Roth accounts and then variable annuities, which provide access to better investment options and tax-deferred compounding of your investment dollars. Roth accounts have the added bonus of tax-free withdrawal of your investment earnings. (See Book 6 for details on retirement accounts.)

WARNING

Life insurance tends to be a mediocre investment at best. The insurance company generally quotes you an interest rate for the first year; after that, the company changes the rate annually. If you don't like the future interest rates, you can be penalized for quitting the policy. Would you ever invest your money in a bank account that quoted an interest rate for the first year and then penalized you for moving your money within the next seven to ten years?

"Cash value policies are forced savings."

Many agents argue that a cash value plan is better than nothing — at least it's forcing you to save. This line of thinking is silly because so many people drop cash value life insurance policies after just a few years of paying into them. You can accomplish "forced savings" without using life insurance. Any of the retirement savings accounts mentioned in Book 6 can be set up with automatic monthly transfers. Employers offering such a plan can deduct contributions from your paycheck — and they don't take a commission! You can also set up monthly electronic transfers from your bank account to contribute to mutual funds.

"Life insurance is not part of your taxable estate."

If the ownership of a life insurance policy is properly structured, the death benefit is free of estate taxes. This part of the sales pitch is about the only sound reasoning that exists for buying cash value life insurance. Under current federal laws, you can pass on $12.92 million ($25.84 million for a married couple) free of federal estate taxes. But even if you have that large of a nest egg, you have numerous other ways to reduce your taxable estate.

Making your decision

Insurance salespeople aggressively push cash value policies because of the high commissions that insurance companies pay them. Commissions on cash value life insurance range from 50 to 100 percent of your first year's premium. Insurance salespeople, therefore, can make *eight to ten times more money* (yes, you read that right) selling you a cash value policy than they can selling you term insurance.

Ultimately, when you purchase cash value life insurance, you pay the high commissions that are built into these policies. As you can see in the policy's cash value table, you don't get back any of the money that you dump into the policy if you quit the policy in the first few years. The insurance company can't afford to give you any of your money back in those early years because so much of it has been paid to the selling agent as commission. That's why these policies explicitly penalize you for withdrawing your cash balance within the first seven to ten years.

Because of the high cost of cash value policies relative to the cost of term, you're more likely to buy less life insurance coverage than you need — that's the sad part of the insurance industry's pushing of this stuff. The vast majority of life insurance buyers need more protection than they can afford to buy with cash value coverage.

WARNING

Cash value life insurance is the most oversold insurance and financial product in the history of the financial services industry. Cash value life insurance makes sense for a small number of people, such as business owners who own a business worth at least $10+ million and don't want their heirs to be forced to sell their business to pay estate taxes in the event of their death. (See the later section "Considering the purchase of cash value life insurance.")

REMEMBER

Purchase low-cost term insurance and do your investing separately. Life insurance is rarely a permanent need; over time, you can reduce the amount of term insurance you carry as your financial obligations lessen and you accumulate more assets.

Buying term insurance

Term insurance policies have several features from which to choose. The following sections cover the important elements of term insurance so you can make an informed decision about purchasing it.

Selecting how often your premium adjusts

Term insurance can be purchased so your premium adjusts (increases) annually or after 5, 10, 15, or 20 years. The less frequently your premium adjusts, the higher the initial premium and its incremental increases will be. (Keep in mind that as you get older, the risk of dying increases, so the cost of your insurance goes up.)

The advantage of a premium that locks in for, say, ten years is that you have the security of knowing how much you'll be paying annually for the next ten years. You also don't need to go through medical evaluations as frequently to qualify for the lowest rate possible. The disadvantage of a policy with a long-term rate lock is that you pay more in the early years than you do on a policy that adjusts more frequently. In addition, you may want to change the amount of insurance you carry as your circumstances change. Thus, you may throw money away when you dump a policy with a long-term premium guarantee before its rate is set to change.

Policies that adjust the premium every five to ten years offer a happy medium between price and predictability.

Ensuring guaranteed renewability

Guaranteed renewability, which is standard practice on the better policies, assures that the policy can't be canceled because of poor health. Don't buy a life insurance policy without this feature unless you expect that your life insurance needs will disappear when the policy is up for renewal.

Deciding where to buy term insurance

A number of sound ways to obtain high-quality, low-cost term insurance are available. You may choose to buy through a local agent because you know them or prefer to buy from someone close to home. However, you should invest a few minutes of your time getting quotes from one or two of the following sources to get a sense of what's available in the insurance market. Gaining familiarity with the market can prevent an agent from selling you an overpriced, high-commission policy.

TIP

Here are some sources for high-quality, low-cost term insurance:

- **USAA:** This company sells low-cost term insurance directly to the public. Contact USAA by phone at 800-531-8722 or visit `www.usaa.com/inet/wc/insurance_life_level_term`.
- **Insurance agency quotation services:** These services provide proposals from the highest-rated, lowest-cost companies available. Like other agencies, the services receive a commission if you buy a policy from them, which you're under no obligation to do. They ask questions such as your date of birth, whether you smoke, some basic health questions, and how much coverage you want. Services that are worth considering include:
  - **AccuQuote:** Phone 800-442-9899; website `www.accuquote.com`
  - **ReliaQuote:** Phone 800-940-3002; website `www.reliaquote.com`
  - **Term4Sale:** Phone 888-798-3488; website `www.term4sale.com` (This company doesn't sell life insurance but can provide quotes and refer you to three agents in your area who do.)

Insurance on You: Life, Disability, and Health

Considering the purchase of cash value life insurance

WARNING

Don't expect to get objective information from the typical salesperson who sells cash value life insurance. Beware of insurance salespeople masquerading under the guise of self-anointed titles, such as estate-planning specialists or financial planners.

As we discuss earlier in this chapter, purchasing cash value life insurance may make sense to consider if you expect to have an estate-tax "problem." However, cash value life insurance is just one of many ways to reduce your estate taxes.

Among the best places to shop for cash value life insurance policies are:

- **USAA:** Phone 800-531-8722; website www.usaa.com/inet/wc/insurance_life_permanent
- **Ameritas Direct:** Phone 800-555-4655; website www.ameritasdirect.com

TIP

If you want to obtain some cash value life insurance, tread carefully with local insurance agents. Most agents aren't as interested in educating as they are in selling. Besides, the best cash value policies can be obtained commission-free when you buy them from the sources in the preceding list. The money saved on commissions (which can easily be thousands of dollars) is reflected in a much higher cash value for you.

Getting rid of cash value life insurance

REMEMBER

If you were snookered into buying a cash value life insurance policy and you want to part ways with it, go ahead and do so. But don't cancel the coverage until you first secure new term coverage. When you need life insurance, you don't want to have a period when you're not covered (Murphy's Law says *that's* when disaster will strike).

Ending a cash value life insurance policy has tax consequences. You generally must pay federal income tax on the amount you receive in excess of the premiums you paid over the life of the policy. Because some life insurance policies feature tax-deferred retirement savings, you may incur a 10-percent federal income tax penalty on earnings withdrawn before age 59½, just as you would with an IRA. Before withdrawing the cash balance in your life insurance policy, consider checking with the insurer or a tax advisor to clarify what the tax consequences may be.

TIP

You can avoid federal income tax early withdrawal penalties and sidestep taxation on accumulated interest in a life insurance policy by doing a tax-free exchange (also known as a section 1035 exchange) into a no-load (commission-free) variable annuity. The no-load mutual-fund company through which you buy the annuity takes care of transferring your existing balance.

Preparing for the Unpredictable: Disability Insurance

As with life insurance, the purpose of disability insurance is to protect your employment income. The only difference is that with disability insurance, you're protecting the income for yourself (and perhaps also your dependents). If you're completely disabled, you still have living expenses, but you probably can't earn employment income.

We're referring to long-term disabilities. If you strain your back while reliving your athletic glory days and you wind up in bed for several days, it likely won't be a financial disaster. But what if you were disabled in such a way that you couldn't work for several years? This section helps you figure out whether you need disability insurance, how much to get, and where to find it.

Deciding whether you need coverage

Most large employers offer disability insurance to their employees. Many small-company employees and all self-employed people are left to fend for themselves without disability coverage. Being without disability insurance is a risky proposition, especially if, like most working people, you need your employment income to live on.

If you're married and your spouse earns a large enough income that you can make do without yours, consider skipping disability coverage. The same is true if you've already accumulated enough money for your future years (in other words, you're financially independent). Keep in mind, though, that your expenses may go up if you become disabled and require specialized care.

For most people, dismissing the need for disability coverage is easy. The odds of suffering a long-term disability seem so remote — and they are. But if you suffer bad luck, disability coverage can relieve you (and possibly your family) of a major financial burden.

Most disabilities are caused by medical problems, such as arthritis, heart conditions, hypertension, and back/spine or hip/leg impairments. Some of these ailments occur with advancing age, but more than one-third of all disabilities are suffered by people under the age of 45. The vast majority of these medical problems cannot be predicted in advance, particularly those caused by random accidents.

WARNING

If you think you have good disability coverage through government programs, you'd better think again:

- **Social Security disability:** Social Security pays long-term benefits only if you're not able to perform any substantial, gainful activity for more than a year or if your disability is expected to result in death. Furthermore, Social Security disability payments are quite low because they're intended to provide only for basic, subsistence-level living expenses.
- **Workers' compensation:** Workers' compensation (if you have such coverage through your employer) pays you benefits if you're injured on the job, but it doesn't pay any benefits if you get disabled away from your job. You need coverage that pays regardless of where and how you're disabled.
- **State disability programs:** Some states have disability insurance programs, but the coverage is typically bare bones. State programs are also generally not a good value because of the cost for the small amount of coverage they provide. Benefits are paid over a short period of time (typically only up to a year).

Determining how much disability insurance you need

You need enough disability coverage to provide you with sufficient income to live on until other financial resources become available. If you don't have much saved in the way of financial assets and you want to continue with the lifestyle supported by your current income if you suffer a disability, get disability coverage to replace your entire monthly take-home (after-tax) pay.

TIP

The benefits you purchase on a disability policy are quoted as the dollars per month you receive if disabled. So, if your job provides you with a $3,000-per-month income after taxes, seek a policy that provides a $3,000-per-month benefit.

If you pay for your disability insurance, the benefits are tax-free (but hopefully you won't ever have to collect them). If your employer picks up the tab, your benefits are taxable, so you need a larger benefit amount.

In addition to the monthly coverage amount, you also need to select the duration for which you want a policy to pay you benefits. You need a policy that pays benefits until you reach an age at which you become financially self-sufficient. For most people, that's around age 65 to 67, when their Social Security benefits kick in. If you anticipate needing your employment income past your mid-60s, you may want to obtain disability coverage that pays you until a later age.

If you crunch some numbers and find that you're within five to ten years of being financially independent or able to retire, five-year and ten-year disability policies are available. You may also consider such short-term policies when you're sure that someone (for example, a family member) can support you financially over the long term.

Identifying other features you need in disability insurance

Disability insurance policies have many confusing features. Here's what to look for — and look out for — when purchasing disability insurance:

- **Definition of disability:** An *own-occupation* disability policy provides benefit payments if you can't perform the work you normally do. Some policies pay you only if you're unable to perform a job for which you are *reasonably trained.* Other policies revert to this definition after a few years of being own-occupation. Own-occupation policies are the most expensive because there's a greater chance that the insurer will have to pay you. The extra cost may not be worth it unless you're in a high-income or specialized occupation and you'd have to take a significant pay cut to do something else (and you wouldn't be happy about a reduced income and the required lifestyle changes).
- **Noncancelable and guaranteed renewable:** These features ensure that your policy can't be canceled because of your falling into poor health. With policies that require periodic physical exams, you can lose your coverage just when you're most likely to need it.
- **Waiting period:** This is the "deductible" on disability insurance — the time between the onset of your disability and the time you begin collecting benefits. As with other types of insurance, you should take the highest deductible (longest waiting period) that your financial circumstances allow. Longer waiting periods significantly reduce the cost of the insurance and eliminate the hassle of filing a claim for a short-term disability. The minimum waiting period on most policies is 30 days. The maximum waiting period can be up to one to two years. Try a waiting period of three to six months if you have sufficient emergency reserves.
- **Residual benefits:** This option pays you a partial benefit if you have a disability that prevents you from working full-time.
- **Cost-of-living adjustments (COLAs):** This feature automatically increases your benefit payment by a set percentage annually or in accordance with changes in inflation. The advantage of a COLA is that it retains the purchasing power of your benefits. A modest COLA, such as 3 to 4 percent, is worth considering.

» **Future insurability:** A clause that many agents encourage you to buy, future insurability enables you to buy additional coverage regardless of health. For most people, paying for the privilege of buying more coverage later is not worth it if the income you earn today fairly reflects your likely long-term earnings and spending desires. You may benefit from the future insurability option if your income is artificially low now and you're confident that it will rise significantly in the future. (For example, you just got out of medical school and you're earning a low salary while being a resident.)

» **Insurer's financial stability:** You should choose insurers that'll be here tomorrow to pay your claim. That said, don't obsess over the stability of the company; benefits are paid even if the insurer fails, because the state or another insurer will almost always bail out the unstable insurer.

Deciding where to buy disability insurance

The place to buy disability insurance with the best value is through your employer or professional association. Unless these groups have done a lousy job shopping for coverage, group plans generally offer a better value than disability insurance you can purchase on your own. Just make sure that the group plan meets the specifications discussed in the preceding section, especially any limitations of benefit amounts or stricter qualification terms, which are found on some group plans.

WARNING

Don't trust an insurance agent to be enthusiastic about the quality of a disability policy your employer or other group is offering. Agents have a conflict of interest when they criticize these options, because they won't make a commission if you buy through a group.

If you don't have access to a group policy, check with your agent or a company you already do business with. But tread carefully when purchasing disability insurance through an agent. Some agents try to add all sorts of extra bells and whistles to policies to pump up the premium along with their commission.

Getting the Care You Need: Health Insurance

Almost everyone needs health insurance, but not everyone has it. Some people in the past were denied coverage or couldn't afford the coverage they were offered. Other people who could afford health insurance chose not to buy it because they believed that they were healthy and weren't going to need it. Others who opted not to buy health insurance figured that if they ever really needed healthcare, they'd be able to get needed care. To a large extent, they're right. But people without health insurance generally put off getting routine care, which can lead to small problems turning into bigger and costlier ones.

Mandating health insurance: The Affordable Care Act

The Patient Protection and Affordable Care Act (informally known as Obamacare) and the Health Care and Education Reconciliation Act enacted comprehensive healthcare reform in the United States.

Employer group health plans are subject to these rules:

- Plans offering dependent coverage must offer coverage to adult children up to age 26. The coverage isn't taxable to the employee or dependent.
- Plans must provide preventive care without cost-sharing and must cover certain child preventive care services as recommended by the government. This rule applies only to new group health plans.
- Employers must offer minimum essential coverage to full-time employees or make nondeductible payments to the government.
- Plans must remove all annual dollar limits on participants' benefit payments. They may not impose lifetime limits.
- Plans must limit cost-sharing and deductibles to levels that don't exceed those applicable to a health-savings-account-eligible, high-deductible health plan.
- Plans must remove all preexisting condition exclusions on all participants.
- Plans may not have waiting periods of longer than 90 days.

Higher-income taxpayers are now hit with higher tax rates on their investments as well as higher Medicare tax rates to help pay for Obamacare. Taxpayers with total taxable income above $200,000 (for a single return) or $250,000 (for a joint return) from any source are subject to a 3.8 percent tax on the *lesser* of the following:

- Their net investment income (for example, interest, dividends, and capital gains)

» The amount, if any, by which their modified adjusted gross income exceeds the dollar thresholds

Taxpayers with earned income above $200,000 (for a single return) or $250,000 (for a joint return) are subject to an additional 0.9 percent Medicare tax (in other words, rising from 1.45 percent to 2.35 percent) on wages in excess of those amounts. Employers aren't required to match the payment of this incremental increase, which is applicable only to the employee.

Choosing the best health plan

Before Medicare (the government-run insurance program for the elderly) kicks in at age 65+, odds are that you obtain your health insurance through your employer. Be thankful if you do. Employer-provided coverage eliminates the headache of having to shop for coverage, and it's usually cheaper than coverage you buy on your own.

Whether you have options through your employer or you have to hunt for a plan on your own, the following sections cover the major issues to consider when selecting among the health insurance offerings in the marketplace.

Major medical coverage

You need a plan that covers the *big* potential expenses: hospitalization, physician, and ancillary charges, such as X-rays and laboratory work. If you're a woman and you think that you may want to have children, make sure your plan has maternity benefits.

Choice of healthcare providers

Plans that let you use any healthcare provider you want are becoming less common and more expensive in most areas. Health maintenance organizations (HMOs) and preferred provider organizations (PPOs) are the main plans that restrict your choices. They keep costs down because they negotiate lower rates with selected providers.

HMOs and PPOs are more similar than they are different. The main difference is that PPOs still pay the majority of your expenses if you use a provider outside their approved list. If you use a provider outside the approved list with an HMO, you typically aren't covered at all.

TIP

If you have your heart set on particular physicians or hospitals, find out which health insurance plans they accept as payment. Ask yourself whether the extra cost of an open-choice plan is worth being able to use their services if they're not part of a restricted-choice plan. Also be aware that some plans allow you to go outside their network of providers as long as you pay a bigger portion of the incurred medical costs. If you're interested in being able to use alternative types of providers, such as acupuncturists, find out whether the plans you're considering cover these services.

Don't let stories of how hard it is to get an appointment with a doctor or other logistical hassles deter you from going with an HMO or PPO plan. These setbacks can happen in plans with open choice, too. The idea that doctors who can't get patients on their own are the only ones who sign up with restricted-choice plans is a myth. Although HMO and PPO plans do offer fewer choices when it comes to providers, surveys show that customer satisfaction with these plans is as high as it is for plans that offer more choices.

Lifetime maximum benefits

Health insurance plans specify the maximum total benefits they'll pay over the course of time you're insured by their plan. Although a million dollars may be more money than you could ever imagine being spent on your healthcare, it's the minimum acceptable level of total benefits. With the cost of healthcare today, you can quickly blow through that if you develop major health problems.

The Affordable Care Act has generally required health plans to do away with lifetime maximums. If you're shopping for a noncompliant plan, ideally choose a plan that has no maximum or that has a maximum of at least $5 million.

Deductibles and co-payments

TIP

To reduce your health insurance premiums, choose a plan with the highest deductible and co-payment you can afford. As with other insurance policies, the more you're willing to share in the payment of your claims, the less you have to pay in premiums. Most policies have annual deductible options (such as $250, $500, $1,000, and so on) as well as co-payment options, which are typically 20 percent or so.

When choosing a co-payment percentage, don't let your imagination run wild and unnecessarily scare you. A 20-percent co-payment doesn't mean that you have to come up with $20,000 for a $100,000 claim. Insurance plans generally set a maximum out-of-pocket limit on your annual co-payments (such as $1,000, $2,000, and so on); the insurer covers 100 percent of any medical expenses that go over that cap.

TIP

For insurance provided by your employer, consider plans with low out-of-pocket expenses if you know you have health problems. Because you're part of a group, the insurer won't increase your individual rates just because you're filing more claims.

Most HMO plans don't have deductible and co-payment options. Most just charge a set amount — such as $25 — for a physician's office visit.

Guaranteed renewability

The Affordable Care Act generally requires health insurers to continue your plan coverage regardless of any changes in your health. You want a health insurance plan that keeps renewing your coverage without you having to prove continued good health. If good health could be guaranteed, you wouldn't need health insurance in the first place.

SAVING ON TAXES WHEN SPENDING ON HEALTHCARE

If you expect to have out-of-pocket medical expenses, find out whether your employer offers a flexible spending or healthcare reimbursement account. These accounts enable you to pay for uncovered medical expenses with pre-tax dollars. If, for example, you're in a combined 30-percent federal and state income tax bracket, these accounts allow you to pay for necessary healthcare at a 30-percent discount. These accounts can also be used to pay for vision and dental care.

Be forewarned of the major stumbling blocks you face when saving through medical reimbursement accounts. First, you need to elect to save money from your paycheck prior to the beginning of each plan year. The only exception is at the time of a "life change," such as marriage, spouse's job change, divorce, a family member's death, or the birth of a child. You also generally need to use the money within the year you save it, because these accounts contain a "use it or lose it" feature. (Some employer plans now allow a $500 carryover; check your plan's details.)

Health savings accounts (HSAs) are another option, especially for the self-employed and people who work for smaller firms. To qualify, you must have a high-deductible (at least $1,500 for individuals; $3,000 for families) health insurance policy; then you can put money earmarked for medical expenses into an investment account that offers the tax benefits — deductible contributions (up to $3,850 for single taxpayers and $7,750 for families) and tax-deferred compounding — of a retirement account. And unlike a flexible spending account, you don't have to deplete the HSA by the end of the year: Money can compound tax-deferred inside the HSA for years. Begin to investigate an HSA through insurers offering health plans you're interested in or with the company you currently have coverage through.

You may also be able to save on taxes if you have a substantial amount of health-care expenditures in a year. You can deduct medical and dental expenses as an itemized deduction on Schedule A to the extent that they exceed 7.5 percent of your adjusted gross income. Unless you're a low-income earner, you need to have substantial expenses, usually caused by an accident or major illness, to take advantage of this tax break.

Buying health insurance

In addition to traditional insurance agents, numerous states operate health insurance exchanges that offer health plans that comply with the Affordable Care Act. To see if your state offers a health insurance exchange, visit `www.healthcare.gov/marketplace-in-your-state/`. If you live in a state without its own exchange, you can enroll in one at `www.healthcare.gov`.

You can buy many health plans through agents, and you can also buy some directly from the insurer. When health insurance is sold both ways, buying through an agent usually doesn't cost more.

TIP

If you're self-employed or you work for a small employer that doesn't offer health insurance as a benefit, get proposals from the larger and older health insurers in your area. Larger plans can negotiate better rates from providers, and older plans are more likely to be here tomorrow.

Many insurers operate in a bunch of different insurance businesses. You want those that are the biggest in the health insurance arena and are committed to that business. Nationally, Blue Cross Blue Shield, Kaiser Permanente, Aetna, UnitedHealth, CIGNA, Assurant, and Anthem are among the older and bigger health insurers.

TIP

Also check with professional or other associations that you belong to, because plans offered by these groups sometimes offer decent benefits at a competitive price due to the purchasing power clout that they possess. A competent independent insurance agent who specializes in health insurance can help you find insurers who are willing to offer you coverage.

Health insurance agents have a conflict of interest that's common to all financial salespeople working on commission: The higher the premium plan they sell you, the bigger the commission they earn. So an agent may try to steer you into higher-cost plans and avoid suggesting some of the strategies in the preceding section for reducing your cost of coverage. (Good agents can help guide you to the best plans that cover preexisting conditions and offer the lowest costs for your medications. Be sure to provide them with this information and compare options carefully.)

Understanding subsidies

Qualifying for a subsidy depends on your family income and how many children you have. Subsidies are available to qualified individuals and families whose incomes fall in the range of 100 percent to 400 percent of the poverty line (assuming they buy a policy on a government exchange). To be eligible for a subsidy, you may not have access to affordable health insurance coverage through an employer (including a family member's employer) and not be eligible for coverage through Medicare, Medicaid, the Children's Health Insurance Program (CHIP), or other forms of public assistance. The income thresholds vary based upon zip code — check out the handy subsidy calculator at `www.kff.org/interactive/subsidy-calculator/`.

TIP

If you're self-employed and end up receiving subsidies, be careful to keep track of your earnings. If you end up making more than you thought you would in a given year, you can end up having to pay back part of your subsidy. Of course, the reverse is also true: If you make less than expected, you may receive a refund.

Coping with higher health insurance prices

Here are a few tips for health insurance shoppers to make the most of their spending:

- **Be patient, shop around, and do your homework.** Talk to insurers and agents. Spend some time on the computer; the ACA marketplace website is `www.healthcare.gov`. Ask friends and colleagues what they're doing. Although you do need to be mindful of enrollment deadlines, you don't want to rush into what is an important financial decision.
- **If you go with a marketplace bronze plan, consider one that is compatible with a health savings account (HSA).** A bronze plan may be best for people who are generally healthy. These have the lowest premiums. Of course, they also have the highest deductibles, which means that in the event you do get sick, you'll have to cover more of your costs out of pocket. And that is why it's important to select a bronze plan that's compatible with an HSA (not all of them are). HSAs are a great tax-saving strategy, and now that deductibles are so high, they make more sense than ever. After all, if you have to

have a high deductible anyway, at least getting the tax break on the out-of-pocket expenses you have to pay makes sense.

- **Do what you can to get and stay healthy.** Chances are you'll now be paying more out of pocket for nonpreventative care, so good health should be your top priority. Of course, health insurance is needed because some conditions are unpreventable, but you can affect plenty of others with lifestyle improvements. Obviously, if you smoke, stop now; smoking is the only "preexisting condition" health insurance companies are allowed to charge you more for. But it's also important to eat healthfully, exercise, and lose weight if you need to. The healthier you are, the less you'll need to seek medical care — and the less you'll have to pay out of pocket for your care.

DEALING WITH MEDICAL CLAIMS HEADACHES

If you sign up for a health plan that has deductibles and co-payments, make sure you review the benefits statements your insurer sends you. Errors often pop up on these statements and during the claims filing process. Not surprisingly, the errors are usually at your expense.

Make sure that your insurer has kept accurate track of your contributions toward meeting your plan's annual deductible and maximum out-of-pocket charges. Also, don't pay any healthcare providers who send you bills until you receive proper notification from the insurance company detailing what you are obligated to pay those providers according to the terms of your plan. Because most insurance companies have negotiated discounted fee schedules with healthcare providers, the amount that a provider bills you is often higher than the amount they're legally due as per the terms of their contract with your insurer. Your insurer's benefits statement should detail the approved and negotiated rate once the claim is processed. Providers are due only the discounted fees they agreed to with your insurer.

Haggling with your health insurer is a real pain, and it usually happens after you rack up significant medical expenses and may still not be feeling well. But if you don't stay on top of your insurer, you can end up paying thousands of dollars in overpayments. If you're overwhelmed with an avalanche of claims and benefits statements, you may want to consider using a health insurance claims processing service. You can get a referral to firms that engage in this line of work by visiting the Alliance of Claims Assistance Professionals website at www.claims.org.

Looking at retiree medical care insurance

Medicare, the government-run health insurance plan for those age 65 and over, is a multi-part major medical plan. Enrollment in Part A (hospital expenses) is automatic. Part B, which covers physician expenses and other charges, including home healthcare coverage; Part C, supplemental Medicare coverage (sold through private insurers); and Part D, for prescription drugs (provided through private insurers), are optional. Supplemental insurance policies, also known as Medigap coverage, may be of interest to you if you want help paying for the costs that Medicare doesn't pay.

Closing Medicare's gaps

Medigap coverage generally pays the deductibles and co-payments that Medicare charges. For the first 60 days of hospitalization, you pay $1,600 total out of your own pocket. If you have an unusually long hospital stay, you pay $400 per day for the 61st through the 90th day, $800 per day for the 91st through the 150th day, and all costs beyond 150 days. Clearly, if you stay in a hospital for many months, your out-of-pocket expenses can escalate; however, the longest hospitalizations tend not to last for many months. Also note that Medicare's hospitalization benefits refresh when you're out of the hospital for 60 consecutive days.

If you're unable to pay for the deductibles and co-payments because your income is low, making a long hospital stay a financial catastrophe for you, *Medicaid* (the state-run medical insurance program for low-income people) may help pay your bills. Alternatively, Medigap insurance can help close the gap.

TIP

Check with your physician(s) to see whether they charge a fee higher than the one listed on Medicare's fee schedule. If your physician does charge a higher fee, you may want to consider going to another physician if you can't afford the fee or if you want to save some money. (But don't drop your current doctor before finding another who accepts Medicare and you as a patient. Many doctors are not accepting Medicare patients.) Medicare often pays only 80 percent of the physician charges that the program allows on its fee schedule.

The biggest reason that elderly people consider long-term care insurance is that Medicare pays only for the first 100 days in a skilled nursing facility. Anything over that is your responsibility. Unfortunately, Medigap policies don't address this issue, either.

Long-term care insurance

Insurance agents who are eager to earn a hefty commission often tell you that long-term care (LTC) insurance is the solution to your concerns about an extended stay in a nursing home. Don't get your hopes up. Policies are complicated and filled with all sorts of exclusions and limitations. On top of all that, they're expensive.

The decision to purchase LTC insurance is a trade-off. Do you want to pay thousands of dollars annually, beginning at age 60, to guard against the possibility of a long-term stay in a nursing home (or possibly to pay for in-home assistance if you qualify)? If you live into or past your mid-80s, you can end up paying $100,000+ on an LTC policy (not to mention the lost investment earnings on these insurance premiums).

People who end up in a nursing home for years on end may come out ahead financially when buying LTC insurance. The majority of people who stay in a nursing home are there for less than a year, though, because they either pass away or move out. Medicare pays for the bulk of the cost of the first 100 days in a nursing home as long as certain conditions are satisfied. Medicare pays for all basic services (telephone, television, and private room charges excluded) for the first 20 days and then requires a co-payment of $200 per day for the next 80 days. First, the nursing-home stay must follow hospitalization within 30 days, and the nursing-home stay must be for the same medical condition that caused the hospitalization. When you're discharged from the nursing home, you can qualify for an additional 100-day benefit period as long as you haven't been hospitalized or in a nursing home in the 60 days prior to your readmission.

If you have relatives or a spouse who will likely care for you in the event of a major illness, you definitely should *not* waste your money on nursing-home insurance. You can also bypass this coverage if you have and don't mind using retirement assets to help pay nursing-home costs.

WARNING

Even if you do deplete your assets, note that you have a backup: Medicaid (state-provided medical insurance) can pick up the cost if you can't. However, be aware of a number of potential drawbacks to getting coverage for nursing-home stays under Medicaid:

- **Medicaid patients are at the bottom of the priority list.** Most nursing homes are interested in the bottom line, so the patients who bring in the least revenue — namely Medicaid patients — get the lowest priority on nursing-home waiting lists.
- **Some nursing homes don't take Medicaid patients.** Check with your preferred nursing homes in your area to see whether they accept Medicaid.
- **The states may squeeze Medicaid further.** Deciding which medical conditions warrant coverage is up to your state. When budgets tighten, some states are disallowing certain types of coverage.

If you're concerned about having your stash of money wiped out by an extended nursing-home stay and you have a strong desire to pass money to your family or a favorite charity, you can start giving your money away while you're still healthy.

(If you're already in poor health, legal experts can strategize to preserve your assets and keep them from being used to pay nursing-home costs.)

TIP

Consider buying LTC insurance if you want to retain and protect your assets and it gives you peace of mind to know that a long-term nursing-home stay is covered. But do some comparison shopping, and make sure that you buy a policy that pays benefits for the long term. A year's worth (or even a few years' worth) of benefits won't protect your assets if your stay lasts longer. Also be sure to get a policy that adjusts the daily benefit amount for increases in the cost of living. Get a policy that covers care in your home or other settings if you don't need to be in a high-cost nursing home, and make sure that it doesn't require prior hospitalization for benefits to kick in. To keep premiums down, also consider a longer exclusion or waiting period — three to six months or a year before coverage starts.

You may also want to consider retirement communities if you're willing to live as a younger retiree in such a setting. After paying an entrance fee, you pay a monthly fee, which usually covers your rent, care, and meals. Make sure that any such facility you're considering guarantees care for life and preferably has a continuum of care levels available. Also verify that it accepts Medicaid in case you deplete your assets.

Making sense of Medicare's prescription drug program

As if there weren't enough confusing government programs, Uncle Sam created yet another that began in 2006 — the Medicare (Part D) prescription drug plan. Here are some key facts you need to know about these somewhat complicated plans, which are offered through private insurers:

- Plans make the most sense for those who expect to spend more than $5,000 annually on prescription drugs.
- If you choose not to enroll when you're first eligible and then later enroll, you'll be charged a penalty equal to 1 percent of the national average Part D premium for each month that has elapsed since you were first eligible to participate. You pay this penalty for as long as you're in the plan.
- If you're on the fence about enrolling, consider starting with a low-premium plan that then gives you the right to transfer into a higher-cost and better-coverage plan without paying the late enrollment penalty.
- Visit `www.medicare.gov` for helpful information on drug plans and how to select one. For example, click on the Formulary (drug) Finder to identify specific insurer plans that cover your current medications or your anticipated future medications. AARP's website, `www.aarp.org`, also has plenty of information and resources to find out more about these plans.

IN THIS CHAPTER

» Reviewing renter's and homeowner's insurance

» Assessing automobile insurance

» Understanding umbrella (excess liability) insurance

Chapter 4

Covering Your Assets: Home, Auto, and Umbrella Insurance

Chapter 3 of Book 2 discusses the importance of protecting your future income from disability, death, or large unexpected medical expenses. You should also insure major assets that you've acquired: your home, your car, and your personal property. Protect these assets for two reasons:

- **Your assets are valuable.** If you were to suffer a loss, replacing the assets with money out of your own pocket can be a financial catastrophe.
- **A lawsuit can drain your finances.** Should someone be injured or killed in your home or because of your car, a lawsuit could be financially devastating.

This chapter explains why, how, and for how much to insure your home, personal property, and vehicle. We also discuss excess liability insurance.

Insuring Your Home

When you buy a home with a mortgage, most lenders require you to purchase homeowner's insurance. But even if they don't, you're wise to do so, because your home and the personal property within it are worth a great deal and would be costly to replace.

As a renter, damage to the building in which you live isn't your immediate financial concern, but you still have personal property you may want to insure. You also have the possibility (albeit remote) that you can be sued by someone who's injured while in your rental.

When shopping for a homeowner's or renter's policy, consider the important features in the following sections.

Dwelling coverage: The cost to rebuild

How much would it cost you to rebuild your home if it were completely destroyed, for example, in a fire? The cost to rebuild should be based on the size (square footage) of your home and its amenities. Neither the purchase price nor the size of your mortgage should determine how much *dwelling coverage* you need.

If you're a renter, rejoice that you don't need dwelling coverage. If you're a condominium owner, find out whether the insurance the condo association bought for the entire building is sufficient.

TIP

Be sure that your homeowner's policy includes a *guaranteed replacement cost* provision. This useful feature ensures that the insurance company will rebuild the home even if the cost of construction is more than the policy coverage. If the insurance company underestimates your dwelling coverage, it has to make up the difference.

Unfortunately, insurers define guaranteed replacement cost differently. While some companies pay for the full replacement cost of the home, no matter how much it ends up costing, most insurers set limits. For example, some insurers may pay up to only 25 percent more than the dwelling coverage on your policy. Ask your insurer how it defines guaranteed replacement cost.

If you have an older property that doesn't meet current building standards, consider buying a *rider* (supplemental coverage to your main insurance policy) that pays for code upgrades. This rider covers the cost of rebuilding your home, in the event of a loss, to comply with current building codes that may be more stringent than the ones in place when your home was built. Ask your insurance company what your basic policy does and doesn't cover. Some companies include a certain amount (for example, 10 percent of your dwelling coverage) for code upgrades in the base policy.

Personal property coverage: For your belongings

On your homeowner's policy, the amount of personal property coverage is typically derived from the amount of dwelling coverage you carry. Generally, you get personal property coverage that's equal to 50 to 75 percent of the dwelling coverage. This amount is usually more than enough. Some insurers allow you to customize this personal property amount, which may save you money as most people need less than 50 to 75 percent of their dwelling coverage.

Regarding riders to cover jewelry, computers, collectibles, and other somewhat costly items that may not be fully covered by typical homeowner's policies, ask yourself whether the out-of-pocket expense from the loss of such items would constitute a financial catastrophe. Unless you have more than several thousand dollars' worth of jewelry or computer equipment, skip such riders.

Some policies come with *replacement cost guarantees* that pay you the cost to replace an item. This payment can be considerably more than what the used item was worth before it was damaged or stolen. When this feature is not part of the standard policy sold by your insurer, you may want to purchase it as a rider, if available.

As a renter or condominium owner, you need to choose a dollar amount for the personal property you want covered. Tally it up instead of guessing — the total cost of replacing all your personal property may surprise you.

TIP

Make a list of your belongings — or even better, take pictures or make a video — with an estimate of what they're worth. Keep this list updated; you need it if you have to file a claim. Retaining receipts for major purchases may also help your case. No matter how you document your belongings, don't forget to keep the documentation somewhere besides your home — otherwise, it can be destroyed along with the rest of your house in a fire or other disaster.

Liability insurance: Coverage for when others are harmed

Liability insurance protects you financially against lawsuits that may arise if someone gets injured on your property, including wounds inflicted by the family's pernicious pup or terrible tabby. (Of course, you should keep Bruno restrained when guests visit — even your cranky in-laws.) At a minimum, get enough liability insurance to cover your financial assets — covering two times your assets is better. Buying extra coverage is inexpensive and well worth the cost.

The probability of being sued is low, but if you are sued and lose, you can end up owing big bucks. If you have substantial assets to protect, you may want to consider an umbrella, or excess liability, policy. (See the later section "Protecting against Mega-Liability: Umbrella Insurance.")

Liability protection is one of the side benefits of purchasing a renter's policy — you protect your personal property as well as insure against lawsuits. (But don't be reckless with your banana peels even if you get liability insurance!)

Flood and earthquake insurance: Protection from Mother Nature

You should purchase the broadest possible coverage when buying any type of insurance. The problem with homeowner's insurance is that it's not comprehensive enough — it doesn't typically cover losses due to earthquakes and floods. You must buy such disaster coverage separately.

If an earthquake or flood were to strike your area and destroy your home, you'd be out tens (if not hundreds) of thousands of dollars without proper coverage. Yet many people don't carry these important coverages, often as a result of some common misconceptions:

- **"Not in my neighborhood."** Many people mistakenly believe that earthquakes occur only in California. We wish this were true for those who live in the other 49 states, but it's not. In fact, one of the strongest earthquakes in the United States occurred in the Midwest, and known (though less active) fault lines lie along the East Coast. The cost of earthquake coverage is based on insurance companies' assessment of the risk of your area and property type. You shouldn't decide whether to buy insurance based on how small you think the risk is. The risk is already built into the price.

  An estimated 20,000 communities around the country face potential flood damage. Like earthquakes, floods are not a covered risk in standard homeowner's policies, so you need to purchase a flood insurance rider. Check with your current homeowner's insurer or with the insurers recommended in this chapter. The federal government flood insurance program (`www.floodsmart.gov`) provides background information on flood insurance policies.

» **"The government will bail me out."** The vast majority of government financial assistance is obtained through low-interest loans. Loans, unfortunately, need to be repaid, and that money comes out of your pocket.

» **"In a major disaster, insurers would go bankrupt anyway."** This is highly unlikely given the reserves insurers are required to keep and the fact that the insurance companies *reinsure* — that is, they buy insurance to back up the policies they write. Also, state regulatory agencies facilitate the merging of faltering insurers into strong entities.

People who have little equity in their property and are willing to walk away from their property and mortgage in the event of a major quake or flood may consider not buying earthquake or flood coverage. Keep in mind that walking away damages your credit report, because you're essentially defaulting on your loan.

TIP

You may be able to pay for some of the cost of earthquake or flood insurance by raising the deductibles (discussed in the next section) on the main part of your homeowner's/renter's insurance and other insurance policies (such as auto insurance). You can more easily afford the smaller claims, not the big ones. If you think flood or earthquake insurance is expensive, compare those costs with the expenditures you would incur to completely replace your home and personal property. Buy this insurance if you live in an area that has a chance of being affected by these catastrophes. To help keep the cost of earthquake insurance down, consider taking a 10-percent deductible. Most insurers offer deductibles of 5, 10, or 20 percent of the cost to rebuild your home. Ten percent of the rebuilding cost is a good chunk of money. But losing the other 90 percent is what you want to insure against. (For most people, a 20-percent deductible is too high.)

Deductibles: Your cost with a claim

REMEMBER

The point of insurance is to protect against catastrophic losses, not the little losses. By taking the highest deductibles you're comfortable with, you save on insurance premiums year after year, and you don't have to go through the hassle of filing small claims.

Special discounts

You may qualify for special discounts on your policy. Companies and agents that sell homeowner's and renter's insurance don't always check to see whether you're eligible for discounts. After all, the more you spend on policy premiums, the more money they make! If your property has a security system, you're older, or you have other policies with the same insurer, you may qualify for a lower rate. Be sure to ask.

Also, be aware that insurers use your credit score as a factor in setting some of your insurance rates. They do this because their studies have shown that folks who have higher credit scores tend to have fewer accidents and insurance claims. See Chapter 3 in Book 1 for how to assess and improve your credit reports and scores.

Buying homeowner's or renter's insurance

Each insurance company prices its homeowner's and renter's policies based on its own criteria. So the lowest-cost company for your friend's property may not be the lowest-cost company for yours. You have to shop around at several companies to find the best rates. The following list features companies that historically offer lower-cost policies for most people and have decent track records regarding customer satisfaction and the payment of claims:

- **Amica:** Although Amica has good customer satisfaction, its prices are high in some areas. You can contact the company by calling 800-242-6422 or checking out the company's website at www.amica.com.
- **Auto-Owners:** Not just for insuring autos, this company offers home insurance too. Check your local phone directory for agents, call 517-323-1200, or visit www.auto-owners.com.
- **Erie Insurance:** This company does business primarily in the Midwest and Mid-Atlantic. Check your local phone directory for agents, call 800-458-0811 for a referral to a local agent, or visit the company's website at www.erieinsurance.com.
- **GEICO:** You can contact the company by calling 800-841-2964 or visit www.geico.com.
- **NJM Insurance:** Offers insurance in Connecticut, Maryland, New Jersey, Ohio, and Pennsylvania. Contact the company at 800-232-6600 or visit www.njm.com.
- **State Farm:** Check your local phone directory for agents, call 844-803-1573, or visit www.statefarm.com.
- **USAA:** This company provides insurance for members of the military and their families. Call the company at 800-531-8722 (or visit its website at www.usaa.com) to see whether you qualify.

Don't worry that some of these companies require you to call a toll-free number for a price quote. This process saves you money because these insurers don't have to pay commissions to local agents hawking their policies. These companies have local claims representatives to help you if and when you have a claim.

TIP

A number of the companies mentioned in the preceding list sell other types of insurance (for example, life insurance) that aren't as competitively priced. Be sure to check out Chapter 3 in Book 2 for the best places to buy these other types of coverage if you need them.

Some state insurance departments conduct surveys of insurers' prices and tabulate complaints received. Look up your state's department of insurance phone number in the government section of your local phone directory or visit the National Association of Insurance Commissioners' website at `content.naic.org/state-insurance-departments` to find links to each state's department of insurance site.

Auto Insurance 101

Over the course of your life, you may spend tens of thousands of dollars on auto insurance. Much of the money people spend on auto insurance is not spent where it's needed most. In other cases, the money is simply wasted. Look for the following important features when searching for an auto insurance policy.

Bodily injury/property damage liability

As with homeowner's liability insurance, auto liability insurance provides insurance against lawsuits. Accidents happen, especially with a car. Make sure you have enough bodily injury liability insurance, which pays for harm done to others, to cover your assets. (Coverage of double your assets is preferable.)

If you're just beginning to accumulate assets, don't mistakenly assume that you don't need liability protection. Many states require a minimum amount — insurers should be able to fill you in on the details for your state. Also, don't forget that your future earnings, which are an asset, can be garnished in a lawsuit.

Property damage liability insurance covers damage done by your car to other people's cars or property. The amount of property damage liability coverage in an auto insurance policy is usually determined as a consequence of the bodily injury liability amount selected. Coverage of $50,000 is a good minimum to start with.

COPING WITH TEEN DRIVERS

If you have a teenage driver in your household, you're going to be spending a lot more on auto insurance (in addition to worrying a lot more). As soon as you decide to allow your teenager to drive, you can take a number of steps to avoid spending all your take-home pay on auto insurance bills:

- **Make sure your teen does well in school.** Some insurers offer discounts if your child is a strong academic achiever and has successfully completed a driver's education class.
- **Get price quotes from several insurers** to see how adding your teen driver to your policy affects the cost.
- **Have your teenager share in the costs of using the car.** If you pay all the insurance, gas, and maintenance bills, your teenager won't value the privilege of using your "free" car.

Uninsured or underinsured motorist liability

When you're in an accident with another motorist and they don't carry their own liability protection (or don't carry enough), *uninsured or underinsured motorist liability coverage* on your policy enables you to collect for lost wages, medical expenses, and pain and suffering incurred in the accident.

REMEMBER

If you already have comprehensive health and long-term disability insurance, uninsured or underinsured motorist liability coverage is largely redundant. However, if you drop this coverage, you do give up the ability to sue for general pain and suffering and to insure passengers in your car who may lack adequate medical and disability coverage.

To provide a death benefit to those financially dependent on you in the event of a fatal auto accident, buy term life insurance (see Chapter 3 in Book 2).

Deductibles

To minimize your auto insurance premiums and eliminate the need to file small claims, take the highest deductible you're comfortable with. (Most people should consider a $500 to $1,000 deductible.) On an auto policy, two deductibles exist: collision and comprehensive.

» *Collision* applies to claims arising from collisions. (Note that if you have collision coverage on your own policy, you can generally bypass collision coverage when you rent a car.)

» *Comprehensive* applies to other claims for damages not caused by collision (for example, a window broken by vandals).

As your car ages and loses its value, you can eventually eliminate your comprehensive and collision coverages altogether. The point at which you do this is up to you. Insurers won't pay more than the book value of your car, regardless of what it costs to repair or replace it. Note that the purpose of insurance is to compensate you for losses that are financially catastrophic to you. For some people, this amount may be as high as $5,000 or more — others may choose $1,000 as their threshold point.

Special discounts: Auto edition

You may be eligible for special discounts on auto insurance. Don't forget to tell your agent or insurer if your car has a security alarm, air bags, or anti-lock brakes. If you're older or you have other policies or cars insured with the same insurer, you may also qualify for discounts. And make sure that you're given appropriate "good driver" discounts if you've been accident- and ticket-free in recent years.

TIP

Before you buy your next car, call insurers and ask for insurance quotes for the different models you're considering. The cost of insuring a car should factor into your decision about which car you buy, because the insurance costs represent a major portion of your car's ongoing operating expenses.

Little-stuff coverage to skip

Auto insurers have dreamed up all sorts of riders, such as towing and rental car reimbursement. On the surface, these riders appear to be inexpensive. But they're expensive given the small amount you'd collect from a claim and the hassle of filing.

Riders that waive the deductible under certain circumstances make no sense, either. The point of the deductible is to reduce your policy cost and eliminate the hassle of filing small claims.

Medical payments coverage typically pays a few thousand dollars for medical expenses. If you and your passengers carry major medical insurance coverage, this rider isn't really necessary. Besides, a few thousand dollars of medical coverage doesn't protect you against catastrophic expenses.

Buying auto insurance

TIP

You can use the homeowner's insurers list in the earlier section "Buying homeowner's or renter's insurance" to obtain quotes for auto insurance. In addition, you can visit AAA/Auto Club on the web at `www.aaa.com/auto` and find your nearest AAA/Auto Club by entering your zip code.

Protecting against Mega-Liability: Umbrella Insurance

Umbrella insurance (which is also referred to as *excess liability insurance*) is liability insurance that's added on top of the liability protection on your home and car(s). If, for example, you have $700,000 in assets, you can buy a $1 million umbrella liability policy to add to the $300,000 liability insurance that you have on your home and car. Expect to pay a couple hundred dollars — a small cost for big protection. Each year, thousands of people suffer lawsuits of more than $1 million related to their cars and homes.

TIP

Umbrella insurance is generally sold in increments of $1 million. So how do you decide how much you need if you have a lot of assets? You should have at least enough liability insurance to protect your assets and preferably enough to cover twice the value of those assets. To purchase umbrella insurance, start by contacting your existing homeowner's or auto insurance company.

IN THIS CHAPTER

» Cutting insurance costs

» Making the most of Medicare

» Saving big bucks on prescriptions

» Caring for your teeth, eyes, and ears

Chapter 5

Getting Quality Healthcare for Less

Whether it's small acts or big lifestyle changes, you could save thousands of dollars in healthcare costs by taking action today. Here's to your health — and healthy cost savings!

Saving on Healthcare and Insurance

Try the following tips for potentially big savings on medical bills and insurance:

» **Read your bills carefully.** Eight out of ten medical bills contain errors, so check to be sure you're not being overcharged. Always ask for itemized bills. If you have lots of bills, another option is to call in a medical bill negotiator to review your bills for errors and overcharges, and potentially save thousands of dollars.

- **Stay in your plan's network.** Most health insurance plans offer in-network and out-of-network coverage. If you stay within the network of providers your plan offers, you can save big on out-of-pocket expenses.
- **Review your health insurance coverage every year.** Your coverage may change from one year to the next, so it's important to review it during your open enrollment period. Changes can affect your monthly premiums, copays, deductibles, the services covered by your insurance, and the list of doctors who participate in the insurer's network. Avoid costly surprises come January 1.
- **Need surgery? Research cost-cutting alternatives to hospitals, such as outpatient facilities.** The fees for a doctor and anesthesiologist may be similar, but typically, outpatient centers charge a fraction of the fee that hospitals charge.
- **Several weeks before a procedure, call your insurer and provider to confirm coverage.** Verify that the procedure and providers involved in your care — such as a physician and anesthesiologist — are in your network and covered by your plan. If they're not all in-network, consider using another provider.
- **Enroll in a flexible spending account at work and pay thousands of dollars of out-of-pocket health bills with pretax dollars.** Expenses such as premiums, copays, deductibles, dental work, and eyeglasses qualify. Check with the Internal Revenue Service for qualifying expenses.

  WARNING

  Plan carefully, though. FSAs have a use-it-or-lose-it penalty, meaning if you contribute more than you use, you forfeit the excess contribution.
- **Get help in disputes.** You have appeal rights when your insurance company denies a medical claim or pays less than you think it should. Most states have a consumer assistance program that can help you file appeals and resolve disputes.

TIP

- **Find assistance if you're a veteran.** The Department of Veterans Affairs (VA) Caregiver Support Program offers clinical services to caregivers of eligible and covered veterans enrolled in the VA healthcare system. The program's mission is to promote the health and well-being of family caregivers who care for U.S. veterans, through education, resources, support, and services. Find details at `www.caregiver.va.gov`, or call 855-260-3274 toll-free.

Here's another tactic to consider: Negotiate hospital bills even if you have insurance. Hospitals will often offer a discounted rate, especially if you pay cash. If you haven't met your deductible, the discounted price may cost you less than you'd pay out of pocket with insurance. Contact the billing department at the hospital or medical practice to get the process started, and be sure to follow these guidelines:

- **Get the data.** Figure out how much you can afford to pay, then look up the average cost for the procedure or treatment you underwent. Consider checking Valenz Bluebook (www.valenzhealth.com/solutions/member-experience/valenz-bluebook/) or FAIR Health Consumer (www.fairhealthconsumer.org/), websites where you can check typical prices in your area for a procedure or course of treatment.

  If you're on Medicare, take a look, too, at what it pays for a procedure and the rate your health plan pays for the service at in-network facilities (visit www.medicare.gov/procedure-price-lookup/). If you were balance-billed because out-of-network providers took part in your treatment without your knowledge (and charged you the balance between their fee and what insurance covered), these figures can serve as starting points for negotiation.

- **Consider "prompt pay."** Sometimes a medical provider will accept far less money if you agree to pay immediately. A doctor may rather work to reach a settlement than get nothing.

  TIP

  If it's late in the year, you may have a better chance of striking a deal, some experts say, because hospitals, doctors, and other providers may be more open to negotiation when their financial offices are trying to close out the annual books.

- **Ask for an installment plan.** If you can't negotiate the bill down, ask the provider whether you can set up an interest-free payment schedule. It's important to know going in what you can afford to pay monthly and for how long. If you make your initial payments in full and on time, the billing office may be willing to reconsider a discount or write-off on the rest of the bill.

- **Get professional help.** When your bill is very high or you've exhausted your ability to negotiate on your own, think about hiring a professional, such as a medical billing advocate or an attorney who specializes in medical billing disputes. You can ask your state's bar association for a referral. (Visit www.findlaw.com/hirealawyer/choosing-the-right-lawyer/state-bar-associations.html.)

  Medical billing advocates work with patients to review bills for errors and negotiate lower costs. There are both for-profit and nonprofit advocates. The Patient Advocate Foundation, for example, does this work for free, but only if you have a chronic, life-threatening, or debilitating medical condition that has been diagnosed.

  Professional advocates either charge an hourly fee or take a percentage of what they save you.

TIP

In looking for a billing advocate, focus on the person's level of expertise. Many previously worked at insurance companies or in the billing offices at hospitals or medical practices; their websites should comprehensively list their skills, experience, and credentials. You can search for billing advocates in the online directories of industry groups such as the National Association of Healthcare Advocacy (www.nahac.com/), the Alliance of Professional Health Advocates (aphadvocates.org/), and the Alliance of Claims Assistance Professionals (claims.org/).

Maximizing Your Medicare Benefits

If you use Medicare (or you're nearly eligible to sign up for Medicare), consider using the following cost-saving ideas:

- **Sign up for Medicare at the right time.** If you are nearing Medicare eligibility, you have a window to sign up. If you miss this window, your monthly Medicare premiums may be higher. For help with your Medicare questions, check out AARP's *Medicare For Dummies* (published by Wiley).
- **Take advantage of the free services Medicare offers, such as many preventive tests and screenings.** Be sure you meet the conditions for free services: You must go to a doctor who accepts the Medicare-approved cost as full payment, and you must observe any time limits for the test, such as once a year.

  Free Medicare services include your annual wellness visit. This appointment gives you time with your doctor to look at long-term health needs and goals. Research shows that people who have them are more likely to get recommended influenza, pneumonia, and shingles vaccines, to receive recommended colon- and breast-cancer screenings, and to get a cholesterol check.

  REMEMBER

  Keep in mind that a "wellness" visit by any other name would not be free. You can have a free "wellness" doctor visit once a year covered by Medicare, if you ask for it by that name. But if you ask for a "physical" — a more comprehensive exam — you'll be charged full price.
- **Check with Medicare before buying health equipment.** The federal health insurance program often pays part of the cost for walkers, canes, wheelchairs, and hospital beds.
- **Shop every year for a new Medicare plan.** Open enrollment runs from October 1 through December 7. Prices and providers change often, so compare plans and change your enrollment at medicare.gov.

- **See whether you qualify for the Medicare Savings Programs, federally funded programs administered by states, to help pay Medicare Part A and B premiums.** Find out more at `www.medicare.gov/medicare-savings-programs`.

Cutting Your Prescription Costs

If the prices of your prescriptions are soaring, the following pointers may help you cut costs:

- **Check your drugs.** Put all your medications — prescription, over-the-counter, even supplements and vitamins — into a bag and take them to your doctor's appointments. Ask whether you need them all. Many people are overprescribed, especially if they see several doctors for different medical issues. Having your meds reviewed periodically is also good for your health.
- **Consider generics.** Authorized generics are made by the manufacturer of the brand-name version and have the same active and inactive ingredients. Thousands are on the market, including epinephrine pens and hepatitis C treatments. Insurance coverage varies, so check first.
- **Get a free prescription discount card through AARP Prescription Discounts provided by the OptumRx program.** The card can be used to save on all FDA-approved medications at 66,000-plus participating retail pharmacies such as CVS Pharmacy, Walgreens Pharmacy, and Walmart Pharmacy. Visit `aarp.org/rx-discounts`.
- **Ask your pharmacist about the best deal.** Congress banned pharmacist "gag clauses" — which prohibited pharmacists from voluntarily informing patients that their prescription medication may cost less if paid for directly instead of through insurance. That just means you have to ask; pharmacists aren't required to offer information about the best price without being asked.
- **Use a pharmacy discount card.** A growing number of insurers, pharmacies, and other companies offer pharmacy discount cards that may get you as much as 80 percent off the list price of prescription drugs — making them more affordable if you don't have drug coverage or if your copay, coinsurance, or other insurance-backed cost is too high. Shop around online to find the best deal on the drugs you take.
- **Head to the supermarket or your favorite discount chain.** Some supermarket and discount chains offer common medications for free. If your deductible is $10, for example, you'll save $120 a year on just one 30-day

prescription. Ask the pharmacy department at your local stores which medications, if any, they offer for free. Often, you only need a doctor's prescription to qualify.

- **Got a long-term condition that requires prescription meds? Ask for a 90-day supply** and make a single copay every three months instead of one every 30 days.
- **Use patient assistance programs.** Many of these pharmaceutical and medical device company-funded programs expanded during the pandemic. Check `needymeds.org/pap` for a list of current programs.

REMEMBER

- **Take your medications regularly.** It's important to take your medications exactly as prescribed. You can avoid costly hospital visits that often result from skipped doses.
- **Get help on drug costs.** Medicare beneficiaries may qualify for the Extra Help program to cover prescriptions. You can potentially save thousands of dollars a year. Apply at `socialsecurity.gov/extrahelp` or call 800-772-1213.
- **Go to the Medicine Assistance Tool** at `https://medicineassistancetool.org/`. Patients who qualify can save hundreds of dollars.
- **Prices vary significantly from pharmacy to pharmacy, so do some research.** To save up to 80 percent, try RxSaver or GoodRx — either the app or the website — that lets you search prescriptions, find prices near you, and get coupons to present at the pharmacy.
- **If you're taking a brand-name drug regularly, check the drugmaker's website** to see whether it offers a coupon or discount card that can save you money.
- **For some meds, skip your insurance.** Ask your pharmacist about the retail price of your prescription medication; it may be cheaper to pay that price.
- **If you're a Medicare recipient, shop every year for your Medicare Part D plan, too.** Note that your expenses can be a lot lower if you buy prescription drugs from a pharmacy that your Part D plan calls "preferred" — meaning the pharmacy has agreed to charge reduced copays. Call your plan for preferred pharmacies in your area.

Taking Care of Your Teeth

Don't forget about your dental care! Here are some tips for saving money at the dentist:

- **No dental insurance? Look into dental practice memberships.** These plans may give you a set number of cleanings, exams, and X-rays for a discounted annual fee, plus a discount on fillings and other services. You can save $100 a year or more over the price of routine care. Your dentist may also be more inclined to negotiate more expensive procedures.
- **Talk to your dentist about X-rays.** If you aren't at higher-than-normal risk for cavities, you may need dental X-rays only every two to three years, says the American Dental Association.
- **Invest in prevention.** An in-office fluoride varnish or home treatment with a prescription toothpaste can repair eroded tooth enamel and stop early tooth decay from becoming a full-fledged cavity, which can save you money on a filling.
- **Find out whether you qualify for free dental care at `dentallifeline.org/our-state-programs/#DDS`.** Donated Dental Services provides older adults with free comprehensive dental treatment. It operates through a volunteer network of more than 15,000 dentists and 3,400 dental labs across the United States.
- **Visit a community health clinic that offers reduced-cost or free dental care to people with low incomes.** Visit `https://findahealthcenter.hrsa.gov/` to find a center near you and check to see whether it offers dental care. There may be a wait list, so apply early.

Looking for Savings on Eye Care and Glasses

To start cutting your eye care costs, understand the features available for eyeglasses, and whether they're worth the extra cost.

- **High-index lenses:** Thinner, lighter, and more comfortable than regular lenses, they're a great choice for those with strong prescriptions — helping you avoid the "Coke bottle" look.
- **Polycarbonate lenses:** A type of high-index lens, they are highly durable (up to 10 times more impact resistant than average plastic), are scratch-resistant, and have built-in UV protection.
- **Photochromic lenses:** These lenses react to ultraviolet (UV) light, staying clear indoors and darkening in sunlight. This option is an economical add-on, good

for those who don't want to carry around a pair of prescription sunglasses — with the caveat that they won't darken inside cars because windshields filter out the UV rays that trigger the color change. They also can be a smart choice for older patients, who may be beginning to get cataracts and need to protect their eyes from UV light.

TIP

Different brands have different levels of darkness and reaction times, so take time to comparison shop.

» **Progressive lenses:** Doing bifocals one better, these lenses offer three prescriptions in one lens — up close and at a distance, with an intermediate distance (say, for computer viewing) in the center — allowing you to see all distances. They gradually change from each prescription, as you move your eyes down and up. This makes them a nice option for those who want only one pair of full-time glasses. They don't have that line across the lens you'll get with bifocals. Some people, though, have difficulty adjusting to them, including going up and down stairs.

» **High-definition (digital) lenses:** These lenses are to your eyes what high-definition (HD) technology is to TV. Based on a digital scan of your eyes, digital lenses can give you even crisper, clearer vision than conventional lenses.

WARNING

Take note: They generally cost up to 25 to 30 percent more than conventional glasses of the same material and design, and may only offer a slightly better view.

» **Anti-glare coating:** This add-on, often bundled with high-index and HD lenses, eliminates reflections from the surfaces of your lenses. That means more light is able to get through, enhancing the quality of your vision by doing away with annoying distractions — such as glare and halos many people see when driving at night. It also improves the look of your glasses: By reducing the glare bouncing off the surface of your lenses, they look practically invisible. On the downside, the anti-glare coating can get scratched or, over time, begin to peel off.

Frames, which can range from a few bucks to hundreds or even thousands of dollars, can be a big part of your total cost. Whether you're looking for standard plastic or pricey titanium wire frames, it pays to comparison shop. And when it comes to designer frames, you shell out more, but that doesn't mean the product is better.

» **Online retailers:** Companies like EyeBuyDirect, GlassesUSA, Warby Parker, and Zenni Optical have been giving the brick-and-mortar stores a run for their money — especially during the COVID pandemic, when many people preferred to shop from home. Many online stores have virtual try-on tools to help you get a good fit. (Warby Parker even allows you to try on five pairs at home, for free.) You can find a huge selection of well-made eyewear for under $150, though adding extras such as impact-resistant lenses with antireflective coating will drive up the price.

Online retailers can also be a good way to nab discount designer frames as well as inexpensive ones (a search on Zenni uncovered a $6.95 pair of basic prescription rectangular glasses with anti-scratch coating and UV protection).

TIP

If you're going to be wearing your glasses full time, it may pay to get professionally fitted. Check the return policy, in case you're not satisfied. Some online retailers offer no-questions-asked returns; others may offer another pair instead. And, if you have vision insurance, be sure the website accepts it (not all do).

REMEMBER

To buy online, you need a valid prescription and your pupillary distance (PD) measurement, which is the distance in millimeters between your pupils or from your pupils to the center of your nose bridge. This indicates where the company filling your prescription needs to place the optical center (or "sweet spot") of vision in the lenses, so you can see clearly. Many online retailers offer ways to determine your PD, including virtual eye exams. Apps may be able to do it, or you can ask your eye doctor to include it as part of an eye exam. Online suppliers typically place the spot in the geometric center of the lens, but sometimes the spot doesn't match your line of sight, and your vision will be affected.

- **Chain retailers and independent opticians or optometrists:** You may want to go this route if you have a strong or complicated prescription (if you wear progressive lenses, for instance). At retailers or independent opticians or optometrists, they can fit your frames and check to see exactly where you're looking through the lenses to find the PD, so they can be aligned precisely in the frames.

  An optometrist (a doctor who performs routine eye exams and fits glasses) or optician (a technical specialist in fitting glasses) can help you select a pair that flatters your face shape and walk you through options for lenses.

  Walmart Vision Center and Costco Optical both have licensed optometrists on-site and are likely to offer specs at much lower prices than you find at boutique opticians. The same goes for the big-chain vision centers, such as America's Best, LensCrafters, and Pearle Vision, which offer seasonal sales (savings of at least 20 percent on a pair of eyeglasses) and BOGO deals.

Here are a few other cost-saving pointers for eye care:

- **Get free eye care if you're retirement age.** People over 65 may be eligible for a free eye exam and care through the American Academy of Ophthalmology's EyeCare America program. Find out more at `aao.org`.

- **Keep your eyes peeled for price-match guarantees.** Or try on glasses at a store, jot down the style number of the frames you fancy, and then search for a website that sells the same ones for less. You can also ask for a price break. It never hurts to ask for a discount or special deal on a second pair.
- **Enjoy savings if you're an AARP member.** Members and their families receive exclusive discounts at participating retailers and independent provider locations nationwide, as well as online, through AARP Vision Discounts provided by EyeMed. You save 50 percent on prescription lenses with the purchase of a frame at LensCrafters, 30 percent on a complete pair of glasses (frames and lenses) at `Glasses.com`, and $10 on a complete pair of glasses at Target Optical. Visit `aarp.org/vision-discounts`.

Hearing Better for Less

Know what to look for when you buy hearing aids. The following guidelines can help:

REMEMBER

- **The words "over-the-counter (OTC) hearing aid" on the package:** This is the FDA-regulated designation that says you're purchasing actual hearing aids and not some type of amplification device. Several models may also carry the designation "Self-Fitting OTC Hearing Aid."
- **Requirements for smartphones:** Many, but not all, OTC hearing aids require users to download and use an app on their smartphone. For details about types compatible with your phone — some work only with iPhones, not Androids — you'll have to go to the maker's website or read the material inside the package.
- **A 30-day (or more) return policy:** The Hearing Loss Association of America recommends choosing devices with a generous return policy. It can take several weeks to know whether new hearing aids work for you, in part because your brain has to acclimate to all the new sounds you hear.

  You want to allow yourself time to get used to wearing a hearing aid and testing it out in different environments. Check out how different tips, domes, or petal sizes feel on models that have them, and which types feel more comfortable. Soundly founder Blake Cadwell, who wears hearing aids, says to make sure you have at least 45 days to check them out.

  You also want to ask about what kind of support is available after the trial expires, including the cost of replacing a damaged or lost hearing aid.

- **Added features:** More expensive OTCs work with telecoils, which pick up signals sent directly to your hearing aids in movie theaters and concert halls. Others may come with Bluetooth options that enable you to stream phone calls and other media wirelessly through your hearing aids.

  Different hearing aid manufacturers market different features: models with more powerful speakers, processors, or directional microphones that can focus on the person you're talking with; features that can filter out background noise; and hearing aids that exploit the latest artificial intelligence technologies.

  Some hearing aids can automatically adjust to different volumes at different frequencies. Premium models let you customize your hearing profile, typically via Bluetooth and a smartphone app.

- **Rechargeable versus battery-powered:** Choose a power option that allows you to wear hearing aids during all your waking hours. Your brain needs to receive input consistently to acclimate to the new device. More expensive models tend to include rechargeable batteries and sometimes wireless charging options. Generally, less expensive hearing aids require you to periodically replace the batteries.

TIP

- **A look that you like:** Hearing professionals say wearing your hearing aids regularly is crucial to making the most of them and may even protect hearing from further loss. So buying a look that you are comfortable with is important. Some hearing aids fit behind the ears or stick out some, while others sit inside your ears and have barely visible threads that help you remove the hearing aids.

Here are a few additional pointers for cutting costs on hearing aids and accessories:

- Hearing aids can sell at a retail markup of up to 117 percent. But those prices can be flexible. In one survey, about half of the 14 percent of people who haggled got a better deal. Or buy online: It can save you over $1,000 per pair.
- If you have mild to moderate hearing loss, you may benefit from the new over-the-counter hearing aids, which are thousands of dollars cheaper than traditional prescription hearing aids. To find out more, see AARP's *Hearing Loss For Dummies* (published by Wiley).
- Save 20 percent on hearing aids and 15 percent on accessories with AARP Hearing Solutions provided by UnitedHealthcare Hearing. Members also get a hearing test at no cost and personalized support through a large nationwide network of hearing providers. Visit `aarp.org/hearing-solutions`.
- Take a confidential hearing test by phone once a year for free. The test is an independent and scientifically validated hearing screen test developed with funding from the National Institutes of Health. Visit `aarp.org/hearing-test`.

IN THIS CHAPTER

» Figuring out what and how to save

» Considering Section 529 plans and Coverdell Education Savings Accounts

» Evaluating other savings options

» Tallying what goes into your education bill

» Surveying costs for different schools

Chapter 6

Saving for Education Costs

You may have just found out that you're pregnant. Maybe you're at the point where the college catalogs are beginning to accumulate on your dining room table. Or perhaps your family is somewhere in the middle, with your children out of diapers but not yet into calculus. Wherever your family falls in the age spectrum, one thing is certain: Either in your immediate family or in your extended one, we all want our children to receive the best possible education for their needs. That may mean public schools all the way, private schools at some point, trade schools, or apprenticeships. The options are endless, but so may be the potential cost.

And therein lies a problem: Although your child can receive a primary and secondary education without incurring significant added expense in your budget (unless you consider details like your local parents' group's fundraisers), there is very little that's free in the way of post-secondary education. For most of us, the privilege of helping your child obtain that degree or learn a trade comes with a hefty price tag. If you've already explored the costs of a post-secondary education, you know that the numbers often are large; if you haven't yet experienced the pleasure, rest assured that the amounts in question will likely take your breath away.

In solving any problem, you need to remain calm and focused on the task at hand. That's where this chapter may help — by making you methodically look at the current state of your education savings, helping you leave your misconceptions about saving at the door, and showing you ways to begin or increase savings. After you convince yourself that you're able to save something and you actually begin to put some money away, you've won a major victory; everything that follows will be easier. Just keep in mind that saving now will create opportunities and open doors for your children in the future.

Doing the Numbers

Up until now, crunching the numbers and figuring out what you think college will cost has usually been where you begin and end your exploration of the topic of how to pay for future educational costs. But after you resolve to start saving and you take the projected costs and create a plan to save for that amount, it's time to take this exercise a bit more seriously.

Figuring out the costs

Depending on the size of your family and your expectations, adding up the cost of a college education can be a fairly straightforward calculation, or it may become quite involved.

REMEMBER

Be realistic about the capabilities and ambitions of your future student and your ability to pay.

Your straight-A student may have to scale back on their dreams of MIT if your budget, including amounts you can add from your current and future earnings, only goes as far as your local state college. (However, they may want to seriously consider applying for some scholarship aid.)

Likewise, there's little point in saving for an Ivy League education if your child has plans to open their own auto repair shop. And clearly, the more children you're educating, the thinner your resources may be stretched per child. (Although, depending on how closely spaced your children are in age, this situation may actually work to your advantage if you need to apply for financial aid.)

Finding resources to help you save

No matter how late you may begin saving specifically for future college costs, the entire weight of doing so doesn't necessarily need to rest solely on your shoulders, nor do you need to begin to save from nothing.

You may have other resources you haven't even thought of — for example, family, friends, or even the students themselves earning money through scholarships and part-time jobs. Just because these are your children, you may not have to come up with the full amount of their education costs from your pockets alone.

Saving efficiently

Too many people equate saving for the future with current deprivation. For most people, living expenses currently equal (or even exceed income), and they may not have money left over in the family budget for saving. Clearly, if you fit into this category, you're not going to be able to save unless you make some changes in your life. Chapter 4 in Book 1 shows you some relatively painless adjustments that will maximize the amount of money you can shave from your current budget while minimizing the effect on your life.

Exploring Section 529 Plans

Most believe that saving money is a good undertaking, and the federal government is prepared to back up that philosophy with a variety of savings programs that contain built-in tax incentives, some of which you may already be using (tax-deferred retirement plans, anyone?). One of these types of incentive savings plans is the Qualified Tuition Program, or Section 529 plan, which is designed solely to save for college or any other type of qualified education, either tax-exempt or tax-deferred, depending on a number of factors. Like almost everything else the government cooks up, though, Section 529 plans aren't as simple to navigate as everyone selling these plans would have you think.

REMEMBER

Although you may come across many variations of 529 plans, all have the following component parts:

- **The plan owner:** The *plan owner* is the person who sets up the plan (and who, presumably, makes contributions into it, although other people can make contributions into a plan that isn't their own). Depending on the plan you're interested in starting, you may need to be a resident of the plan state.
- **The designated beneficiary:** The *designated beneficiary* is the potential student for whom the plan owner (who doesn't need to be related to the designated beneficiary in any way) intends to provide an education. The plan owner names this person when they set up the account. You can change the designated beneficiary over the account's lifetime, but the account must always have a designated beneficiary. Like the plan owner, and dependent

upon the state plan you invest in, the beneficiary may have to be a resident of the plan state to qualify as a designated beneficiary, at least at the time you first open the account. Of course, if you invest in a private plan rather than a state-sponsored plan, there is no residency requirement.

- **The plan administrator:** The *plan administrator* is the entity (state, private, or educational) under whose auspices the plan exists. In many cases, especially in prepaid tuition plans, the plan administrator is also the plan manager (see the next item in this list). The plan administrator lays out the rules that are specific to that plan, including how much may be contributed, what sorts of investments are allowed, when contributions may be made, whether plans are open to only resident owners and beneficiaries, or if all may participate.
- **Plan manager:** Many Section 529 plans (particularly savings plans) are invested in a variety of mutual funds. Because states aren't in the mutual fund business, they farm this work out to mutual fund companies. These companies (and states that actively manage investments) are the *plan managers*; they're responsible for the actual investing of your money.

Following the rules

WARNING

Section 529 of the Internal Revenue Code is long, complex, and not for the faint of heart. Still, savings accounts that fall under its regulations can be a fantastic way to save for future educational expenses. However, to make it work, you have to understand its requirements; there's little point in setting up one of these accounts if you don't cross your t's and dot your i's just like the IRS wants. Remember, the IRS doesn't have a category of "close, but no cigar." Either your account will qualify under the regulations for tax deferrals or exemptions, or it won't. And if it doesn't, the consequences may be costly.

REMEMBER

In order for a Section 529 plan to qualify under the IRS's rules, it must meet the following criteria:

- Contributions may be made only in cash, including checks, money orders, or payroll deductions, but not in stocks, bonds, or real estate.
- After a contribution is made into a specific plan, you have limited ability to direct the investments. You may, however, change plans once each year.
- You may not pledge the account's value as security against any sort of loan.
- The plan or program you invest in must provide each designated beneficiary a separate accounting.

- You can't contribute more into an account, or group of accounts, for the benefit of a single designated beneficiary than the beneficiary will use in the payment of qualified education expenses. Sorry, but you have to try to estimate this amount. There's no hard and fast rule about how to make this calculation.

When you contribute to a Section 529 plan, you're not allowed any federal income tax deduction for the amount of your contribution (unlike many sorts of retirement plans, which defer income tax not only on the accrued earnings in the account but also on your contributions). Depending on your state (and if you use its plan), you may get a current state income tax deduction for part or all of your contribution each year, or you may receive a tax credit.

After your money is safely tied up in a Section 529 plan, the interest you earn on it isn't taxed until *distributions* (amounts of money you take out of the plan to pay your student's expenses) are made to your designated beneficiary. And if you use distributions from these plans to pay the qualified education expenses of a student at an eligible educational institution (these are the IRS's words), accrued earnings generally aren't taxed at all.

REMEMBER

In other words, a Section 529 plan allows you to save for education and exempts or defers income tax on the accrued earnings until the designated beneficiary begins taking distributions from the plan.

At this point, you may be thinking that the only educational institutions that these plans are qualified to pay for are colleges and universities. Not true. Qualified institutions include all primary, secondary (up to $10,000 per year per student, and only for tuition), and post-secondary schools that are eligible to participate in U.S. Department of Education financial aid programs, including many vocational and technical schools, community colleges, and even some apprenticeship programs. (Daycare and nursery schools do not qualify, despite their sometimes exorbitant costs.) Eligible institutions don't need to be located in the United States; many foreign colleges and universities qualify. The standard here is that the schools must be eligible. They don't actually have to participate in these financial aid programs. Check with the institutions you or your student are interested in to ensure they qualify. In addition, up to $10,000 of 529 plan qualified distributions may be used toward payments of outstanding federal student loans.

Making your money work for you

Creating a successful savings plan involves more than following the rules, although compliance with the rules is a big part.

TIP

If you and your student expect they will attend either a state college or university or a community college, the first place to look is at prepaid tuition options in your state or the state in which your student plans to attend school. But if you see only private options, out-of-state public universities, or a graduate/professional school career in the future, you may want to look only at the savings plans offered by all states run by mutual fund companies. Or you could take a look at the Private College 529 Plan, which covers tuition at about 300 private universities around the country. Finally, you could look at a combination of the two.

After you complete your research and decide what plan you want to invest in, you can obtain an application, complete it, and send it off with a check to open your account (or wire the money directly from your bank through an ACH [American Clearing House] transfer). Applications for all plans are available on the Internet. States will also snail mail applications for the non-tech savvy among us. If you're investing in a plan that may only be purchased through a financial advisor, obtain the application directly from that person (who'll probably be more than helpful in filling it out, as well). Also, be sure to obtain (and keep) a prospectus for your plan and the plan agreement, which outlines all the rules and regulations governing your plan.

No matter what state's plan you invest in — whether directly with the state or through an advisor — the application process is quite straightforward. You need to provide the information for the plan owner, the designated beneficiary, a successor owner, and parent or guardian information (if the designated beneficiary is a minor child).

After you complete your application and send it off, you need to get down to the serious business of making your 529 plan grow. And, although you'd like to think that the stock and bond markets will rocket skyward, multiplying the value of your initial investment so rapidly (and securely, of course) that you'll never have to add any more money to your account, you really do need to be sensible here. Unless you can sock away the full amount your student will likely need when you set up the plan, you have to make additional contributions for this to work. Opening a plan and making an initial investment is only the start of saving enough to send your designated beneficiary to school. Consistent savings is the rest of the equation.

You can add money to a 529 plan in three ways:

- » Periodically send money, either through an ACH transfer, writing a check, using a money order, a cashier's check, or even travelers' checks.
- » Schedule automatic withdrawals from your bank account on a weekly, monthly, quarterly, or annual basis.
- » Make contributions through payroll withholdings.

REMEMBER

You're a big factor in determining whether your savings program flies or falls. Understanding the various ways your savings may earn money and the different investment options available is an important piece of creating the substantial savings you'll need to see your children through college.

Checking Out Coverdell Accounts

If the world of tax-deferred/tax-exempt savings accounts were an ice cream parlor, Coverdell Education Savings Accounts (ESAs) may be rum raisin. Rum raisin may not be the most popular flavor, but it might be just what you want on a particular day. Not surprisingly, many people prefer Coverdell accounts when shopping for a place and a way to save money for college. Coverdell accounts provide a wider range of investment options and increased control over the account, and certain expenses qualify for tax exemption under Coverdell rules that aren't under Section 529 requirements. Whatever your reasons, Coverdell ESAs may be just the account flavor you want today.

Understanding the rules and regulations

Internal Revenue Code Section 530, covering Coverdell ESAs, follows hot on the heels of Code Section 529 (those government sorts are sticklers for going in order). In it, you find all the rules, regulations, and other assorted gobbledygook that govern these sorts of accounts. These accounts (created by Congress) allow you to save now for future educational expenses, whether primary, secondary, or post-secondary, of a designated beneficiary.

You can invest money in Coverdell accounts in a variety of ways: stocks, bonds, money market accounts, certificates of deposit, and so on, although you may not invest in life insurance policies. Under the Coverdell rules (and unlike Section 529 rules), if you designate yourself the one responsible for all decisions on this particular account (also known as the *responsible adult,* who must be the parent or legal guardian of the minor child), you keep control of the money and make all the investment decisions for your child's account. Over the years, the investments will hopefully earn significant income through interest, dividends, and capital gains, until the account is closed.

You pay no income tax on the income when it's earned. As distributions are made from these accounts to your designated beneficiary for qualified educational expenses, the income portion of the distribution is not taxed, either to you or to your student.

REMEMBER

A Coverdell ESA must be opened in writing, and you need to designate a beneficiary when you create it; you aren't allowed to take an already existing account and decide that it's now the Coverdell account for your student. Money that you contribute to the account is held by a trustee or custodian, which must be a bank, mutual fund company, or any other entity that's approved by the Internal Revenue Service (IRS).

Getting the most from your Coverdell account

You've probably discovered by now that successful savings involve far more than sticking your money in a passbook savings account at your local bank. And, while your investment options are seriously limited inside a Section 529 plan, you have far more latitude in investment decisions when you open a Coverdell ESA.

First, you need to decide where, exactly, you want to open your account. Unlike Section 529 plans, states don't get involved in Coverdell accounts; accordingly, you have many more options to choose from and need to make many more decisions.

REMEMBER

While you're in the process of choosing a bank, savings and loan company, or other institution, you need to focus on two essential items:

- The range and variety of investments that the account can offer
- The cost to you annually, upfront, or both to set up and administer the account

You also need to decide whether to invest in a *self-directed account* (one in which you decide on individual investments, including stocks and bonds, to invest in) or one in which you have a choice of mutual funds, bank certificates of deposit, and/or money market funds. Clearly, in the self-directed account, you bear more of the risk personally because you're making all the investment decisions by yourself (unless you hire, at your own cost, an advisor to select what you should buy and when to buy). If you choose to go the mutual fund route, even if your investments do poorly, you can still lay some of the blame on the fund manager. Still, a bad investment is a bad investment. Your account loses money regardless of who made the decisions of what — and what not — to buy.

TIP

If this is your first venture into the world of investing, you may want to open your account in an institution that limits your investment options or hire someone to make these decisions for you in a self-directed account. If you don't want to go to the expense of hiring an investment advisor, leaving the actual investing of your money in the hands of the mutual fund managers may give you a greater comfort level than choosing your own investments, especially when you're just beginning. A wise approach may be to ease yourself in and make safer (although maybe not as lucrative) choices at first. As you gain confidence in your own abilities, you always have the option to change to other options, such as investing in individual stocks and bonds. On the other hand, if you're making money and happy with your investments, don't think you must keep searching for a better mousetrap. You never need to apologize to anyone for making money, even if you didn't make as much money as you could have.

But Wait, There's More! Assessing Other Saving Options

People went to college and private schools long before the Internal Revenue Code, and parents and grandparents saved for those costs even when tax deferrals and/or tax exemptions weren't around. You can save money in many other ways, some even specifically for college. Even though they may not be as tax advantageous as Section 529 plans and Coverdell ESAs, they may make perfect sense in your overall savings plan. And if you're not able to save enough to cover the full cost, all is still not lost: Various scholarships, grants, and loan programs are available to cover any shortfall you may have between what you saved and the cost of your child's education. Here are some options to consider:

- **Rediscovering U.S. Savings Bonds:** Whether you're able to save only relatively small amounts, you're uncertain about your potential student's future plans, or you love the safety and security found only in U.S. Savings Bonds, you may find that this is an attractive way to save for future college expenses and still take advantage of some tax exemptions on the interest earned on your bonds.
- **Saving for education the old-fashioned way:** It may seem strange to even think this, but the trade-off for taking advantage of the income tax breaks available through Section 529 plans and Coverdell ESAs is that you're guaranteeing that you will use that money to pay for qualified educational expenses. If only all of life were so certain and so sure.

  REMEMBER

  You may be hesitating over how much to save in these plans — or whether to save at all — because of your great uncertainty over your child's future plans. When you save in traditional investment and savings accounts, you eliminate that uncertainty because you're not tied to using your savings in any one way. Of course, in exchange for that freedom to spend your savings as you will, you lose any opportunity to defer or exempt tax on your earnings, but if your world is an uncertain place, you may find that's a small price to pay.

» **Putting your faith in a trust fund:** For most people, the phrase "trust fund" brings to mind visions of great wealth and privilege; in other words, it has nothing to do with you. And that picture couldn't be further from the truth. If you save money in any form, then you're a potential candidate to create and fund a trust.

» **Saving in your retirement accounts:** Using retirement funds to pay for college usually isn't the best savings strategy to pay for these costs. In certain limited circumstances, however (such as when parents are older or you face unplanned educational expenses), it may make some sense to access funds from a retirement account to pay qualified educational expenses.

» **Accessing your home equity:** If you (or you and the bank) own your home, you may be sitting on a larger nest egg than you ever considered. A combination of rising home values and shrinking mortgage loan balances has created a large pool of equity for many people, equity that may be made available to fund educational expenses.

» **Using cash value stashed in your whole life insurance policies:** You may have been paying premiums for years on whole-life policies without ever considering the considerable cash value accumulated inside the policy. And, if you took out those policies because you wanted to make sure that the money would be there, in case you weren't, for your children to go to college, this cash value can be used to help your child go to the school of their choice.

» **Identifying sources of free money:** Not every potential student is an academic genius or a future first-round NFL draft pick, but you don't necessarily need to conclude that your child won't qualify for scholarships and grants.

» **Borrowing to fill in the gaps:** You're obviously reading this because you don't want to have to resort to borrowing money to pay for your children's college costs. Still, it's not the end of the world if you do.

Dissecting the Total Bill

Because tuition is usually the highest cost for both private schools and colleges, many people make the mistake of saving *only* for tuition. But other costs, such as housing (if your student is living away from home), books, and supplies, can account for a large chunk of your child's expenses — a large enough chunk that you should include those costs in your savings plan.

The following sections explain what costs you should start saving for and give you an idea of how much those costs are.

REMEMBER

Although we cover the major education costs here, they aren't the only costs you may encounter as you try to give your child the most suitable education for them. Although we don't suggest you start saving for a beer fund, be prepared to pay for other items, such as parking permits, transportation, health insurance, and a movie ticket or a new pair of jeans.

Tackling tuition

Tuition refers to probably the largest cost for college: the fees for actual instruction. For the academic year 2025–2026, the average tuition costs for a public university averaged $11,950 for an in-state student and more than $31,880 for an out-of-state student. Room and board added $13,900 to those numbers. The numbers for private four-year universities are much direr: average tuition was a lofty $45,000, and average room and board costs totaled $15,920.

Inflation for school tuition isn't capped at whatever the current inflation rate is for the country. Depending on a number of factors, tuitions sometimes outstrip the inflation rate. Other times, such as during the COVID pandemic, tuition actually dropped. Keep in mind, though, that the number of years tuition has dropped is far outweighed by the number of years it has increased.

If you want your child to attend private schools for all or some of their primary and secondary years, you have many options. Of course, the cheapest, by far, is public education, which is available to all students regardless of where they live. However, all public educations are not created equal, and if you're not living in a tony suburb of a major city that cherishes education, you may decide that private education is the way to go. Average tuition costs for a private education vary widely. If you can access a parochial school, the tuition will be much lower than if you board your child at a posh academy in leafy New England. Once again, the choice is yours.

These numbers may seem insurmountable, especially if you're entering the savings game fairly late; however, some relief may be available. Only a small percentage of students (and their families) pay the top-dollar price for college, and even some aid is available for private schools. Many schools and universities offer huge amounts of outright grants and other forms of financial aid (other than loans, although those are available to all), and scholarships and grants for secondary and post-secondary schools from other sources may be available.

TIP

If you're fairly certain your child will attend a public college, you may want to investigate whether your state offers a Section 529 prepaid tuition plan to help you pay for those upcoming tuition bills. Even if you can't save for tuition costs in one of these plans, saving money in any Section 529 savings plan or Coverdell

Education Savings Account will allow your college savings to grow faster than conventional savings accounts. These plans and accounts are covered earlier in this chapter.

REMEMBER

Up to $10,000 per year is available from 529 plans and Coverdell ESAs to pay private primary or secondary school tuition. This money may only be used for tuition and not for any other ancillary costs of that education, such as room and board, computer equipment, or other fees required. Still, if you have a well-funded plan already set up and you find that the local public school isn't serving your student's best interests, using these plans to pay for qualified tuition at a private school is now an option. In addition, many states now allow up to $10,000 lifetime to repay already existing student loans or pay for apprenticeship programs that were previously excluded from 529 and Coverdell plans' qualifying distributions.

Accounting for housing

You may come from a family who assumes that all those going on to higher learning will receive their post-secondary education at the local campuses. And you may fully expect when your student reaches that point, they will live at home. If so, you can probably skip this part, although you should be stashing some money away for good, reliable transportation, whether that means a car, bus, or subway fare.

If, on the other hand, you suspect that your student won't be satisfied going to the local schools (or if your area doesn't really have many post-secondary offerings), you need to add the cost of housing into your savings plan — either college-owned housing or local rental real estate.

College-owned housing

Most colleges provide some sort of room and board options in the form of on-campus or university-owned housing, and they gladly tack those fees onto the tuition bill. Because most university-owned housing is mandatory for all non-commuting students for at least the first year or two, if you plan on sending your child to college, these costs must factor into your savings plan. For 2025-2026, average college-owned housing and a basic board plan cost between $13,900 and $15,920. Where your college falls in this range depends on a few factors, such as the following:

- **Location:** Generally, city schools tend to have higher housing costs than schools out in the country.
- **Size:** Generally, larger colleges tend to have higher housing costs than smaller colleges.

» **Number of students in a room:** If your child insists on having a room all to their lonesome, expect to pay a premium for that privilege. Generally speaking, the more students crammed into a single room, the less you're likely to pay for your student.

TIP

Room and board charges paid directly to an eligible school (the school will be happy to tell you if it's eligible) can be paid by using tax-free distributions from your Section 529 and/or Coverdell plans. Remember, though, if you're paying for room and board for a private secondary school, this is not a qualified expense and, therefore, is not eligible for payment from either a 529 or Coverdell plan.

Local rental properties

Although colleges and universities attempt to expand their student populations, many fail to increase their own housing to meet the increased number of students, pushing more students into the local housing market. In areas where rental units are being added, this isn't a problem; the rental units increase at a rate equal (hopefully) to the number of students seeking housing. However, many older cities have very limited rental housing, and the increased number of students seeking it has forced prices up sharply. So, if you plan to rent an apartment or house for your student, costs become more variable, making it more difficult to predict how much you may need to save for your student's housing needs.

REMEMBER

The cost of a rental is only the cost of the rental — it may not include utilities (heat in the northern states and air conditioning in the southern states can both be very expensive), and it certainly doesn't include food. You need to add the cost of any utilities not included, plus money for food or a meal ticket at the university, to accurately compare your costs to the university's room and board plan.

Check the amount of room and board the college considers a "qualified education expense." (You can often find this information buried on its website, or just phone one of the college's financial aid officers.) The money you spend on rent to a non-university landlord can be paid using tax-free distributions from your Section 529 and Coverdell plans. However, if you spend more than the college's estimated amount of room and board on a non-university landlord, you may want to pay the excess some other way. Distributions taken from your Section 529 and Coverdell plans in excess of "qualified expenses" are subject to income tax and a 10 percent penalty.

Factoring in books and supplies

Okay, so you know you've saved enough for tuition and room and board, but the need for money doesn't stop once you unload the SUV on the first day of orientation. After your student is at school, they need to buy books and other supplies and won't know which books and supplies they need until after the first few days of school.

The costs for books and supplies aren't insubstantial. You need to figure on saving at least an additional $1,000 per year for books, plus $500 to $1,000 for other supplies, such as lab coats, protective glasses, notebooks, or even pens and pencils. In comparison to the tuition and room and board fees, this amount may not seem huge, but it's still substantial. Over the course of four years, that bill can be anywhere from $6,000 to $8,000.

TIP

Unlike tuition costs, which the university sets, and housing and food costs, which are set either by the university or by the conditions in the local economy, you can somewhat control how much your student spends on books and supplies. Your student can purchase used copies of most books and then resell them when they're through with them, or they can rent them for the semester or the year, returning the book after the final exam has been taken. Supplies, such as notebooks, don't need to have the university or college crest on them in order to function properly. Finally, the cost of computers has come down considerably since computers became the order of the day. All these costs can be paid for using qualified distributions from either 529 or Coverdell plans, provided you have the receipts to substantiate the distributions.

WARNING

Ignore this category at your peril. There is little point in saving enough money to send your student to the school of their choice and then leaving them in the lurch without the tools to access the education offered.

Looking into the Costs of Various Types of Schools

No matter where your student decides to attend college, you have to pay for the tuition, books, and supplies, plus you have to come up with a solution to the housing question. But because you may need a crystal ball to figure out where your child plans to attend college, the next piece of the puzzle isn't quite as straightforward — estimating the tuition and fees you need to save for. However, after you have an idea of what type of school your student plans to attend — or if your student is either recently or not yet born — you can begin some significant planning for the future by planning for the type of school you *hope* they will attend.

If you plan for your child to attend either a private primary or secondary school (or both), factor in the smaller of the $10,000-per-year or actual tuition fees of the desired school into your savings calculations. Failure to do this could result in you running out of funds before your student completes their education.

To make that planning a little easier — short of a crystal ball — we give you some real numbers to work with in this section for each type of school your child may attend.

Enrolling in career and vocational training schools

Smaller, more specialized schools, such as career and vocational training schools, train students in very specific areas for very specific careers, such as funeral services, dental hygiene, piano tuning, or even bartending. So do apprenticeships. The cost of these programs (which may exist independently of or be attached to community colleges or even four-year colleges) tends to be much smaller than your typical college.

TIP

Do your research before enrolling in any post-secondary school, whether purely vocational, combined vocational and academic, entirely academic, or an apprenticeship. Tuition costs run the spectrum from several thousand to tens of thousands of dollars per year. The education you get from the more expensive option may not be any better than what you can obtain at a less costly institution. Typically, public two-year schools are less expensive than public four-year schools, and private for-profit schools cost more than private, not-for-profit schools, but exceptions exist. Keep in mind that if you can commute to school from home, doing so is always less expensive than moving to another place and adding housing and food costs to your education budget.

Taking community college and continuing education classes

Almost every city of any size has at least one community college, an institution of higher education that gives college-level learning without the college-level price. In addition, many large universities have a continuing education division that provides much the same function as a community college, including the lower cost.

REMEMBER

Don't assume that because you can't afford an Ivy League college through the normal channels that you also can't afford to take courses in the continuing education division. Tuition at Harvard University in 2022-2023 was $57,261; per-course fees at the Harvard Extension were $1,980 for most courses that count toward an undergraduate degree. A full-time course load at either school is four to five courses per semester, which means you can attend Harvard University and pay the higher price, or Harvard Extension at approximately one-third the cost. Both schools award degrees from Harvard University.

Tuition costs for community colleges cover a range. You pay the most in the northeast and the mid-Atlantic states and the least in the west. But none of these fees will completely break the bank, especially because you're not required to take a full course load but can take one or two courses a semester if that suits you and your budget.

In addition, 19 states currently provide free tuition to qualifying community college students: Arkansas, California, Connecticut, Delaware, Hawaii, Indiana, Kentucky, Maryland, Massachusetts, Missouri, Montana, New York, Nevada, Oklahoma, Oregon, Rhode Island, Tennessee, Virginia, and Washington State.

While these states don't provide the ancillary costs of education, such as books and computers, room and board, or transportation, if you qualify, this is a very cost-effective way to get the first two years of a four-year degree under your belt, allowing you to use any funds you specifically saved for education to be used in those last two years. Remember, the name on your degree comes from the college or university you graduate from, even if you only attended that institution for three semesters (usually the shortest amount of time a school allows you to attend in order to receive your degree from them).

WARNING

Funds from all education savings plans can be used to pay either community college or continuing education tuition, provided the school you attend is an eligible institution. However, in order to pay for housing using savings from these plans, you need to be at least a half-time student. Be aware of this and vigilant. A mistake here costs you income tax on the distribution and a 10 percent penalty.

Going for a four-year public education

Each state has its own public university/college system. Because state universities are larger than colleges and offer much more programming, they tend to be considerably more expensive than state colleges. If your student has a very clear idea of where they're going in life, it will be most cost-effective if you can find that program at a state college rather than a state university, especially for in-state students.

Unlike public elementary and secondary schools, public universities and colleges aren't funded totally by tax dollars (and may actually be funded very little by tax dollars). However, state-run colleges and universities are one of the best bargains around, especially for in-state students. Any state subsidy, no matter how small, is better than no state subsidy for keeping costs down, and this is reflected in the size of tuition bills.

Getting your education in private

Public education may be the cornerstone on which our country is built. However, a vast network of private schools is available at every level for those who can afford to pay. And because no college education is free (unless you look at the U.S. military academies, where the payment is in kind), all schools that don't rely on public subsidies are referred to as *private*. Private universities can refer to various types of institutions, from Ivy League schools to hundreds of private four-year institutions throughout the country. Each of these colleges and universities offers a unique educational opportunity, as well as a unique price tag.

Overall, prices are high — and climbing higher every year — and no relief is in sight. The schools set tuition and room and board fees, and there is no public oversight. Furthermore, college presidents and trustees retain their jobs based on how well their institutions are doing financially — if it takes tuition hikes to keep it that way, that's just too bad.

TIP

If your savings are a bit lacking when the time comes to start forking over tuition payments, the smartest way to look for a private school may be to shop by endowment rather than the tuition ticket price. (An endowment is the amount of money that the school has invested, with the income available for building projects, professors' salaries, and tuition grants.) Schools with large endowments usually devote a large percentage of the earnings from the fund to outright grants, awarded based on need. Some schools with extraordinary endowments now provide free tuition to students from low-income families, and tuition is capped at no more than 10 percent of income for students from families earning $75,000 to $150,000.

IN THIS CHAPTER

» Understanding how student loans are different

» Knowing your options

» Finding special help for military personnel

Chapter 7

Handling Student Loans

Student loans are hard to live with and, for many, hard to live without! Few question the value of a post-secondary education, whether it is in a technical field, for a skilled trade, or for a four-year (or more) degree. More education frequently yields a better, fuller life as well as more income. But with the cost of education rising fast and the job market always unpredictable, there is a growing disconnect between the cost and the benefit.

This disconnect is demonstrated by the default rate of student loans, which has been on an upward trend. New research indicates that as of April 2025, 31 percent of student loan borrowers with a payment due are in "late-stage delinquency," or over 90 days past due on payments, and that nearly one-quarter of all borrowers are in or approaching loan default, which occurs after 270 days of missed payments.

So, how do you get the benefits you want and need without the risk of owing more than you can pay? This chapter is just what you're looking for, with our favorite heads-up advice to keep you moving in the right direction.

Understanding How Student Loans Work

The way that student loans are reported often catches people off guard. What most of us didn't know when we were in school is that, depending on how your education is funded, you may have a new loan every semester. That equates to up to two loans per year, or a total of eight smaller loans hitting your credit report instead of just one big one, even though you may pay them all with one check each month. When you start repaying the loans, each of them will reflect being paid on time (or not).

WARNING

All this activity can build your credit score, but failing to pay can sink you big time if you end up defaulting.

Another unique feature of student loans is that they are not normally dischargeable in a Chapter 7 bankruptcy. A student loan is a commitment that follows you until you honor it, regardless of how long it takes.

The next sections discuss how to handle default and the collection process along with finding repayment options that work for you.

Dealing with the prospect of default

Before you can be late on your loan, you have to have used up your grace period (the length of time you have after leaving school before you have to make your first payment). Determining when you have used up your grace period can be complex. Each type of loan may have a different grace period. For example, if you have a federal Stafford loan, your grace period is six months. Federal PLUS loans can be based on when they were issued (see `https://studentaid.gov/plus-app/` for more info). Check your loan documents or contact your lender to find out when your grace period runs out.

REMEMBER

Here are some simple steps that may help keep you out of trouble:

- **Keep in communication with your lender or servicer.** If you move, tell them. Being hard to find isn't a plus. If they send you a letter or an email, read it. Ignoring a potential problem only allows it to grow more serious.
- **Find out which plans are available to you.** Federal loans are usually based on a ten-year repayment plan. If you can't or don't want to have that big of a bite taken out of your earnings, change your repayment plan. Extending your payments costs you less each month but more over time.
- **If you have a private loan, contact your lender for forbearance options.** Private loans are different from federal loans and are not eligible for income-based repayment or other federal plans, deferments, or forgiveness. Your private lender may offer other types of forbearance plans, but expect to pay for them.

- **Look to community banks and credit unions for refinancing options of private student loans.** An example is the cuGrad Private Student Loan Consolidation program (`https://consolidation.custudentloans.org`), which can be used to refinance and consolidate existing private student loan debt into one payment at a lower monthly rate.

WARNING

Interest accrues on all types of loans during forbearances and on some types of loans during deferment, increasing your total debt. Be sure you understand your contract.

Handling the collection process

After you know the stakes are high, you want to handle any collection process quickly. The key to minimizing damage from a defaulted student loan is to take action right away. Private student loans may charge off in as few as 120 days rather than the traditional 180-day timeline for normal loans. Early action can enable you to handle loan issues quickly with the servicer rather than a collection agency. Servicers are more likely to work with you to come up with a solution that works for both you and the lender.

Federal student loans offer alternatives to help you get through a financially challenging period and avoid the prospect of default altogether. Contact your loan servicer or Federal Student Aid (800-433-3243; `www.studentaid.gov`) at the first sign you may have difficulty making a payment and they can discuss alternatives with you. Here are two of the most common alternatives:

- **Forbearance:** While in forbearance, your loan payments are temporarily suspended or reduced. However, interest continues to accrue, so be sure you understand the terms of the agreement.
- **Deferment:** When a loan is placed in deferment, your payments are suspended and with certain federal loans, such as subsidized loans, interest usually does not accrue during the deferment, although that isn't universal. Unsubsidized and most private loans continue to accrue interest, so you'll need to be prepared to handle it when the deferment period ends.

These tools may help you avoid defaulting or even becoming late with your payments if you act soon enough.

TIP

Before you contact the loan servicer, organize your thoughts. Treat this as a very important job interview. Explain coherently why you weren't able to pay — medical issues, job loss, pay reductions, armed-service call-up, or family emergency — and propose a realistic repayment amount that you are able to justify based on your budget.

REMEMBER

Collectors are not obligated to offer you the best repayment terms you can get. They just want to get as much money from you as fast as they can. A loan servicer is much more likely to steer you to programs that will keep you out of collections, but you have to act fast.

Quick action also means that any delinquencies will be early, which typically gives you more options to get on top of the situation.

Identifying the best repayment option for you

A huge number of repayment programs are available, and they change all the time. Be sure to check out the big sites that deal with them, such as Federal Student Aid (`https://studentaid.gov/manage-loans/repayment/plans`) and FinAid (`www.finaid.org`).

Even if you've defaulted, federal loans provide two key ways to get back on track:

- **Loan rehabilitation:** You can make a series of affordable, agreed-upon monthly payments — often as low as $5 to $20 — over nine to ten months. After you've finished making payments, the default status is removed from your credit report (though the history of missed payments remains).
- **Loan consolidation:** You can combine your defaulted loans into a new direct consolidation loan, provided you agree to enter an income-driven repayment plan. This doesn't erase the default from your credit report, but it does stop collection efforts and helps you regain good standing more quickly.

Both options can restore eligibility for federal benefits like income-driven repayment plans (Income Based Repayment, Income Contingent Repayment, Pay As You Earn, and Saving on a Valuable Education), deferment, or additional financial aid if you return to school.

WARNING

If you qualify for student loan forgiveness, you may have to pay income tax on any amount that is forgiven.

Finding a Way Out

In most cases, your loans are yours to have and to hold until you pay them back or expire trying. However, on some occasions student loans may be forgiven, canceled, or discharged. The next sections cover loan forgiveness and bankruptcy.

Gaining student loan forgiveness

Different rules govern Direct Loans, Perkins Loans, and Federal Family Education Loans (FFEL). Be sure to know which rules apply to your loans. Following is a summary of the types of loan absolution that are available.

- **Total and Permanent Disability Discharge:** Like the name says, this discharge is for those who have been permanently disabled by military service or those receiving Social Security Disability. You also qualify if your physician certifies that you have a condition that has prevented substantial gainful activity for at least five years, or if your condition is expected to continue for five years, or you are expected to die.
- **Death Discharge:** This one comes into play if you die even for parent PLUS loans. No life, no loan. However, for some private student loans with a cosigner, the cosigner may be responsible for the debt, especially for loans taken out before, not after November 20, 2018, under the Economic Growth, Regulatory Relief, and Consumer Protection Act.
- **Discharge in Bankruptcy:** See the later section "Taking your loans to bankruptcy."
- **Closed School Discharge:** Direct Loans and FFEL are forgiven only if your school folds.
- **False Certification of Student Eligibility and Unpaid Refund Discharge:** To qualify for this discharge, your school has to have messed up in a major way, such as approving your loan for a degree in law enforcement when you have a felony record disqualifying you as a law enforcement.
- **Teacher Loan Forgiveness:** This discharge may be yours if you have taught full-time in a low-income elementary or secondary school or educational service agency for five consecutive years. Only $17,500 of your subsidized or unsubsidized loans are forgiven. PLUS loans cannot be included.
- **Public Service Loan Forgiveness:** If you work in a specified public service job or nonprofit and make 120 payments on your Direct Loans (beginning after October 1, 2007), the remaining balance that you owe may be forgiven.
- **Perkins Loan Cancellation and Discharge:** Federal Perkins Loans (last issued in 2017) may be canceled if you perform certain types of public service or are employed in certain occupations. Generally, each complete year of service gets a percentage of your loan canceled. Occupational categories include volunteers in the Peace Corps or ACTION program (including VISTA), teachers, members of the U.S. armed forces (serving in areas of hostility), nurses and medical technicians, law enforcement and corrections officers, Head Start workers, child and family services workers, and professional providers of early intervention services.

You can find more information at https://studentaid.gov/manage-loans/forgiveness-cancellation.

Taking your loans to bankruptcy

Because the value of your education can't be repossessed, a student loan generally can't be wiped out in a bankruptcy. Due to the limited time a Chapter 13 bankruptcy runs for, student loans are rarely paid in full in a Chapter 13 filing, so be aware that interest often will continue to accrue, and you could end up increasing the amount you owe if you terminate a Chapter 13 bankruptcy filing early. Trying to get rid of student loan debt through a bankruptcy is difficult and perilous, but in some cases it can be done.

Most debtors do not qualify to discharge (eliminate) student loan debt in a Chapter 7 unless you can prove to the court that repaying your student loans would cause you undue hardship. This provision is known as the *hardship exemption*. One size doesn't fit all, and the criteria can vary by court.

Here are some factors the court may look for:

- **Poverty:** Based on your current income and expenses, you can't maintain a minimal standard of living for yourself and your dependents if you are forced to repay your loans.
- **Persistence:** Your current financial situation is likely to continue for a significant part of the repayment period.
- **Good faith:** You have made a good-faith effort to repay your student loans.

REMEMBER

If you have a Health Education Assistance Loan (HEAL), your loan is more than seven years past due, and repayment would impose an "unconscionable" burden on your life, you may be able to get a discharge. A qualified attorney can advise you on your chances for a discharge.

Managing Your Loans Now and Later

Remember, federal student loans are real loans, just like car loans or mortgages. You must repay your student loans even if your financial circumstances become difficult. Your student loans cannot be canceled because you didn't get the job you expected or you didn't complete your education (unless you qualify for a specific relief program, as explained in the earlier section "Gaining student loan forgiveness").

The next sections cover strategies to lower your bill while you're still in school and ways to keep up with your loans after you get out.

Lowering your bill while you're in school

There is no need to let the bill for your student loans grow while you're in school. Unless you have a subsidized loan, interest accrues and accumulates during the term of your education. Consider these strategies to reduce or eliminate your interest buildup.

- **Pay your interest as it accrues.** For students trying to save money on unsubsidized federal loans and private student loan debt, one solution is to make payments of at least the new interest that accrues during the in-school and grace periods. There are no prepayment penalties on federal and private student loans, so you can make interest-only payments. When making a payment, include a note asking for the payment to be applied to interest.

  TIP

  If you have both subsidized and unsubsidized student loans, specify that the extra payment should be applied to the unsubsidized loans.

  Paying off interest early not only saves you money, but also enables you to get used to working with your student loan servicer and helps you establish a relationship for successful repayment. It also gets you in the habit of making payments. Plus, you may get some tax benefits! As much as $2,500 in interest paid on student loans may be deductible on your federal income tax return. This may result in a refund that you could use to prepay a portion of your loan to lower the cost of your loan even further. Sweet! See IRS Publication 970 (`www.irs.gov/publications/p970`) for details.
- **Pay both interest and principal.** Doing so gives you all the benefits listed in the preceding section, plus it reduces your principal, which seriously lowers your future payments.
- **Work a little to save a lot.** You don't need a full-time job to make a big difference in future loan payments. If you can earn only $57 per month (or $13.25 a week, or $1.89 a day), you can pay all the interest that will accrue on a typical $10,000 unsubsidized Stafford loan throughout four years of college and your six-month grace period. This means you can get your diploma owing only $10,000 instead of $13,060 (your principal plus interest). And don't forget, you may get a fat tax deduction as a bonus for deducting the interest you pay on your loans each year.

Keeping up with your loans after you're out

You need to make payments to your loan servicer. Each servicer has its own process, so check with your servicer if you aren't sure how or when to make a payment. You are responsible for staying in touch with your servicer and making your payments, even if you do not receive a bill. It's your job to know who services your loan(s). Check your account at `https://studentaid.gov` to confirm who your current servicer is and how to make payments.

REMEMBER

Even if you don't receive a bill, you're still responsible for staying in touch with your servicer and making your payments on time.

A lot of repayment plan options are available; see the summary in the earlier section "Identifying the best repayment option for you." How much you have to pay and for how long depends on the plan you choose, so it's critical that you understand and act on your options. We strongly suggest that you figure your real repayment amount, using the loan simulator at `https://studentaid.gov`, under each plan before you pick one. A wide range of repayment plan options is available, including the new SAVE Plan (which replaced REPAYE in 2023) and several other income-driven repayment (IDR) plans.

You may be able to consolidate your loans. Understand what consolidating means for you and how it may affect your future payments. You may also want to consider loan forbearance or deferment to temporarily reduce or postpone payments if you go back to school, join the military, or experience a hardship.

You may qualify for discharge, cancellation, or forgiveness in certain circumstances that are covered earlier in this chapter. Keep in mind that in most cases, interest continues to accrue during these periods, which can increase the total cost of your loan.

WARNING

Although student loans do offer generous terms, the danger here is that many young people just out of school don't have much experience budgeting and living on their own. You may find yourself in a real-live "grown-up" job with a salary that makes you feel like a millionaire, and you may start spending like a millionaire, too. Without tools such as a spending plan, you may quickly lose control of credit and debt and find negative items being added to your credit report. See Book 1 as well as Chapter 1 in Book 3 for tips on creating a budget so you're sure to have the money to pay your loan.

Setting Limits during the Planning and Application Process

Beware of passion and peer pressure. Deciding your financial limits early in the game saves you from the emotions that are sure to surface as you narrow down your choices. Begin by setting a value for the earnings you're expecting to get in the field you plan to enter. Don't know your career choice yet? Then we strongly suggest that you minimize loans until you do. Consider community colleges. Like buying a house before you know where you'll be working or what you can afford, buying an expensive education without knowing what type of job or salary you're likely to get is a mistake.

TIP

Shop around with different types of lenders, including the government, nonprofit sources such as your state student loan authority, private lenders, banks, and credit unions. Give extra points to those lenders that keep and service the loans they originate. Keep Parent PLUS Loans and cosigning to a minimum.

Getting Help If You're in the Military

The GI Bill (`https://benefits.va.gov/gibill`) offers substantial benefits to service personnel who qualify. More than one program is available, and programs typically offer tuition, books, and housing allowances. Be sure to check your eligibility before you take on any student loan debt. Here are three simple steps to consider:

- **Reduce your interest rates.** Currently serving active-duty personnel are eligible to have interest rates lowered to 6 percent on *all* student loans taken out prior to active-duty military service under the Servicemembers Civil Relief Act (SCRA; formerly the Soldiers and Sailors Act). The SCRA provides protections for military members as they enter active duty and includes items such as rental agreements, security deposits, prepaid rent, evictions, installment contracts, credit card interest rates, mortgage interest rates, mortgage foreclosures, civil judicial proceedings, automobile leases, life insurance, health insurance, and income tax payments. It also provides benefits to dependents. Ask your loan servicer how to apply.
- **Opt for Income-Driven Repayment (IDR) and Public Service Loan Forgiveness (PSLF).** These are two great options to repay federal student loans. IDR plans tie the amount of your monthly payment to your income and family size. PSLF can forgive any remaining balance on federal student loans after you make ten years of on-time qualified payments while working full-time in public service, such as active-duty military service or service with the government or certain nonprofit organizations.

  Begin IDR as soon as possible so that every payment you make is a qualifying monthly payment. Make 120 qualified monthly payments, and the balance of your loan can be forgiven.

» **Manage your private loans.** After you choose options for your federal loans, remember that private loans don't qualify for IDR or PSLF. Postponing payments on private loans through deferment or forbearance may give you short-term relief if you're having trouble making ends meet. The terms and conditions of these payment plans vary, but for most private student loans interest continues to accrue after you suspend your payments. This means that your debt grows while you wait. You may be better off paying back your private loans if you can afford it. If you can't afford to repay your loans while you're on active duty, ask your servicer about interest-only payments instead.

TIP

If you run into trouble keeping up with your payments, contact your Judge Advocate General, the VA Education Call Center (888-442-4551), or Student Loan Ombudsman (`https://studentaid.gov/feedback-ombudsman`; 800-433-3243) for assistance.

3
Dealing with Debt and Credit

Contents at a Glance

IN THIS CHAPTER

» Examining different kinds of debt

» Erasing debt

» Steering clear of accumulating more debt

Chapter 1

Tackling the Debt You Owe

In this chapter, we look at the different types of debt to help you create a budget for paying debt off. We discuss how to rank the importance of each debt so you can create a payoff plan that works with your budget, and we share tips anyone can use to keep themselves from accumulating more debt. It's all fun and games when you come home with something shiny until you have to pay it back.

REMEMBER

The illusion that you're a terrible person if you have debt is a common misconception. In fact, many personal finance gurus even suggest that if you have debt, you shouldn't enjoy your life until you pay that debt off in full. Ignore them. Debt happens to everyone at one time or another, and you don't deserve a lower quality of life than the person down the street.

Looking at the Different Types of Debt

You acquire *debt* when you borrow a certain amount of money intending to pay it back. People can take on debt, but so can companies, corporations, and even countries. Heck, as of this writing, the United States is more than $38.6 trillion in the hole, according to U.S. Debt `Clock.org`.

Different types of debt affect your credit score in different ways. You want different types of debt paid off in full on your credit report so lenders can see that you're a trustworthy applicant capable of paying off a loan. You *do not* want open or delinquent accounts all over the place. In the following sections, we review the different types of debt so you can get organized and pay these monsters off.

REMEMBER

You often see people refer to debt as being "good" debt or "bad" debt.

- *Good debt* typically provides a return on your investment. Student loans are considered good debt because you're using them to secure a college degree, which helps increase your earning potential. Another example of good debt is a home loan because your home can appreciate in value over time, enabling you to sell for a profit.
- *Bad debt* is anything you've borrowed that doesn't further your finances; you can think of bad debt as anything that decreases your net worth over time, usually with depreciating assets. This type of debt includes auto loans (because cars lose their value) and credit cards.

Student loans

Student loan debt is money you borrow for costs associated with higher education, such as tuition, textbooks, laptops, and living expenses. If you attend a trade school, additional expenses can apply. For example, you may need specific tools if you go into automotive repair or a stethoscope if you're a medical assistant.

These types of debts are considered *unsecured installment loans*. When a debt is *unsecured*, you aren't providing any collateral to the financial institution (or lender). An *installment loan* means that you'll pay back the loan at regular intervals, but the payment amount may change based on the type of interest rate you have (that is, a fixed rate versus an adjustable rate). Student loan debt can be recalculated depending on the type of loan and repayment plan. The interest rates on a student loan can be fixed or graduated (the rate increases as income increases). The lender determines the frequency of payments, which can vary but usually occur once a month over several years. Repayment starts six months after graduation, a span known as a *grace period*.

You can receive either a federal loan from the U.S Department of Education or a private loan through a bank or alternative lender. Private loans are much harder for a younger student to obtain because these loans are typically based on your credit score and credit history. Federal loans, on the other hand, require you to complete the Free Application for Federal Student Aid (FAFSA). Each of these types of loans has different requirements as well as pros and cons, such as income-based repayment options or the ability to refinance at a lower rate.

TIP

We highly encourage everyone who hasn't started their higher ed journey yet to at least fill out the FAFSA. A lot of schools award grants and scholarships based on the information you provide. You can find the online application at `studentaid.gov`.

Credit cards

Credit card debt is money you borrow from a financial institution or company through a line of credit. A *line of credit* is a preselected amount of money you can access at any time as long as you don't exceed the available funds. The length of time to pay back the money is typically a month. After the month is over, the funds you borrowed acquire interest, which means you have to pay back more than what you had initially borrowed in the first place.

Credit cards, like student loans (see the preceding section), may be unsecured. If a credit card is secured, the lender wants you to put some skin in the game by providing some collateral such as paying a hefty fee or providing a cash deposit when you open the account. The lender doesn't keep the collateral forever — usually a year, sort of like a deposit. After you've established a history of making your payments on time, it refunds your collateral and moves you to an unsecured line of credit.

Along with being unsecured or secured, credit cards are also known as revolving debt. *Revolving debt* enables you to borrow money and pay it back, only to repeat the cycle again and again with no end date. Credit cards can also come with perks such as free travel, cash back, and discounts meant to keep you using your credit card again and again. When you use credit cards responsibly, you can take advantage of these perks without spending additional money if you pay your card off in full every month.

Home and auto loans

Unlike the student loan and credit card debt in the preceding sections, which can slowly creep up on you, purchasing a home or automobile can cause you to acquire a large amount of debt at one time. New cars can start at $20,000 and go up from there. Homes typically go for hundreds of thousands of dollars and, depending on the location, sometimes even more! We don't have that type of cash lying around, and we're going to assume you probably don't either.

Home loans

Mortgages, like student loans, are considered installment debt. When you're approved for a mortgage, the bank that has approved your financing sets up an arrangement with you to pay back the loan over time — usually 15 or 30 years. Still, the exact arrangement depends on your lender and other factors, such as what type of loan you're approved for, interest rates, and whether you have a down payment.

Mortgages are considered secured debt. A lender knows it's getting its money back no matter what when helping you finance a home. So if you end up short one month and can't pay your mortgage, no sweat — to the lender, not you. You'll have to pay when it shows up on your credit report. However, after you're 120 days late, the lender will start the foreclosure process and take the house back. Sure, it would've made more money if you had fulfilled the loan's terms, but it's still getting something out of the deal.

WARNING

Please pay your mortgage. You don't want a foreclosure on your credit report! Foreclosures can prevent you from finding a new place to live, even when you're just looking to rent. This costly mistake can cost you thousands of dollars for years to come. See Chapter 2 in Book 2 for details on handling a mortgage meltdown.

Auto loans

If you don't have enough cash to purchase a vehicle outright, you need a bank or credit union to finance you with an auto loan. Suppose you're buying a car through a dealership. In that case, its finance department reviews options with you based on your credit history and whether you're providing a down payment or a trade-in. Dealerships usually have preferred lenders they work with. You can choose to finance with them or look at your bank for finance options.

Auto loans are secured loans you pay off in installments. Because it's an installment loan, you make monthly payments over a timeline, usually no more than six years. Six-year loans are more common when you're purchasing a brand-new car versus an older model because the loan amount tends to be more significant. Auto loans also come with collateral, which is why they're secured. If you don't make your payments, the lender can take the vehicle in a process called *repossession*. It finds someone else to buy your car and then sticks you with the difference of what's still left on your loan. This process happens in a much shorter time frame than a home foreclosure (see the preceding section), but can you imagine? You're getting up to get a coffee one day, and then *bam!* Your car is gone!

Miscellaneous debt

If you've read the preceding sections, you may be thinking, "I owe someone money, but you haven't even mentioned it yet!" Never fear, for this section talks about other types of debt you may need to include in your budget.

Government agencies

Child support, outstanding taxes, any debt owed to agencies besides the IRS, and any excess unemployment payments are all debt that falls into this category. Debt owed to the government is serious business. In fact, unpaid debt can lead to many repercussions, such as having your paycheck garnished or, in some cases, losing your driver's license.

The United States Department of Treasury's Financial Management Service operates the Treasury Offset Program, also known as the TOP. The TOP allows federal and state agencies to collect money however they see fit, such as by garnishing your wages through your employer or taking the money out of your tax refund. Your employer has no choice but to abide, which means a relatively smaller paycheck.

WARNING

Don't forget your property taxes. This bill is just as important as paying your mortgage. When your property taxes become delinquent, the state where the property is located can sell your property even if you own the home that's located on it. If you need assistance, ask your mortgage lender if you can open an escrow account.

Court-ordered debt

Specific crimes such as unpaid parking tickets, breaking traffic laws, and more severe ones such as misdemeanors and felonies carry a fine. Fines cost money and hopefully discourage you from committing the crime again. You usually pay this type of debt to the court, where a judge presides over your case. You may also be asked to pay court fees and, if applicable, restitution toward a victim.

Overdue bills turned over to collection agencies

Unpaid bills that go to a collection agency show up on your credit report to haunt you. Evictions, utility bills, and outstanding lines of credit from places such as department stores all fall in this bucket.

REMEMBER

Bills you'd rather ignore don't go away, as much as you want them to, which is why your budget helps you figure out where the money to pay them comes from.

Medical bills

Medical debt includes any services you receive from your provider, testing, bloodwork, and hospital stays. It can even include medication and transportation to receiving medical care, such as a ride in an ambulance. Many insurance companies charge high premiums, and despite the 2010 passage of the Affordable Care Act (or ACA), many Americans still struggle to afford healthcare coverage.

Some employers cover part of the insurance premiums, but others don't. Even if you have health insurance, you're expected to pay what's known as a deductible before your health insurance provider covers any of the bill.

Personal loans

You can also take out what's known as a personal loan from a bank or another financial institution. *Personal loans* are unsecured loans from a lender that you pay back in monthly payments or installments. Weddings, trips, and holidays are some reasons we see people take out personal loans.

Loans from friends or family

Sometimes loans don't come from a bank but from a friend or family member. These loans typically have no interest rate or payment schedule because the lender provides the money in good faith that you'll eventually pay them back.

Paying Off Your Debt

Your debt may seem overwhelming, and you may wonder what the purpose of creating a budget is when you have so many other bills to pay. But a budget is a money plan that tells your money where to go, not the other way around. If paying off debt is going to be a part of your budget, pull up a seat. In the following sections, we discuss how to pay off your debt so you can eventually start putting your money toward your other financial goals.

REMEMBER

There's no right way to pay off your debt. Just like everything else about you, your debt is unique. You have different financial responsibilities than others do and vice versa. Your debt repayment plan will be different if you have kids or take care of an older family member. It will also look different based on your income and current expenses. That's why mapping out where your money goes, as we explain in Chapter 1 of Book 1, is so important. After you ace that step, you can strategize toward making your debt repayment plan.

Compiling a list of your debt

The first step to tackling debt repayment is to compile a debt assessment by making a list of the different types of debt you currently have. You need to see all this information in front of you so you aren't forgetting anyone you owe money to. You can include an amount as small as owing your spouse $5 for a coffee or as large as your mortgage. For each debt, be sure to log into your account online to make a note of the following details:

- **The company the debt is owed to, the amount owed, and the due date for payment:** If you haven't made payment arrangements, make a note of that, too.
- **Type of debt:** Is this debt your mortgage, car loan, or an unpaid bill? Look over the list in the earlier section "Looking at the Different Types of Debt" if you're unsure how to categorize it. You can also leave a reminder to ask someone or even call the company to which you owe the debt.
- **Secured or unsecured debt:** Both can be harmful to your credit report if you don't pay, but this information is important because secured debt usually means that you have some type of collateral the lender can confiscate if you don't pay the debt on time. The collateral can be vital to your and your family's survival if it's an auto or home loan. Unsecured debt has no collateral at stake.
- **Revolving loan or installment loan:** With an installment loan, you already have a payment arrangement in place. After you pay off revolving debt, you can always borrow more.
- **Any pressing circumstances related to the debt:** A pressing circumstance may be a garnished paycheck or the threat of a suspended driver's license. We'd even go so far as to say that any tension between you and a friend or family member over a loan is a pressing issue.

Next, you should reorganize the information in either a spreadsheet or in a notebook. First, list the name of the creditor, the type of debt, the payment amount, the due date, the interest rate or APR (annual percentage rate), and the total amount still owed. If an account has a payoff amount listed anywhere, you can add it as a note. Figures 1-1 and 1-2 are two formatting examples of a debt assessment.

	A	B	C	D	E	F
1	**Creditor**	**Type of Debt**	**Payment Amount**	**Due Date**	**APR**	**Amount Still Owed**
2	Bank of America	Mortgage	$1,978.55	1st of every month	4.50%	$345,231
3	Credit Union	Personal Loan	$150	5th of every month	3%	$2,450
4	Credit Union	Auto Loan	$497	10th of every month	3%	$16,679
5	SoFi	Student Loan	$358	15th of every month	7%	$28,766
6	Capital One	Credit Cards	$179	20th of every month	19%	$2,023
7	American Express	Credit Cards	$67.44	25th of every month	15%	$786
8	Mastercard	Credit Cards	$97	30th of every month	18%	$877
9	Dr. Smith	Medical Bill	$50	30th of every month	0%	$350

FIGURE 1-1: A debt assessment spreadsheet.

Debt Total, January

Creditor (Debt Type)	Payment Amount / Due Date / APR	Amount Still Owed
BOA (Mortgage)	$1,978.55 / 1st every month / 4.50%	$345,231
Credit Union (Personal)	$150 / 5th every month / 3%	$2,450
Credit Union (Car)	$497 / 10th every month / 3%	$16,679
SoFi (Student)	$358 / 15th every month / 7%	$28,766
Capital One (CC)	$179 / 20th every month / 19%	$2,023
Amex (CC)	$67.44 / 25th every month / 15%	$786
Mastercard (CC)	$97 / 30th every month / 18%	$877
Dr. Smith (Medical)	$50 / 30th every month / 0%	$350

FIGURE 1-2: A debt assessment compiled on a notebook page.

Considering different payoff methods

What does a debt payoff plan even look like? Well, you can keep doing what you're doing now and pay your monthly payments. Or you can try one of these three main debt payoff methods:

- The snowball method
- The avalanche method
- The fireball method

REMEMBER

If making the minimum payments is where you are right now in your money journey, that's okay. You'll eventually work your way to where your financial goals enable you to pay off more of your debt. For example, you may pay your monthly car payment without trying to pay it off because you have other priorities. You're not a bad person for not wanting to pay off your debt faster than you have to.

The snowball method

The *snowball method* works like this: You pay your regular debt payments, and then anything extra you can come up with to pay on your debt goes toward the smallest one first. You then continue this process until your smallest debt is paid off. The goal of the snowball method is to keep you consistent with your debt repayment by motivating you with small wins. When you continually succeed in any area of your life, it's easier to stay on track consistently. Consistency is what's going to enable you to achieve your goals.

Using your debt assessment from the previous section, arrange your debts from smallest amount owed to largest amount owed. It may look like Figure 1-3 or Figure 1-4.

	A	B	C	D	E	F
1	**Creditor**	**Type of Debt**	**Payment Amount**	**Due Date**	**APR**	**Amount Still Owed**
2	Dr. Smith	Medical Bill	$50	30th of every month	0%	$350
3	American Express	Credit Cards	$67.44	25th of every month	15%	$786
4	Mastercard	Credit Cards	$97	30th of every month	18%	$877
5	Credit Union	Personal Loan	$150	5th of every month	3%	$2,450
6	Capital One	Credit Cards	$179	20th of every month	19%	$2,023
7	SoFi	Student Loan	$358	15th of every month	7%	$28,766
8	Credit Union	Auto Loan	$497	10th of every month	3%	$16,679
9	Bank of America	Mortgage	$1,978.55	1st of every month	4.50%	$345,231

FIGURE 1-3: A debt spreadsheet organized by the amounts still owed.

Debt Total, January

Creditor (Debt Type)	Payment Amount / Due Date / APR	Amount Still Owed
Dr. Smith (Medical)	$50 / 30th every month / 0%	$350
Amex (CC)	$67.44 / 25th every month / 15%	$786
Mastercard (CC)	$97 / 30th every month / 18%	$877
Credit Union (Personal)	$150 / 5th every month / 3%	$2,450
Capital One (CC)	$179 / 20th every month / 19%	$2,023
SoFi (Student)	$358 / 15th every month / 7%	$28,766
Credit Union (Car)	$497 / 10th every month / 3%	$16,679
BOA (Mortgage)	$1,978.55 / 1st every month / 4.50%	$345,231

FIGURE 1-4: Debt compiled on a notebook page, organized by the amount still owed.

For example, say your first smallest debt is a bill you owe the dentist. It's $350, and you're currently paying $50 a month. Your next smallest bill is a credit card for $786, and you're paying $50 on this one as well.

You're able to cut some expenses in your budget, which frees up $100 per month (good job!), and you decide to put this money toward debt. Throw the extra $100 on top of the regular $50 payment and pay the dentist bill in full within two months.

Now you have an extra $150 a month in your budget to use toward debt repayment (the $100 you freed up in expenses, plus the $50 you were putting toward that dentist's bill). You can apply this $150 toward your next smallest debt, your credit card. When your next payment is due, you pay $200 rather than the regular payment of $50. You snowballed your old debt payment amount toward another debt payment amount. This approach is going to enable you to pay off this debt faster, too.

WARNING

The one con with this debt repayment strategy is that you pay more interest over time. Paying more in interest and other fees means you're paying more money in the long run than you would with something like the avalanche method, which is discussed in the following section. But if using the snowball method means you're motivated to actually stick to your debt repayment strategy, that trade-off may be okay for you.

The avalanche method

If you'd rather save money and possibly get out of debt faster, then the avalanche method may be a better fit for you than the other methods in this chapter. The *avalanche method* requires you to focus on paying down your debt by homing in on your interest rather than the amount owed. The longer you take to pay a creditor back, the more interest your loan accrues. Depending on the type of debt you have, the interest can fluctuate and collect on different amounts of money at different times.

Using your debt assessment from earlier in this chapter, organize your creditors from the highest to lowest interest. Figures 1-5 and 1-6 show two formatting examples that use the avalanche method.

Look at the creditors with the highest interest rates, which looks like this:

1. Credit card 1 at 19 percent with a $179 monthly payment
2. Credit card 2 at 18 percent with a $97 monthly payment
3. Credit card 3 at 15 percent with a monthly payment of $67.44

	A	B	C	D	E	F
1	**Creditor**	**Type of Debt**	**Payment Amount**	**Due Date**	**APR**	**Amount Still Owed**
2	Capital One	Credit Cards	$179	20th of every month	19%	$2,023
3	Mastercard	Credit Cards	$97	30th of every month	18%	$877
4	American Express	Credit Cards	$67.44	25th of every month	15%	$786
5	SoFi	Student Loan	$358	15th of every month	7%	$28,766
6	Bank of America	Mortgage	$1,978.55	1st of every month	4.50%	$345,231
7	Credit Union	Personal Loan	$150	5th of every month	3%	$2,450
8	Credit Union	Auto Loan	$497	10th of every month	3%	$16,679
9	Dr. Smith	Medical Bill	$50	30th of every month	0%	$350

FIGURE 1-5: A debt spreadsheet organized by APR.

Debt Total, January

Creditor (Debt Type)	Payment Amount / Due Date / APR	Amount Still Owed
Capital One (CC)	$179 / 20th every month / 19%	$2,023
Mastercard (CC)	$97 / 30th every month / 18%	$877
Amex (CC)	$67.44 / 25th every month / 15%	$786
SoFi (Student)	$358 / 15th every month / 7%	$28,766
BOA (Mortgage)	$1,978.55 / 1st every month / 4.50%	$345,231
Credit Union (Personal)	$150 / 5th every month / 3%	$2,450
Credit Union (Car)	$497 / 10th every month / 3%	$16,679
Dr. Smith (Medical)	$50 / 30th every month / 0%	$350

FIGURE 1-6: Debt organized by APR on a notebook page.

You cleared up an extra $100 in your budget for debt repayment. Because you're paying the most interest on your credit card, you focus on that bill first. Rather than paying $179 on credit card 1, you're now paying $279. After you pay off that credit card, you then move onto the next credit card. You take that $279 and apply it to the monthly credit card payment until that debt is gone. You repeat the process with the remaining credit card until the balance is paid off. Then you continue onto lower interest debts such as your student loan and so on until you've paid everything off.

If you don't have a problem with consistency, this payoff method may work for you. You're paying off your debt at a much faster rate than before while also paying less money overall. Depending on the type and amount of loan, you don't always have small wins along the way, so this debt payoff method requires you to be patient. But saving money is always a win because you can then apply that cash to your budget somewhere else.

The fireball method

Though debt is still debt at the end of the day, the fireball method, coined by SoFi, enables you to categorize your debt to pay it off on a timeline that works for you. This method plays off the snowball method covered earlier in this chapter.

First, refer to your debt assessment from earlier in the chapter and categorize your debt as either good or bad. (Check out the earlier section "Looking at the Different Types of Debt" for more on this distinction.)

Figures 1-7 and 1-8 show the two formatting examples to categorize good and bad debt.

	A	B	C	D	E	F
1	**Good Debt**					
2	**Creditor**	**Type of Debt**	**Payment Amount**	**Due Date**	**APR**	**Amount Still Owed**
3	SoFi	Student Loan	$358	15th of every month	7%	$28,766
4	Credit Union	Auto Loan	$497	10th of every month	3%	$16,679
5	Bank of America	Mortgage	$1,978.55	1st of every month	4.50%	$345,231
6						
7	**Bad Debt**					
8	**Creditor**	**Type of Debt**	**Payment Amount**	**Due Date**	**APR**	**Amount Still Owed**
9	Capital One	Credit Cards	$179	20th of every month	19%	$2,023
10	Mastercard	Credit Cards	$97	30th of every month	18%	$877
11	American Express	Credit Cards	$67.44	25th of every month	15%	$786
12	Credit Union	Personal Loan	$150	5th of every month	3%	$2,450
13	Dr. Smith	Medical Bill	$50	30th of every month	0%	$350

FIGURE 1-7: A spreadsheet separating good and bad debt.

Then arrange each list of debt from smallest amount owed to the largest amount owed. Figures 1-9 and 1-10 show two formatting examples that use the fireball method.

Debt Total, January — Good

Creditor (Debt Type)	Payment Amount / Due Date / APR	Amount Still Owed
Credit Union (Car)	$497 / 10th every month / 3%	$16,679
SoFi (Student)	$358 / 15th every month / 7%	$28,766
BOA (Mortgage)	$1,978.55 / 1st every month / 4.50%	$345,231

Debt Total, January — Bad

Creditor (Debt Type)	Payment Amount / Due Date / APR	Amount Still Owed
Dr. Smith (Medical)	$50 / 30th every month / 0%	$350
Credit Union (Personal)	$150 / 5th every month / 3%	$2,450
Capital One (CC)	$179 / 20th every month / 19%	$2,023
Mastercard (CC)	$97 / 30th every month / 18%	$877
Amex (CC)	$67.44 / 25th every month / 15%	$786

FIGURE 1-8: A written list separating good and bad debt.

	A	B	C	D	E	F
1	**Good Debt**					
2	**Creditor**	**Type of Debt**	**Payment Amount**	**Due Date**	**APR**	**Amount Still Owed**
3	Credit Union	Auto Loan	$497	10th of every month	3%	$16,679
4	SoFi	Student Loan	$358	15th of every month	7%	$28,766
5	Bank of America	Mortgage	$1,978.55	1st of every month	4.50%	$345,231
6						
7	**Bad Debt**					
8	**Creditor**	**Type of Debt**	**Payment Amount**	**Due Date**	**APR**	**Amount Still Owed**
9	Dr. Smith	Medical Bill	$50	30th of every month	0%	$350
10	American Express	Credit Cards	$67.44	25th of every month	15%	$786
11	Mastercard	Credit Cards	$97	30th of every month	18%	$877
12	Capital One	Credit Cards	$179	20th of every month	19%	$2,023
13	Credit Union	Personal Loan	$150	5th of every month	3%	$2,450

FIGURE 1-9: A spreadsheet arranging bad and good debt by amount owed.

Debt Total, January — Good		
Creditor (Debt Type)	Payment Amount / Due Date / APR	Amount Still Owed
Credit Union (Car)	$497 / 10th every month / 3%	$16,679
SoFi (Student)	$358 / 15th every month / 7%	$28,766
BOA (Mortgage)	$1,978.55 / 1st every month / 4.50%	$345,231

Debt Total, January — Bad		
Creditor (Debt Type)	Payment Amount / Due Date / APR	Amount Still Owed
Dr. Smith (Medical)	$50 / 30th every month / 0%	$350
Amex (CC)	$67.44 / 25th every month / 15%	$786
Credit Union (Personal)	$150 / 5th every month / 3%	$2,450
Mastercard (CC)	$97 / 30th every month / 18%	$877
Capital One (CC)	$179 / 20th every month / 19%	$2,023

FIGURE 1-10: A written list arranging bad and good debt by amount owed.

Now focus on your bad debt, paying off your smallest loan first. Like the snowball method, you'll still be making your minimum payments, but any extra money goes toward eliminating your smallest debt first. After you pay it off, you apply that payment amount to your next highest debt. Unlike the snowball method, you're focused on only your bad debt for now.

After you take care of the bad debt, you then turn to your good debt. But instead of throwing all the money you were applying toward your bad debt to the good debt, you put it toward your savings goals, such as paying for a down payment on a house. Essentially, you're starting a new snowball for your good debt. Because you're still paying off your good debt, this method encourages you to work on your other goals simultaneously. Most people take advantage of this time to work on catching up on retirement. Wherever you put the money, this method can help you determine what debt you should take care of first while motivating you with small wins.

REMEMBER

The only issue with this method is the significance of designating something as good or bad. People often associate the word *bad* with shame, and personal finance shouldn't be shameful. You don't always choose to take out bad debt; sometimes things happen, such as medical emergencies, car repairs, and sick pets.

Applying additional strategies

You can implement a variety of other strategies to help pay your debt off even faster.

Make a debt payoff settlement

When you fall behind while paying your debt, you become delinquent. Your creditor may work with you to get back on track, but if it sees no progress, it eventually gives up and, in the case of unsecured debt, sells your debt to a collection agency.

Debt sold to collection agencies shows up on your credit report, so you want to avoid this scenario as much as possible. But if you're stuck with a collections bill, call the agency and see whether you can settle for less than the amount you owe. Collection agencies don't really have people banging down their doors to pay their debt, so they're more likely to work with you and accept an amount less than you owe.

A collection agency will most likely accept half of what you owe. Say you have a creditor $500 debt in collections. When you have $250 to part with, call the agency and ask to speak to someone about a settlement offer. First, kindly thank them for taking your call and for being patient with you while you get your financial affairs in order. Next, acknowledge the fact that you do owe them money and ask whether they'd be willing to settle your account today if you could make a cash payment.

If they say yes, great! Ask them for an amount they're willing to accept and then go from there. You always ask what they can do first because they may come back with a lower amount than you had originally thought to offer. After you agree on a payoff amount, ask to receive it in writing via email so you can pay while still on the phone.

REMEMBER

After you've received confirmation in writing, go ahead and make your payment. Make sure to ask for a receipt via email and also by mail. Keeping detailed records of payment is important; selling someone's debt from collection agency to collection agency is a common practice, and you don't want to have to pay for the same debt mistake twice.

Negotiate with creditors

You don't have to wait for your debt to end up being turned over to collections to negotiate with your creditors. If you have a bill such as medical debt, call the medical provider to see what it can do. A lot of doctor's offices enable you to settle your bill for an agreed-upon portion because getting a small guaranteed payment is better than never receiving any payment.

Some medical providers, like hospitals, have financial relief departments. The financial relief department assigns a case worker to look over your medical bills along with your finances to see whether you qualify for assistance. Depending on the amount, they may agree to put you on a payment plan or waive the debt entirely.

TIP

To find a nonprofit hospital located closest to you, type "nonprofit hospital (city you're currently located)" into an online search engine. You can then filter results to find one that meets your needs.

When you have medical emergencies, try to seek medical care at a nonprofit hospital. By law, nonprofit hospitals must offer financial assistance programs. You can also call your local community resource center to see whether any other organizations in your area can help with medical assistance.

Ask about hardship programs

If you have credit card debt that you need assistance with, ask your creditor whether it offers any payment assistance. Some credit card companies have hardship programs that can allow you to go on a monthly repayment plan with more affordable payments. They may also lower any fees or interest you currently pay for a few months. Circumstances that can qualify for hardship include but aren't limited to divorce, death of a loved one, loss of job, or health issues.

TIP

Your other creditors may offer financial assistance programs as well. Some creditors offer a pause on payments by extending the length of your loan. Other options can include moving your payment due date into the future to give you some time to catch up.

REMEMBER

Asking for help can hurt your pride. But you know what? It shouldn't. Instead of being sad or ashamed you had to ask for help, be proud. It takes a strong person to know when they need help, and it takes an even stronger person to ask out loud. Needing help is okay, and your finances will be better off, too!

Use balance transfers

Another strategy you can look into is opening a new credit card for a balance transfer. A *balance transfer* is when you move your debt from one creditor to a new creditor for a lower interest rate. Sometimes the interest rate on a balance transfer is as low as 0 percent. The goal of the balance transfer is to save you money in finance fees by offering you a low rate for a predetermined time period. You may also be able to move other types of debt with the balance transfer, such as an auto or personal loan.

To apply for a credit card that offers a balance transfer, you most likely need to have a credit score of 670 or above. Note that your credit score can range from 300 to 850. The higher the credit score you have, the better.

WARNING

Make sure you're aware of the terms and conditions of your new balance transfer credit card. With balance transfers, your 0 percent APR typically only lasts 12 to 18 months. After that, your credit card balance starts collecting interest on the debt you've transferred over. The whole point of a balance transfer is to save money on fees and interest, so take advantage of it as much as possible. Also, make sure you know what if any circumstances, such as making a late payment, may cause you to lose your 0 percent interest rate.

If you're approved, double-check how the debt is transferred over. A creditor may contact the other creditors directly on your behalf to pay your debt off, or it may expect you to take care of it on your own. Make sure to transfer the debt incurring the highest interest rate first so you can take advantage of the lower interest rate as much as you can.

Make extra payments

If, after creating your budget, you find yourself with extra money, consider using it to make extra payments on your debt. One way to approach this strategy is by making a payment that's applied to the loan principal, such as on a mortgage.

When you pay extra on your mortgage, you can ask your loan provider to apply the money to your loan principal. Every time you pay additional money to your loan principal, you're paying less interest. By lowering the amount you owe directly, you lower the amount you pay over time in financing fees. You can even accomplish this goal by splitting up your monthly mortgage payment and applying half every two weeks. By using this tactic, you're making 13 payments a year rather than 12. ***Note:*** Not all creditors allow extra payments to go to the loan principal, so always research the terms of your loan.

TIP

If you're interested in seeing how you can apply this strategy to your situation, check out the extra payments calculator from Freddie Mac. This calculator enables you to input different payment amounts across different scenarios. It shows you that even small additional payments here and there can add up over time. Find the calculator at `myhome.freddiemac.com/resources/calculators/extra-payments`.

Use financial windfalls

Using any *windfalls* (unexpected money) you receive can help you get out of debt faster. Because you already cover your expenses, put that extra money to work.

If you get a bonus or overtime pay, put it on your car loan. Taking advantage of extra money you weren't expecting can help get you ahead further than you think.

TIP

If you feel the urge to use that windfall to treat yourself, consider the 80-20 rule. Apply 80 percent of your windfall toward your debt and then keep the remaining 20 percent for fun. This approach is great because you're taking care of business, but you're still making fun a priority. Prioritizing fun is one way to keep you motivated on your debt journey.

Avoiding Accumulating More Debt

Paying your debt off is important, but so is keeping yourself from getting into more debt. Incurring more debt is easy to do and can happen quickly. However, you can be proactive while keeping your budget intact.

Here are a few tips to keep in mind when you're reviewing your debt and debt repayment:

- **Know your rights.** Before you speak to any debt collector or creditor, be aware of the questions they can and can't ask. Also beware of illegal debt collection practices, such as contacting you by phone after you asked them to stop. Check out the Fair Debt Collection Practices Act for more information: `www.federalreserve.gov/boarddocs/supmanual/cch/fairdebt.pdf`.
- **Check your budget to ensure the amount you can pay toward your debt.** Don't promise an amount you can't pay.
- **Make a list of debts you want to negotiate.** Refer to the earlier section "Considering different payoff methods" for information on compiling a debt assessment.
- **Call your collector.** Use the following phone script for reference:

  "My name is [insert your name], and I am calling to discuss my current account status. I know I'm late, but I am currently facing an unforeseen financial hardship that has affected my finances, including this account. I would like to see what we can do to help bring my account to good standing. Can we discuss what my options are? Is it possible to arrange a payment plan?"

  REMEMBER

  If you are arranging a payment plan, always be sure to get it in writing and do not offer to pay more than you can realistically afford based on your current budget.
- **Make sure you get the settlement agreement in writing.** Before you hand over the case, ensure you've received the debt repayment agreement in

writing, even if that's email, from the debt collector. Also document what time your phone call took place and to whom you spoke.

» **Stick to the repayment plan.** Follow through with your end of the agreement. If you don't, the collector can then decide that you must pay the full amount, and it probably won't be willing to work with you on a settlement again.

Look into refinancing options

If your student, auto, or mortgage loan has a high interest rate, consider refinancing to save money. When you *refinance* a loan, you take out a newer loan with better terms and conditions to pay off an old loan. By refinancing a loan, you can have smaller monthly payments while paying less money overall with a better interest rate. This option is great if you have a good credit score.

TIP

If you don't have a high credit score, look to see what you can do to improve your rating. Make sure you pay your debt on time and work hard to lower your *credit utilization rate* (how much of your available credit you're using).

As you improve your credit score, more financial products become available. Eventually, you'll be able to find a loan with better terms than what you're currently paying.

Save an emergency fund

Emergency funds are crucial to keeping you out of debt. When people don't have the money to cover a financial emergency, they often charge it to a credit card or take out a loan. This scenario can turn into a nasty cycle of endless debt repayment that keeps you from achieving your financial goals. Having an emergency fund enables you to have the money available to keep emergencies from derailing your budget.

You can also avoid some emergencies if you plan ahead in your budget and take time for regular maintenance and screenings. Go to Chapter 4 in Book 1 for a more in-depth discussion about becoming a saver.

Say no to credit card offers

REMEMBER

If you're trying to pay off debt, stay away from store credit cards and other in-house financing options. This type of consumer financing can keep you stuck in the cycle of charging for an item you don't need because you're "saving" money. If saving money is what you're after, look up discount codes on the Internet. You can find a coupon for just about everything out there if you search hard enough.

Another great way to stay away from credit when working on debt repayment is to pay in cash from your bank account. Instead of using your credit card, pay with your debit card, which is deducted from your account. Go through any online retailers you use and update your payment information. This step ensures you're using your budget to pay for your purchases and not relying on credit.

WARNING

Please keep in mind that there is a higher fraud risk when using your debit card. Banks can only offer so much in terms of fraud protection, unlike credit card companies.

Invest in the right insurance

One way to keep yourself out of debt is to have adequate insurance for your health, car, and home. Insurance is an important tool for protecting both you and your finances. Instead of having to take care of a financial emergency all on your own, an insurance policy can help you weather the cost (after you pay a deductible or co-pay). Insurance doesn't have to be expensive, either. Both online and in-person insurance brokers can offer you great deals and rates.

Health insurance is expensive, but going without insurance can cost more. Medical bills are one of the main reasons people declare bankruptcy. If you don't have health insurance and need major surgery, you can be hundreds of thousands of dollars in debt before you even know it. A lack of health insurance can also cost you your quality of life. Without health insurance, you may not have adequate preventive care — care that can help you avoid having serious medical issues in the future — or be able to fill the prescriptions you need.

REMEMBER

You should also consider life insurance, short-term and long-term disability insurance, and long-term care if you're close to or in retirement. And don't forget Fido. If you're a pet owner, you need pet insurance. See Chapters 3 and 4 in Book 2 for details on different types of insurance.

IN THIS CHAPTER

» Puncturing some credit myths

» Establishing credit when you're first starting out

» Avoiding common mistakes of credit newbies

» Identifying credit issues for immigrants and first-time credit users

» Knowing some special credit rules for students and military members

Chapter 2

Starting or Restarting Your Credit in Real Life

Credit isn't an American invention. It's been around in one form or another since ancient Roman times. Modern consumer credit, however, is as American as apple pie. Taking off after the GIs returned from World War II, credit has been among the most prolific of financial services. Life without it is almost unimaginable today, but if you're among those starting over or just getting started, getting the credit you need may be easier said than done. Those starting over because of divorce or the death of someone you've shared a life with can find the process to be a stressful endeavor, while credit newbies such as those new to the United States and high school or college graduates may wonder where to start. You may find yourself feeling like you're looking through a shop window but can't find the door to get in.

This chapter is your point of entry. We help you understand why a good credit history and financial-services relationships are essential to getting the credit you need. Your confidence gets a boost when we show you the size and importance to lenders of the underbanked market (meaning people whose financial needs aren't being met), so you know just where you stand. We also debunk some credit myths that you may have brought with you from another country or may have been taught right here at home by well-meaning but misinformed parents or friends. We include help for young people as well, with sections for students, grads, and military members. Take your seat at the table and help yourself to a big piece of the American dream: credit.

Debunking Misinformation about Banking and Credit

Depending on your culture, what you've seen on social media, or what your friends, family, or other sources may have told you, you may not have an accurate understanding of how credit really works. However, with a few tips, you'll find that using credit can increase your enjoyment of life and all it has to offer.

REMEMBER

The following list debunks some commonly held misconceptions about banking and credit:

- **You need to be rich to be treated well at a bank.** Not so. Adding new customers is a top priority for banks, and the size of your account, no matter how small your deposits may be, doesn't determine your value as a customer. Banks know that many big depositors start out small and increase their deposits over time. If a bank doesn't respect you on your terms, take your money to a competing bank.
- **Using cash is safer than using credit or debit cards.** A lost or stolen card is protected against misuse by another person (most have a liability of $50 or less); lost or stolen cash is gone. Plus, purchasing with cash never builds the credit history you need for a credit score.
- **You can't build a credit history if you have only a consular ID or a green card and not a Social Security number.** Not true. You can establish a credit history and use credit without a Social Security number.
- **Banks aren't safe places to put money because they can fail, causing you to lose all your money.** Not so. All depository institutions (like banks) are insured by the full faith and credit of the U.S. government for up to $250,000 per depositor. No one has ever lost a penny of money that was insured in an FDIC or NCUA federally insured depository account.

- **Bank accounts are unsafe because currency can decrease in value or become worthless overnight.** When you deposit money into a U.S. bank, it's deposited in dollars. The dollar, though subject to fluctuations in value, is the most stable and trusted currency in the world. So it's safe!
- **The government may nationalize your bank and your account.** If the financial crisis taught people anything, it's that the government wants to support, not own, banks.

The following sections explain why you need credit and why it's safe. We hope that this information eases any anxiety you may have.

Why you need credit

What's your definition of the good life? A good job, a safe place to live, a car, some financial security, and a good education for your kids? The reality of life in the U.S. is that having good credit is important in accomplishing goals such as these.

Start with that good job. Chances are that at some point you have to compete with others for a good position. Many employers check your credit history to see whether you're reliable or you have distracting financial issues at home before making an offer. People can lie about their experience (Resume Lab says that about 70 percent of applicants lie on their resumes), and they can pretend to be nice during an interview, but a good credit history is tough to fake. As one employer put it, "When you think about it, people who have good credit keep their promises and are responsible, so it makes sense that if their credit is good, they may be more honest." So, all other things being equal, the job may go to the candidate with the better credit history. It's important to understand that employers don't get your credit scores, just the credit reports (with your permission).

The same thing happens when you try to rent an apartment, buy insurance, or apply for a college loan. In all these circumstances, the person making the decision may check your credit history as part of the qualification process. Being underbanked and relying on cash may knock you out of the race. It pays to understand how to build good credit and use the banking and financial system to your advantage.

Why credit is safe

The credit industry didn't become the huge and powerful entity that it is today without addressing the question of safety. The federal government has put many regulations and safeguards in place over the last several years to ensure the safety and fair treatment of credit users. As a result, you have access to one of the fairest and most market-driven credit systems in the world. The following laws play a major role in protecting borrowers in the U.S.:

- **The Fair Credit Reporting Act (FCRA)** gives you lots of rights when it comes to how your credit is reported and what you can do to correct mistakes. It also gives you rights and remedies in the event of identity theft.
- **The Fair Debt Collection Practices Act (FDCPA)** spells out what third-party bill collectors can and can't do when they try to collect a debt. If they step over the line, you can sue them.
- **The Equal Credit Opportunity Act (ECOA)** prohibits credit discrimination on the basis of race, color, religion, national origin, sex, marital status, age, and whether you get public assistance. Creditors may collect this information, but they can't use it to decide whether to give you credit or how to set your credit terms.
- **The Credit Card Accountability, Responsibility, and Disclosure Act (CARD Act)** protects you from unfair credit card billing practices. Major protections spell out notification requirements, grace periods, fees, interest rate changes, restrictions on student cards, and more.
- **The Dodd-Frank Wall Street Reform and Consumer Protection Act** established an independent consumer financial protection bureau within the Federal Reserve to protect borrowers against abuses in mortgage services, credit card services, payday lending, and credit counseling.
- **The Truth in Lending laws** ensure that you won't find any hidden surprises when you borrow money. All the costs of borrowing must be spelled out for you before you sign a contract.

RECOGNIZING WHAT'S NOT IN YOUR CREDIT HISTORY

With all the information available to companies, the government, and others, you may think that your credit report houses a huge dossier about your every movement. To clarify: A credit history is nothing more than a snapshot of your financial life to date.

Keeping track of the information that can make or break your chances of getting credit may seem mind-boggling. The good news is that most of the information sent to the credit bureaus is by people with whom you choose to do business.

Recently consumers have been allowed to have positive information added to their reports with products like Experian Boost (`www.experian.com/consumer-products/score-boost.html`). And even then, not all your information is reported. Some companies and service providers, such as doctors, hospitals, and grocery stores, don't report credit activity at all.

You have the right to dispute out-of-date or inaccurate information in your credit report. These provisions are detailed in the FCRA, which is spelled out at `www.congress.gov/108/plaws/publ159/PLAW-108publ159.pdf`.

Obtaining Credit: Starting Out on the Right Foot

You're ready to begin building your own credit, but you're not quite sure where to start. They say that a journey begins with a single step, which just goes to show how wrong people can be. The journey actually begins when you have a destination in mind. Then, after packing your lunch and other essentials, you take that first step. You build up a credit history over a period of time. How much time depends on how active you are and which scoring model is used to rate your credit file.

Don't fret, though. This section walks you through the steps to help you begin your credit journey down the right path.

WHY BANKS WANT TO DO BUSINESS WITH YOU

Why do banks do anything? To make money, of course. With hundreds of millions of dollars in profits at stake from tens of millions of unbanked and underbanked people like you, some of the biggest and best names in the financial-services industry would love to have you as a long-term customer. Why do they like long-term customers? You guessed it: They're more profitable. Why do they like you? Because the Federal Deposit Insurance Corporation (FDIC) estimates there are about 25 million households who either don't use banks at all or use banking services and products on a very limited basis. Selling something new to someone you know is much easier than selling

(continued)

(continued)

to a stranger. So banks really do want to get to know you and get your business, although at times you may not know it from the way they act.

Now that you know you're a valued and valuable customer in a large market segment that banks want to do business with, you should expect to be treated well, respected, and, yes, maybe even spoiled just a little. Anything less and you can just move on to the next player, who may know better how to treat a valuable customer like you.

Establishing a credit file without a Social Security number

You don't need a Social Security number to start building your credit report. In fact, a frequent misconception is that to establish a credit history, and thereby a credit score, you need a Social Security number, a driver's license, or a voter registration card. None of these items is required to establish a successful and envious credit record.

REMEMBER

When a credit bureau receives new account data, the bureau matches the data with the following items:

1. Your name
2. Your birthdate
3. Your address
4. Your Social Security number

No number? No problem. The bureaus can use plenty of other matching points to get your information into the right file. But being consistent is important! For example, make sure to spell your name exactly the same way every time you apply for or use credit.

Setting goals before you set out

Figuring out what your goals are prior to seeking credit is an important step, especially for the underbanked and those new to credit. Writing down your goals enables you to see what you need to do financially to achieve success.

To begin setting goals, you (and your partner, if you have one) should follow these steps:

1. **Set aside some uninterrupted time to dream about the future you want.**

   TIP

   Allow at least an hour, and set an end point so that you finish before you are exhausted. You can always come back to this step later after some reflection.

2. **Write down some short-term (one year or less), intermediate-term (one to five years), and long-term (more than five years) goals.**

   Typical goals include beginning to save this year, beginning to save next year, getting out of debt in a year, and rebuilding bad credit. Other goals may be to get some financial education on topics such as investing, children's college savings accounts, and retirement accounts.

   TIP

   Writing down your goals serves two purposes: It clarifies what you're talking about, and it makes your goals seem more real.

3. **Make a list of the actions you need to take to reach each goal.**

   For example, if you want to get a better apartment and a new job, how do you do so? Good credit can help. A smart first step is to get a free copy of your credit report at `www.annualcreditreport.com` and make sure that it's accurate. Dispute and remove any inaccuracies or out-of-date items to improve your credit. Consider adding utility payment histories and banking information using programs such as Experian Boost (`www.experian.com/consumer-products/score-boost.html`) or asking for a score using UltraFICO (`www.fico.com/ultrafico`), which enhances your score by considering checking, savings and money market savings data. Then make sure to make your payments on all your accounts on time. It's simple, but it works. Chapters 1 and 2 in Book 1 have more suggestions about budgeting and goal setting.

4. **Track your progress.**

   Reviewing your progress toward your goals periodically is not only an incentive to keep up the good work but also an opportunity to celebrate your interim successes.

Starting a relationship with a financial institution

The saying "That's as good as money in the bank" means that it's as good as it gets. Having money in the bank is a good thing; it is the situation you want to be in. If you don't have a relationship with a bank or credit union, we can't stress enough how important this relationship is to your ultimate success. You want to develop a relationship with a bank by setting up at least a savings or checking account, not just so you have a place to take out a loan or get a titanium credit card to impress your friends, but because you need a place to put the money you earn but don't spend right away. Saving is essential to your success.

WARNING

Spending everything you make or using credit to supplement your income is a recipe for disaster. There's no substitute for savings when life throws you a curve-ball. Without savings, even life's little bumps are enough to hold you back on your journey to financial success. Chapter 4 in Book 1 has tips for becoming a saver.

Why you need to save

Everything is going okay. The money that comes in goes out, and your debt is under control. You may be a little short at the moment and your credit card balances may be building, but you figure that will end as soon as you get that promotion in six months. Then your car muffler falls off and costs $500 to repair, your tooth breaks at lunch and you need $1,200 for a crown, and your roommates tell you that they're moving out and you have to pay the rent on your own. Where does the money come from if you have no savings?

You can use credit if you have any left. But if you do, you may be paying a high interest rate and getting closer to your card limit, your credit score may be dropping, and your minimum payment may now be huge.

Without access to credit or savings, you have fewer choices. You may have to carpool, have the tooth removed rather than crowned, and be forced to move to less-expensive housing. That's why you need savings; credit and good luck alone are never enough for you to be financially successful.

How to get started saving

Fortunately, starting to save is easy and painless as soon as you get going. The key is not to focus on how you're going to save six months' worth of living expenses, which could test even a saint. What you can do is start with a small savings program but make it automatic.

To get started saving, take the following steps:

1. **Go to a nearby bank or credit union and ask about automatic deposit savings and checking accounts.**

   You probably don't have much to put away, at least right now, but that's okay. Limited funds are no excuse for not saving. Tell the bank that you don't want to pay any fees because you'll be using automatic deposit. If the bank charges a fee, go to another bank or credit union. Banks and credit unions usually waive all fees for people who save regularly through payroll deductions.

2. **After you open two accounts, one checking and one savings, go to your human resources or payroll department at work and say that you want your pay automatically deposited into these two accounts.**

For example, you want all your take-home pay minus $5 (or more if you can) put into checking and the remaining $5 (or more) put into your savings account. At the end of the first pay period, you will have saved $5. Not a huge sum, but you're starting a habit that will grow and add up with time.

TIP

If direct deposit isn't available through your employer, you can have your bank automatically transfer money monthly from your checking account to your savings account as soon as your paycheck is deposited.

3. **When you get that next raise, bonus, or promotion, have half the increase automatically deposited into your savings account.**

   Now you're making a smart financial move — increasing your savings by putting away the extra money from your raise before you have an opportunity to spend it! Do the same thing for tax refunds and other windfalls. In no time you'll have a cushion that can get you over life's bumps without stretching your credit or damaging your credit history!

REMEMBER

To secure your financial future, stop cashing paychecks and start automatic savings. You owe it to yourself, your family, and your future.

Using prepaid and reloadable cards

While you are building your credit, you may want to consider using prepaid and reloadable cards as alternatives to using cash. They're neither credit cards nor debit cards; rather, they exist somewhere in between. You deposit money onto the cards at locations throughout the nation and then use them as you would a credit or debit card. But they don't build your credit history or score.

REMEMBER

The following list outlines the major advantages of prepaid and reloadable cards:

- You can use money without getting mugged for the cash in your pocket.
- You need no credit record or credit check — just your name, address, and phone number and the ability to pay a one-time fulfillment fee. Non-U.S. citizens can provide an alternative form of ID, such as a driver's license, passport, or alien registration. Funds may post to your account within 30 minutes.
- Prepaid cards offer convenience, easy availability, guaranteed approval, and other features that can make them ideal substitutes for credit cards.
- You can use prepaid cards online, over the phone, and in many other places, just like a credit card or debit card.
- Prepaid cards can help with financial discipline and the building of good financial habits.

Fattening up your credit file

If your credit file is underweight, you're not alone. Today, 49 million U.S. adults — nearly 20 percent of credit-eligible consumers — come back from credit inquiries to the major bureaus either as no-hits or as *thin files* (files with too little data in them to receive a credit score).

If you fit this category, don't worry. You can take action to build your credit muscle. The following options work well for credit newbies and underbanked individuals.

Taking out a passbook loan

A *passbook loan* is a loan that the bank makes using your own money as security. It may sound strange, but if you open a passbook savings account at a bank or credit union and use it as security for the loan, the bank still charges you interest (low interest, thank heavens) and reports the loan repayment to the bureaus. Faster than you can say "Super Prime," you're adding positive history to your file and improving your score.

TIP

Check with your bank or credit union to make sure that it reports the loan to at least one, and preferably all three, of the major credit-reporting bureaus. If it doesn't, request that it do so. If the bank is unwilling to report the loan to at least one of the bureaus, take your business elsewhere.

Continuing to use your foreign credit card if you have one

You may be surprised to find out that foreign credit history may not carry over and can't be imported into your U.S. credit file. However, you can still use your impeccable overseas credit experience to your advantage. You can either continue to use your foreign credit card or get a letter from a multinational bank extolling your virtues so that the local underwriters will approve you for an American credit card that is reported to the American credit bureaus.

TECHNICAL STUFF

Global scoring is expected in the future; in fact, FICO claims a proven global score that's accurate in many countries except France *(quelle surprise!)*. However, while the global score is being used in many countries, it isn't used in the U.S. yet.

Getting a secured credit card

A secured card is a cross between a credit card and a prepaid card. After you establish a savings account and build up the balance, you can ask the bank to give you a credit card backed by your deposit in the bank. You may qualify for a credit line in excess of the amount you have in savings.

TIP

Many credit issuers eventually move you to a traditional credit card after a period of successful payment. The best part is that, unlike most prepaid cards, most secured cards are reported to at least one of if not all of three major credit bureaus and can help you build a history and a credit score. Shop around for the best terms; many secured credit cards have high interest rates and fees.

Here's how to get and use a secured card:

1. **Contact your bank or credit union to find out whether it offers secured credit cards, or look online for an issuing bank.**

   WARNING

   Watch out for annual processing or maintenance fees. You can get secured credit cards for free — you just have to look around for banks or credit unions that offer them.

2. **Deposit the funds to be used as security for the card.**

   Be sure that the account is FDIC or NCUA insured.

3. **Use the card for purchases, making sure that you can pay the balance each month.**

   You don't need to use the card a lot. Just make a few purchases each month.

4. **Make on-time payments every month.**

5. **Ask that an alternative score (such as FICO Score XD) be used to score your application for credit.**

   FICO Score XD is a one-time snapshot that obtains positive and negative landline, cell phone and cable data from the National Consumer Telecom and Utilities Exchange (NCTUE), and public record and property data from LexisNexis Risk Solutions to generate a score for those who may have a thin file (very little data) or only stale information in their credit reports.

REMEMBER

Getting a credit score takes a few months or more of credit use. The two major credit score providers, FICO and VantageScore, require different amounts of payment history to generate a score. Also, you need more than a score to, well, score a card! Lenders are hyper-nervous about potential losses. New accounts are an unknown, so the lender will look at your credit report and income information in detail to decide whether it should grant you credit.

Avoiding high interest, fees, and scams

Unfortunately, being new to something leaves you vulnerable to abuse by people who know the rules better than you do. Abuses perpetuated on credit newbies have been around forever and aren't about to go away. This section lists several that you're likely to run into, along with some guidelines on how to handle them.

Payday loans

When you have a job but you don't have savings or credit but you have an unexpected expense, what do you do? An entire industry has arisen to answer this question. *Payday lenders* charge a very high interest rate or fee for a short-term loan guaranteed by your next paycheck. The fee is based on the amount of your paycheck, and you must supply the lender with a signed check for the date the loan is due.

WARNING

It's not unusual for a person seeking such a loan to need additional money after the lender cashes the postdated check. This can start a vicious cycle of high-fee, high-interest loans rolling over or piling up with no practical way to pay them off. Payday lenders don't report your loan experience to the credit bureaus, so you receive no credit history–building benefit.

If you must use a payday lender, look for one that's a member of INFiN (`https://infinalliance.org`). Members subscribe to a code of conduct and may offer extended repayment terms if you can't pay back a loan as scheduled.

Refund anticipation loans (RALs)

Refund anticipation loans (RALs) are high-fee loans secured by your tax refund that may, and the operative word here is *may*, get you your refund a week or so earlier than having it direct-deposited after filing your return electronically. The real downside of these loans is that the person who sells you the loan has an incentive to inflate your tax refund to get you to take out a higher loan.

If your actual refund is less than what you borrow, you owe the difference plus a hefty interest rate. A much better idea is to open a bank account and have any refund direct-deposited. You get it fast, free, and with no surprises.

Check-cashing for a high fee

Going to a check-cashing place instead of a bank or credit union is like shopping at the most expensive store in town in the worst possible neighborhood. Check cashers are often located in places that are rife with crime. Why? Because everyone coming out has a pocket full of cash.

A bank or credit union with which you have an account won't charge you to cash your check, and you don't have to take all the cash with you when you leave — you can deposit it in your savings and checking accounts.

Instant credit rating

WARNING

Credit repair companies may offer you a new identity or a repaired credit rating for only a few hundred dollars. Don't spend the money. The new identity is often illegal, and instant credit repair doesn't exist.

Foreign bank accounts

WARNING

Occasionally, you may receive a letter or email saying that you've been chosen (lucky you!) to help a rich foreign person get some money into the U.S. and that you'll receive a fat percentage of the amount for your small trouble because you're trustworthy. Most of these communications come from Nigeria, but they can originate anywhere. Don't do it!

Overcoming Credit Fears and Mistakes

Everyone makes mistakes, even lenders and credit bureaus. A mistake needn't be a big deal if you deal with it quickly.

As a person new to credit and maybe even new to the United States, you may be a tad scared of having to deal with credit and the problems that can come along with it. Bill collectors aren't above using threats of deportation or imprisonment if they think that doing so will help them collect a bill. The truth is, they can't legally do either. You won't be deported and you won't go to jail, no matter what they say. These companies only get paid for collecting the money due their employers. If they actually deported you or put you in jail, they wouldn't get their money!

If you're a credit newbie or have had a problem with your credit (including checking overdrafts), keep these basic tips in mind for dealing with mistakes:

- **Don't delay.** Credit and debt problems don't improve with age. If you're proactive and make an effort to resolve a problem before you receive a call, you'll get a much better reception and improve your chances of a favorable resolution.
- **Review your statements when and however you get them and challenge anything you don't understand or remember.** You can correct errors, but often there are time limits. And what may look like an error may turn out to be evidence of identity theft.

TIP

If you overdraw your checking account, be sure to contact the bank as soon as you find out. The objective is to work out a solution before the bank reports the overdraft to one of the specialty credit bureaus. Having this kind of a negative mark on your report can make it difficult or even impossible to open a checking account for up to several years afterward.

TIP

At `www.dummies.com/go/creditrepairkitfd6e`, you can find a sample letter to send to your creditor when you see an error on a billing statement.

- **Do everything in writing.** You may resolve simple problems over the phone, but to protect your rights in a dispute, you need to document your case in writing or by saving online dispute materials in a file. If you really want a problem fixed, keep good records.
- **Keep track of contacts.** Keeping notes on who promised what to whom not only keeps you from making more mistakes but also tells the other person that you know what you're doing. So when the manager says that this is the first time you called, you can say, "You are mistaken; I called on these occasions, and I spoke to these people, who told me these things."
- **Keep cool and calm.** Nothing can derail your effort to resolve an error faster than raising your voice. After you escalate the volume, you'll be directed to someone who does "loud" professionally, or you'll be politely ignored. Either way, you lose. Call back if you need to, but don't lose control.
- **Safeguard your identity.** Identity theft is a serious and growing crime that can take years to unravel and cost thousands of dollars to fix. Guard your personal identification, mail, computer passwords, and bank account information. Shred financial mail. If you invite people into your home, be sure to put away your financial statements and checkbook. You wouldn't leave $20 bills all over the floor and furniture. The same applies to financial information.

Qualifying for First-Time Cards and Lending

This section looks at how credit impacts two major and basic consumer credit instruments that most people need when they get started on life's journey: credit cards and loans. You may think that you know how these instruments work, but methods have changed because of the COVID-19 pandemic, regulations such as the CARD Act, and the 2008 financial meltdown that threatened banks with failure due in large part to lax underwriting standards.

Getting a credit card

Getting credit for the first time used to be easy. All you had to do was drive to your nearest gas station and fill out an application for a gas card and then wait for the mail to arrive with your new plastic. If you were a city dweller who didn't drive, the trip may have been on foot to a department store, which would often grant credit on the spot. Both types of credit were relatively easy to get, and they reported your credit history to the three bureaus so that you built a credit history quickly. More and more department store and gas cards are tightening their standards to reflect credit conditions. You can try for cards issued by banks that use a national transaction network such as Visa. Though these cards are more versatile and powerful than their earlier counterparts, they're also harder to get. Getting that first card now requires a new approach.

To begin with, you need a credit history. But how do you get a credit history without credit? Three of the most popular ways are to use someone else's credit, supply your own data, or use a secured credit card.

Using other people's credit

In most instances, when you use another person's credit, the other person is a family member or a person with whom you have an emotional attachment. Why? Because using someone else's credit can be dangerous to that person if you mess up. Only someone who really likes you is willing to risk helping you get started.

You can piggyback on another person's credit in two ways. The most popular way is to be added to the person's account as an authorized user. The other way is to have the person cosign for you.

- **Becoming an authorized user:** Being named an *authorized user* on someone's credit account enables you to have their specific account history reported on your credit report while you use a card for which the other person is solely financially responsible. The card statement goes to the account owner, they pay the credit card company, you pay the card owner, and the card's credit history is reported in both your and the owner's files.

  WARNING

  Problems with this approach can arise if you overcharge and the account owner has to ask you for more money than you have available, which can cause a rift between you.

- WARNING

  Cosigning: Cosigning on an account is more often than not a recipe for disaster, and we usually don't recommend it. The statement for a cosigned account doesn't go to the cosigner, so unless you share the information, the cosigner has no idea what's happening to the account. Often, the cosigner first hears of a problem when a collector calls and demands an overdue payment. Unfortunately, if you make late payments, the delinquency history appears on the cosigner's credit report, and negative information stays on the cosigner's credit history for a full seven years.

If you decide to go the cosigning route, we suggest that as the borrower, you commit to paying this bill before almost any other. You also need to have the courage to keep your cosigner informed of any changes in your financial picture, especially if you may be late on a payment.

Supplying your own data

In the past, the only way information could get to your credit report was via a creditor. Using products such as Experian Boost (www.experian.com/consumer-products/score-boost.html), you can add your own information drawn from utility payments or banking accounts. Rent payment history can be added by using Boost, Self (www.self.inc) or Boom (www.boompay.app/renters).

Using secured cards

A secured card looks and works just like a credit card but is backed by a cash deposit at the bank that issues the card. Typically, your deposit qualifies you for a credit card with a limit equal to that deposit amount. As a result, limits on secured cards tend to be low, but the real value here is to establish a credit history so that you can get an unsecured card and reallocate your deposit to a better purpose, such as your emergency savings account.

TIP

You can find and compare secured cards on a number of websites. Some options include Bankrate (www.bankrate.com/credit-cards/building-credit/best-secured-cards/) and Nerd Wallet (www.nerdwallet.com/best/credit-cards/secured). You want to balance services, fees, and interest rates to find the best card for you.

Using savings for credit

Most banks and credit unions are happy to, in effect, lend you your own money. If you accumulate some savings in a passbook account, you can use the savings to secure an installment loan of the same or a lesser amount. Needless to say, with 100 percent collateral in cash for the loan, the interest rate should be very low. Make sure that the loan is reported to the credit bureaus so that you build your credit as you pay the money back.

FAIRNESS IN CREDIT

For decades, minorities were disadvantaged in accessing credit fairly. The reality is that, today, most lenders are racially blind when it comes to credit decisions. But stereotypes and prejudices exist on both sides of the lending desk when a person has to apply for a loan in person.

Before applying for a loan, review your credit report for errors or out-of-date data, and know your credit score and what loan terms you're qualified for. That way, you know if you're being fairly treated.

Considering Credit for Students and Military Members

At first blush, students and military members may not seem similar. However, as a credit grouping, they share some commonalities. For example, both have relatively limited means, a high number of younger members, a susceptibility to scams, and laws designed to protect them. And bankruptcy doesn't work as well for students or military members as it does for the general population.

The following sections show you the protections offered under the CARD Act and Dodd-Frank legislation, as well as the impact of the Servicemembers Civil Relief Act. You also find practical advice tuned to the unique needs of students and military members.

Giving credit to students

Most young people entering college or technical school have been brought up using their parents' credit cards. They'd sooner be without their cellphones than do without a credit card. But after they cross that line from authorized son or daughter user to customer, they're exposed to all the pluses and minuses of the credit industry.

Imagine new drivers getting behind the wheel with no driver's education, no insurance, no speed limit, and no police to tell them to slow down. Not a pretty picture, is it? This scenario applies to students and credit, and this section helps you avoid crashing your credit and maybe your immediate future with some insights and suggestions for students and their parents.

Checking out the CARD Act

The Credit Card Accountability, Responsibility, and Disclosure Act of 2009 (CARD Act) aimed to bring about more responsible lending and borrowing and foster more accountability in debt management. The CARD Act set rules to stem the tide of heavily indebted students who often have to drop out of school, work full-time jobs while studying to pay off credit card debts, or enter the job market with damaged credit that can interfere with finding a job. Key provisions include:

- **Proof of income:** Under the law, if you're under the age of 21, you must show proof that you can repay any credit card debt you may incur.
- **Cosign requirement:** If you don't have sufficient income, you need to find someone who does to cosign on the account.
- **Credit limit regulations:** Card companies can no longer offer a preapproved credit limit just because you're a student. Limits have to be based on your independent ability to repay, or you need a cosigner. And if you have a cosigner, the cosigner must approve limit increases in writing.
- **Fewer sign-up incentives:** Card issuers can't turn your head with sign-up rewards such as free T-shirts, pizza, or electronics. The law also prohibits credit card companies from hitting you up on school property. They must remain a specified distance away from campuses. However, they can set up shop at other locations favored by students.
- **Account management assistance:** Your statement must tell you how long it will take to pay off your balance if you make only the minimum payment. It must also allow you at least 21 days to make a payment and your due date has to be the same day of the month, every month.

WARNING

Any law has its loopholes, and the CARD Act is no exception when it comes to protecting students from credit card schemes.

- The CARD Act doesn't allow credit card issuers to market their cards on campus, but they may operate just over the edge of campus.
- Older students have been buying beer for younger students forever, so cosigning for a student under 21 is nothing new.
- Students need to show income to get a card, and some applications may allow student loan proceeds to be counted as income.
- Income verification beyond filling out the application can be spotty for young adults who may not file their own tax returns.

Practicing student credit etiquette

TIP

No, you don't need white gloves or a tie to practice credit etiquette. But if you're new to having your own credit and being responsible for the consequences, here are some basic rules for keeping your credit neat and tidy, regardless of how messy your roommate is:

- **Don't apply for a credit card you don't need.** Every time you apply for a card, it counts against your credit score, whether you're approved or not.
- **It's okay to leave your socks lying around, but not your credit cards or billing statements.** Misuse and identity theft happen to students, too!
- **Lend a shirt, your car, or your cash to a friend, but never lend your credit card.** You're fully responsible for anything your friend does with your card. Anything!
- **Decide what you consider to be an emergency worthy of using your credit card before one happens to you.** If you can wear it, eat it, or drink it, it isn't an emergency!
- **Stick to one low-interest-rate card and charge only what you can afford to pay in full each month.** If you must use more than one card, pay off the card with the highest interest rate first, and make at least the minimum payment on the other(s), on time.
- **Before you charge an item, reflect on whether you can pay it off at the end of the month.** If you know that you would have to carry the balance over, estimate how long you would need to pay it off before swiping. If the answer is more than 90 days, seriously reconsider buying the item!

Following military credit rules

The United States owes a tremendous debt of gratitude to those who volunteer to defend this country and way of life. Not surprisingly, Americans take a dim view of those who take advantage of soldiers and sailors during their term of service. Life is complicated enough in the service without having financial concerns distract you from your mission. This section discusses some of the rules of engagement between the military and the financial-services sector.

Enlisting with credit issues

In addition to meeting rigorous moral character standards, those seeking to join the military undergo a background check that includes a review of their credit history. Uncle Sam doesn't want to give you a loan; he wants to make sure that you don't have existing financial problems, because you're not likely to overcome those difficulties on recently enlisted pay.

Serving with credit issues

Credit problems happen in the military as well as in civilian life. Military personnel have extra protections under the law known as the Servicemembers Civil Relief Act. They're entitled to enhanced protection from eviction, auto lease cancellation penalties, high interest rates, and being summoned to a court hearing while serving.

TIP

A program sponsored by the U.S. Department of Defense, Military OneSource (`www.militaryonesource.mil`) offers financial counseling if you're having financial difficulties. Military OneSource also offers confidential resources and support for service members and their families on a wide range of topics. In-person financial counseling sessions are available at no cost to active-duty, National Guard, and Reserve members and family members, as well as deployed Department of Defense civilians and their families.

Financial counseling over the phone is provided by the financial management team located within the Military OneSource call centers. This team is made up of highly qualified certified financial counselors.

Counseling includes education and coaching in the areas of:

- Budgeting
- The creation of a realistic action plan using specific, manageable steps
- Housing (prepurchase, foreclosure prevention, and reverse mortgage)
- Credit and active-duty alerts
- Debt management
- Debt collections
- Financial-related deployment issues
- The Servicemembers Civil Relief Act (SCRA)
- Payday loans, title loans, and rent-to-own

To reach Military OneSource, call 800-342-9647 from inside the U.S., 800-342-6477 from outside the U.S., or 484-530-5747 for an international collect call, or go to `www.militaryonesource.mil`.

For active or former military service personnel or their families who need help but prefer not to use a government program, financial counseling is available at no cost through Military Reconnect (`www.moneymanagement.org/education/military`), a program offered nationally by the nonprofit Money Management International.

IN THIS CHAPTER

» Figuring out whether you need credit assistance

» Finding free mortgage help, credit counseling, and legal advice

Chapter 3

Getting Help with Your Credit

Where does bad credit come from? The credit fairy? Bad credit karma? No, it comes from overextending your finances and falling behind on your debt payments. Sometimes things happen outside of your control (such as a flat tire) that can take you over the edge if you're just making ends meet. Yes, other factors make up a credit score, such as the length of your credit history and whether you have shown that you can handle a variety of types of credit. But nothing whacks your credit score and report like being delinquent on payments or having to file for bankruptcy because your credit is hopelessly overextended.

FICO and VantageScore, the two main producers of credit scores, count late or missed payments as the most damaging factors to your score. And bankruptcy, the logical result of credit or debt gone wild, is the negative on your credit report from which it takes the longest to recover. After you fall behind, lenders are very hesitant to lend money or change loan terms to help you catch up. So the only legitimate way to get rid of bad credit is to get your spending and income in sync and then make all your debt payments on time, as agreed.

Doing so can be easier said than done, so you may need some help. Getting help from someone with lots of experience is a smart thing to do. Getting it for free is even better. Yet many people avoid seeking help for money or credit problems. Why? Because getting the wrong help can just make matters worse. After all, haven't you been taught that when an offer is too good to be true, it usually is?

In this chapter, we help you sort through the conflicting and overblown claims for help that you find in the media. We also include valuable insights to help you decide which problems you can handle on your own, when to turn to others for assistance, and where to get the help you need.

Knowing Whether You Need Help

If you're asking yourself whether you need to get some outside advice or help, you're no doubt feeling some pressure, even if it's only a squeeze. This is a very personal decision with one or two exceptions, which are covered in the following sections.

Gauging your need for outside assistance

REMEMBER

To help decide whether outside assistance is right for you, ask yourself — and include your partner if you're not in this alone — a few simple questions:

- **Are you stressed out?** You know you need to get some help when:
  - You screen your calls to avoid creditors.
  - You argue with your partner about money or credit.
  - Your sleep is interrupted because of financial worries, and you don't look forward to greeting the day in the morning.
- **Are you (or you and your partner) being pulled in multiple directions regarding possible solutions?** You may be unsure about which approach to use:
  - Increasing income to support your current bills and future goals
  - Decreasing expenses to bring your lifestyle in line with your present income
  - Getting a loan to pay off debt or reduce payments
  - Filing for bankruptcy (see Chapter 5 in Book 3)

- **Are you dealing with multiple creditors or multiple problems?** You probably can use outside help if:
  - More than two or three collectors or creditors have you on speed dial.
  - You have many problems (financial, employment, medical, and/or marital) creating stress in your life at the same time.
- **Are you more than one month late on your mortgage payment?** No matter what else is going on, you need to see a counselor now! A delay or the runaround from your servicer can cost you:
  - Thousands of dollars
  - Your credit
  - Your home (see Chapter 2 in Book 2 to avoid a foreclosure)
- **Are you thinking that bankruptcy may not be so bad for your credit?** Get professional, nonprofit counseling before you decide; otherwise, you may not know:
  - Whether bankruptcy can solve your problems or make them worse
  - Whether other alternatives exist that may be less damaging to your credit
- **Are you new to credit or to the United States and can't seem to break into the financial mainstream but don't know what to do next?** You can benefit from help if:
  - You don't understand how credit works.
  - You need to establish credit.
  - You want to get started on your own version of the American Dream as soon as possible (see Chapter 2 in Book 3 for more info).

Handling situations on your own

The following sections outline three credit situations that you can probably resolve without much help.

REMEMBER

To solve any credit/debt problem, you need to:

- Identify the cause of the problem and resolve to fix it
- Know how much money you have to work with
- Act quickly

Credit cards

If you can't make this month's credit card payment, or if you missed a payment already, you need to take action. As long as you know what you can afford and you don't mind explaining your situation over the phone, you can get quick results. Here's what to do: Call the toll-free customer service number and explain who you are, what happened, and how you'd like to handle the situation. If you need a break from making payments, say so. If you can make up the missed payments over the next month or two, make an offer. Just make sure that you can make good on your offer.

TIP

Be sure to ask the customer service representative not to report your account as late to the bureaus. This decision is up to the credit card company; often, the company is willing to go along with the request as long as you keep your end of the bargain.

If you're polite and proactive and you contact the credit card company before the company contacts you, this approach establishes you as a good customer who needs and deserves special consideration — much better than a customer who is behind in payments, doesn't call, and may be a collection risk.

WARNING

Be careful about asking that a payment be stretched out for more than a month or two. If you need three months to catch up, you may get it — or even qualify for a longer hardship program — but the creditor may close your account, which hurts your credit. Also, don't be surprised if the company asks you to pay more than you think you can. The company doesn't know the details of your situation. Do *not* agree to anything you don't think you can deliver. Making promises that you can't keep won't help when you can't follow through. Explaining why you need an exception is much better than caving in. If you can't agree on a plan, ask to talk to a supervisor — they may have more authority to bend the rules.

Mortgages

If you're behind on your mortgage payment, but you're within the grace period allowed in your mortgage loan documents (typically 10 to 15 days from your contractual due date) and you have the money to make up the shortfall, send it in or transfer the payment electronically from your bank account. If you're past the grace period, what you need to do to catch up depends on the state in which you live.

Say you haven't yet made your payment of $1,000 from last month. This month you can send in only $500 extra with your $1,000 payment. So you're short $500, right? Wrong. You may be behind the full $2,000 if the bank doesn't accept either payment because you didn't catch up in full. Or the bank may apply the extra $500 to this month's principal payment rather than to last month's deficit. The gist is, if you aren't far behind and you can catch up in one shot, do it. Otherwise, don't delay — see the later section "Considering credit counseling" and get help.

WARNING

Mortgage lenders count delinquency occurrences differently than credit card issuers. As soon as you're one day beyond the grace period, mortgage lenders consider you late, back to the original, contractual, non-grace due date. After you're 90 days late from the contractual due date (not the grace period), all the rules change, and you're in serious danger of a foreclosure! (Check out Chapter 2 in Book 2 to find out what a foreclosure can do to your credit and how to avoid it.) Also, be mindful that some banks have shorter grace periods for mortgage holders who don't have bank accounts with them.

Student loans

Getting some breathing room on a student loan isn't difficult if you have a qualifying reason for being unable to pay, especially if it's a federally guaranteed student loan. Unemployment, a low-paying job, illness, a return to school — any of these reasons may qualify you for a short-term waiver, but only if you give the loan servicer a call before you get into a default situation. Student loan people usually cooperate as long as they think you're playing it straight with them.

REMEMBER

If you don't think that you have enough money to catch up on your payments, you may have an alternative: The money may be hidden in your financial budget clutter. The first step in addressing a financial problem is to maximize your income and minimize your expenses. A spending plan (or budget) helps you with that. Only a real spending plan that accounts for at least 90 percent of your income and expenses will help; rough guesses don't yield the results you need. Turn to Chapter 2 in Book 1 for more on budgeting.

Identifying Help You Can Get for Free

Many sources promising financial advice and help, including debt settlement firms, debt reduction companies, debt-erasing lawyers, for-profit credit counselors, credit-monitoring services, and credit repair companies, charge one way or another. And despite the ads that seem to promise better credit and relief from debts, collectors, and even the IRS, only three sources (covered in the following sections) provide truly helpful, truly free assistance for those with credit or debt problems:

» **Housing and Urban Development (HUD)-certified mortgage counselors:** Mortgage counselors can obviously help you with mortgage issues. They're experts at helping people decide whether to stay in their homes and then making the decision work in the best way possible.

- **Nonprofit credit counseling agencies:** We're big fans of good credit counselors for a number of reasons: They're free, they take the time to tailor solutions to your situation, they're well trained, and their mission in life is to help, pure and simple. The main things they deal with are goal setting, identifying the sources of problems and solutions, and budgeting (the foundation of everything financial).
- **Pro bono lawyers:** Because credit and collections are governed by laws, and because life isn't always fair, the time may come when you need an attorney. But if you're broke or quickly getting there, paying for an attorney may not be possible. Pro bono lawyers work for little or nothing.

WARNING

Celebrity financial gurus may be entertaining and sometimes motivational, but they can't take the time to understand your situation. Plus, you can't get important follow-up advice to fine-tune your options and actions. Online influencers offer still more generic help that may give you ideas but rarely actual solutions.

Getting help with your mortgage

Home mortgage debt is different from all other types of debt and can be very complicated. We strongly urge you to use a professional to make sure that you don't make costly and damaging credit mistakes. Here are a few places to look for professionals:

- **Money Management International (MMI):** MMI is the largest full-service nonprofit credit counseling organization in the United States. It has been helping families and individuals since 1958 and is licensed in every state. It offers HUD, as well as student loan and bankruptcy counseling. It has a Better Business Bureau rating of A+. It's a member of the National Foundation for Credit Counseling and the Financial Counseling Association of America and is accredited by the Council on Accreditation. You can reach MMI at 866-889-9347 or `www.moneymanagement.org`.
- **BALANCE:** BALANCE is a nonprofit credit counseling and financial education agency, serving families nationwide. Since its incorporation in 1969, BALANCE has helped hundreds of thousands of individuals and families overcome their financial challenges and reach their goals. BALANCE is a national HUD-certified housing counseling intermediary agency and accredited by the Council on Accreditation. Its mission is to provide comprehensive financial housing counseling and education programs aimed at helping consumers achieve financial independence through debt reduction, home ownership,

and improved money management skills. For assistance, call 888-456-2227 or go to www.balancepro.org.

- **995Hope:** This organization is an alliance among counselors, mortgage companies, investors, and other players. It helps distressed homeowners work out mortgage problems so that they can stay in their homes. The folks at 995Hope know the ropes, have access to decision makers, and can help you with the necessary paperwork for free. They help you understand your options, prepare your application, and work with your mortgage company. The U.S. Department of the Treasury and the U.S. Department of Housing and Urban Development back this alliance. For help, call 888-995-4673 or go to www.995hope.org.
- **State housing authorities:** Every state has a housing authority. These organizations offer help to first-time homebuyers and homeowners in crisis, referrals to counseling, and sometimes funds to cure a delinquency. You can find the housing authority in your state or community at www.ncsha.org/housing-help.
- **Legal/document review:** One of your last resorts is to have an attorney review your loan documents. Some documents may have been drawn or executed incorrectly and may be challenged in court. A pro bono attorney may be able to help you for free. See the later section "Working with an attorney."

Considering credit counseling

A legitimate, certified credit counselor may offer just the help you need to get a handle on your financial problems. A nonprofit credit counseling agency serves as an objective party to help you see your financial situation without emotion and fear clouding your vision. In addition, a trained and certified counselor may be able to offer you some credit education, personalized budgeting advice, and a custom-tailored plan to get you out of debt — all for nothing or next to nothing.

Recognizing debts credit counseling can help with

REMEMBER

Although credit counseling can help in a variety of circumstances, it really shines in five situations. So, if you find yourself dealing with any of the following scenarios, get some outside advice pronto, before matters get further out of hand.

- **Mortgage default:** The rules are complex, the dates are often inflexible, and the servicers are often paper pushers who waste your time until a foreclosure is imminent. Many credit counselors, but not all, are HUD-certified mortgage counselors who can get to the right people faster than you and can lead you through a complex process based on a lot of experience and special access to decision makers.

- **Multiple bill collectors:** You can handle one or two collectors, but when you get to five, ten, or even more, conflicting demands can be impossible to balance.
- **Joint credit problems:** Credit problems are exacerbated when you share them with someone who doesn't see things the way you do. An outside, dispassionate point of view can make all the difference.
- **Debts that are backed by assets:** Loans for cars, houses, and boats are all secured by assets. If you don't or can't pay, the lender can repossess and sell your car, home, or boat. If you don't pay your credit card bill, the lender doesn't have any collateral that it can take, because it has no security beyond your word and your willingness to pay as agreed. As a general rule, the more security lenders have, the less willing they are to work with you to solve what they see as your problem.
- **Bankruptcy:** You must get credit counseling before you can file for bankruptcy. Be sure to pick a good agency that does a lot of this stuff. The agency should be fast, efficient, and cost-effective, or you may run into problems and delays later on. (See Chapter 5 in Book 3 for more info.)

In all these situations, you stand to benefit from talking to a professional who can help you with experience, resources, and a clear and unbiased outside view of your situation that you can't get when you're stuck in the middle.

Knowing what a credit counseling agency can offer you

Although no magic wand exists to make all your financial problems disappear, a good, certified credit counselor can offer thoughtful and useful solutions. Expect more than one option for resolving matters, including some options you won't like. Your counselor can give you a balanced perspective of what you need to do, how long it will take, and what resources are available to help you along the way. Your counselor will probably discuss bankruptcy as well as other solutions.

- **Goals for the future:** A good credit counselor offers solutions with your future goals in focus. A solution that works for you not only deals with current issues but also takes into account how you see your future. For example, if you're planning to buy a house, get a security clearance at work, or send your triplets to college in five years, that future goal affects which courses of action best fit your needs.
- **Improved communication with your family:** For about 70 percent of the more than a million people who bare their souls to credit counselors each year, advice and direction are all they need. One unexpected by-product of credit counseling is improved financial and other communication. For many

couples and families, the credit counseling session is the first time they openly communicate about goals, spending priorities, and even secrets such as hidden debts.

» **A plan that works for you:** Expect to have a customized action plan when you finish with credit counseling. An action plan has to fit the way you live, or you won't follow it. A comfortable budget designed with your spending and saving style in mind is more likely to be effective.

An often overlooked aspect of using nonprofit credit counseling agencies is that they know a lot about other community resources that may be able to help. Doing due diligence before making referrals to community, legal, and other resources is part of a good agency's service.

REMEMBER

The credit counseling process isn't something you can breeze through in 15 minutes, because the plan you walk away with is tailor-made for you and your financial situation. Many nonprofit credit counseling agencies have the ability to provide a full online or phone credit counseling experience. Be prepared to take the time to go through the details and make sure you follow up with any requests so that you get a comprehensive plan of action.

» **Periodic checkups:** Expect some fine-tuning to adjust to changes down the road. Although your counselor anticipates bumps in the road as much as possible when developing your plan, the counselor can't foresee the future. Murphy's Law applies to financial and credit problems in spades. Not only can things go wrong, but with limited financial resources, every bump in the road feels much worse.

Ongoing involvement with your credit counseling agency as you navigate this credit repair journey helps you stay the course. Expect the agency to make it easier for you by giving you the names, email addresses, and phone numbers of people to contact beyond the agency for more help. You should be able to ask your counselor for additional suggestions and referrals as you go along, although most people, when they have a workable plan in hand, are often capable of handling the execution of the plan on their own.

Finding a great credit counseling agency

Here are some details to look for in a quality credit counseling organization:

» 501(c)(3) tax-exempt status

» Accreditation by a national independent third-party accrediting organization, especially the Council on Accreditation or ISO 9000

» A willingness to spend at least 45 to 60 minutes with you, and more if needed — and for free

THE VALUE OF AN INTERMEDIARY

You may wonder why a credit counseling agency has to serve as an intermediary as part of a debt management plan. Why can't the agency just set up the plan and leave you to follow it on your own, without paying the agency a monthly fee? The answer is twofold:

- **Most people hit a bump or two in the repayment road.** Through its ongoing involvement, your credit counseling agency can explain your situation to the creditor dispassionately and professionally. Many plans would blow up at the first misstep without a trusted intermediary to smooth strained communications.
- **Creditors want the credit counseling agencies involved.** Creditors can easily reach agencies for questions, the agencies' checks don't bounce, and the agencies don't get excited and yell over the phone the way consumers and creditors have been known to do, thereby calming down the whole repayment process. Additionally, they can provide welcome guidance to you during the repayment plan and help coach you to financial wellness.

» A willingness to offer help the way you're most comfortable receiving it — in person, by phone, or via the Internet

TIP

Here are a couple of national organizations that can help you find a reputable credit counseling agency:

» **The National Foundation for Credit Counseling:** www.nfcc.org; 800-388-2227

» **The Financial Counseling Association of America:** www.fcaa.org; 800-450-1794

Deciding on debt management plans

For about 25 percent of those who turn to credit counselors, more than advice is prescribed. In these cases, in addition to an action plan, a debt management plan is recommended. A *debt management plan* (sometimes called a *debt repayment plan*) requires that the agency act as an intermediary, handling both communications and payments on your behalf for a small monthly fee. This plan includes revised payments that:

» Are acceptable to all your creditors

» Leave you enough money to handle your living expenses

- Generally get you out of debt in two to five years, although payments may be amortized over as much as seven years

Debt management plans are an alternative to bankruptcy and often go by other names, such as a *workout plan, debt consolidation,* or an *interest-rate-reduction plan.* A debt management plan offers all these benefits and perhaps a lot more. Here's how it works: When creditors realize that you can't meet the original terms of your credit card or other loan agreements, they also realize that they're better off working with you through your credit counselor. Under a debt management plan, your creditors are likely to be open to a number of solutions that are to your advantage, including:

- Stretching out your payments so that the combination of *principal* (the amount you originally borrowed) and interest pays off your balance in 72 months or less
- Changing your monthly payment to an amount you can afford to pay
- Reducing your interest rate and/or any fees associated with your loan
- Refraining from hounding you day and night with collection calls

Why would creditors be willing to do these things for you? Because if they don't, and you really can't make the payments, they'll spend a lot more money on collections than they'd give you in concessions. Plus, if you file for bankruptcy, your creditors may *never* get their money.

REMEMBER

The critical point here is that the creditor has to believe you can't make the payments as agreed. But how does the creditor believe that without staking out your home? The creditor generally takes the word of the nonprofit credit counseling agency you go to for help. Still, being lenders, creditors check your credit report from time to time while you're on a debt management plan to make sure that you haven't opened new lines of credit.

Sounds like a good deal: lower interest rates and smaller payments. Well, a debt management plan isn't a free lunch. The minuses may include:

- A potentially negative impact on your credit report, depending on how your creditors report your credit counseling account (although just being in a debt management plan doesn't affect your credit score)
- Restricted access to credit during the term of the plan
- Difficulty changing credit counseling agencies after you begin a debt management plan

STEERING CLEAR OF DEBT SETTLEMENT PLANS

Debt settlement isn't the same as credit counseling or a debt management plan. It's sometimes advertised as a way to save money, but it can be one of the most expensive methods of all! In a debt settlement plan, you pay money to a company that holds your money without making any payments until the creditor stops hounding you and supposedly is ready to take less than the face value of the debt.

This course of action *severely* damages your credit for years to come. If that's not enough to scare you off, consider this: Often, if you actually get to a settlement, the amount the creditor forgives actually becomes taxable income to you! You guessed it: The IRS wants you to pay taxes on the forgiven amount, which can add up to thousands of dollars due on April 15 to Uncle Sam. And those agents at the IRS don't go away! Even if you later decide to go the bankruptcy route, the IRS still gets its money.

Debt settlement is an unsavory, confrontational business. Our advice: Don't do it! If you must, use a qualified attorney whom you know or one of the new nonprofits offering debt settlement services such as the one offered by MMI (`www.moneymanagement.org/debt-resolution`) to negotiate settlements on your behalf.

REMEMBER

The bottom line is this: If you're in debt crisis or you're concerned that you may be getting close to it, a debt management plan from a good credit counseling agency may be a solution. If you're just shopping for an interest-rate reduction or a consolidation-loan alternative, a debt management plan may *not* be in your best interest.

Working with an attorney

You may be asking yourself if an attorney can possibly be free or low-cost. The answer is yes, if that's what you need. We said *need*, not *want*. If you can't afford an attorney, free or very-low-cost services are available if you know where to find them, and that's what this section is all about.

The phrase *pro bono* comes from the Latin and means "for the public good." Pro bono lawyers exist in most firms; they can be the very same lawyers who charge well-heeled clients hundreds of dollars an hour but will help you for little to nothing. The trick is to find one.

TIP

Here are some suggestions for finding free legal help:

- **Legal Services Corporation (LSC):** LSC is the largest provider of civil legal aid for those who can't afford it. LSC is a nonprofit corporation that supports 132 legal aid programs through more than 900 offices throughout the United States. It offers a variety of help, including cases involving family law, housing and foreclosure issues, and consumer issues such as protection from lenders, debt management, and bankruptcy. LSC serves consumers who are at or below 125 percent of the poverty level. Visit `www.lsc.gov` or call 202-295-1500.
- **Local bar association:** Your local bar association can help you find the help you need for what you can afford to pay. The American Bar Association has a consumers' guide to legal help on its website to help you find such resources in your state; see `www.americanbar.org/groups/legal_services/flh-home` or go directly to `www.abafreelegalanswers.org` to get your questions answered.
- **LawHelp:** LawHelp (`www.lawhelp.org`) helps low- and moderate-income consumers find free legal aid programs in their communities and provides links to other social service agencies.
- **American Bar Association:** All branches of military personnel, veterans, and their families can find access to ABA resources at `www.americanbar.org/groups/legal_services/milvets`.

REMEMBER

A qualified attorney can handle anything a mortgage counselor or credit counselor can. The big difference is that most attorneys don't deal with credit situations every day. As a result, they'll probably take longer to get to the same place than someone who deals with hundreds or thousands of these cases every month. So although you can make a versatile tool fit most situations, sometimes you're better off with one designed specifically for the job at hand — especially when it comes to mortgage issues.

IN THIS CHAPTER

» Keeping your financial information secure

» Watching for signs of identity theft

» Taking action in the event of identity theft

» Using credit safely after identity theft

Chapter 4
Combating Identity Theft

Identity theft doesn't involve someone dressing like you and copying your hairstyle. It's much simpler than that. The cyber-criminal simply acquires and uses the myriad data associated with your name to become you, electronically and financially. But how does an identity thief get this valuable data about you? Often by buying data stolen in a data breach, hacking into your computer, breaking into your home, stealing your mail, or even sifting through receipts and personal information found in your trash can.

In this chapter, you discover the important steps you need to take to protect yourself, your identity, and your credit from identity theft. You also find guidance on repairing the damage if it does occur.

Looking at the Growing Threat of Identity Theft

The Identity Theft Resource Center (the premier nonprofit resource for identity theft victims) helps close to one million people a year deal with this insidious crime. Today's ID thieves are often part of organized crime organizations located in foreign countries that recruit and pay full-time employees to use the latest artificial intelligence (AI) technology to piece together separate pieces of your identity from many sources to establish a fraudulent identity or scam users on social media. As more people go online, and more data is exposed in data breaches (or through other means), companies and industries are coming together to raise security standards and become more diligent about protecting your privacy. However, despite the best of efforts, according to LifeLock, data on virtually every American over the age of 10 may have been compromised in the last several years by data breaches or unauthorized attacks that hijacked personal information.

Depending on what information the thief steals from you, they may use your favorite credit card or open new credit card accounts in your name. They may buy a car using your credit, rent an apartment and leave you to pay the damages, order furniture, and stay a week at the Ritz in Buenos Aires — all while posing as *you*. They may even use your child's Social Security number to open accounts. Of course, the thief makes no payments on any of the debts. The negative credit activity is reported on the victim's credit report, and if the thief is lucky — and you aren't — you may not discover them living it up and wrecking your credit rating for months (or even years, in the case of children's stolen data). You may discover that your identity has been stolen only when you apply for a line of credit and are rejected, or when you receive a flurry of aggressive calls from collection agencies for not paying bills of which you aren't even aware.

After you discover the ID theft, you can defend yourself and prove that the fraudulent accounts aren't yours, but the process can be expensive and may take a long time to resolve. Fortunately, as the problem has become worse, the timeframes and investment to correct the issues have become less burdensome and quicker to resolve. A 2023 report from the Identity Theft Resource Center (ITRC) showed that 71 percent of consumers who reported identity misuse were able to resolve it within a month. However, the IRS's processing of Identity Theft Victim Assistance (IDTVA) cases are averaging 506 days in 2025.

In 2024, the Federal Trade Commission (FTC) reported more than 1.1 million cases of identity theft. And in an era of AI-driven scams, experts expect that number to continue to climb.

REMEMBER

If you receive a data breach notice, take the following immediate actions:

- Freeze your credit and place a fraud alert on your credit report.
- Change the password of any impacted account and any account where you use the same password to unique passwords to prevent all of your accounts from being compromised.
- Set up passkeys (such as a fingerprint) where available.
- Set up multi-factor authentication if you can't create a passkey.
- Sign up for any credit monitoring or identity restoration services offered.

TIP

Go to the Identity Theft Resource Center (`www.idtheftcenter.org/recover`) for help setting up a recovery plan or the Federal Trade Commission at `www.identitytheft.gov`. The FTC has sample letters you can use right away at `www.identitytheft.gov/Sample-Letters/dispute-credit-card-charges`.

Keeping Thieves at Bay

Your identity may be stolen by a stranger. Then again, as often happens, it may be stolen by someone you know and willingly let into your life, such as a friend, relative, or coworker. To reduce your chances of falling victim to identity theft, make sure that you protect your personal information. In short, don't leave financial or confidential documents out in the open, leave computer screens open but unattended when you are online, or use passwords that are easy to find, guess, or access.

New solutions are also being brought to market to help you protect yourself. These services analyze every consumer's unique breach history to prescribe personalized actions that protect your identity and credit. Monitoring your credit activity and signing up for texts when transactions are made are just a few steps that can help.

The following sections walk you through some simple steps you can take to reduce the chances of your identity being stolen.

USING A CREDIT MONITORING SERVICE

Here are some factors to consider when choosing a credit monitoring service:

- Look for services that offer features such as dark web monitoring, fraud alerts, credit monitoring (across multiple bureaus), insurance coverage, and restoration services.
- Choose a service that most aligns with the specific types of threats you're most concerned about.
- Compare pricing of different services to fit your budget.
- Consider the quality of customer support offered.
- Choose a service with a user-friendly interface and instructions.

Finally, read the fine print. This goes without saying, but we're saying it anyway!

Getting on the technology train

One of the easiest ways to protect yourself is to simplify bill-paying, information transfers, and financial transactions by performing them all securely and electronically. Having bills and statements delivered to your password/passkey-protected computer is much safer than having them delivered to your mailbox outside your home.

We recommend that you do a quick once-over of your account activity weekly or have preset dollar-level alerts emailed or texted to you. For example, you can arrange for transactions that exceed $100 to generate an email or text automatically. Virtually every financial institution now offers text messages that can be sent for every purchase over a certain amount. Set your alert level so that it doesn't result in dozens of notices but does catch the transactions you're most concerned about. That way, you can spot a problem early and you won't have to spend a day or two trying to resolve it.

TIP

People who take the time to balance their checking accounts can skip that often frustrating step if they can just confirm their balance online!

WARNING

Take precautions when conducting business via the web. As long as you use only secure websites and ensure that you're protected by a firewall, you're much better protected than you are with snail mail. (See the next section for info on determining whether a website is secure and see the later section "Safeguarding your computer data" for a few words on firewalls.)

Looking out for phishing scams

Phishing occurs when a stranger pretending to be someone you trust (for example, a Facebook friend, a state-operated electronic toll biller, a credit card company, or a representative of your bank) emails you and asks you to confirm critical information about your account — for example, by replying with your password or Social Security number.

REMEMBER

Phishing scams are increasing and becoming more sophisticated. Bottom line: Think twice before replying to any unsolicited requests or giving out your personal information over the Internet. As with phone solicitations, don't give out your personal information unless *you* initiate the transaction. You can find out more about preventing Internet fraud, securing your computer, and protecting your personal information by visiting `www.onguardonline.gov`.

Here are some do's and don'ts that can help keep you and your personal info safe:

- **Do be suspicious of any email with urgent, exciting, or upsetting requests for personal financial info or money.** The sender is using your emotions to stimulate an immediate, illogical response to the request. Pay special attention to any website addresses or domain names that are included. If it doesn't look right, don't click the link.
- **Do protect your passwords and turn on two-factor authentication (2FA) when it's available.** Don't share your passwords over the phone, in texts, or by email. Legitimate companies will *never* ask you for your password. Using 2FA requires a password and typically a code that's texted or emailed to you or generated by an authenticator app such as Google Authenticator, which you install on your smartphone. If you write down your passwords, keep them locked up on your computer or in a safe and out of plain sight. Consider using a password manager such as Bitwarden (`https://bitwarden.com`), currently with an option for free security, or 1Password (`www.1password.com`), which enables you to generate very long, random passwords (ones so strong you would never be able to remember them); you can (and should) create a different password for every website you visit, but you only have to remember one master password to access all the passwords you created.

  TECHNICAL STUFF

  Why a different password for every site? Because, that way, if one website gets hacked and your password is compromised, the hacker can't use that same password to log in to your email account, your credit card company, your bank, and so on.

- **Don't give out personal or financial info unless you're certain of the source and you can confirm that the link is secure.** You can tell that you're on a secure website if the site's address begins with `https://` rather than `http://`. A secure site encrypts data as it's being transmitted, which is especially important when you're entering personal information.

  WARNING

  Email is almost *never* secure, which means that you should never email your credit card number, Social Security number, or other personal info to anyone, even someone you're sure you can trust. This is particularly important if you're using a general hosting provider (such as Gmail or Hotmail, for example). Those emails are stored and backed up in files that you don't want holding your account numbers.

- **Don't respond to emails that aren't personalized or that have your name misspelled.** If the message has your name wrong or doesn't include your name at all, chances are high that it's a fraud.
- **Don't click links in email messages to find out what the great offer is unless you know you signed up for that service.** If you click the link, you may end up downloading spyware onto your computer, and your security may be compromised.

- **Don't unsubscribe to emails unless you know that you subscribed in the first place.** Some phishers send you emails hoping that you'll respond or unsubscribe, thereby confirming that your email address is valid. Just block and delete them.
- **Do be careful of emails pretending to be from companies you do business with.** For example, you may periodically get emails that look like they're from banks you use, but the emails lack the detailed logo or look and feel of the real companies, or they ask you to update information that you know the banks already have.
- **If you suspect that you're being phished, do report the fraud to the Federal Trade Commission at `https://reportfraud.ftc.gov/` and file a complaint with the Internet Crime Complaint Center (IC3) by going to `www.ic3.gov`.** The IC3 is a partnership among the FBI, the National White Collar Crime Center (NW3C), and the Bureau of Justice Assistance (BJA). The IC3 website not only lets you report suspected Internet fraud but also provides disturbing statistics about this growing crime.

Safeguarding your computer data

You need to safeguard your computer so that it doesn't give up its secrets without a fight. Here are some pieces of advice to keep your computer (and your identity) safe:

- Use a unique username and *passphrase* (12 to 20 characters long) or passkey for online accounts and set your computer so that this information is required in order to log on. You can also use a screensaver that has a password so that if you walk away from your desk for a certain period and the screensaver comes on, you need to enter a password to get back to your desktop.
- Don't keep a list of your passwords under your keyboard or near the computer. That's the equivalent of leaving your house key under the doormat.
- Use a digital wallet.
- Make sure your social media profiles are set to private; avoid posting anything publicly.
- Opt for multi-factor authentication (MFA) whenever possible.
- Never click on unexpected pop-ups in your browser or on your device or links in unknown emails, texts, or social media posts. Instead, go straight to the source when verifying an email, text, or social media post.
- Don't leave your laptop, smartphone, or tablet out where it can be picked up. Whether at home, in a hotel, in your favorite coffee shop, or at work, if you're

not in the same room as your device, put it away out of sight. When you're in the same room as others, if you're offline, anyone in the room can see your information. If you're online, especially with a Wi-Fi connection, your computer can be hacked and your data stolen, or you can be observed for sensitive information such as passwords. Lock your computer when you walk away, even if it's in your own house. Would you leave a $100 bill lying around? The same consideration applies here.

» Use antivirus and spyware protection programs to keep key loggers off your computer. Make sure you keep your antivirus and spyware protection programs up to date. *Key loggers* are programs that send to a crook any information you type while on your computer, including your credit card numbers, usernames, passwords, Social Security number, and so on.

» Make sure to delete all personal information on your computer if you decide to get rid of it. Your best bet is to reformat your hard drive, which wipes it clean and gets rid of everything. You may want to reformat your drive more than once to do a thorough job of permanently erasing data. (Check with your computer manufacturer to find out how to scrub your hard drive.)

WARNING

Please don't use your kid's or pet's name or birthday as your password. These things are easy for someone who knows you to guess.

KNOWING THE DIFFERENCE BETWEEN A PASSWORD AND A PASSKEY

Passwords are a combination of letters, numbers, and symbols that you create and remember. They're susceptible to phishing and often reused across multiple accounts. Passwords are typically stored on the website's or app's servers, which can be vulnerable to data breaches.

Passkeys are generated by the system (or stored in a password manager) and are unique for each website or app. They're linked to a device and they often require biometric verification (fingerprint, face scan, or PIN) for login, making them highly resistant to phishing and brute-force attacks. Passkeys are tied to a specific device and cannot be used on other devices without authorization, adding another layer of security. Finally, passkeys don't use a password and are designed to be more secure and user-friendly than passwords, providing a simpler and more robust way to access online accounts.

Keeping passwords secret

A testament to the trusting nature of Americans is that if you want to know something personal or secret about them, all you have to do is ask. But if you use a password, you'd be wise to keep your computer password secret because it protects you from others — even trusted coworkers — accessing your personal information. To make sure that you don't get taken advantage of, follow these suggestions:

- **Don't give anyone your password.** If the guy in the next cubicle wants to be helpful, you can enter your password for him.
- **If you have to give out your password, perhaps to a family member or a tech support person, be sure that you trust the source, and then change your password immediately.** And by immediately, we mean right after you give out your password. Don't wait until the next day or the next week.

REMEMBER

Avoid giving confidential information to friends, acquaintances, or even your kids. They may not be identity thieves, but they sure are great, naive sources of information.

Protecting your mail

The fact that tampering with the U.S. mail is a federal crime doesn't seem to deter identity thieves from helping themselves to the contents of people's mailboxes.

TIP

Following are some easy ways to reduce your exposure to mail fraud:

- **Move as much of your financial business online as you can.** Doing so helps you avoid delivering information to the waiting hands of the criminal scouting your unattended mailbox. Mailboxes can be targets of theft, particularly when mailbox stations are shared with other neighbors.
- **Explore alternatives to your unlocked, end-of-the-driveway mailbox.** Consider using a post office box or a locked mailbox that accepts mail (not unlike the old slot in the door).
- **Don't mail checks or financial information from your home mailbox.** Use a post office mailbox or bring your mail to work with you. (Don't forget the stamps, or the boss may cancel your work identity.)
- **Ask your bank to hold new check orders and pick them up at the bank.** Check reorder boxes are easy to spot with a trained eye. You wouldn't send cash through the mail; don't send checks, either.

» **If you're away for a day or more, have someone pick up your mail or, better yet, have the post office hold it until you return.** Don't let it sit in your mailbox overnight.

Storing financial data in your home

You may believe that your financial information is safe inside the sanctuary of your home, no matter where it's located. Unfortunately, even in your home, securing your documents and personal information by keeping them out of sight is best. Your information is still accessible to anyone who may gain access to your inner sanctum, friend or foe.

Keep all confidential, financial, and legal documents and information in a secure place — a strong box, a locked desk drawer, or a locked file cabinet. Doing so ensures that your valuable data is safe from prying eyes and sticky fingers, and you benefit from having all critical information in one place in case you need to access it quickly.

TIP

Purchase a good crosscut shredder and shred all financial documents that contain account numbers (including savings, checking, credit card and medical statements) before you discard them. Don't overlook all those preapproved offers for credit you receive, either. Look for a shredder that takes multiple sheets of paper, is easy to use, and can be emptied without making a mess. Why? Because you're more likely to use it if it meets these criteria. Also, if it's not easy to empty, the shredded confetti-like material will try to fly all over the place when you dump it.

Putting your credit information on ice

Frozen margaritas, frozen yogurt, frozen credit? The option to freeze your credit to keep it from being used by identity thieves is available to everyone. In fact, many financial institutions also offer you the opportunity to "freeze" your card or "lock" your account or card, if needed. This prevents purchases from being made until you want to make a purchase or you locate the card that fell inside the cushion on your couch. If you lock a card, though, make sure you remember to unlock it before you make that next purchase.

The concept is similar with your credit report: You can freeze, or lock up, your credit information at the major credit bureaus (meaning that your credit report won't be available for new creditors to view) so that anyone who's looking to extend credit has to ask you to thaw (unlock) your file. Freezing your credit information seriously hampers an identity thief from opening credit in your name without your knowledge because few lenders extend credit without a credit report in hand.

REMEMBER

When deciding whether to freeze your credit information, the main consideration is whether you value access to instant credit more than you fear your personal information being misappropriated. Only you know the answer to that question. Because it takes so little effort and time to freeze and thaw a credit report, our recommendation is freeze, baby, freeze!

WARNING

Of course, the freeze-your-credit-info strategy isn't foolproof. Thieves can still pirate and abuse existing accounts by using such tactics as swiping your mail, changing your address from Peoria to Las Vegas, and getting replacement cards issued. So a freeze may help protect you from having someone obtaining fraudulent credit in your name, but it may not protect your *money*, although hopefully you'd notice a problem before it got too far out of hand. Given the low personal level of liability on credit cards, your monetary losses shouldn't be significant.

The bottom line of a freeze is as follows:

- All the bureaus allow you to freeze your credit files regardless of the laws in your state.
- Freezing doesn't prevent abuse of existing accounts.
- Thawing an account online, via an app, or by phone takes less than an hour and may keep impulse or sale purchases from happening — which can be a good thing or a bad thing, depending on how you look at it.

TIP

If you're not into the idea of freezing your credit file, consider a fraud alert. It's like an account "chill" rather than a hard freeze in that it requires only enhanced verification of identity. To place an alert, contact any of the big three credit bureaus. The bureau you contact will automatically forward your request to the other two big credit bureaus for action. For details, see the later section "Sending out a fraud alert."

Shielding your credit card number

One of the easiest ways to safeguard your identity is to ensure that thieves don't have access to your credit card numbers. Luckily, this task has been made a lot easier. Electronically generated receipts for credit card and debit card transactions do not include the card's expiration date or more than the last five digits of the card number. Virtually all credit card issuers print only partial account numbers on statements as well.

TIP

You can find out more about the Fair Credit Reporting Act (FCRA) safeguards at the Federal Trade Commission website (`www.ftc.gov/sites/default/files/documents/reports/40-years-experience-fair-credit-reporting-act-ftc-staff-report-summary-interpretations/110720fcrareport.pdf`).

SAFEGUARDING ACTIVE-DUTY MILITARY PERSONNEL

While on duty outside the United States, military personnel — as well as their families at home — may lack the time or means to monitor their credit. After all, calling TransUnion about an error isn't exactly a high priority when defending our freedoms, and families back home can understandably get distracted and let their guard down when a loved one is serving overseas. So it seems only fair that while soldiers are protecting their country, their country should protect them from credit problems. Thanks to the FCRA Act, active-duty military personnel can place an *active-duty alert* on their credit reports as a way to notify potential creditors of possible fraud.

If you're in the military and away from your usual base or deployed, place an *active-duty alert* on your credit report by contacting any of the three major credit-reporting bureaus (don't bother contacting all three bureaus, because the one you contact will notify the other two). You are required to provide proof of identity, which may include your Social Security number, name, address, and other personal information. As a bonus, you can ask for free credit monitoring from the three bureaus when you ask for the alert.

The active-duty alert stays on your credit report for at least one year. It helps minimize the risk of identity theft by requiring that a business take reasonable care to verify your identity before issuing you credit. However, if you're in a distant land trying to keep the peace, verifying your identity may not be feasible. So before you leave your base or home for active duty, be sure to appoint a personal representative and provide that person's contact information to the credit bureau. If you don't, a creditor only has to "utilize reasonable policies and procedures to form a reasonable belief" before granting credit to someone claiming to be you. Be sure to appoint someone you trust!

With an alert in place, lenders have to take further steps before issuing additional credit cards or changing your limits. When you place the alert, you can get an additional free credit report in addition to the annual report you're already entitled to. Plus, your name is removed from preapproved offer lists for credit cards, insurance, and loans. To lessen the chances of an identity theft, you can place additional alerts if your deployment is to last longer than a year. (To delete an alert, just contact one of the bureaus; it will notify the others of your desire to deactivate the alert.)

If your contact information changes before your alert expires, update it or have your representative do so.

You may also want to examine the Servicemembers' Civil Relief Act (SCRA), which is a federal law that provides protections for military members as they enter active duty.

(continued)

(continued)

The SCRA's benefits and protections include an interest rate cap on financial obligations incurred prior to military service, the ability to stay civil court proceedings, protections in connection with default judgments, protections in connection with residential (apartment) lease terminations, and protections in connection with evictions, mortgage foreclosures, and installment contracts such as car loans. For more information on SCRA, go to `www.consumerfinance.gov/consumer-tools/educator-tools/servicemembers/the-servicemembers-civil-relief-act-scra` or for the entire act see `www.govinfo.gov/content/pkg/PLAW-108publ189/pdf/PLAW-108publ189.pdf`.

Catching Identity Thieves in the Act

If your identity is stolen, you may not notice it for days, weeks, or even months. It may take years for a child's stolen identity to be recognized. If a thief sets up a phony identity at another address and you don't get the bills, you may not know about the crime until the debts go bad and a collector finds you. Called *skip tracers*, these collectors look for people who don't pay their bills and then move — which is what they'll consider you until you straighten matters out.

The IRS may contact you if your identity is stolen. In recent years, fake tax returns filed by identity thieves became common. As a result the IRS has tightened its procedures and now you can request a PIN number for added tax return protection. If the IRS finds a fraudulent tax return filed in your name, they will issue you a PIN automatically. The IRS uses your Social Security number (SSN) to make sure that your tax filing is copacetic, and that if you are due a refund you get it. A notice or letter from the IRS could alert you that someone else is using your SSN.

WARNING

The IRS doesn't initiate contact with taxpayers via email, text, or social media message. If you get an email that claims to be from the IRS, do not reply or click any links it may contain. Instead, forward it to `phishing@irs.gov`.

By being vigilant, you can spot signs of identity theft. Vigilance can make all the difference between a minor and a major crime. The following sections introduce you to some key indications of identity theft so that you can be on the lookout for them.

TIP

Some homeowners insurance policies automatically include a level of identity theft protection. If it's not already part of your policy, you can usually add it as a relatively inexpensive endorsement.

PREDICTING IDENTITY THEFT

The FCRA demands that financial institutions establish procedures to attempt to spot identity theft *before* it occurs. Predicting identity theft may seem as farfetched as calling in a psychic on a missing person's case. But like our trusty weather forecasters who look to the skies for clues to tomorrow's weather, financial prognosticators are writing programs to look for specific activity in your financial records that may indicate a problem. In fact, several credit card companies now tout their own programs to fight identity theft. American Express, Visa, MasterCard, and other companies are making efforts to spot fraud and theft as quickly as possible. A change in pattern, fraud information, or type of spending may trigger an alert to your phone or email if you have an alert in place. Alerts are free and easy to set up.

Certain events — such as a change of address, a request for a replacement credit card, or efforts to reactivate a dormant credit card account — may trigger a fraud alert. Be patient if you get declined for a purchase. The intent is to protect you from fraud, and a quick phone call can usually set things straight. That said, you can only do so much to protect yourself from identity theft. Even with prevention programs in place, you may not know about the problem until after the fact.

Watching for early-warning notices

To help spot identity theft early on, the FCRA requires creditors to give you what may be called an *early-warning notice* (and it may be the first sign of a problem). When credit is used within 30 days of a missed, late, or partial payment or other type of default, you must be sent a one-time notice letting you know that this information is being sent to the credit bureau(s) to which the creditor reports data. This notice has to be sent by collection agencies, too, as long as they report to a credit bureau.

REMEMBER

Do your part by closely monitoring your credit reports, bank account statements, and credit card statements.

An early-warning notice means that something bad is in your account history, and if it's reported to a credit bureau, it has a negative effect on your credit and score. Whether or not it's reported, it's lurking out there. Before negative information is reported, the early-warning notice may look something like this:

> *We may report information about your account to credit bureaus. Late payments, missed payments, or other defaults on your account may be reflected in your credit report.*

After negative information has been reported, the notice may look like this:

> *We have told a credit bureau about a late payment, missed payment, or other default on your account. This information may be reflected in your credit report.*

REMEMBER

The wording makes it sound as though the bad information may not show up. It will, and it probably already has. Make sure you're reviewing your account statements every month so that you can spot and dispute any suspicious transactions. Regular monitoring can eliminate some additional steps and reduce additional fraud activity on your account.

So what do you do if you get a notice? Immediately contact the issuer and find out what's going on. The issuer will be as interested as you are in shutting down a thief, so you can expect cooperation and maybe even a thank-you for acting quickly.

Getting early warnings from the IRS

What's worse than having your identity stolen? Having it stolen and used to cheat the IRS. If someone uses your Social Security number (SSN) to get a job, their employer will use the stolen identity to report any earned income to the IRS using your SSN. Because you don't know about it, you won't report those earnings, thereby failing to report all your income from the IRS's point of view. You'll receive a notice or letter saying that you failed to report income.

Also, if someone uses your SSN to file for your tax refund before you file, that person may get your refund instead of you.

TIP

If you think that someone used your SSN to get a job or a tax refund — or the IRS sends you a notice or letter indicating a problem — contact the IRS immediately. Specially trained agents work with you to file your tax return, get you any refund you are due, and protect your IRS account from identity thieves in the future. The IRS will want a copy of your police report or an IRS Form 14039, Identity Theft Affidavit (available at `www.irs.gov/pub/irs-pdf/f14039.pdf`), as well as proof of your identity, such as a copy of your Social Security card, driver's license, or passport.

Contact the IRS Identity Protection Specialized Unit at 800-908-4490.

In addition, ensure you take these additional steps outside of the IRS:

- Report incidents of identity theft to the Federal Trade Commission at `www.consumer.ftc.gov` or to the FTC Identity Theft Hotline at 877-438-4338 or TTY 866-653-4261.

- File a report with your local police.
- Contact the fraud departments of the three major credit bureaus:
  - Equifax: www.equifax.com, 800-525-6285
  - Experian: www.experian.com, 888-397-3742
  - TransUnion: www.transunion.com, 800-680-7289
- Close any accounts that have been tampered with or opened fraudulently.

The IRS sends you a six-digit identity protection PIN (IP PIN) to prevent someone else from filing a tax return using your Social Security number (SSN) or individual taxpayer identification number (ITIN). The IP PIN is known only to you and the IRS. It helps verify your identity when you file your electronic or paper tax return.

After you're a confirmed victim of tax-related identity theft and you've resolved your tax account issues, the IRS mails you a CP01A Notice with your new IP PIN each year.

TIP

As a precautionary measure, you may get an IP PIN as a proactive step to protect yourself in advance from tax-related identity theft. Anyone with an SSN or an ITIN can get an IP PIN including individuals living abroad. Find out more at www.irs.gov/identity-theft-fraud-scams/get-an-identity-protection-pin.

Handling a collections call

If you're the victim of identity theft, you may receive a collections call, likely a demanding and unpleasant one, from a collector insisting on payment for an overdue account — an account that the collector is certain you owe but that you've never heard of. What should you do? The FACT Act amendment to the FCRA, designed to address identity-theft issues, states that you need to tell the collector very clearly that you didn't make the purchase and that you believe your identity may have been stolen.

After you tell the collector that you believe your identity may have been stolen, the collection agency is required by law to inform the creditor. You're also entitled to a copy of all the information the collection agency or creditor has about this debt, including applications, statements, and the like, as though this really were your account or bill. Request your copy before the collector gets off the phone or in your written response if the collection activity is in the form of a letter.

The best part is that as soon as you notify the creditor or collector that the debt is the work of an identity thief, the debt can't be placed for collection or sold to another collector.

Detecting unauthorized charges

Are you among the many people who just look at the amount due on your monthly statement and pay it? Or is your credit card bill automatically paid from your bank account and you check the details later? In either case, you may be paying for purchases you didn't make, and more importantly, you may be missing an opportunity to stop a thief!

Take the time to review your statements to ensure that all the charges are legitimate. Set a reminder to alert you to check your statement in detail on a regular basis. Remember, you have a limited time to dispute an error. Plus, an identity thief is faster than the proverbial speeding bullet! So, don't delay checking your statements, or you may be in for quite a surprise.

TIP

Don't rely on your memory as you review your statement. Keep all credit card receipts in a convenient place, at least until you receive, verify, and pay your bills.

REMEMBER

If you see any unauthorized charges on your statement, call the card issuer's customer service number and get the details. You may have to dispute the charge, but that's no big deal. Also, the representative may see some indication of identity theft. That happened to us — we saw a stray charge and called the credit card company, and the customer service rep recognized it as fraud right away. Make the call.

Being denied credit or account access

Rejection is always a painful thing, but it's especially painful when you're rejected because of something you didn't do. If you're rejected for credit, you should always ask why and what information they reviewed to make the decision. Order a copy of your credit report and look for evidence of identity theft (accounts you never opened and/or activity you don't recognize). You can get a free copy of the credit report used to deny your application in addition to the free annual reports you get normally.

WARNING

Another sign of identity theft is receiving a notice that you've been rejected for credit that you never asked for. Take this notice seriously. Someone may be applying for credit in your name.

You may try to access an ATM and get a denial message. If this happens, contact your bank immediately to determine whether it's the result of identity theft.

Noticing missing account statements

Your monthly bank statement is really late. Hmm . . . now that you think of it, you didn't receive a statement last month, either. Yes, we know this was one of your birthday wishes, but the real reason you're not hearing from your creditors may be more sinister. It could mean that an identity thief has changed your address in order to use your bank account, hoping that you won't notice for a few months.

TIP

Create a system to remind yourself when statements are due and bills must be paid. This way, you're more likely to stay on top of your payment schedule and be alerted when something is amiss. Paying bills and getting statements online instead of by snail mail makes it harder on thieves (and easier on you).

TO BUY OR NOT TO BUY, THAT IS THE QUESTION

Identity theft protection is a service offered by specialized security companies for a fee (sometimes a flat fee) that helps safeguard personal information such as your Social Security number and bank details, from being misused by criminals. They monitor your accounts and your personal information to detect fraud, give you fraud alerts for suspicious activity, and help with identity restoration, including sometimes insurance to cover the costs of restoring your identity and finances. The best services include credit monitoring along with ID theft protection by monitoring your credit reports and scores and alerting you to any changes or if something seems amiss, such as creditor inquiries or the opening of a new account.

The decision to pay a company to monitor your credit and identity can be daunting. The last thing most of us need is another monthly expense. In most cases, you can do almost everything yourself, for free, that an identity theft prevention company can do. What do they really do?

Consider this analogy recently from an industry executive: If you own a pet, should you pay someone to wash and groom it, or do it yourself? If you have the time and inclination, you can save a buck and do it yourself. However, you're still not out of the woods! If you pay someone for the grooming service, you still need to care for the pet to keep it healthy and see a vet for an annual checkup or shots. So whether you pay or do it yourself, you still need to do all the things mentioned in this chapter.

So, should you buy protection or not? No service can completely stop someone from stealing or using your information. But there are some things a monitoring service can

(continued)

(continued)

do that you can't. Identity monitoring companies are essentially data aggregators and detectors. They leverage relationships with credit bureaus and other data providers, along with advanced technology for scanning the dark web and public records to make sure your identity (credit card details, Social Security number, or the like) hasn't surfaced in a civil or criminal record in some faraway jurisdiction to create a comprehensive picture of your exposed personal information. The information they look for can include, but is not limited to, your Social Security number, driver's license number, credit and debit card numbers, email addresses, usernames, and passwords. This kind of widespread monitoring would be nearly impossible for a single person to do manually. When they find something, they alert you so you can act quickly to stop or lessen any potential damage. Also, paid monitoring services are often combined with remediation services.

Still not sure? Here are three free options to explore:

- The Identity Theft Resource Center has a free service called Breach Clarity that can help you understand the type of information exposed in a specific breach and what actions you can take to deal with it. Find out more at `www.idtheftcenter.org/victim-help-center`.
- Experian offers the Dark Web Triple Scan. You can use it for free, but Experian will try to get you to upgrade to its paid service. Check it out at `www.experian.com/consumer-products/free-dark-web-email-scan.html`.
- The website Have I Been Pwned (`https://haveibeenpwned.com`) lets you check to see if one of your accounts has been compromised in a breach simply by providing your email address.

Taking Fast Action When Identity Theft Occurs

If your identity has been stolen or you believe that it has (you don't need a smoking gun, video, or a ransacked room to act), do everything in the following sections as soon as possible. Most of the places you need to contact are either available online or open 24 hours a day, so a late-night call won't bother anyone.

Communicating with the right people

You may read different advice on who to contact *first* when you believe your identity has been compromised or stolen. Some sources say to begin by reporting the crime to the police to establish a formal record, others suggest that you call your creditors, and still others say to notify the credit bureaus. Our advice is to begin in one of two places, depending on your circumstances:

- If your existing bank or credit accounts have been compromised, contact your financial institution or creditors first.
- If you find out about accounts you've never heard of and didn't open, contact the credit bureaus first.

Either way, don't wait long between the two contacts.

TIP

As you pick up the phone or visit a website, do one more task: Start documenting everything that happens from now on. You want dates, times, names, badge numbers, phone numbers, and so on. Documentation is critical because, unfortunately, this situation may go on for a long time and require a lot of calling and writing to resolve. Don't trust your memory or count on people to call you back when they say they will. You'll help yourself out by writing down the facts and promises or by printing out verification documents and confirmation emails if using automated, online assistance.

TIP

To report identity theft and create a recovery plan, go to `www.identitytheft.gov`. The website also includes an area that's helpful if you've been a victim of identity theft on your unemployment benefits. Other helpful information regarding sample letters, dealing with debt collectors, and accessing records may be useful to you, including the following:

- **Dispute letter for credit card charges:** `www.identitytheft.gov/Sample-Letters/dispute-credit-card-charges`
- **Dispute letter for ATM/debit card transactions:** `www.identitytheft.gov/Sample-Letters/dispute-debit-card-transactions`
- **Identity theft letter to a credit bureau:** `www.identitytheft.gov/Sample-Letters/identity-theft-credit-bureau`
- **Request letter for getting business records related to identity theft:** `www.identitytheft.gov/Sample-Letters/request-records-related-identity-theft`
- **Identity theft letter to a debt collector:** `www.identitytheft.gov/Sample-Letters/identity-theft-debt-collector`

TIP

Be sure to check out the nonprofit Identity Theft Resource Center (`www.idtheftcenter.org`). Formed in 1999, the Identity Theft Resource Center (ITRC) is the "go-to" national nonprofit in the United States for providing live, direct identity crime advice and victim assistance at no cost. You can communicate, chat, or speak to a real dedicated professional who knows the ins and outs of dealing with and containing identity theft. Go to `www.ftc.gov/idtheft` for prevention tips and free resources.

Canceling your cards

If your credit or debit cards have been compromised, call the card issuers, ask for the fraud department, and have the cards canceled immediately. You can find the phone number on your monthly statements, in your terms-and-conditions brochure, or on the card issuer's website or mobile app on your phone. If you have the card, look for the toll-free customer service number on the back of the card.

A small comfort: Your liability on stolen credit card accounts is relatively low — just $50 maximum per card, and it may even be $0. However, you still need to contact all your creditors as quickly as possible so that the thief doesn't continue to rack up charges in your name or open new accounts.

WARNING

For ATM and debit cards, your maximum liability is different and can be much, much higher. It's $50 if you report the loss within 48 hours of noticing it, but the liability can be $500 or even the full amount of your accounts (including any overdraft protection) if you delay too long.

Getting in touch with the credit bureaus

If you call or visit the fraud assistance websites of just one of the three major credit bureaus (Equifax, Experian, or TransUnion) to report identity theft, a one-year *fraud alert* is placed on all three of your credit files within 24 hours. A fraud alert often makes it more difficult for a thief to get credit in your name because it alerts creditors to follow certain procedures to protect you. (See the later section "Sending out a fraud alert" for more info.)

TIP

Fraud alerts aren't foolproof, and compliance by lenders may not be foolproof either. You may prefer to lock a door rather than just close it. So, we advise putting a *credit freeze* on your credit reports in addition to a fraud alert until you know how severe the identity theft damage is (we explain how to place a freeze earlier in this chapter). A "frozen" credit report means a creditor cannot pull your credit report to issue new credit without your express permission. You can always thaw your accounts later.

You can also add a *victim's statement* or *extended victim's statement* to your credit report. These statements inform the people who view your report that the information in your file has a potential problem and that they should be wary of making any decisions based on that information. Most creditors take strong notice of this fact and won't issue new credit in your name.

WARNING

Adding a victim's statement to your report may motivate creditors to suspend existing accounts that weren't affected until they can determine that you're safe again, which may keep you from using your accounts until you can speak with the creditors.

After you notify the credit bureau of your situation, you receive a free credit report from each of the bureaus. Be sure to keep a copy of all reports. (Store them with those copious notes you're taking.)

Contacting the Federal Trade Commission

The Federal Trade Commission (FTC) supports an entire department that handles identity theft issues. The folks in the identity theft clearinghouse don't follow up on individual cases, but they play an important role in looking for patterns and accumulating statistics that help everyone concerned with stopping identity theft.

Call the FTC's Identity Theft Hotline at 877-438-4338 (877-ID-THEFT) or go to `www.identitytheft.gov`. You can report and gain access to information to create your recovery plan, obtain sample forms, understand how to deal with debt collectors and browse the steps of the recovery plan for each impacted area (credit cards, student loans, and bankruptcy, if one has been filed in your name).

Notifying the police

If you call the sheriff, will he flip on his blue and red lights and tear around town to find the thief? Not exactly. But a crime has been committed, so you need to call the police and report it. Plus, some of the people you'll be dealing with (creditors, insurers, and bureaus) may require a police report to take action.

The police report is also a way for others in the process to get a straight, consistent story from a third party about what happened and when. You have less difficulty convincing a collector if you can send an official police report to bolster your story. Be sure to get a copy of the report as soon as it's available or at least get the report number for reference.

Here's how the police reporting process works:

1. **Contact your local police station if you suspect that someone is using your identity.**

   You don't need legal proof to prove your claim; it's your identity, and your suspicion is enough to file a police report.

2. **File the report, providing all the facts and circumstances.**

   Supply all account numbers and other relevant information. No standard form or procedure exists; each police department has its own.

3. **Get the police report number with the date, time, police department, location, and name of the officer writing the report.**

   You likely need to provide this info when dealing with insurance claims, credit card companies, or lenders or collectors to clear your account.

4. **Be persistent but polite if the police seem reluctant to take your statement.**

   All states require police departments to file reports for identity theft victims. If your local police are reluctant to file a report, you can remind them that, without a police report, credit bureaus may not block fraudulent items on your credit report, and the lack of a formal police report may inadvertently help a crook.

   TIP

   If your police department still is reluctant to file a report, contact your state's attorney general's office (you can find contact info at `www.naag.org`) for assistance.

Alerting the post office

Many identity theft cases result from unauthorized and illegal access to information via the U.S. mail. Tampering with the mail is a federal crime. If you're a victim of identity theft and think that your mail may have played a role, contact the U.S. Postal Inspection Service and report your concerns. Call 877-876-2455 or report it by going to `www.uspis.gov/report` and clicking Identity Theft.

Protecting your identity through the FACT Act

The Fair and Accurate Credit Transactions Act (the FACT Act or FACTA) has numerous provisions for businesses, credit bureaus, and you. An entire book could be written on the topic, but in essence, the FACT Act was designed to bolster the Fair Credit Reporting Act (FCRA) and address issues surrounding incomplete or inaccurate credit reporting, including new safeguards for identity theft. It creates benefits for consumers and requires anyone making credit decisions about you to tell you the information they relied upon when making their decision. This safeguard enables you to determine whether there is erroneous information that needs to be disputed or corrected.

TIP

For more information on the FCRA and the FACT Act, go to `www.congress.gov/108/plaws/publ159/PLAW-108publ159.pdf` for a copy of the full act.

The following highlights the consumer-oriented, identity theft–related provisions of the act that are most informative or useful:

- You're entitled to at least one free credit report each year from each of the three credit bureaus. Currently, the three bureaus are offering a free look at your credit reports every week if you like. You can often get additional reports if you file a fraud alert (see the next section) or an active-duty alert. Specialty reporting agencies, such as insurance and landlord reporting services, must also give you a free report if you ask.
- Information based on an account that you've reported as fraudulent or that you've shown to be inaccurate or incomplete cannot be reported to a bureau.
- Businesses must cooperate with you to help clear your name in the event of identity theft. They must provide copies of records about goods or services that they provided to the thief. Businesses may require a police report and may take up to 30 days to comply.
- You may place a 12-month fraud alert, a 7-year extended fraud alert, and a 1-year military active-duty alert on your credit file. We recommend that you also freeze your reports until you feel all the issues have been handled successfully. For more information on placing fraud alerts on your credit file, check out the following resources:
  - **Information on active duty alerts from the FTC:** `www.consumer.ftc.gov/articles/0273-active-duty-alerts`
  - **Fraud and active duty alerts from Equifax:** `www.equifax.com/personal/credit-report-services/credit-fraud-alerts`
  - **Identity theft help from Experian:** `www.experian.com/help/identity-theft-victim-assistance.html`
  - **Fraud alert information from Experian:** `www.experian.com/fraud/center.html`
  - **Fraud alert information from TransUnion:** `www.transunion.com/fraud-alerts`
- You may block or ask that any fraudulent trade lines be suppressed on your credit report if you reported the crime to a police department or law enforcement agency. (See the later section "Blocking fraudulent credit lines.")
- You may request that your Social Security number be truncated (shortened) on your credit report and communications in case it falls into the wrong hands. And credit report users can't just throw your used reports into the trash. They have to dispose of the reports in a legally sanctioned manner.
- Businesses must truncate your credit card number on credit card receipts. In other words, your restaurant receipt shouldn't show your entire credit card number — just the last four or five digits.

Sending out a fraud alert

As we mention earlier in this chapter, contacting the credit bureaus is one of the first steps you should take when you discover an identity theft. When you contact them, you have the opportunity to place a fraud alert and a victim's statement in your file. These two items indicate to those who view your report that the request for credit they received recently may not actually be from you. The creditor should contact you before approving a subsequent request for a new account or a change to an existing account.

REMEMBER

A fraud alert is placed on your account for one year. Any new activity, including your own, is researched and reported to you. So if you open new credit lines during this time, you may notice a slower-than-normal approval process. It's worth the extra red tape to ensure that you and your identity are protected.

If you aren't sure whether your identity has been stolen but you know that the information necessary to steal it has been compromised, consider an initial fraud alert. When you're sure of the theft, file an *extended alert* on your credit report. An extended alert lasts seven years. Why use an extended alert? Say that your hospital's network is hacked, and the hacker gets access to patients' Social Security numbers, birthdates, and credit information. The thief may not sell or use your information right away; he may save it for future use. The extended alert covers a long enough period to prevent the information from being used to open an account, say, next year.

An extended alert can be a bit of a nuisance. After you place an extended alert on your credit file, potential creditors are required to contact you, or meet with you in person, before they issue new credit in your name. Still, an extended alert warns you of any suspicious activity even after you've forgotten about the original event that triggered you to establish the alert in the first place.

TIP

A small silver lining: After you put an extended fraud alert on your file, you're entitled to two more free copies of your credit report from all three bureaus at any time during the next 12 months.

Blocking fraudulent credit lines

"Block that line" may sound like a football cheer, but blocking can be a powerful tool. Be sure to request that the bureaus block (suppress data on) any lines of credit that you believe are fraudulent. You'll have to provide information about the account you want blocked and a copy of your valid police report or state-approved identity theft form. This prevents those accounts from being sold, transferred, or placed for collection. In addition, ask the credit bureaus to remove any inquiries on your record as a result of those fraudulent lines. Those inquiries can hurt your credit score.

Finally, ask the credit bureaus to notify anyone who may have received reports over the last six months with the erroneous information and inquiries on them. Doing so helps alert creditors and other interested parties to the situation — and can save your reputation.

Getting and Using Credit after Identity Theft

As with any theft, break-in, or personal attack, as a victim of identity theft you likely feel traumatized, fearful, and angry. You may want to avoid any experience with credit and borrowing in the future.

But recognize these feelings for what they are — feelings — and do not give up altogether. After all, credit — though it certainly can be abused and exploited — is a powerful and sometimes indispensable tool that can help you achieve personal and financial goals that you may not be able to achieve otherwise. We strongly suggest that you adopt a strong offense and move forward with your personal goals. Whether you're planning to buy a house or a car or you're simply taking advantage of a retailer's offer for 10 percent off with a new credit account, don't be afraid to use credit to your advantage. This section outlines some steps that you can take to get your credit going again without putting yourself at renewed risk for identity theft.

SAFEGUARDING YOUR IDENTITY AFTER IDENTITY THEFT

Here are some tips for steps to take after identity theft:

- Beef up your online protection for shopping, banking, and credit card transactions.
- Get copies of your credit reports, review them, correct any errors, and then freeze them.
- Use a unique username and password to access each of your online accounts.
- Enable multifactor authentication.

(continued)

(continued)

- Enable *biometric authentication* (facial recognition or fingerprint) to access your accounts if offered.
- If possible, set up unique security questions where only you would know the answer.
- Add a unique PIN code or passcode (different than the last four digits of your Social Security number) for your bank account that must be given in order to speak with a representative. Store the PIN or passcode in a secure place if you can't remember it.
- Ensure that any documents with your full debit or credit card number are stored in a locked, fireproof safe or shredded with a cross-cut shredder.
- Only use your debit or credit card on known, secure websites or at trusted establishments.
- When swiping your card in a card reader, particularly at gas stations and ATMs, ensure the card reader is secure. If you aren't sure, go inside to swipe your card. Inspect the card reader and surrounding area. Look for a loose or bulging card slot, mismatched colors or materials, or a damaged security tape or seal.

Closing and reopening your accounts

Whether your accounts were broken into, stolen, or just sniffed at, change all your user IDs, passwords, and account numbers. Unfortunately, fraudsters have had success in accessing information like this over the years. In many cases, your account may need to be closed and reopened, and your cards or account numbers may need to be reissued. Doing so may be a hassle, but if you've been a victim of identity theft, you already know the meaning of *hassle*.

Here's a list of which accounts may need to be reissued:

- **Bank accounts:** When your information is compromised, you never know if or when trouble will pop up. Changing the account numbers results in dead ends for a thief. Place alerts on your accounts so that you're informed when transactions occur. This can be helpful so that any transaction that may be created or authorized will trigger an alert to you and you can contact the creditor immediately.
- **Credit card accounts:** When you contact the card companies, they'll ask you for proper identification. (This is good — you *want* them to be suspicious!) They're used to closing accounts and reopening new ones quickly and painlessly. You should reopen only those accounts that you use. If you haven't used a card in two years, you may begin to wonder why it's taking up space in your wallet or sock drawer.

» **Other accounts:** Contact your Internet service provider, telephone service provider, and utility companies to alert them of the identity theft and to get new account numbers.

Virtually all financial institutions are pretty good at dealing with this issue today and have processes in place to monitor activity with a heightened sensitivity.

Altering your PINs and passwords

When you reopen your bank accounts, change your personal identification numbers (PINs), too. And when you access money at ATMs or in public places, make sure that no one can see you enter the PIN. Getting close to the machine may block the sight of someone across the street using binoculars or a camera with a telephoto lens. (Yes, thieves really *do* go that far.)

In the United States, most credit cards have been converted to chip cards, a small square component of technology on the card that increases its security and technology that enables you to make a charge by tapping your card (a contactless transaction) on a reader rather than swiping it or inserting it into the reader. The adoption of mobile wallets, such as Apple Pay and Google Pay, has yielded additional security features. This method enables you to keep your accounts on your phone and use the contactless feature of your mobile wallet.

TIP

For online access to bank, credit card, bill-paying, and investment accounts, switch to a *pass phrase* instead of a password. A pass phrase uses a short series of words like *Smokey-is-a-cut1e* instead of a single password. Pass phrases tend to be longer and harder to crack. Include some capital letters, numbers, and nonletter characters for additional strength. A password manager such as Bitwarden (`https://bitwarden.com`) can add security by remembering all your very long unique passwords for you.

Changing your Social Security number and driver's license number

If you can't seem to shake the damage done by identity theft (because new occurrences keep popping up or collectors keep landing on you like mosquitoes), you may need to take more serious action. Consider contacting the Social Security Administration to inquire about getting a new Social Security number.

WARNING

Getting a new Social Security number is a huge pain for everyone. Imagine all the places you've used your old number. If you go this route, you need to change all your records yourself. For more information, visit the Social Security website at `www.socialsecurity.gov` or call 800-772-1213 (800-325-0778 TTY for the hearing impaired). They also refer online reports of identity theft to `www.identitytheft.gov`, which enables you to report the identity theft and get a recovery plan.

You won't be the first person who had to take this step. Besides the storied federal witness protection program, Social Security numbers are changed for domestic violence victims and others when warranted. But with all the emphasis on national security, changing your number isn't easy.

A few circumstances can prevent you from changing your Social Security number. You can't get a new Social Security number if:

- You've filed for bankruptcy.
- You intend to avoid the law or your legal responsibility.
- Your Social Security card is lost or stolen, but there's no evidence that someone else is using your number.

REMEMBER

Be sure to document everything. This dog can have a very long tail. You may need to dig up documentation a year or two after you thought all the dust had settled. Good written records, with names and dates, are a godsend.

While you're at it, go to the Department of Motor Vehicles and get your driver's license number changed, especially if someone is using yours as an ID.

IN THIS CHAPTER

» Establishing the pros and cons of bankruptcy

» Discovering the eligibility requirements for filing bankruptcy

» Understanding the process of filing for bankruptcy

» Rebuilding your credit after bankruptcy

Chapter 5
Considering Bankruptcy

Bankruptcy used to be easy. You decided that you were so far in over your head in debt that you had no hope of digging out, and you went to see an attorney, who made your debts disappear. In 2005, new and more restrictive bankruptcy laws were enacted to reduce the significant losses and abuse of the old bankruptcy system. Although the bankruptcy laws changed, the option to file bankruptcy is still available, if needed, and its use is on the rise again. What hasn't changed, however, is our firm opinion that bankruptcy should be your last resort.

Still, bankruptcy can be a cure for over-indebtedness that threatens to deprive you and your family of the hope for a prosperous financial future. A fresh start is the intent of the law, and, when done correctly and for the right reasons, that's exactly what you get. Either way, you have to decide whether the hit to your credit for cleaning up your finances is worth it.

With credit playing an increasingly important role in most Americans' financial lives, understanding the damage a bankruptcy will do to your future is essential. But how do you know whether bankruptcy is right for your situation? How do you know which type or chapter of bankruptcy you qualify for and which bills you'll still be responsible for after you file?

This chapter gives you an accurate and unbiased picture of how bankruptcy law works, helping you figure out whether bankruptcy makes sense, which type of bankruptcy is best for your situation, and how to minimize a bankruptcy's effects on your credit. Sometimes people go into bankruptcy without a full understanding of the consequences or they file for the wrong reasons; instead of providing them with a fresh start, it places them in situations that impact their lives more and for longer than anticipated. However, this chapter can help you see past the legal fine print and consider what may be the most important financial decision you make in the next seven to ten years.

Deciding Whether Bankruptcy Makes Sense for You

WARNING

Declaring bankruptcy is a big decision that affects your life, your self-esteem, and your confidence for seven to ten years or even longer. It creates a condition that redefines your credit report, lowers your credit score, and may also cause issues for future credit and employment.

Both financial and quality-of-life components may factor into your decision to file for bankruptcy. The benefits gained may outweigh the damage to your credit. If your wages are about to be garnished because of your inability to pay a bill — perhaps a totally unexpected medical bill — do you allow your family to suffer the financial consequences for years, or seemingly forever? More than half of those who file bankruptcy have large uninsured or underinsured medical expenses. In other words, bankruptcy is a major life event, so you want to consider it very seriously. Don't get us wrong — bankruptcy may absolutely just be the best choice if you've suffered some serious financial setbacks. Before rushing into the decision to file, we strongly advise you to invest time in carefully weighing all your options before you take the plunge.

Deliberating the bankruptcy decision

When facing this decision, you may already be feeling more pressure than you thought you could bear, but it's a great time to take a step back and evaluate your situation. Can you do anything more to help meet your obligations? Is there any hope of finding a solution that's acceptable to both you and your creditors? If you answered no to both questions, you're on the right track in considering bankruptcy. That being said, have an objective third-party professional evaluate the situation.

Before you make the final decision, review the points in the following sections.

Be sure that bankruptcy will actually solve your financial crisis

Getting rid of all your debts and making those annoying collection calls go away may solve your current problems, but if the real problem is too much spending and not enough income, declaring bankruptcy will just be a short-term fix with long-term consequences. Likewise, bankruptcy won't help if you've been using credit to supplement your income for basic living expenses. More significant behavioral changes will be required.

Understand the consequences of your decision on your near-term goals

Ask yourself how this decision will affect your chances of buying a home, getting married or divorced, or getting a job. Think about your goals for the next ten years, and understand the impact that a bankruptcy would have on those goals. Bankruptcy is a big step, and its consequences may affect you for years to come. Don't make the decision based only on immediate events without considering the future impacts, because that would be a mistake.

Consider all your options

Make a list of other ways to deal with your debts. Can you increase your income? Reduce your expenses? Stretch out your payments? Sell some possessions to pay your bills until your situation improves?

TIP

Find good resources in your community to help you evaluate all your options, such as Legal Aid (`www.lsc.gov/what-legal-aid/find-legal-aid`), the National Foundation for Credit Counseling (`www.nfcc.org`), 995Hope (`https://995hope.org`), and Money Management International (`www.moneymanagement.org/bankruptcy-counseling/faq`).

Talk to a good credit counselor

You are required to meet with a credit counselor within six months of filing for bankruptcy even if you've met with one before. Expect this visit to give you options; an analysis of your spending and income, including a written budget; and an action plan. This consultation goes a long way toward answering the question of whether bankruptcy will help you. See Chapter 3 in Book 3 for more on credit counselors.

Get a professional legal opinion

Find a lawyer who has a great deal of experience in bankruptcy law. Find out whether you qualify for bankruptcy and, if so, which chapter. Make sure you understand what bankruptcy can and can't do for you. Ask about alternatives, including settlements and statutes of limitations. Also ask about the pros and cons of filing for bankruptcy on your own. Called *pro se*, the law allows you to represent yourself, and in some courts with sympathetic judges, doing so can be a money-saver. (In other courts, it can be a disaster.) An experienced lawyer is the best person to guide you here.

Friends, family, or close coworkers who had a satisfying experience with an attorney are good sources of referrals. Often even one of their attorneys has a connection to a good bankruptcy attorney. We're not suggesting that you shout from the rooftop or blast it on social media, but someone who has already experienced the bankruptcy process may be a good referral source.

TIP

Online resources can also be helpful, but make sure you look for good, credible resources. Here are a few that you may want to check out:

- National Association of Consumer Bankruptcy Attorneys (`www.nacba.org`)
- `Lawyers.com` (`www.lawyers.com`)
- American Bankruptcy Institute (`https://bankruptcyresources.org`)

If you used a lawyer to handle other issues, ask for a referral to someone who specializes in bankruptcy. Don't use your cousin, the real estate lawyer. Get a pro. You have to live with any mistakes made here for years.

Talk to your creditors

If you're considering a bankruptcy, let your lenders know and ask if they can offer you a repayment plan. Keep in mind that you have to be able to afford this plan. Don't expect too much, but talking to your creditors is always worth a shot.

Consider the requirements of the current bankruptcy laws

Here's a brief summary of the most impactful provisions that may help you decide whether a bankruptcy is worth pursuing in your situation (for details on how to qualify for Chapter 7 and Chapter 13 bankruptcies, see the later section "Qualifying and Filing for Bankruptcy"):

- **Passing a means test is required to be eligible for Chapter 7.** Except in limited circumstances, your net income has to be below the median income in your state of residence to file for liquidation of your debts in a Chapter 7.

» **You're required to get credit counseling from an "approved nonprofit budget and credit counseling agency" before you can file.** The Executive Office of the U.S. Trustee provides a master list of approved agencies from which you may choose. You can find out who's on the list by contacting the clerk of the court where your bankruptcy is to be filed, either by going to the U.S. Department of Justice website (`www.justice.gov/ust/eo/bapcpa/ccde/cc_approved.htm`) or by talking to your attorney. Counseling may be offered by phone, online, or in person.

» **After you file, you must complete a course in financial management before you're discharged from bankruptcy.** You may contact the same provider for this requirement as for the credit counseling requirement, or you can use a different provider. You can find a list of approved providers at `www.justice.gov/ust/eo/bapcpa/ccde/de_approved.htm`.

» **You're limited in what you can buy immediately before filing.** Having made the decision to file, you're prevented from going out and spending up a storm or taking out cash advances and then not having to pay. Generally, the limits apply to the 90 days preceding your filing.

» **You have to wait a long time after getting a discharge for bankruptcy before you can get another one.** The law requires eight years between Chapter 7 bankruptcy discharges, two years between Chapter 13 bankruptcies, six years between a Chapter 13 and a Chapter 7, and four years between a Chapter 7 and a Chapter 13.

» **Your *homestead exemption* (how much equity in your home you can keep out of your filing and keep for yourself) is limited by state law.** In addition, if you acquired your home less than 40 months before filing, you're allowed a maximum exemption of $200,000 as of April 2025, regardless of your state's exemption allowance. Check for updates to this number as it adjusts from time to time.

» **Under Chapter 13 bankruptcy, you're allowed to spend only what the IRS guidelines allow.** The rest of your disposable income must be included in the plan, and every year you have to document your income and expenses to see whether you can pay more (or less).

» **Your attorney must certify that what you say in the documents you submit to the court is true.** The truth, the whole truth, and nothing but the truth.

» **You still may owe some past and future debts.** These debts include taxes (incurred in the last three years, unfiled, or filed late), domestic support, restitution and fines for drunk-driving injuries and other criminal offenses, and student loans. Courts are extremely reluctant to discharge student loans, and the general policy is not to discharge them. Rarely, some older student loans can be discharged; if an "undue" hardship condition exists, you file a separate motion with the bankruptcy court and then appear before a judge to explain your hardship.

- **Domestic-support obligations are a priority debt that you must pay.** A *priority debt* takes precedence over other debt payments you owe and is paid completely. However, the *bankruptcy trustee* (the person appointed by the court to administer your Chapter 13 plan) gets administrative fees before any money goes to any other creditor or person.
- **You may be evicted if you don't pay your rent after you've filed for bankruptcy.** Bankruptcy creates a time stamp on the debts that you have up to that date. New debts or defaults on new or ongoing credit obligations after filing bankruptcy are not included.
- **You must provide your most recent tax return to your creditors if they ask for it.** Before you can finalize your bankruptcy, you need to give your creditors information about your financial status so they can see that you can't afford to pay what you owe. If you're filing for Chapter 13, you must provide your tax returns for the last four years.

Find a small circle of people who care about you

Although these people may not be professionals, they know you and may offer important perspectives. You don't have to agree with them, but their guidance may be helpful. Avoid visiting with someone who would be personally affected by your choice (such as a person you owe money to, someone who owes you money, or a dependent).

Be intentional

REMEMBER

Given your current financial state, will your mindset allow you to use bankruptcy as a fresh start? Consider your goals; weigh the options offered by your creditors, your credit counselor, and your lawyer; and consider the advice of others who care about you. Now you're ready to decide what's best for your future and your peace of mind. Whatever you decide to do, make sure it's the best decision you can make based upon the information that you have. If you don't like what you see, go through the process until you do, and then do what you think is in your best interest. Don't wait too long to make a decision, though. Sometimes the hardest decision may be the best one.

Adding up the pluses and minuses

Like anything in life, bankruptcy is neither all good nor all bad. The following sections explain the benefits of bankruptcy, as well as the harsh reality of bankruptcy's consequences.

The silver lining of filing bankruptcy

Here are some of the positives that bankruptcy can do for you:

- **You get a fresh start.** The collection activity stops. The fees and penalty rates stop. In fact, in a Chapter 7 bankruptcy, virtually all your debts may go away. Without the ability to put a stop to the madness of credit gone awry, some people would never — and we mean *never* — be able to live a normal life again. Bankruptcy can enable that to happen.
- **You get credit education.** The bankruptcy law says that anyone who files is required to get some credit education. This is an opportunity to look back at what happened and reset your financial and credit course going forward. If you take full advantage of this opportunity, you'll walk away with a much better sense of how to manage your financial life, which means that you'll be less likely to end up back where you started.

The darker side of filing bankruptcy

As you can probably guess, filing bankruptcy may create some pretty heavy consequences, too. Here are the major ones:

- **You may still owe money.** Bankruptcy may not wipe out *all* your debt. Some debts don't go away, even though you'd like them to, and you must pay them in full. The debts that typically don't disappear are
  - Federal, state, and local taxes
  - Child support
  - Alimony
  - Student loans (except in very limited circumstances)
  - Money owed as a result of drunk driving and other criminal offenses, such as willful injury or damage to people and property
- **Your credit score will be affected for years.** Bankruptcy is a major negative on your credit report that appears as a public record in your file as well as in your account history for up to ten years. Worse, it causes your credit score to stay depressed longer than a normal delinquency does. Good credit can plunge by 200 points. Declare bankruptcy and you're likely to see your score drop to the lowest 20 percent of all credit scores. Ouch!
- **Borrowing money becomes more difficult.** When lenders see a score in the lowest percentile, your interest rates and terms escalate. In a tight credit market, lenders may decline to give you credit at any price.

WARNING

Some lenders, however, specialize in loaning to people with bad credit. They're delighted to see you; the fact that you've just gone bankrupt is a big plus in their eyes. Why? Because under the law, you can't file a Chapter 7 bankruptcy again for eight long years. So, although lenders get to charge you high interest rates as a risky borrower, you can't avoid repaying them by playing the bankruptcy card. If you fall behind, you can run, but you can't hide. These lenders are very good at collecting overdue accounts. The bottom line: Avoid these lenders at all costs. If you must borrow shortly after a bankruptcy, use a reputable lender.

- **Renting an apartment may become more complicated.** Many landlords use credit reports to approve tenant applicants. They may refuse to rent to you, require a cosigner, or demand a larger deposit if they see a bankruptcy.
- **Insurance costs may rise.** A bankruptcy may cost you more in insurance premiums, particularly for homeowner's and auto insurance. The insurance mavens and their actuarial elves love credit reports. All those dispassionate numbers lend themselves to justifying rate increases much more than real claims do. So even if you have no claims, expect your premiums to go up. Some states don't allow credit to be a factor in setting rates, but many do.
- **Employment searches may be more difficult.** There have been some changes in employers utilizing credit reports over the years with recent health and privacy concerns, but many employers still do credit or financial checks on candidates. If you're job hunting, ask questions during the interview to understand the process. As a practical matter, some licenses won't be given to people who've filed for bankruptcy, and security clearances can be denied.
- **Your self-image and confidence may suffer.** Bankruptcy can take its toll, because like it or not, a great deal of the way many people view themselves is wrapped up in their financial persona. Most people think of themselves as responsible adults, and they've been taught that responsible adults pay their bills and keep their promises. Even though you know that filing for bankruptcy is okay and that you have no choice in the matter, you may find that you have an unexpected internal conflict to deal with.

Considering a debt management plan first

One of the stops you're required to make on the road to getting help from the bankruptcy courts is a credit counseling agency. The court recognizes the value of the work done by these agencies by requiring that a court-approved agency review your financial circumstances (*before* you file). The idea is that you'll get an unbiased assessment of your financial condition and that you may, upon reflection, find other alternatives to handle your debt.

Understanding what a debt management plan is

One of the services provided by the credit counseling industry is the debt management plan. You begin with an individually tailored spending plan that you create with the help of a credit counselor. A *debt management plan* uses the equivalent of your disposable income after actual expenses and reallocates some or all of your income to pay your creditors. Many creditors require that you be able to pay off the balance in a hypothetical 72 months to allow the account to be placed under a debt management plan. The average plan is set up for three to five years but in practice may be completed in about two years. (For more on debt management plans, turn to Chapter 3 in Book 3.)

Seeing how a debt management plan differs from bankruptcy

Under a debt management plan, the money left (if any) after you pay your living expenses and your creditors is yours to use as you see fit. If you file Chapter 13 bankruptcy, however, all your disposable income goes toward paying off your creditors. The amount you get to use for living expenses with minor adjustments comes from less-than-generous IRS guidelines.

Unlike the terms of a Chapter 7 or a Chapter 13 bankruptcy, a debt management plan is a voluntary arrangement between you and your creditors, by using the credit counseling agency as an intermediary. You can walk away from a debt management plan at any time and still file for bankruptcy. Or, if you're on the receiving end of a windfall, you can pay off your creditors and be done with it.

Of course, your creditors don't have to accept the terms of the debt management plan, whereas they *have* to accept a court-ordered repayment plan if you file bankruptcy. That said, most creditors do accept debt management plans because they know that you'll be off to the courthouse to file bankruptcy if they say no. Additionally, if a creditor refuses to negotiate with a credit counselor, the court can order that the uncooperative creditor's debt get a 20-percent haircut.

REMEMBER

Whereas a Chapter 7 bankruptcy liquidates many debts, a Chapter 13 bankruptcy forces creditors to accept a lower payment over a set period that may not cover all that you originally owed. The difference between what you owe and what you pay under Chapter 13 is what the creditors lose. They also can't charge interest or fees under Chapter 13. A debt management plan allows the creditors to collect interest charges, although many creditors reduce the rate to one that's more affordable and reflects your circumstances and your desire to repay the debt.

Perhaps one of the biggest differences between a Chapter 7 or Chapter 13 bankruptcy and a debt management plan is the effect on your credit score.

- Bankruptcy has a large negative impact on your score, which affects your ability to do lots of the things we mention earlier in this chapter for years after the *end* of your bankruptcy.
- A debt management plan, on the other hand, doesn't have the same negative impact on your credit score. In fact, many creditors don't report to the credit bureaus that your account is being handled by a credit counseling agency. Those that do report it to the bureaus report it as a description of the account (for example, credit card, real estate mortgage, or credit counseling), not as a payment history item (such as "pays as agreed" or "X days late"). Payment history items are included in calculating your credit score, but account descriptions are not. Further, your credit report shows the credit counseling account description only until you pay off the account or decide to discontinue the plan, at which point the notation is removed.

More good news: Even while you're enrolled in a debt management plan, the FICO scoring system doesn't subtract any points. That's right — your credit score isn't affected just by being in a plan. A credit counseling notation on your file is perceived as neutral, not a negative or public-record item.

REMEMBER

If you decide to try the debt management-plan route rather than a Chapter 13 and the debt management plan doesn't work out for you, you can always file for bankruptcy without a waiting period. We suggest that when you get your mandatory counseling on the road to bankruptcy, you explore making a debt management plan work for you. You, your credit, and your score may be glad you did.

Understanding Bankruptcy, Chapter and Verse

Filing for bankruptcy is a very serious decision for which you need to be armed with all the information you can find. Why? Because for all the problems a bankruptcy solves, it can create many more if you make a mistake. As with many laws, bankruptcy laws may seem like a secret code. Besides being long and written in legalese, these laws contain mysterious chapters with numbers — 7, 11, 12, and 13 — rather than names. What do the chapters really mean, and which one is right for you? That's what this section is all about.

In basic terms, the reason for filing bankruptcy is to seek the protection of the court from your creditors. It's that simple. If you can't pay what you owe on your own, now or in the foreseeable future, call in the judge, and the judge will handle your collectors.

The courts allow many different types of bankruptcy, identified as chapters with numbers. The variety of options reflects the variety of solutions needed for different situations. One size doesn't fit all. A farmer's problems and needs differ significantly from a corporation's. A Chapter 12 bankruptcy, for example, enables farmers to reorganize their debt and keep their farms. Meanwhile, a Chapter 11 bankruptcy provides for reorganization, usually by a corporation, to keep a business running and repay creditors over time.

REMEMBER

Among all the various chapters, two are most commonly used by consumers who find themselves unable to come to agreement with or to meet contractual payments with their creditors:

- **Chapter 7:** Also known as *liquidation,* this is the most popular form of bankruptcy. It may require you to give up some assets (the liquidation part), but it gets you out of almost all your liabilities.
- **Chapter 13:** Often referred to as *wage-earner bankruptcy,* this form of bankruptcy allows you to keep most of your assets and pay back what the judge rules you can afford over a period of time, usually three to five years, under court supervision and protection.

Regardless of which chapter you file, our final advice is to make sure that bankruptcy will truly solve your problems — the problems you have today, the problems you'll have tomorrow, and the complications of dealing with the financial, employment, and insurance systems in the future.

Qualifying and Filing for Bankruptcy

After reviewing the previous sections, you may determine that bankruptcy is the best or only viable solution for your financial situation. But you still need to see whether you qualify for bankruptcy. Both Chapter 7 and Chapter 13 bankruptcies have eligibility requirements, which are covered in the following sections.

TIP

For a look at the rules, refer to the bankruptcy code filing procedures chart at `www.dummies.com/go/creditrepairkitfd6e`.

Qualifying for Chapter 7

If qualified, under a Chapter 7, you receive relief from virtually all your debts, with a few exceptions, and you get it fast — like the same day (unlike a Chapter 13, which may take up to five years before you get a discharge).

Passing the means test

The first hurdle in moving forward with Chapter 7 bankruptcy is meeting the means test (www.justice.gov/ust/means-testing). If you have too many means (that is, too much money), you can't declare Chapter 7. And the courts won't take your word for it; you have to prove that your income really is what you say it is. If your income over the last six months is above the applicable median for your state of residence, you can't file for Chapter 7. The amounts allowed are updated annually.

TIP

See www.legalconsumer.com/bankruptcy/means-test for a good means-test calculator, which includes the latest revised means test forms.

If your income is above your state's median, don't give up just yet. Next, you want to determine whether you have excess monthly income of more than $166.66 to pay $10,000 of debt over five years. So what counts as excess income? To find out, you have to use the spending guidelines approved by the IRS. Allowable expenses are shown at www.justice.gov/ust/eo/bapcpa/20200501/bci_data/median_income_table.htm. An updated chart with the allowable expenses for each state can be found under the heading "Median Family Income Based on State/Territory and Family Size." The IRS guidelines may be very tight for you.

Using the IRS allowable expenses as a guide, if you *fail* the means test, the best you can do is to file under Chapter 13.

If you have less excess monthly income than the magic number of $166.66 after IRS expense allowances, you may proceed to the next hurdle: Do you have excess income that, over the next 60 months, will account for at least 25 percent of your debt? If the answer is no, you can pass go and file for Chapter 7. If not, you likely go directly to Chapter 13.

TIP

Tithing — giving money to your church — is allowed in both Chapter 7 and Chapter 13 bankruptcies. You may donate up to 15 percent of your gross income and have it count as an expense that may lower your income. Donating to your church may just help you make the numbers work to become eligible for a Chapter 7 rather than a Chapter 13.

Receiving required counseling

At some point during the six months before you file for bankruptcy, you have to receive counseling and get a certificate from a court-approved nonprofit credit counselor. The counselor may file the certificate directly with the court on your behalf.

TIP

The Office of the U.S. Trustee has a website (`www.justice.gov/ust/credit-counseling-debtor-education-information`) that lists approved agencies.

Credit counseling costs are on a sliding fee scale. They are free if your income is below 150 percent of the poverty level for your family size. Otherwise, up to $50 is considered reasonable. Credit counseling and debtor education services are now widely available online and often offer flexible scheduling options, making this hurdle easier to clear for filers.

REMEMBER

Just because the court has approved the counseling agency doesn't make it the right one for you, so exercise caution when selecting. (See Chapter 3 in Book 3 for guidance in choosing a credit counselor.) You want someone who has a good track record and has electronic-certificate-issuing capability. Why? Because if the counselor makes a mistake or the certificate is delayed in getting to you, or you lose it, you could face costly delays in getting this matter successfully concluded.

Qualifying for Chapter 13

The strict guidelines to qualify for filing a Chapter 7 bankruptcy mean that some people qualify only to file Chapter 13. The requirements for counseling and proof of income are the same for both types of bankruptcy. Although you must take the same means test, the outcome leads to different results.

Chapter 13 differs from Chapter 7 in that, after establishing your income and deducting allowable expenses, you must use the remainder of your excess monthly income to repay your debt. *Excess* is defined by subtracting the IRS allowable expenses from your income (see the earlier section "Passing the means test").

Just as with Chapter 7, those filing for Chapter 13 bankruptcy must establish that their family income is either below or above the median for their state. If your total income is above the state median, your excess income gets disposed of (paid to your bankruptcy trustee, who forwards it to your creditors) for the next five years, unless you can show that you can pay off 100 percent of the debt in less than 60 months. If your total income is below the state median, your excess income may be paid to your creditors over the next three years. The rest of the debt that you owe to your creditors goes unpaid, and no interest accrues on any of the accounts involved. You also want to understand any tax implications as creditors forgive that debt.

TIP

If you file for Chapter 13 bankruptcy, the court requires full disclosure of all debts, not just what appears on your credit report. So, even medical debt that has been removed from your credit report must be listed in your bankruptcy schedule. Failing to list medical debt, or any other unsecured debt, can cause problems, including dismissal or non-dischargeability of those debts.

REMEMBER

The current bankruptcy law is intended to require those who can afford to make payments toward their debt to do so.

FILING, THEN BACKING OUT

If you decide that bankruptcy isn't for you *after* you file your court papers, you can ask the court to dismiss your case before you get your discharge. For example, say you file a Chapter 7 and then find out that you have to give back that 3-carat diamond ring you gave your sweetie recently. Or in the case of a Chapter 13, maybe you've been making payments and eating peanut butter for a month and can't go on. Or, looking on the bright side, perhaps you get a windfall inheritance from a rich uncle and can pay off the Chapter 13 in one fell swoop.

No matter what the reason, you can call the whole thing off and get a dismissal. Keep in mind, however, that the credit-reporting bureaus pick up the record of your bankruptcy filing and report it, even if you stop the process without getting out of any debts. The bureaus must report that the filing was dismissed, but the record of your filing a bankruptcy stays on your credit report and continues to lower your score for the remainder of the reporting period (up to ten years). Both you and your creditors have the same rights and remedies as you had before you filed your bankruptcy case.

If you ask for a dismissal, you won't be the first to do so. In fact, the law has a specific section that deals with people who not only change their minds but also change them back again. Perhaps after you back out of the bankruptcy to save the diamond ring, your creditors turn up the collection heat to the point where you'd gladly give them the ring and your grandfather's watch if they'd just leave you alone.

Here's how the change works the second time around: In your first filing, after you file the paperwork with the courts, you receive an automatic *stay* (or suspension) of collection activity on the part of your creditors. The length of time for the collection stay can vary depending on the type of debt or action pending, but generally it's in place until you discharge your debts (that is, get rid of them). But if you change your mind, ask for a dismissal, and then change your mind and refile a second time within one year of the original filing, the automatic stay (the stopping of all collection activity) is for only 30 days. So you have to get all your testing, counseling, and paperwork done in the 30-day period or the collectors and foreclosers return in force. If this is your third such filing in a year, you don't get *any* stay unless the court orders it.

In other words, when you file for bankruptcy, do your best to make sure that it's a decision you can live with for the long haul.

When you're comfortable that filing bankruptcy is what you want to do, you can stop all collection activity by telling your creditors and/or collectors of your intent. Go to `www.dummies.com/go/creditrepairkitfd6e` for a sample notification letter declaring your intent to file bankruptcy.

Managing Your Credit after a Bankruptcy

Declaring bankruptcy is more of a hassle than it used to be, and qualifying for relief is definitely harder. But if you take the bankruptcy plunge, don't think that you're out of the woods. You still have to live with the effects of bankruptcy on your credit report and your credit score, as well as the barriers that your new status creates. You're likely to discover that bankruptcy has an impact on your insurance rates and your ability to get hired or licensed. Your bankruptcy status remains on your credit report as the mother of all credit negatives for up to ten years, and that's a long time.

So how do you get a handle on your credit future post-bankruptcy? You rebuild your credit as quickly as possible, and you use credit carefully as you go forward. This section shows you how to do so.

Telling your side of the story

Now that your credit report shows a bankruptcy and will continue to show it for a long time, expect the matter to come up periodically in a number of life's scenarios. You need to be ready with an explanation of what happened, what you did about it, and why it won't happen again. Work on a short statement that describes your valid reasons for filing for bankruptcy. Businesspeople and potential lenders who have access to your credit report want to know your reasons to help them decide whether to extend you credit or do business with you in general.

REMEMBER

This statement *isn't* the 100-word statement discussed in Chapter 3 of Book 1 that you can attach to your credit report. This is a verbal statement that you make when you're doing anything that requires other parties to review your credit report (applying for a loan, applying for a job, and so on). Be proactive and tell them about your bankruptcy before they see your credit report, but only if you're sure they'll be looking at it. (Why raise the issue if they would never know about it otherwise?)

Like the statement you use to explain why you left your last employer, a tight and targeted statement explaining your bankruptcy may be important. Whatever your circumstances were, your explanation may put a positive spin on the truth. It's short, sweet, and rehearsed. Having it at the ready enables you to convey yourself as confident, professional, and reliable.

TIP

Although it's rare for one debt to push you over the edge, a single traumatic event such as a divorce, layoff, or illness is easier for a lender, employer, or landlord to accept. Something that's beyond your control is a plus. Your efforts to pay the debts or deal with collectors are only of interest to you. All you need to convey is that you reviewed all other solutions. End the short statement with some words of wisdom, such as "I've learned a lot from this experience" or "I've become better at saving money as a result." Here's an example of a tight little speech that takes less than two minutes to share:

> When you look at my credit report, you'll see a bankruptcy there. It's not something I'm proud of, but because of an illness, I ended up with $100,000 in medical bills. I felt terrible about having to declare bankruptcy, but I had no choice. I have increased my insurance coverage and savings so that this will never happen again. I certainly learned a painful lesson, but that's all behind me now.

REMEMBER

Your speech needs to be honest and apply specifically to your unique situation.

BEWARE OF SOLICITATIONS

After you declare bankruptcy, you'll likely face a flurry of solicitations and telemarketing calls from companies that receive notices of your filing. Many businesses use bankruptcy notices as mailing lists for the high-cost credit products or scams that they sell.

Read the fine print on any solicitations, and be suspicious of a company that's eager to give you a new start. You're very vulnerable from both a personal and a financial perspective. This may be a good time to opt out of the credit bureau prescreening process and direct marketing programs that a lot of solicitors use to send you preapproved offers. If you want your name and address removed from mailing lists obtained from the main consumer credit-reporting agencies, go to `www.optoutprescreen.com` or call 888-567-8688. The Association of National Advertisers can provide information about opting out of lists produced by companies that subscribe to their mail and telephone preference services. Contact the ANA at the following address:

DMAchoice

Consumer Preferences

P.O. Box 900

Cos Cob, CT 06807

You can find out more at www.ana.net/content/show/id/thedmaorg-redirect.

Include the following information with your request:

- The date
- Your first, middle initial, and last name (including Jr., Sr., III, and so forth)
- Your current address

Check out the credit bureau sample opt-out letter at www.dummies.com/go/creditrepairkitfd6e, which is recommended by the Federal Trade Commission. Be sure to send your letter to all three credit bureaus.

It wouldn't hurt to make sure you're included in the Federal Trade Commission's National Do Not Call Registry as well: www.donotcall.gov.

Reaffirming some debt

As part of your bankruptcy rights, you can request to keep some of your debt if you can show the court that you can afford to pay it. After all that trouble to relieve yourself of the terrible burden, isn't keeping some of your debt sort of like going through a knock-down divorce and remarrying your spouse? Well, people do both, and here's why.

Believe it or not, keeping some debt (and its associated credit lines) has some benefits. This approach is technically called *reaffirmation.* For starters, having some ready credit available when you walk out of the courthouse may be a good idea. Also, a chunk of your credit score is based on longevity of accounts. Keeping an old account with a positive credit history may help you rebuild your credit score.

TIP

If you decide to keep some of your debt, make sure that you really *can* afford to pay. And more importantly, if the debt is in the form of a credit card, be sure that the terms of the card, including your original unused credit limit and interest rate, don't change because of the bankruptcy.

Repairing your credit score

Your credit score is likely to suffer dramatically from a bankruptcy. The better your score originally, the more it drops. If you had terrible credit before, a filing may not cause such a big drop. Either way, you'll likely have a very low credit score for a very long time unless you take positive action to improve it.

Here's how the factors that influence your credit score are influenced by a bankruptcy:

- **Timeliness of payments:** This category may be heavily affected, especially if yours is among the nearly one-third of all bankruptcies that happen with no prior delinquencies. After you get new credit, be sure to make all your payments on time or the full balance, every time.
- **Amount and proportion of credit used:** In a bankruptcy, you or your lenders close most of your accounts. Your available credit drops to $0 in most cases. As you reestablish credit, expect low limits at first. Try not to carry balances over 20 percent of your limit for best score improvement results.
- **Length of time you've been using credit:** Here again, your score is damaged, because the history on your open accounts stops at your filing. Negative accounts typically drop off your record in seven years, although the public bankruptcy record may remain listed for up to ten years. Positive accounts are reported for at least ten years and sometimes longer.
- **Variety of accounts:** Chances are you're left with only secured debt such as mortgages, student loans, or car loans. All your revolving and retail accounts may be gone, which means that you don't have the variety of accounts that helps boost your credit score. Consider a secured credit card or a passbook loan to restart your revolving or installment credit history.
- **Number and types of accounts you've opened recently:** After the bankruptcy, you may have more activity here than usual as you attempt to reestablish your credit. And your score will fall. (The more inquiries you create for new accounts or changes, the lower your score.) To minimize damage, don't apply for more accounts than you need.

TIP

A helpful tactic is to take steps over time to improve your credit in each of these five areas. And don't forget that creditors don't necessarily report to all three credit bureaus. Now more than ever, you want to make sure that your good creditor experiences get onto *all* your credit reports. Ask a potential creditor whether it reports all your information to all three bureaus. If it doesn't, try to get credit from another creditor that does. Also, look into nontraditional credit reporting products, such as Experian Boost, that add phone bills, utilities, and more to muscle up your credit profile.

Follow these tips to increase your credit score as much as you can in the aftermath of your bankruptcy:

- **Keep one or two of your older and lower-balance cards or lines of credit open by reaffirming them.** See the preceding section for more information.
- **Apply for a secured credit card.** This type of account uses a deposit to secure or guarantee that you will make the payments. Most report to the credit bureaus as any other credit card would, but be sure to ask the issuer whether the card you choose is reported.
- **Open a savings account, and then take out a "credit builder" loan against it to demonstrate that you can make those fixed payments on time every month.** Again, make sure that the lender reports the loan to the credit bureaus.
- **Add rent, utility, cell phone, and cable payments to your credit report using a service such as Experian Boost or Boom.**

Establishing new credit

Yes, you can probably get new credit soon after you come out of bankruptcy. In fact, establishing new lines of credit could be the first step in improving your credit score. However, make sure you aren't creating debt you can't handle if you can't pay it off each month. You'll face some challenges as you pursue new credit opportunities. For example, you'll discover that the best loans at the most attractive terms and interest rates may not be available to you. Instead, you may find that you're being pursued by loan-shark types that make Jaws look like a guppy (see the earlier sidebar "Beware of solicitations").

WARNING

Be extra careful about committing to new lines of credit, especially payday loans (see Chapter 2 in Book 3). Not only are you a target for unscrupulous lenders who specialize in post-bankruptcy loans, but also — now more than ever — you're vulnerable to slipping back into an out-of-control borrowing situation. You don't want to get trapped in debt again. New credit is okay as long as it's part of a plan to rebuild your rating, you're 100 percent confident that you can handle the payments, and it fits into your spending plan.

Moving forward with a game plan

Moving forward with a plan is very different from moving forward *without* one. Although plans may not always work out exactly as you want them to, plans give you the direction, motivation, and tools to achieve your financial ends, and they help you realize when you're drifting.

TIP

Begin by paying close attention in the post-bankruptcy education class you must attend as a springboard for your future. You may feel that this class is a waste of time, but it isn't. Then, if you didn't create a spending plan when you first went to the credit counseling agency (as you were required to do before filing for bankruptcy), work with your counselor to develop a detailed spending plan that includes saving for financial goals.

A credit counselor will work with you to craft a spending plan that not only fits your current needs but also enables you to set aside money for emergency savings and savings for those goals you want to achieve in the future. This plan tells you how much money you can comfortably spend each month and helps you make sure that you're spending only on those things that you've consciously decided to spend your money on. No impulse buying for you. That money will be allocated to other choices you make — like a college fund, a vacation fund, or a retirement account.

4

Boosting Your Income with Triple Compounding

Contents at a Glance

IN THIS CHAPTER

» Exploring different types of investment assets for triple compounding

» Understanding the importance of risk management in triple compounding

» Determining your ability, willingness, and confidence to take a risk

» Checking out different types of risks in the three triple-compounding phases

» Getting a handle on the time value of money

Chapter 1
Understanding the Basics of Triple Compounding

Gone are the days when you could go to college, get a good job, and retire comfortably on your government-backed retirement account. But there is good news: Building a comfortable retirement is now easier than ever, so it's no wonder the number of millionaires in the United States has tripled in the past decade. Nearly 6 percent of Americans now have more than $10 million net worth. The bad news is that most people are still following the old playbook, and it's failing them.

You may be wondering whether triple compounding is really the winning formula you can use to accelerate your freedom, and you also may be wondering if the results outweigh the risks. Is triple compounding a "too good to be true" buzzword, or can you implement the formula of self-made millionaires and billionaires such as Warren Buffett, Grant Cardone, and Dave Ramsey without taking more risk than you're comfortable with?

Or maybe you're excited to jump on the bandwagon, perhaps because you expect a gigantic *return* (profit) on your investment. That's basically the reward for investing. However, you can't consider return without also looking at risk. *Risk* is the uncertainty surrounding the return you generate. What may represent a high risk for one person may not be as risky for you due to everyone's unique lifestyle and financial circumstances.

This chapter explains how you can start applying the triple compounding framework to your life. You discover the different levels of risk each phase of triple compounding can expose you to and how to measure your exact risk tolerance. You also find an overview of methods you can use to increase your risk tolerance. This way, you get to decide which phase of triple compounding you can start with and manage your risk along the way as you build your triple-compounding system.

Breaking Down the Different Types of Investment Assets

REMEMBER

You can simplify triple compounding into three categories:

- **Generating:** This is income generated from exchanging your time for money.
- **Automating:** This is income generated from a *one-time* investment of time or money that continues generating automatic income indefinitely.
- **Accelerating:** This is income generated from leveraging and combining your skills, money, and time with someone else's assets.

A number of self-made millionaires and billionaires have used the triple compounding system. They have three traits in common:

- They invest in themselves to acquire a success mindset that helps them generate more income.
- They invest in an income-generating extension of themselves, such as their own business or their job, and then they automate that process of generating income. Whether you have a business that automates your income-generation process or you're an employee who can figure out a way to increase your paycheck and commissions each month, you can find a way to generate more income.

- They invest in other people's businesses and talents, whether through direct partnerships or private equity, stocks, and other financial assets.

They then compound all three to officially become a triple compounder! Triple compounders often automate all parts of their system to accelerate their profits without physically being involved.

Investing in yourself

People who want to escape the rat race and achieve financial freedom often overlook the importance of having the right mindset. However, research shows that mindset is the foundation of one's ability to generate wealth.

In fact, in his research and study of the wealthiest people alive during his time, author Napoleon Hill came to two unique conclusions:

- All self-made wealthy people have certain characteristics in common.
- None of the people were born with these characteristics!

Isn't that an amazing insight? Every successful person develops this mindset by investing in themselves. Even though Napoleon Hill and the successful people of his time are all long gone, this stands true.

TIP

All self-made wealthy people admit that they first invested in themselves to acquire the success mindset. That gave them the confidence to bet on themselves so that they could generate more income, which is the first phase of triple compounding. Chapter 2 in Book 4 explains the necessary steps to invest in yourself and develop a wealthy mindset.

Investing in your income-generating extension

The purpose of investing in financial assets such as stocks and cryptocurrency is to make your money work for you. But you can't make money you don't have work for you!

WARNING

Investing in external assets such as stocks and cryptocurrency before investing in yourself to generate income involves huge risks. When you buy stocks without actually having money you already generated, you're borrowing money to buy. Due to the volatile nature of such financial assets, investing with money you don't have can cause you to lose the little you may have and more. This reason is exactly why 96 percent of retail traders *lose* money in the stock market. Find out about different risks and how to manage them later in this chapter.

Before starting to invest in online financial markets or other people's businesses, you must make sure of two factors:

- You're generating an income.
- Your income is higher than your expenses.

Now, you may say, "I'm already working three jobs and can barely make ends meet. How can I do this without burning out even more?"

You must become *resourceful*.

TIP

You have so many temporary pursuits you can do to become resourceful and invest in yourself or in your extension. Here are some examples:

- Getting gig work, such as driving for Uber, delivering for Uber Eats or DoorDash, or doing personal shopping for Instacart or Shipt
- Babysitting
- Waiting tables or being a barista
- Writing AI prompts for ChatGPT (it can pay $30K per year as a side gig)
- Mowing your neighbor's lawn

TIP

You're not trying to find something that will become your career. You're just trying to find ways to generate more income quickly. You want to reach your ultimate goal faster, as if you're using a bridge. Chapter 3 in Book 4 outlines the five income-generating categories you can consider.

Investing in external assets

External assets are the final type of asset you need to invest in to complete your triple-compounding system. When you already invested in yourself as an asset and invested in your income-generating extensions such as your career, your business, or even side gigs as a steppingstone, you can start accelerating your triple compounding by investing in external assets. This means leveraging other people, businesses, or even governments' investment in themselves without having to be directly involved in the value creation. Here are some examples of what this can include:

- Stocks
- Crypto
- Foreign exchange (forex)
- Options
- Index funds
- Real estate
- Private equity
- Venture capital
- Insurance
- Alternative investments

Read Chapters 4 and 5 in Book 4 for information about different types of external assets you can add to your triple-compounding system.

Putting it all together: Compounding the three types of investment assets

The word *compounding* essentially means "to put together." You first invest in your most important asset: yourself. Then you do your first compounding (1X) by also investing in your income-generating endeavor. Next, you do your second compounding (2X) by investing in external assets to accelerate your financial growth. At this point, you completed the first round of three investment types, so you get to compound it by investing in yourself again (3X) to unlock your next level of financial growth.

REMEMBER

As Tony Robbins says, if you're not growing, you're dying. Similarly, if your money isn't growing, it's also dying. Triple compounding is the most complete framework to ensure that you're on the right path to reaching your fullest potential, both personally and financially.

Measuring Exactly Where You Are Now

Your current *risk tolerance* is your personal ability, willingness, and confidence to take a risk. This helps you decide exactly how much you should start with and get an idea of what type of investments you should go for so that you can invest with confidence and minimize your risk.

Although most people associate their risk tolerance only with their own personal willingness to take a risk, the truth is, there's more to the story. You can't simply assume you have a low risk tolerance because you're scared of skydiving. You also can't simply assume you have a high risk tolerance because you enjoy gambling in Las Vegas.

REMEMBER

Here are the three factors that collectively determine your real risk tolerance:

- Your *ability* to take a risk
- Your *willingness* to take a risk
- Your *confidence* in the asset you're planning to invest in

Measuring your risk tolerance is the most important and foundational step you must take before starting your triple-compounding journey.

WARNING

Not taking this step is the reason why 96 percent of traders lose money in the markets. They blindly follow the market noise without having a plan that is the exact fit for their ability and their willingness to take a risk.

TIP

You can find a free risk management toolkit to implement the steps in this chapter by attending the free Triple Compounding Masterclass at `www.triplecompounding.com`.

Calculating Your Ability to Take a Risk

Your ability to take a risk shows you your exact current financial strength minus any emotions or psychological factors.

You have different ways of calculating your financial ability so that you can basically become your own financial advisor and never have to rely on someone else for your financial statements. The following sections focus on the two most important financial numbers you need to know to get a feeling about how you're doing:

- **Your current financial snapshot:** This is what Wall Street pros call a balance sheet, but it's really just a snapshot of your current financial situation.
- **Your cash flow diary:** Wall Street pros call this the statement of income and expenses, which is actually not as intimidating as their other lingo. It tells you how much money you're making *(income)* and how much you're spending *(expenses)* over a specific period.

Summing up your assets

We get into it without going into too much geeky stuff. Get a piece of paper and write down everything that you own that can be categorized as an asset.

An *asset* is anything you own that has value — something that can make you money now or in the future. You are the most valuable asset there is. You're priceless and not up for sale. So, for this exercise, we leave you out of the equation and only focus on assets that you can put a monetary value on, including the following:

- **Cash and equivalents:** Money in your bank's savings or checking account, anything you have in money markets (which is like a financial waiting room where people and institutions park their cash temporarily while earning a little interest), and cash under your mattress (hopefully in a safe place!)
- **Investments:** Stocks, bonds, mutual funds, real estate, retirement accounts such as your 401(k), IRA, and education savings — anything that grows in value or pays you income
- **Physical assets:** Houses, land, cars (sometimes), gold, luxury handbags, watches, jewelry, furniture, boats, private jets, collectibles — items that can be sold for cash
- **Business assets:** Equipment, patents, trademarks — stuff that helps a business make money

TIP

Calculating your assets can also be an awesome family dinner discussion! Use this exercise to open the dialogue with your family in a fun way. How fun is it to go through all the stuff that you own? And you may even find things you completely forgot about that you can now use to increase your risk tolerance!

Taking note of your liabilities

After you get a general understanding of the total value of your current assets, you can move on to get a general understanding of your current liabilities — that is, everything that you *owe*.

REMEMBER

Although most people consider liabilities to be bad things, you need to know that not all debt is bad. *Good debt* is the type of leverage wealthy people use to become wealthy! Here's how to tell the difference between bad debt and good debt:

- **Bad debt:** This debt is a liability on something that doesn't make you money. It is when you go into debt to buy items such as luxury bags, a car that depreciates in value, televisions, and all the other goods people go into debt for to give the appearance of having more money than they actually do.

The goal is to avoid compounding bad debt, which is a burden on wealth.

- **Good debt:** This is known as funding or leverage. It's money you may owe to acquire an asset that grows in value. For example, your investment in this book, even if you had to leverage the bank's money to get it, is actually an asset. Because this is going to put you and your family on the trajectory of taking control of your finances and making your money work for you, your initial investment in the book will keep on compounding for years to come as you become financially free.

  The goal is to leverage funding to create wealth. Leverage is the means to get to wealth. In fact, if it wasn't for leverage, most self-made millionaires and billionaires wouldn't even have had the chance to get started.

Although good debt is indeed better than bad debt, when measuring your ability to take a risk, you must add both good and bad debt under your liabilities column.

Evaluating your net worth

REMEMBER

After you have a rough draft of your good debt and bad debt as described in the preceding section, use a calculator to add all the values of your combined assets and the value of your combined liabilities. Then you're ready to calculate your net worth, which uses this formula:

Net Worth = Total Assets – Total Liabilities

All you have to do is punch in the total value of your assets from the first column and then subtract the total value of your liabilities that you got under the second column.

Your *net worth* is your financial scorecard — a simple way to measure how much you're really worth (in money, not personality!).

This number is going to be your first clue in your capital analysis and your risk tolerance. Here's an example:

> If you own a house worth $500,000, have $50,000 in savings, and have $100,000 in investments, your assets total *$650,000*.
>
> If you also have a mortgage of $300,000, student loans of $50,000, and $10,000 in credit card debt, your liabilities total *$360,000*.
>
> $650,000 – $360,000 = $290,000
>
> Your net worth is *$290,000*.

REMEMBER

If your net worth is positive by a lot, then your ability to take a risk is higher. If it's negative by a lot, and most of your liabilities are considered bad debt, then your risk tolerance is lower. If it's break-even or somewhere in between, then your risk tolerance is somewhere in between.

REMEMBER

Measuring your net worth gives you an insight into your current financial situation at any given time. You need to recalculate your net worth at least once per year or anytime something major happens in your life, such as if you receive an inheritance, get married, or make a huge lump-sum investment such as buying a house.

Tracking your income

The next step in calculating your ability to take a risk is tracking your cash flow in a diary. To figure out the healthiness of your cash flow, you first need to identify all sources of income you receive during a specific period. Write them all down under an income column. You can go by a monthly or a yearly basis.

REMEMBER

Use the same time frame in all three columns of your cash flow diary.

Some examples of income include the following:

- **Your salary or wages:** This is money you earn from your job.
- **Your rental income:** This is income gained from any properties you own.
- **Your business income:** This can include dividends and interest payments. If you have periodic capital gains income through swing trades or options trades, you can include them here. Flip to Chapter 3 in Book 4 to find out more about all the different ways you can generate income from within your investment portfolio.
- **Side hustle or freelance income:** For example, you can include all commissions from affiliate marketing as well as what YouTube, TikTok, and Instagram pay you for content.
- **Government benefits:** If you're retired or receive any type of government benefits such as Social Security, unemployment benefits, or food stamps, you can include them here.

TIP

If you are fresh out of college, just got fired, or are disabled with no income, you can put a big zero right there and not stress.

REMEMBER

The purpose of this exercise isn't to make you feel bad. It's just to give you a solid understanding of where you stand financially. Also, you can find many alternative methods to increase your income. Flip to Chapter 3 in Book 4 to review some of the most common approaches.

Reviewing your expenses

Tracking your income may be exciting, but you can't consider income without also looking at your expenses. To complete your cash flow diary, you must add up your expenses over the same period of time that you calculated your income.

You can create categories for your expenses to make organization easier. Common expense categories include:

- **Housing:** Rent/mortgage, property taxes, and utilities
- **Transportation:** Car payment, insurance, fuel, and public transportation
- **Food:** Groceries and dining out
- **Debt payments:** Credit cards and loans
- **Healthcare:** Insurance premiums and medical expenses
- **Entertainment and leisure:** Movies, cable and streaming services, dining out, and your hobbies
- **Savings and investments:** Any money you're putting away to save or invest over a set period of time
- **Miscellaneous expenses:** Clothing, gifts, and personal care

Figuring out your bottom line

REMEMBER

The number that is going to contribute to your risk tolerance is your net income. This is the money you actually get to keep after all the bills, taxes, and other costs are paid. It's also called your *bottom line* because it's the final number after all the financial math is done. You can calculate your net income by subtracting your total expenses from your total income:

Total Income – Total Expenses = Net Income

If you have a positive net income, you can call yourself "cash flow positive," which indicates that you are living within your means and have a higher risk tolerance.

A negative net income is called "cash flow negative," which suggests that you are spending more than you earn, so your risk tolerance is lower.

REMEMBER

You may be upset because your expenses are currently more than your income and savings. Or you may be super happy because you were a big saver or had lucrative side hustles that you may have even forgotten about, so you feel great about where you stand. There is no shame in either. The point of this is not to get you down or to fill you up with overconfidence. The point is simply to open your eyes so that you can take measured risks as you build your triple-compounding system.

Measuring Your Willingness to Take a Risk

The second component of your risk tolerance is your willingness to take a risk. This can depend on your age, family situation, health, and life cycle. For example:

- Between the ages of 25 and 45, you're probably more growth-oriented. But even then, big life events can change your risk tolerance. For example, you may have been more willing to take a risk before you became a parent.
- Between the ages of 45 and 60, you may identify as conservative and more protection oriented.
- Some people see the years above 60 as their retirement years, so they may be concerned about generating income and protecting what they have — or maybe they are thinking about gifting to their grandchildren.

REMEMBER

Age-based risk tolerance is very popular among traditional financial advisors, but your age alone shouldn't dictate your investment strategy. In fact, a person's willingness to take a risk has a lot to do with how they view themselves, their identity, and their skills rather than their age or personality. The cool news is that by adopting a new identity, you can change your willingness to take a risk and potentially say hello to your more financially secure future self. Chapter 2 in Book 4 can help you discover how to embody your future self now.

Measuring Your Confidence

The third factor determining your overall risk tolerance is your confidence in the asset you plan to invest in. This certainly applies to investing in yourself. If you have a habit of keeping your word to yourself, you will trust yourself more to follow through with the commitments you make to yourself.

REMEMBER

Your self-confidence is directly impacted by your ability or disability to keep your promises to yourself. Just as you gain trust in someone who always keeps their word to you, you can establish trust with yourself when you keep your word to yourself.

When investing in assets other than yourself, especially when investing in external assets such as stocks and cryptocurrency, you can use a method that's called the *Confidence Compass* — two questions that you ask yourself. Your honest answers typically reveal your exact level of confidence in the asset you're buying and the price you're paying for it.

Here are the two confidence compass questions:

- If I invest at this price and the price drops by 50 percent tomorrow, will I freak out?
- If I *don't* invest at this price and its price *skyrockets* by 50 percent tomorrow, will I beat myself up?

Of course, both scenarios kind of suck, but you have to be really honest with yourself as to which scenario sucks more and adjust your investment strategy accordingly. If you freak out, beat yourself up, or panic, in most cases, your confidence in this asset is low. You can increase your confidence in a financial asset by researching more about it.

TIP

You can use similar confidence compass questions when deciding whether to sell an asset. Here's an example:

- If I sell at this price and the price goes up by 50 percent tomorrow, will I regret selling too early?
- If I *don't* sell at this price and its price *drops* by 50 percent tomorrow, will I beat myself up for not selling at a higher price?

Digging into Different Kinds of Risk

Risk is a part of life — especially when it comes to money. Whether you're investing, trading, running a business, or just deciding where to park your cash, you're always balancing risk and reward.

Don't let risk frighten you. After all, life itself is risky. Knowing your risk tolerance helps you decide what kind of risk you can confidently take so that you can reap the rewards while being able to sleep peacefully at night. Not all risk is equal. The following sections describe the various types of triple-compounding risks.

Compounding risk

Compounding is a powerful tool — when it works in your favor. The same rule of compounding can come and bite you in the butt if you use it in reverse. *Reverse compounding* is when, instead of earning with compounding, you're paying. Common compounding risks include

- **Bad habits multiplying:** If you repeatedly make poor financial choices (such as overspending or ignoring your investments), those mistakes compound over time.
- **Debt spirals:** High-interest debt compounds just like investments — but in the wrong direction. The longer you ignore it, the bigger it gets.
- **Market downturns:** A downturn can erase your compounded gains if your investments are heavily exposed to risk without proper diversification.
- **Interest rate cuts:** A news headline as harmless as "interest rates have dropped" can lower your ability to compound interest, especially if you parked all your money in places that promise high-interest payments.
- **Inflation:** When the price of everyday shopping, such as groceries, continues to go higher, you're compounding in reverse by having to pay more for the same goods month after month. Inflation means your money doesn't buy as much as it used to. So, if your money is sitting under your mattress, you're exposing yourself to compounded devaluation of your money.

Investing risk

Whether you're investing in yourself, your career, or external assets, there's always a risk that you will not only gain the rewards you hoped for but also lose everything you have!

WARNING

This risk is why it's so important that you first measure your own ability and willingness to take a risk using the risk calculation methods shared earlier in this chapter. Here are some investing risks to be mindful of:

- **Financial risk:** The financial risk of investing is that you can lose your money. This type of risk is the most obvious because companies do go bankrupt, cryptocurrency projects can go bust, and no matter how awesome you are as a value asset, your investment in yourself may not turn out as you had hoped. Check out Chapters 4 and 5 in Book 4 to explore how you can manage this risk by choosing your investments wisely.

- **Market risk:** All the Wall Street pros and other market participants' mood changes cause the financial markets, such as stocks and crypto, to go up and down like a roller coaster.
- **Security risk:** Scams! Hacking! Theft! Impersonators pretending to be experts reach out to individuals and promise the world. They're getting better at it every day, and with the progress of artificial intelligence, this problem can only worsen. Make sure that you triple-check everyone online before handing over your money.

Some assets have higher risks than others. For example, investing in yourself is always a lower risk, because even if you don't succeed on your first try, the knowledge you gain is invaluable. If you persist, you will eventually gain the rewards. Other investment assets such as stocks and crypto have higher risks.

Trading risk

Trading is like investing on steroids. It's faster, riskier, and — if you're not careful — it can burn through your money quicker than a bad weekend in Vegas.

If, based on the previous sections in this chapter, you discover you have a low or medium risk tolerance, then you may want to consider avoiding trading and stick to investing instead. Although traders aim to make quick profits, they face unique risks such as the following:

- **Volatility risk:** This is the risk of unexpected market movements. Though volatility can be a good thing, it can sometimes also catch you off guard due to a sudden move in the opposite direction from what you expected. If you aren't prepared for the market volatility, you can lose the money in your trading account.
- **Hype risk:** This is the danger of making investment decisions based on excitement, speculation, or media buzz rather than on solid fundamentals. When a stock, cryptocurrency, or asset becomes trendy, prices often surge — not because of real value, but because of fear of missing out (FOMO). The problem? What goes up fast often comes crashing down even faster.
- **Leverage risk:** Borrowing money to trade (margin trading) can amplify gains but also wipe out your account if the trade goes south.
- **Tax risk:** Profits from selling stocks, options, or crypto held for less than one year are taxed as short-term capital gains, which are treated as ordinary income. This means you can be paying anywhere from 10 percent to 37 percent in taxes (depending on your income bracket) versus a lower long-term capital gains tax rate of zero percent, 15 percent, or 20 percent for investments held over a year.

REMEMBER

The media thrives on creating fear emotions. That is how they make money, because people are more likely to click on negative headlines. Before falling for the market noise, arm yourself with knowledge of the specific asset you're considering adding to your triple-compounding system. You have plenty of opportunities to make lots of money in the markets. Be patient and acquire the right knowledge instead of betting on the hype. An investor who trades on the hype probably doesn't even have an investment strategy — unless you call gambling a strategy!

Business risk

As you find out earlier in this chapter, the second investment asset of your triple-compounding system is typically an extension of you, which is your business. Entrepreneurs and business owners face a different kind of financial risk. Unlike investing in stocks, where you can buy and sell shares of companies that *other people* control, running a business gives you full control, but it also ties up your time, money, and energy. Here's where matters can go wrong:

- **Cash flow risk:** A business can be profitable on paper but still struggle if cash isn't flowing in at the right time.
- **Competition risk:** A great business idea doesn't guarantee success — especially if competitors have a better offer or marketing system.
- **Operational risk:** Mistakes in management, hiring, or supply chains can cripple a business before it even takes off.

Tax risk

For an average person, taxes are one of the highest expenses. You also have potential financial or legal consequences you need to watch out for. Here are some examples:

- **Noncompliance risk:** This happens when taxpayers fail to meet their tax obligations, whether by accident or on purpose. Examples include filing taxes late, underreporting income (even unintentionally), and failing to pay taxes owed, leading to interest and penalties that will then reverse-compound.
- **Audit risk:** This is the chance of being selected for a tax audit, which can be stressful, time-consuming, and costly. You can get audited for reporting large deductions or business losses that seem unusual, claiming excessive tax credits, and frequent changes in income that raise red flags with tax authorities.

- **Investment tax risk:** This is the risk that taxes will reduce investment returns more than expected. Investors pay taxes on capital gains and pay even more if they sell stocks within a year of purchasing them (short-term gains). Dividend taxes can also eat into stock market earnings.

TIP

Tax-efficient investing, business structuring, and estate planning can minimize tax burdens. A tax advisor or Certified Public Accountant (CPA) can help you avoid costly mistakes.

Missed opportunity risk

Not all risks involve losing money. Sometimes, the biggest risk is *not acting at all.* Although playing it safe feels comfortable, staying on the sidelines can cost you in the long run.

Although most people think taxes or their mortgage is their biggest expense, the truth is, your biggest expense is not knowing how to accelerate your financial freedom. If you spent the past year thinking about learning a new skill to generate more income or starting to invest, then you have already missed out on a year of compounding.

Here's a list of some nonmonetary risks you could be compounding that will negatively impact your future net worth:

- **Missed-out compounding:** The biggest component of compounding is time. The best time to start compounding was 20 years ago. The second-best time is today. Figure 1-1 demonstrates the importance of time in basic compounding.
- **Being too conservative:** Avoiding all risk can mean missing out on high-growth opportunities.
- **Fear of change:** Holding onto a failing business, job, or investment out of fear can keep you stuck.
- **Ignoring financial education:** The biggest missed opportunity? Not learning how money works and how to make it work for you.

TECHNICAL STUFF

If, instead of purchasing every new high-end iPhone and accessories released since 2007, you had invested that same amount of money (about $1,600 per year) in Apple stock, reinvested dividends, and optimized your purchasing price, your investment could have been worth more than $640,000 in 2025.

Now you may be saying, "But I didn't start when I was 19! What to do now?" With compounding, you need time on your side. To accelerate this process and make up for the time you lost, you need triple compounding.

FIGURE 1-1: The importance of time in compounding.

Source: Adapted from Triple Compounding

Understanding the Time Value of Money

A fundamental principle in triple compounding is the time value of money (TVM). Certified financial planners (CFPs) rely on this concept to make investment decisions, calculate retirement needs, and determine how much money should be saved today for future goals.

Understanding TVM shouldn't be limited to financial planners. This needs to be taught in schools, and if you're serious about becoming financially secure, you must start playing around with it.

Simply put, TVM means that a dollar today is worth more than a dollar in the future because money has the potential to grow over time through investing or earning interest. Understanding TVM helps you create a unique triple-compounding system for yourself and make better financial decisions, whether you're planning for retirement, saving for a house, or comparing different investment options.

Breaking down TVM

REMEMBER

The time value of money is based on two key ideas.

- **Money today can earn interest or be invested:** If you have $1,000 today and invest it at a 5 percent annual return, it will grow to $1,050 in a year. If you wait a year to receive that $1,000, you miss out on the growth.

- **Inflation erodes purchasing power:** Over time, the cost of goods and services rises. If inflation is 3 percent per year, that $1,000 will buy less next year than it does today.

Because of these factors, money has different values depending on when you receive it. You can use TVM to compare financial choices and evaluate investment returns.

The five key components of TVM

You can use TVM formulas based on the following five key variables:

- **Present value (PV):** How much money you have today (or the current value of a future sum)
- **Future value (FV):** How much money will be worth in the future after interest or investment growth
- **Interest rate (r or i):** The rate at which money grows (also called the discount rate or required rate of return)
- **Number of periods (n):** The number of years (or time periods) over which the money grows
- **Payments (PMT):** Any regular contributions or withdrawals (such as savings deposits or loan payments)

After you decide on these five variables, you can use websites such as `www.calculatorsoup.com/calculators/financial/future-value-annuity-calculator.php` to calculate the following:

- How much you need to save today for a future goal
- How an investment will grow over time
- The impact of different interest rates on financial outcomes

Making up for the time lost

Many people believe that if they didn't start investing early, they've missed their chance at financial freedom. But although starting early is ideal, starting late is still better than never. This is where triple compounding comes in. You can use the TVM formula to see how you can accelerate your retirement even if you start late.

The case study in Figure 1-2 shows the retirement outcome for Lisa and Mark, both 50 years old with zero retirement savings. They both want to retire at 65, but only one of them makes smart, consistent choices to reach $1 million.

Details	Lisa (Disciplined Saver)	Mark (Minimal Saver)
Starting Age	50	50
Retirement Goal	65	65
Starting Savings	$0	$0
Monthly Contribution	$3,155	$500
Investment Return	7% annually	7% annually
Investment Period	15 years	15 years

Source: Adapted from Triple Compounding

FIGURE 1-2: Making up for lost time — Lisa's and Mark's case study.

Lisa uses triple compounding to hit her $1 million retirement goal, whereas Mark contributes less and hopes for the best. Specifically, Lisa realizes she started late but makes up for lost time by investing $3,155 per month in a diversified portfolio that earns 7 percent annually.

Using the TVM calculator to solve for FV, Figure 1-3 shows how Lisa makes up for lost time without even employing higher-risk investment methods covered in Chapter 4 of Book 4 and which could increase her rate of return.

Age	Lisa's Investment Value ($3,155/month)	Mark's Investment Value ($500/month
50	0	0
55	$225,875.6	$35,796.45
60	$546,082.57	$86,542.4
65	$1,000,016.05	$158,481.15

Source: Adapted from Triple Compounding

FIGURE 1-3: Results based on Lisa's and Mark's case study.

This example is proof that starting late isn't the problem; inaction is. Lisa proved that even at 50, you can still hit $1 million by making consistent, disciplined contributions. After you determine your risk tolerance, you get to choose the way that you feel comfortable with accelerating your financial freedom. In Lisa's case, she didn't increase her rate of return and only focused on increasing her contributions.

Mark started investing, but he didn't contribute enough, and he didn't increase his rate of return, and that cost him his financial freedom.

IN THIS CHAPTER

» Developing a vision for your future self

» Mastering your subconscious mind and reframing your past

» Making decisions that help you succeed

Chapter 2
Investing in Yourself

If you have nails and a hammer without having the mental/creative/physical capacity to use them, you can't build anything. You have to have a skillset and, more importantly, a mindset to accompany your toolset, or you won't get results. You need to become the person who can use the toolset. Tripling your income, tripling your net worth, tripling your abundance has everything to do with investing in yourself.

Tools alone and knowledge alone won't help you become financially free. That's why, in this chapter, we spend some time helping you develop the mindset that enables you to use the toolset and to develop the skillset to become a triple compounder. Would that be cool with you? Yes? Then, keep reading.

REMEMBER

The number one factor in accelerating your success is to invest in the most important asset you can ever access, which is *yourself*. How can you be an asset? Because regardless of the general economic conditions of the country or what is going on geopolitically, you will always have access to *you*! If you become your own most important value asset, you can get dropped off in the middle of a desert, and you'll come up with a way to create value, create something out of nothing, and make the world around you a better place.

Developing a Vision

Before you can build wealth, achieve financial freedom, or leverage triple compounding, you need a clear, compelling picture of the future you want to create. Author Napoleon Hill called this *Definiteness of Purpose* — knowing exactly what you want and refusing to settle for anything less. Dr. Benjamin Hardy, coauthor of *10X Is Easier than 2X* (Hay House Business, 2023), takes it further, arguing that achieving a 10X vision is actually easier than a small 2X goal because it forces you to eliminate distractions and focus only on what truly matters.

Here are just a few reasons why having a crystal-clear vision is crucial for your financial success:

- **Your mind needs a target.** Just like a GPS needs a destination, your brain works better when it has a clear financial goal.
- **Clarity eliminates distractions.** A strong vision helps you say *no* to things that don't align with your long-term success.
- **Big goals create big energy.** A 10X vision excites and motivates you far more than a 2X goal ever can.

REMEMBER

When developing your vision, be as specific as you can. Don't just say, "I want to be rich." Instead, define a number and say it in the present tense: "I have a $5 million investment portfolio and work only 10 hours a week in 2035."

TIP

As you develop your vision, write down your six-month, one-year, five-year, and ten-year goals and place them somewhere you can see every day. Here are some methods to consider:

- **Create a vision board.** This is a visual representation of your goals, dreams, and ideal future. It's a collage of images, words, and symbols that reflect what you want to achieve in your life — whether in wealth, career, relationships, health, or personal growth. Spend at least 30 seconds per day viewing your vision board.
- **Set reminders on your phone.** You can create notifications on your phone's calendar that pop up your goals, affirmations, and purpose every day at a certain time.
- **Create a future journal and read it every day.** Whenever you're working on a brand-new vision, take time to write a journal with the vision and the rules and principles that you know will help you achieve it. You can then either record yourself and listen to it every day or get your phone to read the text while you're driving, going for a walk, or working out.

Mastering Your Subconscious Mind

Your subconscious mind is the hidden powerhouse behind achieving your desired future. Your wealth starts in your mind before it appears in your investment portfolio. That is why it's crucial that you change your identity first and transform your mindset before you start your journey. When you do this, you can make decisions from the perspective of your future self and get on the right path to achieve your goal.

REMEMBER

Your subconscious mind runs your financial habits on autopilot, and it influences your financial identity. If you grew up thinking "money is hard to earn" or "wealthy people are unethical," your subconscious will keep you playing small and prevent you from becoming wealthy to fit in your idea of "ethical."

Here's how to reprogram your subconscious mind to attract more wealth:

- **Feed it the right input.** Don't just repeat financial affirmations. Get yourself in a state of gratitude and watch yourself become how you *feel.*
- **Control your environment.** Surround yourself with wealth-minded people and cut out negative financial influences. Your subconscious mind absorbs the mindset of the people around you, and the news steals your attention and fuels fear. Both keep you from achieving abundance.
- **Take action that reinforces your new identity.** If your vision is to have a $5 million portfolio, start making investment moves like someone who already has it.

When your subconscious believes you are wealthy, your actions will naturally align to make it true.

Tapping into your imagination

If your vision is your destination and your subconscious is the engine, then your imagination is the fuel that helps you solve financial challenges and create wealth-building opportunities.

Zoroastrianism, one of the world's oldest belief systems, produced the ancient Persian proverb, "Good thoughts, good words, good deeds." This idea emphasizes that your inner world (thoughts), your spoken intentions (words), and your external actions (deeds) must be in harmony to create a righteous and fulfilling life.

In modern terms, this principle aligns with the power of mindset, language, and action in shaping your reality — especially in creating wealth and abundance.

REMEMBER

Your thoughts, words, and actions determine whether you attract or repel opportunities, financial success, and abundance. The mind is a creative force, and when you master these three elements, you become the architect of your financial destiny.

Becoming your future self now

One of the most powerful ways to accelerate your financial success is to embody your future self today. Try the following exercise as a way to facilitate this transformation into your future self.

1. **Center yourself.**

   Breathe in deeply, hold the breath for a moment, and slowly exhale. Let any tension in your body melt away. Slowly close your eyes and tilt your eyes toward the center of your forehead.

2. **Consider the future date you're stepping into.**

   For example, say, "It is July 21, 2035," and calculate how old you will be on this specific date.

3. **View the world from your future-self perspective.**

   With your eyes closed, look to your left, to your right, in your hands, and in front of you. Envision what your future self sees. Specifically, what stands out that shows you have achieved your dream? Maybe it's a number in your bank account. It could be an award hanging on your wall. It could be that special someone you're sharing the good news with. It could be the view from your dream home.

4. **Feel your future self.**

   With your eyes closed, answer this question: "Now that my dreams have come true, how do I feel?" The answer may put a smile on your face or a tear in your eyes.

5. **Anchor the feeling.**

   With your eyes closed, scan your body to find where you're feeling these emotions the most. You may be feeling a tingling in your tummy, in your throat, or on your cheeks. Tap on the area where you feel the most tingling. Then take a deep breath to anchor. When you're ready, slowly open your eyes and bring yourself back to the present moment.

TIP

You may be thinking, "I thought this book was about serious compounding stuff. What in the voodoo is this stuff about?" You don't have to understand exactly how this works just as you don't need to know how electricity works to still benefit from your fridge, microwave, and computer. Many successful people, including Tony Robbins, Mr. Beast, Oprah Winfrey, Richard Branson, and even Lady Gaga, practice these same principles!

Overcoming resistance

Have you ever noticed that every time you get excited about a new goal or commit to doing something that you know will help you grow, you feel or experience something that holds you back? Sometimes it's fear. Other times, it's skepticism. It may also be that something actually happens in your life to prevent you from moving forward, such as getting into an argument with your spouse!

In his book, *The War of Art* (Black Irish Entertainment, 2012), Steven Pressfield describes this thing that holds you back as the *resistance.* He defines it as the invisible force that blocks you from achieving your goals. Every time your emotional mind comes up with a new goal to be excited about, the resistance comes and hits you to see if you're for real.

Here are the different forms of resistance you may experience once you step into your future self, as described in the previous section:

- Self-doubt
- Procrastination
- Fear
- Distractions
- Self-sabotage

REMEMBER

Resistance shows up whenever you try to level up — when you start a business, invest seriously, write a book, commit to a financial plan, or start your triple-compounding journey. It often disguises itself as logical excuses — such as *I need more research, I'll start next year*, or *What if I fail?* Resistance will always try to stop you, but the fact that it's there means you're doing something important. So, if you feel resistance when taking bold financial steps, take it as a sign you're on the verge of a breakthrough — and push forward anyway.

Pressfield argues that resistance is strongest right before a breakthrough, which means the bigger your goal (such as financial freedom), the stronger the resistance. Here are some methods you can use to overcome resistance:

- **Act first, feel ready later.** The best way to beat resistance is action — even small steps. Start investing, automate savings, and refine as you go.
- **Commit to daily progress.** Even if it's just one investment move a day, consistency weakens resistance.
- **Identify your excuses and challenge them.** Whenever you catch yourself delaying action, ask: *Is this Resistance talking?*
- **Embody your future wealthy self.** Think and act as if you're already financially free. Make decisions from abundance, not fear.

Reframing Your Past

Stepping into your future self is fun and all, but sometimes, the thing that's holding you back is your past. If you haven't taken care of your past, stepping into your future may become harder.

Can you think of a traumatizing experience in your past that is still haunting you to this day, and you feel like it's preventing you from moving forward? Maybe it's a mistake you made. Or a mistake someone else made that impacted you.

The following sections teach you a *reframing* skill that enables you to turn your past "trauma" or failures into steppingstones for success.

Becoming better, not bitter

Dr. Benjamin Hardy explains a phenomenon in his book, *Be Your Future Self Now* (Hay House Business, 2022). Your future self is not limited by your past. It's shaped by how you choose to frame it.

REMEMBER

Stuff that happened to you in the past can really mess with your head if you let it. You need to realize that it's not about what happened. The important detail is the story you tell yourself about it — the frame you put around it. Your toughest times can teach you the most if you're open to it. Owning your experiences, instead of being owned by them, lets you create a story that helps your future. You can be *bitter* about an experience, or you can put a *better* frame around it.

Here's an exercise to help you reframe your past:

1. **Identify a past financial mistake or regret.**

   Maybe you missed an investment opportunity, overspent, or avoided managing money altogether. Or maybe you fell for a scam or media hype and lost all your money. Write the mistake down.

2. **Change the story you tell yourself.**

   Is there any way you can give a new positive meaning to your tragic experience? Think of at least one new way of reframing your past experience positively. Can you find a lesson? Or maybe even a blessing?

3. **Use your new story to build your compelling future.**

   Instead of using your past as an excuse, use it as evidence that you're evolving.

TIP

You can ask yourself:

- How can I use my past experiences to make better financial decisions now?
- What strengths did those struggles develop in me?

You may have become more resilient, resourceful, or determined. These are assets that can help you become a triple compounder.

REMEMBER

Instead of carrying the weight of regret, remind yourself that life is happening *for* you, not *to* you. Every challenge, every setback, every financial misstep was never meant to break you; it was meant to build you. The struggles weren't roadblocks; they were lessons disguised as obstacles, sharpening your resilience, wisdom, and financial intelligence. Add the following sentence to your daily mantra and witness your life change for the better:

The universe is conspiring in my favor.

Avoiding the fly's strategy

Have you ever heard that to succeed, you need to "try harder"? Okay, here's another question. Have you ever seen a fly at your window, trying super hard to fly *through* the glass?

Picture that scenario in your head right now. The fly keeps flapping and flapping, but it's just not producing a result. Basically, the fly's big plan is "I'll give it all I've got!" But that plan isn't working out. Even though the fly tries its best, it won't get through that window.

The saddest part? There's an open door right across the room! Instead of switching up its game plan, the fly is just being stubborn, sticking to what's not working. No one's forcing the fly to keep at it, but it's stuck on the idea that trying harder is the way to win.

REMEMBER

Just trying harder with what doesn't work isn't the answer. If you keep doing the same thing over and over, expecting different results, you're probably setting yourself up for disappointment. This doesn't mean you should sit on your butt doing nothing. You *do* need to work hard. But your effort needs to go toward things that are proven to work. If that little fly had a big fly mentor to model flying through the open door, the little fly wouldn't die.

The cool thing is, in your job, in your business, in your investments, in your bank account, in your life, you're not a gazillion steps away from achieving what you desire. You're likely three to five tweaks away from setting yourself up to reach that million-dollar portfolio that can compound and enable you to live your lifestyle after you decide to retire.

Developing a Decisive Nature

The word *decision* is rooted in the Latin word *decidere,* which is the combination of two words:

> *de = off*
>
> *caedere = cut*

To *decide* means to *cut off* everything except the circumstances that matter most.

This idea goes hand in hand with triple compounding, which requires you to cut off 80 percent of who you are and what you're doing right now and hone in on and automate the 20 percent that matters most. Making decisions is a very important component in your triple-compounding journey.

REMEMBER

Becoming decisive in nature is one of the most critical traits for achieving success, wealth, and financial freedom. Indecision is the enemy of progress. It keeps you stuck in analysis paralysis; you second-guess every move while opportunities pass you by.

Successful people make decisions quickly and change them slowly. Unsuccessful people take forever to decide and then change their minds quickly. When you're looking for financial freedom, you've got to evaluate your investments through the eyes of wealthy people. Ultimately, you have two resources for investing: your time and your money. What's more important?

REMEMBER

Most people would answer time, and some may say "time is money." Here's the truth: Time is *infinitely* more valuable than money. You can always make more money, but you can never make more time.

Self-made wealthy people become financially free because they spend as much money as possible to save as much time as possible. Why? Because the most important ingredient in compounding is *time*.

William Clement Stone, a self-made multimillionaire, entrepreneur, and co-author of *Success Through a Positive Mental Attitude* (Prentice Hall, 1960), built his fortune by embracing a simple yet powerful mantra: "Do it now."

He believed that *procrastination is the killer of opportunity* and that success belongs to those who take immediate, decisive action rather than waiting for the "perfect moment." That's why he made himself and all his employees say, "Do it now," a hundred times a day!

REMEMBER

Every time you hesitate, you allow resistance to creep in. (Read about resistance earlier in this chapter.) The faster you act, the faster you build momentum and the faster you step into financial freedom.

TIP

When you think about your next move — whether it's investing, starting a business, or making a big decision, ask yourself, "What would my future self want me to do?" Then, do it right away.

Surrounding Yourself with Like-Minded People

Your environment shapes your reality. If you want to build wealth, achieve financial freedom, and step into your 10X future, you must surround yourself with people who think bigger, act bolder, and are already living at the level you aspire to reach. Napoleon Hill called this the *Mastermind Principle* — the idea that success accelerates when you align yourself with those who elevate your thinking.

TIP

Success leaves clues. Instead of figuring everything out on your own, study the habits, mindset, and strategies of the people who have already achieved what you want.

- How do they think about money?
- What daily actions do they take?
- What risks do they embrace that others avoid?

Surrounding yourself with wealth-minded people — especially other triple compounders — rewires your subconscious beliefs about what's possible. You start thinking, acting, and making decisions like someone who is already financially free because that's who you're becoming.

IN THIS CHAPTER

» Using savings to generate income

» Working a job to generate income

» Earning from your portfolio to generate income

» Operating businesses to generate income

» Accelerating your triple compounding

Chapter 3
Investing in Your Income-Generating Extensions

If you feel like you're late to the compounding game, there's only one way to catch up and speed your way to financial freedom: maximize your contributions. Chapter 1 of Book 4 breaks down the math of the time value of money (TVM). Your ability to compound wealth is directly tied to how much you put in. The more you contribute, the faster your money grows.

But here's the challenge: You can't contribute more if you don't earn more. That's why this chapter is all about expanding your income-generating extensions — the revenue streams that fuel your compounding engine. By increasing your income and positively influencing your cash flow, you're not just making more money; you're unlocking the ability to take higher-calculated risks, access better investment opportunities, and grow your wealth exponentially without losing sleep at night.

REMEMBER

There's no such thing as truly passive income — not even if you win the lottery. In fact, one-third of lottery winners declare bankruptcy within five years, not because they didn't have enough money but because they never learned how to keep it growing. Even if you hit a financial jackpot, you won't stay ahead unless you're constantly investing in yourself, your income-generating extensions, and external assets.

Every financial milestone unlocks the next goal. Growth isn't just about money. It's about momentum. If you're not growing, you're dying. And if your money isn't growing, it's dying, too. Conversely, if you work through Chapter 1 in Book 4 and discover that you aren't cash-flow positive, what comes in this chapter is even more important.

Generating with Savings

No, saving some money by giving up your morning latte will not make you a millionaire. But if you free up some cash and then use that cash to generate more cash, you're no longer just saving; you're compounding your wealth. The following sections show you some easy ways you can generate income by saving on things that no longer give you joy. So, you won't be diminishing the quality of your life while finding money to contribute to your triple-compounding system.

Cutting the waste

Cutting waste is the easiest way to find money. Brainstorm all the things in your life that you could eliminate or reduce to cut your expenses and enter them in a table like the one shown in Figure 3-1. For example, fly on a weekday rather than a weekend, cut down on the daily Pumpkin Spice Frappuccino, go out to matinée movies instead of evening shows, pack a lunch for work, and so on. These are small things that add up over time.

Now determine how much each of these items/activities cost. Fill in the amount for each and multiply it by the number of times per week you indulge in this expense to get a reality check about how much you are spending. Then ask yourself, on a scale from 0 to 10 (with 0 being none and 10 being extremely pleasurable), how much joy do you get from each of these items? Write this in the last column for each item.

CUT THE WASTE: FIND MONEY

ITEM/ ACTIVITY	COST	ITEMS PER WEEK	TOTAL COST (Cost of item x #time per week)	LEVEL OF ENJOYMENT (0-10)

FIGURE 3-1: Cut the waste — find money.

Source: Adapted from Triple Compounding

TIP

Associate in your body the feeling of absolute financial freedom. How will it feel to be able to do whatever you want, wherever you want, whenever you want, with whomever you want? What will you be able to enjoy, have, do, be, or give? Now consider whether the expense you included on your list will give you more joy or take you further away from your financial goals?

REMEMBER

Decide which is more important: the joy you receive from the items on your list or the feeling of absolute financial freedom. Also remember that life is a balance. You don't have to cut out everything you enjoy; rather, cutting the waste is about giving you more choices by reducing the things that truly do not give you proportional levels of joy.

Circle or mark at least three things in the list that you're resolved to eliminate from the list. How much money will this save you over the course of the next year?

This is found money.

WARNING

This is not about saving money and wasting it on something else that wouldn't accelerate your financial freedom. Here's a quick pop quiz:

- What are you *not* going to spend this found money on? Another liability.
- What are you going to do with it instead? Contribute it to your triple-compounding system.

Eliminating liabilities

A liability is anything that takes money out of your pocket without generating income. That means your $5,000 Chanel bag, your leased car, or even that expensive couch that just sits there — they're all liabilities if they're not making you money. Although these purchases may seem harmless, they add up and compound over time, creating a negative wealth effect instead of fueling your financial growth.

REMEMBER

Every dollar you're *not* spending on liabilities is a dollar that can be invested and compounded into more wealth. For example, the less you pay for your car lease each month, the more money you have to invest. That compounded income generation doesn't just stop there. It double-compounds as that money grows inside your portfolio, creating even more wealth.

TIP

It's time to shift your mindset. Every dollar you free from liabilities is a dollar that can be put to work. Small financial decisions, when compounded, create massive long-term wealth. Start redirecting your cash into income-generating assets today. Flip to Chapter 1 in Book 4 to discover the difference between good and bad liabilities.

Stopping reverse compounding

The previous sections show how to invest in yourself, cut waste, eliminate liabilities, and generate income with savings — but you have one more silent wealth killer to stop: reverse compounding.

Reverse compounding happens when unnecessary fees and costs eat away at your wealth, compounding in someone else's favor instead of yours. It's what happens with the hidden fees inside your 401(k), IRA, and other retirement accounts. Most people don't even realize how much they're losing as, over time, these fees can add up to millions of dollars in lost growth.

Now, you may be wondering, *Should I ditch my 401(k)?*

Not necessarily. The only time we would consider keeping a 401(k) is if our employer offers a match — because that's free money. Even then, we would take control of it and manage it by using the triple-compounding method that Book 4 covers. That way, you can maximize returns, minimize fees, and eliminate reverse compounding wherever possible.

WARNING

401(k)s have layers of hidden fees — so many that even most financial advisors don't fully understand them.

Figure 3-2 reveals the ways that you're reverse-compounding without realizing it. Many of these stealth costs add up to over 28 percent compounded over time, which means you could be losing millions of dollars over your lifetime.

Things You Could Be REVERSE Compounding

Bad Debt	Ignoring Maintenance	Poor Tax Planning	Leveraged ETFs
401K Hidden Fees	High-Expense Ratio Mutual Funds	Lifestyle Inflation	Non-Traded REITs
Late Fees	Actively Managed Funds	Annuities with High Fees	Private Equity Hidden Fees

FIGURE 3-2: Sneaky ways reverse compounding can occur.

Source: Adapted from Triple Compounding

TIP

If you stop reverse-compounding, you instantly free up more cash, increase your risk tolerance, and accelerate your triple-compounding strategy.

So, ask yourself: Do you want to be a reverse compounder or a triple compounder? The choice is yours, but once you see what's at stake, the answer becomes obvious.

Using leverage

Chapter 1 in Book 4 breaks down the differences between bad and good debt. Bad debt is a liability that "reverse-compounds" against you — eating away at your portfolio and trapping you in financial stagnation. Good debt, on the other hand, is why 99 percent of businesses exist today. It's the tool successful entrepreneurs, investors, and corporations use to build real wealth.

If you're in a city right now, look out your window. What do you see? Hotels, car dealerships, malls, restaurants.

Now, here's a question for you: How many of those businesses do you think were built with cash that was sitting under a mattress?

Almost none. Maybe 1 percent.

The truth is that nearly every successful business and investor uses debt strategically. They don't take on debt just to survive; they use it as leverage to build income-generating assets.

REMEMBER

Becoming debt-free is not the first step in your financial freedom journey. Most people believe that the first step to financial freedom is paying off all their debt. They focus on getting rid of their car loans, student loans, or mortgages, thinking that once they're "debt-free," they'll finally be in control. The hard truth is that *debt-free is still zero.*

If your only goal is to get out of debt, you're working incredibly hard just to get back to nothing — to a neutral financial position. You may feel relieved after you're debt-free, but relief isn't the same as freedom. And while you're focused on paying off every dollar, you're missing out on the most valuable asset you have: time.

The key isn't just eliminating debt. It's learning how to use leverage to your advantage.

Three smart ways to borrow money that can generate more wealth for you are:

- **Borrow money to start a business** that creates cash flow and pays off debt.
- **Use the bank's money** if borrowing is cheaper than using your own money.
- **Leverage credit card rewards** to generate cash back and investment funds.

If you're earning 40 percent on your money and the bank is offering you a loan at 10 percent, should you use your own money to pay for something? No. If you use your own money, it's costing you 40 percent in opportunity cost. But if you borrow at 10 percent, your real cost is only 10 percent, and your money keeps earning 30 percent more.

That's why wealthy people use leverage strategically. They leave their money in income-generating investments and use cheap money from banks to pay for what they need. Let your money work for you. Borrow at a lower cost and keep your cash compounding.

If you can't pay your credit cards off every month, the solution isn't avoiding credit. It's borrowing the right way, building a business, and generating cash flow to eliminate bad debt while continuing to leverage good debt to your advantage.

WARNING

Using bad debt can negatively impact your risk tolerance. See Chapter 1 in Book 4 to calculate your ability to take a risk.

REMEMBER

Most people use debt to look rich instead of becoming rich. They put vacations, designer bags, and luxury cars on credit to impress people. They finance a lifestyle instead of financing income-producing assets. But once you shift your mindset and learn how to use debt as a tool, you stop playing defense and start playing offense. You start compounding your way to financial freedom instead of just escaping debt.

The real question isn't *Should I avoid debt?* The real question is *Am I using debt to build wealth or just to survive?* When you use leverage wisely, you multiply your money, expand your compounding system, and accelerate your financial freedom faster than you ever thought possible.

Developing a spending plan

Most people create a spending plan (also known as a budget) with one goal: cutting expenses to avoid running out of money. But as a triple compounder, your spending plan shouldn't just be about saving money; it should be designed to make you money.

A wealth-building spending plan prioritizes cash flow, investments, and assets that generate income so that every dollar you spend has the potential to grow. Instead of just tracking where your money is going, you're going to redirect it into things that bring money back to you and turn your spending into a powerful tool for financial freedom. Here are a few ways you can create a wealth-building spending plan:

- **Categorize your spending into assets versus liabilities:** If it's not generating income, you should question it.
- **Question every purchase:** Ask yourself, *Does this expense get me closer to financial freedom, or is it just a liability?*
- **Use a percentage-based system:** For example, dedicate 50 percent of your budget to necessities, 30 percent to income-generating investments, and 20 percent to fun.

REMEMBER

Most people create spending plans to avoid going broke, but if you want to achieve financial freedom, your spending plan needs to be designed to generate income, not just cut costs. The goal isn't to spend less just for the sake of spending less; it's to spend smarter.

Cutting portions

If you know anything about marketing, you know that most stores deliberately price their largest portion only slightly higher than the medium one, so your brain automatically thinks, *Why not just go for the bigger one?* It feels like you're getting more value for your money.

The reality is that you're not saving money. You're spending more for something you don't actually need.

Not only is this bad for your body, but it is also bad for your income. If you're serious, portion. This doesn't just apply to food portions. It applies to the following ways that every company gets you to spend more without you realizing it:

- **Streaming services** bundle extras you don't actually use into higher-priced plans.
- **Gym memberships** offer "premium" packages when a basic plan would work just fine.
- **Retailers** push "Buy More, Save More" deals that just make you buy items you wouldn't have purchased otherwise.

REMEMBER

Every time you opt for the bigger portion, you're spending more without increasing value. That extra $2, $5, or $10 here and there may seem insignificant, but small amounts compound over time. You're giving that money away instead of putting it to work for you.

REMEMBER

When you cut portions strategically, you free up hundreds, even thousands of dollars a year. You can reinvest and compound that money into income-generating assets and serve your triple-compounding system to accelerate your freedom.

Here's an example: say you save $5 per day by cutting unnecessary spending. If you invest that $5 daily into an index fund earning 10 percent annually, you'll have $113,000 in 30 years — just from skipping the up-sized meal or premium subscription. That's real money that can go toward your triple-compounding system, including your investment portfolio, income-generating business, or passive income stream.

Avoiding paying cost of convenience

Companies make millions — sometimes billions — because 97 percent of people are willing to pay a premium for convenience, even when that convenience adds no real value to their lives or financial future.

Most people overpay, not because they have to, but because they hesitate. They "sleep on it" when making a decision and think they're being careful by doing so. In reality, they're just delaying and letting opportunities slip away.

Here's the truth: For most decisions, no matter how long you think about it, the facts don't change, but the cost usually goes up. This is another reason why successful people like William Clement Stone are committed to "doing it now," as explained in Chapter 2 of Book 4.

The following are some of the most common ways people overpay for convenience to their own financial detriment:

- **Booking flights at the last minute:** Buying flights within a week of departure can cost two to three times more than booking months in advance.
- **Shopping at convenience stores:** Markups on everyday items are often 50 percent to 100 percent higher than buying the same products in bulk at a grocery store.
- **ATM fees:** Transactions that cost $3 to $5 at non-network ATMs compound into hundreds per year — just to access your own money.
- **Food delivery services:** Between delivery fees, service charges, tips, and marked-up menu prices, a meal delivered to your door can cost significantly more than picking it up yourself.
- **Precut fruits and vegetables from grocery stores:** You're paying up to three times more for something you can prep yourself in minutes.
- **Bottled water instead of a reusable filter:** Spending $2 per bottle daily equals $730 per year, when a $50 water filter can last all year.
- **Light bulbs that aren't energy efficient:** Traditional bulbs cost more in electricity over time compared to LEDs, which last longer and use less power.

TIP

Time is infinitely more valuable than money, but that doesn't mean that paying for every convenience is a good investment. Some conveniences save time and are worth the cost, but most are simply draining your financial future. Every time you overpay for convenience, ask yourself these questions:

- Am I really getting value, or just avoiding a small inconvenience?
- Is this saving me significant time, or is it just feeding into my resistance?
- If I invested this money instead, how much could it compound over time?

Generating More Income from Your Current Job

If you have a job right now, you already have a built-in opportunity to generate more income without starting a business or taking on side hustles. The key? Adding more value. The more valuable you become to your employer, the more leverage you have to increase your salary, commissions, and bonuses. Here are some ideas for how to earn more at your job:

- **Add more value with new skills:** Invest in yourself by learning new skills that increase your worth to the company. If you can solve bigger problems, streamline processes, or improve efficiency, you become indispensable.
- **Change positions within your company:** Knock your KPIs (key performance indicators) out of the park, take on bigger responsibilities, and position yourself for a promotion or leadership role.
- **Earn commissions:** If your company offers performance-based pay, invest in sales, negotiation, and marketing skills to maximize your earnings. The better you are at driving revenue, the more you can compound your commissions.

You can also learn automation skills, organizational strategies, or even financial compounding techniques that make you an even greater asset. As a result, you gain the ability to negotiate better pay, higher bonuses, and improved benefits.

REMEMBER

The key strategy for earning more money is figuring out how to add more value. Is it possible to earn twice as much money in the same amount of time? Three times as much? Ten times as much? The answer is yes, if you add two, three, or ten times the value. You need to bring value equivalent to what you're asking for. You can't do the bare minimum and expect a raise. This means becoming so valuable that your employer can't afford to lose you.

Your income reflects the value you create. The faster you increase your value, the faster you can multiply your earnings without working more hours.

So, the question isn't *How can I make more money?* It's *How can I add so much value that my income grows automatically?*

Generating from Your Portfolio

The definition of *making your money work for you* is creating income by investing in external assets in your investment portfolio. You have several ways to make your portfolio work for you right now, producing cash flow that can be reinvested, saved, or used to fund other income-generating activities.

The following sections point out some of the most effective ways to generate passive or semi-passive income from your portfolio.

Earning interest on your investments

One of the safest ways to generate income from your portfolio is through interest-bearing assets: investments that pay you simply for parking your money in them. This type of investment is especially popular when interest rates are high because it enables you to earn a steady return with minimal risk. Here are some examples:

- **High-yield savings accounts:** These offer better interest rates than traditional bank accounts, keeping your money liquid while earning returns.
- **Bonds and treasury securities:** Government bonds, municipal bonds, and corporate bonds pay fixed interest over time.
- **Money market funds:** These funds invest in short-term, low-risk securities and provide steady, reliable interest income.

REMEMBER

The time it takes to generate substantial income by earning interest is long. Interest alone won't make you rich unless you have significant capital invested. However, it's a safe way to earn while protecting your money from inflation.

Generating income with dividend stocks

Dividend stocks pay out a portion of their profits to shareholders regularly (monthly, quarterly, or annually). This creates a steady income stream, even when the stock price fluctuates. The risk level with this method is low to moderate, but without higher investment, you won't see meaningful returns, and it takes a while to generate substantial income.

Some of the best dividend-paying assets include the following:

- **Blue-chip stocks:** Large, stable companies such as Coca-Cola, Alphabet (Google), Microsoft, and Procter & Gamble consistently pay dividends.

- **Dividend ETFs (exchange-traded funds):** Funds such as Vanguard Dividend Appreciation ETF (VIG) or Schwab US Dividend Equity ETF (SCHD) hold multiple dividend-paying stocks to reduce risk while still generating income.
- **REITs (Real Estate Investment Trusts):** These pay high dividends from real estate income without requiring you to buy physical property.

TIP

Dividends can compound over time if you reinvest them into more shares, making them a powerful source of long-term passive income. Flip to Chapter 4 in Book 4 to explore different types of stocks.

Swing trading for short-term gains

As explained in Chapter 4 of Book 4, swing trading involves buying and selling stocks, ETFs, or crypto over days or weeks to capitalize on short-term price movements. Unlike long-term investing, this strategy focuses on momentum, trends, and technical analysis, which means that you can generate substantial income in a short time, but the risk is high.

To be successful in swing trading, you need:

- **Risk management:** Knowing how to create a unique investment strategy that matches your risk tolerance. Read Chapter 1 in Book 4 to find out all about risk management.
- **Emotional control:** Not making impulsive decisions based on market fluctuations.
- **Chart reading skills:** Understanding the price action of an asset on the charts.

WARNING

Swing trading can generate quick profits, but it requires active monitoring, experience, and discipline to prevent big losses.

Earning crypto rewards through staking

Cryptocurrency (crypto) is a digital or virtual currency that uses cryptography for security and operates on decentralized blockchain networks. Unlike traditional currencies issued by governments (such as the U.S. dollar or the euro), cryptocurrencies are not controlled by any central authority, such as a bank or government. *Cryptocurrency Investing For Dummies* by Kiana Danial (Wiley) dives deep into all the ways you can grow your portfolio with cryptocurrency investing.

One of the ways to earn with cryptocurrency is by *staking* — a process where you lock up your crypto to support blockchain networks and earn rewards.

Popular staking options include:

- **Ethereum (ETH):** Earn rewards by staking ETH on the Ethereum 2.0 network.
- **Cardano (ADA), Solana (SOL), and Polkadot (DOT):** These offer staking rewards through various blockchain validators.
- **Stablecoin staking:** Platforms such as Aave, BlockFi, or Binance offer interest on stablecoins like USDC and DAI, reducing volatility risks.

WARNING

Staking is a great way to earn passive income in the medium term, especially if you have a high-risk tolerance. However, the value of your crypto is still subject to market risks.

Generating income with options trading

Options trading enables you to generate income even when the stock market moves sideways. Unlike buying stocks, options let you profit from price movement without owning the underlying asset.

Two common strategies for income generation are:

- **Selling covered calls:** If you own 100 shares of a stock, you can sell a call option and get paid a premium, regardless of whether the option gets exercised.
- **Selling cash-secured puts:** If you want to buy a stock at a lower price, selling a put enables you to earn a premium while waiting for the stock to drop.

WARNING

Options trading can provide immediate cash flow, but the risk level is high, so without proper risk management, it can lead to significant losses. See Chapter 4 in Book 4 to find out more about options.

Generating with Businesses

One of the most powerful ways to generate income is through businesses. Real magic can happen when you add automation, accelerating your triple-compounder system even further.

When we say, "investing in business," we don't mean starting a company from scratch (although that's an option). You can generate income by leveraging other people's businesses, partnering with existing systems, or enhancing what you're already doing. Whether you work for someone else, run your own business, or are just getting started, there's a way to increase your cash flow right now.

And the best part? You can stack these income streams over time, making each dollar work harder for you.

TIP

Having your own business unlocks an ocean of tax loopholes that save you even more money.

The following sections cover different ways you can generate income through business.

Becoming a contractor: Monetizing your skills as a freelancer

Not everyone wants to build a company, but that doesn't mean you can't profit from your expertise. You can offer services such as the following to other businesses that already exist and generate income as a contractor:

- **Freelancing and consulting:** Provide specialized services such as writing, coding, design, or marketing.
- **AI and tech services:** Businesses are willing to pay for AI-generated solutions, such as writing AI prompts for ChatGPT or building automation workflows.
- **Virtual assistance and operations management:** Many companies need help with back-end systems, website building, and event management.

REMEMBER

If you're already skilled in a particular area, you don't need to reinvent the wheel — just offer what you know to people who need it.

Becoming an affiliate: Getting paid to share what you love

You don't have to create a product to generate business income. You can promote products you already use and love through affiliate marketing.

Affiliate marketing is a performance-based marketing strategy in which you earn a commission by promoting another company's products or services. Instead of creating your own product, you recommend and sell products you trust, using a unique referral link. When someone makes a purchase through your link, you earn a percentage of the sale.

REMEMBER

One of the biggest advantages of affiliate marketing is that you don't need to create your own product. You're simply promoting an existing product or service. Unlike traditional businesses, start-up costs are minimal because you don't have to worry about inventory, shipping, or customer support. The income potential is also highly scalable. The more traffic and sales you generate, the more passive income you can earn over time.

Affiliate marketing works in virtually any niche, whether you're passionate about finance, health, beauty, tech, or business. It's a flexible and profitable income stream for anyone willing to put in the effort. Here are some affiliate marketing examples:

- As a finance blogger, you can earn commissions by recommending investment courses.
- As a YouTuber, you can review tech gadgets and links to Amazon's affiliate program.
- As a business coach, you can promote software tools and get paid per sign-up.
- As a fashionista, you can earn commissions by recommending your favorite skincare routine and fashion brands.

Earning income through insurance strategies

Insurance isn't just about protecting wealth. It can also be a powerful tool for generating income and building long-term financial security. You have two key ways to profit from insurance strategies:

- Leveraging whole life insurance for wealth building and passive income
- Becoming an insurance agent and earning commissions

Both of these methods enable you to use the insurance industry to your financial advantage — whether by growing your own money tax-free or earning a steady income helping others protect and grow their wealth.

TIP

No matter the economy, people always need insurance, which means steady income opportunities. Top insurance agents easily earn six figures, and some even make seven figures per year.

Creating your own business

If you want full control over your income, financial freedom, and the ability to scale without limits, creating your own business is one of the most powerful wealth-building moves you can make. Unlike a job, where your earnings are capped by salary limits, running a business enables you to control how much you make, how you grow, and how you invest your profits.

Starting your own business requires vision, action, and persistence, but the rewards can be life-changing. Whether you're looking to replace your 9-to-5 income, build a side hustle, or create generational wealth, launching a business can put you on the fast track to financial independence.

REMEMBER

All of the income-generating ideas in this section can be applied to your own business.

Most millionaires own businesses because business ownership enables you to scale income, automate systems, and invest profits into wealth-building assets.

Creating your own business is a fundamental phase of the triple-compounding system. As a business owner, you can reinvest your earnings in the following ways:

- **Tax loopholes and write-offs:** Business expenses reduce taxable income.
- **Investing in income-generating assets:** Stocks, real estate, and other wealth-building tools.
- **Scaling and automating:** Hiring teams and leveraging technology to increase revenue.

Buying another business

Although starting a business from scratch is an exciting challenge, it requires time, effort, and often years of trial and error. But what if you could skip the start-up phase and step directly into a cash-flowing business that's already built, already making money, and just needs someone to take it to the next level?

That's exactly why buying an existing business can be one of the fastest ways to generate income and grow your wealth.

Many established businesses already generate revenue and profit, so you start earning from day one instead of waiting years for a start-up to become profitable.

For others, you can bring your up-to-date marketing and AI skills to old businesses, serve their existing customers with your updated offers, and take the business to the next level.

And the best part? You don't have to go knock on the doors of the businesses in your town to see if they're willing to sell. There are platforms dedicated to helping buyers connect with sellers. Here are a few:

- `BizScout.com`: Lists Boomer-owned businesses for sale, many of which are profitable but need a new owner
- `Flippa.com`: A marketplace for buying digital businesses, websites, and online stores
- `EmpireFlippers.com`: Specializes in cash-flowing online businesses like e-commerce, Software as a Service (SaaS), and content sites
- `BizBuySell.com`: A massive marketplace for brick-and-mortar businesses, franchises, and local service businesses

TIP

Before buying a business, ask yourself the following questions:

- **Is the business profitable?** Check financial statements to ensure steady revenue and cash flow.
- **Does it align with my skills or interests?** If you have experience in a particular industry, buying a business in that space can help you scale faster.
- **Can I improve or automate it?** Look for businesses where you can increase efficiency, improve marketing, or streamline operations to boost profits.
- **Why is the owner selling?** Understand the seller's motivation. Are they retiring? Facing competition? Losing money? Make sure the business doesn't have hidden problems.
- **What financing options are available?** You don't always need to pay cash upfront. You can use seller financing, Small Business Administration (SBA) loans, or investor funding to acquire the business.

Finding money with tax loopholes

Most people think that they need to earn more to build wealth, but what if you could keep more of what you already make — legally? The tax code is filled with loopholes that business owners and investors use to lower their taxable income, keep more cash, and accelerate wealth-building. If you're not taking advantage of tax strategies, you're giving away money that could be working for you.

The wealthy don't pay less in taxes because they cheat the system. They use the system to their advantage. You can, too.

REMEMBER

The rich don't work harder; they work smarter. Wealthy people use legal tax strategies to redirect their income toward investments that generate even more tax advantages.

Here are some of the most common ways you can save on taxes:

- Deduct business expenses (turn everyday costs into write-offs)
- Use real estate for tax-free wealth growth
- Pay yourself tax-free with the proper business structure
- Hire your children for your business, pay them tax-free, reduce your taxable income, and keep wealth inside your family

See Book 5 to explore different tax strategies that you can discuss with your accountant.

IN THIS CHAPTER

» Clarifying your risk tolerance and defining your portfolio goals

» Choosing an asset allocation that reflects your triple-compounding goals

» Investing in cryptocurrency

Chapter 4
Investing in Online External Assets

Most people hear the word *compounding* and instantly think of investing in external assets — stocks, real estate, crypto, or gold. But here's the truth: This is actually Phase 3 of the triple-compounding method.

Why is it last? Because investing in external assets is about making your *money* work for you, and you can't make money work if you haven't made any yet. That's why you start with the other two phases: Phase 1, investing in yourself (read Chapter 2 of Book 4) and Phase 2, investing in your extensions (read Chapter 3 of Book 4).

After you complete those two phases, you're ready to put your money to work in external assets — and that's where the third compounder kicks in.

This chapter introduces you to some of the most popular online-accessible external assets — from Wall Street favorites to new digital opportunities — and explains how to decide which ones deserve a place in your triple-compounding portfolio. You don't need a financial advisor, trust fund, or market predictions to start investing in external assets. But you do need a process.

REMEMBER

The goal of external investing is not to beat the market. It's to build a life of financial peace, freedom, and choice — on your terms.

Considering Your Risk Tolerance

Before you choose any external asset to invest in, you need to check in with a critical piece of your financial profile: your risk tolerance. You can calculate your exact ability and willingness to take a risk in Chapter 1 of Book 4, but here's a quick refresher tailored specifically for external investing.

REMEMBER

Risk tolerance is more than just your gut feeling. It's a combination of three factors:

- Your *ability* to take a risk (your current financial strength)
- Your *willingness* to take a risk (your mindset, goals, and life stage)
- Your *confidence* in the asset you're planning to invest in

All three of these factors directly shape how much volatility, loss, or uncertainty you can handle, especially when the markets turn against you. You should figure out exactly where you currently stand so that you can align your investments with your personal situation.

TIP

Before investing in any external asset, ask yourself these questions:

- If this asset dropped by 50 percent, would I panic or hold steady?
- If this asset soared by 50 percent and I hadn't invested, would I regret it?

Your honest answers reveal your true confidence level.

Although traditional advisors often adjust portfolios based on the investor's age alone, your identity, education, and emotional resilience are just as important. As Warren Buffett puts it, "Risk comes from not knowing what you're doing."

REMEMBER

Knowing your risk tolerance upfront doesn't just help you pick the right assets; it helps you avoid emotional decisions when markets get bumpy.

WARNING

Skipping this step is one of the top reasons investors lose money. They chase returns without a plan that matches their tolerance, goals, and circumstances.

In the rest of this chapter, you find out how to evaluate each external asset class through the lens of risk, reward, and suitability so you can invest with clarity instead of guesswork.

Considering Your Portfolio Goals

After you clarify your risk tolerance, the next question is, *What is the purpose of your portfolio?*

This is where intentional analysis comes into play. In this step, you define exactly *why* you're investing in external assets and what outcomes you're looking to achieve.

In other words, are you investing for long-term wealth? Early retirement? Passive income? Saving for a down payment? Legacy building? Your intentions shape everything, from the assets you choose to the strategy you use to manage them. Without clear portfolio goals, you risk chasing shiny objects or reacting emotionally to short-term market movements.

Here are a few common portfolio goals to consider:

- **Wealth accumulation:** Building long-term wealth through steady growth. This often includes a mix of stocks, exchange-traded funds (ETFs), and real estate held over many years.
- **Income generation:** Earning steady payouts from dividends, rental income, or bonds. This goal is common for those who are preparing for or already in retirement.
- **Capital preservation:** Protecting the money you've already earned, often with lower-risk assets such as Treasury bonds, dividend stocks, or precious metals.
- **Aggressive growth:** Taking on higher risk for the chance at higher reward. This may include growth stocks, options trading, or early-stage investments.
- **Tax efficiency or legacy planning:** Structuring your portfolio to minimize taxes or pass on wealth to future generations.

TIP

If you're not sure what your goals are, think in terms of milestones. Do you want to replace the income from your employment? Retire early? Buy your dream house in five years? The more clarity you have, the better your portfolio can support that vision.

REMEMBER

The most successful investors aren't chasing random returns; they're building a system that supports their lives. A portfolio without a goal is like a GPS without a destination.

WARNING

If you copy someone else's strategy without knowing their goals, you could end up with a portfolio that's totally wrong for you. It's not about what's "hot." It's about what's *right* for you.

Selecting Your Asset Allocation

After you clarify your risk tolerance and your portfolio goals, it's time to answer the million-dollar question: *Where should you actually put your money?* This is where *asset allocation* comes in — the strategic mix of different asset types you include in your portfolio to balance risk and reward.

Your allocation acts as your portfolio's blueprint. It determines how much of your money goes into stocks versus bonds, real estate versus crypto, or index funds versus private equity. A well-crafted allocation reflects your personal financial goals, timeline, and comfort level with volatility — not what's trending on social media.

Asset allocation is more important than individual investment picks. In fact, research shows it accounts for more than 90 percent of a portfolio's long-term performance.

TIP

Think of asset allocation as building a plate at a buffet. If you pile it with only one type of food (or asset), you will get either bored or sick. A smart portfolio includes a healthy variety.

REMEMBER

There's no perfect one-size-fits-all formula. Your asset mix should evolve as your goals, income, and risk tolerance change.

The following sections break down the most common *online* asset classes — starting with stocks — and explain how to decide which ones align with your goals, risk tolerance, and freedom timeline. To find out about offline assets that you can add to your triple-compounding system, turn to Chapter 5 in Book 4.

Stocks

Stocks are one of the most popular — and accessible — external assets in any portfolio. When you buy a stock, you're buying a tiny slice of a publicly traded company. If the company grows, your slice becomes more valuable. If it pays dividends, you also get a piece of the profits along the way.

In triple compounding, stocks play a critical role because they offer both *growth potential* and *passive income* opportunities, depending on the type of stock you choose.

Not all stocks are created equal. Some are undervalued and overlooked. Others are pumped up by hype. Some are consistent income generators. Others are built to ride economic trends. The five common stock types you're likely to encounter are

- **Value stocks:** Often overlooked, sometimes underpriced, but full of potential. These are the kinds of companies Warren Buffett loves.
- **Dividend stocks:** Steady income generators that pay you just for holding them.
- **Pump-and-dump stocks:** Flashy, risky, and often manipulated. These may look tempting but are usually traps.
- **Cycling stocks:** Follow predictable economic trends and can be powerful tools if you know when to ride the wave.
- **Growth stocks:** High-risk, high-reward companies with the potential for rapid price appreciation.

The following sections walk you through each of these stocks to explain how to evaluate whether they deserve a spot in your portfolio.

TIP

Just like you diversify your income sources in the first two phases of triple compounding, you also want to diversify the types of stocks you invest in to balance stability, growth, and opportunity.

REMEMBER

Buying a stock means buying into a business. So, before you invest, ask yourself: *Would I be proud to own this company?*

Value stocks

Value stocks are the underdogs of the investing world; they're companies that are often trading for less than they're really worth. They may be out of the spotlight, temporarily struggling, or simply misunderstood by the market. But for investors who know how to spot them, they can offer incredible long-term upside.

This is the style of investing Warren Buffett made famous. He looks for businesses with strong fundamentals that are on sale — not because they're broken but because the market hasn't caught up to their true value yet.

You can think of value stocks as Black Friday deals on quality companies. The trick is knowing the difference between a deal and a dud.

What makes a company a *value stock?* Buffett says to approach stock picking as if you're buying the *entire company.* Would you want to own the whole thing and be proud to call yourself the CEO? That mindset changes everything. Consider the following when picking stocks:

- The stock price is low compared to its earnings, sales, or assets. Two popular ratios used to measure this are
  - **P/E (price-to-earnings) ratio:** Shows how much investors are paying for each dollar of a company's earnings. A low P/E may signal a bargain *or* a business in trouble.
  - **P/B (price-to-book) ratio:** Compares the stock price to the company's book value (what the company is worth on paper). A lower P/B often suggests the stock is undervalued.
- The company still shows strong fundamentals: solid cash flow, brand strength, or a competitive edge.
- It may be in a boring or "unsexy" industry the market has temporarily overlooked.
- The business is stable but currently undervalued due to market fear, economic cycles, or negative headlines.

You can take it one step further. Instead of getting lost in short-term financial reports and thousands of quarterly earnings statements, you can look for a different kind of signal. You can ask, *Is this company making the world better?*

REMEMBER

As a triple compounder, you don't just buy stocks you heard about from your brother-in-law and hope for the best. You buy the *right* ones and hold onto them with intention — not just to avoid unproductive screen-scrolling but to build a system that compounds both financially and energetically.

Here's what to look for in a true value asset.

- **Category kings:** Companies that dominate their niche
- **Efficiency creators:** Businesses that help people do things better, faster, and cheaper
- **Mission-driven brands:** Companies that do good for humankind

TIP

Published growth trends, profit margins, and P/E ratios matter, but not as much as understanding how a company creates long-term value. The goal isn't to predict the next quarter. It's to invest in companies that *last*.

REMEMBER

A value stock doesn't rise overnight. But over time, when the market catches up to its true worth, it can deliver consistent and compounding returns, especially when paired with dividends.

Dividend stocks

Imagine getting paid just for owning something. That's exactly what dividend stocks do, and they're a great alternative to renting out real estate because there's much less hassle involved in earning. These are shares of companies that distribute a portion of their profits to shareholders — usually every quarter. It's one of the most accessible forms of passive income and a core component of many triple compounders' portfolios.

Dividend stocks are especially popular among people who want

- Steady, predictable income
- Lower volatility compared to growth or hype stocks
- The ability to reinvest dividends and compound wealth over time

These companies are often well established, profitable, and stable — think blue-chip companies such as Coca-Cola, Johnson & Johnson, or Procter & Gamble. Although their value may not double overnight, they tend to be resilient during market downturns and offer a level of consistency that many investors appreciate.

The best part? Dividends can be automatically reinvested, enabling you to compound your returns over time without lifting a finger.

Here's why dividend stocks are great inside a triple-compounding system:

- They align beautifully with Phase 3, investing in external assets, especially when paired with automation.
- You can set up DRIPs (dividend reinvestment plans) that buy more shares for you every time a dividend is paid.
- They can supplement your income in retirement — or sooner if you build your portfolio with intention.
- Reinvested dividends can significantly boost long-term returns, even if the stock itself doesn't grow much.

WARNING

Not all dividend stocks are created equal. Some companies pay high dividends because they're desperate to attract investors. If a yield looks too good to be true, it may be. Always check the company's health and dividend payout ratio.

REMEMBER

The goal of dividend investing isn't just income. It's *compound income* — income that grows on autopilot when you reinvest it smartly. Dividend stocks are like your portfolio's loyal employees. They keep working and paying you — even while you sleep.

You can discover the amount of dividend a company pays on websites such as Yahoo! Finance (`https://finance.yahoo.com/`).

Pump-and-dump stocks

If value stocks are the wise old sages and dividend stocks are your loyal employees, pump-and-dump stocks are the shady restaurant customers who promise the world and disappear before the check arrives.

These are stocks that get artificially inflated — *pumped* — through hype, manipulation, or social media buzz only to be *dumped* after enough unsuspecting investors buy in. The result? The stock price crashes, leaving latecomers holding the bag.

You've probably seen this happen in real time, even if you didn't realize it. A stock skyrockets overnight because of a viral Reddit thread, a social media influencer, or a "leaked" stock tip and then drops like a rock days (or even hours) later. The problem isn't just volatility. It's that the price has nothing to do with the company's actual value.

Signs of a pump-and-dump stock include

- Massive price spikes with no news or fundamental reason
- Heavy promotion on forums, in chat rooms, or in spammy newsletters
- A small, low-volume stock that's easy to manipulate
- Sudden surges in volume followed by silence

WARNING

Pump-and-dumps are common in penny stocks, microcaps, and even crypto, especially when there's low liquidity and low regulation. If it feels like gambling, it probably is.

TIP

Just because a stock is being talked about online doesn't mean it's a scam, but hype should never be your reason to invest. The moment you hear, "It's going to the moon!" ask yourself, "Based on what, exactly?"

REMEMBER

Triple compounders don't fall for shortcuts or speculation. They build portfolios based on real companies, real value, and long-term vision. They don't invest in hype. They invest in purpose.

Cycling stocks

Some stocks move in waves — and not the kind you catch at the beach. These are called *cycling stocks* (or *cyclical stocks*), and they tend to rise and fall in sync with the economy.

When the economy is booming, people spend more on things such as travel, new cars, and fancy furniture, so companies in those industries thrive. But when the economy slows down, those same companies often see a drop in profits, and their stock prices usually follow.

This isn't necessarily a bad thing. In fact, if you understand how business cycles work, cyclical stocks can be a powerful addition to your triple-compounding strategy, especially as part of your long-term plan.

Common examples of cycling stock industries include

- Travel and hospitality (such as airlines, hotels, and cruise lines)
- Automotive and transportation
- Retail and luxury goods
- Construction and home improvement
- Energy and materials (such as oil, gas, and metals)

How do you know when to buy cycling stocks? It starts with understanding where the economy is in its cycle.

- **Early expansion:** People are cautiously optimistic; markets start to rise.
- **Full-blown boom:** Spending is high; cyclical stocks usually perform best.
- **Slowdown or recession:** Spending pulls back, and these stocks tend to drop.

REMEMBER

Although cyclical stocks rise and fall with the economy, defensive stocks do the opposite. These are companies that tend to remain stable even during economic downturns — think groceries, utilities, and healthcare. Many defensive stocks also pay consistent dividends, which can help cushion the blow when cyclical stocks are taking a hit.

TIP

Because of their predictable behavior during market cycles, many cyclical stocks make excellent swing trading candidates. Their price movements often follow patterns that technical traders can spot and capitalize on — whether that means holding for a few days, weeks, or months.

Growth stocks

If value stocks are the slow-and-steady types, *growth stocks* are the overachievers. These are companies that are expanding fast, disrupting industries, and reinvesting most of their profits (if they even have profits yet!) to keep growing even faster.

Growth stocks are typically not cheap because investors are betting on the company's *future potential* rather than its current financials.

Think of tech giants such as Apple, Amazon, or Tesla in their earlier days. These were once high-risk bets, but over time, they proved their growth trajectory. Today's growth stocks may be in sectors such as

- Artificial intelligence
- Clean energy and electric vehicles
- E-commerce and cloud computing
- Biotechnology
- Fintech and emerging markets

WARNING

Unlike dividend stocks, most growth stocks don't pay dividends. Instead, they reinvest everything back into innovation, hiring, or expansion. That means the only way you make money is through *capital appreciation*, the stock price going up.

Here's why growth stocks can be powerful inside a triple-compounding portfolio:

- They have the potential to significantly outperform the market — if you choose wisely and time your entry right.
- They're ideal for younger investors or anyone with a longer time horizon and a higher risk tolerance.
- When paired with more stable assets, they can give your portfolio the "rocket fuel" that accelerates long-term returns.

TIP

Growth stocks often look overpriced on paper (they usually have high P/E ratios), but that's because the market is pricing in future earnings. Your job is to determine whether those expectations are realistic or hyped.

You can combine growth stocks with value investing, meaning that you buy growth stocks when their price temporarily drops due to market sentiment.

REMEMBER

Growth stocks tend to be more volatile than cycling or value stocks, especially in down markets. That doesn't make them bad; it just means you need a strategy, not just hope.

When chosen wisely, growth stocks can transform your portfolio over time, but they're not lottery tickets. They're businesses that need time and execution to fulfill their potential.

Forex

Forex — short for foreign exchange — is the largest and most liquid financial market in the world. It's where global currencies are bought, sold, and traded 24 hours a day, five days a week.

In forex, you're not buying physical currency. You're trading currency pairs — such as EUR/USD or USD/JPY — speculating on how one currency will move in relation to another.

If you've ever traveled abroad and exchanged money, you've already participated in the forex market on a much smaller scale.

Here's what makes forex unique:

- It's the most liquid market in the world — trillions of dollars traded daily.
- It runs 24/5 across global time zones.
- It uses leverage, meaning you can control a large trade size with a relatively small amount of money.
- Currency values are influenced by interest rates, inflation, economic reports, and geopolitical events.

Although the potential for profit is real, so is the potential for loss, especially when leverage is involved. That's why most retail traders who jump into forex without a plan end up losing money.

TIP

If you're going to explore forex, treat it like a skill — not a slot machine. Study the fundamentals, learn technical analysis, and start small. Forex can be an active, short-term income strategy that complements your long-term portfolio, but only if you have rules and discipline in place.

WARNING

Leverage can magnify gains, but it also magnifies losses. Don't risk more than you can afford to lose and never trade with money meant for bills or savings.

Options

Options are one of the most misunderstood and misused financial tools out there. When used strategically, they can *protect* your portfolio or *amplify* your returns. But when used recklessly, they can wipe out your account faster than you can say "theta decay."

An option is a contract that gives you the right — but not the obligation — to buy or sell an underlying asset (usually a stock) at a specific price, within a specific time frame.

Two main types of options are

- **Call options:** Give you the right to *buy* a stock at a certain price (useful when you think the price will go up).
- **Put options:** Give you the right to *sell* a stock at a certain price (useful when you think the price will go down).

Options aren't new. What most people don't realize is this: Options were originally invented as a risk management tool rather than a get-rich-quick strategy.

When used wisely, options can do the following:

- Generate income through strategies such as covered calls
- Hedge against market drops with protective puts
- Boost returns with less capital compared to buying full shares
- Add flexibility to your overall investing approach

Options are like power tools: They're amazing in skilled hands and dangerous in untrained ones. The reality is that most beginners dive into options without a strategy and end up chasing short-term gains using high-risk, high-leverage bets such as weekly options, zero-DTE plays, or meme-stock hype trades. *Zero-DTE* (zero days to expiration) refers to options contracts that expire on the same day they're traded, making them extremely high-risk and time-sensitive. They're often used by advanced traders for fast, speculative bets.

WARNING

Options can expire worthless. That means you can lose 100 percent of what you paid for the contract. Always manage your risk and never trade options without understanding the Greeks (as in delta, theta, and implied volatility).

When used intentionally, options can be a powerful tool inside your triple-compounding portfolio and give you leverage with control. But when misused, they turn into nothing more than educated gambling.

Index funds

If forex and options are the fast lane of investing, index funds are the scenic route. For many triple compounders, index funds are the *sweet spot* between simplicity, safety, and long-term growth.

Index funds are investment funds — usually structured as ETFs (exchange-traded funds) or mutual funds — that track a specific market index. That means instead of picking individual stocks, you invest in an entire basket of companies that represent a segment of the market.

One of the most well-known examples is the S&P 500 index fund, which includes 500 of the largest publicly traded companies in the U.S., including Apple, Microsoft, Amazon, and Google.

When you invest in an index fund, you get

- **Instant diversification:** One fund gives you exposure to hundreds (sometimes thousands) of companies.
- **Low fees:** Because index funds are passively managed, they're way cheaper than traditional mutual funds.
- **Minimal effort:** You don't need to research individual companies or time the market. You set it, forget it, and let it grow.

Index funds are especially powerful for

- Beginner investors
- Busy professionals who want to automate
- Long-term wealth builders who value steady, compounding growth over hype
- Retirement accounts such as IRAs and 401(k)s

TIP

Index funds are one of the few investments even Warren Buffett recommends for everyday investors. He's said that if he could only give one piece of advice to most people, it would be, "Put 90 percent of your money in a low-cost S&P 500 index fund."

REMEMBER

In triple compounding, you don't just chase excitement; you also build stability. Index funds can anchor your portfolio while other assets give you room to grow and explore. You can dive into the world of ETFs with the latest edition of *Exchange-Traded Funds For Dummies* by Russell Wild (published by Wiley).

REITs

If you want to invest in real estate without fixing toilets, chasing down tenants, or worrying about broken HVAC systems, then you need to know about real estate investment trusts (REITs).

A REIT is a company that owns, operates, or finances income-generating real estate, and it's legally required to pay out at least 90 percent of its taxable income to shareholders in the form of dividends. That means you, the investor, get regular cash flow without ever owning or managing a property yourself.

REITs are kind of like real estate mutual funds. You buy shares (often through the stock market), and in return, you get exposure to a portfolio of properties — sometimes hundreds — ranging from apartment buildings and office parks to malls, hospitals, and even cell towers.

Two main types of REITs are

- **Publicly traded REITs:** Bought and sold just like stocks or ETFs through your brokerage account. These are the most liquid and beginner-friendly.
- **Private or non-traded REITs:** Offer access to different kinds of real estate but may have higher fees, less transparency, and longer lock-up periods.

REITs are a powerful fit for your triple-compounding strategy because they offer

- **Passive income** through consistent dividends
- **Diversification** across property types and locations
- **Liquidity** because you can buy or sell shares easily
- **Low barriers to entry** because you don't need $100,000 or a mortgage to get started

TIP

You can invest in REITs with as little as $100. Some popular ones even pay monthly dividends, which is great for automating your passive income stream. However, just because a REIT pays a high dividend doesn't mean it's healthy. Use the same fundamental analysis you would with a stock. Look at occupancy rates, management quality, debt levels, and payout ratios.

WARNING

REITs are still tied to the real estate market. If commercial property values drop or vacancy rates spike, your investment can lose value. Always diversify your income streams, even within real estate.

TIP

Find out more about REITs in *REITs For Dummies* by Brad Thomas (published by Wiley).

Unlocking Cryptocurrency

Cryptocurrency is one of the most hyped — and misunderstood — asset classes in modern investing. It's volatile, unregulated, and polarizing. But for triple compounders who know how to approach it strategically, it also offers unique opportunities for growth, diversification, and long-term freedom.

The following sections show you how to explore it as one of your external investment options. For more information, check out the latest edition of *Cryptocurrency Investing For Dummies* by Kiana Danial (published by Wiley).

Defining cryptocurrency

So, what is *cryptocurrency*, really? It's a decentralized form of digital money that operates without a central bank, powered by *blockchain* technology — a decentralized digital ledger that records transactions across a network of computers in a secure, transparent, and tamper-proof way.

Unlike traditional currencies such as the U.S. dollar or the euro, most cryptocurrencies have a fixed supply and are controlled by code, not governments. That makes them potentially resistant to inflation and government interference. Bitcoin and other decentralized assets offer something many traditional systems can't: freedom and control over your own money.

Here's why cryptocurrency can be a compelling part of your external asset strategy:

- It diversifies your portfolio beyond traditional assets such as stocks and real estate.

- It may provide capital appreciation through price growth (if chosen and timed wisely).
- Some cryptos allow for yield generation, such as staking or earning interest.
- It can serve as a potential hedge against inflation and currency risk.
- It fuels emerging technologies like decentralized finance (DeFi), non-fungible tokens (NFTs), and the metaverse.

  NFTs are unique digital assets stored on a blockchain representing ownership of something unique, such as art, music, or virtual collectibles. *Metaverse* is a virtual, interconnected digital world where people can interact, work, play, shop, and invest using avatars, often powered by blockchain, cryptocurrencies, and virtual reality technologies.

WARNING

Before you get starry-eyed, here's the truth: crypto is not magic. It comes with serious risks — from volatility and scams to regulatory uncertainty and tech vulnerabilities. Crypto is not about getting rich overnight. It's about getting smart, intentional, and strategic about how you enter this space — as you do with any other asset class.

REMEMBER

The price of a coin may catch headlines, but what really matters is what's *behind* that coin: the blockchain, the use case, the adoption, and the community. In other words, don't invest in symbols; invest in substance.

WARNING

If you don't understand how a crypto project works, don't invest in it. It's your protection against being the exit liquidity for someone else's pump-and-dump.

Understanding coins, altcoins, and tokens

Before you go crypto shopping, it's important to understand the difference between coins, altcoins, and tokens because they're not interchangeable.

- **Coins:** These are digital assets that operate on their own independent blockchain. Examples are Bitcoin (BTC), Ethereum (ETH), and XRP.
- **Altcoins (short for "alternative coins"):** These include any coin that isn't Bitcoin. Most run on their own blockchains and offer specific use cases beyond just "digital money."
- **Tokens:** These are digital assets that don't have their own blockchain. Instead, they operate on top of an existing blockchain network. Ethereum and Solana are examples. Tokens can represent anything: ownership in a project, access to a platform, or even digital art.

TIP

Think of coins as the infrastructure and tokens as applications built on top of that infrastructure.

Bitcoin

Bitcoin is where it all began. Launched in 2009 by the mysterious Satoshi Nakamoto, Bitcoin (BTC) was the first-ever cryptocurrency. It remains the largest, most recognized, and most widely held digital asset in the world.

But Bitcoin isn't just a first mover. It's the foundation of the entire crypto ecosystem. For many investors, it still serves as the "digital gold" of the 21st century.

Bitcoin was created as a decentralized alternative to government-issued currencies. It runs on its own blockchain, has a fixed supply of 21 million coins, and is not controlled by any central bank, government, or corporation. This makes it immune to inflationary policies that devalue traditional currencies over time.

Here's why many triple compounders consider Bitcoin an essential part of their external asset allocation:

- It's seen as a **store of value,** similar to gold, especially during times of currency debasement or economic uncertainty.
- It's **scarce** by design, with only 21 million coins ever to exist — a feature that increases its appeal as digital hard money.
- It's **borderless and permissionless,** meaning you can send it to anyone, anywhere, without a bank or intermediary.
- It's becoming **more mainstream,** with adoption by companies, hedge funds, and even governments.

Although Bitcoin is no longer the fastest or most innovative crypto out there, it's the most battle-tested and widely adopted. For many, it serves as the entry point to crypto and the core holding in a diversified digital portfolio.

TIP

If you're new to cryptocurrency, Bitcoin is a great place to start. It's the least risky of the bunch — not because it's safe but because it's proven. Owning Bitcoin doesn't mean betting on a trend. It means investing in a system of money that's decentralized, deflationary, and global.

WARNING

Bitcoin can still be extremely volatile. Don't invest more than you can afford to hold through wild price swings.

Altcoins

Altcoins are any cryptocurrencies that aren't Bitcoin. Some try to improve on Bitcoin's limitations. Others launch entirely new ecosystems around smart contracts, DeFi, and next-gen tech.

Here's a breakdown of three of the most important altcoins in the market at the time of writing:

- **Ethereum (ETH):** Ethereum introduced the concept of smart contracts, enabling developers to build decentralized apps (dApps) that run without middlemen. Ethereum is used to pay for transactions and services on the Ethereum network.

  Blockchain: Ethereum

  Primary use: Smart contracts, dApps, DeFi, NFTs

- **Solana (SOL):** Solana is built for speed. It can process thousands of transactions per second thanks to a unique system called proof-of-history (PoH). It's popular among developers building fast, scalable applications in gaming, NFTs, and finance, including Web3 apps (applications that use blockchain technology to give users more ownership and control).

  Blockchain: Solana

  Primary use: High-speed DeFi, Web3 apps, NFTs

- **XRP (Ripple):** XRP focuses on cross-border payments, aiming to make international money transfers faster and cheaper. It's not mined like Bitcoin; instead, it uses a consensus protocol that reduces transaction time and energy usage.

  Blockchain: XRP Ledger

  Primary use: Global payments and remittances

TIP

Altcoins can offer more upside than Bitcoin, but they also come with more complexity and risk. Evaluate both the vision and viability of each project.

WARNING

Just because a coin is "cheaper" doesn't mean it's a better deal. Price per coin means nothing without understanding market cap, supply, and utility.

Tokens

Tokens are digital assets created and hosted on an existing blockchain. The most common platform for tokens is Ethereum, but others such as Solana, BNB Chain, and Avalanche also support them.

Unlike coins, tokens don't function as native currency for their networks. Instead, they represent

- Access to a product or service (utility tokens)
- Ownership or voting rights in a project (governance tokens)
- Real-world assets such as dollars or gold (stablecoins)
- Unique digital collectibles (NFTs)

Here are some common types of tokens:

- **Utility tokens:** Give you access to services, discounts, or tools on a crypto platform
- **Governance tokens:** Enable you to vote on decisions related to a decentralized project
- **Stablecoins:** Pegged to traditional currencies such as the USD (for example, USDC, USDT) to reduce volatility
- **NFTs:** Represent ownership of unique assets such as art, music, or in-game items

TIP

Tokens are like apps on your phone, where the blockchain is the operating system. You don't need to build a new operating system to build something useful. You just need to use the tools already available.

REMEMBER

Many of the most exciting projects in crypto aren't coins; they're tokens. But their value depends on adoption, not hype.

Staking

If you've ever wished your crypto could earn income while you sleep — without having to sell it — staking may be your new favorite strategy.

Staking is the process of locking up your cryptocurrency to help support the operations and security of a blockchain network. In return, you earn rewards, usually in the form of more crypto. It's kind of like earning interest at a bank but for participating in a decentralized system.

You can stake certain cryptocurrencies that run on proof-of-stake (PoS) or delegated proof-of-stake networks. Popular staking coins include Ethereum, Solana, Cardano, and Polkadot.

Here's how staking works in simple terms:

1. **You commit your crypto to the network.**
2. **Your funds are used to validate transactions and keep the blockchain secure.**
3. **You get rewarded with more of that crypto in exchange for your contribution.**

TIP

Think of it as renting out your crypto's energy to help keep the lights on in the blockchain — and getting paid for it.

Benefits of staking include the following:

- **Passive income:** Your crypto earns while you hold.
- **Compound growth:** Many platforms let you automatically restake your rewards.
- **Network support:** You're helping the ecosystem stay secure and decentralized.

TIP

You don't need to run your own validator node to stake. Many exchanges, such as Coinbase, Kraken, or Binance, let you stake your crypto with just a few clicks. Also, staking rewards vary, depending on the coin and platform, and some require lock-up periods. Always check the terms before committing your funds.

WARNING

Staked assets are still exposed to market volatility. If the price of the coin drops, your staked rewards may not make up for the loss. Staking is not risk-free, but it *is* a way to put idle crypto to work.

Non-fungible tokens

Non-fungible tokens (NFTs) are one of the most talked-about applications of blockchain technology. At their core, NFTs are unique digital assets stored on a blockchain that represent ownership of something that is one of a kind. That "something" can be anything: art, music, event tickets, virtual land, digital fashion, or even a tweet.

Unlike cryptocurrencies such as Bitcoin or Ethereum, NFTs are not interchangeable. One Bitcoin is always equal to another Bitcoin. But each NFT is different, which is what makes it non-fungible.

The technology behind NFTs has real potential — and it goes way beyond just digital art. Here are a few real-world applications that are already in motion.

- **Art and collectibles:** Digital artists can now sell and track ownership of their work with authenticity built in.
- **Gaming:** Players can buy, sell, or trade in-game assets — such as characters or weapons — as NFTs.
- **Memberships and access:** Some NFTs serve as digital keys to communities, events, or perks.
- **Real estate and identity:** Long-term, NFTs can represent deeds, IDs, or other legal documents.

If you're wondering whether NFTs belong in a triple compounder's portfolio, consider this: They're *not* must-haves, but they *can* be an interesting part of your strategy if you understand their utility, scarcity, and creator value.

WARNING

The most valuable NFTs tend to have strong communities, real-world use cases, or connections to influential creators or brands. If you're just buying random images hoping they'll go to the moon (skyrocket), you're gambling, not investing.

NFTs are powered by smart contracts, and most live on blockchains such as Ethereum, Solana, or Polygon. If you're already exploring those ecosystems, NFTs may be a natural next step.

WARNING

The NFT space is still speculative and unregulated. Many projects are driven by hype, and scams are common. Don't invest in an NFT just because someone else made money on it. Invest because you understand the asset and believe in the long-term value.

IN THIS CHAPTER

» **Understanding the pros, cons, and cash flow potential of real estate**

» **Diving into private equity**

» **Discovering physical asset strategies — from precious metals to crypto cold wallets**

» **Reinforcing your triple-compounding flywheel by reinvesting profits intentionally**

Chapter 5
Investing in Offline External Assets

Most people think of investing as something that happens online — buying stocks, crypto, or options with a few taps on a screen. And although those digital markets are powerful tools (see Chapter 4 in Book 4), they're not the only way to grow your wealth.

There's a whole other category of external assets that live in the physical world — things you can touch, own, or operate in real life. These are called *offline assets*, and for many triple compounders, they create a second layer of security, income, and long-term growth.

This chapter is your guide to the most common offline investment vehicles, including

- Real estate, from flipping to rentals to commercial buildings
- Private equity, including venture capital and growth equity
- Funds of funds, for diversified exposure to private markets

» Other tangible or hybrid asset classes that don't rely on market apps or online trading platforms

In this chapter, you find out how to spot the opportunities that make sense for your goals, your time, and your energy — and avoid the ones that tie you down or drain your bandwidth.

TIP

Offline assets are often slower to move but more stable in the long term. They can be your portfolio's foundation while your online investments provide speed and flexibility.

REMEMBER

The goal isn't to copy what other people are investing in. The goal is to create a personalized, resilient portfolio that supports your entire wealth-building flywheel.

Building Wealth with Real Estate

Real estate is one of the oldest — and most trusted — ways to build wealth. From generational landlords to HGTV-style flippers, people have long turned to property as a way to generate income, hedge against inflation, and create long-term financial security.

Here's some good news: You don't have to buy a house to invest in real estate.

Whether you want to roll up your sleeves and flip properties, collect passive rental income, or own a slice of the real estate market through real estate investment trusts (REITs), which are covered in Chapter 4 of Book 4, there's an option for every risk level, budget, and lifestyle.

Your goal as a triple compounder is not just to own "stuff." It's to create automated, intentional income that grows with time. Real estate can do exactly that, if you choose the right strategy for your season of life.

The following sections break down the most common ways investors tap into real estate as an external asset:

» **House flipping:** The fast-paced, high-risk way to profit from undervalued properties

» **Rental properties:** A steady stream of cash flow — and headaches, if you're not careful

- **Residential real estate:** Properties where people live, from single-family homes to vacation rentals
- **Commercial real estate:** Larger-scale investments such as office buildings, shopping centers, and industrial warehouses

REMEMBER

Real estate can build real wealth, but it's not passive by default. You need a strategy that matches your energy, risk tolerance, and time capacity.

REMEMBER

You don't need to buy a house to get into real estate. Thanks to modern tools such as REITs and crowdfunding platforms, there are more accessible ways to get started than ever before.

House flipping

House flipping may be the most glamorous — and most misunderstood — real estate strategy out there. Thanks to TV shows and influencer reels, it's easy to think that flipping a home is just a quick trip to Home Depot and a few weekends of DIY magic.

But here's the truth: Flipping real estate is a full-time business, not a passive investment. And unless you know what you're doing (or have a team who does), it can cost you far more than you make.

Flipping involves buying a property at a discount, fixing it up, and reselling it for a profit — ideally in a short period of time. It's all about timing, margins, and speed. The longer you hold the property, the more it eats into your potential profits.

Some flippers do all the work themselves. Others outsource everything and manage the project like a business. Either way, success in flipping comes down to one detail: your numbers.

Before you ever swing a hammer (or hire someone who does), you need to know the following:

- The purchase price
- Your renovation budget
- Expected selling price (after repair value, or ARV)
- All holding costs (loan interest, taxes, insurance, utilities)
- Closing costs and commissions
- Your profit margin

Your profit margin is the most important consideration. Many pros aim for at least 20 percent to 30 percent net profit after all expenses.

REMEMBER

Flipping is not triple compounding unless it's systematized. If you treat it like a one-time hustle, you're just buying yourself a part-time job. If you treat it like a business — with teams, checklists, and automation — it can be a powerful wealth-building tool. Also, it works best in hot markets that have low inventory and high buyer demand. But those same markets can also be the riskiest if things turn.

WARNING

Underestimating repair costs is the number one reason flippers lose money. Always estimate high on your budget and build in extra time. Renovation delays are more common than you think. For more information, check out the latest edition of *Flipping House For Dummies* by Ralph R. Roberts with Joe Kraynak and Kyle Roberts (published by Wiley).

Rental properties

Rental properties are one of the most popular ways to turn real estate into a recurring income stream. The idea is simple: buy a property, rent it out, and collect monthly payments. Although the income can be passive, the work involved *usually isn't* — especially in the beginning.

When done right, rental properties can offer

- Monthly cash flow from tenants
- Long-term appreciation of the property
- Tax benefits such as depreciation and mortgage interest deductions
- Leverage from controlling a large asset with a relatively small down payment
- A hedge against inflation because rent prices often rise with inflation

WARNING

But the truth is that owning rental properties can also mean late-night plumbing emergencies, broken leases, and months with no income if a tenant leaves or stops paying.

That's why successful rental investing requires more than just buying a cute house in a nice neighborhood. It takes the following:

- Careful location analysis
- Accurate cash flow projections

- Smart property management, whether you do it yourself or hire help
- Legal awareness of tenant rights, leases, and eviction rules

Being a landlord is not the same thing as being a passive investor. If you want rental properties to support your triple-compounding lifestyle, you need to build systems or delegate them.

TIP

You don't have to start with a multi-unit building. Some of the best rental portfolios start with one small, cash-flowing, single-family home. Focus on properties that are cash-flow positive from day one — not just "potentially profitable in a few years."

WARNING

If your mortgage, taxes, and maintenance costs are higher than your rent income, your property is bleeding money rather than building wealth. Never assume appreciation will bail you out.

Residential real estate

Residential real estate includes any property where people live: single-family homes, condos, duplexes, townhouses, and small apartment buildings (typically four units or fewer). This property is often the first stop for new real estate investors because it feels more familiar and accessible than commercial properties.

Residential properties tend to be more stable than commercial, especially in uncertain markets. People always need a place to live, regardless of what the economy is doing. And if you pick the right neighborhood, residential rentals can provide steady cash flow, long-term appreciation, and tax advantages.

Here are some common ways that investors earn with residential real estate:

- **Long-term rentals** (traditional landlord-tenant model)
- **Short-term rentals** (Airbnb, Vrbo, and so on)
- **House hacking** (living in one unit and renting out the others)

Residential real estate is typically easier to finance and manage than commercial, and there's a wider pool of buyers if you ever decide to sell.

TIP

Start with what you know. If you live in a certain type of home or area and understand what renters want there, that insight can give you an edge as an investor.

REMEMBER

You're not just investing in a property; you're investing in a community. Pay close attention to school zones, crime rates, job growth, and local amenities.

WARNING

Buying in the wrong neighborhood — or underestimating property taxes, vacancies, or maintenance — can turn a residential "deal" into a money pit. Run the numbers and don't get emotional.

Commercial real estate

Commercial real estate includes income-producing properties used for business purposes: office buildings, retail centers, warehouses, apartment buildings with five or more units, hotels, and even storage facilities.

This property is where the *big money* is made in real estate, but it often requires more experience, capital, and risk management than residential real estate. Commercial leases tend to be longer, tenants may cover more of the operating costs (known as triple-net leases), and the valuation of these properties is based on income potential, not just comparable sales.

Commercial real estate can be incredibly rewarding when done right, by providing the following:

- Higher income potential due to multiple units or higher rents
- Economies of scale (especially with multifamily or mixed-use buildings)
- More professional tenants because businesses are often more predictable than individual renters
- Stronger long-term appreciation if the area is growing

But this space also comes with more risk. A vacant storefront or large commercial unit can cost you thousands per month if it sits empty.

TIP

If you're interested in commercial real estate but not ready to buy a strip mall, you can get exposure through REITs (see Chapter 4 in Book 4), crowdfunding platforms, or syndications.

WARNING

Lenders often require higher down payments (20 percent to 30 percent or more) and stricter approval for commercial loans. Make sure that you understand the numbers and have a solid team in place.

Investing in Private Equity

Private equity is one of the most powerful — but least understood — external asset classes in the investing world. It's where the ultra-wealthy often play: investing in private companies before they go public (if they ever do) and earning returns through business growth, acquisitions, or eventual exits.

Unlike stocks or REITs (covered in Chapter 4 of Book 4), private equity investments aren't traded on public exchanges. That means they're less liquid, harder to access, and usually come with higher minimums. But for investors who qualify, private equity can offer higher returns, more control, and a deeper connection to the companies they support.

Private equity can take many forms, including

- Direct investments in start-ups or growing businesses
- Venture capital funding early-stage companies with high growth potential in exchange for partial ownership
- Private equity funds managed by firms that pool money from investors
- Angel investing in early-stage companies
- Crowdfunding platforms that allow smaller investors to access private deals

The following sections look at common types of private equity investments you may come across, whether you're a retail investor exploring crowdfunding platforms or an accredited investor ready to dive deeper.

Venture capital

Venture capital is private equity at the start-up stage. Venture capital focuses on high-risk, high-reward investments in early-stage companies — usually in tech, biotech, or disruptive industries.

Venture capitalists typically invest in exchange for equity (ownership), and they expect that most of their investments will fail but that one or two big winners will more than make up for the losses.

As an everyday investor, you may not have access to top venture capital funds. However, thanks to platforms such as SeedInvest, Republic, and StartEngine, you can now invest small amounts into vetted start-ups and get a front-row seat to innovation.

TIP

Venture capital investing is like planting seeds. Some won't grow, some will shoot up fast, and a few may become a forest. Only invest what you can afford to let sit and grow for years.

Growth equity

Think of this as the "teenage" phase of private investing. *Growth equity* investors fund companies that are past the start-up stage but need capital to expand, enter new markets, or restructure operations.

Unlike with venture capital, the companies they invest in often have proven revenue and are looking to scale — not just survive.

As an investor, growth equity lets you tap into businesses that are less risky than raw start-ups but still offer potential for a big upside. Some crowdfunding platforms, syndicates, and small business funds offer access to these kinds of deals.

TIP

Growth equity is ideal for investors who want to support expansion-stage companies with a clear use of funds and a path to profitability.

Buyouts and private acquisitions

Buyouts are the heavyweight class of private equity. *Buyouts* involve purchasing a controlling interest in a company, often using a mix of investor money and debt (called a leveraged buyout or LBO).

Buyout firms typically target mature businesses with steady cash flow, cut costs or boost performance, and sell them later at a profit.

Although this kind of investing is mostly reserved for institutional or accredited investors, some fractional platforms and private equity funds of funds are starting to open the door to smaller investors.

TIP

Private equity buyouts aren't about quick flips. They're about improving businesses over time and getting paid well for the patience.

Funds of funds

If you like the idea of private equity but don't want to pick individual companies or deals, a fund of funds may be your entry point. These are professionally managed portfolios that invest in multiple private equity funds — kind of like the private investing version of a mutual fund. Instead of betting on one company or one manager, you get exposure to a broader pool of deals, strategies, and industries.

Some funds of funds are available only to accredited investors, but a few platforms and retirement plans offer access to retail investors through structured products or lower minimums.

WARNING

Funds of funds are great for diversification, but they often come with extra layers of fees, so make sure that the access is worth the cost.

REMEMBER

You may not know exactly which companies are in the portfolio, so always look for transparency around fund strategy, past performance, and lock-up periods.

Getting into private equity without billions

You don't need to be a billionaire to get into private equity anymore. Platforms such as AngelList, Republic, and StartEngine have lowered the barrier for both accredited and nonaccredited investors.

WARNING

Private equity is *illiquid*, meaning that your money may be tied up for five to ten years. And yes, many private companies fail. Never invest more than you can afford to lose, and always do your due diligence.

Private equity isn't for everyone. But for triple compounders who've built stable income streams, solid investments, and a long-term financial vision, it can be an exciting next-level play.

Investing Old School: Physical Precious Metals

If real estate is the dinner-party flex of offline investing, and crypto is the rebel genius, then physical precious metals are the grandparents. Quiet. Old school. And still incredibly valuable.

For thousands of years, people have stored wealth in gold, silver, and other metals. Why? Because unlike currencies or companies, these elements never go to zero. They don't rely on CEOs or central banks. They just *are*. In a world of digital everything, holding real, tangible gold in your hand can feel oddly grounding — and strategic.

The following sections uncover what to know before adding shiny metals to your triple-compounding portfolio.

Understanding the role of metals in your portfolio

Precious metals aren't designed to skyrocket like stocks or crypto. They're built to hold value when everything else feels shaky. This reason is why many investors use metals as

- A hedge against inflation
- A safe haven during economic downturns or global crises
- A diversifier that moves differently than the stock market

Gold and silver won't make your net worth explode, but they can help keep it from imploding.

REMEMBER

Metals don't produce income. They don't pay dividends. You don't "scale" gold. Their job is to preserve, not multiply. And that's okay.

Choosing among gold, silver, and other metals

The two most common metals for individual investors are gold and silver:

- **Gold:** The classic. It is more stable, more expensive, and easier to store large amounts of value in a small space.
- **Silver:** Cheaper and more volatile. It takes up more space but gives you more flexibility for smaller transactions.

Other options such as platinum and palladium exist, but they're more industrial and less common for everyday investors.

TIP

If you're just getting started, most people begin with silver (for affordability) or small gold bars and coins (for compact value).

Buying and storing precious metals

When it comes to buying physical metals, you've got a few options:

- **Bars and coins:** These are the most common. You can buy them online or from local dealers.

- **Jewelry:** This isn't ideal for investing because the markup is high, and resale is tricky.
- **Vaulted storage:** Some companies let you buy metals that they store for you in secure vaults (think Brinks or the Royal Canadian Mint).

TIP

If you take delivery yourself, store it in a safe or safety deposit box — not under your mattress or next to your cookie jar.

WARNING

Watch out for collector coins or fancy packaging. Unless you're a collector, stick to bullion-grade metals from reputable dealers with clear pricing.

Avoiding the "shiny object" trap

Precious metals are great for stability, but they can't do the heavy lifting of wealth-building alone. They don't compound, and they don't generate cash flow. They just *sit there and sparkle.*

So, although they absolutely belong in a well-rounded offline asset strategy, they're more like your portfolio's fireproof vault — not your growth engine.

REMEMBER

Think of gold as your seatbelt, not your engine. It won't drive your wealth forward, but it'll help keep you safe if things crash.

Using Crypto Hard Wallets: The Offline Side of Your Digital Assets

You may be surprised to see crypto in a chapter on offline external assets. After all, crypto lives online, right?

Yes — but also no.

In Chapter 4 of Book 4 and in the latest edition of *Cryptocurrency Investing For Dummies* by Kiana Danial (Wiley), you discover how to buy, trade, and evaluate digital currencies such as Bitcoin, Ethereum, and other cryptocurrencies. That's the *online* side of crypto investing.

There's another side most beginners overlook, and it's one of the most important things you can do as your crypto portfolio grows: Take your assets offline. This is where cold wallets, also known as hard wallets, come in.

Hot wallets versus cold wallets

When you first buy crypto, your coins are usually stored in a *hot wallet* — a digital wallet connected to the internet. These are often hosted by exchanges (such as Coinbase or Binance) or exist as apps and browser extensions (as in MetaMask).

Hot wallets are easy to use, convenient for frequent trading, and ideal for beginners and small balances. But they also come with risk: If someone hacks your exchange, you lose access. If the platform freezes withdrawals (yes, this has happened), your money is stuck. And if you fall for a phishing scam, your assets can be drained in seconds.

Consequently, serious investors eventually move to *cold wallets* — offline tools that keep your private keys completely disconnected from the internet.

REMEMBER

Cold wallets may be digital in nature, but their storage, security, and setup are completely offline. That makes them part of your external asset protection strategy, especially after your crypto holdings start to grow.

Cold wallets have the following benefits:

- Let you be your own bank
- Add a layer of security most online users never consider
- Keep your freedom fund safe from tech glitches, platform shutdowns, or centralized control

REMEMBER

Cold storage is not about making your crypto do more. It's about keeping what you already built safe. If you're building serious wealth in crypto, a cold wallet isn't optional. It's essential.

Popular cold wallets

Here are three of the most trusted and widely used cold wallet options:

- **Ledger:** One of the most popular hardware wallets, Ledger offers the Nano S Plus and Nano X, both of which support hundreds of coins and tokens. The Nano X even has Bluetooth, so you can manage your assets from your phone.
- **Trezor:** This is another OG in the crypto space. The Model One and Model T are both easy to use, beginner-friendly, and support major cryptos. The Model T has a touchscreen for extra security and simplicity.

- **Bitkey:** A newer option from Block (formerly Square), Bitkey is designed to simplify self-custody for everyday users. It includes a hardware device *and* a mobile app, making cold storage more intuitive without compromising on safety.

TIP

If you're holding crypto as part of your long-term Phase 3 triple-compounding strategy, at least a portion of your coins should be stored offline.

Protecting your crypto with paper

Surprised to see *paper* in a section about crypto? You're not alone. Most people think crypto belongs in the metaverse — not in a manila envelope.

But despite the high-tech nature of digital currency, one of the oldest, most low-tech tools in the crypto world is still one of the most secure: the paper wallet. A paper wallet is the most low-tech cold storage method. You generate a private and public key, print it out, and keep that paper somewhere safe, such as a safe deposit box or fireproof safe.

Pros of a paper wallet include that it's completely offline, so there's no hacking risk. It's also free to create a paper wallet.

Cons of a paper wallet are that it's easy to lose, damage, or misplace. Also, if anyone finds your paper, they have access to your crypto. Of course, you also have the downside that a paper wallet doesn't support modern features such as staking or smart contracts.

REMEMBER

Paper wallets are best suited for truly long-term holding. Think of them like a physical treasure map. If you go this route, protect it like gold.

TIP

If you create a paper wallet, store backup copies in separate, secure locations. Fire, flood, or forgetfulness can wipe out your entire portfolio.

Adding Your Investment Profits to Your Triple-Compounding System

Investing in external assets isn't just about watching your net worth grow. It's about feeding the entire triple-compounding machine. The profits you generate from stocks, crypto, real estate, or private equity don't exist in isolation. When reinvested intentionally, they can fund new skill-building (compound 1X), expand your systems and teams (compound 2X), or roll back into your portfolio for accelerated returns (compound 3X).

Every dollar earned — from a dividend payout, a rental income stream, or an exit from a private deal — becomes fuel. The more you circulate it through your triple-compounding strategy, the faster you create *true financial freedom* — not just bigger numbers on a spreadsheet.

TIP

Think of every external asset profit as a decision point: Will this money buy you more time, more leverage, or more long-term growth? Triple compounders choose all three — on purpose.

WARNING

Don't let these assets sit in isolation. If you don't funnel the profits back into your triple-compounding system, they become dead weight.

5 Dealing with the Tax Man

Contents at a Glance

IN THIS CHAPTER

» Preparing your own tax return

» Interacting with the IRS and their website

» Understanding the pros and cons of tax-preparation software and websites

» Hiring help: Preparers, EAs, CPAs, and tax attorneys

Chapter 1

Tax Return Preparation Options and Tools

By the time you actually get around to filing your annual income tax return, it's too late to take advantage of many tax-reduction strategies for that tax year. And what can be more aggravating than, late in the evening on April 14 when you're already stressed out and unhappily working on your return, finding a golden nugget of tax advice that works great — if only you'd known about it last December!

If you're now faced with the daunting task of preparing your income tax return, you're probably trying to decide how to do it with a minimum of pain and taxes owed. You have several options for completing your return. The best choice for you depends on the complexity of your tax situation, your knowledge about taxes, and the amount of time you're willing to invest.

Going It Alone: Preparing Your Own Return

You already do many things for yourself. Maybe you cook for yourself, do home repairs, or even change your car's oil. You may do these tasks because you enjoy them, because you save money by doing them, or because you want to develop a particular skill.

Sometimes, however, you hire others to help you do the job. Occasionally, you may buy a meal out or hire someone to make a home improvement. Plenty of folks have a service garage change the oil in their car and perform other needed services. And so it can be with your annual income tax return — you may want to hire help, but you may end up, like many people, preparing your own return.

REMEMBER

Doing your own income tax return is an especially good option if your financial situation does not change much from year to year. You can use last year's return as a guide. You may need to do some reading to keep up with the small number of changes in the tax system and laws that affect your situation. Given the constant changes to various parts of the tax laws, you simply can't assume that the tax laws that apply to your situation are identical from one year to the next just because your situation is the same.

A benefit of preparing your own return includes the better financial decisions that you make in the future by using the tax knowledge you gain from learning about the tax system. Most tax preparers are so busy preparing returns that you probably won't get much of their time to discuss tax laws and how they may apply to your future financial decisions. Consider doing tax planning late in the year when you can still apply recommendations and when preparers aren't buried under returns they're preparing like they are in the spring.

Last, but not least, doing your own return should be your lowest-cost tax-return-preparation option. Of course, we're assuming that you don't make costly mistakes and oversights and that the leisure time you forego when preparing your return isn't too valuable!

Taking Advantage of IRS Publications

In addition to the instructions that come with the annual tax forms that the good old Internal Revenue Service (IRS) provides you with every year, the IRS also produces hundreds of publications that explain how to complete the myriad tax forms various taxpayers must tackle. These booklets are available in printed form, through the IRS's website (`www.irs.gov`; see the later section "Internal

Revenue Service" for more on what the site has to offer), or by mail if you simply call and order them from the IRS (800-829-3676). Additionally, the IRS provides answers to common questions through its automated phone system and through live representatives.

If you have a simple, straightforward tax return, completing it on your own using only the IRS instructions may be fine. This approach is as cheap as you can get, costing only your time and patience. And with electronic filing, you can even side-step the minimal photocopying expenses, and postage to mail the completed tax return.

WARNING

One danger in relying on the IRS staffers for assistance is that they have been known to give wrong information and answers. When you call the IRS with a question, be sure to take notes about your phone conversation, thus protecting yourself in the event of an audit. Date your notes and include the name of the IRS employee (and office location and employee number) with whom you spoke, what you asked, and the employee's responses.

In addition to the standard instructions that come with your tax return, the IRS offers some publications such as the following:

- **Publication 17:** *Your Federal Income Tax (For Individuals)* is designed for individual tax-return preparation.
- **Publication 334:** *Tax Guide for Small Business (For Individuals Who Use Schedule C or C-EZ)* is for (you guessed it) small-business tax-return preparation.

These guides provide more detail than the basic IRS publications. To access or request these free guides, visit the IRS website at `www.irs.gov` or call them at 800-829-3676. (Actually, nothing is free. You've already paid for IRS guides with your tax dollars!)

The IRS also offers more in-depth booklets focusing on specific tax issues. However, if your tax situation is so complex that this book (and Publications 17 and 334) can't address it, you need to think long and hard about getting help from a tax advisor or from one of the other sources recommended in the later section "Hiring Help."

TIP

IRS publications present plenty of rules and facts, but they don't make it easy for you to find the information and advice you really need. The best way to use IRS publications is to confirm facts that you already think you know or to check the little details. Don't expect IRS publications and representatives to show you how to cut your tax bill.

Perusing Tax-Preparation and Advice Guides

Privately published tax-preparation and advice books are invaluable when they highlight tax-reduction strategies and possible pitfalls — in clear, simple English. Such books help you complete your return accurately and save you big money. The amount of money invested in a book or two is significantly smaller than the annual cost of a tax expert.

TIP

The latest edition of *Taxes For Dummies* by Eric Tyson and Chris Eck (published by Wiley) covers the important tax-preparation and planning issues that affect the vast majority of taxpayers. A minority of taxpayers may run into some nitpicky tax issues caused by unusual events in their lives or extraordinary changes in their incomes or assets. That book may not be enough for those folks. In such cases, you need to consider hiring a tax advisor, which we explain how to do later in this chapter (see the section "Hiring Help").

Using Software

If you don't want to slog through dozens of pages of tedious IRS instructions or pay a tax preparer hundreds of dollars to complete your annual return, you may be interested in tax preparation software that can help you finish off your IRS Form 1040 and supplemental schedules. If you have access to a private computer, tablet, or even a smartphone, tax-preparation software can be a helpful tool.

Tax-preparation software also gives you the advantage of automatically recalculating all the appropriate numbers on your return if one number changes — no more painting out math errors with a little white brush or recalculating a whole page of figures because your dog was sleeping on some of the receipts. (Just don't let your cat walk on your keyboard or another family member use the computer before saving your return!) The best tax-preparation software is easy to install and use on your computer, provides help when you get stuck, and highlights deductions you may overlook.

WARNING

Before plunking down your hard-earned cash for some tax-preparation software, know that it has potential drawbacks. Here are the big ones:

- **Garbage in, garbage out.** A tax return prepared by a software program is only as good as the quality of the data you enter into it. Of course, this drawback exists no matter who actually fills out the forms; some human tax preparers don't probe and clarify to make sure that you've provided all the right stuff, either. Tax software programs also may contain glitches that can lead to incorrect calculating or reporting of some aspect of your tax return.

- **Where's the beef?** Some tax software gives little in the way of background help, advice, and warnings. This lack of assistance can lull you into a false sense of security about the completeness and accuracy of the return you prepare.
- **Think, computer, think!** Computers are good at helping you access and process information. Remember that your computer is great at crunching numbers but has a far lower IQ than you have!

TIP

TurboTax, H&R Block Tax Software, and TaxSlayer are among the leading programs, and they do a reasonable job of helping you through the federal tax forms. One way to break a tie between good software options is considering price — you may be able to get a better deal on one software package.

Procrastinating also offers some benefits, because the longer you wait to buy the software, the cheaper it generally gets — especially when you buy it after filing for an extension. (You may also want to examine whether the tax software you buy can import the data from the checkbook software you've been using to track your tax-deductible expenses throughout the year.)

Accessing Internet Tax Resources

In addition to using your computer to prepare your income tax return, you can do an increasing number of other tax activities via the Internet. The better online tax resources are geared more to tax practitioners and tax-savvy taxpayers. But in your battle to legally minimize your taxes, you may want all the help you can get! Use the Internet for what it's best at doing — possibly saving you time tracking down factual information or forms.

WARNING

On the Internet, many websites provide information and discussions about tax issues. Take advice and counsel from other Internet users at your peril. Don't depend on the accuracy of the answers to tax questions that you ask in online forums. The problem: In many cases you can't be sure of the background, expertise, or identity of the person with whom you're trading messages.

The following sections describe some of the better sites out there.

Internal Revenue Service

When you think of the Internal Revenue Service — the U.S. Treasury Department office charged with overseeing the collection of federal income taxes — you probably think of the following adjectives: bureaucratic, humorless, and stodgy. Difficult as it is to believe, the IRS website (`www.irs.gov`) is reasonably well organized and relatively user-friendly.

The IRS site also has links to state tax organizations, convenient access to IRS forms (including those from prior tax years), and instructions. To view and download forms from the IRS site, start browsing at `www.irs.gov/forms-instructions`.

You can complete your tax forms online at the IRS site. The IRS site even features a place for you to submit comments on proposed tax regulations, with a statement that, "Although we cannot respond individually to each email, we do appreciate your feedback and will consider your comments as we revise our tax products." Is this the IRS we know and love?

You find plenty of other useful things to do on the IRS website such as the following:

- Create an online account to access your tax information and historical data (including via transcripts).
- Make online payments, such as quarterly estimated tax payments. The lowest cost way to do this is through an electronic payment from your bank account (no charge) or via a personal debit card ($2.15).

  WARNING: Do not pay your taxes with a personal credit card because you will get whacked with a 1.75 percent service charge of the tax amount paid.
- Check your refund status and access other recent tax perks.

GOING PAPERLESS AND PAYING YOUR INCOME TAXES ELECTRONICALLY

It's "old school" to keep paper records and paper copies of your income tax returns.

It's "old school" to mail in your completed income tax returns and to send in a paper check if you owe income taxes quarterly and/or when it's time to submit your complete annual returns to the federal government and state government if you live in a state with a state income tax.

If you like doing things the "old-school" way, that's a good enough reason to keep doing them that way.

There is, however, an alternative. The IRS and state governments enable you to register an account on their income tax websites through which you can pay your income taxes and obtain records as needed. And there are many ways today to submit completed income tax returns electronically.

The benefits of going the electronic route include no papers to keep track of and organized or possibly perused by nosy people in your home or office. It's also quicker to file and pay that way and get your refund if you're due one.

Just be sure that if you're submitting payments electronically, you are on the relevant official federal or state website. Beware of scams and fraudsters!

Research

Most tax research sites have information that is of greater interest to tax and other financial professionals. That said, here are some tax websites that may be of some interest or use to you:

- **Tax Foundation:** For lots of insightful research and data on taxes, visit taxfoundation.org/.
- **Congressional tax doings:** If you really have nothing better to do with your time, check the government sites with updated information on tax bills in Congress: The Joint Committee on Taxation (www.jct.gov/) and the Ways & Means Committee (waysandmeans.house.gov).
- **Wolters Kluwer:** This professional service firm's website (www.wolterskluwer.com/en/tax-and-accounting) is geared toward tax and legal professionals who need to keep up with and research the tax laws. Access to most of the site's resources comes by subscription only.

Tax preparation sites

A number of websites enable you to prepare federal and state tax forms and then file them electronically. Many of these sites enable you to prepare and file your federal forms for free if you access their site through the IRS website. Just go to www.irs.gov and click on any link for "Free File" (or visit www.irs.gov/filing/free-file-do-your-federal-taxes-for-free) to see whether you qualify. If you access a tax preparation site directly instead, you may have to pay a fee for a service that would be free through the Free File program.

TIP

If you're simply after the tax forms, plenty of the sites mentioned in this section offer such documents for free, as do public libraries and post offices.

Hiring Help

Because they lack the time, interest, energy, or skill to do it themselves, some people hire an auto mechanic to handle the servicing of their car. And most people who hire an auto mechanic do so because they think that they can afford to hire such a person.

For some of the same reasons, some people choose to hire a tax preparer and advisor. By identifying tax-reduction strategies that you may overlook, competent tax practitioners can save you money — sometimes more than enough to pay their fees. They may also reduce the likelihood of an audit, which can be triggered by blunders that you may make. Like some auto mechanics, however, some tax preparers take longer, charging you more, and not delivering the high-quality work you expect. As with an auto mechanic, you may not even be aware that the person you've hired to help with your income taxes isn't very competent or ethical because you're not an expert in their area.

Deciding whether you really need a preparer

Odds are quite good that you can successfully prepare your own income tax return. Most people's returns don't vary that much from year to year, so you have a head start and can hit the ground running if you get out last year's return, which hopefully you retained a copy of!

Preparing your own return may not work as well whenever your situation has changed in some way — if you bought or sold a house, started your own business, or retired, for example.

Don't give up and hire a preparer just because you can't bear to open your tax-preparation booklet and get your background data organized. Even if you hire a tax preparer, you still need to get your stuff organized before a consultation.

TIP

As hard and as painful as it is, confront preparing your return as far in advance of April 15 as you can so that if you feel uncomfortable with your level of knowledge, you have enough time to seek help. The more organizing you can do before hiring a preparer, the less having your return prepared should cost you. Avoid waiting until the last minute to hire an advisor — you won't do as thorough a job of selecting a competent person, and you'll probably pay more for the rush job. If you get stuck preparing the return, you can get a second opinion from other preparation resources discussed in this chapter.

Looking at different types of preparers

If you decide to seek out the services of a tax preparer/advisor, know that tax practitioners come with various backgrounds, training, and credentials. One type of professional isn't necessarily better than another. Think of them as different types of specialists who are appropriate for different circumstances. The four main types of tax practitioners are unenrolled preparers, enrolled agents, certified public accountants, and tax attorneys.

Unenrolled preparers

Among all the tax practitioners, *unenrolled preparers* generally have the least amount of training, and more of them work part-time. H&R Block is the largest and most well-known tax-preparation firm in the country. In addition, other national firms such as Jackson Hewitt and plenty of mom-and-pop shops are in the tax-preparation business.

The appeal of preparers is that they're relatively inexpensive — they can do basic returns for $200+. The drawback is that you may hire a preparer who doesn't know much more than you do! As with financial planners, no national regulations apply to tax-return preparers, and no licensing is required, although this may change in the near future. Currently, though, in most states, almost anybody can hang out a tax-preparation shingle and start preparing. Most preparers, however, complete some sort of training program before working with clients.

TIP

Preparers make the most sense for folks who don't have complicated financial lives, who are budget-minded, and who dislike doing their own taxes. If you aren't good about hanging onto receipts or don't want to keep your own files with background details about your taxes, you definitely need to shop around for a tax preparer who's going to be around for a few years. You may need all that paperwork stuff someday for an audit, and some tax preparers keep and organize their clients' documentation rather than return everything each year. (Can you blame them for keeping your records after they go through the tedious task of sorting them all out of the shopping bags?) Going with a firm that's open year-round may also be safer, in case tax questions or problems arise. (Some small shops are open only during tax season.)

Enrolled agents (EAs)

A person must pass IRS scrutiny to be called an *enrolled agent* (EA). This license enables the agent to represent you before the IRS in the event of an audit. The training to become an EA is longer and more sophisticated than that of an unenrolled preparer. Continuing education also is required; EAs must complete an average of 24 hours of continuing education per year to maintain their licenses, which are renewed every three years.

Enrolled agents' prices tend to fall between those of a preparer and a certified public accountant (discussed in the next section). If you require tax return preparation and related advice and representation, and nothing more (no corporate audits or production of financial reports), an enrolled agent can provide the expertise you need for a reasonable cost.

TIP

The main difference between enrolled agents and CPAs and attorneys is that EAs work exclusively in the field of taxation, which makes them more likely to stay attuned to the latest tax developments. Not all CPAs and attorneys do. In addition to preparing your return (including simple to complex forms), good EAs can help with tax planning, represent you at tax audits, and keep the IRS off your back. You can find names and telephone numbers of EAs in your area by contacting the National Association of Enrolled Agents (`taxexperts.naea.org/expertdirectory`). NAEA members have an even higher standard for continuing education requirements, totaling 30 hours per year.

Certified public accountants (CPAs)

Certified public accountants (CPAs) go through significant training and examination to receive the CPA credential. To maintain this designation, a CPA must complete at least 40 hours' worth of continuing education classes every year.

As with any other professional service you purchase, CPA fees can vary tremendously. Expect to pay more if you live in an area with a high cost of living, if you use the services of a large accounting firm, or if your needs are involved and specialized.

TIP

Competent CPAs are of greatest value to people completing some of the more unusual and less user-friendly tax forms/schedules, such as K-1 for partnerships. CPAs also are helpful for people who had a major or first-time tax event during the year, such as the childcare tax-credit determination. (Good EAs and other preparers can handle these issues as well.)

WARNING

Whenever your return is uncomplicated and your financial situation is stable, hiring a high-priced CPA year after year to fill in the blanks on your tax returns is a waste of money. A CPA once bragged he was effectively making more than $500 per hour from some of his clients' returns that required only 20 minutes of an assistant's time to complete.

Paying for the additional cost of a CPA on an ongoing basis makes sense if you can afford it and if your financial situation is reasonably complex or dynamic. If you're self-employed and/or file many other schedules, hiring a CPA may be worth it. But you needn't do so year after year. If your situation grows more complex one year and then stabilizes, consider getting help for the perplexing year and then using other preparation resources discussed in this chapter or a lower-cost preparer or enrolled agent in the future.

If you desire more information about CPAs in your area, contact the local organization of CPAs in your state. To locate your state's group, visit the American Institute of Certified Public Accountants listing of state CPA associations and useful state tax links at `www.surgent.com/resources/state-societies-list/`. If you're considering hiring a CPA, be sure to ask how much of the person's time is spent preparing individual income tax returns and returns like yours.

Tax attorneys

Unless you're a super-high-income earner with a complex financial life, hiring a tax attorney to prepare your annual return is prohibitively expensive. In fact, many tax attorneys don't prepare returns as a normal practice. Because of their level of specialization and training, tax attorneys tend to have high hourly billing rates — $300 to $400-plus per hour isn't unusual, and some attorneys in a major metropolitan area have crossed the $1,000-per-hour threshold.

Tax attorneys sometimes become involved in court cases dealing with tax problems, disagreements, or other complicated matters, such as the purchase or sale of a business. Other good tax advisors also can help with these issues.

WHO'S BEST QUALIFIED — EA, CPA, OR PREPARER?

Who is best qualified to prepare your return? That really depends on the individual you want to hire. The CPA credential is just that, a credential. Some people who have the credential will try to persuade you not to hire someone without it, but don't always believe this advice.

Some tax-preparation books perpetuate the myth that only a CPA can do your taxes. In one such book, in a chapter about choosing a tax preparer entitled "How to Prepare for Your Accountant," the authors say, "Choosing an accountant isn't something that should be done casually. There are more than 300,000 certified public accountants." These authors then recommend that you ask a potential preparer, "Are you a certified public accountant?" (As you may have guessed, the firm behind the book is a large CPA company.)

What about all the non-CPAs, such as EAs, who do a terrific job helping prepare their clients' returns and tax plans throughout the year?

If you can afford to and want to pay hundreds of dollars per hour, hiring a large CPA firm can make sense. But for the vast majority of taxpayers, spending that kind of money is unnecessary and wasteful. Numerous EAs and other tax preparers are out there doing outstanding work for less.

REMEMBER

The more training and specialization a tax practitioner has (and the more affluent the clients), the higher the hourly fee. Select the one who best meets your needs. Fees and competence at all levels of the profession vary significantly. If you aren't sure of the quality of work performed and the soundness of the advice, get a second opinion.

Finding Tax Preparers and Advisors

TIP

The challenge for you is to locate a tax advisor who does terrific work, charges reasonable fees, and thus is too busy to bother calling to solicit you! Here are some resources to find those publicity-shy, competent, and affordable tax advisors:

- **Friends and family:** Some of your friends and family members probably use tax advisors and can steer you to a decent one or two for an interview.

- **Coworkers:** Ask people in your field what tax advisors they use. This strategy can be especially useful if you're self-employed.
- **Other advisors:** Financial and legal advisors also can be helpful referral sources, but don't assume that they know more about the competence of a tax person than you do. Beware of a common problem: Financial or legal advisors may simply refer you to tax preparers who send them clients.
- **Associations:** EAs and CPAs maintain professional associations that can refer you to members in your local area. See the relevant sections earlier in this chapter.

Never decide to hire a tax preparer or advisor solely on the basis of someone else's recommendation. To ensure that you're hiring someone who is competent and with whom you can work well, please take the time to interview at least two or three prospective candidates.

IN THIS CHAPTER

» Knowing you maintain the burden of proof

» Understanding the benefits of keeping good records

» Knowing what to do when records aren't available

» Using the Cohan Rule

Chapter 2
Getting and Staying Organized

Do you want to make your tax preparation easier and make sure you claim every deduction you're entitled to? Would you like to survive an IRS audit and not pay additional tax, interest, or penalties? Do you want to save money by not paying tax preparers $50 to $200 or more an hour to organize your stuff?

Then keep good records!

WARNING

If you're like most people, you probably aren't a good bookkeeper. But without good records, you may be in trouble, especially if you're ever audited. Furthermore, some tax preparers and accountants love to see you walk into their offices with lots of receipts. Knowing that they can charge you a hefty hourly fee and then turn around and pay someone else $20 an hour to organize your receipts brightens their day and fattens their firm's bottom line.

Compiling tax records is one of life's many challenges, but it doesn't need to be one of the awful ones. Look at this step as an opportunity to connect with your past — you may find not only tax records for the most recent year, but you may also find old report cards or to-do lists from five years ago (that still have unfinished business). Taking the time to rummage is often worth it. You may finally be able to itemize your deductions this year, but first you need to be able to produce those charitable receipts, medical bills, and mortgage and real estate tax bills.

In this chapter, you discover tried and proven ways of keeping track of everything you need to survive — not only this tax-preparation season, but also in future tax situations.

Maintaining the Burden of Proof

Perhaps you can easily imagine yourself the night before an IRS audit wondering how you're going to support your claim for all those business expenses. Do you know what happens when you're audited and you can't document your claims? First, you get socked with additional tax and interest. Then come the penalties — and the IRS has a lengthy list of them.

To deal effectively with the IRS, you need documentation, because the tax laws place the burden of proof primarily on the taxpayer. Do you think this policy means that you're guilty until proven innocent? Unfortunately, it does, but don't let that depress you. Remember that you need to produce documentation only if you're audited. Even if you're not being audited, you still should organize your records now.

If you are audited and lack the tax records that you need to support your case, don't throw in the towel. This chapter shows you how to overcome such a problem — just in case you failed Recordkeeping 101.

Keeping Good Records

Tax records pose a problem for many people because the IRS doesn't require any particular form of recordkeeping. In fact, the IRS recommends, in general terms, that you keep records only to file a "complete and accurate" return. Need a bit more detail? Read on.

Ensuring a complete and accurate tax return

In case you don't feel like flipping through countless pages of government instructions on what constitutes a "complete and accurate" return, you may want to check out several common problem areas at a glance and the types of records normally required.

Itemized deductions

REMEMBER

Receipts, receipts, who's got the receipts? If you're planning on itemizing your deductions on Schedule A, you need the numbers to calculate your deductions and to prove your claims in case you're audited. Here's a list of expenses you want to have proof that you paid in the order you find them on Schedule A:

- **Medical expenses:** Keep all your receipts and make sure you get receipts for all services that you receive during the year, including transportation fares to and from the doctor's office. The list of allowable medical deductions is long and fairly inclusive, and as healthcare costs continue to rise faster than most people's salaries, more and more people will find they can take a medical deduction.
- **Mortgage interest payments:** You should receive a record of these payments, which are documented on Form 1098, from the bank that holds your mortgage.
- **Real estate taxes:** Keep a copy of your real estate tax bill, and either the canceled checks, a receipt from your city or town, or a line item on your Form 1098 (if your mortgage company pays your taxes for you).
- **Personal property taxes:** Keep a receipt for your excise tax bill.
- **State and local income taxes:** Hang on to copies of your canceled checks if your bank still gives you back your checks. If you pay your state income taxes electronically, the state's website will have an electronic record of your payments.
- **Charitable deductions:** For donations in excess of $250 (per donation), keep a written receipt or letter from the charity that states the amount and nature of your donation. For donations under $250 (per donation), make sure you have a credit card receipt, canceled check, notation on a bank statement, or a receipt from the charity if you want to claim that deduction.
- **Casualty or theft losses:** You just never know when your number will come up in the burglar lottery, or you'll drop your diamond ring down the garbage disposal. If you don't have your receipts, don't despair, though; you have other ways to prove this deduction. Check out the later section "Casualty losses."

TIP

You may be rejoicing to find that you don't have enough deductions to itemize this year, so you can trash all your receipts now. And you may also be assuming that the same will be true next year. Keep in mind, though, that your finances — and your tax situation — can do funny things from year to year; be sure to hang on to your receipts so that you keep all your deduction options open down the road.

Dependent expenses

If you plan to claim someone other than your qualifying child as a dependent, you need to be able to prove (if you're audited) that you provided more than 50 percent of that person's total support. The length of time that you provide the support doesn't mean anything — it's the total cost that matters. So be ready to show how much you paid for your dependent's lodging, food, clothes, healthcare, transportation, and any other essential support stuff. (See Chapter 3 in Book 5 for the rules for claiming dependents and the definition of a qualifying child.)

Car expenses

If, for the business use of your car, you choose to deduct the actual expenses rather than the standard mileage rate, you need to be able to show the cost of the car and when you started using it for business. You also must record your business miles, your total miles, and your expenses, such as insurance, gas, and maintenance. You need a combination of a log and receipts, of course!

Home expenses

If you own your home, you not only need to keep track of your mortgage and real estate tax payments, but you also need to keep records of your purchase price and purchase expenses, plus the cost of all the improvements and additions you make over time (save your receipts, please!). Although you may not be selling your house this year, when you do, you'll be thankful you have all your receipts. If you rent a portion of your house or you run a business from it, you'll also need your utility bills, general repair bills, and housecleaning and lawn-mowing costs in order to calculate your net rental income or your home office expense.

Business expenses

The IRS is especially watchful in this area, so be sure to keep detailed proof of any expenses that you claim. This proof can consist of many items, such as receipts of income, expense account statements, and so on. So make sure that you hang on to the bill or receipt for every expense you incur.

Setting up a recordkeeping system

The tax year is a long time for keeping track of records that you need (and where you put them) when the filing season arrives. The following sections discuss using technology to help with these chores along with more old-school options for doing so.

Diving into digital

A number of financial software packages enable you to keep track of your spending for tax purposes. Just don't expect to reap the benefits without a fair amount of upfront and continuing work. You need to figure out how to use the software, and you need to enter data for it to be useful to you come tax time. Don't forget, though, that you still need your statements/receipts to back up your claims; in an audit, the IRS may not accept your computer records without verifying them against your statements/receipts.

TIP

If you're interested in software or an app, consider Quicken or GoodBudget. Or you may want to explore a more business-oriented program, such as QuickBooks, Xero, or FreshBooks for your small-business accounting. Whichever software or app you choose, make certain it allows you to do everything you need it to, such as keep track of your stock portfolio, pay your bills, balance your checking account, and, best of all, get help with tabulating your tax information. Just remember that the package tabulates only what you enter. So if you use the software to pay your monthly bills but neglect to enter data for things you pay for with cash, for example, you won't have the whole picture.

Keeping it classic

TIP

If you'd rather not use technology for your income tax recordkeeping system, consider these old-school ways that have stood the test of time:

- If you like simple, invest in an accordion file. You can buy one with slots already labeled by month, by category, or by letters of the alphabet, or you can make your own filing system with the extra labels — all this can be yours for $10 to $15.
- If $10 to $15 is too much, you can purchase dozens of those manila file folders for about $5. Decide on the organizational method that best fits your needs, and get into the habit of saving all bills, receipts, and records that you think you can use someday for your tax purposes and for things that affect your overall financial planning. This basic advice is good for any taxpayer, whether you file a simple tax return or a complicated Form 1040 with numerous supplemental schedules. Remember that this plan is only minimal, but nevertheless is much better than the shoebox approach to recordkeeping.
- If your financial life is uncomplicated, then each new year you can set up one file folder that has the year on it (so in January 2027 you establish your 2027 file). During the year, as you receive documentation that you think you'll use in preparing your return, stash it in the folder. Come springtime 2028, when you finally force yourself to sit down and work on your return, you have everything you need in one bulging file.

WATCH OUT FOR STATE DIFFERENCES

Although the IRS requires that you keep your records for only three years, your state may have a longer statute of limitations with regard to state income tax audits. Some of your tax-related records may also be important to keep for other reasons. For example, suppose that you throw out your receipts after three years. Then the fellow who built your garage four years ago sues you, asserting that you didn't fully pay the bill. You may be out of luck in court if you don't have the necessary documentation showing that you paid.

The moral: Hang on to records that may be important (such as home improvement receipts) for longer than three years — especially if a dispute is possible. Check with a legal advisor whenever you have a concern, because statutes of limitations vary from state to state.

» If you're a 1040 user and a real perfectionist, you can arrange your records in a file according to the schedules and forms on which you'll report them. For example, you can set up folders such as these:

  - **Schedule A:** Deductible items (such as mortgage interest, property taxes, and charitable contributions)
  - **Schedule B:** Interest and dividend income stuff
  - **Schedule D:** Documents related to buying, selling, and improving your home, and the sale and purchase of investments such as stocks and bonds

  You 1040 filers have so many options that you truly need to take the time to figure out your return so that you can anticipate your future tax needs.

Deciding when to stash and when to trash

REMEMBER

One of the most frequently asked questions is how long a taxpayer needs to keep tax records. The answer is easy — a minimum of three years. That's because the statute of limitations for tax audits and assessments is three years. If the IRS doesn't adjust or audit your 2023 tax return by April 15, 2027 (the three years starts running on April 15, 2024), it missed its chance. On April 15, 2027, feel free to celebrate another auditless year with a "Shredding the 2023 Tax Year" party. (If you filed after April 15 because you obtained an extension of time to file, you must wait until three years after the extension due date rather than the April 15 tax date. The same is true when you file late — the three-year period doesn't start until you actually file your return.)

TIP

However, we must add one point to the general three-year rule: Save all records for the assets that you continue to own. These records can include purchase records for stocks and bonds, automobiles, your home (along with its improvements), and expensive personal property, such as jewelry, photography equipment, or computers.

Some taxpayers take the practical step of videotaping their home and its contents, but if you do, make sure that you keep that record outside your home. Uploading such files to the cloud or emailing them to yourself would do the trick.

WARNING

In situations where the IRS suspects that income wasn't reported, IRS agents can go back as far as six years. And if possible tax fraud is involved, forget all time restraints!

Reconstructing Missing Tax Records

Our experience shows that the number-one reason taxpayers must cough up additional tax when they're audited is lousy recordkeeping. They don't get themselves into this situation by fabricating deductions, but rather because most taxpayers aren't very good bookkeepers and they fail to produce the records that properly substantiate the deductions they have a right to claim.

When taxpayers misplace tax records or simply don't save the ones that they need to be able to prove the deductions they're allowed under the law, all is not lost. Other ways exist for gathering the evidence that establishes what was actually spent, but obtaining the necessary evidence may prove time-consuming. And yet, when you consider the other option — paying additional tax, interest, and penalties on disallowed deductions from an audit where you can't prove what you spent — your time and energy are typically amply rewarded. The following sections describe some ways to reconstruct lost or forgotten records.

Property received by inheritance or gift

The starting point for determining whether you made or lost money on a sale of a property is the property's *tax basis*. (Remember, to the IRS, *property* can be more than just real estate; it also includes stocks, bonds, cars, boats, and computers.)

Tax basis is an IRS term for cost. Your basis usually is what you paid for something.

However, the rules for determining the tax basis for property you inherited or received as a gift are different. Because you don't know the cost of the inheritance, the tax basis for determining the taxable gain or loss on the property you inherited is the fair market value of the property on the date of the titleholder's death. For property received as a gift, the tax basis is either the donor's cost or the fair market value on the date you received the gift.

The best time for determining your basis in either a gift or an inheritance is when you receive that gift or inheritance, not years later after people who may have that information have long since forgotten or even died. If you know the basis of the property you've received, either through a gift or an inheritance, because you have access to either the Gift Tax Return (Form 709), the Estate Tax Return (Form 706), or because your Uncle Joe told you upfront what your basis is in this property, great! When you sell the property, you're all set with your initial basis information, and calculating your gain or loss is a matter of simple math.

If, on the other hand, Uncle Joe hasn't been so accommodating, and the relevant estate or gift tax returns aren't available, you're not out of luck, but you'll need to do some research on your own.

If there has been no estate tax return prepared for an estate, you're responsible for establishing the date-of-death value for your inheritance. You can use four methods to compute your tax basis: newspaper ads, local real estate board and broker records, the property's assessed value, and the *Consumer Price Index* (CPI). (You know the CPI: It tells you that what cost $10 five years ago this past month costs $50 this month. Seriously, it probably costs $12, and the CPI is an official government measure that tells how much prices increase over time.)

Researching newspaper ads

The Internet is also a wonderful resource for current and prior values. Many newspapers enable you to access their archives online. Local libraries often have such access and necessary subscriptions if that would be easier or less expensive for you. What you're seeking is a copy of the newspaper published on the approximate date for which you're trying to establish the value.

TIP

If a piece of real estate exactly like yours wasn't offered for sale at that time, you may have to find an ad for one as close as possible in description to yours and simply estimate the price. For example, suppose that you're trying to figure out how much Aunt Jessica's farm was worth when she left it to you in 1990. You now want to sell the 100-acre farm and farmhouse, and you're searching for its value in 1990. You check out some 1990 ads from the *Daily Bugle* and find

- An ad showing a house and 50 acres for $75,000
- An ad showing a house and 60 acres for $85,000

Because the farm with ten more acres was selling for $10,000 more, assume that an acre was worth around $1,000. The IRS, should you ever be audited, would likely find your assumption reasonable. Therefore, Aunt Jessica's farm has 40 more acres than the one selling for $85,000, so you can figure that the value of the farm in 1990 was about $125,000 ($85,000 + $40,000).

TIP

If you do get audited, the IRS generally won't accept the statement that you looked up this information. Remember, IRS agents act as if they come from Missouri (the Show-Me state — in case you were absent from school the day your fifth-grade teacher lectured on state nicknames). If you go to all the trouble to visit the library, make sure you come away with a photocopy of the paper's real estate section and the real estate pricing data we just discussed. The IRS requires documentation, especially when you use an alternative method to establish something's value.

Consulting local real estate board and broker records

If your trip to the library or local newspaper office comes up short, try the local real estate board or a real estate broker (one may owe you a favor or want your business). Individual brokers or local real estate boards usually keep historical data on property sold in their respective areas. Again, you may have to estimate selling prices if you don't find a property exactly like yours.

Obtaining assessed values

The assessed-value method may uncover the most accurate estimate of a property's value. Because property taxes are collected on the basis of assessed values, try to obtain the property's assessed value on the date you're interested in. With that information and the percentage of the fair market value that the tax assessor used in determining assessed values, divide the percentage into the assessed value to come up with the market value.

TIP

You can obtain assessed values for property (and the percentage of the fair market value of property assessed in its vicinity) from the government office that receives or collects property taxes, which you can usually find in the courthouse of the county where the property is located. Don't forget to get a copy of this information. For example, if the assessed value was $27,000 and the percentage of the fair market value at which the property was assessed was 30 percent, the fair market value was about $90,000 ($27,000 ÷ 30 percent).

Using the Consumer Price Index (CPI)

Unlike baseball, when you're assessing the value of real estate, you're not out on three strikes. When all else fails, use the CPI method. For example, say you sold a tract of land for $300,000. If the CPI has tripled since you inherited it, your tax basis would be about $100,000.

REMEMBER

Determining the property's acquisition date depends on how you acquired the property. If you inherited it, the acquisition date is the date of the previous owner's death. If the property was a gift, the acquisition date is the date the property originally was purchased by the person who gave you the gift.

CPI data is available on the internet at the Consumer Price Index page of the Bureau of Labor Statistics website (`www.bls.gov/cpi/home.htm`).

WARNING

If you use the CPI to value real estate, don't be surprised if the IRS doesn't accept your valuation without some further adjustment. That's because historically real estate prices have risen at higher rates than the CPI in many major metropolitan areas.

Securities received by inheritance or gift

Establishing a stock or a bond's price on a particular date is much easier than coming up with the value of other property, especially if the stock or bond is traded on a major securities exchange.

When you inherit a stock or bond, your tax basis usually is the value of the stock or bond on the deceased's date of death. Sometimes an estate — to save taxes — uses a valuation date that is six months after the date of death. If you receive the security as a gift, you often have the added task of establishing the date when the donor acquired the security, because you normally must use the value on that date (including any commission expense). Not to confuse you, but sometimes you must use the value on the date you received the gift.

You can contact the transfer agent to find out when the stock was acquired. The transfer agent is the company that keeps track of the shares of stock that a company issues. Your investment brokerage firm can tell you how to locate the transfer agent, or you can consult the *Value Line Investment Survey,* which you can find at most local libraries.

TIP

A number of investing websites such as Yahoo! Finance (`https://finance.yahoo.com/`) provide free historical stock pricing data going way back. Also, consider checking with the investment firm where the securities were (or are still) held. The firm may be able to research this information — maybe even for free.

Improvements to a residence

How many homeowners save any of the records regarding improvements that they make, even when those expenditures are substantial? Not nearly enough. Why? Because improvements to a home quite often are made during a multi-year and sometimes even multi-decade span, and saving records for that many years is a lot to ask of anyone. For example, landscaping expenditures — one tree or bush at a time — can really add up.

The point of counting every tree and bush and other improvement to your home sweet home is to raise the basis, or total investment, that you have in your residence so that you can reduce your taxable profit when you sell.

Although the tax laws eliminated the fiendish recordkeeping requirements for sales in which a profit of $500,000 or less for couples filing jointly and $250,000 for singles is realized, for sales above these amounts you still need records to prove, for example, that you didn't make more than these threshold amounts ($500,000/$250,000). And if you buy a house today, say for $350,000, you don't know what the sales price will be in 10, 20, 30, or more years when you finally sell it. Here's hoping it's $1 million plus. So tax records are still important.

TIP

Before you estimate how much you spent on residential improvements, you first have to determine what improvements you spent the money on. This step is necessary because if you can't document the amount spent, you at least can establish that an improvement was made. Your financial records for your bank and credit card accounts likely document payments made to home improvement contractors you hired over the years. Photos you've taken over the years may also document important improvements you've made to your home and property.

TIP

If you can't get a receipt from the contractor who made improvements to your home, hike down to the county clerk's office to obtain a copy of the Certificate of Occupancy (the house's birth certificate, so to speak), which shows what your house consisted of when it was built. Records at the county clerk's office also reveal any changes in the house's assessed value as the result of improvements you made, along with any building permits issued. Any of these documents can clearly establish whether improvements were made (assuming, of course, that you did obtain the proper permits for these improvements).

When original invoices, duplicate invoices, or canceled checks aren't available, obtain an estimate of what the improvement would cost now, and then subtract the increase according to the CPI (as explained in the earlier section "Using the Consumer Price Index (CPI)"). This procedure can help establish a reasonable estimate of what the improvement originally cost.

Casualty losses

A casualty loss is probably the most difficult deduction to establish. Few people consistently save receipts on the purchase of personal items, such as jewelry, clothing, furniture, and so on. If the casualty loss occurred because of a fire or hurricane, any receipts that you may have had were probably destroyed along with your property. Although a police, fire, or insurance company report establishes that a casualty loss was sustained, how do you establish the cost of what was stolen or destroyed? The answer: with a little bit of luck and hard work.

For example, the value of an expensive necklace that was stolen was once established by using a photograph that showed the taxpayer wearing the necklace. The taxpayer then obtained an appraisal from a jeweler of the cost of a similar necklace.

TIP

Although you can prove to the IRS that you have enough money to afford the lost or stolen item, the IRS also needs proof that you had the item in your possession. For example, suppose that your $10,000 Rolex watch is stolen (we feel for you). To make the IRS folks happy, you must prove two details:

- That you can afford the Rolex, which your total income from your tax return can prove.
- That you had the Rolex, which can be established by a statement from a friend, a relative, or an acquaintance asserting that you actually owned the item. If the Rolex was a gift, a statement from the giver also helps. Perhaps you had your watch repaired or cleaned in recent years but lack a receipt for that — the store that performed the service can document your ownership.

You can use an appraisal from the Federal Emergency Management Agency (FEMA) if you obtained a disaster loan as evidence for tax purposes to claim a casualty loss.

Business records

If business records have been lost or destroyed, you can often obtain duplicate bills from major vendors. You shouldn't have a great deal of trouble getting copies of the original telephone, utility, rent, credit card, oil company, and other bills. Reconstructing a typical month of automobile use can help you make a reasonable determination of the business use of your automobile. If that month's use approximates an average month's business use of an auto, the IRS generally accepts such reconstructed records as adequate substantiation.

Using duplicate account statements

If all your business income was deposited in a checking or savings account or investment firm account, you can reconstruct that income from those bank or investment firm statements. Although banks usually don't charge for copies of bank statements, they do charge for copies of canceled checks. You can generally access your account records online without charge.

Understanding the Cohan Rule

Before we end this chapter, we must tell you about the case of George M. Cohan and the resulting Cohan Rule. It's the story of one person's victory over the IRS, and it may inspire you to defend your own rights as a taxpayer. Even if some of the rights that taxpayers earned because of his victory have been eroded over the years, Cohan's battle for the right to estimate deductions still has repercussions today.

In 1921 and 1922, George M. Cohan deducted $55,000 in business-related travel and entertainment expenses. The IRS refused to allow him any part of these entertainment and travel deductions on the grounds that it was impossible to tell how much Cohan spent because he didn't have any receipts to support the deductions he claimed.

Cohan appealed to the Second Circuit Court of Appeals, and, in 1930, the court established the rule of approximation. The court instructed the IRS to "make as close an approximation as it can, bearing heavily, if it chooses, upon the taxpayer whose inexactitude is of his own making." (Isn't "inexactitude" a lovely way of saying "no records"?)

For more than 30 years, the Cohan Rule enabled taxpayers to deduct travel and entertainment expenses without having to substantiate what they spent. Taxpayers had only to establish that it was reasonable for them to have incurred travel and entertainment expenses in the amount they claimed they spent.

REMEMBER

Congress changed the law regarding travel, use of a car, and entertainment expenses in the early 1960s. Since that change, taxpayers no longer can deduct travel or entertainment expenses without adequate substantiation.

The Cohan Rule still applies, however, to other expenses for which records aren't available. Under the Cohan Rule, the Tax Court routinely allows deductions based on estimates for the following deductions:

- Petty cash and office expenses
- Delivery and freight charges
- Tips and business gifts
- Cleaning and maintenance expenses
- Small tools and supplies
- Casualty losses (fire, flood, and theft losses)

For some expenses, obtaining receipts for what you spend is impractical, if not downright impossible. Petty cash and tips are just two examples of such expenses.

WARNING

The Cohan Rule doesn't mean that you can stop keeping receipts and simply use estimates. You must have a valid reason for relying on the Cohan Rule, such as impracticability or lost or destroyed records. In fact, taxpayers have had penalties assessed against them for not attempting to obtain duplicate records that were lost when they moved, and for periodically destroying all business records immediately upon the filing of their tax returns. One court held that the unexplained loss of corporate records carries a strong presumption that the records would have prejudiced the taxpayer's position.

IN THIS CHAPTER

» Understanding the differences among the 1040 tax forms

» Deciding on a filing status

» Filing a return for children or for someone who has died

» Answering questions about where, when, why, and how to file

Chapter 3

What Kind of Taxpayer Are You?

You have to make some key decisions before grabbing those good ol' tax forms and marking them up. Even though you're anxious to begin, read the relevant portions of this chapter first. We explain some important issues you must resolve each tax year before you knuckle down to complete your return.

REMEMBER

Here's an old saying from a wise man — the father of one of us. He said, "Son, there are two kinds of payments in the world you should avoid: too early and too late." That kind of advice also applies to filing your taxes. Filing taxes late leads to IRS interest and penalties; paying your taxes too early, or withholding too much, is simply an interest-free loan to the federal government. Thanks for the advice, Dad.

What Rendition of 1040 Shall We Play?

The days of the so-called "long form" (Form 1040), "short form" (Form 1040-A), and the ever-popular Form 1040-EZ are history, and new forms have replaced them. No, the size of a tax return hasn't shrunk down to a postcard — politicians almost never make tax forms simpler. The new forms have fewer lines but more confusion, and if you're filing on paper, the information is spread over more sheets of paper. There are forms in Spanish, forms with larger print, and well, just forms. No matter which version of Form 1040 you use, the line numbers are all the same, which helps to simplify the explanations of where to put something, even if it does nothing to simplify the tax code.

The one positive change that does simplify things for many taxpayers is that the standard deduction is greatly increased, which is beneficial to the majority of taxpayers; far fewer people now need to complete Schedule A for Itemized Deductions.

Form 1040

Unless you or your spouse is over age 64, the regular Form 1040 is the one you'll most likely use. It's filled with all the biographical information you've come to know and love that inhabits every tax form you've ever filed, including your name (and your spouse's, if you have one of those), address, Social Security numbers for you and your spouse, and your list of dependents and their Social Security numbers.

The Form 1040 then starts listing out different forms of income, such as wages, interest, dividends, IRA distributions, pensions and annuities, Social Security benefits, and capital gains or losses. It's only after you get to this point in your return that the fun and games really begin, with the introduction of Schedules 1, 2, and 3.

You may feel a bit intimidated by these Form 1040 schedules, but don't be: All the IRS has done is moved much of the information that used to be on the old (pre-2019) Form 1040 off the Form 1040 itself, and it has now taken up residence on these three schedules, which were introduced in the 2019 tax filing season.

If your financial situation isn't particularly complex, you may not need to use any of these schedules, but if you need to use any or all of them, here's what they include:

- **Schedule 1, Additional Income and Adjustments to Income:** Here is where you report things such as taxable state tax refunds; alimony received; business income or loss; other gains or losses; income or losses from rental real estate, royalties, partnerships, S Corporations, estates, and trusts; farm income or loss; unemployment compensation; net operating losses; gambling income; cancellation of debt; the foreign earned income exclusion; taxable distributions from Health Savings Accounts; Alaska Permanent Fund distributions; jury duty pay; prizes and awards; and income from hobbies. Actually, the list goes on even longer, but we won't bore you with all that now.

The second page of Schedule 1 is where you put all your deductible adjustments to income, which run the gamut from educator expenses to alimony paid, IRA, HSA, and Archer MSA deductions; student loan interest deduction; the 50 percent deduction for self-employment tax; the deduction for the cost of health insurance for self-employed people; and so on. Once again, the list of adjustments is long.

- **Schedule 2, Additional Taxes:** Annual tax return filings not only cover income taxes, but also a plethora of additional taxes to which you may be subject, and Schedule 2 is where you report them. The most popular ones include self-employment tax, additional taxes paid on non-qualified distributions from IRA and other tax-favored accounts, household employment taxes, additional Medicare taxes for high-income individuals, and the net investment income tax. As with Schedule 1, we're just scratching the surface with these additional taxes here.
- **Schedule 3, Additional Credits and Payments:** This is the schedule you may adore if you qualify for some of these credits. These credits include the child tax credit, the foreign tax credit, education credits, retirement savings credits, residential energy credits, and an entire cornucopia of additional nonrefundable and refundable tax credits to which you may be entitled.

TIP

If English isn't your first language but Spanish is, and if you feel intimidated by dealing with the forms and instructions in English, you'll be happy to know that more and more forms and instructions have been translated into Spanish by the IRS. Form 1040, 1040-SR, and Schedules 1, 2, and 3 are all available in Spanish.

Form 1040-SR

If you or your spouse is age 65 or older, you no longer file the standard Form 1040; now, the IRS has created a form especially for you, Form 1040-SR (U.S. Tax Return for Seniors). Instead of a two-page form, you now get the exact same form but with larger print so it takes up three pages. Those of us with diminishing eyesight would like to thank the IRS for their consideration.

As with Form 1040, once you move beyond very basic forms of income, you need Schedules 1, 2, and/or 3 to complete all the parts of your return. The IRS has not increased the print size on these Schedules. Maybe as IRS agents age, they'll see the wisdom of providing large print versions of all forms and schedules.

Form 1040-NR

Form 1040-NR (U.S. Nonresident Alien Income Tax Return) gets a little trickier, and it doesn't apply to most of us. This form is only used by people who are non-resident aliens with U.S.-sourced income from a trade or business, or who are filing for someone who is a nonresident alien. So, a Canadian citizen, for example, who owns rental real estate in Florida would be required to file Form 1040-NR to report the rental income or loss from that property. So would that same Canadian who works for a company across the border in a border state, such as Minnesota, Washington, or North Dakota.

Once again, Schedules 1, 2, and/or 3 can be used with Form 1040-NR if your circumstances warrant it.

WARNING

Don't try to use Form 1040-NR if you are a U.S. citizen or green card holder who lives outside the United States. If you fall into that category, your form of choice will be either Form 1040 or Form 1040-SR.

CAN I ITEMIZE? SHOULD I ITEMIZE? AND WHAT THE HECK ARE ITEMIZED DEDUCTIONS?

Deductions are just that: You subtract them from your income before you calculate the tax you owe. (Deductions are good things!) To make everything more complicated, the IRS gives you two methods for determining the total of your deductions: itemized and standardized deductions. You get to pick the method that leads to the best solution for you — whichever way offers greater deductions. If you can itemize, you should, because it saves you tax dollars.

The first method — taking the standard deduction — requires no thinking or calculations. For most people, taking the standard deduction is generally the better option. And the good news is that far more people now can and do claim the standard deduction because it was nearly doubled by the Tax Cuts and Jobs Act, which took effect in 2018 and increased further due to the 2025 passage of the One Big Beautiful Bill. The standard deduction for married couples filing jointly for tax year 2025 rises to $31,500. For single taxpayers and married individuals filing separately, the standard deduction rises to $15,750 for 2025, and for heads of households, the standard deduction will be $23,625 for tax year 2025. These amounts increase annually with inflation.

Some deductions — some moving expenses, the penalty for early withdrawal from savings, and so on — are available even if you don't itemize your deductions.

If you are paying on a large mortgage, have high medical expenses, or give a substantial amount to charity, you may be better off itemizing your deductions. Recent tax legislation eliminated some itemized deductions, so if you were used to itemizing because of large payments you made to investment advisors, or you had unreimbursed employee business expenses, we're so sorry, but those are no longer deductible on your federal return. Neither is the cost of this book, although we still think you'll find it helpful even without the deduction.

Choosing a Filing Status

When filing your return, you must choose the appropriate filing status from the five filing statuses available. You select a status by checking the appropriate box directly below your name on page 1 of Form 1040, where it says "Filing Status":

- Single
- Married filing jointly
- Married filing separately
- Head of household
- Qualifying widow(er) with dependent child

REMEMBER

Each filing status has its own tax rates. As a general rule, you pay the lowest tax if you're able to file jointly or as a qualifying widow(er). Those individuals who are married filing separately pay tax at the highest rate. However, like every rule, a few circumstances exist in which married filing separately saves couples money, as you find out later in this chapter. In addition, you can select a different filing status every year. For example, because you filed jointly last tax year doesn't mean you automatically have to file that way this tax year.

Single

Most people who aren't married file as *single*. The IRS doesn't recognize couples living together as being married for filing purposes.

However, if you were widowed, divorced, or legally separated by the end of the tax year (December 31, 2025) and provided support to dependents, such as children or an elderly parent, you may be able to save yourself some tax dollars by filing as *head of household* or as a *qualifying widow(er)*. You can find out more in the upcoming sections "Head of household" and "Qualifying widow(er) with dependent child."

Married filing jointly

If you're married, you probably share many things with your spouse. One of the more treasured tasks you get to share is the preparation of your annual tax return. In fact, this may be the one time during the year that you jointly examine and combine your financial information. Let the fireworks begin!

For your 2025 return, you're considered married if you got married by or were still married as of the end of the tax year — December 31, 2025. In some rare instances, married folks can save money by filing their taxes as *married filing separately.* This somewhat oddball status can be useful for couples who have large differences between their two incomes and can claim more itemized deductions by filing separately. See the later section "Married filing separately" to determine whether you can save money by filing separately.

REMEMBER

If you file a joint return for 2025, you may not, after the due date for filing, amend that return to change to a married filing separately filing status. You're "jointly" stuck!

You can file jointly if you meet any of the following criteria:

- You were married as of December 31, 2025, even if you didn't live with your spouse at the end of the year.
- Your spouse died in 2025, and you didn't remarry in 2025.

  If your spouse died during the year, you're considered married for the entire year, providing you didn't remarry. You report all your income for the year and your spouse's income up to the date of their death.
- Your spouse died in 2024 before you filed a 2025 return. If you're filing jointly in 2025, but your spouse died in either 2025 or before you managed to file your return in 2026, you're exempt from the "both must sign" rule. Only you are required to sign the return. After your name, write the words, "surviving spouse."

You and your spouse may file jointly even if only one of you had income or if you didn't live together all year. However, you both must sign the return, and you're both responsible for seeing that all taxes are paid. That means if your spouse doesn't pay the tax due, you may have to.

TIP

If you signed that joint return, but are either unaware of what's on it, or someone (your spouse) has exerted pressure on you to sign that return, you may be a candidate for the *Innocent Spouse Rule*. This rule can, in some instances, relieve a spouse who was unaware of their spouse's shenanigans from sharing joint responsibility for what is owed.

SPOUSES WHO ARE NONRESIDENT ALIENS OR DUAL-STATUS ALIENS

If one spouse is a nonresident alien and doesn't pay U.S. income taxes on all of their income, regardless of the country (or countries) in which it's earned, then the couple may not choose the married filing jointly tax status.

The same is true when your spouse is a dual-status alien — that is, if during the year, your spouse is a nonresident as well as a resident. You may file jointly under these circumstances:

- If you were married as of December 31, 2025, even if you didn't live with your spouse at the end of 2025.
- If your spouse is a nonresident alien, or if either of you are dual-status aliens, you can make a special election to file jointly. IRS Publication 519 *(U.S. Tax Guide For Aliens)* explains how to make this election.

A couple legally separated under a divorce decree may not file jointly. On the other hand, if one spouse lived away from the home during the entire last six months of the tax year (July 1 through December 31), the remaining spouse, if taking care of dependents, may be able to file under the more favorable head of household status (see the later section "Head of household").

TIP

Although this suggestion is decidedly unromantic, if you're considering a late-in-the-year wedding, especially in December, you may want to consider the tax impact of tying the knot so soon. A considerable number of couples pay higher total taxes when they're married versus when they were single. On the other hand, what spells commitment more than sending money to the IRS with the one you love?

Married filing separately

The vast majority of married couples would pay more taxes if they chose to file separate returns. The IRS won't stand in the way of your filing separate returns. However, by filing separately, you may be able to avoid the marriage penalty and save on your combined tax bill. To determine whether filing separately is to your benefit, figure your tax both ways (married filing jointly and married filing separately).

TIP

Besides saving money, another reason you may choose to file separately is to avoid being responsible for your spouse's share of the joint tax bill whenever you suspect some kind of monkey business (for example, your spouse is underreporting taxable income or inflating deductions).

If your marriage is on the rocks, married filing separately may be the way to go. Remember, if you both sign that tax return, you're both on the hook for any amounts due. Even if the tax owed may be solely due to your soon-to-be ex-spouse's income, if said spouse refuses to pay the bill, you may have to. This is a case where paying a little more upfront can save you a whole lot down the road.

TIP

Even though married filing separately on your federal return may work out to be the same as filing jointly, don't overlook the possibility that by filing that way you may save state taxes.

If you file separately, be aware that the following restrictions may apply:

- You can't take the standard deduction if your spouse itemizes deductions. Both spouses must itemize their deductions, or both must claim the standard deduction.
- You can't claim the credit for child and dependent care expenses in most cases. The amount of income you can exclude under an employer dependent care assistance program is limited to $2,500 instead of the $5,000 by filing jointly.
- You can't claim a credit for qualified adoption expenses unless you are legally separated or living apart from your spouse during the last six months of the year, and the eligible child lived with you for more than half of 2025.
- You can't take the earned income credit.
- You can't exclude from your taxable income the interest you earned from series EE U.S. Savings Bonds issued after 1989, even if you paid higher education expenses in 2025.
- You can't take the credit for being elderly or disabled unless you lived apart from your spouse for all of 2025.
- You may have to pay more tax on the Social Security benefits you received in 2025.
- You usually report only your own income, exemptions, deductions, and credits. Different rules apply to people who live in community property states.
- You can't deduct interest paid on your student loan.
- If you own and actively manage real estate, you can't claim the passive loss exception.

- You can't claim the American Opportunity Credit, the Hope Scholarship Credit, and the Lifetime Learning Credits.
- You can't claim the $7,000 IRA deduction for a nonworking spouse. And you may not be able to deduct all or part of your own $7,000 IRA contribution if your spouse is covered by a retirement plan.
- You can't transfer funds from a traditional IRA to a Roth IRA.
- Your capital loss limit is $1,500 instead of $3,000.

Instead of filing separately, you may be able to file as a head of household if you had a child living with you and you lived apart from your spouse during the last six months of 2025. See the later section "Head of household" for more information.

For many, the choice between filing jointly and filing separately comes down to a simple matter of dollars and cents — which leads you to pay the least tax? For many married couples, the fact that you're married means that you're paying higher taxes than if you and your spouse shacked up and filed as single taxpayers. Welcome to the so-called *marriage penalty*, which is the annual additional tax you pay for being married.

If you and your beloved fall into the marriage penalty category, you may be able to limit the amount of your penalty by filing as married filing separately. Take the time to prepare three returns — two separate and one joint — and see which filing status produces a lower tax bill for you and your honey. We know it's a time sink, so you may want to purchase a computerized tax program that does the number crunching for you. (See Chapter 1 in Book 5 for software recommendations.)

Married couples most likely to save tax dollars filing separately are those who meet both of the following criteria:

- Couples who have two incomes
- Couples who have hefty deductions for medical expenses, miscellaneous itemized deductions, or casualty losses

If you fall under this umbrella, by all means complete the three tax returns to determine which filing status works best for you.

Table 3-1 shows an example of how the same income and the same deductions can be used to obtain a very different result when you compare a joint return with two separate returns. In this example, you earn $75,000, your spouse earns $65,000, and your spouse has a casualty loss of $13,000. If you file a joint return, the two of you lose that deduction because casualty losses can't be deducted until they reach at least 10 percent of your income, in this case $14,000. But if you and your spouse file separate returns, your spouse is entitled to a $6,500 deduction, because the loss is $6,500 — 10 percent of your spouse's income ($13,000 – $6,500 = $6,500). For the purpose of this illustration, the $100 nondeductible portion of casualty loss and the rate reduction credit aren't being considered.

TABLE 3-1

Filing Jointly versus Separately: A Sample Couple

	Jointly	Husband	Wife
Gross income	$140,000	$75,000	$65,000
Casualty loss	$13,000	$0	$13,000
Less 10 percent of income	($14,000)	($0)	($6,500)
Deductible casualty loss	$0	$0	$6,500
Taxes (state, local, real estate, personal property, and so forth)	$5,000	$3,000	$2,000
Mortgage interest	$9,500	$9,500	$0
Charitable contributions	$5,000	$5,000	$0
Total itemized deductions	$19,500	$17,500	$8,500
Taxable income	$120,500	$57,500	$56,500
Tax	$17,125	$7,958	$7,737

Amounts may vary slightly depending on whether you use the tax tables or the rate schedules.

Filling out both joint and separate returns and comparing them is worth doing the numbers. For example, in Table 3-1, the sample couple saves a total of $1,430 by filing separately. Their combined separate tax bill comes to only $15,695 instead of $17,125.

REMEMBER

If you think you could have saved money in a previous year by filing separately, sorry. There's nothing you can do about it now. After you file a joint return, you can't turn back the clock and change it to separate returns. On the other hand, if you and your spouse filed separately, you can (within three years from the due date of your return or two years from the date the tax was paid) file an amended return and switch to filing jointly. You may want to do this if, when audited, some of the deductions you and your spouse claimed were disallowed, or if you get an insurance recovery greater than you expected, reducing the amount of the casualty loss. If you're making estimated tax payments during the year, it doesn't matter whether you make joint or separate payments. You can still file your actual return however you choose and divide the estimated tax payments in accordance with the rule for joint refunds.

Head of household

The rules for who may file as a head of household are fairly straightforward, extremely specific, and only apply if you were unmarried, or separated and considered unmarried at the end of the year, and you paid more than half of the cost of maintaining a home (see Table 3-2 to compute that figure) that either:

- Was your parent's main home for the entire year, provided you can claim your parent as your dependent. Unlike every other dependent relationship, your parent doesn't have to live with you in your own home to qualify as your dependent, but can still be in their own residence, whether it's the old family homestead, an apartment of their own, an assisted living situation, or even a nursing home.
- You lived in for more than half of the year (temporary absences, such as for school, vacation, or medical care, count as time lived in your home) with any of the following:
  - Your qualifying child (which we explain in the later section "Defining Who Is a Qualifying Child").
  - Any other person you can claim as your dependent.
  - Your qualifying married child, but only if that child doesn't file a joint income tax return with their spouse, and only if that child is a U.S. citizen, U.S. national, or a resident of the United States, Mexico, or Canada (an exception is made for certain adopted children).

  You can't claim head of household status on the basis of a person who is your dependent only because they lived with you for the entire year, or because you're entitled to claim that person as a dependent under a multiple support agreement.

REMEMBER

Emotional estrangement doesn't qualify as living apart for head of household status. In a Tax Court case on this topic, a couple became estranged but continued to reside in the same dwelling. The court rejected the idea that emotional estrangement equated to actual separation. Living apart requires geographical separation and living in separate residences.

TABLE 3-2 How to Compute the Cost of Maintaining a Home

	Amount You Paid	Total Cost
Property taxes	$______	$______
Mortgage interest expense	$______	$______
Rent	$______	$______
Utility charges	$______	$______
Upkeep and repairs	$______	$______
Property insurance	$______	$______
Food consumed on the premises	$______	$______
Other household expenses	$______	$______
Totals	$(a)______	$(b)______
Subtract Total (a) from Total (b) and enter here		($______)

Note: If you paid more than half of the total cost of maintaining a home, you qualify for head of household status.

In the case of a birth or death of a dependent, you must have provided more than half the cost of keeping up a home that was that person's home for more than half the year; if the person wasn't alive that long, they must have been a member of your household during the period of the tax year that they were alive.

REMEMBER

The cost of keeping up a home doesn't include clothing, education, medical expenses, vacations, life insurance, or transportation. These are personal support items that are taken into account to determine whether you're entitled to claim the larger standard deduction for the support of a dependent.

Qualifying widow(er) with dependent child

If you meet all five of the following tests, you can use the tax table for married filing jointly:

- Your spouse died in 2023 or 2024, and you didn't remarry in 2025.
- You have a child, stepchild, adopted child, or foster child whom you can claim as a dependent.
- This child lived in your home for all of 2025. Temporary absences, such as for vacation or school, count as time lived in your home.
- You paid more than half the cost of keeping up your home for this child.

» You could have filed a joint return with your spouse the year your spouse died, even if you didn't actually do so. (But you can't claim an exemption for your deceased spouse.)

If your spouse died in 2025, you may not file as a qualifying widow(er) with a dependent child. But see whether you qualify for filing jointly and refer to the later section "Filing a Return for a Deceased Taxpayer." And if you can't file as a qualifying widow(er) with a dependent child, see whether you can qualify as a head of household. If you don't meet the rules for a qualifying widow(er) with a dependent child, married filing a joint return, or head of household, you must file as single.

For example, suppose that a mother with children died in 2022, and the husband hasn't remarried. In 2023 and 2024, he kept up a home for himself and his dependent children. For 2022, he was entitled to file a joint return for himself and his deceased wife. For 2023 and 2024, he may file as a qualifying widow(er) with dependent children. After 2024, he may file as head of household if he qualifies. If he doesn't qualify, he files as single.

Counting your dependents

The number of dependents you have, whether qualifying children or other dependents, can impact a slew of income tax credits you may be entitled to take, including the child tax credit, the additional child tax credit, the earned income tax credit, and all the education credits (American Opportunity Credit and Lifetime Learning Credit). Your dependent's deductible expenses can also impact the tax you pay, since you're the one actually paying that person's medical bills.

If you're a traditional family with both parents married to each other, and minor children, and you're all living together in the United States, this calculation is easy — your minor children are your dependents. In the middle of the first page of your Form 1040, in the section marked "Dependents," enter their full names, Social Security numbers, and their relationship to you, and tick the appropriate box for either qualifying for the child tax credit or the credit for other dependents. Presto, you're done.

If you're part of a nontraditional family, you may have to work a little harder to determine who is, and who isn't, your dependent (see the next section). But please, persevere — each dependent that you claim can put money into your pocket in the form of nonrefundable and refundable tax credits.

Deciding who is your dependent

You can claim a dependent if the person in question is your qualifying child (see the later section "Defining Who Is a Qualifying Child"). You're also allowed to claim a qualifying relative as your dependent if you provide more than half of that person's support, if they can't be claimed as a dependent on anyone else's tax return, and if they pass the five dependency tests. (Don't forget that if you claim someone, that person can't claim a personal exemption on their own tax return.)

TIP

Qualifying relative is a pretty broad term and can include people who are not related to you by blood or marriage. If, for example, a friend lives with you, has no income of their own, and you provide all their support, you may find that they qualify as your dependent. Run through all the rules in the following sections to see if they pass the tests. And to make it even easier, the IRS website has a terrific Interactive Tax Assistant (ITA) at `www.irs.gov/help/ita/whom-may-i-claim-as-a-dependent`.

Okay, you may open your booklets and begin the tests now. In order for a person other than your qualifying child to be your dependent, they must meet all five of the following tests.

Test 1: Member of your household or relative

Your dependent must either live with you for the entire year as a member of your household or must be related to you by blood or marriage. The required relationships are very specific, so that your parents' siblings qualify on the relationship part of this test, but their children, your cousins, need to live with you for the entire year.

If you file a joint return, you don't need to show that a dependent is related to both you and your spouse. The dependent only needs to be related to one of you.

REMEMBER

Temporary absences are ignored. If a person is placed in a nursing home for constant medical care, the absence is also considered temporary.

Here are some more details you may need to consider:

- **Death or birth:** A person who died during the year but was a member of your household until death meets the member of your household test. The same is true for a child who was born during the year and was a member of your household for the rest of the year. A child who was born and died in the same year qualifies, but a stillborn child doesn't. The child must have been born alive — even if for just a moment — to qualify as a dependent.
- **Violation of local law:** A person doesn't meet the member of your household test if your relationship violates local law.
- **Adoption:** Before the adoption is legal, a child is considered your child if they were placed with you for adoption by an authorized adoption agency (and the child must have been a member of your household). Otherwise, the child must be a member of your household for the entire tax year to satisfy this test.

» **Foster care:** A foster child or adult must live with you as a member of your household for the entire year to qualify as your dependent. However, if a government agency makes payments to you as a foster parent, you may not list the child as your dependent.

» **Employees:** Your nanny or live-in housekeeper doesn't qualify for this test. Living with you may be a requirement of their job, but it doesn't meet the member of the household test.

Test 2: Married person

If your dependent is married and files a joint return, unless the purpose of filing that return is to claim a refund, you can't take this person as an exemption.

Test 3: Citizen or resident

The dependent must be one of the following:

» A U.S. citizen or U.S. resident alien

» A resident of Canada or Mexico

» Your adopted child who isn't a U.S. citizen but who lived with you all year in a foreign country

You can't claim a person who isn't a U.S. citizen or resident and lives abroad (in a country other than Canada or Mexico) as a dependent.

CHILDREN OF DIVORCED OR SEPARATED PARENTS

The parent who had custody of the child for the largest number of nights is the one entitled to claim the child as a dependent — provided that both parents together paid more than half of the child's support.

A noncustodial parent can claim the child if any of the following apply:

- The custodial parent gives up the right to claim the child as a dependent by signing Form 8332, Release of Claim to Exemption for Child of Divorced or Separated Parents.

(continued)

(continued)

The form allows for the release of a child for a single year, a number of years, or all future years. The noncustodial parent must attach this form to the return.

- A decree or separation agreement signed after 1984 provides that the noncustodial parent is unconditionally entitled to claim the child as their dependent, and the custodial parent isn't. You must list the child's name, Social Security number, and the number of months the child lived in your home. You also must attach a copy of the cover page of the decree or agreement with the custodial parent's Social Security number written next to their name, along with the page that unconditionally states that you can claim the child as a dependent. Don't forget to attach a copy of the signature page of the decree or agreement.
- A decree or separation agreement signed before 1985 provides that the noncustodial parent is entitled to the exemption, and that this parent provided $600 or more toward the child's support.

Note: If you fail to pay child support in the year it's due but pay it in a later year, it isn't considered paid for the support of your child in either year.

Even if you can't claim a child because your ex-spouse is claiming the child, you still can claim the child's medical expenses, and you're entitled to the Child and Dependent Care Credit if you're the custodial parent. When the child reaches the age of majority, the custodial parent rules no longer apply. The parent who provides more than 50 percent of the child's support is entitled to the exemption.

Note: The special rules for divorced or separated parents also apply to parents, whether married or not, who lived apart at all times during the last six months of the year. In such situations, you either have to provide more than half the support of the child or enter into a multiple support agreement (Form 2120).

Test 4: Income

The dependent's gross income must be less than $5,200. Gross income counts all taxable income, but doesn't include nontaxable income, such as welfare benefits or nontaxable Social Security benefits. Income earned by a permanently and totally disabled person for services performed at a sheltered workshop school generally isn't included for purposes of the income test.

Of course, there are exceptions. Your qualifying relative can have a gross income of $5,200 or more under one of the following conditions:

- » The person was under the age of 19 at the end of 2025.
- » The person was under the age of 24 at the end of 2025 and was also a student.

REMEMBER

Your qualifying relative is considered a student if they're enrolled as a full-time student at a school during any five months of 2025. A school includes technical, trade, and mechanical schools. It doesn't include on-the-job training courses or correspondence schools.

WARNING

Students just graduating college (or high school if they choose to work full-time after that) generally want to claim themselves on their tax returns in the year they leave school. But beware! For people graduating at any time from May through December, that dependency claim rightly belongs with the parent, not the child. Be sure to remind your graduating senior that they're still your dependent this one last year.

Also, be aware that most storefront tax preparation services fail to ask all the questions they should or explain what the questions mean, so if your student has filed their return through one of these services, chances are good that they've tried to claim themselves. When you attempt to file your return electronically, it will be rejected if someone has already claimed that Social Security number; to fix this, you'll have to file your return on paper, and your dependent will have to amend their return.

Test 5: Support

You must have provided more than half of your qualifying relative's total support in 2025 to claim that person as your dependent. If you file a joint return, support can come from either spouse. If you remarried, the support provided by your new spouse is treated as support coming from you. For exceptions to the support test, see the sidebar "Children of divorced or separated parents."

Support includes food, a place to live, clothing, medical and dental care, and education. It also includes items such as a car and furniture, but only if they're for the dependent's own use or benefit. In figuring total support, use the actual cost of these items, but figure the cost of a place to live at its fair rental value. Include money the person used for their own support, even if this money wasn't taxable. Examples are gifts, savings, Social Security and welfare benefits, and other public assistance payments. This support is treated as not coming from you.

Total support doesn't include items such as income tax and Social Security taxes, life insurance premiums, or funeral expenses. A person's own funds aren't considered support unless they're actually spent for support. For example, your mother received $2,400 in Social Security and $400 in interest. She paid $2,000 for rent and $400 for recreation. Even though her income was $2,800, she spent only $2,400 for her own support. If you spent more than $2,400 for her support, you can claim her as a dependent because you provided more than half her support.

TIP

Even if you didn't pay more than half of a dependent's support, you may still be able to claim this person as a dependent if all five of the following apply:

- You and one or more eligible persons paid more than half of the dependent's support. An *eligible person* is someone who could have claimed the dependent but didn't pay more than half of the dependent's support.
- You paid more than 10 percent of the dependent's support.
- No individual paid more than half of the dependent's support.
- Dependency tests 1 through 4 are met.
- Each eligible person who paid more than 10 percent of support completes Form 2120, Multiple Support Declaration, and you attach this form to your return. The form states that only you will claim the person as a dependent for 2025.

Securing Social Security numbers for dependents

You must list a Social Security number for every dependent in the "Dependents" section on the face of Form 1040, column (2). If your dependent was born and died in 2025 and didn't have a Social Security number, write "Died" in column (2). No Social Security number, no deduction, and no right to claim head of household status.

TIP

If you're in the process of adopting a child who is a U.S. citizen or resident and can't get a Social Security number until the adoption is final, you can apply for an adoption taxpayer number (ATIN) that you can use instead of a Social Security number. To get one, file Form W-7A, Application for Taxpayer Identification Number for Pending U.S. Adoptions.

Filing for Children and Other Dependents

Even if you're able to claim someone else (your child, your grandchild, and so on) as a dependent on your return, that person may have to file their own income tax return in the following circumstances:

- The dependent had unearned income (generally, income other than wages, income from self-employment, and tips), and the total of that income exceeds $1,350.

- The dependent had earned income in 2025 on which income tax has been withheld.
- The dependent had no unearned income but had earned income that exceeds $15,750.
- The dependent had both earned and unearned gross income that exceeds the larger of (a) $1,350 or (b) the earned income up to $15,750 plus $450.

For example, suppose that your teenager has interest income of $600 and salary from a summer job of $4,500. This dependent doesn't need to file because the total income was less than $15,750, and their unearned income (interest) is less than $1,350. If your teenager had no unearned income but earned $2,000 from a summer job, they wouldn't have to file either because the earned income was under $15,750, unless income tax was withheld, and they wanted to request a refund.

TIP

But here's an important point: Your dependent, who isn't going to have a tax liability in the first place, doesn't need to have income tax withheld from their paycheck. Instead, have that dependent claim an exemption from income tax when completing Form W-4. If the dependent didn't claim an exemption on Form W-4, they must file to get back the tax that was withheld from their paychecks. Remember, though, when they reach $15,750 in income, withholding will have to start, and a new W-4 must be filed with the employer.

You may encounter another wrinkle in the IRS rules for this exemption from withholding to apply — the teenager's investment income (interest) can't exceed $450. If it does, they can't claim an exemption from withholding if their total income exceeds $1,350. There's no such thing as being too young when introducing your kid to convoluted tax laws.

TIP

A new Form W-4 needs to be filed for each year your child is exempt, and after your child is no longer exempt, a fresh Form W-4 should be filed, indicating the number of exemptions they will be claiming for withholding purposes.

Congress continues to fiddle with the *kiddie tax* (tax on a child's income that's taxed at their parents' highest marginal tax rate) that applies to all children under age 19 and to children who are full-time students under the age of 24 unless they're providing more than half of their own support. The kiddie tax kicks in after your child hits $2,700 of unearned income in 2025.

Defining Who Is a Qualifying Child

In case you were wondering, there is a uniform definition for who, exactly, is a qualifying child for the following tax benefits:

- Dependency exemptions
- Head of household filing status
- The earned income credit (EIC)
- The child tax credit
- The credit for child and dependent care expenses

For your child to qualify for any of these benefits, they need to meet the age test, the relationship test, the residency test, and the support test. If they don't meet the requirements of all these tests, unfortunately they aren't your qualifying child in the eyes of the IRS.

Age test

For your child to qualify under the age test for dependency exemptions, head of household filing status, and the earned income credit, they must be under the age of 19 at the end of the year or under the age of 24 if a full-time student for some part of each of five months during the year (not necessarily consecutive). No age test applies for a child who is permanently and totally disabled.

REMEMBER

To qualify for the child tax credit, your child must be under age 17 by the end of the tax year.

To be eligible for the child and dependent care credit, your child must be under age 13, or permanently and totally disabled. For the purpose of this credit only, expenses you incur *and* pay for that child in the year of their 13th birthday before that birthday can be used to claim the credit; expenses incurred after that birthday can't, even if you made payment before their 13th birthday.

Relationship test

The child must either be your child, adopted child (even if the adoption isn't yet final), stepchild, eligible foster child (any child placed with you by an authorized placement agency, or by a judgment, decree, or any other court order), brother, sister, stepbrother, stepsister, or the descendent of one of these relatives.

Residency test

Your qualifying child must live with you for more than half of the year. Although the days don't have to be consecutive, they do need to add up to at least 183. Temporary absences for school, vacation, military service, medical reasons, or for detention in a juvenile detention center don't count as time away from you.

REMEMBER

"Days" actually doesn't mean days at all; instead, you need to count the number of nights they spend with you.

An exception is made for children who are born during the tax year, provided that they lived with you for the entire period they were alive. So, a child who is born on December 30, 2025, is your qualifying child, even though they may not make it home from the hospital until January 1, 2026. An exception is also made for a child who dies during the year and for a child who is kidnapped, provided that the kidnapper isn't related.

Finally, the children of divorced or separated parents qualify under the rules set out in the earlier sidebar "Children of divorced or separated parents."

Support test

To meet the standards of this test, your child must not have provided at least half of their own support. Calculate how much your child spent on their share of housing costs (including rent, utilities, furnishings, and repairs, but not mortgage interest, insurance, or real estate taxes), on clothing, on food, on education, and on medical and dental bills not reimbursed by insurance. Also add vacations and travel, and any other miscellaneous expenses that your child paid for their benefit. Then compare this number against the total cost of that child's share of these items. If the amount your child paid is less than 50 percent, you meet this test.

TIP

If you're having some difficulty in figuring out whether your child qualifies under the support test, use the nifty worksheet in IRS Publication 501 *(Dependents, Standard Deduction, and Filing Information)*.

Filing a Return for a Deceased Taxpayer

When someone dies, a separate taxpaying entity is created — the decedent's estate. If the estate has more than $600 in income or has a beneficiary who is a nonresident alien, the executor or administrator for the estate (the person responsible for winding up the decedent's financial affairs) must file Form 1041, U.S. Income Tax Return for Estates and Trusts. This filing is in addition to the decedent's final tax return.

Suppose the decedent died before April 15, 2026, without having filed their 2025 tax return. The executor is responsible for filing a tax return for that individual for 2025 (a complete year) and for 2026, which isn't due until April 15, 2027. For example, if someone died on April 1, 2026, a return must be filed for 2025, and a final return for 2026 must be filed by April 15, 2027, reporting all the deceased's income and deductions for the period January 1, 2026, through April 1, 2026.

If a decedent died in 2025, you must allocate their income based on what was earned and received prior to and including the date of death, and what was received after the date of death. Income received prior to death is reported and taxed on the decedent's final Form 1040; after the date of death, all income received is reported on the Form 1041 for the estate. The good news is that even though you report only part of the year's income on the Form 1040, you get to deduct the full amount of the decedent's standard deduction if you're not itemizing.

If the surviving spouse didn't remarry in the same year as the death, a joint return can be filed. The surviving spouse reports their income and deductions for the entire year and the deceased's up to the date of death. If you remarry in the same year that your spouse dies, you can file jointly with your new spouse, but not with your deceased spouse. Your deceased spouse's filing status will revert to "married filing separately."

Medical expenses paid within one year of the decedent's death must be deducted on the decedent's final return; an estate can't take this type of deduction on its Form 1041. If you've already filed that last return, and then you pay more bills (within the one-year time limit), you may amend that final return (by filing IRS Form 1040X), take the larger medical deduction, and receive a refund.

If the deceased owned E or EE Savings Bonds and chose not to report the interest during their lifetime, the tax on the interest must be paid by the survivor unless an election is made to report the interest on the decedent's final return. Doing so may make sense if the deceased died early in the year and had little income and large deductions.

Either the surviving spouse or the executor can sign the deceased's final personal income tax return. Write "DECEASED," the decedent's name, and the date of death at the top of page 1 of the 1040. If you are using tax software, make sure to include the date of death in the program so the return produces the appropriate diagnostics.

TIP

Please be aware that, while the IRS encourages everyone to file their tax returns electronically, when you are dealing with the final 1040 for a deceased person, even if it is joint with their spouse, that return, including any extension, may have to be filed on paper. Please make sure that, when you mail the return to the appropriate IRS office, you send it via Certified Mail. You want to make certain that, if the IRS loses that return, you have proof that you timely filed it.

If the deceased's final Form 1040 isn't joint with the surviving spouse and a refund is due, the person who is receiving the refund must also file Form 1310, aptly named "Statement of Person Claiming Refund Due a Deceased Taxpayer." Who said the IRS wasn't any good with words? And, Form 1310 must be filed on paper, even if you can figure out how to file the final return electronically. Our general rule is that, if any part of the return needs to be filed on paper, file the entire return on paper. That way, hopefully all the pages stay together, and the IRS has everything they need to process the refund.

Check out *Estate & Trust Administration For Dummies*, by Margaret Atkins Munro, EA, and Kathryn A. Murphy, Esq. (Wiley), for complete information on how to fill out the decedent's final Form 1040 and prepare Form 1041 for the estate.

Must You File?

Yes, you must file a tax return when your income exceeds the amount for your age and filing status, as shown in Table 3-3.

TABLE 3-3 When You Must File

Marital Status	Filing Status	Age*	Filing Required When Gross Income Exceeds
Single, divorced, legally separated	Single	Under 65	$15,750
		65 or older	$23,750
		65 or older and blind	$25,750
	Head of household	Under 65	$23,625
		65 or older	$31,625
		65 or older and blind	$33,625
Married with a child and living apart from spouse during last six months of 2025	Head of household	Under 65	$23,625

(continued)

What Kind of Taxpayer Are You?

TABLE 3-3 ***(continued)***

Marital Status	Filing Status	Age*	Filing Required When Gross Income Exceeds
		65 or older	$31,625
		65 or older and blind	$33,625
Married and living with spouse at end of 2025 (or on date of spouse's death)	Married (joint return)	Under 65	$31,500
		65 or older (one spouse)	$39,100
		65 or older (both spouses)	$46,700
		65 or older (both spouses) and blind (one spouse)	$48,300
		65 or older (one spouse) and blind (one spouse)	$40,700
		65 or older (both spouses) and blind (both spouses)	$49,900
	Married (separate return)	Under 65	$15,750
		65 or older	$23,350
		65 or older and blind	$24,950
Married and not living with spouse at end of 2025 (or on date of spouse's death)	Married (separate return)	Under 65	$15,750
		65 or older	$23,350
		65 or older and blind	$24,950
Widowed before 2025 and not remarried in 2025	Single	Under 65	$15,750
		65 or older	$23,750
		65 or older and blind	$25,750
Qualifying widow(er) with dependent child		Under 65	$31,500
		65 or older	$45,100
		65 or older and blind	$46,700

* *If you turn 65 on January 1, 2026, you're considered to be age 65 at the end of 2025.*

When to file

If you don't file your tax return by April 15, 2026, you'll have to pay penalties and interest. If you live or work outside the United States, your filing deadline is June 15, 2026.

If you know that you can't file by April 15, you can get an automatic six-month extension of time to file — until October 15, 2026 — by filing Form 4868, Application for Automatic Extension of Time to File U.S. Individual Income Tax Return. Keep in mind that you must file this form by April 15, 2026. If you pay all or a portion of what you think the balance due is using either the IRS Direct Pay, the EFTPS (Electronic Federal Tax Payment System), or a credit or debit card to pay the balance owed for 2025, you don't have to separately file Form 4868; it's done automatically for you when you choose "extension payment" as the type of payment you're making. You can also obtain extensions of time to file by using your personal computer and a tax software program. The choices are endless, so don't blow the April 15 filing date.

If you're living outside the country, you're not required to file Form 4868 until June 15, 2026, which is the due date of your return. Form 4868 for taxpayers living abroad extends the due date to October 15, 2026.

WARNING

Filing an extension of time to file doesn't extend the time to pay. You'll be charged interest and a late payment penalty of 0.5 percent a month on your unpaid balance if you don't pay at least 90 percent of your tax by April 15, 2026. And with the recent rise of interest rates, paying interest is starting to hurt. Current interest rate on tax underpayments in 2025 is 7 percent.

If you don't file

You can end up crushing rocks. Remember, Al Capone didn't go to prison for running rackets; he went to the big house for tax evasion. Realistically, though, it's more likely that you'll be assessed penalties that make crushing rocks seem like a stroll in the park. Annually, the IRS prosecutes only 5,000 individuals (you can't call them taxpayers) for tax evasion. Some 80 percent are members of organized crime or drug dealers, and the balance is made up of high-profile individuals and others. You don't want to be one of the others.

If you don't file, based on the information reported to the IRS by your employers, the IRS either prepares a substitute return and assesses a late filing penalty of 25 percent, a late payment penalty of 0.5 percent a month to a maximum of 25 percent plus interest (and possibly a 75 percent fraud penalty), or issues a summons for you to appear with your tax records so that the IRS can use those records to prepare a more accurate return. Interest and penalties are charged whichever way the IRS decides to proceed. Bottom line, you should file your return to avoid the late filing penalty even if you are unable to pay any taxes that may be due.

Where to file

The IRS website (`www.irs.gov/filing/where-to-file-paper-tax-returns-with-or-without-a-payment`) lists the specific address to which you should send your forms. So does your instruction booklet. Just look for the "Where To File" link in the "Resources" section.

How to file

You have a couple of ways to get the forms — and the check, if necessary — to IRS Central: You can file the old-fashioned way through the U.S. Postal Service, or you can file electronically.

Electronic filing

Although electronic filing became the most popular form of tax filing for the first time in 2005, we still need to define it, especially for that last 10 percent who insist on doing it the old-fashioned way, on paper and by mail (for tax year 2023, about 94 percent of all individual returns were filed electronically). You or the company that offers this service files your return securely and encrypted over the internet.

Through a link on the IRS web page (`www.irs.gov/filing/free-file-do-your-federal-taxes-for-free`), a group of software companies are offering free online tax filing. Why are they doing this? To ensure that the IRS doesn't jump into the online tax filing market with a competitive product. If free electronic filing sounds too good to be true, you're probably right. We have experienced that when someone offers something for nothing, usually a gimmick is involved. Some companies may have something up their sleeves and try to solicit you for their financial services or products. Others only offer a stripped-down version of their regular software for free — if your taxes are more complicated, they're happy to sell you the necessary software to prepare your return (the electronic filing remains free). Another catch we noticed is that, although they'll file the federal return for free, you need to pay a fee to file your state return.

Each participating software company has set its own eligibility requirements for free filing. Generally, those requirements are based on age, adjusted gross income

(AGI), eligibility to claim the earned income credit, state residency, and active-duty military status (if applicable). Each company has a description of the criteria for using its free service.

The advantage of electronic filing is that you may get your hands on your hard-earned refund in about ten days, which is approximately three weeks faster than by mail. Also, you can have your refund deposited directly into your bank account. Your state return gets filed along with your federal return at the same time. One transmission does it all.

Some tax preparation firms not only prepare and electronically file your return, but they also loan you money based on the projected amount of the refund. These clever loans are called *refund anticipation loans.*

WARNING

Our principal objection to these refund anticipation loans is that they're too pricey. Some tax preparation firms can arrange for an on-the-spot loan for the amount of your refund.

Filing by mail or other private delivery service

REMEMBER

Face it, many taxpayers, whether by choice or through necessity, still do it the old-fashioned way, with a trip to the post office on April 15. If you're one of those taxpayers who feels the job isn't done right without that postmark on the upper right-hand corner of the envelope, you need to consider the following:

- Make sure you have proof of mailing. For the post office, that means a certified mail receipt. And remember, there are no post offices that stay open until midnight on April 15 anymore. You have to be inside the post office door by 5 p.m. to get that all-important April 15, 2026, postmark. Filing electronically buys you time until midnight on deadline day!
- If you choose to use a private delivery service, you need to know that only certain types of deliveries (such as DHL, FedEx, and UPS) provide you with adequate proof (in the form of dated receipts) should the IRS question whether you have timely filed.

6

Retiring Comfortably

Contents at a Glance

IN THIS CHAPTER

» Understanding how a 401(k) plan helps you

» Getting to keep your employer's contribution

» Benefiting from investment pros

» Keeping your money safe

» Avoiding potential problems

Chapter 1
Checking the Benefits of a 401(k)

In the 40-plus years 401(k) plans have been available, millions of Americans have used them to save for retirement. Because Social Security alone won't provide adequate retirement income and fewer companies offer a traditional pension plan, 401(k)s have become an essential part of the average worker's retirement plans.

Even young people, for whom retirement is normally low on the priority list, have jumped on the retirement savings bandwagon. They're the smart ones, because in some respects, how long you save is more important than how much you save.

The 2008 market crash caused 401(k) plans to come under fire because owners saw large drops in their accounts. Some blamed the 401(k) itself, but that's like blaming the messenger who brings you bad news. Those who didn't panic and kept making their usual 401(k) contributions have done well. If you take the time to understand and follow basic investing principles, your 401(k) can grow into a nest egg that can help you retire comfortably.

REMEMBER

The beauty of a 401(k) is that it makes saving easy and automatic, and you probably won't even miss the money you save.

How much your 401(k) will be worth when you retire depends on a number of factors, such as how much you contribute, what investments you choose, what return you get on those investments, whether your employer makes a contribution, and whether you withdraw money early.

Realizing What a 401(k) Does for You

A 401(k) plan lets you put some of your income away now to use later, presumably when you're retired and not earning a paycheck. This procedure may not appeal to everyone; human nature being what it is, many people would rather spend their money now and worry about later when later comes. That's why the federal government approved tax breaks for 401(k) participants to enjoy now. Uncle Sam knows that your individual savings are going to be an essential part of your retirement, and he wants to give you an incentive to save.

When you sign up for a 401(k) plan, you agree to let your employer deposit some of the money you earn into the plan as a pre-tax contribution, Roth after-tax contribution, or a combination of the two, instead of paying it to you. (You always pay tax on contributions before they go into a Roth account.) Your employer may even throw some money, known as a *matching contribution,* into your 401(k). You don't pay federal income tax on any of this money except the Roth contribution until you withdraw it. (Find out about matching contributions in the upcoming section "Gets you matching funds from your employer.")

WARNING

Of course, there's a catch. Some 401(k) plans don't allow you to withdraw money while you're still working. Even if your plan does allow withdrawals, if you're under 59½ years old, those withdrawals can be difficult and costly.

The following sections cover the benefits of what a 401(k) does for you.

Lowers how much tax you pay

A 401(k) lets you pay less income tax in two ways:

- **Lower taxable income:** You don't have to pay federal income tax on the money you contribute with pre-tax contributions to your 401(k) plan until you withdraw it from the plan.

REMEMBER

If you're making contributions to a Roth 401(k), you must pay tax now on the amount you put into the plan.

- **Tax deferral:** You don't pay tax on your 401(k) investment earnings each year. You pay tax on your pre-tax contributions, any employer contributions, and your investment gains on these contributions only when you make withdrawals.

  The investment gains on your Roth contributions are never taxed if you follow the rules.

The government provides these big tax breaks in an attempt to avoid having a country full of senior citizens who can't make ends meet. (Nice to know the government's looking out for seniors, huh?)

Lower taxable income

The money you contribute to a 401(k) except for Roth contributions reduces your *gross income* or *taxable income* — and lowers your pay before tax and some other deductions. When you have lower taxable income, you pay less of the following income or wage taxes:

- **Federal taxes:** These taxes increase as your taxable income increases.
- **State taxes:** Many states impose their own income or wage taxes, depending on the state.
- **Local/municipal government taxes:** Many local and municipal governments also have income or wage taxes.

In every state except Pennsylvania, you aren't required to pay state income tax on your 401(k) contributions if you opt for pre-tax contributions. Your contributions are also exempt from most local wage taxes. Check with your local tax authorities if you're not sure what the rules are.

TECHNICAL STUFF

Taxes that you can't avoid paying because everybody has to pay them on gross income (including 401(k) contributions) are Social Security/Medicare (FICA) and unemployment (FUTA) taxes. The only way to avoid these taxes is if you're a sole proprietor and set up a plan funded with employer contributions rather than employee salary-reduction contributions.

Check the following hypothetical to see how you save money when you contribute some of your pay pre-tax to a 401(k). Consider the following hypothetical example:

- Your gross pay is $3,000 each pay period.
- You're in the 22 percent federal tax bracket.
- Your state income tax is 2 percent, your local income tax is 1 percent, and your FICA taxes are 7.65 percent.
- You don't live in Pennsylvania, so contributions you make to a 401(k) plan are exempt from federal, state, and local tax.

You have the option to contribute to a retirement plan. Table 1-1 shows the difference to your bottom line when you choose to participate. The right side shows what happens when you hypothetically make a 6 percent, or $180, per paycheck pre-tax contribution to a 401(k) plan. Your FICA/FUTA taxes remain the same, but other taxes are lower because they're based on a lower income (your gross income minus your retirement contribution). Here's how it breaks down.

TABLE 1-1 Take-Home Pay without and with 401(k) Contributions

	Without 401(k) Contributions	With 401(k) Contributions
Gross pay	$3,000	$3,000
Retirement contribution	$0	$180
Federal income tax withheld	$350	$310
State income tax withheld	$60	$56
Local wage tax withheld	$30	$28
FICA taxes withheld	$230	$230
Take-home pay	$2,330	$2,196

You invested $180 for your retirement, but your take-home pay is reduced by only $134. For the time being, you're up $46 that would otherwise have gone to the government. You don't have to pay these taxes until you withdraw your money from the plan.

REMEMBER

Another way of looking at it: Without a 401(k) plan, taxes eat away the money you can save.

Say you want to put 10 percent of your earnings into retirement savings. You earn $75,000 per year, so you want to set aside $7,500 for your retirement fund. Your total tax rate is 32.65 percent — 22 percent federal income tax plus 7.65 percent FICA plus 2 percent state income tax plus 1 percent local wage taxes — so it takes almost 16 percent of your gross income, or $11,136, to have 10 percent left to invest for retirement.

You have to earn $11,136 in order to have $7,500 left after paying taxes — bummer. The following table lays out this scenario:

Pre-tax earnings required	$11,136
Federal income tax	– $2,450
State/local wage tax	– $334
FICA taxes	– $852
Amount left to save	$7,500

Now assume that your employer offers a 401(k) plan, and you can save the $7,500 pre-tax in your 401(k) account. In this case, the only tax you have to pay at the time you make the contribution is FICA. As a result, you need to earn only $8,121 in order to be able to contribute $7,500 to the 401(k) plan — $7,500 plus the 7.65 percent FICA tax, which is $621. Check out the difference:

Pre-tax earnings required	$8,121
Federal income tax	$0
State/local wage tax	$0
FICA taxes	– $621
Amount left to save	$7,500

Without a 401(k) plan, it takes you $11,136 in pre-tax income to save $7,500 after taxes. When you can save pre-tax money in your 401(k), it takes only $8,121 to save the same $7,500. In other words, with a 401(k), it costs less of your current earnings to save the same amount. Pretty good deal, don't you think?

Even better, you can also avoid the $621 FICA taxes if you are self-employed and set up an employer-funded plan. That means you only need $7,500 to invest $7,500 into a retirement account.

TIP

Some plans allow you to make *after-tax* contributions that aren't Roth contributions. You don't get the initial tax break of lower taxable income, but you do benefit from deferring taxes on your investment earnings. The earnings are taxable when they are withdrawn with this type of after-tax contribution.

Tax deferral

In addition to the income tax savings on your contributions, you also save when it comes to paying tax on your investment earnings.

The gains in your 401(k) aren't taxed annually, as they would be in a regular bank savings account, a personal mutual fund account, or a *brokerage account* (which you may use to buy and sell stocks and other investments). With a 401(k), you defer paying taxes on your investment earnings until you withdraw the money.

Figure 1-1 shows how tax-deferred compounding lets your money grow faster than it would in a taxable account. It compares the results of investing $7,500 at a 9 percent return in a tax-deferred account with investing $5,050 in a taxable account ($5,050 = $7,500 less income tax) at a 9 percent return.

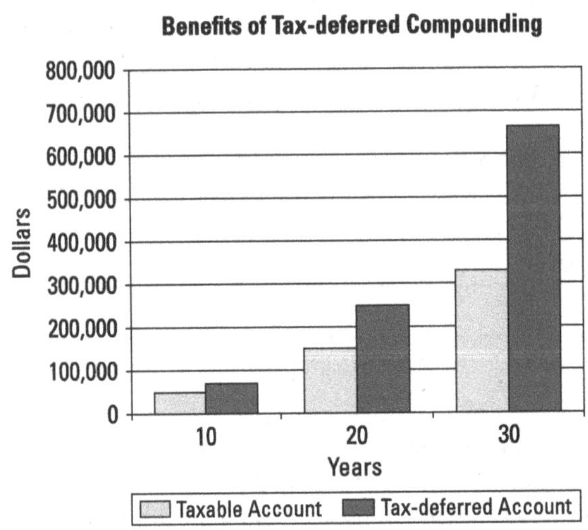

FIGURE 1-1: Positive impact of tax-deferred compounding.

© John Wiley & Sons, Inc.

Gets you matching funds from your employer

Whoever said there's no such thing as a free lunch didn't know about *employer matching contributions* — money that your employer contributes to your 401(k) if you contribute to the plan. (Not all employers make this type of contribution, but many do.)

The most common formula is for the employer to put in 50 cents for every dollar you contribute up to 6 percent of your salary. Employers may make higher (dollar-for-dollar, for example) or lower (25 cents on the dollar, for example) matching contributions and may match higher or lower percentages of salary. There's no set rule, and some employers are more generous than others. But after an employer sets the formula for the matching contribution, it must meet the commitment until it amends the *plan document* unless the document permits the employer to make variable employer matching contributions. (The plan document is the official document detailing the plan's rules.)

So, if your employer puts in 50 cents for every dollar you put in up to 6 percent of your salary, the most your employer will contribute is half of 6 percent, or 3 percent of your salary. You get this full 3 percent only if you contribute 6 percent or more of your salary.

For a concrete example, say you earn $50,000 a year. Six percent of your salary is $3,000. For every dollar you contribute to your 401(k) plan up to $3,000, your employer will contribute 50 cents. So, if you contribute $3,000, your employer contributes an additional $1,500, and you end up with $4,500 after only contributing $3,000 of your own money. However, if you contribute only $1,000, your employer contributes just $500, and you miss out on $1,000 in employer contributions.

How much will your employer contribute if you put in $4,000? If you answered $2,000, or 50 percent of your contribution, unfortunately you're wrong. If you contribute $4,000, your employer still only contributes $1,500 if the matching funds apply only to $3,000, or 6 percent of your salary.

You can also include your employer's contribution when determining how much you should be saving for retirement. Suppose you earn $50,000 and want to put aside 10 percent in your 401(k). If your employer contributes up to 3 percent of your salary as a match, you need to contribute only 7 percent of your salary to achieve your 10 percent savings goal. You pay no taxes on the 3 percent employer contribution until you withdraw it from the 401(k), so the math works out as follows:

Your contribution of 7 percent	$3,500
Employer 3 percent matching contribution	± $1,500
Total contribution	= $5,000

TIP

An employer matching contribution gives you an incentive to save, and it can give your savings a powerful boost. It makes sense for you to contribute at least the full amount that your employer will match.

You typically have to work for your employer for a certain period of time before you can leave the company without losing your employer's contributions. Find out about that in the upcoming section "Vesting: When Your Employer's Contribution Is Yours to Keep."

REMEMBER

The employer matching contribution can be the single most important feature of your 401(k) plan. The more you get from your employer, the less you have to save out of your own paycheck to achieve an adequate level of retirement income. In fact, if your employer offers a matching contribution, make sure that you contribute enough to your plan to get it all. If you don't, this money will be lost to you. Keep in mind that it's easier to contribute the amount needed to get the full employer matching contribution if you utilize pre-tax rather than Roth contributions.

Some employers make what's called a *variable* or *discretionary matching contribution* — a hybrid of profit-sharing and matching contributions. You have to contribute to your 401(k) to get it, as with an ordinary matching contribution, but the amount of the contribution varies at the discretion of your company. For example, the amount of your matching contribution may depend on the success of your company from one year to the next.

Makes room for a little something extra: Employer non-matching contribution

Some employers contribute to their employees' 401(k) accounts (or to another plan) whether the employee contributes or not in what's called a *non-matching contribution*. For example, your employer may deposit a profit-sharing contribution into the 401(k) on your behalf, either alone or in addition to a matching contribution. In a good year, for example, your employer may contribute 5 percent of each eligible employee's pay as a profit-sharing contribution, plus a 25 percent of 401(k) deferral or 50 percent of 401(k) deferral matching contribution. You get the 5 percent no matter what, but you only get the additional matching contribution if you put some of your salary into the plan. In a bad year, the company may only make the matching contribution and forgo the profit-sharing contribution, or it may even forgo both contributions!

A company may also make *a non-matching employer contribution* that's not based on its financial results. The employer may contribute a specific percentage of your pay each year — typically between 3 and 5 percent — regardless of whether the company does well. A non-matching employer contribution is frequently used when a company has discontinued a defined-benefit pension plan in favor of a defined-contribution arrangement including a cash-balance plan.

Automatic contributions may also be made in what's called a *Safe Harbor 401(k)* or a *Qualified Automatic Contributions Arrangement* (QACA). These are two types of 401(k) plans that don't have to pass certain federal nondiscrimination tests that are part of the law governing 401(k)s. As a matter of fact, if your employer sets up a brand-new plan, you will likely be automatically enrolled in the new plan at a set rate, then subject to an annual automatic escalation of your deferral percentage. If you are automatically enrolled into a plan, you can always change your deferral to a different amount.

Enables you to save without tears

A big benefit of signing up for your 401(k) plan is that you don't have to think about the fact that you're saving. "Out of sight, out of mind" is what happens to most people — they don't even miss the money because it's taken out of their paycheck before they have a chance to spend it.

REMEMBER

This semi-forced savings is one of the most valuable benefits of 401(k) plans. The payroll deduction has the power to convert spenders into savers. Most people are unable to save over a long period of time if they have to physically write the check or make the deposit each pay period. Saving becomes the last, not the first, priority. Many participants have said that the 401(k) has helped them save thousands of dollars that they otherwise would have spent carelessly.

TIP

Increasing your 401(k) contributions if you get a raise or a bonus is a good idea. In fact, do it right away so that you don't get used to spending the extra money.

Vesting: When Your Employer's Contribution Is Yours to Keep

When your employer puts money into your 401(k) plan, that money doesn't necessarily belong to you right away. Most companies require that you stay employed with them for a certain amount of time before the contributions *vest*, or are yours to keep if you leave your job. They use this requirement to encourage you to stay on the job.

The employer contributions are generally deposited in the account right away, earning a return on your behalf even before they vest. If you leave your job before the employer contributions vest, you forfeit those contributions plus any earnings on them.

REMEMBER

The contributions you make from your salary are always yours to keep, and you can take them with you when you leave. Vesting applies only to contributions made by your employer.

Your employer can't make you wait forever to vest. There are maximum lengths of time for matching and non-matching contributions. What are they? Keep reading to find out.

Vesting of employer contributions

Employer contributions, whether matching or non-matching, must generally become yours to keep in one of the following two ways:

- All at once on a specified date within three years
- Gradually over six years

The first method is known as *cliff vesting*. With this method, you go from 0 to 100 percent vested after three years of service, at the most (the period can be shorter). The second is called *graded vesting*, or *graduated vesting*. With this method, you must go from 0 to 100 percent vested by increases of 20 percent over a period of six years at the most.

Table 1-2 shows a comparison of the two vesting schedules, looking at the maximum number of years of service that an employer can generally require.

TABLE 1-2 **Longest Allowed 401(k) Matching Contribution Vesting Schedules**

Years of Service	Cliff	Graduated
Less than 2	0%	0%
2 but less than 3	0%	20%
3 but less than 4	100%	40%
4 but less than 5	100%	60%
5 but less than 6	100%	80%
6 or more	100%	100%

An employer may choose a faster vesting schedule and may even choose to have your matching contributions 100 percent vested at all times.

Making exceptions

A few other situations may cause immediate vesting of matching and non-matching employer contributions no matter how many years you have worked at the company. These situations are as follows:

- If your employer terminates your 401(k) plan
- If you reach normal retirement age (an age defined by the plan, but usually age 65)
- If you die before you leave the company
- If you become disabled, as defined in the plan
- If you're among a substantial portion (such as more than 20 percent) of plan participants who are laid off due to the closing of a plant or division, or are otherwise part of a large layoff
- If your employer needs to make contributions to pass one of the nondiscrimination tests for a regular 401(k)

TECHNICAL STUFF

Employer contributions to a Safe Harbor 401(k) must be fully vested at all times. Employer contributions to a QACA 401(k) must be fully vested after two years.

To find out which rules apply to you, check your summary plan description.

Letting the Pros Work for You

Have you ever wished that you could hire a professional money manager to handle your investments? A 401(k) lets you take a step in that direction by offering *mutual funds.*

Mutual funds are investments that let you pool your money with the money of hundreds or thousands of other investors. An investment expert called the *fund manager* decides how to invest all this money, trying to get the best return on your investment based on the fund's *investment objectives.* Because the fund manager invests your money along with the money contributed by other investors in the fund, they have more money to invest and can spread it around to different companies or sectors of the economy. This *diversification* helps reduce the amount of risk that you take with your investments.

What does this mean for you? If you choose your fund carefully, you benefit from a professional money manager who's seeking the best return for the fund's investors, based on the fund's investment objectives.

In most cases, your employer is responsible for choosing the mutual funds (and any other investments) offered by your 401(k) plan. More than 8,000 mutual funds are registered in the United States. If your employer does a good job of narrowing the offering down to a handful, it can save you a lot of time.

Rather than rely on choices made by their employer, however, some investors prefer to choose their own investments, such as individual stocks, mutual funds, or other investments that aren't included in their plans. Some 401(k) plans offer a *brokerage window* that enables you to choose your own investments. But you generally pay an extra fee if you use this feature.

You have the sole responsibility as an IRA investor for deciding where to invest your IRA contributions.

Protecting Your Money

Investing money always involves some risks, but money in a 401(k) plan is protected in some ways that money in an ordinary savings account, brokerage account, or IRA isn't. The following sections explain the safeguards.

Meeting minimum standards

A federal law called ERISA, the Employee Retirement Income Security Act, governs 401(k) plans. Passed in 1974, ERISA sets minimum standards for retirement plans offered by private-sector companies. Some nonprofits also follow ERISA rules, but local, state, and federal government retirement plans, as well as church plans, don't have to.

ERISA requirements include:

- Providing information to you about plan features on a regular basis, including a *summary plan description* outlining the plan's main rules, when you enroll in the plan and periodically thereafter.
- Defining how long you may be required to work before being able to sign up for the plan or before employer contributions to the plan are yours to keep if you leave your job.

- Detailing requirements for the *plan fiduciary,* essentially including anyone at your company or the plan provider who has control over the investment choices in the plan. (A fiduciary who breaks the rules may be sued by participants.)

REMEMBER

This last point, *fiduciary responsibility*, is important to understand. Essentially, it means that anyone who has a decision-making role in your 401(k) plan's investments is legally bound to make those decisions in the best interests of the plan participants (you and your coworkers), and not in the best interest of the company, the plan provider, or the fiduciary's cousin Joe. For example, the committee in charge of choosing a 401(k) provider shouldn't choose Bank XYZ just because the company president's cousin runs the bank.

But this doesn't necessarily mean that you can sue your employer if your 401(k) doesn't do well. (Keep in mind that lawsuits are often costly and won't endear you to your employer.) If you lose most of your money because you make bad investment decisions or the stock market takes a nosedive, but your employer has followed ERISA rules, your employer isn't liable. Your employer may gain limited protection through something called *404(c)*. Without going into too much detail, Section 404(c) of ERISA requires your employer to provide you with specific information about your plan, including information about the investment options, and allows you to make changes in your investments frequently enough to respond to ups and downs in the market. In return, you assume liability for your investment results.

Avoiding losses in bankruptcy

Many people wonder whether their 401(k) money is at risk if their employer goes out of business. The answer is usually no, with a few caveats:

- If the money is in investments that are tied to your employer, such as company stock, and the employer goes bankrupt, you may lose your money. (This is a compelling argument for you to limit the amount of your 401(k) that you invest in a single stock.)
- In the case of fraud or wrongdoing by your employer or the trustee of the 401(k) account, your money may be at risk. (The trustee would be personally liable to return your money, but that's no help if they have disappeared.)

  These situations are rare; what's more, your employer is required to buy a type of insurance — a *fidelity bond* — when it sets up the plan that may enable you to recoup at least some of your money in the event of dishonesty. (Fidelity bonds generally cover 10 percent of the amount in the entire plan, or $500,000, whichever amount is smaller.)

» Part of your money may be lost if your employer goes out of business or declares bankruptcy before depositing your contributions into the trust fund that receives the 401(k) money that is deducted from your paycheck.

REMEMBER

Federal law says that if you declare personal bankruptcy, your creditors generally can't touch your 401(k). They may be able to get at your other savings, but your 401(k) should be protected. Exceptions include if you owe money to the IRS or if a court has ordered you to give the money to your ex-spouse as part of a divorce settlement. In both of those cases, your 401(k) money is vulnerable.

Watching Out for Potential Pitfalls

The tax advantages you get with a 401(k) have a flip side: rules. Rules about when you can take your money out, whether you have to pay a penalty, and even what you can invest in. All of these are out of your control after you decide to contribute to a 401(k) plan. The following sections tell you what pitfalls to watch out for.

Earning more may mean contributing less

If you earn enough to qualify as a highly compensated employee, your contributions to your 401(k) plan may be limited to only a few percent of your salary. Many 401(k) plans are required to pass *nondiscrimination tests* each year to make sure that highly paid employees as a group aren't contributing a lot more to the plan than their lower-paid colleagues. In requiring these tests, Congress is looking out for the little guy and gal. Chapter 4 in Book 6 explains how these tests work and who qualifies as "highly compensated."

Being at the mercy of your plan

A well-administered, well-chosen, flexible 401(k) plan can be a wonderful benefit. A poorly administered plan with bad investment choices and little flexibility can be a nightmare. There are stories of companies that don't invest employee contributions on time or that take money from the plan; companies that don't let employees contribute the maximum permitted; and companies where employees pay useless fees for a plan because the managers who set it up were incompetent, uninformed, or even criminals.

REMEMBER

In most cases, the tax benefit of a 401(k) is a good enough reason to take advantage of the plan offered by your employer. However, if the investments offered by the plan are truly bad, the fees charged are exorbitant, or the administration of the plan is questionable, you may be better off investing your retirement money elsewhere until you have a better 401(k).

IN THIS CHAPTER

» Starting with IRA basics

» Opening an IRA

» Keeping an eye on your money

» Changing locations

Chapter 2

Retiring Your Way: IRAs

Individual retirement arrangements (also known as individual retirement accounts), or IRAs, came into being through provisions added to the internal revenue code (IRC) in 1978. These provisions encourage you and every other American worker to save money for retirement. Tax advantages sweeten the pot, and automatic deductions can make saving nearly painless.

This chapter clues you in to the types of IRAs available, finding the place to put your funds, keeping track of your money, and moving it if necessary.

Looking at the Basics of Your IRA

An IRA is a special type of savings and investment account that helps you save for retirement by providing specific tax advantages. Federal law limits the amount you can contribute during 2026 to an IRA (or to all your IRAs combined, if you have several) to $7,500 in a single year plus a $1,100 catch-up contribution if you're at least age 50. The IRS reviews the limits annually and may update them. Your contributions are invested and grow tax-free until you withdraw them. All the money you withdraw is taxable except for a Roth IRA. Withdrawals from a Roth IRA aren't taxable if you follow the rules.

REMEMBER

The primary reason for tax advantages that accompany IRAs is to encourage you to save for retirement, so taking funds out before then can be financially painful. If you withdraw funds from your traditional pre-tax IRA before you're 59½ for any other than a few approved expenses, you pay a 10 percent penalty.

As well as saving for retirement, you can use IRA savings for select other purposes — buying your first home or adding a child to your family, for example. If you withdraw money for a specific, approved reason, you must pay tax on the amount you withdraw from a traditional IRA but you don't have to pay a penalty tax. If you take money out for other than approved purposes, you're liable for taxes and penalties.

The financial bite for taking money from a Roth IRA isn't as harsh as from a traditional IRA, although you are liable for taxes on the portion of the investment gains you must withdraw if your Roth IRA is less than five years old. A pro-rata portion of the investment gains must be withdrawn and will be taxable if the Roth IRA is less than five years old, but there isn't an early withdrawal tax penalty. Read on for information on the different types of IRAs.

Historically, IRAs haven't been connected to employers, but that's changing. Some states are requiring employers that don't offer a retirement plan to start offering one. Most states have or will have state-run payroll-deduction IRA plans to make it easier for employers to meet these mandates. Oregon has what's known as the OregonSaves state-run payroll-deduction IRA plan, and a growing number of employees are enrolled in this plan.

Small employers including solo entrepreneurs, family businesses, and gig workers have a number of IRA options. These options include the SEP IRA and SIMPLE IRA, which are two types of employer-sponsored plans — and self-employment plans.

TIP

For more information about IRAs, take a look at IRS Publication 590-A, Individual Retirement Arrangements, which you can download for free from the IRS website at `www.irs.gov/pub/irs-pdf/p590a.pdf`. (The IRS home page is `www.irs.gov`.)

Staying traditional

Most IRA holders have traditional IRAs because (as their name suggests) they've been around for a while — since 1974.

You can make two types of contributions to a traditional IRA:

- **Deductible:** You can deduct your contributions from your income for tax purposes.
- **Nondeductible:** You guessed it — you *can't* deduct your contributions. (Who said this financial stuff was complicated?)

With both types of contributions, you don't pay income tax on your earnings until you withdraw money from the account. You owe income tax when you withdraw the untaxed portion at retirement. With deductible contributions, you owe tax on the contributions plus the earnings. With nondeductible contributions, you owe tax only on the earnings. As you can imagine, if you make both types of contributions to an IRA, you need to keep meticulous records in order to know what's what when you start withdrawing the money, which can be many years from now.

The deductible IRA is a better deal because you get the extra tax break of being able to deduct your contributions from your taxable income. The catch is that if you have a 401(k) or any other employer-sponsored tax-qualified plan, you can deduct your contributions to an IRA only if your income is below certain limits. (*Income* means modified adjusted gross income (MAGI), which is your gross income minus certain deductions as defined in detail in IRS Publication 590-A.)

REMEMBER

Even if you participate in a 401(k) plan, you're allowed to use earned income to contribute to an IRA — earned income is the only acceptable source for IRA contributions. Your spouse can contribute as well even if they don't work. The only question is whether your contributions will be deductible.

A traditional IRA is typically used for making pre-tax contributions. After-tax contributions to this type of IRA are unusual and are usually made by high-income earners who aren't eligible to make Roth IRA contributions. Individuals who aren't covered by an employer-sponsored retirement plan can reduce their taxes by making pre-tax contributions.

Touching on Roth IRAs

You can't deduct your contributions to a Roth IRA, so in that sense, it's like a nondeductible traditional IRA. The advantage of a Roth is that the amount you contribute grows without being taxed, and you don't pay tax on your investment earnings — ever.

As long as you follow all applicable rules, your money grows tax-deferred in the account, and you can withdraw it tax-free at retirement.

REMEMBER

You may wonder why anyone would bother with nondeductible contributions to a traditional IRA, where you have to pay tax on withdrawals, when they can have a Roth IRA. Good question. The answer is that you can't contribute to a Roth IRA if your income is over a certain limit.

Benefiting from a spousal IRA

A spousal IRA is available to a spouse who doesn't work for pay and who checks the "married, filing jointly" box on their tax form. The togetherness doesn't hold for the actual IRA, though: The spousal IRA must belong solely to the spouse and cannot be in a jointly held account.

If neither spouse is covered by an employer-sponsored retirement plan, a couple can double the amount of their tax-deductible IRA contributions. If you fit this category, you can contribute between $15,000 and $17,200 to an IRA depending on your age and the age of your spouse. The $7,500 regular and the $1,100 catch-up contribution limits apply to each spouse. A spouse under age 55 can contribute $7,500 and a spouse 55 or older can put in $8,600. One spouse under and one over age 55 results in a $16,100 combined limit.

The money contributed to the spousal IRA can come from any source — the employed spouse's income, other savings, and so on. However, the contribution can't exceed the employed spouse's earned income.

Starting an IRA for a child

You can set up a traditional or Roth IRA for a child or grandchild provided the child has earned income — so, one thing toddlers can't charm their way into. A parent or other adult can open a custodial traditional or Roth IRA account for a child anywhere IRAs are offered.

REMEMBER

Contributions to an IRA that benefits a child can't exceed the amount of income the child earns.

If you open an IRA account to benefit a child, you have control of the account, including how it is invested and administered, until the child becomes an adult at age 18 or 21, depending on the state. Anyone can contribute to the account. For example, you can contribute to your favorite niece's account and so can her parents. Just check to make sure that total contributions don't amount to more than she earned.

WARNING

You can withdraw funds but only for the benefit of the child. And if you take money out of the IRA, you may create taxable income for the child.

TIP

A Roth IRA is the way to go for a custodial IRA for a child if the child doesn't pay any income tax or is taxed at the lowest tax rate. Also investing aggressively in an attempt to achieve a higher investment return makes sense assuming the time horizon is at least 10 to 20 years. Having funds growing for 50 or more years without any withdrawals would be even better. The potential for early withdrawals also makes a Roth IRA a good option because you can take money out of it for any reason any time after the account is five years old. If the child is over age 59½ when the funds are withdrawn, neither the principal *nor* the earnings are taxable.

Keep in mind that an early withdrawal from a Roth IRA isn't totally painless because a pro-rata portion of the investment earnings is taxable, and an early withdrawal penalty tax will apply unless the withdrawal is for one of the reasons that qualifies as an exception (see IRS Publication 590-A for exception rules).

Offering to open and contribute to such an account may encourage a child to earn some income and can also help a young adult discover how to save and invest.

Setting Up Your IRA

Your first step in starting an IRA is selecting a financial institution where your contributions will be deposited and invested. To qualify for the tax advantages, your IRA must be held by a qualified custodian or trustee. The number of possibilities is almost endless because banks, insurance companies, credit unions, mutual fund companies, brokerage firms, and some other entities are considered qualified to offer IRAs.

In choosing the institution in which to invest your IRA money, you need to decide how much investment choice and what level of service you want.

With virtually all major financial institutions offering IRAs, you can invest IRA funds in any legal, traditional investment vehicle. *Traditional* means stocks, bonds, certificates of deposit (CDs), exchange-traded funds (ETFs), and other publicly traded securities.

Along with brokerage firms, just about any financial organization can now sell you stocks and bonds, including banks and insurance companies. If you buy a mutual fund from a bank, keep in mind that it's not guaranteed or insured like other more traditional bank investments, such as certificates of deposit (CDs) or plain old savings accounts.

Nontraditional investments include everything else you can legally invest in, including real estate; gold, silver, and other precious metals; and cryptocurrencies. You need to find a special custodian for nontraditional investments and open a separate account.

TIP

Having all your IRA investments in a single traditional or Roth IRA is strongly recommended in order to make it easier to track and manage them.

Deciding where to invest your money

Seeking help from someone you respect is a good idea if you have little-to-no investment experience. Check with family members or friends who have experience and are people you can trust. Asking an accountant, an investment advisor, or another individual you respect is another possibility.

All entities that offer IRAs are tightly regulated. You don't invest in the actual entity where you open your IRA unless you're investing in CDs and/or some annuity products.

Your major consideration is how you want to invest your IRA savings, which is a difficult question if you're not an experienced investor.

Please note that one type of financial organization isn't safer than another. Some IRA investors think they receive FDIC (Federal Deposit Insurance Corporation) protection when they use a bank to house their IRA account. This is true only when you buy the bank's CDs. You don't get FDIC protection when you open your IRA at a bank and invest in mutual funds. Other investment firms such as Vanguard, Fidelity, and Charles Schwab also offer FDIC-backed CDs.

WARNING

A 48-year-old woman had taken her bank's advice and invested in two mutual funds. The investments dropped in value by more than 35 percent during the 2008 meltdown, and she was deeply troubled by this because she thought banks were a safe place to invest. She didn't realize that the mutual funds weren't guaranteed investments. Keep in mind that stocks, bonds, and mutual funds involve the same level of risk whether you buy them from a bank, stockbroker, or other financial institution.

TIP

Spend time getting familiar with the organization you're considering before you open an account:

- Visit websites to see how easily you can find useful information about the type of account you want to open, and get basic investment information.
- Call the technical support number a couple of times to test the quality of support they provide.

Setting up your account where you have access to a broad range of investments is recommended. You want a range that includes both low-risk investments and those with growth potential. Having a wide range of investments available gives you the ability to stick with the institution you select for the long term.

Consider one of the top-brand mutual fund companies such as Vanguard, Fidelity, and T. Rowe Price. Charles Schwab and other discount brokerage firms are also a good option. These entities give you access to their own brand of mutual funds plus the option to utilize a brokerage account. A brokerage account enables you to buy stocks, bonds, CDs, ETFs, and so on.

WARNING

Don't invest your contributions where you pay a front-end fee or a back-end surrender charge. Avoiding these types of investments enables you to move your IRA to another organization if you feel the need.

Opening your account

The easiest way to open your account is online unless you're dealing with a local institution. You must decide which type of account you want to open — a traditional or Roth IRA — and you are required to name your beneficiaries.

You can send money to be invested after the account is open.

Starting with lower-risk investments isn't a bad idea until you accumulate a meaningful account balance, such as $10,000. At that point you are in a better position to invest more broadly.

REMEMBER

A huge advantage 401(k)s offer is to take money out of your paycheck each pay period. For most workers, having semi-forced savings is an easy way to become successful long-term savers. You can do the same thing with a personal IRA by having money transferred directly from your bank account to your IRA each pay period or every month.

Maintaining Your IRA

REMEMBER

You don't need to follow any specific requirements to keep your IRA ticking along. However, paying attention to a few issues makes sense:

» **Keep your beneficiaries up-to-date.** This detail may be easy to forget when an important life change occurs.

- **Track your investments and the value of your account.** Don't hover over your investments — you don't want to overreact to the daily ups and downs of the investment markets. You just want to keep an eye on them from afar. Your account should contain investments you're comfortable holding for the long haul, but there are times when a change may be advisable.

When you reach your late 30s/early 40s, you need to start devoting more time to overseeing your retirement savings. You want to pay closer attention to the quality of your investment options; the fees you pay; your current and possible future tax situation; and how much access you have to your money, especially without a tax penalty. You need to also be realistic about your ability to:

- Save each paycheck or month without it being taken off the top each pay period
- Keep your sticky hands off the money each time an emergency happens

TIP

You can spend time at the end of each year reviewing your retirement accounts. It's easier to do this if you have only one account or have multiple accounts at the same place — a traditional and Roth IRA, for example.

Moving Your IRA

You may want to move your IRA to a different financial organization at some point for any number of reasons. Perhaps the investment results have been okay, but you aren't satisfied with the service you receive. You may have made a bad decision when you picked your financial organization initially, or the size of your account may have grown to a point where you want to make investments that aren't offered by your current financial institution.

Changing to a new financial organization isn't hard, but it requires some time. You need to open an account with the new entity and then provide the transfer instructions to the old entity. You can probably retain most of your current investments even if you transfer to another financial organization, although this isn't always the case. For example, if you want to move your IRA to Fidelity and keep your current Vanguard fund investments, you may not be able to do so.

TIP

The transfer must occur via a direct transfer from the old entity to the new one. Ask your agent at the new entity whether they can manage the transfer process. The major financial organizations are all able to offer a broad range of investments, but they may not have all the ones that you want. Check before you start the transfer process.

IN THIS CHAPTER

» Understanding reverse mortgage basics

» Considering costs and payment choices

» Shopping for the best reverse mortgage

Chapter 3

Paychecks from Your House: Reverse Mortgages

If you own a home, a reverse mortgage allows you to tap into its *equity* (the difference between the market value of your home less the mortgage debt owed on it) to supplement your retirement income — while you still live in your home. Because these mortgages are so different from what most people expect, it generally takes a while for the most basic information about them to make sense. Even experienced financial professionals are often surprised to find out how these loans really work, how different their costs and benefits can be, and what you have to look out for.

Are you full of questions about these types of mortgages perhaps for yourself or for a senior relative? If so, this chapter gives you the lowdown on reverse mortgages and helps you figure out whether they're right for you.

Grasping the Reverse Mortgage Basics

A *reverse mortgage* is a loan against your home that you don't have to repay as long as you live there. In a regular, or so-called *forward* mortgage (the kind we discuss throughout the rest of this book), your monthly loan repayments make your debt go down over time until you've paid it all off. Meanwhile, your equity is rising as you repay your mortgage and as your property value appreciates.

With a reverse mortgage, by contrast, the lender sends you money, and your debt grows larger and larger as you keep getting cash advances (usually monthly), make no repayment, and interest is added to the *loan balance* (the amount you owe). That's why reverse mortgages are called *rising debt, falling equity* loans. As your *debt* (the amount you owe) grows larger, your *equity* (that is, your home's value minus any debt against it) generally gets smaller. However, your equity could increase if you're in a strong housing market where home values are rising nicely.

TIP

If your financial goal is to preserve the equity in your home, you may be able to conservatively structure your reverse mortgage so you limit the amount of equity you pull out of your property to the estimated increase in home values anticipated over future years. Predicting future real estate appreciation is of course an inexact science. But real estate values do generally rise over time, and you may find that if you're modest in the amount of money you receive from the lender, you won't have eroded your home equity as much as you thought.

Reverse mortgages are different from regular home mortgages in two important respects:

- To qualify for most loans, the lender checks your income to see how much you can afford to pay back each month. But with a reverse mortgage, you don't have to make monthly repayments. Thus, your income generally has nothing to do with getting a reverse mortgage or determining the amount of the loan.
- With a regular mortgage, you can lose your home if you fail to make your monthly repayments. With a reverse mortgage, however, you can't lose your home by failing to make monthly loan payments — because you don't have any to make!

TIP

A reverse mortgage merits your consideration if it fits your circumstances. Reverse mortgages may allow you to cost-effectively tap your home's equity and enhance your retirement income. If you have bills to pay, want to buy some new carpeting, need to paint your home, or simply feel like eating out and traveling more, a good reverse mortgage may be your salvation.

This section focuses on the ABCs of reverse mortgages and helps clarify any confusion you may have.

Considering common objections

Most older homeowners contemplating a reverse mortgage have worked hard for many years to eliminate their home's mortgage in order to own their home free and clear. After what they've gone through, the thought of reversing that process and rebuilding the debt owed on their home is troubling. Furthermore, reverse mortgages are a newer type of loan that few people have encountered and understand. And most of today's reverse mortgage borrowers are low-income, single seniors who have run out of other money for living expenses. Some people think reverse mortgages are only a last resort, but that isn't true.

Can you lose your home?

It's not too surprising that folks who don't fully understand reverse mortgages often have preconceived notions, mostly negative, about how they work. Seniors with home equity often erroneously think that taking a reverse mortgage may lead to being forced out of their homes or ending up owing more than the house is worth.

Seniors taking out a reverse mortgage won't be forced out of their home. Nor will they (or their heirs) end up owing more than their house is worth. Federal law defines reverse mortgages to be *nonrecourse loans*, which simply means that the home's value is the only asset that can be tapped to pay the reverse mortgage debt balance. In the rare case when a home's value does drop below the amount owed on the reverse mortgage, the borrower isn't on the hook for the extra debt. The lender assumes that risk.

WARNING

As detailed later in this chapter (see the section "When do you pay the money back?"), not keeping current with all your property expenses, such as your property taxes, community association dues/fees and/or special assessments, homeowners insurance, and proper maintenance can trigger your reverse mortgage going into default and requiring payoff. When a loan is called due and payable, the reverse mortgage borrower or the borrower's estate needs to repay only the lesser of either the loan balance or 95 percent of the home's appraised value at that time.

Would a home equity loan or second mortgage work better?

Some people who are intimidated by having to understand reverse mortgages wonder whether it would be simpler to get a home equity loan or a new mortgage that allows them to take some equity out of their home. The problem with this strategy is that you have to begin paying traditional mortgage loans back soon after taking them out.

For example, suppose that you own a home worth $200,000, with no mortgage debt. You decide to take out a $100,000, 15-year mortgage at 7 percent interest. Although you'll receive $100,000, you'll have to begin making monthly payments of $899. No problem, you may think; you'll just invest your $100,000 and come out ahead. Wrong!

Most seniors gravitate toward safe bonds, which traditionally may yield in the neighborhood of 5 percent — a mere $416 of monthly income — an amount far short of your monthly mortgage payments. If you were to invest in stocks and earn the generous average return of 10 percent per year, which is by no means guaranteed, your returns would amount to more — $833 per month — but still not enough to cover your monthly mortgage payment. (We should also note that most income from stocks and bonds is taxable at both the federal and state level. By contrast, reverse mortgage payments you receive aren't taxable.) Advantage: reverse mortgage.

Here's another big drawback of taking out a traditional mortgage to supplement your retirement income. The longer you live in the house, the more likely you are to run out of money and begin missing loan payments, because you drain your principal to supplement inadequate investment returns and cover your monthly loan payment. If that happens, unlike with a reverse mortgage, the lending institution may foreclose on your loan, and you can lose your home.

Who can get a reverse mortgage?

Of course, reverse mortgages aren't for everyone. As we discuss later in this chapter (see the section "Deciding Whether You Want a Reverse Mortgage"), alternatives may better accomplish your goal. Also, not everyone qualifies to take out a reverse mortgage. Specifically, for you, to be eligible for a reverse mortgage, the following conditions apply:

- You must own your home. In the early years of reverse mortgages, as a rule, all the owners had to be at least 62 years old. Now, in a couple, you may qualify for a reverse mortgage if one person is at least 62 years of age and the other person is younger than that. However, such a couple will qualify for lower reverse mortgage money due to the younger spouse because "life expectancy" is part of the calculation.
- Your home generally must be your *principal residence* — which means you must live in it for more than half the year.

- For the federally insured *Home Equity Conversion Mortgage (HECM)*, your home must be a single-family property, a two- to four-unit building, or a federally approved condominium or planned-unit development (PUD). Reverse mortgage programs will lend on mobile homes with foundations that meet the U.S. Department of Housing and Urban Development (HUD) guidelines but won't lend on cooperative apartments. Borrowers must now also complete financial counseling with a HUD-approved agency.
- If you have any debt against your home, you must either pay it off before getting a reverse mortgage or, as most borrowers do, use an immediate cash advance from the reverse mortgage to pay it off. If you don't pay off the debt beforehand or don't qualify for a large enough immediate cash advance to do so, you can't get a reverse mortgage.

One final and important point about qualifying for a reverse mortgage: Lenders are required to perform a financial assessment analyzing the prospective borrower's financial situation, including credit history and monthly income and expenses. Lenders pay particular attention to whether borrowers have enough cash flow to pay their ongoing property expenses including property taxes, community association dues/fees and/or special assessments, homeowners or flood insurance, and all operating costs (municipal or utility liens) and maintenance/repair bills. If borrowers have little wiggle room in their monthly budget, lenders may require a "set-aside" fund to ensure payment of property taxes and home insurance, and this set-aside fund reduces how large a reverse mortgage the borrowers can get. The amount of this set-aside fund may also vary depending on the age of the reverse mortgage borrowers.

How much money can you get and when?

The whole point of taking out a reverse mortgage on your home is to get money from the equity in your home. How much can you tap? That amount depends mostly on your home's worth, your age, and the interest and other fees a given lender charges. The more your home is worth, the older you are, and the lower the interest rate and other fees your lender charges, the more money you should realize from a reverse mortgage.

- For all but the most expensive homes, the federally insured Home Equity Conversion Mortgage (HECM) generally provides the most cash and is available in every state.
- In general, the most cash is available for the oldest borrowers living in the homes of greatest value over current debt (net equity) at a time when interest rates are low. On the other hand, the least cash generally goes to the youngest borrowers living in the homes of lowest value (or with high current debt) at a time when interest rates are high.

The total amount of cash you actually end up getting from a reverse mortgage depends on how it's paid to you plus other factors. You can choose among the following options to receive your reverse mortgage money:

- **Monthly:** Most people need monthly income to live on. Thus, a commonly selected reverse mortgage option is monthly payments. However, not all monthly payment options are created equal. Some reverse mortgage programs commit to a particular monthly payment for a preset number of years. Other programs make payments as long as you continue living in your home or for life. Not surprisingly, if you select a reverse mortgage program that pays you over a longer period of time, you generally receive less monthly — probably a good deal less — than from a program that pays you for a fixed number of years.
- **Line of credit:** Instead of receiving a monthly check, you can simply create a line of credit from which you draw money by writing a check whenever you need income. Because interest doesn't start accumulating on a loan until you actually borrow money, the advantage of a credit line is that you pay only for the money you need and use. If you have fluctuating and irregular needs for additional money, a line of credit may be for you. This is also the preferred way to access funds if your financial goal is to limit the equity you pull from your home to its increase in value. The size of the line of credit is either set at the time you close on your reverse mortgage loan or may increase over time. Generally, during the first 12 months, you can receive up to — but no more than — 60 percent of the maximum loan allowed.
- **Lump sum:** The third, and generally least beneficial, type of reverse mortgage is the lump-sum option. When you close on this type of reverse mortgage, you receive a check for the entire amount that you were approved to borrow. Lump-sum payouts usually make sense only when you have an immediate need for a substantial amount of cash for a specific purpose, such as making a major purchase or paying off an existing or delinquent mortgage debt to keep from losing your home to foreclosure. Ironically, but also a blessing, when your financial troubles are caused by falling behind on your mortgage payments, you can get a reverse mortgage to tap the remaining equity in your home to assist in resolving your immediate pending foreclosure.
- **Mix and match:** Perhaps you need a large chunk of money for some purchases you've been putting off, but you also want the security of a regular monthly income. You can usually put together combinations of the preceding three programs. Some reverse mortgage lenders even allow you to alter the payment structure as time goes on. Not all reverse mortgage programs offer all the combinations, so shop around even more if you're interested in mixing and matching your payment options.

When do you pay the money back?

As discussed in the earlier section "Considering common objections," some reverse mortgage borrowers worry about having to repay their loan balance. Here are the conditions under which you generally have to repay a reverse mortgage:

- When the last surviving borrower dies, sells the home, or permanently moves away. "Permanently" generally means that the borrower hasn't lived in the home for 12 consecutive months.
- Possibly, if you do any of the following:
  - Fail to pay your property taxes
  - Fail to timely pay all community association dues/fees and/or special assessments
  - Fail to keep up your homeowners or flood insurance
  - Let your home fall into disrepair

  If you fail to properly maintain your home and it falls into disrepair, the lender may be able to make extra cash advances to cover these repair expenses. Just remember that reverse mortgage borrowers are still homeowners and therefore are still responsible for taxes, HOA financial obligations, insurance, and upkeep.

What do you owe?

The total amount you will owe at the end of the loan (your loan balance) equals:

- All the cash advances you've received (including any used to pay loan costs)
- Plus all the interest on them — up to the loan's nonrecourse limit (the value of the home)

If you get an adjustable-rate reverse mortgage, the interest rate can vary based on changes in published indexes. The greater a loan's permissible interest rate adjustment, the lower its interest rate initially. As a result, you get a larger cash advance with this type of loan than you do with loans that have higher initial interest rates.

You can never owe more than the value of the home at the time the loan is repaid. True reverse mortgages are *nonrecourse loans*, which means that in seeking repayment the lender doesn't have recourse to anything other than your home — not your income, your other assets, or your heirs' finances.

Even if you get monthly advances until you're 115 years old, even if your home declines in value between now and then, and even if the total of monthly advances becomes greater than your home's value — you can still never owe more than the value of your home. If you or your heirs sell your home to pay off the loan, the debt is limited by the net proceeds from the sale of your home.

How is the loan repaid?

How a reverse mortgage is repaid depends on the circumstances under which the loan ends:

- If you sell and move, you most likely pay back the loan from the money you get from selling your home. But you can pay it back from other funds if you have them.
- If the loan ends due to the death of the last surviving borrower, the loan must be repaid before the home's title can be transferred to the borrower's heirs. The heirs may repay the loan by selling the home, using other funds from the borrower's estate, using their own funds, or by taking out a new forward mortgage against the home.

As lenders have discovered, not all reverse mortgage borrowers end up living in their homes for the rest of their lives. Some folks who originally plan to live in a particular house forever subsequently change their minds. Others develop health problems that force them to move. So it makes sense to plan for the possibility that you may sell and move some day. How much equity would be left if you did?

If, at the end of the loan, your loan balance is less than the value of your home (or your net sale proceeds if you sell), then you or your heirs get to keep the difference. The lender doesn't get the house. The lender gets paid the amount you owe on the reverse mortgage, and you or your heirs keep the rest of the house's proceeds of sale.

TIP

If you take the loan as a credit line account, be sure to withdraw all your remaining available credit before the loan ends. You have access to the money sooner that way, and the amount could be more than otherwise may be left. For example, a growing credit line could become greater than the leftover equity if the home's value decreases.

What's the out-of-pocket cost of getting a reverse mortgage?

The out-of-pocket cash cost to you with a reverse mortgage is usually limited to just two modest items. First is an application fee that covers a property appraisal (to see how much your home is worth). Second is a minimal credit check (to see whether you're delinquent on any federally insured loans).

Other costs, including the loan origination fee, can be financed with the loan. This means you can use reverse mortgage funds advanced to you at closing to pay the costs due at that time and later advances to pay any *ongoing costs*, such as monthly servicing fees. The advances are added to your loan balance and become part of what you owe — and pay interest on.

What are the other reverse mortgage costs?

The specific cost items vary from one program to another. Many of them are of the same type found on forward mortgages: interest charges, origination fees, and whatever third-party closing costs (title search and insurance, surveys, credit report, inspections, document, courier and recording fees, escrow fees, and property taxes) are required in your area. And don't forget about the federally required counseling fee for HECM loans (see the upcoming section, "Counseling").

Two other costs unique to some reverse mortgages are the monthly servicing fee, which can cost up to $35 per month, and a reverse mortgage insurance premium, which can cost up to 2 percent of the home's value up front.

In addition to the upfront insurance charge, there is also an annual mortgage insurance premium of 0.5 percent of your reverse mortgage balance. This ongoing premium accumulates and the upfront insurance premium is owed and paid once your loan ends and is paid back.

TIP

Within the federally insured Home Equity Conversion Mortgage (HECM) program, the costs that may be different from one lender to another are the origination fee, the servicing fee, third-party closing costs, and the interest rate. To get the best deal, compare these specific costs.

It's difficult to evaluate or compare the true, total cost of reverse mortgages because that amount ultimately depends on the following:

- How long you end up keeping the loan
- The cash advances you receive during the loan
- The interest rate charged on the loan
- Your home's value when the loan is over

You can, however, compare the costs of different reverse mortgages by evaluating each loan's total annual average loan cost, also known as the total annual rate. We give you more information about that in the following section.

What's the total annual rate?

The total annual rate on a reverse mortgage includes all the loan's costs. On any given loan, total annual rates depend on two major factors: time and appreciation.

Total annual average rates are generally greatest in the early years of the loan and decrease over time, for two reasons:

- The initial fees and costs become a smaller part of the total amount owed as years go by.
- The likelihood increases that the rising loan balance will catch up to — and then be limited by — the nonrecourse limit the longer you have the loan.

Total annual rates also depend on changes in a home's value over time. The less appreciation, the greater the likelihood that a rising loan balance will catch up to — and then be limited by — the home's value. On the other hand, when a home appreciates at a robust rate, the loan balance may never catch up to (and be limited by) it.

If you end up living in your home well past your projected life expectancy or your home appreciates at a lower rate than anticipated, you may get a true bargain. But if you die, sell, or move within just a few years, the true cost could be quite high due to the upfront costs of securing the reverse mortgage.

When deciding to go with a reverse mortgage, you simply can't avoid the fundamental risk that the true cost could end up being quite high. You just have to understand the risk in general, assess the potential range of total rates on a specific loan, and decide whether the risk is worth the benefits you expect to get from the loan.

Just remember, total annual rates aren't really comparable to the interest rates quoted on forward mortgages because:

- Total annual rates include all the costs.
- Reverse mortgages require no monthly repayments.
- Reverse mortgages can provide an open-ended monthly income guarantee or a guaranteed credit line (which may grow larger).

- You can never owe more than your home's worth, even if its net value is less than what your loan balance would otherwise have been.

How do reverse mortgages affect your government-sponsored benefits?

Social Security and Medicare benefits aren't affected by reverse mortgages. But Supplemental Security Income (SSI) and Medicaid are different. Reverse mortgages will affect these and other public benefit programs under certain circumstances:

- Because they don't count as income, loan advances on a reverse mortgage generally don't affect your benefits if you spend them during the calendar month in which you get them. But if you keep an advance past the end of the calendar month (in a checking or savings account, for example), it counts as a *liquid asset.* If your total liquid assets at the end of any month are greater than $2,000 for a single person or $3,000 for a couple, you could lose your eligibility. These federal limits currently are not indexed and have not been increased since 1989.

WARNING

- If anyone in the business of selling annuities has tried to sell you on the idea of using proceeds from a reverse mortgage to purchase an annuity, you need to know that annuity advances reduce SSI benefits dollar for dollar and can make you ineligible for Medicaid. So, if you're considering an annuity and if you're now receiving — or expect that someday you may qualify for — SSI or Medicaid, check with the SSI, Medicaid, and other program offices in your community. Get specific details on how annuity income affects these benefits.

Shopping for a Reverse Mortgage

Reverse mortgages give you a new retirement financial option that previous generations of homeowners didn't have. These loans can provide an important new source of retirement cash — without requiring you to leave your home or to make loan payments for as long as you live there.

But you have to proceed carefully. What you don't know about reverse mortgages *can* hurt you. The most important — and perhaps surprising — facts you need to understand are these:

- You may get a lot more cash from one reverse mortgage program than from another.

- The true cost of one program may be much greater than the cost of another.
- A program giving you significantly more cash may also cost less than any other.
- To find the program that works best for you, you have to take both of the following into account:
  - How much total cash would be available to you in growing versus flat credit lines
  - The comparative total annual rate on competing loans
- Lenders offering a variety of plans may try to sell you one plan versus another because they make more money on it.

REMEMBER

Reverse mortgages are a specialty loan product that requires loan officers to receive training to be eligible to work on a reverse mortgage. Most loan officers (even the best ones with decades of experience) don't work with reverse mortgages. When you decide to apply for a reverse mortgage, ask enough questions to make sure the loan officer has done dozens of reverse mortgages. You don't want a loan officer figuring out reverse mortgages on your loan!

Making major choices

Which reverse mortgage plan — if any — would work the best for you?

- The federally insured Home Equity Conversion Mortgage (HECM) is most likely to provide more cash at a lower cost, especially if you want a credit line or if you own your home jointly with a spouse or other person. But be aware that $1,249,125 is the maximum loan limit allowed on a HECM as of 2026.
- Consider shopping these private reverse mortgage providers — American Advisors Group, Finance of America Reverse Mortgage, Longbridge Financial, and Paramount Residential Mortgage Group — especially if you own a higher value property. Private reverse mortgage providers aren't subject to the same regulations and loan limits as HECM providers.

Although HECM may be more likely to provide significantly more cash at a lot lower cost on the credit lines most consumers prefer, the best plan for you depends on your specific situation. So you need to consider *all* your reverse mortgage options. That's especially important if you:

- Want a monthly loan advance only
- Live in a home worth substantially more than the average

In the later section "Deciding Whether You Want a Reverse Mortgage," we give you additional considerations to ponder when thinking about whether a reverse mortgage is your best option.

Counseling

To get a HECM reverse mortgage, you must complete a counseling session with a HUD-approved counselor. Visit `answers.hud.gov/housingcounseling/s/?language=en_US` to find approved counselors in your area or call 800-569-4287. Reverse mortgages can get complicated quickly, and most folks find them challenging to fully understand. So having to complete counseling before committing to a reverse mortgage is a good thing.

Counselors ask ten core questions during each session to be sure borrowers understand the basics of reverse mortgages. To "pass" the counseling session, the prospective borrowers must answer at least five of the ten questions correctly. If they can't, they may need to go back for more sessions. Counseling fees are reasonable and typically cost about $200, although they may vary based on the borrowers' financial situation and may even be waived for lower-income folks.

Deciding Whether You Want a Reverse Mortgage

Only you can decide what a reverse mortgage is worth to you. The value probably mostly depends on your purpose for the money, such as the following:

- Increasing your monthly income
- Having a cash reserve (credit line account) for irregular or unexpected expenses
- Paying off debt that requires monthly repayments
- Repairing or improving your home
- Getting the services you need to remain independent
- Improving the quality of your life (perhaps fulfilling some of your bucket list items)

One approach is to consider a major alternative: selling your home and moving to a less expensive form of housing. Think about the following questions:

- How much money could you get by selling your home?
- What would it cost you to buy and maintain or rent a new one?
- How much could you safely earn (that is, without exposing yourself to excessive risk) on sale proceeds not used for a new home?
- Could you tolerate living in the same home or even in that separate but all-too-close "Granny flat" with your relatives?

Thanks to continued innovation in the mortgage industry, you could sell your current home, buy a different one, and, at the time of purchase, take out a reverse mortgage. To be eligible for a "HECM for Purchase," which enables you to buy a home in part using proceeds from a new reverse mortgage, you generally need to make a significant down payment (50-plus percent of the purchase price), and the reverse mortgage finances the rest. You'd do this in place of making an all-cash purchase.

IN THIS CHAPTER

» Making sure you have enough to enjoy retired life

» Choosing the amount to save

» Saving relative to when you'll retire

Chapter 4
Determining How Much to Save

So you're retired. No more 9 to 5, no more boss to answer to, no more commute, no more meetings . . . and no more paycheck. Even though you no longer get a paycheck, you still have expenses, and that's why you started saving for retirement all those years ago — or yesterday. This chapter gives you the tools to use to fund your retirement.

Improving Your Chances of an Ideal Retirement

Investing in a retirement plan or an IRA (individual retirement account) can mean the difference between merely surviving retirement and actually living it up.

REMEMBER

Most financial planners suggest that you'll need at least 70 to 80 percent of your pre-retirement income to maintain your lifestyle in retirement. But many people may need closer to 100 percent, or more.

WARNING

Some people think their Social Security benefits alone will be enough to cover their retirement needs. The unfortunate fact is you shouldn't rely on Social Security to finance your retirement. Financial security during retirement requires income from a variety of sources. Social Security was never intended to be the sole source of retirement income for Americans.

After you retire, you have to manage your nest egg so that you don't run out of money before you die. Chapter 5 of Book 6 looks at ways to make your money last after you retire.

Deciding How Much of Your Salary to Put Aside

How do you decide what percentage or dollar amount to put aside for your retirement? To begin with, you need to consider several factors:

- Whether you can enroll in an employer-sponsored retirement plan
  - If yes, the plan documents prompt you for decisions.
  - If no, you need to become the captain of your own retirement plan by starting an IRA. See Chapter 2 in Book 6 for info on IRAs.
- The government's restrictions on contributions to IRAs and 401(k)s
- Your own plan's restrictions
- Your budget's limitations
- The amount you need to get the full employer matching contribution

The following sections help with all these issues.

Making use of your salary deferral agreement

When you enroll in a 401(k) plan, you fill out a *salary deferral agreement*. Salary deferral refers to the pre-tax amount of your pay that you want your employer to put in the 401(k) plan rather than in your paycheck. It probably also gives you the option to make after-tax Roth contributions.

The form may require you to select a percentage of salary to contribute, or it may ask for a dollar amount. In fact, it may even give you a choice, such as the one shown in Figure 4-1. What's the difference? Take a look:

- The percentage of salary is easy because it's the same no matter how many pay periods you have. If you want to contribute 10 percent of your pay, you simply list "10%" on the form.
- For a dollar amount, you need to figure out the total amount you want to contribute for the year and then divide it by the number of pay periods. Say you get paid twice a month. If you earn $50,000 and you want to put $3,000 a year into your 401(k), you list "6%" on the form. This amount results in a $125 per pay deduction ($3,000 divided by 24 equals $125).

SECTION I - Salary Deferral Election

Participant should complete A or B.

A. ☐ I **elect to contribute** the following pay to the Plan each pay period:

☐ ________________% **OR** ☐ $________________

B. ☐ I **elect NOT to contribute** to the Plan.

SECTION II - Salary Deferral Election of Bonuses and Commissions

I elect ☐ **to apply** ☐ **not to apply** the percentage or fixed dollar amount specified in Section I(A) above to any bonuses and/or commissions I may receive as compensation.

FIGURE 4-1: Sample 401(k) salary deferral form.

If you work irregular hours or earn variable pay such as overtime, bonuses, or commissions, contributing a percentage of pay means a variable amount is deducted each pay period.

TIP

Some employers won't let you include overtime or other forms of non-base pay as compensation for the purposes of contributing to a 401(k). In this case, contributions may be based only on your base pay or something less than your total compensation.

REMEMBER

The most important step is to start contributing as soon as you're eligible. Even if you only contribute 1 percent of your salary to begin with, it's a start. After you're in the habit of saving, it gets easier and easier. But if you put it off, it only gets harder.

Measuring your plan's maximums

Your 401(k) plan isn't allowed to let you contribute more than the federal limits, but it probably restricts you to less because there are other things that must be deducted from your pay including federal and state income taxes, local wage taxes, and Social Security. Your plan may also have a priority that will be followed due to other deductions for medical coverage, charitable donations, and so on. Your employer decides the pecking order for your 401(k) contributions.

Being highly paid means different rules

Under federal law, employers must test their 401(k) plans each year to ensure that no discrimination exists in favor of highly paid employees.

The key question is: How much do you have to earn to qualify as a highly compensated employee, or HCE? The rules are pretty tricky. If you earn less than $160,000 and you don't own more than 5 percent of your company (and you aren't related to, or married to, anyone who does), you aren't highly compensated. If that's the case for you, feel free to skip this section. Otherwise, keep reading — but do a few jumping jacks first to make sure that you're fully alert.

What makes you an HCE?

You're considered highly compensated in a given year if you own more than 5 percent of your company in that year or the previous year. You may also be considered highly compensated in a given year if you earned more than a specified salary in the previous year. Here's a concrete example: You're considered an HCE in 2026 if you owned more than 5 percent of your company in either 2025 or 2026. Also, you *may* be considered an HCE in 2026 if your salary in 2025 is more than $160,000. (We say "may" because a possible exception exists for the salary rule. See the nearby sidebar "Being highly paid but not an HCE" for details.)

The contribution percentages of HCEs are added up as one group, and the contribution percentages of lower-paid employees are added up as a second group. The average contribution percentage of the highly paid employees can't be more than 2 percentage points above those of the lower-paid group. For example, if lower-paid employees as a group contribute an average of 4 percent of salary to the 401(k), highly paid employees can only contribute 6 percent. (The formula is actually more complex, but this example gives you the basic idea.)

Safe harbor and Qualified Automatic Contribution Arrangement 401(k) plans are exempt from these requirements.

BEING HIGHLY PAID BUT NOT AN HCE

If you earn more than the HCE salary limit, you still may not be considered an HCE even if your company has a lot of highly paid employees. A company is allowed to limit its designated HCEs to only the top 20 percent of employees. So, for example, if 40 percent of employees at your company earned more than the $160,000 limit in 2026, your company can choose to designate only the top-paid 20 percent of non-excludable employees as HCEs who may have their contributions capped or receive refunds in 2026. This flexibility doesn't exist with the ownership rule, though. If you own more than 5 percent of the company in 2025 or 2026, you'll be considered an HCE. To make matters more confusing, beginning in 2026, there is a new class of employee called a Highly Paid Individual (different than an HCE). If your 2025 W-2 was greater than $150,000, you are considered a Highly Paid Individual in 2026. If you are over age 50 and are considered part of the Highly Paid Individual group, any catch up contributions you make into your retirement plan must be made as a Roth contribution.

TIP

Highly compensated employees are often referred to as *HCEs*, while lower-paid workers are referred to as *non-HCEs*. This chapter mentions these terms so you are familiar with them if you come across them.

How do HCE contributions work?

If you're highly compensated, your contributions will likely be limited to bring your combined contributions down to an acceptable level (in other words, in line with lower-compensated employees).

Say you're highly compensated and you want to contribute 10 percent for a year in which HCE contributions have to be capped at 6 percent. If your plan is on the ball, you'll find out about the problem early and have your contributions capped at 6 percent.

By the way, there's another way your employer can resolve this problem. Your employer can give an extra contribution to some or all of the lower-paid employees to make up for the discrepancy. This contribution is called a *qualified matching contribution* (QMAC) or *qualified nonelective contribution* (QNEC). If you receive one of these contributions, it must be vested right away. This option is less popular among employers because it costs them extra and it's complicated. (Go figure, right?)

CALCULATING AN HCE REFUND

If your plan fails the nondiscrimination test during any year, refunds will probably be made. The system for determining who gets a refund, and how much it is, is somewhat complicated. First the plan has to determine how far the highly compensated employees were over the limit. Say the lower-paid employees in the plan contributed 4 percent on average, and three highly compensated employees are in the plan. One of the highly compensated employees contributed 8 percent, one contributed 7 percent, and one contributed 6 percent. Their average contribution is 7 percent, which is 1 percent too high. (Because the lower-paid employees contributed 4 percent, the highly compensated employees are limited to 6 percent.)

The HCE who contributed the largest dollar amount (rather than highest percentage of pay) is the first to get a refund. This rule can cause tension among highly compensated employees, because the person who caused the plan to fail by contributing 8 percent isn't the one who has to take a refund.

Another limit may come into play: In 2026, 401(k) contributions and employer contributions generally cannot be based on more than $360,000 of compensation. So, if you earn $400,000 and contribute 5 percent of your salary, your contribution would be limited to 5 percent of $360,000, or $18,000. Any employer match is also calculated using no more than $360,000 of compensation.

Estimating what your budget can afford

Talking about how much you're allowed to put into a retirement plan is fine, but what about how much you can afford to put in? If money is tight, you may be tempted to wait and start saving in a couple of years when you're earning more or have less debt. The problem with that strategy is that the longer you wait to start saving, the harder it gets psychologically. You get used to spending the money you have. Also, by waiting to participate, you lose a lot of potential earnings.

The following example (also illustrated in Figure 4-2) shows how you can cheat yourself big-time by waiting just a few years to start saving.

Ken, Rasheed, and Lisa all earn $50,000 a year. They all decide to contribute 5 percent of their salary, or $2,500, to their 401(k) plans, but over different periods of time. Assuming that each has an average annual return (how much the money increases in value when it's invested) of 8 percent, look at the surprising results:

Advantages of Starting to Save Early Through a 401(k) Plan

	A) KEN waits 8 years to start saving		B) RASHEED starts saving early, quits after 8 years		C) LISA starts saving early and keeps at it!		What you invest and what you earn
Year	Annual Investment	Year end value @ 8%	Annual Investment	Year end value @ 8%	Annual Investment	Year end value @ 8%	
1	$0	$0	$1,250	$1,295	$1,250	$1,295	A – started late 22 years @ $1,250 Total saved $71,827 Amount invested 27,500 Investment return 44,327
2	0	0	1,250	2,694	1,250	2,694	
3	0	0	1,250	4,205	1,250	4,205	
4	0	0	1,250	5,836	1,250	5,836	
5	0	0	1,250	7,598	1,250	7,598	B – started early 8 years @ $1,250 Total saved $71,827 Amount invested 27,500 Investment return 44,327
6	0	0	1,250	9,501	1,250	9,501	
7	0	0	1,250	11,557	1,250	11,557	
8	0	0	1,250	13,777	1,250	13,777	
9	1,250	1,295	0	14,879	1,250	16,174	
10	1,250	2,694	0	16,069	1,250	18,763	C – started early & continued 30 years @ $1,250 Total saved $71,827 Amount invested 27,500 Investment return 44,327
15	1,250	11,557	0	23,611	1,250	35,167	
20	1,250	24,579	0	34,692	1,250	59,271	
25	1,250	43,713	0	50,973	1,250	94,687	
30	1,250	71,827	0	74,897	1,250	146,724	

The figures indicated reflect employee contributions only. In this example, investment return is calculated at 8%. Your own 401(k) investment return may be higher or lower, depending on the performance of the funds offered and how you invested the money in your account.

FIGURE 4-2: Payoffs of saving early in a 401(k).

- Ken waits eight years to begin saving. In years 9 through 30, he contributes a total of $55,000 to the plan ($2,500 × 22 years), and his account balance grows to $143,654. (The extra comes from his 8 percent return, which is reinvested in the account each year without being taxed.)
- Rasheed starts saving right away, but he stops after eight years. He contributes only $20,000 to the plan ($2,500 × 8 years), but because he started earlier, his money has more time to grow through the magic of compounding. He ends up with $149,794 — $6,000 more than Ken after 30 years.
- Lisa saves for the entire 30 years. She contributes only $20,000 more than Ken in total (over the eight years when Ken doesn't contribute), but her $75,000 contribution grows to $293,448 — twice that of Ken's, because her money benefited from compounding for a longer period of time.

You can see that it pays to start saving early and to keep saving. In this example, each person is saving a little more than $200 per month. If that seems like too much for you now, consider contributing a smaller amount. Sometimes that's the best way to get started. For example, consider saving $20 per week, or $1,040 a year.

If you're contributing to a 401(k), you can save $20 while only reducing your take-home pay by about $16 per week, because you save the $20 before paying taxes if you opt for pre-tax contributions, while you get your take-home pay after paying taxes. Just about anyone who's earning $50,000 can probably find a way to save $20 a week. If you keep a record of your nonessential spending for just one week, you may find that eliminating one or two incidentals is easy.

Note that even a small amount of savings makes a big difference over time. That $20 per week invested for 35 years with an 8 percent return can eventually become $180,000! Any employer matching contribution increases this amount (see Chapter 1 in Book 6 for more on employer matching).

TIP

After you start saving, make it a goal to increase your savings rate each year. Perhaps the easiest way to do this is to save more each time you get a raise. If you start by contributing 1 percent of your pay, and you receive a 4 percent pay increase, use part of the raise to increase your contribution rate to 2 percent. Keep doing this each time you get a raise, until you reach a point where your savings plus any employer contribution is likely to provide an adequate level of retirement income.

Building Your Nest (Egg)

You'll probably need at least 100 percent of your income in the year before you retire in order to maintain your standard of living. How much savings will it take to provide this level of income? The answer is a lot.

TIP

Try to save ten times the income that you expect to earn in the year before you retire. This formula is a good starting point if you plan to retire at your Social Security normal retirement age. If you plan to retire earlier, you'll need to save more. If you have a company pension or other sources of income or if you retire later, you may be able to get away with saving a bit less.

If you're retiring in the near future

Assume that you're retiring at the end of this year, and your salary for this year is $50,000. According to the earlier benchmark, you should save $500,000 to hit the ten-times goal.

Sound like a lot of money? It is, but it would provide approximately $30,000 a year of *inflation-adjusted income* (see the nearby sidebar "What goes up — or inflation-adjusted income" for more information) over 25 years, assuming:

- The rate of inflation is 3 percent.
- Only a small cushion remains at the end of 25 years.
- You invest 50 percent of your nest egg in stocks and 50 percent in bonds during this period.

A yearly income of $30,000 may not sound like much, but keep in mind that your taxes will be lower after you retire, and you won't need to save for retirement anymore. Your expenses will likely be less than when you were working. Your income should also be supplemented by your taxable savings and Social Security, giving you an adequate level of retirement income.

WHAT GOES UP — OR INFLATION-ADJUSTED INCOME

What is inflation-adjusted income? *Inflation* is the rate at which prices increase over time. When you plan for the future, you have to plan for prices to go up; otherwise, you'll run out of money too soon. Inflation-adjusted income essentially refers to the *purchasing power* of your money — what your bucks can buy. It means that if over the next 25 years you want to be able to buy what will cost $30,000 today, you'll need significantly more than $30,000.

You can't know for sure what the inflation rate will be. You need to make an assumption. Consider using 3 percent, which is on the low side from a historical perspective but realistic for long-range planning.

The following table shows how much income is needed to keep the buying power of $10,000 over the years. (Using $10,000 makes it easy to adjust to whatever income you think will be right for your situation.) For example, you can calculate that you'll need $60,984 in the 25th year of your retirement to buy what $30,000 will buy in the first year ($20,328 × 3).

Number of Years After You Retire	Annual Income Needed
1	$10,000
2	$10,300
3	$10,609
4	$10,927

(continued)

Determining How Much to Save

(continued)

Number of Years After You Retire	Annual Income Needed
5	$11,255
6	$11,593
7	$11,941
8	$12,299
9	$12,668
10	$13,048
11	$13,439
12	$13,842
13	$14,258
14	$14,685
15	$15,126
16	$15,580
17	$16,047
18	$16,528
19	$17,024
20	$17,535
21	$18,061
22	$18,603
23	$19,161
24	$19,736
25	$20,328

If your retirement is farther off

You may be calling, "Hey, a little help over here . . . I'm not retiring tomorrow, so how do I know how much I'll be earning the year before I retire?" Not to worry. Table 4-1 is here to help. The percentages in the table refer to the assumed annual rate of change.

TIP

Assume that you're 41, and you want to retire when you're 62. You need to project your current income to what you think you'll be earning 20 years from now (at age 61, the year before you retire). Decide on an average rate that you expect your income to increase — say 3 percent. Go down the Number of Years column in Table 4-1 to 20, and over to the 3% column, where you see the factor of 1.80. Multiply your current income, say $50,000, by 1.8, and you see that your expected income at retirement is $90,000. Using the ten-times rule, your desired nest egg becomes $900,000 (10 × $90,000). This is an easy way to get a rough idea of how big a retirement account to build — regardless of your current age or income.

TABLE 4-1 Inflation Adjustment Table

Number of Years	3%	3.5%	4%	4.5%	5%
1	1.03	1.035	1.04	1.045	1.05
2	1.06	1.07	1.08	1.09	1.10
3	1.09	1.11	1.12	1.14	1.16
4	1.12	1.15	1.17	1.19	1.22
5	1.16	1.19	1.22	1.25	1.28
6	1.19	1.23	1.27	1.30	1.34
7	1.23	1.27	1.32	1.36	1.41
8	1.27	1.32	1.37	1.42	1.48
9	1.31	1.36	1.42	1.49	1.55
10	1.34	1.41	1.48	1.55	1.63
11	1.38	1.46	1.54	1.62	1.71
12	1.42	1.51	1.60	1.70	1.80
13	1.46	1.56	1.67	1.77	1.89
14	1.51	1.62	1.73	1.85	1.98
15	1.56	1.68	1.80	1.93	2.08
16	1.60	1.74	1.87	2.02	2.18
17	1.65	1.80	1.95	2.11	2.29
18	1.70	1.86	2.02	2.21	2.41
19	1.75	1.93	2.10	2.31	2.53

(continued)

TABLE 4-1 *(continued)*

Number of Years	3%	3.5%	4%	4.5%	5%
20	1.80	1.99	2.19	2.41	2.65
21	1.86	2.06	2.28	2.52	2.79
22	1.91	2.13	2.37	2.63	2.93
23	1.97	2.21	2.46	2.75	3.08
24	2.03	2.29	2.56	2.87	3.23
25	2.09	2.37	2.66	3.00	3.39
26	2.15	2.45	2.77	3.14	3.56
27	2.22	2.53	2.88	3.28	3.74
28	2.28	2.62	3.00	3.43	3.92
29	2.35	2.72	3.12	3.58	4.12
30	2.42	2.81	3.24	3.74	4.33

Using a retirement calculator

Another way to develop a workable retirement plan is by using one of the many retirement calculators and other tools available on the Internet or through the financial organization that handles your money. Note that each calculator uses different methods and makes different assumptions, so different calculators can produce widely varying results. Check the assumptions each calculator uses to see whether they make sense for you and your situation.

TIP

The major benefit of using a retirement calculator is that it gives you an investment reality check. Will the amount you're saving and the investment mix enable you to accumulate what you need? A good retirement calculator answers this question and also helps you decide how to close any savings gaps. Generally, you can close a gap by increasing your contributions, adjusting your investments to achieve a higher long-term return, or a combination of the two.

If your retirement plan is an IRA, you can use retirement income calculators available online through many financial organizations by doing a simple web search, and AARP (`www.aarp.org/money/retirement/retirement-calculator/`).

IN THIS CHAPTER

» Setting yourself up to live the good life

» Making decisions about your retirement accounts

» Withdrawing required minimums

» Considering taxes

» Managing risk and living your retirement life

Chapter 5

Managing Money in Retirement

Living out your retirement years is supposed to be easy, but it isn't. It takes careful planning even with good professional help. In fact, retirement is similar to running a business. Running a successful business requires having a budget each year. A good business plan includes expected expenses and income for each month of the year. You track both during the year and make adjustments as needed to keep things on track.

This chapter helps you decide what to do with the money in your retirement accounts when you retire from your job, and how to manage it to give you comfort and peace of mind (and maybe even have a little something left over for your heirs).

Looking Forward to Retirement

Did you ever stop to think how much money you'll need in retirement to keep up your current lifestyle? You need to have realistic goals and prepare to be flexible.

The trick is to try to estimate how big a retirement account you'll need and develop a savings plan to try to accumulate that amount. When you retire, you'll have to manage your nest egg so that you don't run out of money before you die. (See Chapter 4 in Book 6 for more information.)

When you retire, your investment job isn't over. In some ways, the job's just beginning. You have to convert your account balance (your *nest egg*) into a healthy income stream that will last the rest of your life. This means that you not only have to decide how to invest your money, but you also have to decide how and when to spend it. Making a bad investment decision or two when you're young is pretty normal and doesn't have to be a tragedy. Losing all your money in one investment and earning nothing on another investment isn't a serious problem if you also have investments that perform well — proving the benefits of diversification.

It's great if you can invest the money in a way that would let you live off the investment income without touching the *principal* (the amount in your nest egg before withdrawing any money), but for most people this isn't possible. You have to spend the principal as well. Spending your account's principal is often referred to as *drawing down* your account. The trick is spending just enough to make life comfortable but not using everything up before you go to the great beyond.

REMEMBER

All the recommendations in this chapter are directed toward individuals, not couples. That's because both you and your spouse need to do your own retirement planning — unless you operate on a combined income. If you and your spouse have joint accounts and a "what's yours is mine" attitude, a combined plan is fine. But keep in mind that, unless you have other resources, both incomes need to be replaced to maintain your lifestyle.

Decisions, Decisions: What to Do with Your 401(k) Money

One of your first decisions as a retiree is what to do with the money in your 401(k). You essentially have two choices with your 401(k):

- Leave it in the plan.
- Take it out of the plan.

Well, okay, the choices are a bit more complicated than that. On the first point, you can leave it in the plan if your vested balance is more than $7,000 (although some plans may still use the older $5,000 limit) and you haven't reached the plan's normal retirement age, usually 65. Leaving your money in your former employer's plan is probably fine if you like the 401(k) plan investments and if you're not going to need the money soon. However, note that the employer can change the plan investments at any time, and you have to go along with it. Also, most plans won't let you take installment payments, so if you need to withdraw some money from the plan, it'll probably be all or nothing.

That brings you to the second option — taking it out of the plan. When you take money out of a 401(k), you have to act carefully to keep taxes and penalties in check. The untaxed amount you take out has to be added on top of your other taxable income for that year.

TIP

The only portion of your account withdrawals that won't be taxable are any Roth contributions you made and the investment income on those contributions. You must have made Roth contributions for at least five years and be over age 59½ to get this tax break. Other withdrawals are taxable, and this additional untaxed income can push you into a higher tax bracket if you have a healthy account balance that you withdraw all at once.

If your plan lets you take installment payments, you can arrange to take out what you need and pay income tax only on that amount each year. (This works until you hit age 73, when you must start taking a *required minimum distribution* each year.) Find out more about these distributions (RMDs) in the later section "Paying Uncle Sam His Due: Required Withdrawals."

However, most 401(k) plans have an all-or-nothing policy — either leave it in the plan or withdraw a *lump sum* (the entire amount). With all-or-nothing plans, the best solution is generally to transfer the money into an IRA to preserve the tax advantage and withdraw money periodically from the IRA as you need it. Again, you pay income tax only on the amounts that you withdraw, which works out to be less than paying tax on the entire amount all at once.

You may also transfer Roth contributions and the earnings on them into a Roth IRA so this portion of your account will continue to grow without being taxed. You can also convert some or all of your untaxed 401(k) account into a Roth IRA.

REMEMBER

What you decide to do, and when you decide to do it, should depend largely on two factors:

- Your age when you leave your employer
- When you plan to start using the money

The following sections explore both points.

Being older can save you money

Your age when you leave your employer is important because it determines whether you have to pay a 10 percent early withdrawal penalty on money you withdraw from the 401(k), in addition to taxes.

If you're at least 55 years old when you leave your employer, you don't have to pay the penalty on money withdrawn from that employer's plan. You still have to pay income tax on the untaxed portion of your account withdrawal, though.

REMEMBER

The exemption from the 10 percent early withdrawal penalty doesn't apply to any untaxed 401(k) money you still have with employers you once worked for but left before turning 55.

If you're under 55 years old when you retire, you will owe a 10 percent early withdrawal penalty on any 401(k) money you withdraw, in addition to taxes. (There are a few exceptions called 72(t) withdrawals, which are explained in the following section.) When you reach age 59½, though, you can withdraw your 401(k) money without a penalty, even if you retired from your employer before age 55.

WARNING

Just to complicate matters, your plan can refuse to let you withdraw money until you are the plan's "normal retirement age," which is often 65. This is unusual but make sure to find out the rules for your plan before you do anything drastic, such as retire.

No matter how old you are, you can avoid the early withdrawal penalty tax by rolling over your untaxed 401(k) money into an IRA. Keep in mind, though, that after it's in the IRA, you'll generally owe a 10 percent early withdrawal penalty on any money you withdraw before you turn 59½. (The mysterious 72(t) withdrawal exception, which is explained in the following section, applies here, too.)

Foiling the dreaded early withdrawal penalty

But what if you need your money before age 55 or age 59½? Here's where the *72(t) withdrawals* (distributions) come into play — you can use them to avoid the early withdrawal penalty. It's called a Section 72(t) distribution because it comes under that section of the Internal Revenue Code. These distributions are a list of exceptions to the penalty, such as being disabled or having medical expenses exceeding 10 percent of your income. However, one of the exceptions, called a *SEPP*, can be used by anyone. (SEPP stands for substantially equal periodic payments.)

When you use SEPP withdrawals, you set up a schedule of periodic payments that continue for five years or until you're 59½, whichever is longer. Monthly, quarterly, semi-annual, annual, or some other form of equal payments work provided you withdraw the same amount each year. (You determine the amount using an IRS formula based on your life expectancy. Several approved methods exist. The simplest is the same one used to determine required minimum distributions, described in the later section "Paying Uncle Sam His Due: Required Withdrawals.") You can set up SEPP payments with your 401(k) if your plan allows these periodic payments. If it doesn't allow them, you can roll your 401(k) balance into an IRA and take the SEPP payments from the IRA.

The three methods for SEPP withdrawals are:

- **The amortization method:** Your annual payment is determined by amortizing your balance over a single or joint (you and your spouse) life expectancy. This method produces the largest and most reasonable amount you can remove. The amount is fixed annually.
- **The minimum distribution (or life expectancy method):** This method uses a dividing factor from the IRS's single and joint life expectancy table. This factor is divided into your annual account balance. The annual withdrawals are likely to vary each year but not substantially. The lowest possible amounts can be withdrawn with this method.
- **The annuitization method:** This option requires using an IRS annuity factor to determine a fixed annual payout that typically falls between the other two methods.

TIP

Use a SEPP to avoid the 10 percent penalty tax if you retire before age 55 and start withdrawals from your 401(k) before age 59½, or if you need to make withdrawals from your IRA before age 59½.

WARNING

If you move your 401(k) money into an IRA, be sure to have it transferred directly. Don't accept a check made out to you personally. If the 401(k) service provider makes the 401(k) check out to you, 20 percent of the amount must be withheld for taxes. You must make up this difference when depositing the money in the IRA; otherwise, the 20 percent withheld will count as taxable income.

Here's an example of a situation requiring SEPP withdrawals. Say you stop working at age 56 and leave your money in your 401(k). Everything's fine for two years, and then you decide you need to withdraw some money. You don't have to worry about the 10 percent early withdrawal penalty because you were at least 55 years old when you left your employer. (A word of caution about this — it doesn't apply if you did not actually retire, but instead changed jobs. Making sure you are following the rules is important and may warrant a discussion with your tax preparer or financial advisor.) However, you still have to think about income tax. If you withdraw the entire 401(k) balance, you'll have a big tax hit. Your employer may allow you to take installment payments from your 401(k) in the amount of your choosing, which would solve your problem. However, if your employer requires you to take a lump-sum withdrawal, what do you do? That's right, roll over the 401(k) into an IRA to preserve the tax advantage.

You have one complication, though. (There's always something.) If you take a distribution from an IRA before you're 59½, you have to pay the 10 percent penalty tax. It doesn't matter that you were over 55 when you left your employer. To get the money out of the IRA without the penalty tax, you need to take a Section 72(t) distribution that must continue for at least five years — until you're 63, in this example.

An alternative is to take a partial distribution from your 401(k) for just the amount you need right away, and roll over the rest of the money into an IRA. For example, assume that you have $200,000 in your account, and you need to use $35,000 before you turn 59½. You can take $35,000 (plus enough money to cover the tax) from your 401(k) plan and transfer the rest of the money directly to the IRA.

TIP

Have the bulk of your savings in an IRA after you retire because IRAs give you greater withdrawal flexibility after age 59½ and more investment flexibility than a 401(k).

Leaving money with your former employer

If you don't need to use any of your 401(k) money for retirement income and your account exceeds $7,000, you can leave the money in your 401(k). Your employer can't force you to take the money out prior to your plan's normal retirement age. Participants who are comfortable with the investments they have in their 401(k) and/or who don't like making decisions are more likely to leave their money in the plan. Those who aren't thrilled with their 401(k) investments usually can't wait to get their money out of the plan and into other investments they think are better.

There is no right or wrong decision. Either arrangement is fine if your 401(k) investments are satisfactory. One thing to note is that money in a 401(k) may have somewhat greater protection from creditors than money in an IRA, depending on your state of residence, should you declare bankruptcy. (IRA protection depends on state law where you live, whereas 401(k) protection is afforded by federal law.)

On the other hand, an IRA offers much greater investment flexibility. An IRA also gives you greater flexibility in naming a beneficiary: You don't have to get your spouse's approval before you can name someone else as beneficiary, as you have to with a 401(k).

TIP

As you decide whether to leave your 401(k) money with your former employer, also consider the fact that the corporate landscape changes constantly. In a continuous merger-and-acquisition climate, consider getting your money out of the 401(k) plan as soon as you can. Not only can former employers be elusive, but they can also change your plan investments at any time. Your money can be moved from one set of investments to another without your approval.

Making Withdrawals from Your IRA

You may hold some or all of your retirement savings in a traditional and/or Roth IRA. You can withdraw money from either type at any time; however, you have tax penalties if you don't follow the rules that exempt you from a penalty tax. The same rules apply to a traditional IRA as to withdrawing untaxed money from a 401(k), so check the earlier section "Foiling the dreaded early withdrawal penalty." ***Note:*** Comments in this section are limited to IRA withdrawals to provide retirement income. You can make IRA withdrawals for other reasons without tax penalty.

Withdrawals from a Roth IRA aren't taxable if your account is at least five years old and you are at least 59½. Otherwise, withdrawing any of the investment income means you pay a 10 percent penalty tax on the investment income. Amounts you contributed to a Roth IRA are never taxable because you already paid tax on this money.

You can also take Section 72(t) distributions known as substantially equal periodic payments (SEPP) from your IRA accounts without tax penalty. This is a way to access the money in these accounts prior to age 59½ to generate retirement income without paying a penalty tax. You must follow an IRS-approved specific schedule. Three different methods are covered in the earlier section "Foiling the dreaded early withdrawal penalty." You must stick with the schedule you select for five years or until you reach age 59½, whichever comes later (unless you are disabled or die). A tax penalty will be applied to all payments you have received up to that point if you vary from the schedule.

REMEMBER

A key issue when you have different types of retirement savings accounts is how to manage them. They're much easier to manage when you combine them into one account or at least into one investment organization. You need to put thought into how to generate the amount of retirement income you currently need and to keep doing so.

Never having to pay tax on the investment gains with a Roth IRA is an important issue because you aren't required to take money out of your Roth IRA during your lifetime. As a result, delaying withdrawals from a Roth IRA is usually a great idea; however, withdrawing some nontaxable money from the Roth IRA and taxable money from a traditional IRA or 401(k) gives you less taxable income.

REMEMBER

Careful planning will also be necessary if your total income will be coming from your retirement savings during the early years of retirement because you either aren't eligible for Social Security (SS) or because you decide to delay taking your SS benefit. Getting help from a good accountant is advisable.

Paying Uncle Sam His Due: Required Withdrawals

You must begin taking your money out of the 401(k) plan and a traditional IRA by the time you're 73. If you're still working for the employer that maintains the 401(k) plan, you don't have to start withdrawing money until you leave that job. (However, if you own more than 5 percent of the company, the age-73 rule applies, even if you're still working.) The government wants to collect tax on your money at some point, which is why you can't leave it in a 401(k) or traditional IRA forever. Roth accounts are different. Withdrawals from a Roth IRA aren't required during your lifetime, and the Roth portion of a 401(k) is also exempt from required minimum distributions during your lifetime.

REMEMBER

The amount that you're required to withdraw each year from your 401(k) or traditional IRA is called your *required minimum distribution,* or RMD. Again, 73 is the magic age when it comes to your first RMD. The requirement kicks in during the year you turn 73, but you have until April 1 of the following year to take the installment. You then have to take required distributions by December 31 of each year.

WARNING

You have a few extra months to take your first required distribution (until April 1), but because that distribution is for the previous year, you still have to take a second required distribution for the current year before December 31 of that same year. Be aware that the withdrawals increase your taxable income for that year. You may not want to put off taking your first withdrawal.

For example, if you turn 73 in 2026, you have to take your first RMD by April 1, 2027. But you can take it in 2026 if you like. Why would you take it in 2026?

Because you'll also have to take a second distribution by December 31, 2027, for the year 2027. If you put off your 2026 distribution until 2027, you'll have a higher taxable income that year, all else being equal. You may also have to pay tax on a larger portion of your Social Security benefit if you have more taxable income.

Calculating your RMD isn't terribly difficult if you have the right information. Be prepared to have the following items at hand:

- **The balance of your retirement account as of December 31 of the year before the one that you're taking the distribution for:** In other words, if you're calculating your 2026 distribution, you need to know your account balance as of December 31, 2025.
- **The IRS life expectancy tables that apply to you and the correct number for your age:** You can find these tables in a supplement to Publication 590-B, "Distributions from Individual Retirement Arrangements (IRAs)," which is available at `www.irs.gov/pub/irs-pdf/p590b.pdf`. Use Table III if your spouse is less than ten years younger than you, if you're single, or if you're married but your spouse isn't your named beneficiary. Use Table II if your spouse is more than ten years younger than you and is your sole beneficiary. Don't worry about Table I — it's for beneficiaries who inherit an IRA.

For example, if you reach age 73 during 2025 and are married, and your spouse is 65, use Table III, provided at `www.irs.gov/pub/irs-pdf/p590b.pdf`. On that table, the distribution period for a 73-year-old is 26.5. You divide your account balance by that number, and the result is your required minimum distribution. Say your account balance on December 31, 2025, is $250,000. Your required minimum distribution is $9,433.96 ($250,000 divided by 26.5). That's how much you have to take out the first year. For the following year, you do a new calculation with your updated account balance and the next distribution period number on the table.

REMEMBER

The trustee, custodian, or issuer that held the 401(k) or IRA at the end of the preceding year must either report the amount of the RMD to you or offer to calculate it for you. This entity must include the date the RMD must be distributed. The report is due by January 31 of the year the distribution is required.

By the way, the rules for calculating required minimum distributions are the same whether your money is in a 401(k) or a traditional IRA. And you can always take out more than the required minimum with no penalty. However, if you take out less, the IRS will fine you 50 percent of the required amount that you didn't withdraw.

Developing a Strategy to Deal with the Tax Man

It would be nice if taxes disappeared when you retired, but unfortunately, they don't. The earlier sections of this chapter talk about minimizing taxes when you first move your money out of your retirement fund, but you need to look at a few other situations, too, which are put forth in the following sections.

Which comes first: Plucking the chicken or emptying the nest egg?

You most likely have some money saved in *taxable* (nontax-advantaged) accounts such as Roth 401(k) contributions or a Roth IRA as well as in your 401(k) or traditional IRA. How do you decide which money to spend first?

Historically, many professional advisors recommended keeping as much money as possible in a tax-deferred account, even during retirement. The rationale was that you would continue to benefit from the fact that no interest, dividends, or gains were taxable while the money was in the account.

But the game changed in 1984 when Congress revised the tax rules regarding Social Security benefits. Although this tax-deferred advantage is still true, you also have to factor in taxation of your Social Security benefits. When you start receiving Social Security, your benefits are taxed if your income is over certain limits. Non-Roth distributions from a 401(k) or traditional IRA are taxable retirement benefits included in the income you must count to determine what portion, if any, of your Social Security benefits are taxable. So, if you take money out of your 401(k) or traditional IRA when you start receiving Social Security benefits, you may have to pay tax on your Social Security benefits.

TIP

Do some basic planning before deciding on your retirement withdrawals, bearing in mind that receiving income over a certain level means you pay tax on your Social Security benefits. You can check the Social Security Administration website at `www.ssa.gov` for updates.

If you retire a few years before taking Social Security benefits, you may want to use up your tax-deferred accounts first, rather than your other savings, per the following example that assumes you:

- Retire at age 60
- Plan to start receiving Social Security benefits when you reach age 62, before you reach your full retirement age
- Have $150,000 of personal savings
- Have $350,000 in your retirement account
- Will need $45,000 of income (after taxes) each of your first two years of retirement (before Social Security kicks in)

You can either use your personal savings or withdraw approximately $50,000 from your retirement account during each of these two years. (Assume that a $50,000 withdrawal will leave you about $45,000 after paying taxes. If you have other taxable income, your tax rate may be higher.) Withdrawing the money from your 401(k) right away will reduce the size of the taxable distributions you'll receive after you become eligible for Social Security. It reduces your taxable income after you start to collect Social Security benefits, so perhaps you won't have to pay as much, or any, tax on your benefits. This option may be a better tax deal than the tax break you receive by keeping more money in your retirement account. And you still have your personal savings available, which you've already paid taxes on.

REMEMBER

You need to do some fairly complex calculations to see what's better in your situation, so you're strongly encouraged to consult an experienced accountant or other qualified advisor who does this type of planning.

Dealing with that darned company stock

You need to consider taxes when you decide what to do with the company stock you may have accumulated in your 401(k) account or other employer-sponsored plan, such as an employee stock ownership plan (ESOP). You get a special tax break when you receive company stock as a distribution. You pay tax only on the value of the stock when it was credited to your plan account, not on its current value. You pay a capital gains tax on the difference whenever you eventually sell the stock. These capital gains taxes are lower than the income taxes you would otherwise pay. Finally, if you pass the stock to your heirs after you die, they won't pay tax on any gains that occurred before it was given to them.

This type of estate planning is feasible only if you don't expect to use the stock during your retirement, and you're willing to take the risk of having a chunk of money tied to one stock for many years.

WARNING

Holding stock in an individual company is much riskier than investing in a number of different investments.

If you roll your company stock into an IRA, you can sell it and diversify into other investments. You have to pay income tax on your eventual withdrawals. If you take your distribution of stock, you must pay tax on the value of the stock when you received it in the plan. You can then sell the company stock, paying only capital gains tax on the gain, and use the money to invest in more diversified mutual funds or a portfolio of stocks. However, returns on these "taxable" investments will be subject to income tax every year. Still, the benefits of diversification probably make either one of these strategies more palatable than holding on to the company stock, unless you really aren't going to need the money during your lifetime.

REMEMBER

Don't let the tax tail wag the dog. Passing company stock on to your heirs is an instance when tax planning for them may get in the way of good investment planning for you.

Managing Your Investments in Retirement

Investing to build up an adequate retirement nest egg takes most people an entire working career. But, believe it or not, managing your investments is even more critical *during* your retirement years, because what took many years to build can go "poof" in an instant, like one of those big soap bubbles kids blow. When you're younger, you can do some really dumb things and still have time to recover. If your investments lose 20 percent or more when you're 30, it's a non-event. When you're 70, it can be a disaster.

REMEMBER

As a retiree, you really have to pay attention to your investments, so that you can convert your retirement account and other resources into an income stream that will last for the rest of your life.

TIP

As you decide how to manage your nest egg during your retirement years, the importance of consulting a professional can't be emphasized enough. This is probably the best investment you can make for your retirement. Ask coworkers, friends, or family members for recommendations on financial professionals in your area. A good resource is `www.napfa.org`, the website of the National Association of Personal Financial Advisors.

Live long and prosper

Maintaining an income stream that will last for the rest of your life is more difficult now than it used to be. A generation or two ago, retirees commonly converted all their available funds into income-producing investments. For most retirees, this meant converting their funds into bank certificates of deposit (CDs). Those who owned stocks typically stuck to the ones that were popular for widows and orphans — in other words, stocks such as utilities that paid high dividends and had a history of steady income with low price fluctuation and modest long-term growth.

Keeping up with inflation wasn't a big deal when the average retiree lived for only 10 to 12 years after retiring. A 3 percent inflation rate reduced the amount of income a retiree can spend by only 23 percent after 10 years.

Today, if you retire during your 50s or early 60s, you need to plan for at least 30 years of retirement income. Your buying power will be reduced by 58 percent after 30 years of inflation at 3 percent. You've probably read that you have to keep some money invested in stocks during your retirement years to help offset the impact of inflation. This advice makes sense because stocks have produced a higher level of return on average than other investments over 20- to 30-year time periods. But you also need to know how much stock, and which types of stock, to own.

Stay practical

WARNING

When you do your retirement planning, don't expect an annual return of 10 percent or higher. Too many 401(k) and IRA investors have come to expect just that during the high-performance 2010s and early 2020s. The stock returns that investors experienced during these years can't continue indefinitely — you can expect a typical market crash. No one knows when the next prolonged, major downturn will occur.

Retirees who were following traditional investment advice during 2008 incurred losses in the 30 percent range. Such a loss shortly after you retire is a horrible way to start your retirement years. More aggressive retiree investors incurred even larger losses.

A $100,000 account that drops to $70,000 due to a 30 percent loss must increase by 43 percent to get back to $100,000. Assume you need to withdraw $4,000 per year from your retirement accounts — the 4 percent generally recommended by investment professionals. You assumed your $100,000 would grow by 6 percent each year. If both happened during the first year of your retirement, you would have roughly $102,000 in your account at the end of the first year. If, instead of a 6 percent gain, you experience a 30 percent loss, your account becomes worth approximately $66,000 after the first year rather than $102,000 — a 55 percent gap from which you most likely will never recover.

It's important to have a plan in place and reserves at the ready in case there is a drop in the market. Read on to find out how to manage your investments when things don't go quite according to plan.

Managing Risk

After all the years you worked hard to reach your retirement goal, you probably want, and deserve, a break that's free of investment stress. But this sort of break isn't possible. At this point, you need to withdraw money from your account to live. The combination of a low or negative return for a couple of years and regular withdrawals can really disrupt your carefully laid plans.

Balancing investments

One way to avoid having to sell stocks when they're down is to invest about 20 percent of your nest egg in low-risk, fixed-income investments, such as a money market fund or short-term bond fund. Hold these investments in your regular IRA or in a separate IRA. Use this money as a special cash reserve fund during down periods. You can tap this fund rather than be forced to sell stocks and bonds when their value is down.

Imagine you have a retirement nest egg worth $250,000. You withdraw 4 percent, or $10,000, for living expenses the first year. The next year you withdraw $10,300 to keep up with 3 percent inflation. Now say the value of your investments drops 10 percent the first year and another 4 percent the second year. Finally, assume that you based your plan on a 6 percent return during your retirement years.

REMEMBER

If you're particularly thrifty, you may think that you don't need to adjust for inflation. Don't fool yourself. You're not living on the same income now that you had 20 or 30 years ago, and you won't want to live on today's income 30 years from now. Some argue that, despite inflation, expenses decrease during retirement years. That's true for some expenses, but medical expenses usually increase, and you may ultimately need to cover the cost of an assisted-living facility. Keeping some of your investments in stock should help you make up the gap that inflation causes.

A 6 percent return may have looked like a sure thing when you retired, but instead the market drops by 14.6 percent during the first year and gains 10.8 percent the second year as it did in 2008 and 2009. Table 5-1 shows returns for a mutual fund with a 47/53 stock/bond mix that was considered appropriate for a retiree early in the 21st century. Table 5-1 shows the fluctuations in value of a $250,000 nest egg in these circumstances, compared to your original investment plan, which assumes 6 percent gains per year.

TABLE 5-1 **How Actual Results Can Differ from Your Plan**

	Beginning Amount $250,000 Your Plan	Beginning Amount $250,000 Actual Results
Withdrawal Year 1	$10,000	$10,000
Withdrawal Year 2	$10,300	$10,300
Investment gain (or loss) Year 1	$14,700	($35,770)
Investment gain (or loss) Year 2	$14,973	$26,507
Ending balance Year 1	$254,700	$204,230
Ending balance Year 2	$259,373	$215,431

The actual results were a 14.6 percent loss during 2008 and a 10.8 percent gain during 2009. If your plan is based on a 6 percent average annual return, this example shows how badly your plan can be disrupted if the year you retire is when the market crashes.

Although no one can predict when the market will go up and down, you do need a predictable stream of income during your retirement years. But withdrawing money when the value of your investments is declining can be gut-wrenching.

Buying an annuity

Buying a fixed-income annuity is an option to consider if you have less than a few million in assets to provide the retirement income you need.

REMEMBER

Many types of annuities are on the market. The only recommended one is a fixed-income annuity that provides a guaranteed monthly income for the rest of your life. A joint life annuity will provide a guaranteed income to both you and a spouse.

The amount you pay to buy a fixed-income annuity depends on your current age, the age when you want the monthly income to begin, and the monthly annuity amount. It costs a lot to buy $1,000 of monthly annuity income when you are age 67 with immediate monthly payments because the insurance company must pay you for the rest of your life — potentially 20 to 30 years.

You can choose from many annuity options:

- Buy one that starts payments when you retire.
- Buy one that doesn't start paying you until you reach an older age such as 75 or 80. Doing so will assure you a guaranteed monthly income at that age, reducing the risk that your nest egg will run dry while you are still living.
- Buy two annuities — one that starts paying when you retire and another one that starts payments during your later years.

A life-income annuity is the reverse of life insurance. With life insurance, you pay premiums each year for a benefit paid to your beneficiaries when you die. This benefit is meant to help replace your lost income. With an annuity you receive monthly benefits for as long as you live. The annuity protects you from living too long. The monthly payments end when you die unless you select one that guarantees an income to a spouse or someone else after you die. You receive the largest monthly benefit if payments end when you die.

WARNING

The biggest risk with a life annuity is incurred if you die shortly after buying it, making the insurance company that sold you the annuity the big winner.

Your health and gene pool are factors to consider before buying a fixed income annuity. You need to judge how likely you are to live into your 80s or 90s based on your health and genes.

TIP

A lot more needs to be considered about this type of annuity than can be covered in this book. "Stan the Annuity Man" has the best information available. Go to `www.stantheannuityman.com` and order his free books to get access to a lot of good information even if you never buy an annuity from Stan.

The amount of annuity income you get varies a bit by state due to state taxes. Annuity rates also change frequently for a variety of reasons, with changes in interest rates the biggest factor. You can buy a larger annuity income when interest rates are higher because insurance companies factor their expected return into their pricing.

Consolidating Your Accounts

Many 401(k) and IRA savers have multiple accounts, often including one or more in former employer 401(k) plans. If this is you, you probably won't be able to say how these accounts are invested. At best, you may be able to name the investment organization where the money is invested.

Having multiple retirement accounts makes it much more difficult to manage your investments and to plan for retirement. You must decide how to structure your withdrawals when you retire to provide the income you need and to satisfy the minimum withdrawal requirements. Having multiple accounts with different financial organizations makes this much more difficult.

The larger and better financial organizations provide investment and other help when you have an account with them. They usually help you transfer money from a 401(k) or an IRA without any additional fee, or you can pay an additional fee to get more extensive help. Such assistance is more effective when you have all or most of your retirement account assets with one organization.

When your money is invested with a major financial organization, you can easily transfer money from your account or accounts into your checking account via electronic transfers as needed. You can have a set amount transferred each month without having to do anything after the process is established. Or you can go online or call in to have money transferred as needed.

TIP

You can also hire an independent firm to take total control of the transfer process. One recommendation is Retirement Clearinghouse. They work directly with the financial institution, making the transfer as stress-free and pleasant as possible. They also don't get paid until the transfer has been completed. Their website is `www.rch1.com`, and the phone number is 866-827-9608.

Tending to Your Nest Egg

Some people think that they'll never run out of money if the amount they withdraw from their retirement account each year never exceeds their investment return. But how can you do this in years when your return is low or negative? Would you be able to live on 1 percent of your account? (Even with an account of $500,000, that's $5,000 for the entire year.)

Achieving an investment return such as 6 percent is not a given every year. Stock returns can be almost nonexistent even during extended periods. Living through one of these longer-term market funks when you're building your nest egg isn't easy — but it's much more painful when you're retired and watching your account shrink. In addition to good planning, a favorable economy during most of your retirement years will certainly help — but of course, you can't control that.

WARNING

The COVID-19 pandemic is a reminder that we have limited control. As a result, we aren't comfortable suggesting that readers approaching retirement or already retired follow traditional investment advice to invest 40 percent in stocks and 60 percent in bonds. Such a mix will leave you exposed to a 20 to 30 percent drop in your account value when the next market drop hits.

Consider moving 50 percent of your holdings into cash because a major meltdown can occur soon based on historical records. You won't earn anything currently, but you shouldn't lose anything on the cash portion unless there is a total economic collapse. If that happens, who knows what will be safe? Such a move should cut your losses in half when the next major and prolonged downturn occurs. You will have the opportunity to invest all or a portion of this money in stocks and bonds after the market drops substantially.

Investors at or after retirement age need to be more concerned about protecting the retirement savings they have rather than pursuing higher investment returns. Buying a fixed income annuity and/or holding a larger than normal portion of your invested assets in cash will provide a greater level of protection. The return on cash investments is crappy currently, but the reduced investment risk may be worth it.

Row, Row, Row Your Boat, Gently Down the Income Stream

Model plans for retirees generally recommend withdrawing only 4 percent per year from their accounts, increasing the withdrawal by 3 percent annually for inflation, and assuming a 6 percent investment return. We agree with such a model except we recommend reducing your expected investment return from 6 percent to 4 percent. Doing so enables you to invest more conservatively and reduce the likelihood of a 20 to 30 percent drop.

Table 5-2 shows how this strategy would have worked for someone who retired during 2008, the year of the last market crash. At the end of 2021, $209,345 of the original $250,000 was left. The account will run dry during 2036 when the payout will have increased to $22,865 and the owner is 94, assuming the owner was 65 in 2008.

TABLE 5-2 Planned Withdrawal Strategy

Year	Beginning Balance	Annual Payout	Investment Return	Year-End Balance
2008	$250,000	$10,000	$9,800	$249,800
2009	$249,800	$10,300	$9,786	$249,286
2010	$249,286	$10,690	$9,758	$248,354
2011	$248,354	$10,927	$9,716	$247,143
2012	$247,143	$11,255	$9,661	$245,549
2013	$245,549	$11,593	$9,590	$243,546
2014	$243,546	$11,941	$9,503	$241,108
2015	$241,108	$12,299	$9,398	$238,207
2016	$238,207	$12,668	$9,275	$234,814
2017	$234,814	$13,048	$9,132	$230,898
2018	$230,898	$13,439	$8,967	$226,426
2019	$226,426	$13,842	$8,780	$221,364
2020	$221,364	$14,248	$8,570	$215,686

REMEMBER

Planning for a 4 percent rather than a 6 percent return frees you to pick investments that have less volatility. To do so, you must be willing to accept less upside potential because protecting rather than growing your investments is more important at this stage of your life. You can do this by investing in one or more mutual funds that have smaller up and down swings.

Table 5-3 shows the actual results rather than a model assuming you retired at the end of 2007 and invested all your retirement savings into a 2010 target date fund. This action would have given you the asset mix considered appropriate for a retiree.

If you were searching for a fund to invest in today, this fund would be attractive if you looked only at the average investment returns posted for this fund because the one-year return is 17.02, the five-year average return is 6.38, and the ten-year average return is 5.66 percent. Investing in this fund would appear to be a great option if you want to achieve a 4 percent average annual return. But the results show you would have had only $133,953 left at the end of 2020. You needed $215,686 at the end of 2020 to be on track with your 4 percent average annual investment return plan. Very scary and much worse for someone who is attempting to get a 6 percent or higher average annual return. These average annual return results show why they aren't helpful when you're deciding how to manage your investments. You need to dig deeper by checking how the funds you are considering performed during the 2008 market crash.

TABLE 5-3 Actual Results for a Target Date Fund

Year	Beginning Balance	Annual Payout	Return Percentage	Gain or Loss	Ending Balance
2008	$250,000	$10,000	–14.6	–$35,770	$204,230
2009	$204,230	$10,300	10.8	$21,501	$215,431
2010	$215,431	$10,927	5.8	$12,178	$216,682
2011	$216,682	$11,255	2	$4,221	$209,648
2012	$209,648	$11,593	5.3	$10,804	$208,859
2013	$208,859	$11,941	2	$4,058	$200,976
2014	$200,976	$12,299	3.5	$6,819	$195,496
2015	$195,496	$12,668	–3.7	–$6,999	$175,802
2016	$175,802	$13,048	3.2	$6,524	$169,278
2017	$169,278	$13,439	5.6	$9,103	$164,942
2018	$164,942	$13,842	–6.1	–$9,650	$141,450
2019	$141,450	$14,258	10.2	$13,701	$140,893
2020	$140,893	$14,686	5.8	$7,746	$133,953

Treating Your Home Like the Asset It Is

When you consider financial resources to fund your retirement, you may also wonder whether to convert your home into an income-producing asset. In some cases, this makes sense, but many people are emotionally attached to their family home and don't want to sell it. You may have to try to take a less emotional look, however, because you may need the equity from your home to achieve a comfortable level of retirement income.

Adding up the expenses

It may be smart to sell your home and use the proceeds to generate income, and then find a place to rent. Why rent if you own a home without a mortgage? Consider that a home is indeed an asset, but it doesn't produce money — it eats it up. It costs a lot of money to live in your home even if you don't have a mortgage. If you own a $300,000 home, your annual costs to maintain it are likely to be pricey:

- Real estate taxes are probably in the $5,000 range.
- Homeowner's insurance may be $1,000, more or less.
- Routine annual maintenance and utilities, such as water, sewer, and lawn care, are probably in the $6,000 range. (Check all your expenditures for a year if these estimates seem high.)
- Periodic repairs, such as a new roof and indoor and outdoor painting or upkeep.

All told, you probably spend at least $12,000 per year for the privilege of owning your $300,000 home — even with the mortgage fully paid. This additional expense is okay if you have adequate retirement income but is less than okay if your retirement resources are limited. The situation is much worse if you still have mortgage payments.

You can probably find a nice place to rent for $1,500 per month in the same area as your $300,000 home. The rental will cost you $18,000 per year compared to the $12,000 it may cost to live in your present home. You're paying a bit more for the rental, but you don't have the hassle of home ownership. Most importantly, you can reinvest the money from the sale of your home and make up the difference. Investing $300,000 at a 4 percent return gives you an additional $12,000 annually, and you have the $300,000 available as needed.

Making use of your equity

A reverse mortgage (covered in Chapter 3 of Book 6) or home equity loan are other ways to tap into your home's value if you really want to stay where you are and in the house you own. *Equity* is the difference between what your home is valued at and the amount you owe on it.

Up-front costs for a reverse mortgage are in the $10,000 to $15,000 range. All you get for those fees are the right to draw against your home equity as needed and no repayment schedule. No repayments are due during your lifetime, and you and your spouse can live in the house for the rest of your lives regardless of how long you live. You must keep up with taxes and maintain the home.

You should delay applying for a reverse mortgage until you need to tap into your home equity; however, apply a year or more before you reach this point because the process takes a while.

WARNING

A reverse mortgage may not be in the best interest of your heirs. They may not have much time to pay off the balance after your death. The mortgage holder's primary interest is to get their money out of the property as soon as possible. Getting a price high enough so your heirs get some money usually isn't a concern.

Obtaining a home equity line of credit is another option to consider rather than selling your home. Do this while you're still working because a bank must approve your request based on your ability to repay the loan. Your income while still working should enable you to get the loan approved.

TIP

Save using your home equity loan until the later stage of your life for repayment reasons. Assume you obtain a $100,000 home equity loan when you're age 65 but don't need to use it until you reach age 80. Assume you start drawing $1,000 per month. One bank requires paying back 2 percent of the loan balance plus interest every month. There's usually no fee or only a small one with this type of loan, but monthly repayments are required, and they will grow if you make $1,000 monthly withdrawals. Eventually you will probably need to sell the home because you won't be able to make the monthly payments.

7
Planning Your Estate and Will

Contents at a Glance

IN THIS CHAPTER

» Understanding what your estate is

» Planning what will happen to your estate

» Realizing that your estate-planning goals are different from other people's

» Stepping onto the critical path for estate planning

» Putting together your estate-planning team

Chapter 1 The Fundamentals of Estate Planning

The protection and control that you need.

No, the above phrase isn't the marketing slogan for a new deodorant. Instead, it expresses the two most important reasons for you to spend time and effort on your estate planning:

- After you die, the government will try to take the portion of your estate that the current tax law says it's entitled to, but you have the opportunity to protect your estate by minimizing that tax bite.
- You want to have as much control as possible over how your estate is divided up. Basically, you want to decide what will happen to your estate rather than have a jumbled set of complicated laws dictate who will get what.

You may have spent time working on a financial plan throughout your life, as well as crafting your retirement plan. Your estate plan accompanies those other two plans and makes up the third leg that supports your life's overall "financial stool."

WARNING

Without a solid estate plan, however, your "financial stool" can't stand on just those two other legs. Even worse, even though you may not be around to witness the complications and damage, all your hard work on your financial and retirement plans could be severely compromised in the absence of a solid estate plan.

Before you can plan your estate, you need to understand what your estate really is. Many people think that for the average non-billionaire, estate planning involves only two steps:

- Preparing a will
- Trying to figure out what inheritance and estate taxes — the so-called "death taxes" — apply (and if so, then how much money will go to the state and federal governments)

But even though wills and death taxes are certainly important considerations, chances are, your own estate planning will involve much, much more.

This chapter presents the basics of estate planning that you need to get started on. In this chapter, we show you why estate planning is every bit as important as saving for your child's college education or putting money away for your retirement. In fact, your estate plan is the continuation and culmination of your personal and family financial planning.

What Is an Estate?

In the most casual sense, your estate is your *stuff* (all your possessions). However, even if your only familiarity with estate planning comes from watching a movie or TV show where someone's will is read, you no doubt realize that you aren't very likely to hear words such as "I leave all of my stuff to . . .." Therefore, a bit more detail and formality is in order, which we provide in this section.

The basics: Definitions and terminology

"All my property."

Think of that phrase when you plan your estate.

What's that, you say? You live in an apartment and don't own a house or a condo or any other real estate (more formally known as *real property*), so you think you don't have any property? Not so fast! In a legal sense, all kinds of items are considered your property, not just real estate, including the following:

- Cash, checking accounts, and savings accounts
- Certificates of deposit (CDs)
- Stocks, bonds, and mutual funds
- Crypto assets such as cryptocurrencies and non-fungible tokens (NFTs)
- Retirement savings in your individual retirement account (IRA), 401(k), health savings account (HSA), and other special accounts
- Household furniture (including antiques)
- Clothes
- Vehicles
- Life insurance
- Annuities
- Business interests
- Jewelry, your baseball card collection, that autographed first edition of *The Catcher in the Rye,* and all the rest of your collectibles

As we discuss in the later section "Property types," your estate consists of all the preceding types of items — and even more — divided into several different categories. (For estate-planning purposes, these categories are often treated differently from each other, but we cover that distinction later.)

The types of property listed almost always have a *positive balance,* meaning that they are worth something, even if "something" is only a very small amount. Of course, an exception may be your overdrawn checking account, which then is actually property with a negative balance. So, your estate also needs to account for debts that need to be subtracted from your asset values, such as:

- » The outstanding balance of the mortgage you owe on your house or a vacation home
- » The outstanding balance on all loans (home equity, car, or student loans)
- » The outstanding balances on your credit card accounts
- » Taxes you owe to the government
- » Any IOUs to people that you haven't paid off yet

REMEMBER

Basically, all debts you have are as much a part of your estate as all the positive-balance items.

Determining your estate's worth

In addition to understanding what your estate is, you also need to know what your estate is worth. You can calculate your estate's value as follows:

1. **Add up the value of all the positive-balance items in your estate (again, your banking accounts, investments, collectibles, real estate, and so on).**
2. **Subtract the total value of all the negative-balance items (the remaining balance of the mortgage on your home, how much you still owe on your credit cards, and so on) from the total of all the positive-balance items.**

The result is the net value of your estate, which you can think of as your "personal balance sheet." In most cases, the result is a positive number, meaning that what you have is worth more than what you owe.

TECHNICAL STUFF

If calculating a *net value* by subtracting the total of what you owe from the total of what you have seems familiar, you're right! In the simplest sense, calculating the value of your estate involves essentially the same steps that you follow when you apply for many different types of loans (mortgage, automobile, educational assistance, and so on).

However, in many cases — including perhaps your own — determining what the parts of your estate are, and what they're worth, can be a bit more complicated than simply creating two columns on a sheet of paper or in your computer's spreadsheet program and doing basic arithmetic. If you're a farmer, for example, you need to figure out the value of your crops or livestock. If you own a small one-person business, you need to calculate what your business is worth. Or perhaps you and six other people are joint owners of a complicated real estate investment partnership; if so, what is your share worth?

For now, another point to keep in mind is that, in addition to what you have right now, your estate may also include other items that you don't have in your possession, but will at some point in the future, such as:

- Any future payments you expect to receive, such as an insurance settlement or the remaining 18 annual payments from that $35 million lottery jackpot that you won a couple of years ago!
- A loan you made to your sibling to help get their business started that they will eventually repay.

TIP

For planning purposes, you also want to consider future inheritances you *may* receive, which *might* be part of your estate when you die (see the nearby sidebar "The ripple effect").

If you're familiar with the business and accounting term *accounts receivable* (what people or businesses owe to you), you need to include your own personal accounts receivable along with your banking accounts and home when figuring out what your estate contains and what your estate is worth.

Defining "estate planning"

One final term to cover is *estate planning*. By definition, estate planning means to plan your estate (of course!). More precisely, you need to follow a disciplined set of steps that we discuss later in this chapter. Why? Because you want to protect as much of your estate as possible from being taken away, and because you want to control what happens to your estate after you die. An estate plan enables you to preserve as much as you can for your *beneficiaries* (family members, lifelong friends, or maybe even your favorite charities).

REMEMBER

Your estate plan typically includes the following:

- Your will
- Documents that substitute for your will, called (big surprise) *will substitutes*
- Trusts
- Tax considerations, with the idea of minimizing the overall amount of taxes you have to pay
- Various types of insurance, such as life insurance and long-term care insurance

» Items related to your own particular circumstances, such as protecting your business or setting aside money to pay for your health care or a nursing home in your later years

If this collection of estate-planning activities seems a bit overwhelming, think of estate planning as a parallel to how you plan your personal finances and investments. Your investment portfolio may be made up of individual stocks, bonds, mutual funds, and exchange-traded funds (ETFs), along with bank CDs or other savings-related investments. And then, within each type of investment, you have further categories (for example, different types of mutual funds) that you may want to use.

REMEMBER

Your investment objective is to sort through this menu of choices and put together just the right collection for your needs. You must also do the same with your estate plan. You need to have the right will and insurance coverage, possibly accompanied by trusts if they make sense for you and your family. You may need additional estate-planning activities and strategies particular to your own needs.

Property types

You can have several types of property within your estate. Make a distinction between these types of property because various aspects of your estate planning treat each type differently. For example, in your will (see Chapter 2 in Book 7), you can use different legal language when referring to various types of property, so remember to keep these definitions and distinctions straight!

THE RIPPLE EFFECT

The old saying "Don't count your chickens before they're hatched" can definitely be applied in estate planning as it relates to future inheritances you're supposed to receive and then, in turn, pass on to others as part of your own estate plan.

For example, your grandparents, parents, and other loved ones (your *benefactors*) may have informed you that they have provided you with an inheritance — money, property, or something else of monetary value — in their own estate plans. However, you know how circumstances in life often change. Changes in a benefactor's circumstances, such as a health issue that requires unplanned health-care costs, can easily eat into or even evaporate your inheritance. Accordingly, when it comes to these future inheritances that are eventually supposed to be heading your way, you need to keep the "uncertainty factor" in mind and make adjustments as necessary in your own estate plan. Essentially, unforeseen changes to the estate of one of your own benefactors could "ripple" into unforeseen changes in your own estate.

Real property

Earlier, we mention one type of property — *real property* — and note that real property refers to various types of real estate, including the following:

- Your *home* (a house, condominium, co-op apartment, or some other type of primary residence that you own)
- A second home (such as a vacation property on a lake or near a ski resort)
- A "piece" of a vacation home, such as a time-share
- Fractional ownership in real estate (through companies such as Pacaso and Arrived)
- Any kind of vacant land, such as a building lot in a suburban development or even agricultural land you may own next to your "main" farm
- Any investment real property that you own either by yourself or with someone else, such as a house you rent out through Airbnb or Vrbo or on your own, or your share of an apartment building

In addition to the actual real property itself, your estate also includes any improvements that you can't even see. For example, if you and three of your friends bought 200 acres of land with the intention of turning that land into a subdivision, and you've spent loads of money on infrastructure — water lines and hookups, sewer lines and hookups, in-ground electricity, and so on — then those improvements (or, more accurately, your share of those improvements) are also considered to be part of your estate along with the original real property itself.

Personal property

In addition to real property, your estate includes *personal property*, which is further divided into two categories:

- **Tangible personal property:** Your tangible personal property includes possessions that you can touch, such as your car, jewelry, furniture, paintings and artwork, and collectibles (baseball and sports cards, autographed first-edition novels, and so on).

  REMEMBER

  Your house is considered to be real property, not tangible personal property, even though you can touch it. Why? Because your house is permanently attached to (and, thus, made a part of) the land upon which it is built.
- **Intangible personal property:** Your intangible personal property consists of financially oriented assets, such as your bank accounts, stocks, mutual funds, bonds, and your IRA.

TIP

Technically, that stock certificate or mutual fund statement isn't actually what you own; it represents your portion of the ownership of some company (in the case of the stock certificate) or your portion of that mutual fund in the companies' stocks in which it invests. Sound confusing? Don't worry — just keep in mind that financially oriented paper assets are typically intangible personal property, while actual possessions are tangible personal property. If you have any doubt as to what category any particular item of your possessions falls into, just ask one of your estate-planning team members.

Types of property interest

For each of the three types of property in your estate — real, tangible personal, and intangible personal — you also need to understand what your interest is.

"Of course, I'm interested in my property," you may be thinking. "After all, it's *my* property, isn't it?"

In the world of estate planning, *interest* has a somewhat different definition than how that word is used in everyday language, or even as the word is often used in the financial world (for example, interest that you earn on a CD or pay on a loan). And more importantly, the specific type of interest in any given property determines what you specifically need to be concerned about for your estate planning.

REMEMBER

Property interest is an essential part of almost all your estate planning, from the words that you put in your will (see Chapters 2 and 3 in Book 7) to how you may set up a trust, for two very important reasons:

- You need to clearly understand what type of interest you have in your property, so you can make accurate decisions about how to handle your property when you plan your estate.
- As you decide what to write in your will and perhaps also set up trusts as part of your estate plan, you need to make decisions about what type of interest in each property that you want to set up for your children, your spouse, other family members, or institutions such as charities.

The two main types of property interest are:

- Legal interest
- Beneficial interest

If you only have a *legal interest* in a property, you have the right to transfer or manage that property but you don't have the right to use the property yourself. For example, consider the very important (and very complicated) subject of trusts that may be an essential part of your estate planning. By way of a very brief introduction to that topic, when you set up a trust you name a *trustee* (a person who manages the trust).

Suppose you set up a trust for your oldest son, Alvin, as part of your estate plan, and you name your aunt, Jackie, as the trustee. Jackie isn't allowed to use Alvin's trust for her own benefit, such as withdrawing $10,000 for a trip to Paris. That's called "Aunt Jackie goes to jail for stealing!" Assuming Jackie does what she's supposed to do — and, more important, doesn't do what she's *not* supposed to do — Jackie has a legal interest in Alvin's trust as the trustee.

Unlike Aunt Jackie, Alvin has the other type of property interest in his trust: a *beneficial interest*, meaning that he *does* benefit from that trust. Basically, you set up that trust to benefit Alvin.

Now, to complicate matters a bit more, two "subtypes" of beneficial interest exist:

- Present interest
- Future interest

If you have a *present interest* (remember that means "present beneficial interest") you have the right to use the property immediately. So, if Alvin has a present interest in his trust that is managed by Aunt Jackie, he may receive payments of some specified amount — for example, $30,000 every three months — from the trust. After Alvin receives the money, he can do whatever he wants with it; the money is his to use, no strings attached.

The other type of beneficial interest — *future interest* — comes into play when someone with a beneficial interest (that person is allowed to benefit from the property) can't benefit right now, but instead must wait for some date in the future.

For example, you can set up the trust described to not only benefit Alvin, but also benefit your other two sons, Simon and Theodore. But you decide to take care of your three sons differently within that same trust. Suppose that after Alvin receives his quarterly $30,000 payments for five years, his payments will then stop, and Simon and Theodore will each begin receiving $30,000 quarterly payments. Essentially, Simon and Theodore have a future interest in the property (the trust) because they can't benefit right now; instead, they benefit in the future.

Complicating factors just a bit more (last time, we promise!), someone with a future interest in property can actually have one of two different types of future interest:

- Vested interest
- Contingent interest

If you have a *vested interest,* you have the right to use and enjoy what you will get from that property at some point in the future, with no strings attached.

TECHNICAL STUFF

In the world of estate planning, the word *vested* means basically the same as it does in the world of retirement plans, stock options, and other financial assets. After you're vested in your company's retirement plan, you have the right to receive retirement benefits according to the particulars of your company's plan, even if you leave your job. Similarly, if you have stock options that have vested, you have the right to "exercise" those options and buy your company's stock at your "strike price." Furthermore, if you want, you can immediately sell those shares for a quick profit if your company's stock price has gone way up.

However, if you have the other type of future beneficial interest — *contingent* — then you have to deal with some strings attached other than the simple passage of time. For example, you may set up that trust for your three sons in such a way that for Simon and Theodore to *realize* that future benefit, each must graduate from college and spend two years in the Peace Corps.

Why You Need to Plan Your Estate

You can, of course, decide to leave what happens to your estate after you die totally up to chance (or, more accurately, the complicated set of state laws that will apply if you haven't done the estate planning that you need to do). But because you're reading this book, chances are, the two fundamental goals of estate planning at the beginning of this chapter — protection and control — are uppermost in your mind.

Taking care of your loved ones and business

But going beyond the general idea of protecting your possessions and being in control, you have some very specific objectives that you're trying to accomplish with your estate planning, such as the following:

» **Providing for your loved ones:** You have people such as your spouse or significant other, children, grandchildren, and parents who may rely on you for financial support. What would happen to that financial support if you were to die tomorrow?

WARNING

Even if you have a "traditional" family (that is, the kind of family typically shown in a 1950s sitcom), financial and other support for family members after you die can get very complicated if your estate isn't in order. But if your family isn't exactly like the one in *Leave It to Beaver,* then you absolutely need to pay attention to all the little details of protecting your family members if you die. Specifically, if your loved ones include former spouses, children living in another household, stepchildren, adopted children, divorced and remarried parents, or an unmarried partner, then you have a lot of decisions to make with regard to your estate and who gets what.

» **Minimizing what your estate will have to pay in estate taxes:** Yes, we know that we said that estate planning involves much more than the inheritance and estate (death) taxes, but make no mistake about it, death taxes are certainly a consideration. Why pay more than you have to? You can take several steps — such as giving gifts while you're still alive — to reduce the value of your estate and, therefore, reduce the amount of death taxes that will have to be paid.

» **Protecting your business:** Politicians love to talk about the small business owner or the family farmer when describing how they're "a friend to the little guy," but the fact remains that if you own a small or medium-size business, such as a retail store or a farm, that business can be turned topsy-turvy if you die without a solid estate plan in place.

Sure, it's human nature to just let things happen. You're very busy with your career and your family. And after all, do you really want to dwell on morbid thoughts such as your own death?

But you really can't take any of your property with you, and you do leave behind people and institutions (charities, foundations, and so on) that you care about along with all your possessions. So, why wouldn't you want to take the time to appropriately match up your property with those people and institutions?

Besides, estate planning is as much about what you do during your life to manage your estate than what happens after you die. Sure, it makes good theater to have a deathbed scene where the aged family patriarch or matriarch dictates what will happen to the vast family fortune, but the place to begin your estate planning isn't on your deathbed! That last-minute approach usually opens up the probability of one or more disgruntled family members trying to overturn your dying words.

More than likely, due to the result of your lack of estate planning, your estate will dwindle away through legal fees and taxes in excess of what should have been paid.

And not to be morbid, but if you were to die suddenly and unexpectedly, you may not even have the "opportunity" for that dramatic deathbed scene. If you haven't done your estate planning, chances are, nobody in your family will have any idea what you want to happen to your estate.

Dealing with taxes

Need more? How about the game that the United States Congress is playing with the federal estate tax? As part of the estate tax laws, you have an *exclusion* — an amount that you may leave behind that is free of the federal estate tax. (The estate tax doesn't kick in until your estate exceeds the exclusion amount.)

Back in 2003, the federal estate tax exclusion had just been set at $1 million. In 2022, however, the estate tax exclusion (the amount of your estate that is protected from being taxed by the federal government) was much, much higher: $12.06 million for an individual and $24.12 million for a married couple! Even better, the estate tax exclusion will continue to increase indexed to inflation until 2026. And given the resurgence of inflation in the early 2020s, that annual exclusion increase will really help you out when it comes to protecting your estate from inflation.

WARNING

Beware though! In 2027, the *sunset* (a commonly used legal and financial term meaning "the end or expiration") of the Tax Cuts and Jobs Act of 2017 will cut those personal and married exclusions by a gigantic 50 percent — or even more because of indexing. This means that an estate that escapes taxes in 2026 because of the generous exclusion could find itself whacked by estate taxes in 2027. But wait, there's more.

In general, estate taxes are an important part of crafting your overall estate plan. But why should you care if your estate value is far below these exclusions? Well, just because the value of your estate is less than the federal tax exclusion levels *now*, or even after the 50 percent cut in 2027, that doesn't mean it always will be. Federal estate tax exclusions are a popular tax issue used as talking points by both Congress and the president as a way to increase tax revenue and make the "wealthy" pay their fair share.

A historical look at some of the estate tax exclusions over the last 20 years highlights that estate tax exclusion amounts are a moving target:

- $1 million in 2003
- $1.5 million in 2005
- $2 million in 2008
- $3.5 million in 2009
- $5 million in 2010

At first glance, it seems that the federal tax exclusions only increase — great news, right? — but the drumbeat continues in Washington to "roll back" these exclusions to much lower numbers. Do we hear $1 million? This is why estate taxes in general, and exclusion amounts in particular, matter so much and why you need to keep an eye on the current exclusions and changes to these exclusion amounts by Congress so you can adjust your estate plan for tax-planning purposes.

The main point for now is that for federal estate-tax purposes, your estate planning is actually a moving target between now and 2027. If you were to die between now (the time you're reading these words) and 2027, the amount of federal estate tax could be all over the map if your estate is very valuable. Now, most people won't try to work "Dying in a specific year" into their estate plans for the sole purpose of saving money on federal estate taxes. But the point is that you really need to stay on top of your estate-planning activities to try to minimize the amount of those taxes.

TIP

Another reason to plan your estate has to do with a mistake that many married couples make with their respective estates. Irrespective of the federal estate tax and varying exclusion amounts, you can leave an unlimited amount of your estate to your spouse free of federal estate taxes.

WARNING

However, sometimes you're better off *not* leaving your entire estate to your spouse, especially if your spouse also has a sizable estate (not only property jointly owned with you, but personal property that only your spouse owns). Why? Because then your spouse (assuming you die first) now has an even *larger* estate, which is then subject to a potentially larger tax liability than if you had done something else with your estate. Basically, your children or whoever else you and your spouse are leaving your respective estates to will likely be stuck paying more in federal estate taxes just because you decided to take the easy step with your estate and leave it all to your spouse.

Many states also impose inheritance and estate taxes that your estate pays in addition to federal estate taxes.

REMEMBER

The answer? You need to proactively conduct your estate planning, take all the matters in this section into consideration, and create a personalized estate plan.

Why Your Estate-Planning Goals Are Different from Your Neighbor's

You are unique.

No, the preceding statement isn't part of the latest feel-good pop psychology designed to boost your self-esteem. Instead, it's a point we want to emphasize to stress why you need to take time to create an individualized estate plan for your own situation. Your financial plan and retirement plans are specific to *your* individual circumstances and needs, right? Well, your estate plan is no different.

Many people finally and grudgingly acknowledge that they need to worry about their estate plans but then take a haphazard, lackadaisical approach to estate planning: a generic fill-in-the-blank will purchased in a stationery store, a cursory review of active insurance policies, and checking to see whose names are listed as beneficiaries on the retirement plan at work. But that's all — everything else will fall into place, right?

And besides, is it really worth putting in any more time and effort beyond those basic tasks? After all, you'll be dead. Why make all that effort for a series of events that will take place after you're gone?

But consider all the factors that make up many different aspects of your life, including the following:

- Your marital status (married, divorced, separated, single, widowed, or unmarried but living with someone)
- Your age
- Your health (Not to be excessively morbid, but if you know that you have a potentially fatal illness, or you're in generally poor health, time is of the essence for your estate planning.)
- Your *financial profile,* such as the property (real and personal) you have and what that property is worth

- Any potentially complicated business or financial situations you have, such as investment partnerships
- Any money you expect to receive — particularly large sums — such as an inheritance, lawsuit settlement, or severance pay from a job you're leaving
- What insurance policies you have, the types of insurance (see Book 2), and the value of each
- If any of your assets are particularly risky, such as stock or stock options in a start-up company that, on paper, is worth millions of dollars, but you can't do anything with those assets for some reason (for example, maybe your stock options haven't fully vested)
- If you have children and, if so, how many, their ages, their respective financial states, and their respective marital statuses
- If you have any grandchildren and, if so, if you want to explicitly take care of them as part of your estate planning or, alternatively, leave it to your children to take care of their own children as part of their own estate planning
- If your parents are still alive and, if so, whether they're still married to each other, if either may have remarried, their financial status (together or, if divorced, separately), and if you need to take care of them
- Your siblings and if you want or need to take care of them as part of your estate planning
- Any other family members (cousins, aunts, uncles, and so on) or even friends that you want to include in your estate planning
- Charities and foundations that you support

Just consider the items in this list — not to mention dozens of others that you can probably think of — and the answers for you and your life. Sure, somewhere in the United States, you can probably find someone else with more or less the same profile as yours, but the point is that no estate plan is a one-size-fits-all plan that you can effortlessly adapt to your situation.

Additionally, even a canned plan that seems to be suitable for your situation may actually be a poor choice after you really dig into the details. Think of the outfit that looks great in an ad but, when you try it on, something just doesn't look or feel right.

REMEMBER

We strongly recommend that you make your credo for estate planning "No shortcuts allowed!" The time, effort, and even expense that you put into developing a solid, comprehensive estate plan will be well rewarded. True, you won't necessarily be alive to fully see the benefits of your efforts, but those people who you care about enough to include in your estate plan likely will be grateful!

The Critical Path Method to Planning Your Estate

Estate planning is a process that can be further divided into multiple steps or activities. Whether in business or in life itself (planning a wedding, for example), most processes tend to take days, weeks, months, or even years from start to finish; rarely does any process happen overnight. All these elements take planning.

You need to treat your estate-planning activities as a process. The process includes a disciplined method created from a set of steps that lead you from a state of *estate-planning nothingness* (that is, you have no estate plan at all) to the point where you have a well-thought-out estate plan in place. We recommend using the *critical path method* to planning your estate.

TECHNICAL STUFF

If you've taken a college business class in operations research, quantitative methods, or a similar topic, you may already be familiar with the critical path method, which is defined as "the most effective way through a series of steps to reach your objectives." In other words, even when you have a seemingly infinite number of possible paths in front of you, you can find one particular path that is the most effective and efficient of all those alternatives.

In estate planning, you're often faced with many side roads when working on your will or setting up a trust. Before you know it, the side road has turned into a detour and your estate plan is in a state equivalent to your car being stuck up to its lug nuts in mud. (If you're automotively challenged, the previous sentence means you aren't going anywhere anytime soon.)

TIP

If the terms *operations research* and *quantitative methods* cause shudders and tremors as you flash back to college courses that you barely passed, simply think of the critical path method as a map. If you're standing on a corner in Winslow, Arizona, and you want to go to Phoenix, Arizona, you can get in your car and, after checking a map, drive approximately 190 miles of interstate highway. Or maybe you don't know the area very well and you're one of those people who never checks a map, so you get in your car and just start driving. First, you head to Los Angeles, then you drive up to San Francisco, then maybe you go over to Chicago, then back to Denver, and then you drive toward Phoenix. ("By the time I get to Phoenix, she'll be on Social Security.")

Anyway, the critical path method is fairly straightforward and includes the following steps:

1. **Define your goals.**

   Before you begin your estate planning, decide what you're trying to achieve. Are you trying to make sure that your spouse has enough income for some period of time (say, five years, or maybe longer) if you were to die suddenly? Are you trying to make sure that your children have enough money for college after you're gone? Is your estate worth upwards of $10 million, and are you trying to protect as much as possible from the eventual federal estate-tax bite?

   As we mention earlier in this chapter, your estate-planning goals are almost certainly different from anyone else's, so make sure you take the time to define exactly what those goals are.

   TIP

   Write down your goals — don't just think about them. Often by actually writing your goals rather than just visualizing them, you get a better handle on how your goals relate to one another, and you make sure that you haven't forgotten anything.

2. **Determine which estate-planning professionals you want to work with.**

   Financial planners, insurance agents, attorneys, and accountants (all of whom we discuss in the next section) can provide valuable guidance and service to you. You need to determine which professionals best help you meet your goals. For example, have an attorney work with you on your will to be sure you meet all your own state's requirements for the will to be legally binding. You may also decide to work with other professionals depending on the complexity of your estate and the particular goals you defined in the previous step.

3. **Gather information.**

   Whether you work with professionals or not (more on this particular decision point in the next section), you need to have as much available information as possible so you know where you are currently in your estate-planning process. You need to ask yourself the following questions:

   1. Do you have a will right now and, if so, when did you prepare that will?
   2. What in your life has changed since you created that will?
   3. What insurance policies do you currently have?
   4. Have any insurance policies expired?
   5. Perhaps most important, what property is in your estate and what is the value of that property?

4. **Develop your action plan.**

   Basically, get ready to do many different activities: Work on your will (create your will if you don't have one, or perhaps update your will if the will is out of date); decide if trusts make sense for you and, if so, choose which ones; figure out what you need to do to protect your business; and so on.

5. **Actually conduct your action plan.**

   People often trip up on this step during their estate planning (or anything else they like to procrastinate on). Take the plans that you developed in Step 4 and actually do them! If you die without a will, complications may arise even if someone in your family finds a sheet of paper on your desk that reads "Step 4: Prepare my will."

6. **Monitor your action plan.**

   You may like going through all the previous estate-planning steps, finishing them, and then just forgetting about them all. But in estate planning, you never really finish. You periodically need to resynchronize your estate plan with any major changes in your life. For example, have you gotten divorced and remarried? You'd better get cracking on those updates! Even less dramatic changes in your life can trigger changes, so your best bet is to double-check everything in your estate plan once a year so you can make sure that all changes to your life, great and small, are reflected in your estate planning in a timely fashion.

   TIP

   You can even tie your "checkup" to an annual occurrence, like your birthday, or the first of the year, or to some other occasion that you won't easily forget. Just add a recurring calendar reminder to your calendar app so you remember.

By following these steps and staying on the critical path, you greatly reduce the chances of taking all kinds of unnecessary and potentially serious detours with your estate planning, and you can typically get through the tasks with a minimum amount of stress.

TIP

Take the initiative to meet with each member of your estate-planning team annually. Or ask someone on the team to remind you annually to review your estate plans — the way your dentist reminds you to come in for a checkup.

Getting Help with Your Estate Planning

You can do all your estate planning by yourself, but you don't have to and, even more importantly, we don't recommend that approach. But can you turn to someone with a job title along the lines of *professional estate planner* for help?

Not exactly. As we mention several times in this chapter, estate planning actually consists of several different specialties or disciplines, and if you want, you can work with one or more people in each of those specialties as part of your estate planning.

The number of people with whom you work largely depends on two main factors:

- How comfortable you are with the overall concepts and mechanics of estate planning
- How complicated your estate is

The material covered in Book 7 can go a long way toward helping you with the first of those two factors. But even if you thoroughly understand little nuances of the clauses to include in your will (see Chapter 2 in Book 7) or the basic types of trusts, you may still want to tap into a network of professionals if your estate is particularly complicated. Sure, you'll spend a bit more money on fees, but in the long run, you're more likely to avoid a horrendously costly mistake (financially, emotionally, or both), particularly if your estate is rather complicated.

Making sure your team is "FAIL" safe

TIP

So, who do you work with? Here's an acronym to help you remember who you need to think about for your estate-planning team: FAIL, which stands for:

- Financial planner
- Accountant
- Insurance agent
- Lawyer

The order of the professionals in this list doesn't indicate any type of priority (that is, your financial planner isn't more important than your accountant) or any type of sequence (such as you must work with your accountant before you work with your insurance agent). The order shown is solely for the purposes of the FAIL acronym to help you remember these different professions and how they may help you.

TIP

You don't necessarily need a full slate of estate-planning professionals on your team. You may, for example, work with your lawyer and accountant. But if you've decided that insurance is only a minimal part of your overall estate plan, then you may not need to work with an insurance agent. Or if you're well versed in investments and financial planning, then you can handle that aspect of your estate plan by yourself and work with team members from the other specialization areas.

STRAIGHT TALK

You need to talk candidly and honestly about personal and sometimes sensitive — or even painful — matters with your estate-planning team. The last thing you want is for your insurance agent to recommend a certain type of insurance policy that the issuing insurance company could invalidate because you hid some important fact that was later found out. And your lawyer needs to thoroughly understand all aspects of your relationships with your family to help you create a will that accurately reflects your wishes. For example, if you really want to cut someone out of your will and leave that person nothing at all, make sure that your lawyer knows that so your will can be constructed appropriately.

WARNING

The best professionals sometimes set things into motion that can have unintentional and less-than-desirable consequences if another member of your estate-planning team isn't aware of what was done. For example, you need to be certain that you understand all the tax implications — federal income, state income, gift, estate, and so on — of a trust that your financial planner recommends and that your attorney sets up. Therefore, your accountant needs to work side-by-side with your lawyer and your financial planner before the trust is created to be sure that no unpleasant tax surprises pop up.

Hiring a financial-planning professional

Because a significant portion of your estate is likely to involve your investments and savings, consider working with some type of financial-planning professional. You can work with a financial-planning professional solely on an advisory basis. If you want, you can make your own decisions about your investments and savings, after consulting with a professional. Your financial-planning professional also can play a much more active role, such as making major decisions for your financial life (with your consent, of course).

Before you decide to work with any financial-planning professional, you need to understand just who these people are, what type of formal training and credentials they have, and how using them relates to your estate planning. All financial-planning professionals aren't created equal, nor do they necessarily have the same background and qualifications.

Certified Financial Planners

Certified Financial Planners (CFPs) provide financial-planning services and general financial advice on a wide range of topics from investments to taxes and from estate planning to retirement planning. CFPs are required to pass college-level courses in a broad range of financial subjects and then a two-day, ten-hour examination. CFPs must also have a bachelor's degree and at least three years of professional experience working with financial-planning clients *or*, without a degree, they must have at least five years of experience doing financial planning.

TIP

You can check with the Financial Planning Association at `www.financialplanningassociation.org` and search for planners by state, city, or zip code. You can find financial planners who have the CFP credentials. You can then verify a planner's CFP status with the CFP Board of Standards at `www.letsmakeaplan.org`. Just enter your location, and the site gives you not just names, but also the specific services they offer — estate planning, tax planning, insurance planning, and so on.

You can regularly check *Money* (`https://money.com`), Kiplinger (`www.kiplinger.com`), and other personal finance publications for the latest information, and even problems and scandals in the profession. Searching online reviews for someone you're thinking about working with is a good way to get an overall consensus about the good, and less good, points about working with a specific financial professional.

Other financial-planning professionals

If your financial life is particularly complicated, you may need to work with several types of financial-planning professionals in addition to a basic financial planner (who may or may not be a CFP).

- Another type of financial-planning professional is the *investment adviser* (IA) or the *registered investment adviser* (RIA). IAs and RIAs specifically advise their clients about securities (stocks, bonds, and so on). Any IA who manages at least $25 million in assets must register with the Securities and Exchange Commission (SEC), and you can check this information out at `https://adviserinfo.sec.gov`.
- *Chartered Financial Analysts* (CFAs) are typically portfolio managers or analysts for banks, mutual funds, or other institutional clients (in Wall Street lingo), but some CFAs also advise wealthy individuals and families who have particularly complicated investment situations. CFAs take a series of examinations covering portfolio management, accounting, equity analysis, and other subjects, and must have at least three years of professional experience in investments. CFAs are also required to sign an ethics pledge every year.
- A *Certified Fund Specialist* (CFS) works with clients on mutual funds. (Some CFSs also provide general financial-planning services.) Examinations and continuing education are required to retain CFS status.

How financial-planning professionals are paid

WARNING

Make sure you clearly understand how your financial-planning professional — CFP or otherwise — gets paid! Some financial-planning professionals get paid on a "fee-only" basis, meaning that they don't receive any commissions for selling you financial products. They're only compensated for advice (basically, they're consultants).

Fee-based financial-planning professionals earn fees not only from the advice they give you, but also from commissions for selling you financial products, while commission-based financial-planning professionals only make money from the products they sell you.

You can certainly find both ethical and unethical people (not to mention competent and incompetent) in either of these categories. However, always pay particular attention to recommendations from fee-based or commission-based financial-planning professionals. Perhaps those investment choices are the perfect match for you, but you need to make that decision, not your financial-planning professional who stands to benefit financially from selling you some type of product.

Knowing what to expect from your accountant for your estate planning

Your accountant can do a lot more for you than fill out your tax returns for the previous year. Businesses use accountants for planning purposes — trying to steer what happens in the future for tax purposes by doing certain steps today. You can work with an accountant on your estate planning for those very same reasons, even if you do your own income taxes and haven't really worked with an accountant before.

Make sure the accountant on your estate-planning team presents you with scenarios of what will likely happen, based on recommendations from other members of your estate-planning team. If your CFP recommends certain investments or insurance products, then what are the tax implications when you die? What are the tax implications if you die tomorrow versus dying ten years from now?

Your accountant can also play a more active role in your estate planning, suggesting certain tactics with an eye toward reducing your overall estate-tax burden, giving gifts in particular.

WARNING

Never do any financial gift giving (as contrasted with birthday gift giving or holiday gift giving) without consulting with an accountant for all the tax implications.

Seek out an accountant who is a Certified Public Accountant (CPA), meaning that the accountant has passed the American Institute of Certified Public Accountants (AICPA) examination.

TIP

You may also consider combining two of the roles on your estate-planning team — the financial-planning and accounting specialists — by working with someone who is a Certified Public Accountant/Personal Financial Specialist (CPA/PFS). In other words, find a CPA who also provides overall financial planning and has passed the PFS exam.

Including your insurance agent

Depending on your particular estate-planning needs, various forms of insurance (life, disability, liability, and other types we discuss in Book 2) may play a key role. Most people who have dependents (particularly a spouse and children) wind up working insurance into their estate plan to meet the "protection" objective of estate planning.

So, consider your insurance agent a part of your estate-planning team. For example, when you discuss life insurance and choose among different types of life insurance policies (see Chapter 3 in Book 2), make sure that your insurance agent is aware of any estate-planning strategies, such as trusts, so you can make sure that your policy beneficiaries are listed correctly.

TIP

Some insurance companies are *agentless*, meaning that, unlike traditional insurance companies, where you have an assigned insurance agent, your contact with the company is through any one of hundreds or even thousands of customer service representatives, almost always over the phone or online. In these situations, ask one of the customer service representatives whether you can speak with or even work with anyone at the company on estate-planning matters. Chances are, the representative will say yes, so even though you don't technically have an insurance agent, you may still have access to short-term estate-planning assistance when you need it.

Working with your attorney

Even though your attorney is last on the list of the members of your estate-planning team (courtesy of the *L* for *lawyer* that we use in our *FAIL* acronym), they could quite possibly be the most important member for one simple reason: Your attorney keeps you from inadvertently making very serious mistakes!

All kinds of problems can trip you up and cause serious headaches in the future (if not headaches for *you*, because you've already died, then headaches for someone you care about). For example:

- How should your will read to make sure that your significant other (to whom you are not married) receives what you want out of your estate?
- How should the deed to your home be written to make sure that your unmarried significant other isn't forced to move if you die first?
- If you have an elderly parent who needs to go into a nursing home, what are the implications to your parent's estate and your own?

Basically, think of your attorney as your scenario-planning specialist. Your attorney takes all kinds of information about you and your estate into consideration. They then present you with options, based on various scenarios, such as your dying suddenly next week (morbid, but definitely an eye-opener for many people when first doing their estate planning) versus your dying at the ripe old age of 134 (courtesy of advanced biotechnology), having outlived everyone else in your family.

Beyond the scenario planning, make your attorney your primary advisor for your will, trusts, legal implications for your business, and pretty much any other legal matter that directly or indirectly relates to your estate planning.

REMEMBER

Don't worry about being overwhelmed by estate-planning legal definitions. It's more important to understand the concepts than worry about learning legal jargon. If you're working with a good estate-planning team, your attorney can handle all the legalese and make sure all your estate documents reflect the proper clauses and conditions, which, in turn, reflect your wishes for your estate.

IN THIS CHAPTER

» Getting your ducks in a row for your will

» Looking at different types and clauses of wills

» Keeping your will safe and making changes down the road

» Ensuring that what you specify in your will remains in effect after you're gone

» Understanding what your current will status is and what the implications are

Chapter 2
Where There's a Will

Your will is the number-one legal weapon you have at your disposal to make sure that your estate is divided and distributed according to your wishes after you die. Basically, think of your will as your voice from beyond the grave to make it absolutely clear who will receive your assets, and to prevent unintended and unpleasant side effects to your well-thought-out estate plan.

But sometimes the best-laid plans of mice and men (well, make that women and men — we've never seen a mouse that has a will) are thwarted by selecting a type of will that is inappropriate or inadequate for the particulars of a given estate or by leaving out key wording that is necessary to make a will valid. And sometimes your will can be 100 percent perfect for you and your estate at one point in your life, but you neglect to keep your will up to date with changes in your life. By not keeping your will updated, your estate and the people you want to take care of after you die can have serious troubles.

You must also take care to keep your will very "matter of fact." You may have seen movies or TV shows where someone uses a will as a from-the-grave statement of love, hate, indifference, generosity, stinginess, or some other emotion. If you use your will in that fashion (something like "To my eldest son, who has always disappointed me his entire life, who never sent me any cards, who married someone I despise, I leave absolutely nothing"), you open the door to all kinds of problems. You can make a mistake in your wording choice that can cause your will to be invalid. Even if your will is letter-perfect, you can open emotional wounds and cause psychological scars that could take years (and lots of expensive therapy!) to overcome. So, in your will, you should stick to — like the detectives on *Dragnet* used to say — "just the facts!"

In this chapter, we focus on the basics of wills necessary to ensure that your will is the most appropriate for your wishes and needs and that your wishes will be carried out.

Planning for Your Will

REMEMBER

We advise that you work with your attorney to create and take care of the technical and legal details of your will. Even the simplest, most straightforward wills are filled with legal terminology. Your attorney has likely prepared hundreds or even thousands of wills. Why not leave the details to someone for whom the legal-speak and technicalities are second nature?

WARNING

You'll find a significant proliferation of prepackaged wills available online. The main selling point to this quick-and-easy, fill-in-the-blanks approach to wills (and trusts) is their relatively low cost — that's why you'll see catchy taglines such as "$99 for All Your Estate Planning Documents." These ready-to-go documents may serve a purpose in some *very* basic estate planning, but as soon as you run across specifics from *your* estate planning that aren't easily met by the off-the-shelf approach, you probably need to shift your focus to having an attorney handle your will. (See the later sidebar "How about a preprinted, ready-to-fill-in will?" in this chapter.)

But before your attorney starts putting anything on paper for your will, you need to consult with them to determine what your major objectives are. Be sure to specifically discuss the following items:

- **What your tax exposure situation is based on your estate's value:** Your estate may have to pay federal estate tax and any state estate or inheritance tax if your estate is worth more than the allowance at which taxes are owed. Your will needs to reflect your overall estate planning, including your tax planning, so both you and your attorney need to clearly understand all tax implications to your estate.

» **Who you want to explicitly take care of:** You can write your will in many different ways to outline to whom you want to give what portions of your estate. However, you need to have a general idea of which family members you want to take care of, such as:
  - Your spouse and children
  - All your children (including adopted children and stepchildren)
  - Only some of your children
  - All your children and all your grandchildren
  - All your children and your brothers and sisters
  - Your parents and your brothers and sisters
  - Only two of your four children and all except one of your sisters
  - Your pets (you can reference "any pets that I have at the time of my death" as a catchall to cover all your future pets)

» **Whether you want some part of your estate (or even all of your estate) to go to one or more charities, foundations, or other institutions:** Later in this chapter, we discuss different ways in which you can divide up your estate among those you want to include in your will.

TIP

The first time you sit down with your attorney, make sure to talk about the value of your estate, the individuals (family members and others) and institutions you want to leave your estate to, and *continuity of care* concerns such as long-term care at home or facility care such as independent living, assisted living, and nursing home concerns. Your attorney will then clearly understand your motivation and can help you prepare a will that accurately reflects your situation and preferences.

BENEFICIARIES VERSUS HEIRS: WHAT'S THE DIFFERENCE?

One of the primary purposes of creating a will is to financially take care of your *beneficiaries*. However, if you fail to properly prepare your will, your *heirs* may wind up with less than expected, or maybe with nothing at all. Legal double-talk? Not exactly. People (such as your family members and friends) and institutions (such as charities) that you take care of in your will are called *beneficiaries*. However, if you don't have a will — or don't have a valid will, as we discuss later in this chapter — the individuals who benefit from your estate are determined by state law and are usually called *heirs* (or *heirs at law*).

In layman's language, the terms *beneficiary* and *heir* are often used interchangeably. However, the two words technically have a significant distinction.

Getting to Know the Different Types of Wills

Before you even think about what wording you should put in your will, you first need to decide which of several types of wills is right for you. The good news is that you can usually stop your search for the perfect type of will with the first type we discuss: the simple will. However, you should be familiar with the other types in case your attorney advises that some unique aspect of your estate makes one of these other types more appropriate.

Simple wills

Almost always, a *simple will* is the will of choice for you. A simple will is a single legal document that applies only to you (unlike a *joint will* for you and your spouse, which we discuss briefly in the next section).

A simple will describes:

- Who you are, with enough information to clearly identify that document as your will.
- The names of your beneficiaries, both people (whether those people are family members or not) and institutions (such as charities), and enough information about the beneficiaries (such as their birth dates to distinguish among multiple family members with the same name, for example) so whoever is reading your will can figure out to whom you're referring.
- The name of the person who you're appointing to be the *executor* of your will. The executor — also called a *personal representative* — is the person who is legally responsible for making sure that your directions are carried out. You also need to appoint a backup executor — or maybe even a backup to the backup — if, for any reason, your designated executor is unable to perform the official duties (sounds like the Miss America Pageant!).

  TIP

  Always check with whoever you specify as an executor or backup executor in your will before putting that person's name in your will. You want to avoid unnecessary complications that may arise if that person is unwilling or unable to serve as your will's executor.
- Your directions as to who will care for your children, pets, or anyone else you're legally responsible for.
- How you want your assets distributed, and to whom, after you're gone.

Your simple will should be *typewritten* (a term that comes from the days of old-fashioned typewriters but that also applies to a printed and produced document by a computer and printer). Other forms of your will, such as those written in your own handwriting or spoken (we discuss both forms briefly in the next section), usually have problems and should be avoided.

Other types of wills

You have other options for your will besides the simple, typewritten will we discuss in the preceding section. Other choices, along with the drawbacks of each, include the following:

- **Joint will:** A single legal document that applies to two people (you and your spouse, for example). Some married couples mistakenly think that they're required to have a joint will or that a joint will is better for them than two simple wills. Indeed, a single joint will may be less expensive to have prepared than two simple wills. However, joint wills are usually a bad idea.

  WARNING

  The primary problem is that most courts treat a joint will as a form of a *contractual will,* which is a will or contract that is irrevocable and can't be changed after one party dies. Therefore, if your spouse dies first and you want to revise the contents of your joint will for estate planning or tax purposes, you probably can't. Joint wills can be problematic, because the death of a spouse can cause a change in your circumstances and how you want to leave your estate to your loved ones. Don't even think about a joint will unless your attorney suggests that some particularly unique aspect of your situation makes a joint will advisable, and then ask your attorney to explain, explain, and explain some more!

- **Mutual will:** A legal document you can use to coordinate your estate planning with someone else, such as your brother. For example, suppose you and your brother want to leave a substantial amount of money to be split among two charities — Charity A and Charity B — that both of you have supported for many years. You can create mutual wills in which:

  - No matter which one of you dies first, 75 percent of either your estate or that of your sibling goes to Charity A, with 20 percent going to Charity B and 5 percent going to some other beneficiary.
  - When the other one of you dies, 50 percent of that person's estate goes to Charity B, with 30 percent going to Charity A and 20 percent designated for some other beneficiary.

  Basically, because you don't have a crystal ball to tell you and your sibling which one of you will die first (and even if you did, would you really want to know?), you both set things up so no matter what happens, Charity A receives a larger amount of money first than Charity B does.

If you think a mutual will is particularly suitable for some unique aspect of your estate, ask your attorney and then proceed with caution.

- **Holographic will:** The technical term for a handwritten will. A holographic will is handwritten and signed by you. A handwritten will doesn't require an attorney to be involved when you prepare this form of will. However, only some states recognize a holographic will as valid, which means that you may think you have a valid will, but in fact you don't.
- **Nuncupative will:** A technical term used to describe a spoken will and has nothing to do with Sister Maria or any of the other nuns from *The Sound of Music.* (Everybody sing along: "How do you solve a problem like Maria's estate planning?") Even though creating a nuncupative will is extremely easy — all you have to do is talk and have someone present to listen — you have many complications and limitations. Some states only allow people who are on their death beds (literally!) — about to die any minute — to use nuncupative wills for last-minute expressions of what they want done with part of their estates. Some states allow only certain types of property or property only up to a certain dollar amount to be transferred with a nuncupative will.

WARNING

Don't use any of the preceding nonstandard types and forms of wills — or any others that may arise in the future.

Choosing Your Will's Contents

Your will is composed of a number of *clauses* that when put together into a single legal document, accurately and precisely represent your wishes for your estate. The clauses in your will fall into three categories:

- **Opening clauses:** These clauses provide basic information about you and also lay the groundwork for the other clauses in your will that follow.
- **Giving clauses:** These clauses follow the opening clauses and comprise the main body of your will, in which your who-gets-what-part-of-my-estate strategy is specified.
- **Ending clauses:** These clauses help to make your will valid by making sure that all statutory requirements have been met.

REMEMBER

However, just like you put together a bicycle, bake blueberry muffins, or do anything else in which you need to combine parts or ingredients together, you need to make sure of three points:

- That you select the right parts or ingredients — or in the case of your will — the right clauses
- That you put those parts, ingredients, or clauses together in the right order, with the right number of each to make sure that the finished product is what you intend it to be
- That you've spent time *seriously* thinking about what you want because these thoughts are the foundation to create your will

If you leave out or mess up just a single essential clause, you can completely change your intentions or even make your will invalid. And because clauses can get very technical with all kinds of legal terminology, have a professional, such as your attorney, prepare your will for you. (See the nearby sidebar "How about a preprinted, ready-to-fill-in will?")

HOW ABOUT A PREPRINTED, READY-TO-FILL-IN WILL?

Many do-it-yourself preprinted will forms are available, and some people use them to save money (as compared to meeting with an attorney and having a will created from scratch). The proliferation of online wills and TV ads for wills costing less than a grocery shopping trip may seem enticing as a shortcut. Chances are, though, your individual needs require you to customize your will to some extent, meaning that in most cases, preprinted will forms won't be quite right for you, even though many of these will forms are advertised as suitable for complicated situations.

Therefore, you most likely have to do at least some customization if you use a preprinted will form. As soon as you begin customizing, you open up the possibility of all kinds of problems. Why? First, you need to be sure that you're satisfying legal requirements specific to your own state; otherwise, your will may not be valid. If you're going to put the time and effort into preparing your will, you certainly want the finished result to be legally binding.

Second, you're better off starting to work on your will with a clean slate rather than preprinted boilerplate language; doing so actually forces you to decide what to include in your will.

(continued)

(continued)

However, if you think that your specific situation is so uncomplicated that a preprinted will form may do the trick — and you really are trying to spend as little money as possible on your will and your estate planning — then we recommend that you at least get an attorney to look over your filled-in will form after you complete it and to advise you if the finished document may have any problems. If you have limited financial resources, you can usually obtain low-cost or even no-cost basic legal assistance within your community; just check around.

Opening clauses

Think of the opening clauses of your will as a preamble in which you provide some basic information to set up the giving clauses that follow. Your will's opening clauses include the following:

- An introductory clause that
  - Clearly identifies you as the maker of the will
  - Explicitly states that you created this document of your own free will (this part is where you write "being of sound mind," as in the movies)
  - Explicitly states that any wills you previously created are no longer valid
- A family statement clause, in which your family members referenced later in your will are introduced
- A tax clause — the structure of your will needs to align with your overall tax strategy for your estate. You can include a tax clause to specifically state how you want taxes to be paid — often out of the *residuary* (everything else) part of your estate, as we discuss later in this chapter. But if you want to specify some other tax strategy in your will, you use the tax clause to state how you want taxes to be paid, by whom, and from what part of your estate

TIP

Your attorney likely has a favorite way of preparing opening clauses, based on hundreds or thousands of wills they've prepared. Still, before your attorney starts writing anything for your will, make sure to discuss your overall strategy. Don't be afraid to speak up, ask questions, and decide what *you* want — this is *your* will, not your attorney's will.

Giving clauses

The heart of your will may contain the giving clauses in which you specify as precisely as possible how your estate is to be divided among your beneficiaries.

In general, you can take one of three different approaches to how you want your estate divided and how the contents of your will's giving clauses will be written:

- You can be extremely general.
- You can be extremely explicit and detailed.
- You can be very explicit about part of your estate and very general about the rest of your estate.

The simplest approach you can take for your will is to basically lump all or almost all your property together, identify the beneficiaries who will share that property, and simply leave all that property to the entire group of beneficiaries to be divided up equally. For example, if you have an estate worth $500,000 that is comprised primarily of bank accounts and stock; your spouse has died before you; you live in a rented apartment and no longer own a home; and you want to divide your estate up equally among your four children, all of whom are still alive, then you can take the be-extremely-general approach and just leave that $500,000 worth of property to all your children, each of whom will get an equal share of your estate.

But suppose you have an estate worth $3 million, a significant portion of which is made up of collectible cars and several vacation homes? And suppose you not only have two living children from your third (and current) wife, but also seven living children from previous marriages, not to mention several stepchildren? And what if you not only want all these children and stepchildren to share in your estate, but also your two sisters, but not your two brothers?

In this example, you must be as explicit as possible in your will about who will receive specific property from your estate. Which child will receive the 1955 Thunderbird? Who will get the 1967 Corvette, and who will get the 1965 Pontiac GTO? Should your sister who works at Apple get your Apple stock and your other sister who works at Tesla get your Tesla stock, or should you give your Apple stock to your sister who works at Tesla and your Tesla stock to your Apple-employed sister to help each sister diversify their respective portfolios? Should Peter Piper pick a peck of pickled peppers and a woodchuck chuck wood, or in the interest of diversification should Peter Piper chuck wood and that woodchuck do the pickled pepper picking? (Just kidding about that last part.)

The third strategy for your giving clauses — somewhere in between very explicit and very general — can be useful if you want to divide most of your estate equally among your children, but you still want to explicitly leave other smaller amounts of your estate to your grandchildren, parents, brothers and sisters, a favorite niece or nephew, or a charity.

So, regardless of which of the three strategies you want to follow, how do you use your will's giving clauses to make it all happen? You can use:

- Real property clauses
- Personal property clauses for intangible and tangible property
- Residuary clause
- Appointment and fiduciary powers clauses

Real property clauses

Your real property — for most people, their home — is often the most significant asset in terms of dollar value that you leave to your loved ones — quite possibly far more valuable than all your personal property put together.

If you want to explicitly leave real property to one or more beneficiaries, you use a *real property clause*, which is a straightforward statement that reveals who is to receive your real property, identifies the property to which you're referring, and names who is to get that property.

WARNING

Often, homes are left to loved ones with the intent to retain the family legacy and continue building generational memories: "This was your grandparents' house, and it will be yours someday, too." The reality is that the real property you leave may not be something that your loved ones have interest in keeping, not to mention take on all the expenses associated with the property — real estate taxes, property insurance, and general upkeep. The real estate taxes alone, especially in coastal cities, can cost tens of thousands of dollars annually, even if that ancestral family home is fully paid off. Just keep in mind that your beneficiaries may not be able to retain the property you want to keep in the family and may sell the property. If you discuss this with your loved ones ahead of time, you can save everybody a lot of heartache (not to mention the guilt over selling your parents' home, which may have been your childhood home) and time by explicitly having your executor sell your house upon your death and distributing the proceeds to your beneficiaries as you predetermine.

Personal property clauses

If you're following the be-very-explicit strategy for your will, then your will must contain personal property clauses specifying what will happen to both your intangible and tangible personal property. In the case of your intangible personal property, such as your stocks and bonds, you can specify who your Apple stock goes to, who your Tesla stock goes to, and who gets your collection of nonfungible tokens (NFTs).

Even though you plan to utilize the partly-general-and-partly-explicit will strategy, you can still use a personal property clause to identify some stock or other intangible personal property that you want to go to someone different. For example, if you're leaving the majority of your $750,000 estate to be divided among your children, but you want to leave each of your five grandchildren $10,000, you can use this strategy.

For your tangible personal property, you can divide up your personal items among your beneficiaries. Very often, you want to specify what will happen to sentimental, small-in-monetary-value-but-large-in-heart-value (whew!) items, such as your grandmother's antique quilt or your great-great-great-great-grandfather's diary that he carried through the Civil War.

The residuary clause

Technically, your will's *residuary clause* covers the leftovers in your estate that you didn't explicitly mention in real property clauses or personal property clauses. The residuary clause gives you and your will a safety net in case you forget to specifically identify some part of your estate in your will. Think of it as an asset catchall clause.

DON'T FORGET YOUR DIGITAL ASSETS

You need to keep in mind any digital assets, why they're different from your other assets, and how to account for them in your will. It isn't sufficient to just list any digital assets you own — Bitcoin, other cryptocurrencies, NFTs, or any other blockchain assets in your will. You need a detailed game plan, because your beneficiaries will need to know not only that you *have* these digital assets, but also how to find and access them. The unique nature of these assets is that they're stored in digital wallets with passwords, private keys, personal identification numbers, codes, or other security protection.

Create a *digital assets memorandum* (DAM) as an accompanying document to your will. You should state in your will that your digital assets information is contained in the DAM that is stored with your other estate planning documentation. As a separate document from your will, you control who sees the DAM's confidential information. The DAM should include specific details and step-by-step instructions on the digital assets, where they're located, how to find them, and any and all passwords or other security measures required to obtain them. Pretend your executor knows nothing about digital assets (which they may not) and explain everything in simple, basic terms. If your instructions are like trying to find the elusive "Where's Waldo" (as in, really difficult to find), redo them in simpler terms.

REMEMBER

Your estate can change over time, and if you haven't updated your will lately, you may have some particular item (often tangible personal property, such as a valuable painting you may have recently acquired) unaccounted for. This is more common than you would think, so the residuary clause is an important clause to include in your will.

However, you can use your will's residuary clause for far more than just the leftovers (actually, your entire estate or the majority of your estate) if your will strategy is to be as general as possible. You simply don't use any other giving clauses to explicitly mention real or personal property (as we describe earlier), which forces your estate into being covered by the residuary clause.

Or if you want to take that in-between approach to your will, you can use specific giving clauses for whatever real property and personal property you explicitly want to give to someone and use a residuary clause to cover everything else.

REMEMBER

No matter what your will strategy is, don't forget to include a residuary clause! Even though you may want your will to be as explicit as possible, you'll almost always have property in your estate that falls into the leftovers category. Make sure to designate one or more beneficiaries to receive those leftovers.

Appointment and fiduciary powers clauses

The section of your will that includes your giving clauses also contains some additional clauses that actually don't have anything to do with how your estate will be divided. You use the *appointment clause* to name the person you've chosen to manage your estate. At the time you prepare your will, you need to decide who you feel is the best person to handle your estate and act as your *personal representative* after you die.

The *fiduciary powers clause* is a companion clause to the appointment clause that gives you the ability to provide your personal representative with powers beyond what may be available in your state statutes.

For example, use the fiduciary powers clause to specify that your personal representative will provide your children with some amount of income on an interim basis until your estate is settled. Another way you can use the fiduciary powers clause is to allow your personal representative to continue operating your solely owned business that still provides income to your estate.

Ending clauses

After you complete the most difficult part of your will — the giving clauses portion, which should reflect your overall will strategy — you need to finish up your work with your ending clauses that include the *signature clause.* The signature clause is where you date and sign your will.

Your will's witnesses also sign the will along with appropriate language that indicates that they witnessed you signing your will and that you executed the will voluntarily and did so of your own free will. (In other words, you weren't coerced or perhaps unconscious with a devious family member putting a pen in your hand to make you "sign" your will. Hey, this would make a good storyline for a movie.)

REMEMBER

Make sure that your will's witnesses are *disinterested parties* who are not beneficiaries in your will.

TECHNICAL STUFF

Most states recognize that a will can be *self-proved,* which is a method of avoiding the requirement of producing witnesses at the time of probate to prove the validity of the signature of the *decedent* (the person who died). In the usual case (with a "non-self-proved will"), the person making the will simply signs the will in the presence of witnesses, who also then sign their names as witnesses. In a self-proved will, however, the signature of the person making the will is acknowledged in addition to being witnessed, and the witnesses also execute affidavits. The necessity of providing witnesses at the time of probate is, therefore, avoided.

Safeguarding Your Will

Here's a quick quiz, and the answer may surprise you: On what single point about wills are estate-planning professionals more likely to passionately disagree?

The answer: whether or not you should keep your will in a safe deposit box.

Some experts contend that you must keep your original, signed will in your safe-deposit box and that you must also make several copies of your will (or have your attorney make several copies) and give a copy to your personal representative. You must also give copies to certain family members or friends (different people than your personal representative) like your children or your brother or sister, for example. Because other people may have copies of your will, it's important to have a separate DAM (see the earlier sidebar "Don't forget your digital assets") so you control who sees the DAM's confidential information.

Other experts argue that your will shouldn't be kept in a safe-deposit box, but rather in a safe at your attorney's office or a fireproof safe at home. The reason for not using the safe-deposit box for your will, they contend, is that after you die, your safe-deposit box may be sealed until probate (depending on what state you live in) or at least be subject to highly restricted access. For example, your safe-deposit box may be accessible only by a person whom you designated on the signature card when you opened the box and only during a visit supervised by a bank official and possibly audited by your attorney or the taxing authorities. And in some states, the only items that can be removed from the safe-deposit box are your will and burial plot deed.

TIP

Our suggestion: Ask your attorney what they recommend and follow those guidelines. If you live in a state where safe-deposit boxes aren't sealed, your attorney may advise you to keep your signed will in your safe-deposit box. But if you live in a state that does seal safe-deposit boxes, you may be advised to keep your signed will with your attorney or at home.

WARNING

You should only keep your will at home if you have a fireproof safe. That stack of to-be-filed receipts, to-be-replied-to-letters, and candy bar wrappers on your desk in your den or a corner of the family room is no place for your will!

Also, regardless of where you safeguard your original will, you must also keep an unsigned copy of your will for yourself so you don't need to touch the original signed copy in your safe-deposit box. If you want to double-check to whom you left a particular item or some other detail in your will, or scribble a possible change that you want to ask your attorney about, you won't risk invalidating your will by damaging or defacing it.

You should also give unsigned reference copies of your will to key family members and others, so your family can start planning for what will happen to your estate.

Of course, if you have a flair for the dramatic and don't want anyone to know what's in your will until after you're dead, you can always do the bad-movie-plot version and give no one a copy at all, but we strongly advise against that approach!

Changing, Amending, and Revoking Your Will

After you have completed your will, you may assume that you're done with it. Even though you've completed the tough process of formally expressing what you want to be done with your estate, you still must keep it up to date. Often, working on your will can be an emotional process for you as you decide who will get your best dishes when three different children and grandchildren have explicitly expressed their interest with comments like, "Boy, I sure do love those plates" at your family dinners. Nevertheless, you've finally made your tough decisions, you want to put the whole process behind you, and you're tempted to simply put your will in a safe place so that someday in the future your "wishes for your dishes" will be carried out.

WARNING

Don't make the mistake of putting your will away and forgetting about it. You must make sure that at all times, the details of your will reflect changes in your life that occurred after you initially executed your will.

TIP

All of your estate planning documentation — wills, trusts, power of attorney — should be reviewed at least annually. Add a recurring calendar reminder to review your will to make sure everything is still up to date and accurately reflects what you want done with your estate.

Why you may need to change your will when something happens

Your will is a dynamic, living document because your life and tax laws are dynamic and ever-changing. Ironically, although a will's intent is to provide for what happens to your estate after you've died, the reality is that your will needs to change as your life changes.

Think about the climactic last scene of some old black-and-white movie, where the stoic attorney reads the deceased's will aloud as the family members gather around to see what rich oil magnate Grandfather has left them. In that last scene, almost everyone is surprised to find out that Grandpa had made changes to his will as family members drifted in and out of favor, and at the time of his passing those who were out of favor receive nothing except a token amount of cash and a stern from-beyond-the-grave lecture (while those family members who Grandpa favored the last time he updated his will are all ear-to-ear smiles).

This classic movie scene can serve to remind you that those shocked family members were probably blindsided because of some change made to the will that they weren't aware of at all. You need to keep this scenario in mind because your life does change — marriages, children, divorces, increases in your estate value, and so forth — and your will may need to change with these life changes.

The reasons you need to change your will vary. The following are typical times to change a will:

- **After a marriage:** You need to include your new spouse in your estate plan.
- **After a divorce:** You most likely want to absolutely, positively, and certainly make changes to the list of what you had previously been planning on leaving to your now ex-spouse.

- **After your spouse's death:** Most likely, you had left a significant portion — or perhaps all — of your estate to your spouse in your will, and now that your spouse has died, you need to update your will to adjust who you now want to leave your assets to.
- **After the death of one of your heirs or dependents:** Suppose your will has specified that a particular person is to receive a specific asset. If that person dies before you do, you need to update your will to reflect who you now want to receive that asset.
- **After you experience a significant change in your estate's value:** For example, your stock holdings may go way up (or way down!). You should now reevaluate who gets what and how much.
- **After any other change in your life that causes you to reevaluate who you want to leave something to:** For example, you become passionate about a specific cause and decide that you want to leave a large portion of your estate to some charity that champions that cause.

WARNING

If the change to your will is triggered by an emotional event, such as being extremely angry with a family member and wanting to write them out of your will, allow yourself some time to clear your head before you act. Make changes or amendments to your will after life changes and not after an emotional reaction that may dissipate over time.

Ways to change your will

You can change your will in one of two ways:

- You can create an entirely new will that supersedes your current will.
- You can change or delete specific parts of your current will, or add new parts, while leaving the rest of your current will unchanged. You do so through a new, separate document and not by directly altering your original will itself.

Each of these two methods has advantages and disadvantages. In most cases, simply creating an entirely new will with the changes, additions, and deletions is what you want to do. Creating an entirely new will is relatively straightforward, especially because your will was most likely prepared with good old standard word-processing software such as Microsoft Word or Google Docs (so your attorney doesn't need to have an entirely new will typed from scratch — with carbon paper for extra copies — like in the olden days before computers).

However, you can also add, change, or delete specific parts of your current will *without* creating an entirely new will through a form called a *codicil*. A codicil is a separate document that adds to your original will.

WARNING

Codicils are often expressed in the context of specifically referenced portions of your will. Because a codicil needs to clearly reference a specific portion of your will that it's amending, ask your attorney to prepare any codicils instead of trying to do them yourself, no matter how simple it may seem to just write or type a couple of lines of text. If you mess up, your codicil most likely won't be valid.

When should you use a codicil?

- When your original will is very long and you want to make only a few, minor changes.
- When your competency at the time of executing the codicil may be challenged. If someone does successfully argue that you were losing your grip in later years, the codicil may be overturned without affecting the will itself.

Protecting Your Loved Ones from Your Unloved Ones

Perhaps your family bears an uncanny resemblance to an episode of *The Waltons* (still showing in reruns on cable!) or maybe a family scene from an old Norman Rockwell painting. Everyone gets along most of the time, and every holiday dinner creates new lifelong memories (sigh!).

Or, on the other hand, maybe your family is more like an episode of a soap opera. Lots of bickering and arguing, one family member not speaking to another for years . . . you know the story. Quite possibly, then, your family consists of loved ones and "unloved ones." Suppose then, that you decide that your unloved ones will receive little or nothing from your estate. If you make that decision and you're willing to live with it (so to speak, because they may not find out your decision until after you died), then you need to be concerned with more than just figuring out how to leave those individuals out of your will. You also need to be concerned with protecting other family members — your loved ones — so that they justly get what you want them to receive without interference from the others who you decide to leave nothing.

WARNING

You may think that the most logical way to not leave anything to unloved ones is to simply leave them out of your will (basically, not to mention them at all), but that may be the worst thing you can do! Why? Because doing so leaves the door wide open for the unloved ones to contest your will by saying they were excluded by accident. ("You know, he was always so distracted, he obviously forgot to mention us. After all, we're blood relatives. Why wouldn't we be in his will?")

Therefore, you need to explicitly state your intentions for your unloved one in your will, no matter how painful it may be to form those words and commit them to paper. Your attorney can help you with the language to include, as well as help you to keep those words as factual and unemotional as possible.

TIP

A simple way to handle the wording problem is to mention the unloved ones in your will, but to leave them only a small or token sum. That way, they can't claim that you overlooked or forgot them and you don't have to explain in your will why they're otherwise excluded.

Still, after you die, those unloved ones may try to overturn your wishes to receive what they feel they rightly deserve from your estate. One way to try to avoid future issues with an unloved one is to add a *no-contest clause* in your will. The no-contest clause, also called an *in terrorem clause* (note the word *terror* as part of the name!), basically says that if your unloved one contests what they were left, they receive — get ready for it — nothing! This is another reason that it's important to at least mention your unloved ones in your will.

WARNING

No-contest clauses are not foolproof, however. Some states have enforceability restrictions on no-contest clauses if there is probable cause for someone to challenge your will. Nevertheless, it's a recommended clause to add to your will, if only as a deterrent for your unloved one to not contest your will.

Figuring Out Your Will Status

When you die, you have one of three *will statuses* depending on whether you have a complete valid will. Your will status may be:

- **Testacy:** All your assets are covered by a valid will, and you're in pretty good shape.
- **Intestacy:** You die, and you don't have a valid will.
- **Partial intestacy:** The "no man's land" (or maybe purgatory?) when only some of your assets are covered by a valid will.

Testacy: When you've nailed everything down

If you have a valid will, you are said to die *testate*. Basically, you have spelled out your intentions completely and legally in your last will and testament and you have attained one of your two primary objectives of estate planning: control. (Your other primary estate-planning objective is protection.)

Not to sound like a commercial for a funeral home or life insurance policy, but when you die testate, you at least die with some peace of mind knowing that your wishes will be followed through, courtesy of the legal system.

Intestacy: When you die with zero "willpower"

Intestacy: the dark side! Being *intestate* means that you die without a valid will. Depending on your particular circumstances, the implications of your intestacy can be far-reaching. Most important, dying intestate results in your estate being distributed through the *laws of intestate succession* (commonly referred to as the *intestate law*) — a technical way of saying that the legal system decides how your estate is distributed. Essentially, your state writes a will for you — not an actual-on-paper physical will, but sort of a virtual will, made up of your state's default clauses that apply to the particulars of you, your family, and your estate.

Now, unfortunately, you have no say whatsoever in how your estate is distributed and who receives it. The intestate succession laws vary by state but are usually similar from one state to another in terms of the primary purpose: basically, to determine who receives your estate. The intestate law establishes a particular next-of-kin priority for distributing your estate. Did you have a spouse? Did you have children? What other relatives are in the picture?

WARNING

But what about other people — specifically, those people who aren't related to you — who you had wanted to take care of? Most likely, they're out of luck if you die intestate. Suppose, for example, you had wanted to leave $100,000 worth of Amazon stock to the family housekeeper who has been with you for years, and who even worked for your parents. Without your having a valid will specifying that desire — and, thus, being intestate — your housekeeper will most likely never receive anything from your estate. (Of course, whoever does wind up with that $100,000 worth of Amazon stock according to the intestate succession laws may later transfer that stock to the housekeeper, as you wanted, but don't count on it!)

WARNING

Also, if you don't have any living family members covered by the state's intestate laws, depending on the state where you live and your particular circumstances, the state's intestate laws could make your state your only beneficiary! Unless you really want to leave your estate to the state where you live, make sure you have a valid will so you don't die intestate!

Partial intestacy: When the vultures start circling

No man's land. Purgatory. Between a rock and a hard place. *Partial intestacy* — when part of your estate isn't covered by your valid will — is an in-between will status, not quite testacy but not quite intestacy either. Very often, forgetting to include a residuary clause (discussed earlier in this chapter) in your will is what causes you to be considered partially intestate when you die.

WARNING

If you've followed all the steps we discuss in this chapter and you've prepared your will, you may be tempted to think that you no longer have to worry about being intestate or partially intestate. Wrong! You may have overlooked some little item in your will that could negate your will completely if a disgruntled family member contests your will's validity.

The result, if that disgruntled person is successful: You may be *rendered* (basically, switched) into intestacy if your will is declared invalid, resulting in your estate being distributed through intestate succession laws — the one thing you wanted to avoid in the first place by having a will! Or you could forget to include the all-important residuary clause. What happens to your collection of 1930s-era baseball player autographs that you neglected to specifically bequeath to someone? Because you're intestate with regard to those autographs, they'll pass to your heirs at law under the intestate law.

TIP

Be sure to periodically consult with your attorney to make sure that your will is complete and current and has been properly signed and witnessed, and you'll increase the likelihood of your will status being testate (which is what you want).

IN THIS CHAPTER

» Understanding the laws that affect or interpret your will

» Grasping the laws that your will can change and what you must do about them

» Comprehending the laws that your will can't change

Chapter 3

What You Can and Can't Do with Your Will

We slightly altered an old saying: "Where there's a will, there's all kinds of laws you need to worry about." (Well, it could be an old saying in legal circles, anyway.)

Even though your will provides you with a fantastic tool to direct what happens to your estate after you die, you don't exactly have a free hand in what you can make your will do for you. A number of state statutes affect or interpret your will and, consequently, the way you transfer assets to others. If you know what these laws provide, you can include appropriate language in your will to amplify or diminish the effect of those statutes.

In this chapter, we discuss those statutes. Keep in mind that because state law — not federal law — governs your will, some of the statutes we discuss in this chapter may not apply to you simply because of where you live. But because you're working with your attorney to create your will (see Chapter 2 in Book 7), don't worry — your attorney is well aware of the particular provisions that affect your will.

Making Your Peace with Statutes That Affect Your Will

Before you start grumbling about those laws or statutes that affect your will, remember that many of them protect your beneficiaries, particularly your spouse and children, so they're not necessarily bad for you and your estate. Think of these statutes as playing cards: You have to play the hand you're dealt, but if you really know your game, you can give yourself an advantage.

For example, what happens if your will specifically states that $100,000 must be left to each of your two children (a total of $200,000), but when you die, your estate is only valued at $150,000? A statute called the *abatement statute* (which we discuss later in this chapter) specifies what happens then.

After you die, who is responsible for paying any death tax that is due? Again, a statute is waiting in the wings to say exactly what will happen.

As you figure out what you want to write in your will (see Chapter 2 in Book 7 for a discussion about the basics of wills), you need to keep the list of the statutes we discuss in this chapter handy for easy reference.

TIP

Some statutes affecting or interpreting wills are complicated, especially when the fine print kicks in. Furthermore, the particulars of these statutes vary from one state to another, so you really need to work with your attorney when you prepare your will, rather than use a general fill-in-the-blank form that quite possibly doesn't address the impact of these statutes on your estate. If you do decide to make use of an online legal site to generate your own fill-in-the-blank form will, you should still run your near-finished will past a qualified estate-planning attorney to ensure that all state statutory requirements are met.

Identifying Statutes That Your Will Can Change

You can write your will in a certain way to address the following statutes:

- **Abatement statutes:** What happens when your estate isn't worth enough to provide what you want to leave your beneficiaries and to meet any debts you have remaining when you die?

- **Ademption statutes:** What happens if some of your property is missing when you die?
- **Anti-lapse statutes:** What happens if certain beneficiaries die before you?
- **Divorce statutes:** Well, these statutes are fairly self-explanatory.
- **Simultaneous death statutes:** What happens if you and someone else die at the same time?

Abatement: There's not enough in the cupboard for everyone

In Chapter 2 of Book 7, we explain how you can specify in your will how much of your estate will go to various beneficiaries.

But what happens if you die and for whatever reason, your estate isn't worth enough to give everybody what you want them to get? Your state's *abatement statutes* come into play.

REMEMBER

Abatement is defined as the process of reducing or lessening something, so you can think of abatement statutes as those laws that say, "Hold on, folks! Your estate doesn't have enough value to go around. Here's what we're going to do." Abatement statutes typically provide for a distribution priority in the event that the assets in your estate are not sufficient to pay all your creditors and to make a full distribution to each of the beneficiaries named in your will. The abatement statutes specify, for example, that property in your estate's *residue* (your "left-overs") may abate — that is, be reduced — before other property you specifically mention in your will.

Check with your attorney to determine how your particular state's abatement statutes work. However, if you're not satisfied with your state's statutory method of abatement, don't panic! Usually, you can make specific provisions in your will to specify how (and in what order) your assets should abate if your estate is not large enough to provide for the payment of all debts (including taxes) and to then carry out your directions for leaving specific dollar amounts or specific items to your beneficiaries.

REMEMBER

Your best strategy to avoid your estate being affected by your state's abatement statutes is to use percentage amounts rather than actual dollar amounts whenever possible in your will.

Suppose you calculate the value of your estate at $200,000, and you want to split that amount equally between your two children. One way to do so is to specifically state in your will that each child receives $100,000.

However, what happens if your estate doesn't grow at all and, instead, shrinks? Maybe some stock you own has declined significantly in value, or maybe you had a lot of medical expenses. Regardless, if your estate is now worth $150,000 and you haven't updated your will to reflect the reduced value of your estate, you have a problem!

But if you used percentage amounts rather than dollar amounts in your will, specifying that 50 percent of your estate goes to each child, you avoid abatement statutes coming into play, even though your estate's value has decreased.

Abatement statutes can also come into play even if you have enough assets in your estate to cover specific dollar amounts you specified for your beneficiaries, but you have outstanding debts that need to be settled when you die. For example, suppose you still have $200,000 worth of cash, stock, and other assets when you die, but you also have $50,000 outstanding on a variety of credit cards and other debts. Your estate isn't worth $200,000 at all, but rather $150,000 — your $200,000 in assets minus the $50,000 in debts.

Can't your family just, shall we say, forget about what you owe? After all, you're dead, right? Sorry. In the probate process, valid creditors' claims must be paid.

REMEMBER

You need to tally up your debts, as well as your assets, when you're figuring out what your estate is worth. Don't forget — otherwise, you may be way off in your calculations of your estate's value compared with what your estate is really worth! Be sure to consider an estimate of probate costs and death taxes as part of your estate's "debt," because those items will also diminish the amount of your estate that will be available to distribute to your beneficiaries.

But what happens if the way you write your will (typically, with specific dollar amounts used throughout) causes abatement statutes to apply to your estate? Basically, the abatement statutes determine how your will's property transfers to your beneficiaries will be reduced, and by how much. In the worst case, some of your property transfers may actually disappear due to the lack of funds available to pay them. That $25,000 to your cousin Jane? Sorry, the money is gone! But why?

State law, rather than federal law, regulates property transfers in wills. States greatly vary in the laws or statutes that affect these transfers. Some states follow the Uniform Probate Code (UPC) regarding wills. More than half of the states in the United States have adopted, in part or in whole, the UPC. The adoption of the UPC enables some uniformity of statutes among states, including abatement statutes.

TIP

In Chapter 1 of Book 7, we mention that one of the primary roles of your attorney on your estate-planning team is to help you with the "what if" scenarios and to help you prevent problems from occurring. When you're working with your attorney on your will, ask about the abatement statutes that apply in the state where you live, and what may happen to your property based on those statutes. And while you're asking, specifically question your attorney to help you prepare your will so abatement statutes won't come into play at all!

Ademption: Some property is missing

Cataloging and valuing your tangible personal property (jewelry, antiques, collectibles, furniture, and so on) can be tedious and frustrating, but you need to take the time to do it as part of your estate planning.

In your will, you can explicitly leave items to someone through a *specific bequest.* For example, you can leave your valuable collection of '50s and '60s baseball cards to your baseball-crazy oldest son, and your collection of autographed first-edition novels to your other son, who is working on his PhD in English literature.

But what happens if you die and the baseball cards or the novels — or maybe both — are, for whatever reason, no longer part of your estate? You may have had to sell some of your property to pay for medical expenses. Or maybe you already gave your baseball cards to your son as a gift with the appropriate gift tax implications while you were still alive, meaning that you've already transferred that property from your estate to his.

Regardless of the reason, if your will refers to property that isn't part of your estate when you die, that property is considered to be missing, or *adeemed,* and the *ademption statutes* apply.

REMEMBER

Ademption statutes concern whether the specific asset in question is in existence when you die. In general, the statutes provide that your "who gets what" direction will fail if you aren't the owner of the asset when you die. However, you also find exceptions to the rule, which may apply in your case, including what happens if you dispose of an asset while incompetent but receive another asset in exchange. Ask your attorney to walk you through the various scenarios that specifically relate to your estate's property.

Ademption statutes vary from state to state and determine whether the beneficiary who can't receive the specific bequest from your will is allowed to still receive something from your estate, and if so, what that beneficiary will receive.

WARNING

So, what can you do to keep ademption statutes at bay? You can include *backup property* for some or all beneficiaries in your will. For example, you can specify that if your baseball card collection worth $50,000 is no longer part of your estate because you wound up selling all your cards on eBay, your son is to receive $50,000 in cash instead. Beware, though: Including backup property in your will can be complicated and have unintended side effects, so work carefully with your attorney on what backup property to use and the wording to use in your will.

Anti-lapse: Someone dies before you do

Anti-lapse sounds like a doddering old relative . . . you know, your "Aunty Lapse." Actually, anti-lapse is your situation when somebody named in your will dies before you do. To cover yourself, you should consider naming a *contingent beneficiary* (your backup beneficiary) for any property distribution in your will by including words such as the following:

> In the event that my named beneficiary for the property listed herein does not survive me, I hereby direct that that my bequest be given to John Doe.

If you don't make your own provisions for contingent beneficiaries, and if your state has an anti-lapse statute, that law dictates who receives the property that is in limbo because of your beneficiary who died. If your state doesn't have an anti-lapse statute, then typically the in-limbo property goes to the beneficiaries you name in your *residuary clause* (that statement names the beneficiaries who get anything you haven't explicitly mentioned in a giving clause; see Chapter 2 of Book 7). Sometimes, though, that is exactly what you want! Be sure to work with your attorney to determine whether naming a contingent beneficiary makes sense.

Divorce: High noon at Splitsville

Nearly everyone has heard the statistic, again and again: Approximately half of all marriages end in divorce. With that large of a target audience, no wonder states have divorce statutes that you need to be aware of for your estate planning.

Your spouse automatically has a claim on part of your estate after you die. If you live in a common-law state, your spouse is entitled to claim a percentage of your assets. If you live in a community-property state, your spouse generally owns half of your property. (We cover common-law and community-property states later in this chapter.)

WARNING

You may not want to change your will right away after you're divorced. For example, you may not have initiated the divorce and you subconsciously think that changing your will is equivalent to acknowledging that your marriage has ended. Therefore, estate-planning procrastination is a natural reaction for the recently divorced.

The good news: In many states, if your marriage has ended, but you resist changing your will to reflect this fact, your estate is protected from claims by your former spouse. The effect is that, typically, your ex isn't allowed to claim their share of your estate if you die after you're officially divorced but before you change your will. But be careful!

REMEMBER

Even with the protection provided by such statutes, you still need to change your will as soon as possible after a divorce to clarify your intentions as to who your beneficiaries are. If your ex isn't one of them, make sure that's what your will reflects. Furthermore, you need to check on all your beneficiary designations that pass outside your will, such as life insurance. Be sure that any and all beneficiary designations are up-to-date, reflecting the beneficiaries you chose.

Simultaneous death: Sorry, but we have to talk about it

REMEMBER

Estate planning can sometimes be a depressing topic because it revolves around the subject of death, and the statutes dealing with simultaneous death are particularly depressing. However, you need to understand the implications to your estate from these statutes if you want to be as comprehensive as possible.

The simplest way to understand simultaneous death statutes is to consider the following situation:

- You and your spouse both die.
- The order of your deaths can't be established. (For example, you and your spouse both die in the same fatal car accident.)
- Your state law determines the order of death for inheritance purposes.

TECHNICAL STUFF

Most states have adopted a form of the Uniform Simultaneous Death Act to deal with simultaneous death situations. This act is based on the assumption that when the transfer of property is dependent on the order of death, the estate is distributed as if each person had survived the other person. For example, if a childless married couple dies in an accident, and for any assets not held jointly or that contain a beneficiary designation, the wife's estate is left to her relatives and the husband's estate is left to his relatives. Why? Because each person is assumed to have survived the other, the act treats the estate distribution as if the other spouse had already passed away, which is actually good news (if you can consider any news in this type of situation as "good"). The same assets don't pass through probate twice (once for each spouse), quite possibly subjecting the estate to double estate taxation and twice as much complication.

To be on the safe side, include a *survival clause* in your will to either confirm or change your state's version of the Uniform Simultaneous Death Act, according to what you and your attorney decide makes sense for you.

WARNING

A survival clause is important in "closely related death" (though not simultaneous death) situations. You effectively "void out" a directive you had made in your will to leave property to someone if that person dies very soon after you do. For example, suppose the same childless couple is critically injured in an accident, but one spouse dies five days before the other. Without a survival clause, property from the spouse who dies first transfers to the surviving spouse and goes through probate, possibly being subjected to death taxes. When the other spouse dies only a few days later, that very same property can once again be subjected to estate taxes. In effect, the estate goes through double taxation that wouldn't have occurred if that couple had died simultaneously.

TECHNICAL STUFF

Typically, however, in most states that have an inheritance or estate tax, when assets pass from one spouse to the surviving spouse, a tax is not imposed.

TIP

To help prevent these complications, specify in your will that your beneficiary must survive for some period of time — 30 or 60 days, for example — after your death before receiving the assets you've specified in your will. If that beneficiary dies very soon after you do, your property will skip over that person and go to someone else, avoiding double probate and possibly double estate taxation.

Living (and Dying) with the Laws That Your Will Can't Change

WARNING

If you prepare a will that conflicts with certain statutes, you risk spending a lot of time and effort only to find out that you've created a will that may not be effective or valid. If, for some reason, you decide to treat your will and your estate like a bad soap opera plot and leave as little as possible to your spouse and children (possibly leaving them in serious financial trouble), your state's statutes may come to the rescue and provide some amount of financial protection for your family.

But even if you aren't deliberately and maliciously trying to hurt your family with what you specify in your will, you still need to be aware of what your state's laws say about what may happen with your estate. Otherwise, you face the very real possibility of preparing what you think is a valid will, but because you've accidentally run aground of one or more of your state's statutes, your will isn't valid at all.

So, read through the following descriptions of statutes so you know what you're dealing with.

Community property

If you live in a community-property state, any property acquired and any income made while you're married is considered to be owned 50 percent by you and 50 percent by your spouse. More important for estate-planning purposes, you're required under those states' *community-property statutes* to leave half of your community property to your spouse.

REMEMBER

Eight states are community-property states: Arizona, California, Idaho, Louisiana, Nevada, New Mexico, Texas, and Washington. Wisconsin has a system similar to community property called *marital property*, and for purposes of our discussion, we lump Wisconsin in with the other eight community-property states.

If you live in a community-property state, all property acquired while you're married is considered community property except for property that you personally receive by a gift or by inheritance, which is considered to be your sole and separate property. For example, your grandmother's inherited wedding ring or the $10,000 cash gift from your aunt to you isn't part of your community property. Additionally, property you owned before you were married is also exempt from being included in community property.

WARNING

Keep your non-community property separate from your community property! You can actually override the "separate stuff" aspect of your non-community property by specifying in writing that you want that property (again, a gift or inheritance) to become part of your community property with your spouse, or by intermixing your non-community property and your community property (for example, by putting your $10,000 cash gift from your aunt into a joint savings account you and your spouse share). If you turn your non-community property into community property, either accidentally or on purpose, you lose your sole control over that property, and the community property statutes take over.

A COMPLICATED COMMUNITY

Community-property laws can be very complicated. For example, property you own before you marry in a community-property state is still considered to be your own. However, income you earn on your own property after you're married may be considered to be community property. For example, if you inherit a farm from your parents before you get married, and then you marry and live in a community-property state, income from that farm may be considered to be community property.

Additionally, you need to be aware of what happens to your estate if you married in a community-property state but later moved to a non-community-property state, or if you purchased investment property in a community-property state but live elsewhere.

You absolutely need to consult with your attorney to see whether community-property statutes apply to any part of your estate, and if so, what those statutes mean to your estate.

Common-law property and spousal elective shares

What if you reside in one of the other 41 states that aren't community-property states? You live in a common-law state, and your spouse still has a claim to some part of your estate, though not the automatic 50 percent specified by community-property statutes. In almost all common-law states, your spouse is provided for through *spousal elective shares,* or the law that permits your spouse to claim some part of your estate.

If you live in Alaska, Florida, Kentucky, South Dakota, or Tennessee, you can elect to opt into a community-property system. You can also identify specific assets to be community property. In three states — California, Nevada, and Washington — domestic partnerships must also legally operate under community-property laws.

TECHNICAL STUFF

A few other states — Arkansas, Kentucky, and Ohio — use the old English concepts called *dower* and *curtesy,* which we discuss in the later section "Homestead allowance: Keeping a house for kiddies and spouse." In all other common-law states, spousal elective shares have replaced dower and curtesy.

Your spouse has the right under spousal elective shares to claim a portion of your estate, with the amount depending on your own state's spousal elective shares statutes. But what about your will? Spousal elective shares are sort of like flipping a coin and calling "Heads, I win, and tails, I win, too."

Your spouse basically gets a choice between accepting the amount you specified in your will or the amount specified in your state's spousal elective shares. If your will specifies that your spouse is to receive more than your state's spousal elective shares specify, then your spouse can accept that higher amount. But if your will specifies a lower amount than your state's spousal elective shares, your spouse can opt for the higher amount specified by law. In doing so, your spouse can cause all kinds of complications to your will.

Spousal elective share amounts vary among states. Under some statutes, your spouse's share is a percentage amount that ranges from 3 percent to 50 percent of your estate, based on how long you were married. Other states' statutes specify an amount equal to some flat percentage of your estate regardless of how long you were married.

TECHNICAL STUFF

In some states, spousal elective shares are based on an *augmented estate* amount rather than your actual estate amount. Basically, certain property that isn't technically part of your estate is added back to your estate's value, and the spousal elective percentage amount is based on this higher, augmented value rather than on your estate's actual value at the time of your death. What's the deal? States that use augmented estate amounts are trying to protect a surviving spouse from that person's husband or wife deliberately trying to reduce the value of an estate and leaving as little as possible to the surviving spouse.

For example, property transfers that you made within a certain period of time before your death may be added back to your estate, along with certain property in which you have ownership with right of survivorship and sometimes life insurance proceeds, retirement benefits, and annuities. When you work with your attorney to understand the spousal elective share laws in your estate, make sure that you also ask if augmented amounts apply to your estate.

WARNING

If you really don't like your spouse, don't use your estate plan to try to punish them by trying not to leave them anything as part of your estate. Your estate-planning attorney isn't the person you should be working with on this problem; try a marriage counselor, or if that doesn't work, ask your estate-planning attorney for a recommendation for a good divorce attorney! Don't complicate or even trash your estate planning by trying to give your spouse a raw deal to make some kind of point. Your entire estate plan may be defeated if your spouse makes that spousal election after your death!

Homestead allowance: Keeping a house for kiddies and spouse

Just as Dorothy discovered in *The Wizard of Oz*, there's no place like home. So, you definitely want your home to be protected after you die. Fortunately, the *homestead-allowance statutes* may take care of your home. Unfortunately, though, only a few states have these statutes.

The purpose of homestead-allowance statutes is to make sure that your spouse and any minor children (under 18 years of age) have a place to live after you die. Your homestead is typically defined as your house and may also include a certain amount of adjacent land. (The legal term you may run across is *curtilage.*) The land aspect of homestead allowances is very important if you live on a farm or any property with a large number of acres.

TECHNICAL STUFF

Homestead-allowance statutes come from the old English common law concepts of *dower* and *curtesy,* and you may come across those terms. (We mention in the previous section that Arkansas, Kentucky, and Ohio laws use dower and curtesy rather than spousal elective shares or community-property statutes.) The purpose of dower and curtesy was to provide a surviving spouse with an interest for the remainder of their life in the real property owned by the spouse who died and, therefore, have somewhere to live. *Dower* is the word used for a wife's interest, while *curtesy* refers to a husband's interest.

Homestead exemption: How the law protects your house from your creditors

Homestead-exemption statutes are closely related to homestead-allowance statutes and apply if your estate needs to pay debts you owe to creditors. If not enough cash is available, the estate is forced to sell off property — real, personal, or perhaps both — to get enough money to pay the creditors. If your estate owes a lot of money for debts, selling off a single high-value item, such as your house, is often easier than trying to sell a lot of smaller items.

So, the homestead-exemption statutes are intended to prevent your surviving spouse and minor children from being kicked out of your home if property does need to be sold to pay creditors.

WARNING

Even with homestead-exemption statutes, your home can still be subject to a forced sale. Think of these statutes simply as a first line of defense rather than an absolutely 100 percent guarantee that your spouse and children can remain in your home if your estate owes a lot of money and that money can't be raised by selling other property from the estate. Therefore, you need to consider the other parts of your overall estate planning, such as life insurance, to help out the homestead-exemption statutes and protect your family and your home.

Exempt property: How the law protects your personal property from creditors

Your estate is composed of various types of property: real property and personal property, including both tangible personal property and intangible personal property.

The two types of homestead statutes that we discuss earlier — homestead allowance and homestead exemption — help to protect part of your real property (your home). However, the vast majority of your intangible personal property (stocks, bonds, and so on) isn't covered by protective statutes and, therefore, may be forcibly sold to satisfy claims from your estate's creditors.

The good news: Some of your tangible personal property (your car, collectibles, jewelry, and so forth) may be protected through *exempt-property award statutes.*

With the homestead statutes, exempt-property award statutes vary among states so you need to talk with your attorney about what types of tangible personal property your state's statutes protect, and how that relates to your estate plan.

Family allowance: Drawing from your estate to protect your family

Your spouse and children may rely on you as the family's breadwinner. And even if you aren't the sole breadwinner, the income you provide to your family may provide a substantial portion of basic care, such as food and shelter, for your family. Therefore, your unanticipated death will often create an immediate financial crisis for your family. But you have several assets, and your will specifies what goes to your family, so you don't have this problem, right?

WARNING

Not necessarily! Your estate may be tied up in the probate process for an extended period of time. Typically, your estate can't make any distributions to your beneficiaries until all debts to your creditors have been paid. Therefore, your family's immediate financial needs, such as the mortgage payment and even paying for utilities and food, may be in jeopardy!

Fortunately, *family-allowance statutes* enable the probate court to provide money for support of your spouse and minor children during the probate process. In fact, family-allowance statutes are one of the only distributions that can be made from your estate without risk before the claims of your creditors are paid.

TIP

The amount of your family's allowance under your state's law may depend on a number of factors, including your estate's size and your family's living expenses. Ask your attorney to inform you what the allowance likely is so you can factor that into your overall estate plan. For example, you may want to set up your gift-giving strategy to transfer cash to your beneficiaries (while you're alive) so they can use it to help cover living expenses during the probate process.

Oops! Taking care of VIPs who aren't in the will

REMEMBER

You must continually update your will as circumstances in your life change, particularly when you get married, give birth, or adopt.

But suppose you get married or have a child and you don't update your will before you die. Are family members who aren't mentioned in your will totally out of the picture when your estate is distributed? (In legal-speak, a spouse or child not included in your estate is called a *pretermitted* or *omitted* heir or beneficiary.)

Pretermitted- or *omitted-heir statutes* help to protect certain family members that you don't mention in your will, but they only apply to your spouse and children. These statutes, which (as you probably expect us to say) vary from one state to another, govern what part of your estate must go to your spouse and children if you procrastinate and don't keep your will up-to-date.

Index

Numerics

A

B

C

D

E

F

G

H

I

J

K

L

N

O

P

Q

R

T

U

V

W

X

Y

Z

About the Authors

Ted Benna is commonly referred to as the "Father of the 401(k)" because he created and gained IRS approval of the first 401(k) savings plan. He has received many citations for his accomplishments including the 2001 National Jefferson Award recipient for Greatest Public Service by a Private Citizen, the 2001 Player of the Year selected by Defined Contribution News, and one of eight individuals selected by *Money* magazine for its special 20th Anniversary Issue Hall of Fame. He was selected by Business Insurance as one of the four People of the Century, was one of ten selected by Mutual Fund Market News for its special 10th Anniversary Issue "Legends in Our Own Time," received the Lifetime Achievement Award by Defined Contribution News 2005, and was the recipient of the Icons and Innovators Award — Investment News 2017. Ted has authored several books including *401(k)s & IRAs For Dummies* and *401(k) — Forty Years Later.*

Steve Bucci has been helping people decode and master personal credit and debt issues for the last 20 years. For more than a decade, he has authored a popular weekly personal finance column for the financial mega-site Bankrate (`www.bankrate.com`). He also writes a weekly column on credit scoring that appears on `CreditCards.com` (`www.creditcards.com`). Steve is also a personal credit coach, speaker, and expert witness. He is the coauthor of *Credit Repair Kit For Dummies,* 6th Edition.

Kiana Danial, former electrical engineer and founder of Invest Diva, is an internationally recognized expert in investing, entrepreneurship, and wealth creation. She is the author of seven books, including the *Wall Street Journal* and *USA Today* bestseller *Million Dollar Family Secrets.*

Through her signature Triple Compounding method, Kiana empowers professionals to take control of their finances and accelerate their path to financial freedom. She is the author of *Triple Compounding For Dummies.*

Chris Eck, CPA, is a highly skilled and dedicated financial professional with over 18 years of experience in the field. Chris is known for his exceptional expertise in providing comprehensive accounting services and strategic financial guidance to clients across various industries. Throughout his career, Chris has cultivated a reputation for his attention to detail and unwavering commitment to delivering accurate and reliable financial information. With a strong foundation in accounting principles, tax law, and financial regulations, he has become a trusted advisor to many businesses and individuals seeking to optimize their finances. He is the coauthor of *Taxes 2026 For Dummies.*

Robert S. Griswold, MSBA, is a successful real estate investor, expert witness, and hands-on landlord/property manager with a large portfolio of residential and commercial rental income properties. He uses print and broadcast journalism to bring his many years of experience to his readers, listeners, and viewers. He is the author of *Property Management For Dummies* and *Property Management Kit For Dummies* and for 15 years was the real estate expert for NBC San Diego, with a regular on-air live-caller segment. Robert was the host of a live weekly radio talk show, *Real Estate Today!*, for nearly 15 years, and he's also the columnist for the syndicated "Rental Roundtable" and "Rental Forum" columns. These popular features are published in dozens of major newspapers throughout the country, and Robert has been recognized twice as the number-one real estate broadcast journalist in the nation by the National Association of Real Estate Editors. He is the coauthor of *Mortgage Management For Dummies.*

Athena Valentine Lent first learned the power of a budget in her early 20s. Once homeless when she was in high school, personal finance was not something her family taught or understood. After acing her own personal budget, she was able to go on to complete an associate's degree in criminal justice from the College of Southern Nevada. She then pursued a dual bachelor's degree in criminal justice and criminology from Arizona State University, as well as a counterterrorism certificate.

Now Athena is an award-winning financial columnist for *Slate* magazine. Her work includes items for BuzzFeed, Prudential, Experian, T. Rowe Price, The College Investor, and Money Under 30, to name a few. She also serves as a community liaison for FinCon, an annual conference for content creators and brands in the financial industry. She is the author of *Budgeting For Dummies.*

Joe Mashinski received his AB from Princeton University and his JD from the Dickinson School of Law at Pennsylvania State University. Joe is an attorney and consulting professional with varied experience ranging from estate planning, alternative investments, and financial services to ERISA compliance. Joe has worked for several start-up ventures in alternative investments, artificial intelligence, and fintech. He is the coauthor of *Estate Planning For Dummies,* 2nd Edition.

Margaret Atkins Munro, EA (who answers to Peggy), is a tax advisor, writer, and lecturer with more than 40 years of experience in various areas of taxation and finance with a mission in life to make taxes understandable. Her practice is concentrated in the areas of family tax, small business, trusts, estates, and charitable foundations. She is a graduate of Johns Hopkins University and has also attended University College Cork (Ireland) and the Pontifical Institute of Mediaeval Studies in Toronto, and she feels that her ability to decipher the language in the Internal Revenue Code derives completely from her familiarity with a variety of obscure medieval languages. Peggy is the author of *529s & Education Savings Plans For Dummies,* 2nd Edition.

Brenda Watson Newmann is a writer and editor dedicated to helping ordinary folks understand complicated topics. She was in charge of editorial content for the mPower Cafe, a leading educational website for retirement investors. Under her direction, the site won accolades including *Forbes* magazine's "Best of the Web." Brenda keeps attuned to the concerns of 401(k) investors through the emails she receives regularly from readers. She frequently writes articles on retirement investing and has been interviewed by media outlets, such as *USA Today* and *Investor's Business Daily*. Brenda began her writing career with The Associated Press and was a foreign correspondent in Germany and Switzerland. She is a graduate of Stanford University and the Johns Hopkins University School of Advanced International Studies. Brenda is the coauthor of *401(k)s & IRAs For Dummies*.

Jordan S. Simon is vice president of asset management at Venture West, Inc., a Tucson, Arizona–based investment firm, where he has worked since 1988. Jordan focuses on real estate investments. He received his BA from the University of Arizona and his MBA from the University of Southern California, where he was the recipient of the Quon Award for outstanding university and community service. He is the coauthor of *Estate Planning For Dummies*, 2nd Edition.

Eric Tyson, MBA, is a bestselling author and syndicated columnist. Through his counseling, writing, and teaching, he equips people to manage their personal finances better. An accomplished freelance personal finance writer, Eric is the author of the national bestsellers *Personal Finance For Dummies* and *Investing For Dummies*, coauthor of *Home Buying For Dummies*, and was an award-winning columnist for the *San Francisco Examiner*. His work has been featured and quoted in hundreds of national and local publications, including *Newsweek*, the *Wall Street Journal*, *Forbes*, *Kiplinger's Personal Finance Magazine*, the *Los Angeles Times*, and *Bottom Line/Personal*; and on Fox, NBC's *Today Show*, ABC, CNBC, PBS's *Nightly Business Report*, CNN, CBS national radio, Bloomberg Business Radio, and Business Radio Network. He's on the web at `www.erictyson.com`. Eric is the coauthor of *Mortgage Management For Dummies* and *Taxes 2026 For Dummies*.

Publisher's Acknowledgments

Executive Editor: Tracy Boggier
Compilation Editor: Georgette Beatty
Managing Editor: Murari Mukundan
Development Editor: Linda Brandon
Copy Editor: Jerelind Charles
Production Editor: Umeshkumar Rajasekhar
Cover Image: Vertigo3d/Getty Images